THE ECONOMICS OF WELFARE

MACMILLAN AND CO , Limited
LONDON · BOMBAY · CALCUTTA · MADRAS
MELBOURNE

THE MACMILLAN COMPANY
NEW YORK · BOSTON · CHICAGO
DALLAS · SAN FRANCISCO

THE MACMILLAN CO. OF CANADA, Ltd.
TORONTO

The Economics of Welfare

THE ECONOMICS
OF WELFARE

BY

A. C. PIGOU, M.A.

PROFESSOR OF POLITICAL ECONOMY IN THE UNIVERSITY OF CAMBRIDGE

MACMILLAN AND CO., LIMITED
ST. MARTIN'S STREET, LONDON
1920

HB
771
P6

PREFACE

THIS volume was originally conceived as a rewritten and revised edition of my *Wealth and Welfare* published in 1912. But the work has grown to such an extent and has come to cover so much more ground that, though considerable sections of *Wealth and Welfare* are incorporated in it, it is essentially an independent book. In writing it I have made use of passages from various earlier books of my own, and also from articles contributed by me to the *Economic Journal, Quarterly Journal of Economics, Nineteenth Century and After* and *Contemporary Review.*

The general plan is as follows. In Part I. it is argued, subject, of course, to a large number of qualifications, that the economic welfare of a community is likely to be greater (1) the larger is the *average* volume of the national dividend, (2) the larger is the *average* share of the national dividend that accrues to the poor, and (3) the less variable are the *annual* volume of the national dividend and the *annual* share that accrues to the poor. Parts II., III. and IV. are devoted to a study of certain principal influences by which the average volume of the national dividend is affected. Part II. deals with the distribution of productive resources in general among different places and occupations; Part III. with various problems connected with the organisation of Labour, and Part IV. with the relation between the national dividend and Government finance. In Part V. the question is raised in what circumstances it is possible for the absolute share of dividend accruing to the poor to be increased by a cause which at the same time diminishes the volume of the dividend as a whole; and the relation of disharmonies of this kind, when they occur, to economic welfare is discussed. Finally, Part VI. is devoted to an investigation of the causes of variability in the national dividend and in the absolute share of the poor and of certain relevant problems of practice.

In preparing the book for the press I have done my best, by restricting as far as possible the use of technical terms, by relegating specially abstract discussions to Appendices, and by summarising the main drift of the argument in an Analytical Table of Contents, to render what I have to say as little difficult as may be. But it would be idle to pretend that the book is other than a severe one. In part, no doubt, the severity is due to defects of exposition. But in part also it is due to the nature of the problems studied. It is sometimes imagined that economic questions can be adjudicated upon without special preparation. The "plain man," who in physics and chemistry knows that he does not know, has still to attain in economics to that first ante-chamber of knowledge. In reality the subject is an exceedingly difficult one, and cannot, without being falsified, be made to appear easy.

In publishing my book at the present time, I have had to face one somewhat special difficulty. The process of printing now takes so long, and legislative and other changes both here and abroad are so numerous and rapid, that some of the legal enactments and general conditions to which I have referred in the present tense are certain, by the time the book is in the reader's hands, to have been superseded. Even an illustration from geometry, which I have employed in the introductory chapter, should now, in the light of the confirmation recently won for Einstein's theory, be expressed somewhat differently! I do not think, however, that the impossibility of being completely up-to-date in a world of continuous change matters very greatly. For the illustrations I have used are not brought forward for their own sake. The service I ask of them is to throw light on principles, and that purpose can be performed as well by an arrangement or a fact that lapsed a year ago as by one that is still intact.

I would add one word for any student beginning economic study who may be discouraged by the severity of the effort which the study, as he will find it exemplified here, seems to require of him. The complicated analyses which economists endeavour to carry through are not mere gymnastic. They are instruments for the bettering of human life. The misery and squalor that surround us, the dying fire of hope in many millions of European homes, the injurious luxury of some wealthy families, the terrible uncertainty overshadowing many families of the poor—these are evils too plain to be ignored. By the knowledge that our science seeks it is possible that they may be restrained. Out of the darkness light! To search for it is the task, to find it, perhaps, the prize, which the "dismal science of Political Economy" offers to those who face its discipline.

A. C. P.

KING'S COLLEGE,
CAMBRIDGE, *June* 1920.

ANALYTICAL TABLE OF CONTENTS

PART I

WELFARE AND THE NATIONAL DIVIDEND

CHAPTER I

CHAPTER II

ix

CHAPTER III

§ 1. For the most part economic causes act upon economic welfare, not directly, but through the national dividend. §§ 2-3. In spite of the paradoxes involved, this is most conveniently taken to embrace only things purchased with money income, together with the services a man obtains from inhabiting a house owned by himself. §§ 4-7. The *national dividend* and the national consumable income are distinguished, and various problems connected with the definition and evaluation of the dividend are examined.

CHAPTER IV

§ 1. Economic welfare is dependent on (1) the average volume, (2) the distribution, and (3) the variability of the national dividend. §§ 2-4. After an analysis of difficulties, a first main proposition is set out as follows : Any cause, which, without the exercise of compulsion or pressure upon people to make them work more than their wishes and interests dictate, increases productive efficiency and, therewith, the average volume of the national dividend, provided that it neither injures the distribution nor augments the variability of the country's consumable income, will, in general, increase economic welfare. §§ 5-7. The bearing on this proposition of various complications and reactions is examined. § 8. A second main proposition is : Any cause which increases the proportion of the national dividend received by poor persons, provided that it does not lead to a contraction of the dividend and does not injuriously affect its variability, will, in general, increase economic welfare. §§ 9-11. Some general considerations bearing on this proposition are examined. §§ 12-16. Certain difficulties connected with the reactions of income upon population are examined. § 17. After a somewhat intricate discussion, a third main proposition is set out : Any cause which diminishes the variability of the national dividend, provided that it neither diminishes its volume nor injures its distribution, will, in general, increase economic welfare. § 18. A fourth main proposition, the practical importance of which is comparatively small, is : Any cause which diminishes the variability of the part of the national dividend accruing to the poor, even though it increases in corresponding measure the variability of the part accruing to the rich, will, other things being equal, increase economic welfare.

CHAPTER V

§ 1. Since the dividend is made up, not of a single sort of commodity, but of many sorts, the quantities of which vary differently, it is desirable so to define a change in the actual heterogeneous dividend.

CHAPTER V

CHAPTER VI

CHAPTER VII

CHAPTER VIII

CHAPTER IX

§ 1. Apart from the qualifying circumstances considered in the preceding chapters, our discussion suggests that State interference with competitive prices must injure the national dividend. This presumption has now to be confronted with the extensive price regulation of the war period. §§ 2-4. An account is given of the problems and practice of price control in the United Kingdom during that period. §§ 5-6. Owing to a variety of causes it is improbable that price control, in the special circumstances of the great war, damaged production to any significant extent. § 7. But there is strong reason to fear that a general permanent policy of control over competitive prices, designed to prevent groups of producers from reaping abnormal profits on favourable occasions, would not be thus innocuous.

CHAPTER X

§ 1. State regulation of prices during the war involved State regulation of distribution also. §§ 2-4. Supplies of material were allocated to different *uses* on the basis of their comparative war urgency; a criterion for which it would be difficult to find a satisfactory substitute in normal times. § 5. Within each use materials were allocated to different *firms* on the basis of their pre-war purchases; an arrangement impossible in normal times. § 6. Finished products were allocated among *ultimate consumers* on the basis of an estimate of their necessary rations. § 7. Arrangements of this kind do not directly affect the volume of the national dividend, though the price regulations to which they are supplementary, as was explained in the preceding chapter, do have this effect.

CHAPTER XI

§ 1. It will presently be necessary to inquire how far the values of marginal trade net products in different uses tend to equality under monopoly. As a preliminary to this inquiry, the conditions which determine the appearance of monopolistic power have to be studied. § 2. Circumstances, which, when the aggregate scale of an industry is given, make it structurally economical for the typical individual establishment to be large, are favourable to the advent of monopolistic power. § 3. So also are circumstances which make it structurally economical for the typical individual unit of business management (embracing, perhaps, a number of establishments) to be large. § 4. So also are conditions under which amalgamation is able greatly to reduce expenses by cutting down competitive advertisement. § 5. So also is the existence of a highly inelastic demand for any commodity, since this implies the possibility of large gains if monopolisation takes place. The influences by which

CHAPTER XV

CHAPTER XVI

PART III

THE NATIONAL DIVIDEND AND LABOUR

CHAPTER I

CHAPTER II

CHAPTER VII

CHAPTER VIII

CHAPTER IX

CHAPTER X

CHAPTER XI

CHAPTER XII

CHAPTER XIII

CHAPTER XIV

CHAPTER XV

CHAPTER XVI

CHAPTER XVII

CHAPTER XVIII

PART IV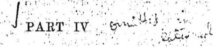

THE NATIONAL DIVIDEND AND GOVERNMENT FINANCE

CHAPTER I

CHAPTER II

CHAPTER III.

CHAPTER IV

CHAPTER V

CHAPTER VI

CHAPTER VII

CHAPTER VIII

CHAPTER IX

CHAPTER X

CHAPTER XI

PART V ✓

THE DISTRIBUTION OF THE NATIONAL DIVIDEND

CHAPTER I

CHAPTER II

CHAPTER III

CHAPTER IV

CHAPTER V

CHAPTER VI

CHAPTER VII

CHAPTER VIII

ences are open to wealthy employers as regards their workpeople, and to wealthy citizens as regards their fellow-townsmen. § 4. They may be further stimulated by a judicious use of honours and decorations. § 5. The expectation of compulsory transferences through taxation tends somewhat to check the contribution which rich people make to the upbuilding of the dividend.

CHAPTER IX

CHAPTER X

CHAPTER XI

CHAPTER XII

PART VI

THE VARIABILITY OF THE NATIONAL DIVIDEND

CHAPTER I

CHAPTER II

CHAPTER XI

CHAPTER XII

CHAPTER XIII

APPENDICES

PART I

WELFARE AND THE NATIONAL DIVIDEND

CHAPTER I

§ 1. WHEN a man sets out upon any course of inquiry, the object of his search may be either light or fruit—either knowledge for its own sake, or knowledge for the sake of good things to which it leads. In various fields of study these two ideals play parts of varying importance. In the appeal made to our interest by nearly all the great modern sciences *some* stress is laid both upon the light-bearing and upon the fruit-bearing quality, but the proportions of the blend are different in different sciences. At one end of the scale stands the most general science of all, metaphysics, the science of reality. Of the student of that science it is, indeed, true that "he yet may bring some worthy thing for waiting souls to see"; but it must be light alone, it can hardly be fruit that he brings. Most nearly akin to the metaphysician is the student of the ultimate problems of physics. The corpuscular theory of matter is, hitherto, a bearer of light alone. Here, however, the other aspect is present in promise; for speculations about the structure of the atom may lead one day to the discovery of practical means for dissociating matter and for rendering available to human use the overwhelming resources of intra-atomic energy. In the science of biology the fruit-bearing aspect is more prominent. Recent studies upon heredity have, indeed, the highest theoretical interest; but no one can reflect upon that without at the same time reflecting upon the striking practical results to which they have already led in the culture of wheat, and upon the far-reaching, if hesitating, promise that they are beginning

3

to offer for the better culture of mankind. In the sciences whose subject-matter is man as an individual there is the same variation of blending as in the natural sciences proper. In psychology the theoretic interest is dominant—particularly on that side of it which gives data to metaphysics; but psychology is also valued in some measure as a basis for the practical art of education. In human physiology, on the other hand, the theoretic interest, though present, is subordinate, and the science has long been valued mainly as a basis for the art of medicine. Last of all we come to those sciences that deal, not with individual men, but with groups of men; that body of infant sciences which some writers call sociology. Light on the laws that lie behind development in history, even light upon particular facts, has, in the opinion of many, high value for its own sake. But there will, I think, be general agreement that in the sciences of human society, be their appeal as bearers of light never so high, it is the promise of fruit and not of light that chiefly merits our regard. There is a celebrated, if somewhat too strenuous, passage in Macaulay's Essay on History : "No past event has any 'intrinsic importance. The knowledge of it is valuable, only as it leads us to form just calculations with regard to the future. A history which does not serve this purpose, though it may be filled with battles, treaties and commotions, is as useless as the series of turnpike tickets collected by Sir Matthew Mite." That paradox is partly true. If it were not for the hope that a scientific study of men's social actions may lead, not necessarily directly or immediately, but at some time and in some way, to practical results in social improvement, not a few students of these actions would regard the time devoted to their study as time misspent. That is true of all social sciences, but especially true of Economics. For Economics "is a study of mankind in the ordinary business of life"; and it is not in the ordinary business of life that mankind is most interesting or inspiring. One who desired knowledge of man apart from the fruits of knowledge, would seek it in the history of religious enthusiasm, of martyrdom, or of love; he would not seek it in the market-place. When

we elect to watch the play of human motives that are
ordinary—that are sometimes mean and dismal and ignoble
—our impulse is not the philosopher's impulse, knowledge
for the sake of knowledge, but rather the physiologist's,
knowledge for the healing that knowledge may help to
bring. Wonder, Carlyle declared, is the beginning of philo-
sophy. It is not wonder, but rather the social enthusiasm
which revolts from the sordidness of mean streets and the
joylessness of withered lives, that is the beginning of economic
science. Here, if in no other field, Comte's great phrase
holds good: "It is for the heart to suggest our problems;
it is for the intellect to solve them. . . . The only position
for which the intellect is primarily adapted is to be the servant
of the social sympathies."

§ 2. If this conception of the motive behind economic
study is accepted, it follows that the type of science that
the economist will endeavour to develop must be one adapted
to form the basis of an art. It will not, indeed, itself be
an art, or directly enunciate precepts of government. It is
a positive science of what is and tends to be, not a normative
science of what ought to be. Nor will it limit itself to
those fields of positive scientific inquiry which have an obvious
relevance to immediate practical problems. For this course
would hamper thorough investigation, and shut out inquiries
that might ultimately bear fruit. For, as has been well said,
"in our most theoretical moods we may be nearest to our
most practical applications."[1] But, though wholly independent
in its tactics and its strategy, it will be guided in general
direction by practical interest. This decides its choice of
essential form. For there are two main types of positive
science. On the one side are the sciences of Formal Logic
and Pure Mathematics, whose function it is to discover
implications. On the other side are the realistic sciences,
such as physics, chemistry, and biology, which are concerned with actualities. The distinction is drawn out in
Mr. Russell's *Principles of Mathematics*. "Since the growth
of non-Euclidean Geometry, it has appeared that pure
mathematics has no concern with the question whether the

[1] Whitehead, *Introduction to Mathematics*, p. 100.

axioms and propositions of Euclid hold of actual space or
not: this is a question for realistic mathematics, to be
decided, so far as any decision is possible, by experiment
and observation. What pure mathematics asserts is merely
that the Euclidean propositions follow from the Euclidean
axioms, *i.e.* it asserts an implication: any space which
has such and such properties has also such and such other
properties. Thus, as dealt with in pure mathematics, the
Euclidean and non-Euclidean Geometries are equally true:
in each nothing is affirmed except implications. All propositions as to what actually exists, like the space we live in,
belong to experimental or empirical science, not to mathematics."[1] This distinction is applicable to the field of
economic investigation. It is open to us to construct an
Economic Science either of the pure type represented by pure
mathematics or of the realistic type represented by experimental
physics. Pure economics in this sense—an unaccustomed sense,
no doubt—would study equilibria and disturbances of equilibria
among groups of persons actuated by any set of motives *x*.
Under it, among innumerable other subdivisions, would be
included, at once an Adam-Smithian Political Economy, in
which *x* is given the value of the motives assigned to the
economic man—or to the normal man—and a non-Adam-
Smithian Political Economy, corresponding to the geometry
of Lobatschewsky, under which *x* consists of love of work
and hatred of earnings. For Pure Economics both these
Political Economies would be equally true; it would not
be relevant to inquire what the value of *x* is among the
actual men who are living in the world now. Contrasted with
this pure science stands Realistic Economics, the interest
of which is concentrated upon the world known in experience,
and in no wise extends to the commercial doings of a
community of angels. Now, if our end is practice, it is
obvious that a Political Economy that did so extend would
be for us merely an amusing toy. Hence, it must be the
realistic, and not the pure, type of science that constitutes the
object of our search. We shall endeavour to elucidate, not any

---

[1] *Principles of Mathematics*, p. 5. I have substituted *realistic* for Mr.
Russell's word *applied* in this passage.

generalised system of possible worlds, but the actual world
of men and women as they are found in experience to be.

§ 3. But, if it is plain that a science of the pure type will
not serve our purpose, it is equally plain that Realism, in the
sense of a mere descriptive catalogue of observed facts, will
not serve it either.   Infinite narration by itself can never
enable forecasts to be made, and it is, of course, capacity to
make forecasts that practice requires.   Before this capacity
can be obtained, facts must be passed upon by reason.   Besides
the brute facts, there must be what Browning calls, "something
of mine which, mixed up with the mass, made it bear hammer
and be firm to file."   It is just the presence of this *something*
which is essential to a realistic science as distinguished from
mere description.   In realistic science facts are not simply
brought together; they are compelled by thought to *speak*.   As
M. Poincaré well writes: "Science is built up of facts as a
house is built of stones; but an accumulation of facts is no
more a science than a heap of stones is a house."[1]   Astrono-
mical physics is not merely a catalogue of the positions which
certain stars have been observed to occupy on various occasions.
Biology is not merely a list of the results of a number of
experiments in breeding.   Rather, every science, through
examination and cross-examination of the particular facts
which it is able to ascertain, seeks to discover the general
laws of whose operation these particular facts are instances.
The motions of the heavenly bodies are exhibited in the light
of the laws of Newton; the breeding of the blue Andalusian
fowl in the light of that of Mendel. . These laws, furthermore,
are not merely summaries of the observed facts re-stated in a
shorthand form.   They are *generalisations*, and, as such, extend
our knowledge to facts that have not been observed, may be,
that have not as yet even occurred.   On what philosophical
basis generalisations of this sort rest we are not here concerned
to inquire.   It is enough that in every realistic science they
are *made*.   As Mr. Whetham, speaking of physics, puts it, any
such science "seeks to establish general rules which describe
the sequence of phenomena in *all* cases."[2]   It is only by

[1] *Science and Hypothesis*, p. 141.
[2] *Recent Developments in Physical Science*, p. 30. The italics are mine.

reference to these general rules that the forecasts, which practice needs, are rendered possible. It is in their fundamental aspect as an organon of laws, and not in their superficial aspect as a description of facts, that the realistic sciences have bearing upon the conduct of affairs. The establishment of such an organon adapted and ready for application to particular problems is the ideal at which they aim.

§ 4. To say this without saying something more, would, however, be very misleading. It is not pretended that, at the present stage of its development, economic science is able to provide an organon even remotely approaching to what it imagines for itself as its ideal. Full guidance for practice requires, to borrow Dr. Marshall's phrase, capacity to carry out quantitative, not merely *qualitative*, analysis. "Qualitative analysis tells the ironmaster that there is *some* sulphur in his ore, but it does not enable him to decide whether it is worth while to smelt the ore at all, and, if it is, then by what process. For that purpose he needs quantitative analysis, which will tell him *how much* sulphur there is in the ore."[1] Capacity to provide information of this kind Economic Science at present almost entirely lacks. Before the application of general laws to particular problems can yield quantitative results, these laws themselves must be susceptible of quantitative statement. The law is the major premiss and the particular facts of any problem the minor. When the statement of the law lacks precision, the conclusion must generally suffer from the same defect. And, unfortunately, the task of setting out economic laws in precise form has scarcely been begun. For this there are three reasons. First, the relations which have to be determined are extremely numerous. In physics the fundamental thing, the gravitation constant, expressing the relation between distance and attractive force, is the same for all sorts of matter. But the fundamental things in the economic world—the schedules expressing the desires or aversions of groups of people for different sorts of commodities and services—are not thus simple and uniform. We are in the position in which the physicist would be if tin attracted iron in the inverse ratio of the cube of its distance, lead in that of the square of its

[1] Marshall, *The Old Generation of Economists and the New*, p. 11.

distance, and copper in some other ratio. We cannot say, as he can of his attractions, that the amount offered or required of every several commodity is one and the same specified function of the price. All that we can say in this general way is that it is *some one* of a specified large family of functions of the price. Hence, in Economics there is not, as in Dynamics, one fundamental law of general application, but a great number of laws, all expressible, as it were, in equations of similar form but with different constants. On account of this multiplicity, the determination of those constants, or to put the matter broadly, the measurement of the elasticities of demand and supply of the various commodities in which economics is interested, is a very large task. Secondly, this task is one in attacking which the principal weapon employed by other sciences in their inquiries cannot be fully used. "Theory," said Leonardo da Vinci, "is the general; experiments are the soldiers." Economic science has already well-trained generals, but, because of the nature of the material in which it works, the soldiers are hard to obtain. "The surgeon dissects a dead body before he operates on a living one, and operates upon an animal before he operates upon a human being; the mechanic makes a working model and tests it before he builds the full-sized machine. Every step is, whenever possible, tested by experiment in these matters before risks are run. In this way the unknown is robbed of most of its terrors."[1] In economics, for the simple reason that its subject matter is living and free men, direct experiment under conditions adequately controlled is hardly ever feasible. But there is a third and even more serious difficulty. Even if the constants which economists wish to determine were less numerous, and the method of experiment more accessible, we should still be faced with the fact that the constants themselves are different at different times. The gravitation constant is the same always. But the economic constants—these elasticities of demand and supply—depending, as they do, upon human consciousness, are liable to vary. The constitution of the molecule, as it were, and not merely its position, changes under the influence of environment. Thus the real injury done to Ireland by

[1] Cecil, *Conservatism*, p. 18.

the earlier English administration of that country was not the destruction of specific industries or even the sweeping of its commerce from the seas. " The real grievance lies in the fact that something had been taken from our industrial character which could not be remedied by the mere removal of the restrictions. Not only had the tree been stripped, but the roots had been destroyed."[1] This malleability in the actual substance with which economic study deals means that the goal sought is itself perpetually shifting, so that, even if it were possible by experiment exactly to determine the values of the economic constants to-day, we could not say with confidence that this determination would hold good also of to-morrow. Hence the inevitable shortcomings of our science. We can, indeed, by a careful study of all relevant facts, learn *something* about the elasticities of demand and supply for a good number of things, but we cannot ascertain their magnitude with any degree of exactness. In other words, our fundamental laws, and therefore inferences from these laws in particular conditions, cannot at present be thrown into any quantitatively precise form. The result is that, when, as often happens, a practical issue turns upon the balancing of opposing considerations, even though these considerations are wholly economic, Economic Science must almost always speak with an uncertain voice.

§ 5. The preceding paragraph has been somewhat of a digression. It has now to be added that, just as the motive and purpose of our inquiry govern its form, so also they control its scope. The goal sought is to make more easy practical measures to promote welfare—practical measures which statesmen may build upon the work of the economist, just as Marconi, the inventor, built upon the discoveries of Hertz. Welfare, however, is a thing of very wide range. There is no need here to enter upon a general discussion of its content. It will be sufficient to lay down more or less dogmatically two propositions; first, that welfare includes states of consciousness only, and not material things; secondly, that welfare can be brought under the category of greater and less. A general investigation of all the various groups of causes by which welfare thus conceived may be

[1] Plunkett, *Ireland in the New Century*, p. 19.

affected would constitute a task so enormous and complicated as to be quite impracticable. It is, therefore, necessary to limit our subject-matter. In doing this we are naturally attracted towards that portion of the field in which the methods of science seem likely to work at best advantage. This they can clearly do when there is present something measurable on which analytical machinery can get a firm grip. The one obvious instrument of measurement available in social life is money. Hence, the range of our inquiry becomes restricted to that part of social welfare that can be brought directly or indirectly into relation with the measuring-rod of money. This part of welfare may be called economic welfare. It is not, indeed, possible to separate it in any rigid way from other parts, for the part which *can* be brought into relation with a money measure will be different according as we mean by *can*, "can easily" or "can with mild straining" or "can with violent straining." The outline of our territory is, therefore, necessarily vague. Professor Cannan has well observed : " We must face, and face boldly, the fact that there is no precise line between economic and non-economic satisfactions, and, therefore, the province of economics cannot be marked out by a row of posts or a fence, like a political territory or a landed property. We can proceed from the undoubtedly economic at one end of the scale to the undoubtedly non-economic at the other end without finding anywhere a fence to climb or a ditch to cross."[1] Nevertheless, though no precise boundary between economic and non-economic welfare exists, yet the test of accessibility to a money measure serves well enough to set up a rough distinction. Economic welfare, as loosely defined by this test, is the subject-matter of economic science. The purpose of this volume is to attempt a partial study of the causes affecting economic welfare in actual modern societies.

§ 6. At first glance this programme, if somewhat ambitious, appears, at all events, a legitimate one. But reflection soon shows that the proposal to treat in isolation the causes affecting one part of welfare only is open to a serious objection. Our ultimate interest is, of course, in the effects

[1] *Wealth*, pp. 17-18.

which the various causes investigated are likely to have
upon welfare as a whole. But there is no guarantee that
the effects produced on the part of welfare that can be
brought into relation with the measuring-rod of money
may not be cancelled by effects of a contrary kind brought
about in other parts, or aspects, of welfare; and, if this
happens, the practical usefulness of our conclusions is wholly
destroyed. The difficulty, it must be carefully observed, is
not that, since economic welfare is only a part of welfare
as a whole, welfare will often change while economic
welfare remains the same, so that a given change in
economic welfare will seldom synchronise with an equal
change in welfare as a whole. All that this means is that
economic welfare will not serve for a *barometer* or *index* of
total welfare. But that, for our purpose, is of no importance.
What we wish to learn is, not how large welfare is, or
has been, but how its magnitude would be affected by the
introduction of causes which it is in the power of statesmen
or private persons to call into being. The failure of economic
welfare to serve as an *index* of total welfare is no evidence that
the study of it will fail to afford this latter information:
for, though a whole may consist of many varying parts, so
that a change in one part never *measures* the change in
the whole, yet the change in the part may always *affect*
the change in the whole by its full amount. If this
condition is satisfied, the practical importance of economic
study is fully established. It will not, indeed, tell us how
total welfare, after the introduction of an economic cause, will
differ from what it was before; but it will tell us how total
welfare will differ from what it would have been if that
cause had not been introduced: and this, and not the other,
is the information of which we are in search. The real
objection then is, not that economic welfare is a bad *index*
of total welfare, but that an economic cause may affect non-
economic welfare in ways that cancel its effect on economic
welfare. This objection requires careful consideration.

§ 7. One very important aspect of it is as follows. Human
beings are both "ends in themselves" and instruments of
production. On the one hand, a man who is attuned to

the beautiful in nature or in art, whose character is simple
and sincere, whose passions are controlled and sympathies
developed, is in himself an important element in the ethical
value of the world; the way in which he feels and thinks
actually constitutes a part of welfare.   On the other hand,
a man who can perform complicated industrial operations,
sift difficult evidence, or advance some branch of practical
activity, is an instrument well-fitted to produce things whose
use yields welfare.   The welfare to which the former of
these men contributes directly is non-economic; that to
which the latter contributes indirectly is economic.   The
fact we have to face is that, in some measure, it is open to
the community to choose between these two sorts of men,
and that, by concentrating its effort upon the economic welfare
embodied in the second, it may unconsciously sacrifice the
non-economic welfare embodied in the first.   The point is
easy of illustration.   The weak and disjointed Germany of
a century ago was the home of Goethe and Schiller, Kant
and Fichte.   "We know what the old Germany gave the
world," says Mr. Dawson in a book published several years
before the war, "and for that gift the world will ever be
grateful; we do not know what modern Germany, the
Germany of the overflowing barns and the full argosies, has to
offer, beyond its materialistic science and its merchandise. . . .
The German systems of education, which are incomparable
so far as their purpose is the production of scholars and
teachers, or of officials and functionaries, to move the cranks,
turn the screws, gear the pulleys, and oil the wheels of the
complicated national machine, are far from being equally
successful in the making of character or individuality."[1]   In
short, the attention of the German people was so concentrated on the idea of learning to *do* that they did not
care, as in former times, for learning to *be*.   Nor does Germany
stand alone before this charge; as witness the following
description of modern England written by an Englishman from
the standpoint of an Oriental spectator.   "By your works
you may be known.   Your triumphs in the mechanical arts
are the obverse of your failure in all that calls for spiritual

[1] *The Evolution of Modern Germany*, pp. 15-16.

insight. Machines of every kind you can make and use
to perfection; but you cannot build a house, or write a
poem, or paint a picture; still less can you worship or
aspire. . . . Your outer man as well as your inner is
dead; you are blind and deaf. Ratiocination has taken
the place of perception; and your whole life is an infinite
syllogism from premises you have not examined to conclusions
you have not anticipated or willed. Everywhere means,
nowhere an end. Society a huge engine and that engine
itself out of gear. Such is the picture your civilisation
presents to my imagination."[1] There is, of course, exaggeration
in this indictment; but there is also truth. At all events it
brings out vividly the point which is here at issue; that efforts
devoted to the production of people who are good instruments
may involve a failure to produce people who are good men.

§ 8. The possibility of conflict between the effects of economic
causes upon economic welfare and upon welfare in general, which
these considerations emphasise, is easily explained. The only
aspects of conscious life which can, as a rule, be brought into
relation with a money measure, and which, therefore, fall
within economic welfare, are a certain limited group of *satisfactions* and *dissatisfactions*. But conscious life is a complex
of many elements, and includes, not only these satisfactions
and dissatisfactions, but also other satisfactions and dissatisfactions, and along with them, cognitions, emotions and
desires. Environmental causes operating to change economic
satisfactions may, therefore, either in the same act or as a
consequence of it, alter some of these other elements. The
ways in which they do this may be distinguished for purposes
of illustration into two principal groups.

First, non-economic welfare is liable to be modified by the
manner in which income is earned. For the surroundings of
work react upon the quality of life. Ethical quality is affected
by the occupations—menial service, agricultural labour, artistic
creation, independent as against subordinate economic positions,[2]

---

[1] Dickinson, *Letters of John Chinaman,* pp. 25-6.
[2] Thus, it is important to notice that machinery, as it comes to be more
elaborate and expensive, makes it, *pro tanto,* more difficult for small men, alike
in industry and agriculture, to start independent businesses of their own. Cf.
Quaintance, *Farm Machinery,* p. 58.

monotonous repetition of the same operation,[1] and so on—into which the desires of consumers impel the people who work to satisfy them. It is affected, too, by the influence which these people exert on others with whom they may be brought into personal contact. The social aspect of Chinese labour in the Transvaal and of the attempt by Australian pastoralists to maintain the convict system, as a source of labour supply,[2] have relevance to welfare. So, too, have the unity of interest and occupation which characterise the farm family as distinguished from the town-dwelling family.[3] In the Indian village "the collaboration of the family members not only economises expenses, but sweetens labour. Culture and refinement come easily to the artisan through his work amidst his kith and kin."[4] Thus, the industrial revolution, when it led the cottager from his home into the factory, had an effect on other things besides production. In like manner, increased efficiency in output was not the only result which the agricultural revolution, with its enclosures and large-scale farming, brought about. There was also a social change in the destruction of the old yeoman class. The human relations that arise out of industrial relations are also relevant. In the great co-operative movement, for example, there is a non-economic side at least as important as the economic. Whereas in the organisation of ordinary competitive industry opposition of interest, both as between competing sellers and as between sellers and buyers, necessarily stands in the forefront, and results at times in trickery and a sense of mutual suspicion, in a co-operative organisation unity of interest

[1] Munsterberg writes "that the feeling of monotony depends much less upon the particular kind of work than upon the special disposition of the individual" (*Psychology and Industrial Efficiency*, p. 198). But, of course, the *ethical effect* of monotony must be distinguished from the unpleasantness of it. This effect is not measured adequately by the money offered as wages. Marshall maintains that monotony of life is the important thing, and argues that variety of life is compatible with monotony of occupation, in so far as machines take over straining forms of work, with the result that "nervous force is not very much exhausted by the ordinary work of a factory" (*Principles of Economics*, p. 263). On the other hand, as Smart observes, "the work of the majority is not only toilsome, monotonous, undeveloping, but takes up the better part of the day, and leaves little energy for other pursuits" (*Second Thoughts of an Economist*, p. 107).
[2] Cf. V. S. Clark, *The Labour Movement in Australia*, p. 32.
[3] Cf. *Proceedings of the American Economic Association*, vol. x. pp. 234-5.
[4] Cf. Muckergee, *The Foundations of Indian Economics*, p. 326.

is paramount. This circumstance has its influence on the general tone of life. "As a member of a society with interests in common with others, the individual consciously and unconsciously develops the social virtues. Honesty becomes imperative, and is enforced by the whole group on the individual, loyalty to the whole group is made an essential for the better development of individual powers. To cheat the society is to injure a neighbour."[1] In the relations between employers and workpeople in ordinary industry the non-economic element is fully as significant. The *esprit de corps* and interest in the fortunes of the firm, which animate the workpeople in establishments where the personal intercourse of employers and employed is cordial, besides leading to increased production of wealth, *is* in itself an addition to welfare. As large-scale industry extended during the eighteenth and nineteenth centuries, employers and employed became more distant in station, and their opportunities of meeting one another diminished. In the wake of this inevitable physical separation there followed a moral separation—"the personal alienation of the employer from his fellow-men whom he engages to work for him in large numbers."[2] This spirit of hostility was an obvious negative element brought about in non-economic welfare by an economic cause; and the partial suppression of it through Boards of Conciliation and Copartnership arrangements is an equally obvious positive element. Nor is this all. It is more and more coming to be recognised that, if one root of "labour unrest" has been dissatisfaction with rates of wages, a second root, also of great importance, has been dissatisfaction with the general *status* of wage-labour—the feeling that the industrial system, as it is to-day, deprives the workpeople of the liberties and responsibilities proper to free men, and renders

[1] Smith-Gordon and Staples, *Rural Reconstruction in Ireland*, p. 240. Cf. the enthusiastic picture which Wolff draws of the general social benefits of rural co-operation on the Raiffeisen plan : "How it creates a desire and readiness to receive and assimilate instruction, technical and general, how it helps to raise the character of the people united by it, making for sobriety, strict honesty, good family life, and good living generally." It has been seen, he says, to produce these effects "among the comparatively educated peasantry of Germany, the illiterate country folk of Italy, the primitive cultivators of Serbia, and it is beginning to have something the same effect among the ryots of India" (*The Future of Agriculture*, p. 481).
[2] Gilman, *A Dividend to Labour*, p. 15.

them mere tools to be used or dispensed with at the convenience of others: the sense, in short, as Mazzini put it long ago, that capital is the *despot* of labour.[1] Changes in industrial organisation that tend to give greater control over their own lives to workpeople, whether through workmen's councils to overlook matters of discipline and workshop organisation in conjunction with the employer, or through a democratically elected Parliament directly responsible for nationalised industries, or, if this should prove feasible, through some form of State-recognised and State-controlled national guilds,[2] might increase welfare as a whole, even though they were to leave unchanged, or actually to damage, economic welfare.

Secondly, non-economic welfare is liable to be modified by the manner in which income is spent. Of different acts of consumption that yield equal satisfactions, one may exercise a debasing, and another an elevating, influence. The reflex effect upon people's characters of public museums, or even of municipal baths,[3] is very different from the reflex effect of equal satisfactions in a public bar. The coarsening and brutalising influence of bad housing accommodation is an incident not less important than the direct dissatisfaction involved in it. Instances of the same kind could be multiplied. The point that they would illustrate is obviously of large practical importance. Imagine, for example, that a statesman is considering how far inequality in the distribution of wealth influences welfare as a whole, and not merely in its economic aspects. He will reflect that the satisfaction of some of the desires of the rich, such as gambling excitement or luxurious sensual enjoyment, or perhaps, in Eastern countries, opium-eating, involves reactions on character ethically inferior to those involved in the satisfaction of primary physical needs,

[1] Cf. Mazzini, *The Duties of Man*, p. 99.
[2] Cf. *The Meaning of National Guilds*, by Bechhofer and Reckitt, *passim.* "The essence of Labour's demand for responsibility is that it should be recognised as responsible to the community, not to the capitalist" (p. 100). The goal of National Guilds "is the control of production by self-governing Guilds of workers sharing with the State the control of the produce of their labour" (p. 285). The fact that schemes of industrial reorganisation on these lines are exposed to serious practical difficulties, which their authors do not as yet seem fully to have faced, does not render any less admirable the *spirit* of this ideal.
[3] Cf. Darwin, *Municipal Trade*, p. 75.

to the securing of which the capital and labour controlled by the demand of the rich would, if transferred to the poor, probably be devoted. On the other hand, he will reflect that other satisfactions purchased by the rich—those, for example, connected with literature and art[1]—involve reactions that are ethically superior to those connected with the primary needs, and still more to those derived from excessive indulgence in stimulants. These very real elements in welfare will, indeed, enter into relation with the measuring rod of money, and so be counted in economic welfare, in so far as one group of people devote income to purchasing things *for* other people. When they do this, they are likely to take account of the total effect, and not merely of the effect on the satisfactions of those people—especially if the said people are their own children. For, as Sidgwick acutely observes: "A genuine regard for our neighbour, when not hampered by the tyranny of custom, prompts us to give him what we think really good for him, whereas natural self-regard prompts us to give ourselves what we like."[2] In these special circumstances, therefore, the gap between the effect on economic welfare and the effect on total welfare is partially bridged. Generally, however, it is not so bridged.

§ 9. There is one further consideration, of the great importance of which recent events can leave no doubt. It has to do with the possible conflict, long ago emphasised by Adam Smith, between opulence and defence. Lack of security against successful hostile attack may involve "dissatisfactions" of a very terrible kind. These things lie outside the economic sphere, but the risk of them may easily be affected by economic policy. It is true, no doubt, that between economic strength and capacity for war there is a certain rough agreement. As Adam Smith wrote: "The

---

[1] Sidgwick, for example, observes after a careful discussion : "There seems, therefore, to be a serious danger that a thorough-going equalisation of wealth among the members of a modern civilised community would have a tendency to check the growth of culture in the community" (*Principles of Political Economy*, p. 523).

[2] *Practical Ethics*, p. 20. Cf. Effertz: "Ce que les intéressés savent généralement mieux que les non-intéressés, ce sont les *moyens* propres à réaliser ce qu'ils croient être leur intérêt. Mais, dans la détermination de l'intérêt le non-intéressé voit généralement plus clair."(*Antagonismes économiques*, pp. 237-8).

nation which, from the annual produce of its domestic
industry, from the annual revenue arising out of its lands,
labours and consumable stock, has wherewithal to purchase
those consumable goods in distant countries can maintain
foreign wars there."[1]   But agreement between economic
and military strength is ultimate and general, not immediate
and detailed.   It must, therefore, be clearly recognised that
the effect upon economic welfare of the policy which a
State adopts towards agriculture, shipping and industries
producing war material is often a very subordinate part of its
whole effect. Injury to economic welfare may need to be
accepted for the sake of defensive strategy. Economically it
is probably to the advantage of this country to purchase
the greater part of its food supplies from abroad in exchange
for manufactured goods, and to keep more than two-thirds
of its cultivated land under grass—in which state comparatively little capital and labour is employed upon it and
correspondingly little human food produced.[2]   In a world of
perpetual peace this policy would also probably be advantageous on the whole; for a small proportion of the population
engaged in agriculture does not necessarily imply a small
proportion living under rural conditions.   But, when account
is taken of the possibility that imports may be cut off by
blockade in war, that inference need not follow.   There can
be little doubt that Germany's policy of conserving and
developing agriculture for many years at an economic loss
enabled her to resist the British blockade in the Great War
for a much longer period than would otherwise have been
possible; and, though there are, of course, alternative means
of defence, such as the establishment of large national grain
stores, it is, from a general political point of view, a debatable question whether in this country some form of artificial
encouragement should be given to agriculture as a partial
insurance against the danger of food difficulties in the
event of war.   This issue, and the kindred issue concerning
materials and industries essential for the conduct of war,

---

[1] Wealth of Nations, p. 333.
[2] Cf. The Recent Development of German Agriculture [Cd. 8305], 1916,
p. 42 and passim.

cannot be decided by reference to economic considerations alone.

§ 10. The preceding discussion makes it plain that any rigid inference from effects on economic welfare to effects on total welfare is out of the question. In some fields the divergence between the two effects will be insignificant, but in others it will be very wide. Nevertheless, I submit that, in the absence of special knowledge, there is room for a judgment of probability. When we have ascertained the effect of any cause on economic welfare, we may, unless, of course, there is specific evidence to the contrary, regard this effect as *probably* equivalent in direction, though not in magnitude, to the effect on total welfare; and, when we have ascertained that the effect of one cause is more favourable than that of another cause to economic welfare, we may, on the same terms, conclude that the effect of this cause on total welfare is probably more favourable. In short, there is a presumption—what Professor Edgeworth calls an "unverified probability"—that qualitative conclusions about the effect of an economic cause upon economic welfare will hold good also of the effect on total welfare. This presumption is especially strong when experience suggests that the non-economic effects produced are likely to be small. But in all circumstances the burden of proof lies upon those who hold that the presumption should be overruled.

§ 11. The above result suggests *prima facie* that economic science, when it shall have come to full development, is likely to furnish a powerful guide to practice. Against this suggestion there remains, however, one considerable obstacle. When the conclusion set out in the preceding section is admitted to be valid, a question may still be raised as to its practical utility. Granted, it may be said, that the effects produced by economic causes upon economic welfare are probably, in some measure, representative of those produced on total welfare, we have really gained nothing. For the effects produced upon economic welfare itself cannot, the argument runs, be ascertained beforehand by those partial and limited investigations which alone fall within the scope of economic science. The reason for this is that the effects upon economic welfare produced by any economic cause are likely to be modified by the non-economic conditions, which, in one form or another, are always present, but which economic science is not adapted to investigate. The difficulty is stated very clearly by J. S. Mill in his *Logic*. The study of a *part* of things, he points out, cannot in any circumstances be expected to yield more than approximate results: "Whatever affects, in an appreciable degree, any one element of the social state, affects through it all the other elements. . . : We can never either understand in theory or command in practice the condition of a society in any one respect, without taking into consideration its condition in all other respects. There is no social phenomenon which is not more or less influenced by every other part of the condition of the same society, and, therefore, by every cause which is influencing any other of the contemporaneous social phenomena."[1] In other words, the effects of economic causes are certain to be partially dependent on non-economic circumstances, in such wise that the same cause will produce somewhat different economic effects according to the general character of, say, the political or religious conditions that prevail. So far as this kind of dependence exists, it is obvious that causal propositions in economics can only be laid down subject to the condition that things outside the economic sphere either remain constant or, at least, do not vary beyond certain defined limits. Does this condition destroy the practical utility of our science ? I hold that, among nations with a stable general culture like those inhabiting Western Europe, the condition is fulfilled nearly enough to render the results reached by economic inquiry reasonably good approximations to truth. This is the view taken by Mill. While fully recognising "the paramount ascendancy which the general state of civilisation and social progress in any given society must exercise over all the partial and subordinate phenomena," he concludes that the portion of social phenomena, in which the immediately determining causes are principally those that act through the desire for wealth, "do *mainly* depend, at least in the first

[1] *Logic*, ii. p. 488.

resort, on one class of circumstances only." He adds that, "even when other circumstances interfere, the ascertainment of the effect due to the one class of circumstances alone is a sufficiently intricate and difficult business to make it expedient to perform it once for all, and then allow for the effect of the modifying circumstances; especially as certain fixed combinations of the former are apt to recur often, in conjunction with ever varying circumstances of the latter class."[1] I have nothing to add to this statement. If it is accepted, the difficulty discussed in this section need no longer give us pause. It is not necessarily impracticable to ascertain by means of economic science the approximate effects of economic causes upon economic welfare. The bridge that has been built in earlier sections between economic welfare and total welfare need not, therefore, rust unused.

[1] *Logic*, ii. pp. 490-91.

CHAPTER II

DESIRES AND SATISFACTIONS

§ 1. IN the preceding chapter economic welfare was taken broadly to consist in that group of satisfactions and dissatisfactions which can be brought into relation with a money measure. We have now to observe that this relation is not a direct one, but is mediated through desires and aversions. That is to say, the money which a person is prepared to offer for a thing measures directly, not the satisfaction he will get from the thing, but the intensity of his desire for it. This distinction, obvious when stated, has been somewhat obscured for English-speaking students by the employment of the term utility—which naturally carries an association with satisfaction—to represent desiredness. Thus, when one thing is desired by a person more keenly than another, it is said to possess a greater utility to that person. Several writers have endeavoured to get rid of the confusion which this use of words generates by substituting for " utility " in the above sense some other term, such, for example, as Professor Pareto's " ophelimity." It may be suggested that, in English writing, " desiredness " would be equally effective and much more readily intelligible. I shall myself employ that term. The verbal issue is, however, a subordinate one. The substantial point is that we are entitled to use the comparative amounts of money which a person is prepared to offer for two different things as a test of the comparative satisfactions which these things will yield to him, only on condition that the ratio between the intensities of desire that he feels for the two is equal to the ratio between the amounts of satisfaction which their possession will yield to him. This condition, however, is not always fulfilled. We are not,

23

of course, here concerned with the obvious fact that people's expectations as to the satisfaction they will derive from different commodities are often erroneous. The point is that, even apart from this, the condition sometimes breaks down. Thus, Sidgwick observes: " I, do not judge pleasures [and the same thing obviously holds of satisfactions other than pleasures] to be greater and less exactly in proportion as they exercise more or less influence in stimulating the will to actions tending to sustain or produce them ": [1] and again, " I do not think it ought to be assumed that intensity of immediate gratification is always in proportion to intensity of pre-existing desire." [2] This consideration obviously has great theoretical importance. When it is recollected that all comparisons between different taxes and different monopolies, which proceed by an analysis of their effects upon consumer's surplus, tacitly assume that demand price (the money measure of desire) is also the money measure of satisfaction, it is apparent that it *may* have great practical importance also. The question whether it has in actual fact great practical importance has, therefore, to be examined.

§ 2. In a broad general way we may, I think, safely answer this question in the negative. It is fair to suppose that most commodities, especially those of wide consumption that are required, as articles of food and clothing are, for direct personal use, will be wanted as a means to satisfaction, and will, consequently, be desired with intensities proportioned to the satisfactions they are expected to yield.[3] For the most general purposes of economic analysis, therefore, not much harm is likely to be done by the current practice of regarding money demand price indifferently as the measure of a desire and as the measure of the satisfaction felt when the desired thing is obtained. To this general conclusion, however, there is one very important exception.

§ 3. This exception has to do with people's attitude toward the future. Generally speaking, everybody prefers present pleasures or satisfactions of given magnitude to future pleasures or satisfactions of equal magnitude, even when the latter are

---

[1] *Methods of Ethics,* p. 126.
[2] *The Ethics of T. H. Green,* etc., p. 340.
[3] Cf. my " Some Remarks on Utility," *Economic Journal,* 1903, p. 58 *et seq.*

perfectly certain to occur. But this preference for present pleasures does not—the idea is self-contradictory—imply that a present pleasure of given magnitude is any *greater* than a future pleasure of the same magnitude. It implies only that our telescopic faculty is defective, and that we, therefore, see future pleasures, as it were, on a diminished scale. That this is the right explanation is proved by the fact that exactly the same diminution is experienced when, apart from our tendency to forget ungratifying incidents, we contemplate the past. Hence, the existence of preference for present over equally certain future pleasures does not imply that any economic dissatisfaction would be suffered if future pleasures were substituted at full value for present ones. The non-satisfaction this year of a man's preference to consume this year rather than next year is balanced by the satisfaction of his preference next year to consume next year rather than to have consumed this year. Hence, there is nothing to set against the fact that, if we set out a series of exactly equal satisfactions — *satisfactions*, not objects that yield satisfactions—all of them absolutely certain to occur over a series of years beginning now, the desires which a man will entertain for these several satisfactions will not be equal, but will be represented by a scale of magnitudes continually diminishing as the years to which the satisfactions are allocated become more remote. This reveals a far-reaching economic disharmony. For it implies that people distribute their resources between the present, the near future, and the remote future on the basis of a wholly irrational preference. When they have a choice between two satisfactions, they will not necessarily choose the larger of the two, but will often devote themselves to producing or obtaining a small one now in preference to a much larger one some years hence. The inevitable result is that efforts directed towards the remote future are starved relatively to those directed to the near future, while these in turn are starved relatively to efforts directed towards the present. Suppose, for example, that a person's telescopic faculty is such that he discounts future satisfactions, which are perfectly certain to occur, at the rate of 5 per cent per annum. Then, instead of being ready to work for next

year, or a year ten years hence, so long as a given increment
of effort will yield as much satisfaction as an equal increment
devoted to work for the present, he will only work for next
year so long as the yield of an increment of effort employed
for that year is 1·05 times, and for ten years hence so long
as it is $(1·05)^{10}$ times, the yield of an increment employed for
the present. It follows that the aggregate amount of economic
satisfaction which people in fact enjoy is much less than
it would be if their telescopic faculty were not perverted, but
equal (certain) satisfactions were desired with equal intensity
whatever the period at which they are destined to emerge.

§ 4. This, however, is not all. Since human life is
limited, such fruits of work or saving as accrue after a
considerable interval are not enjoyed by the person to whose
efforts they are due. This means that the satisfaction with
which his desire is connected is not his own satisfaction,
but the satisfaction of somebody else, possibly an immediate
successor whose interest he regards as nearly equivalent to his
own, possibly somebody quite remote in blood or in time about
whom he scarcely cares at all. It follows that, even though
our desires for equal satisfactions *of our own* occurring
at different times were equal, our desire for future satisfaction
would often be less intense than for present satisfaction,
because it is very likely that the future satisfaction will
not be our own. This discrepancy will be more important
the more distant is the time at which the source of future
satisfaction is likely to come into being; for every addition
to the interval increases the chance of death, not merely
to oneself, but also to children and near relatives and friends
in whom one's interest is likely to be most keen.[1] No doubt,

---

[1] If k be the fraction of importance that I attach to a pound in the hands of
my heirs as compared with myself, and $\phi(t)$ the probability that I shall be alive
t years from now, a certain pound *to me or my heirs* then attracts me now equally
with a certain pound multiplied by $\{\phi(t)+k(1-\phi(t))\}$ *to me* then. This is
obviously increased by anything that increases either $\phi(t)$ or k.

If, through an anticipated change of fortune or temperament, one pound after
t years is expected to be equivalent to $(1-a)$ times one pound now, a certain
$\{\phi(t)+k(1-\phi(t))\}$ pounds of the then prevailing sort to me then attracts me
equally with $(1-a)\{\phi(t)+k(1-\phi(t))\}$ pounds, of the now prevailing sort, to me
then. Therefore, a certain pound to my heirs will be as persuasive to call out
investment now as the above sum would be if I were certain to live for ever, and
always to be equally well off and the same in temperament.

this obstacle to investment for distant returns is partly overcome by stock-exchange devices. If £100 invested now is expected to reappear after 50 years expanded at, say, 5 per cent compound interest, the man who originally provides the £100 may be able, after a year, to sell his title in the eventual fruit for £105; the man who buys from him may be able similarly to get his capital of £105 back with 5 per cent interest after one year, and so on. In these circumstances the fact that any one man would require a higher rate of interest per annum to induce him to lock up £100 for 50 years than he would to induce him to lock up the same sum for one year makes no difference. But, of course, in actual life this device is of very narrow application. As regards investments, such as planting a forest or undertaking drainage development on one's own estate, which can only be accomplished privately, it is not applicable at all; and, even when investment is undertaken by a company, investors cannot seriously expect to find a smooth and continuous market for non-dividend paying securities.

§ 5. The practical way in which these discrepancies between desire and satisfaction work themselves out to the injury of economic welfare is by checking the creation of new capital and encouraging people to use up existing capital to such a degree that larger future advantages are sacrificed for smaller present ones. Always the chief effect is felt when the interval of time between action and consequence is long. Thus, of the check to investment, Giffen wrote: "Probably there are no works more beneficial to a community in the long run than those, like a tunnel between Ireland and Great Britain, which open an entirely new means of communication of strategical as well as of commercial value, but are not likely to pay the individual enterpriser in any short period of time." A number of other large undertakings, such as works of afforestation or water supply, the return to which is distant, are similarly handicapped by the slackness of desire towards distant satisfactions.[1] The

---

[1] In this connection the following passage from Knoop's *Principles and Methods of Municipal Trade* is of interest: "To secure an additional supply of water to a town, ten or more years of continuous work may easily be

same slackness is responsible for that over-hasty exploitation of stored gifts of nature, which must make it harder for future generations to obtain supplies of important commodities. Resources devoted to the development of high-speed vessels that, in order to secure a slightly shortened passage, consume enormous extra quantities of coal; the reckless cutting down of forests; fishing operations so conducted as to disregard breeding seasons, thus threatening certain species of fish with extinction;[1] farming operations so conducted as to exhaust the fertility of the land, are all instances in point. As a palliative of these tendencies it is natural to suggest Government intervention. Nobody, of course, holds that the State should force its citizens to act as though so much objective wealth now and in the future were of exactly equal importance. In view of the uncertainty of productive developments, to say nothing of the mortality of nations and eventually of the human race itself, this would not, even in extremest theory, be sound policy. But there is wide agreement that the State should protect the interests of the future *in some degree.* The whole movement for "conservation" in the United States is based on this conviction. It is the clear duty of Government to watch over, and, if need be, by legislative enactment, to defend the exhaustible natural resources of the country. How far it should itself, either out of taxes, or out of State loans, or by the device of guaranteed interest, press resources into undertakings from which the business community, if left to itself, would hold aloof, is a more difficult problem. The idea, to which a hasty reader of the preceding discussion might perhaps be led, that it should push them all up to the point at which the marginal £ invested yields no interest, is plainly illusory. For though, no doubt, a part of the resources which it would

required. This means that for several years a large amount of capital will be unproductive, thus seriously affecting the profits of the undertaking and making boards of directors very chary about entering upon any large scheme. . . . It is almost inconceivable that a water company would have undertaken the great schemes by which Manchester draws its supply of water from Lake Thirlmere in Cumberland, a distance of some 96 miles ; Liverpool its supply from Lake Vyrnwy in North Wales, a distance of some 78 miles ; and Birmingham its supply from the Elan Valley in Mid Wales, a distance of some 80 miles" (*loc. cit.* p. 38).

[1] Cf. Sidgwick, *Principles of Political Economy*, p. 410.

thus turn to its purposes would otherwise have been devoted to unproductive consumption, another part would have been employed by the owners in occupations yielding the normal return of interest. On the whole, we may conclude that special State stimulation, based on the class of consideration advanced here, should be confined to undertakings which promise a commercial profit, but only after an interval too long to attract private capital in the ordinary way of business.

CHAPTER III

THE NATIONAL DIVIDEND

§ 1. GENERALLY speaking, economic causes act upon the economic welfare of any country, not directly, but through the earning and spending of that objective counterpart of economic welfare which economists call the national dividend or national income. Just as economic welfare is that part of total welfare which can be brought directly or indirectly into relation with a money measure, so the national dividend—the concept has nothing to do with the dividends paid by joint stock companies—is that part of the objective income of the community that can be measured in money. The two concepts, economic welfare and the national dividend, are thus co-ordinate, in such wise that any description of the content of one of them implies a corresponding description of the content of the other. In the preceding chapter, it was shown that the concept of economic welfare is essentially elastic. The same measure of elasticity belongs to the concept of the national dividend. It is only possible to define this concept precisely by introducing an arbitrary line into the continuum presented by nature. It is entirely plain that the national dividend is composed in the last resort of a number of objective services, some of which are rendered through commodities while others are rendered direct. These things may be described at will either as goods and services or as services simply, the choice between the two terms being a matter, not, as Professor Fisher appears to suggest, of principle,[1] but of convenience. It

---

[1] *The Nature of Capital and Income*, pp. 105-6.

is not, however, entirely plain *which part of* the stream of services, or goods and services, that flows annually into being can usefully be included under the title of the national dividend. That is the question which has now to be discussed.

§ 2. The answer which first suggests itself is that those goods and services should be included (double-counting, of course, being avoided), and only those, that are actually sold for money. This plan, it would seem, must place us in the best possible position for making use of the monetary measuring rod. Unfortunately, however, for the symmetry of this arrangement, some of the services which would be excluded under it are intimately connected, and even interwoven, with some of the included services. The bought and the unbought kinds do not differ from one another in any fundamental respect, and frequently an unbought service is transformed into a bought one, and *vice versa*. This leads to a number of violent paradoxes. Thus, if a man hires a house and furniture belonging to somebody else, the services he obtains from them enter into the national dividend, as we are here provisionally defining it, but, if he receives the house and furniture as a gift and continues to occupy it, they do so no longer. Again, if a farmer sells the produce of his farm and buys the food he needs for his family in the market, a considerable amount of produce enters into the national dividend which would cease to enter into it if, instead of buying things in the market, he held back part of his own meat and vegetables and consumed them on the farm. Again, the philanthropic work done by unpaid organisers, church workers and Sunday school teachers, the scientific work of disinterested experimenters, and the political work of many among the leisured classes, which at present do not enter, or, when there is a nominal payment, enter at much less than their real worth, into the national dividend, would enter into it if those people undertook to pay salaries to one another. Thus, for example, the Act providing for the payment of members of Parliament, increased the national dividend by some £250,000 worth. Yet again, the services rendered by women enter into the dividend when they are rendered in exchange for wages, whether in the factory or in the home, but do not enter into it when they are rendered by mothers and wives gratuitously to their own families. Thus, if a man marries his housekeeper or his cook, the national dividend is diminished. These things are paradoxes. It is a paradox also that, when Poor Law or Factory Regulations divert women workers from factory work or paid home-work to unpaid home-work, in attendance on their children, preparation of the family meals, repair of the family clothes, thoughtful expenditure of housekeeping money, and so on, the national dividend on our definition *appears* to suffer a loss against which there is to be set no compensating gain.[1] And it is a paradox, lastly, that the frequent desolation of beautiful scenery through the hunt for coal or gold, the desecration widely wrought by uncontrolled smoke from factories and the injury done to natural beauty by public advertisements must, on our definition, leave the national dividend intact, though if it had been practicable, as it is in some exceptional circumstances, to make a charge for viewing splendid scenery, it would not have done so.[2]

§ 3. Reflection upon these objections makes it plain that they are of a type that could be urged in some degree against any definition of the national dividend except one that coincided in range with the whole annual flow of goods and services. But to adopt a definition so wide as that would be tantamount to abandoning dependence upon the measuring rod of money. We are bound, therefore, either to dispense altogether with any formal definition or to fall back upon a compromise.

[1] It would be wrong to infer from the above that the large entry of women into industry during the war was associated with an approximately equal loss of work outside industry. For, first, a great deal of war work was undertaken by women who previously did little work of any kind; secondly, the place of women who entered industry was taken largely by other women who had previously done little—for example, many mistresses in servant-keeping houses themselves took the place of a servant—and, thirdly, owing to the absence of husbands and sons at the war, the domestic work which women would have had to do if they had not gone into industry would have been much less than in normal times.

[2] The Advertisement Regulation Act, 1907, allows local authorities to frame by-laws designed to prevent open-air advertising from affecting prejudicially the natural beauty of a landscape or the amenities of a public park or pleasure promenade. It is not, we may note in this connection, a decisive argument against underground, and in favour of overhead, systems of tramway power wires that they are more expensive. The London County Council deliberately chose the more expensive underground variety.

The former policy, though there is more to be said for it than is sometimes allowed, would certainly arouse distrust, even though it led to no confusion. The latter, therefore, seems on the whole to be preferable. The method I propose to adopt is as follows. First, in accordance with the precedent set by Dr. Marshall, I shall take, as the standard meaning of the term national dividend, that suggested by the practice of the British Income Tax Commissioners. I therefore include everything that people buy with money income, together with the services that a man obtains from a house owned and inhabited by himself. But "the services which a person renders to himself and those which he renders gratuitously to members of his family or friends; the benefits which he derives from using his own personal goods [such as furniture and clothes], or public property such as toll-free bridges, are not reckoned as parts of the national dividend, but are left to be accounted for separately."[1] Secondly, while constructing in this way my standard definition of the national dividend, I reserve full liberty, with proper warning, to use the term in a wider sense on all occasions when the discussion of any problem would be impeded or injured by a pedantic adherence to the standard use. There is, no doubt, a good deal that is unsatisfactory about this compromise. Unfortunately, however, the conditions are such that nothing better appears to be available.

§ 4. The above conclusion does not complete the solution of our problem. Given the general class of things which are *relevant* to the national dividend, a further issue has to be faced. For the dividend may be conceived in two sharply contrasted ways: as the flow of goods and services which is *produced* during the year, or as the flow which is *consumed* during the year. Dr. Marshall adopts the former of these alternatives. He writes: "The labour and capital of the country, acting on its natural resources, produce annually a certain net aggregate of commodities, material and immaterial, including services of all kinds. This is the true net annual income or revenue of the country, or the national dividend."[2]

---

[1] Marshall, *Principles of Economics*, p. 524.
[2] *Ibid.* p. 523.

Naturally, since in every year plant and equipment wear out and decay, what is produced must mean what is produced on the whole when allowance has been made for this process of attrition. To make this clear, Dr. Marshall adds elsewhere: "If we look chiefly at the income of a country, we must allow for the depreciation of the sources from which it is derived."[1] In concrete terms, his conception of the dividend includes an inventory of all the new things that are made, accompanied, as a negative element, by an inventory of all the decay and demolition of old things. Professor Fisher, on the other hand, placing in the forefront of his argument the proposition that savings are in no circumstances income, claims unequivocally to identify the national dividend with those services, and those only, that enter directly into consumption. According to him, Dr. Marshall's national dividend represents, not the dividend that actually *is* realised, but the dividend that would be realised *if* the country's capital were maintained and no more than maintained. In a stationary state, where the creation of new machinery and plant in any industry exactly balances, and no more than balances, loss by wear and tear, these two things would be *materially* equivalent. The dividend on either definition would consist simply of the flow of goods and services entering into final consumption; for all new materials at earlier stages in the productive process that came into factories and shops would be exactly balanced by the corresponding materials that left them in worked-up products; and all newly created machinery and plant would exactly take the place, and no more than take the place, of corresponding machinery and plant that became worn out during the year. In practice, however, the industry of a country is hardly ever in this kind of stationary state. Hence, it is extremely rare for the two versions of the national dividend to be *materially* equivalent, and it is impossible for them to be *analytically* equivalent. The question how the choice between them should fall is, therefore, an important one.

§ 5. The answer to it, as I conceive the matter, turns upon the purpose for which we intend the conception to be

---

[1] Marshall, *Principles of Economics*, p. 80.

used. If we are interested in the comparative amounts of economic welfare which a community obtains over a long series of years, and are looking for an objective index with which this series of amounts can be suitably correlated, then, no doubt, Professor Fisher's conception is the proper one. It is also much more relevant than the other when we are considering how much a country is able to provide over a limited number of years for the conduct of a war; because, for this purpose we want to know what is the utmost amount that can be squeezed out and "consumed," and we do not premise that capital must be maintained intact. The major part of this volume, however, is concerned, not with war, but with peace, and not with measurement, but with causation. The general form of our questions will be: "What effect on economic welfare as a whole is produced by such and such a cause operating on the economic circumstances of 1920?" Now, it is agreed that the cause operates through the dividend, and that direct statements of its effects must refer to the dividend. Let us consider, therefore, the results that follow from the adoption of Professor Fisher's and Dr. Marshall's conceptions respectively. On Professor Fisher's plan, we have to set down the difference made by the cause to the dividend, not merely of 1920, but of every year following 1920; for, if the cause induces new savings, it is only through a statement covering all subsequent years that its effect on the dividend, as conceived by Professor Fisher, can be properly estimated. Thus, on his showing, if a large new factory is built in 1920, not the capital value of that factory, but only the value of the services rendered by it in 1920, should be reckoned in the dividend of 1920; and the aggregate effects of the creation of the factory cannot be measured without reference to the national dividend of a long series of years. On Dr. Marshall's plan this inconvenient elaboration is dispensed with. When we have stated the effect produced on the dividend, in his sense, for the year 1920, we have implicitly included the effects, so far as they can be anticipated, on the consumption both of 1920 and of all subsequent years; for these effects are reflected in the capital value originally possessed by the factory. The *immediate* effect on consumption is measured by the alteration in the 1920 dividend as conceived by Professor Fisher. But it is through total consumption, and not through immediate consumption, that economic welfare and economic causes are linked together. Consequently, Dr. Marshall's definition of the *national dividend* is likely, on the whole, to prove more useful than the other, and I propose in what follows to adopt it. The entity—also, of course, an important one—which Professor Fisher calls by that name, I shall speak of as the *national income of consumable goods*,[1] or, more briefly, *consumable income.*

§ 6. We have thus achieved a definition which, unsatisfactory as it is, is still reasonably precise, of the concrete content of the national dividend. This definition carries with it certain plain implications as to the way in which that dividend must be evaluated. The first and most obvious of these is that, when the value of a finished product is counted, the value of materials employed in making that product must not be counted also. In the *British Census of Production of 1907* this form of double counting was carefully avoided. The Director described his method as follows: The result of deducting the total cost of materials used, and the amount paid to other firms for work given out, from the value of the gross output for any one industry or group of industries is to give a figure which may, for convenience, be called the "net output" of the industry or the group. This figure "expresses completely and without duplication the total amount by which the value (at works) of the products of the industry or the group, taken as a whole, exceeded the value (at works) of the materials purchased from outside, *i.e.* it represents the value added to the materials in the course of manufacture. This sum constitutes for any industry the fund from which wages, salaries, rent, royalties, rates, taxes, depreciation, and all other similar charges, have

---

[1] For a somewhat different line of criticism, *vide* an article by Professor Flux in the *Quarterly Journal of Economics* for February 1909, to which Professor Fisher replied in the May issue of the same journal. The problem of how to distribute charges between income and capital account from the standpoint of an individual business is well discussed in Cole's *Accounts*, chapter xiii.

to be defrayed, as well as profits."[1] When, however, it is desired to evaluate the national dividend as a whole, these allowances are not sufficient. There is no real difference between the flour which is used up in making bread, and bread-making machinery which is used up and worn out in the process of effecting the conversion. If adding together the flour and the bread in summing the national dividend involves double counting, so also does adding together the machinery and the bread. "Logically," as Dr. Marshall observes, "we ought to deduct the looms which a weaving factory buys as well as its yarn. Again, if the factory itself was reckoned as a product of the building trade, its value should be deducted from the output (over a term of years) of the weaving trade. Similarly with regard to farm buildings. Farm houses ought certainly not to be counted, nor for some purposes any houses used in trade."[2] At first sight it might seem that these considerations could be taken quite fully into account by simply subtracting from the sum of the values of the net products of various industries, as defined in the Census of Production, the value of the annual depreciation, and, therefore, the annual renewal of all kinds of machinery and plant.[3] Thus, if a particular sort of machinery wears out in ten years—Professor Taussig's estimate for the average life of machinery in a cotton mill[4]—it is obvious that the value of the national dividend over ten years falls short of the value of the aggregated net product by the value of this machinery.[5]

---

[1] [Cd. 6320], p. 8.
[2] Marshall, *Principles of Economics*, p. 614 n.
[3] Cf. Flux, *Statistical Journal*, 1913, p. 559.
[4] *Quarterly Journal of Economics*, 1908, p. 342. The report of the *Census of Production* sanctions the view that an average life of ten years may reasonably be assigned to buildings and plant in general (*Report*, p. 35).
[5] In industries where large individual items of assets need replacement at fairly long intervals, it is usual to meet this need by the accumulation of a depreciation fund built up by annual instalments during the life of the wasting asset. For machinery which wears out in about equal quantities every year, Professor Young argues that, provided the renewals and repairs required every year are duly furnished, capital will be maintained intact by that fact alone, and no depreciation fund is necessary (*Quarterly Journal of Economics*, 1914, pp. 630 *et seq.*). It is true that by this method, when the plant has been running for some time, the capital is maintained in one year at the level at which it stood in the preceding year. But

Again, in so far as any sort of crop wastes the productive powers of the soil, the value of the dividend falls short of the value of the aggregated net product by the cost of returning to the soil those chemical ingredients that it removes.[1] Yet again, when minerals are dug out of the ground, a deduction should be made equal to the excess of the value which the minerals used during the year had in their original situation (theoretically represented by the royalties paid on their working), over the value which whatever is left of them possesses to the country after they have been used. If "using" means exporting in exchange for imports that are not used as capital, this latter value is zero. If, on the other hand, it means allowing Nature miraculously to transmute the mineral into something possessing greater value than it had in the mine, then, in order to obtain the value of the national dividend from the value of the aggregated net product, we shall need to add, and not to subtract, something. All this is simple enough. But in fact the problem of evaluating the national dividend is more delicate than this. The concrete content of the dividend is, indeed, unambiguous—the inventory of things made and (double counting being eliminated) services rendered, *minus*, as a negative element, the inventory of things worn

---

Professor Young himself shows that, in static conditions, when a plant has been established for some time, it will normally be about half worn out (*loc. cit.* p. 632). If half-worn-out plant, that is to say, plant half-way through its normal life—is technically of the same efficiency as new plant, this fact does not injure his conclusion. But, in so far as the efficiency of plant diminishes with age, the case is otherwise. If the capital is to be maintained at the level at which it stood *when first invested*, it is necessary, not merely to provide renewals and repairs as needed, but also to maintain a permanent depreciation fund, to balance the difference between the values of a wholly new plant and of one the constituents of which are on the average half-way through their effective life. (Cf. also a discussion between Professor Young and Mr. J. S. Davis under the title "Depreciation and Rate Control" in the *Quarterly Journal of Economics*, Feb. 1915).

[1] Professor Carver writes of the United States: "Taking the country over, it is probable that, other things equal, if the farmers had been compelled to buy fertilisers to maintain the fertility of their soil without depletion, the whole industry would have become bankrupt. . . . The average farmer had never (up to about 1887) counted the partial exhaustion of the soil as a part of the cost of his crop" (*Sketch of American Agriculture*, p. 70). Against this capital loss, however, must be set the capital gain due to the settlement of the land.

out during the year. But how are we to *value* this negative
element ?   For example, if a machine originally costing £1000
wears out and, owing to a rise in the general price level, can
only be replaced at a cost of £1500, is £1000 or £1500 the
proper allowance ? . Nor is this the only, or, indeed, the principal difficulty.   For depreciation is not measured merely by
the physical process of wearing out, and capital is not therefore maintained intact when provision has been made to replace
what is thus worn out.   Machinery that has become obsolete
because of the development of improved forms is not really
left intact, however excellent its physical condition; and
the same thing is true of machinery for whose products
popular taste has declined.   If, however, in deference
to these considerations, we decide to make an allowance
for obsolescence, this concession implies that the value, and
not the physical efficiency, of instrumental goods is the
object to be maintained intact.   But, it is then urged, the
value of instrumental goods, being the present value of
the services which they are expected to render in the
future, necessarily varies with variations in the rate of
interest.   Is it really a rational procedure to evaluate the
national dividend by a method which makes its value in
relation to that of the aggregated net product of the country's
industry depend on an incident of that kind?   If that
method is adopted, and a great war, by raising the rate
of interest, depreciates greatly the value of existing capital,
we shall probably be compelled to put, for the value of the
national dividend in the first year of that war, a very large
negative figure.   This absurdity must be avoided at all
costs, and we are therefore compelled, when we are engaged
in valuing the national dividend, to leave out of account
any change in the value of the country's capital equipment that may have been brought about by broad general
causes.   This decision is arbitrary and unsatisfactory,
but it is one which it is impossible to avoid.   During
the period of the war a similar difficulty was created
by the general rise, for many businesses, in the value
of the normal and necessary holding of materials and stocks,
which was associated with the general rise of prices.

On our principles this increase of value ought not to be reckoned as an addition to the income of the firms affected, or, consequently, to the value of the national dividend.[1]

§ 7. It remains to consider the relation between the national dividend as thus evaluated—an addition, of course, being made for the value of income received from abroad—and the money income accruing to the community. On the face of things we should expect these two sums to be substantially equal, just as we should expect a man's receipts and his expenditure (including investments) to be equal. With proper account-keeping this clearly ought to be so. In order that it may be so, however, it is necessary for the money income of the community to be so defined as to exclude all income that is obtained by one person as a gift against which no service entering into the evaluation of the national dividend is rendered—all allowances, for example, received by children from their parents. This point is, of course, well understood. But certain further implications are less fully realised. Thus, the income of all old-age pensioners must be excluded, or, alternatively, that part of the income of tax-payers which is paid to the State to provide these pensions. So also must income received by native creditors of the State in interest on loans that have been employed "unproductively," i.e. in such a way that they do not, as loans to buy railways would do, themselves "produce" money with which to pay the interest due on them. This means that the income received as interest on War loan—or the income paid to the State to provide this interest—ought to be excluded. Nor is it possible to overthrow this conclusion by suggesting that the money spent on the war has really been "productive," because it indirectly prevented invasion and the destruction of material capital that is now producing goods sold for money; for whatever product war expenditure may have been responsible for in this way is already counted in the income earned by the material capital. Finally, it would seem that income obtained by force or fraud, against which no real service has been

---

[1] For a discussion of this question in its bearing on the Excess Profits Duty, cf. Report of the Committee on Excess Profits.

rendered, ought not to be counted. When the nominal money income of the country has been " corrected " in these various ways, what is left should approximate fairly closely to the value of the national dividend (inclusive of incomes from abroad) estimated on the plan set out above.

CHAPTER IV

THE RELATION OF ECONOMIC WELFARE TO THE NATIONAL DIVIDEND

§ 1. THE national dividend, as it flows into being in any year, is the fruit of the activities of the people working in conjunction with the accumulated results of past activities and with the materials and forces provided by nature. It consists of an indefinite number of parts which are distributed in various proportions among different groups and individuals. Furthermore, both the magnitude of the whole and the magnitude of the separate parts are variable quantities, oscillating about, perhaps a fixed, but more probably a changing average, and differing, therefore, from one year to another. An entity of this kind is far too complex to be handled in its concrete actuality by any scientific machinery of which we are at present possessed. If, therefore, the relation of economic welfare to the national dividend is to be examined with any prospect of success, it is necessary to construct some artificially simplified picture of the dividend, which will leave detail on one side and focus attention on a small number of dominant characteristics. In this book I shall make use of the following "model" conception. First, over any period of, say, a decade, covering a cycle of good and bad years together, the national dividend will possess some definite *average volume*. Secondly, over this period the portion of the dividend accruing to poor persons—the precise definition of what we mean by a poor person need not trouble us—will constitute some definite *proportion of the whole*. Thirdly, both (*a*) the dividend as a whole, and (*b*) the part of it accruing to poor persons *will vary about its average level by a definite average amount.* The purpose of the present chapter is to exhibit in a general way the relations between economic welfare and each of these several characteristic features of the national dividend. It is evident that these relations are never direct, but are always mediated through the income of consumers' goods. Under each head, it will be necessary to bear this fact in mind.

§ 2. Let us begin with the relation between economic welfare and the average volume of the national dividend. Here the necessary mediation through consumable income raises no difficulties. In general, anything that increases or diminishes the average volume of the national dividend will affect the average volume of the national consumable income in the same sense. We need not, therefore, trouble to maintain the distinction between them, but may treat national dividend and consumable income as, for this purpose—not, of course, for all purposes—practically equivalent terms. For economy of language I shall, in fact, adopt this plan. With this understanding it is tempting to maintain that any cause which increases the volume of the dividend, provided that it neither injures its distribution nor increases its variability, will increase economic welfare. But this proposition is not valid. The quantity of economic welfare associated with any volume of the dividend depends, not only on the satisfaction yielded by consumption, but also on the dissatisfaction involved in production. There must, therefore, be some point after which an addition to the resources expended in production, while still adding something to the dividend, would involve a direct loss of satisfaction greater than the indirect gain. Suppose, for example, that the whole community was compelled by law to work for eighteen hours a day, and—which is in fact improbable—that this policy made the national dividend larger. It is practically certain that the satisfaction yielded by the extra product would be enormously less than the dissatisfaction caused by the extra labour. And the same thing is true if extra work is done, not under compulsion, but because some workpeople have formed an erroneous estimate of their own interests. No doubt, in the modern world, apart from military conscription, we have to do, not with forced, but with voluntary labour. No doubt too, hours of labour cannot be carried *far* beyond the point to which the work-people's interests, rightly interpreted, would lead them, without causing a diminution, instead of an increase, in the national dividend. Hence, it is unlikely that we shall often meet in practice with any considerable expansions of the national dividend that are injurious to economic welfare. Still the mere fact that injurious expansions are possible invalidates the proposition suggested above.

§ 3. Nor is the somewhat obvious disharmony just displayed the only one that may arise. It is fairly plain that, if two regions, between which capital or labour have hitherto been unable to move, with the result that a unit of capital or labour in one of them is producing a considerably larger output than a similar unit in the other, are brought into communication, economic welfare is bound to be increased. For hereafter labour (or capital) will be so distributed between the two regions that nothing could be gained by movement, and the amount of labour exercised (or capital created) will be such that the exercise (or creation) of any additional unit would destroy more satisfaction than the product for which it might be responsible could yield. If, therefore, there is to be harmony, it is necessary that the opening up of communication between the two regions shall also cause the national dividend to increase. It can be shown, however, that this need not happen. Working along the lines of an argument developed by Cournot in his chapter on "The Competition of Markets," [1] we perceive that the abolition of obstacles between the two regions *may* cause the aggregate quantity of labour exercised, or capital created, to be *smaller* than it was before. Suppose, for example, that one group of workpeople is assembled at A and another at B; that the marginal hour's work at A yields a much smaller return than the marginal hour's work of similar quality yields at B; and that at both places the return yielded per hour's work is smaller the greater is the quantity of work that is done there. The removal of an obstacle which has hitherto prevented workmen at A from

[1] *Mathematical Theory of Wealth,* ch. xi.; cf. Bowley, "The Mobility of Labour," *Economic Journal,* 1912, pp. 46 *et seq.*

going to B at once causes a migration. Since, after the change, an hour's work both at B and at A yields more return than an hour's work at A formerly yielded, the men who were originally at A may be led to provide more hours' work than they provided before. But the men originally at B, finding that an hour's work there now yields a less return than it used to yield, may be led to provide fewer hours' work than they provided before. It is evident that conditions of demand and supply at A and B *may* be such that the diminution in the amount of work provided by the natives of B will be greater than the increase in that provided by the natives of A; in such wise that the quantity of labour forthcoming in both regions together is made smaller by the removal of the obstacle between them. Suppose again that in agricultural districts the capital employed is yielding a low return, while in manufacturing districts isolated from them it is yielding a high return; that the demand is elastic in the agricultural districts and very inelastic in the manufacturing districts; and that the supply is about equally elastic in the two sets of districts. On these suppositions, after the removal of the obstacles that separated them, say, by the development of banking, the amount of capital made available in manufacturing districts would remain practically unchanged; but the amount made available in agricultural districts would, on account of the increase in cost, be greatly diminished. On balance, therefore, there would be a smaller aggregate of capital than before in the two sets of districts taken together. These examples show that the abolition of obstacles to movement between two districts *may* diminish the aggregate quantity of resources available for production in the two together. Further, mathematical analysis enables us to conclude that, when an obstacle selected at random is removed, an increase and a decrease in the quantity of productive resources that come into being are about equally *probable*, or, if we prefer to put it so, will occur about equally often.[1] This result does

---

[1] When there is no communication between two fields in which productive resources are employed, let the demands for these resources be

$$\phi_1(p_1) \text{ and } \phi_2(p_2)$$

and the supplies

$$f_1(p_1) \text{ and } f_2(p_2).$$

not, of course, imply that an increase and a decrease in the magnitude of the national dividend are about equally probable. For, whether or not the aggregate quantity of resources available for work is diminished, such resources as are available are necessarily employed, on the average, under conditions more favourable to production. Thus, in our example of the two groups of workpeople assembled at A and B, let us suppose that, before the obstacle was removed, x hours' work was forthcoming at A and y hours' work at B, and that, after it is removed, $(x+y-h)$ hours' work are performed at B and no hours' work at A. Then each one of the $(x-h)$ hours now added to the work done at B necessarily yields a larger

---

Then we have the equations

$$\phi_1(p_1)=f_1(p_1) \qquad \text{(I.)}$$
$$\phi_2(p_2)=f_2(p_2) \qquad \text{(II.)}$$

When communication is introduced, we have the equation

$$\phi_1(p_3)+\phi_2(p_3)=f_1(p_3)+f_2(p_3) \qquad \text{(III.)}$$

Let the root of (I.) be a, of (II.) b, of (III.) $a+k$, where k is such that $a+k+h=b$.

Let it be assumed that all the functions involved are linear, so that all differentials beyond the first are equal to zero.

Then it is easily proved that

$$h=\frac{(b-a)(\phi_1'-f_1')}{\phi_1'+\phi_2'-f_1'-f_2'}$$

Hence,

$$a+k=\frac{a(\phi_1'-f_1')+b(\phi_2'-f_2')}{\phi_1'+\phi_2'-f_1'-f_2'},$$

a value intermediate between a and b.

It is also easily proved that the increase in the amount of the factor in question, when communication is opened up,

$$= \{f_1(a+k)+f_2(a+k)\} - \{f_2a+f_2(a+k+h)\}$$
$$= kf_1'-hf_2'$$
$$= \frac{b-a}{\phi_1'+\phi_2'-f_1'-f_2'}\{f_1'\phi_2'-f_2'\phi_1'\}$$

This may be either positive or negative. In order that it may be negative, $\{f_1'\phi_2'-f_2'\phi_1'\}$ must be positive,

$$\text{i.e. } \frac{f_1'}{\phi_1'}>\frac{f_2'}{\phi_2'}$$

If the elasticities of supply of and demand for productive resources in the two fields respectively are written e_1, η_1, e_2, η_2, this condition becomes $\frac{e_1}{\eta_1}>\frac{e_2}{\eta_2}$; or, in other words, the elasticity of supply must bear a higher ratio to the elasticity of demand in the market where, before communication, price was lower, than in the other market. There is, obviously, no reason for thinking that this condition is either more or less likely than not to be fulfilled. Nor would our ignorance be in any way lightened, if the assumption that all the functions involved are linear was abandoned.

product than it would have yielded had it continued to be performed at A. The addition that is made in this way to the efficiency of productive resources will bring about an enhanced product, not only on all occasions when the aggregate quantity of resources is increased, but also on some occasions when it is diminished. Hence, more often than not the removal of an obstacle to movement between two regions will increase the national dividend. It is easy to show, however, that sometimes it will diminish it. Suppose, for example, that in the region, where, before the obstacle is removed, production per unit of labour or capital is larger than in the other, there is not room to employ more than a few further units except at a greatly reduced return. In these circumstances, when the obstacle is removed, the output as well as the capital and labour employed there, will be practically the same (if the demand is perfectly inelastic, *exactly* the same) as before; while capital and labour having been withdrawn from the other region in order to take the place of those units that it is no longer worth while to provide in the first, the output in the other region will be smaller than before. This proves that the removal of the obstacle *may* lessen the national dividend. Since, therefore, it *must* increase economic welfare, there may, or in other words, sometimes will, be disharmony. Some causes that injure the national dividend will increase economic welfare, and *vice versa.*

§ 4. The qualification set out in the preceding section is probably of small importance otherwise than academically. That set out in § 2, however, is obviously of very great importance. For practical purposes it will be sufficient to modify our statement of the relation between economic welfare and the average volume of the national dividend with reference to it alone. Broadly and generally then we may lay down the following proposition: *Any cause which, without the exercise of compulsion or pressure upon people to make them work more than their wishes and interests dictate, increases productive efficiency, and, therewith, the average volume of the national dividend, provided that it neither injures the distribution nor augments the variability of the country's consumable income, will, in general, increase economic welfare.*

§ 5. This proposition, it will be observed, is purely qualitative in form, and states nothing about the quantitative relation between an expansion of the national dividend and additions to economic welfare. To remedy this deficiency completely is, of course, impossible. It is not impossible, however, to throw some further light on the matter. To this end we may begin by leaving out of account the reactions that may be produced by the fact of consumption upon capacity for deriving enjoyment from consumption. When this is done, the familiar "law of diminishing utility" instructs us that a given expansion of the national dividend is likely to be accompanied by a *less than proportionate* increase in economic welfare. This conclusion is, moreover, reinforced by a further consideration. The satisfaction which a man obtains from his economic environment is, in great part, derived, not from the *absolute*, but from the *comparative*, magnitude of his income. Mill wrote: "Men do not desire to be *rich*, but to be richer than other men. The avaricious or covetous man would find little or no satisfaction in the possession of any amount of wealth, if he were the poorest amongst all his neighbours or fellow-countrymen."[1] More elaborately, Signor Rignano writes: "As for the needs which vanity creates, they can be satisfied equally well by a small as by a large expenditure of energy. It is only the existence of great riches, which makes necessary for such satisfaction a very large, instead of a very small, expenditure. In reality a man's desire to appear 'worth' double what another man is worth, that is to say, to possess goods (jewels, clothes, horses, parks, luxuries, houses, etc.) twice as valuable as those possessed by another man, is satisfied just as fully, if the first has ten things and the second five, as it would be if the first had a hundred and the second fifty."[2] Moreover, it is not merely rivalry that is in question. Besides the desire for a good relative position among people, which improvement benefiting all people similarly obviously does nothing to satisfy, there is the nobler desire for excellence for

[1] Posthumous Essay on Social Freedom, *Oxford and Cambridge Review,* Jan. 1907.

[2] *Di un socialismo in accordo colla dottrina economica liberale,* p. 285.

its own sake. "We needs must love the highest when we see it "; we desire, in a measure, that what we have shall be the best of its kind. This desire obviously receives no fuller satisfaction, or, in other words, economic welfare gains nothing, when improvements create a new "best" superior to the old one. Considerations of this order are much more important than is sometimes recognised. An ordinary man's satisfaction does not, of course, depend entirely upon his comparative, but partly at least upon his absolute, income. It cannot be maintained seriously that an increase in the latter will add *nothing whatever* to the satisfactions which constitute his economic welfare.[1] But there is good reason to believe that it will add considerably less to these satisfactions than might have been thought probable at a first careless glance.

§ 6. It remains to take account of the reactions which the fact of consumption may produce on taste. *Prima facie* it would seem that those reactions may enable a given expansion in the average volume of the dividend to augment economic welfare more largely by indirect means than it is able to do directly. Obviously, the amount of economic satisfaction that a community obtains from a given economic environment depends, not only on the environment, but also, in an at least equal degree, upon the mentality of the people concerned. Jevons observed long ago that a small change in wants and tastes might often by itself lead to a very great increase in economic welfare. And he added a characteristic illustration: "While the great Irish famine was at its worst, abundance of salmon and other fish could have been had for the trouble of catching; scarcely any of the starving peasantry would consent to touch it."[2] A similar thought underlies the late Canon Barnett's observation: "Children should be prepared for leisure with as much care as they are prepared for work. Great pains are taken that boys should learn some skill and that girls

---

[1] Lassalle's view, as quoted by Leroy-Beaulieu, that "la situation de chaque classe a toujours pour unique mesure la situation des autres classes dans le même temps" (*Répartition des richesses*, p. 45), is clearly an extravagance, but there may be literal truth in Professor Carver's epigram, "We all spend more in trying to live like our neighbours than in trying to live comfortably" (*Essays on Social Justice*, p. 379). Veblen's *Theory of the Leisured Class* contains a number of acute, if somewhat one-sided, observations upon this matter.

[2] *Principles of Economics*, p. 32.

E

should do needlework, but surely as great pains should be taken that they may develop powers of self-amusement and others' amusement."[1] It follows that, if a cause, which directly increases the output of any of the goods or services contained in the national dividend, thereby indirectly increases people's capacity for deriving satisfaction from these goods and services, it will, to that extent, make an important indirect contribution to economic welfare. And in fact it can be shown that this frequently happens. For in the economic world "infant," or undeveloped, demands are to be found, equally with "infant," or undeveloped, industries. People may be given a taste for a particular thing, or the keenness of their desire for it may be permanently increased, through the temporary use of, or acquaintance with, it. When machines are sent out on trial, or articles presented in sample-packets, or pictures exhibited free to the public, the popular taste for these objects tends to be augmented. When public-houses, or lotteries, or libraries are easily accessible, the taste for drink, or gambling, or literature is not merely gratified, but is also stimulated. When cleanliness, or light,[2] or model dwellings, or model plots of agricultural land are set up, though it is only to be seen, and not owned, by the neighbours, the object lesson may still succeed and make plain superiorities hitherto unrecognised.[3] Thus, "free libraries are engines for creating the habitual power of enjoying high-class literature," and a savings bank, if confined to the poor, is an "engine for teaching thrift."[4] In like

---

[1] *Towards Social Reform*, p. 302; cf. Fisher, *The Nature of Capital and Income*, p. 176.

[2] Cf. Walpole's account of the way in which the introduction of street lamps led to an increased demand for illuminants *within* the neighbouring houses (*History of England*, i. 86). An elaborate method of advertising electric light is quoted in Whyte's *Electrical Industry*, (p. 57). A company undertakes to instal six lamps in a house free of all charge for a six months' trial, the householder paying only for the current that he uses. After the six months, the company undertakes to remove the whole arrangement if the customer so desires.

[3] Cf. Miss Octavia Hill's practice of insisting on the cleanliness of the *staircases* of her houses, and Sir H. Plunkett's account of the Cork Exhibition, 1902 (*Ireland in the New Century*, pp. 285-7).

[4] Jevons, *Methods of Social Reform*, p. 32. It should be noted, however, that Dr. Marshall thinks this order of consideration is of relatively small range. He writes: "Those demands, which show high elasticity in the long run, show a high elasticity almost at once; so that, subject to a few excep-

manner the policy of many German cities, in subsidising theatres and opera-houses and in providing symphony concerts two or three evenings a week at a very small admission fee, is an *educational* policy that bears fruit in increased capacity for enjoyment.[1] No doubt sometimes the increase in taste for one thing is associated with a substantially equivalent decline in taste for another thing that fulfils the same purpose,—*e.g.* wool as against cotton,—and does not, therefore, lead to any appreciable increase in aggregate welfare. But, frequently, as a consideration of the examples cited above will show, there is a genuine creation or development of a new taste. The indirect benefits which are thus conferred upon economic welfare by an increase in the dividend have the further characteristic that they may be permanent, even though the increase in any part of the dividend is itself only temporary. For, peoples' tastes being altered in an enduring manner, they will continue to obtain more satisfaction than they did before, if and when the supply of the commodity they have become trained to like falls again to its original amount.

§ 7. This line of reasoning is, however, subject to an important qualification. It is true that experience of a particular thing will often enable people to get increased satisfaction out of it. But it is at least arguable that, after a point, as growing wealth gives a man command over more and more luxuries, the satisfaction that he gains from each new one is, as it were, taken out of relaxed interest in the others, so that the economic satisfaction which he achieves on the whole is not substantially increased. He may be conceived, in short, as a vessel able, according to his temperament, to "contain" a certain limited amount of economic satisfaction. When satiety point is reached, further new satisfactions can only be admitted at the cost of driving out an equivalent volume of other satisfactions. There can be no doubt that this conception embodies a large element of truth. It need not

---

tions, we may speak of the demand for a commodity as being of high or low elasticity without specifying how far we are looking ahead" (*Principles of Economics*, p. 456).

   [1] Cf. Howe, *European Cities at Work*, pp. 147-50.

be denied that a rich man accustomed to a yacht would be much hurt at the time by having to do without his yacht: but, when he had got accustomed to a new and lower standard of living, provided that it still remained fairly high, it might well be that he would be no less happy than before. *Per contra*, a man accustomed to a standard of living represented, say, by £3000 a year, may well get quite as much satisfaction out of life as another man of similar temperament with £300,000 a year and accustomed to the standard which that income implies. These considerations suggest that the reactions which take place between consumption and taste may, on the whole, lessen rather than augment the beneficial effects which a given expansion of the dividend is likely to have upon economic welfare. It must be noted, however, that they are relevant to a change from riches to greater riches, rather than to one from poverty to less poverty; and, looked at as a whole, every modern nation, when its real income is balanced against its population, is still very poor. Hence, as things actually are, I am inclined to think that the reactions which occur between consumption and taste are likely, on the whole, to make the benefit to economic welfare resulting from a given expansion of the dividend a little larger than it would be if there were no reactions. But this conclusion in the present state of economic science, is, of course, little better than a guess.

§ 8. We now turn to the relation between economic welfare and the proportion of the national dividend accruing to poor persons. Here the distinction between total income and consumed income is more important, because, generally speaking, the richer a man is, the larger proportion of his income he is likely to save, so that, if his total income is, say, twenty times as large, his consumed income may be only, say, five times as large. Nevertheless, it is evident that any transference of income from a relatively rich man to a relatively poor man of similar temperament, since it enables more intense wants to be satisfied at the expense of less intense wants, must increase the aggregate sum of satisfaction. The old "law of diminishing utility" thus leads securely to a second main proposition, which may be stated as follows: *Any cause which increases the proportion of the national dividend received by poor persons, provided that it does not lead to a contraction of the dividend and does not injuriously affect its variability, will, in general, increase economic welfare.* This conclusion is further fortified by the fact that, of the satisfaction yielded by the incomes of rich people, a specially large proportion comes from their *relative* rather than their *absolute* amount, and, therefore, will not be destroyed if the incomes of all rich people are diminished together.[1]

§ 9. It must be conceded, of course, that, if the rich and the poor were two races with different mental constitutions, such that the rich were inherently capable of securing a greater amount of economic satisfaction from any given income than the poor, the possibility of increasing welfare by this type of change would be seriously doubtful. Furthermore, even without any assumption about inherent racial difference, it may be maintained that a rich man, from the nature of his upbringing and training, is capable of obtaining considerably more satisfaction from a given income, —say a thousand pounds—than a poor man would be. For, if anybody accustomed to a given standard of living suddenly finds his income enlarged, he is apt to dissipate the extra income in forms of exciting pleasure, which, when their indirect, as well as their direct, effects are taken into account, may even lead to a positive loss of satisfaction. To this argument, however, there is a sufficient answer. It is true that at any given moment the tastes and temperament of persons who have long been poor are more or less adjusted to their environment, and that a sudden and sharp rise of income is likely to be followed by a good deal of foolish expenditure, which involves little or no addition to economic welfare. If, however, the higher income is maintained for any length of time, this phase will pass; whereas, if the increase is gradual or, still better, if it comes about in such a way as not to be directly perceived—through a fall in prices, for example—the period of foolishness need not occur at all. In any case, to contend that the folly of poor persons is so great that a rise of income among them will not promote

[1] Cf. Rignano, *Di un socialismo,* p. 289.

economic welfare in any degree, is to press paradox beyond the point up to which discussion can reasonably be called upon to follow. The true view, as I conceive it, is admirably stated by Messrs. Pringle and Jackson in their special report to the Poor Law Commissioners : "It is in the unskilled and least educated part of the population that drink continues to hold its ground ; as greater regularity of employment and higher wages are achieved by sections of the working-classes, the men rise in respectability and character. That the drink bill is diminishing, while wages are rising throughout the country, is one of the most hopeful indications of progress we possess."[1] The root of the matter is that, even when, under existing conditions, the mental constitution of poor persons is such that an enlarged income will at the moment yield them little benefit, yet, after a time—more especially if the time is long enough to allow a new generation to grow up—the possession of such an income will make possible the development in them, through education and otherwise, of capacities and faculties adapted for the enjoyment of the enlarged income. Thus, in the long run differences of temperament and taste between rich and poor are overcome by the very fact of a shifting of income between them. Plainly, therefore, they cannot be used as an argument to disprove the benefits of a transference.[2]

§ 10. After all, however, general reasoning of the above type, though perhaps necessary to provide formal justification for our thesis, is not necessary to convince us practically that it is valid. For that purpose it is sufficient to reflect on the way in which, in this country, income is in fact distributed, or rather, since more recent information is not available, was distributed before the war. There are not sufficient data to enable this to be calculated with any degree of accuracy. On the basis, however, of work done by Dr. Bowley,[3] we may

---

[1] Cd. 4795, p. 46.

[2] Similarly, of course, when we are taking a long view, the argument that a reduction in the real income of the rich inflicts a special injury, because it forces them to abandon habits to which they have grown accustomed, loses most of its force.

[3] *Quarterly Journal of Economics*, Feb. 1914, p. 261 ; and *The Division of the Product of Industry before the War*, 1918, pp. 11 and 14.

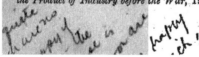

hazard the following rough estimate for the period immediately prior to the war.   The 12,000 richest families in the country received about one-fifteenth of the total national income; the richest *fiftieth* of the population received about one-quarter, and the richest *ninth.* of the population received nearly one-half of that total income.   The remainder of it, a little more than a half, was left to be shared among small independent workers and salary-receivers earning less than £160 a year and practically the whole body of wage-earners.   The table below, giving Dr. Bowley's estimate of distribution among a portion of this last group in 1911, carries the matter a little further.

WEEKLY MONEY WAGES OF ADULT WORKMEN IN ORDINARY

FULL WORK

(INCLUDING VALUATION FOR PAYMENT IN KIND)[1]

Wage.	Number of Men.	Per cent of whole.
Under 15/- . .	320,000 (mainly agriculture)	4
15/- to 20/- . .	640,000	8
20/- to 25/- . .	1,600,000	20
25/- to 30/- . .	1,680,000	21
30/- to 35/- . .	1,680,000	21
35/- to 40/- . .	1,040,000	13
40/- to 45/- . .	560,000	7
45/- and over .	480,000	6

What these figures meant in the concrete is brought out very clearly in the same author's study of the conditions of life in four industrial towns.   Together these towns embrace "about 2150 working-class households and 9720 persons. Of these households 293 or $13\frac{1}{2}$ per cent, of these persons 1567 or 16 per cent, are living in a condition of primary poverty," *i.e.* with incomes so low that, even if expended with perfect wisdom, they could not have provided an adequate subsistence.   " Out of 3287 children who appear in our tables,

[1] From the *Contemporary Review*, Oct. 1911, p. 1.

879, or 27 per cent, are living in families which fail to reach the low standard taken as necessary for healthy existence."[1] Of course since the war the whole scale of money incomes has altered. But the scale of money prices has altered also; and the general forces that produced the state of things depicted above are still at work. In considering how far that state of things is susceptible of remedy by an alteration in the distribution of income, it is essential to recollect that the dominant part of the annual new investments of the country — before the war perhaps 350 millions—and a large part of the expenses of central and local government—over 200 millions—had to be provided out of the larger incomes. Moreover, estimates of money income tend to exaggerate the relative real income of wealthy persons, because these persons are often charged higher prices than poor persons pay for the same services. A number of London shops, for example, discriminate against "good addresses," and hotel charges are also often discriminatory. It has even been suggested that as much as 25 per cent of the money income of the rich, as spent by them, represents no equivalent in real income.[2] In like manner, estimates of money income sometimes make it appear that the real incomes of poor persons are less than they really are, by ignoring discriminations in their favour. Thus Dr. Bowley points out: "A butcher can perhaps raise his prices to his day customers without much affecting the sale, but not to those in the evening. In this case the working class would suffer a smaller rise than the richer class. This consideration applies especially to the very large volume of purchases made late on Saturday night." But, when all qualifications have been made, the figures cited above leave no room for doubt that, so long as the dividend as a whole is not diminished, any increase, within wide limits, in the real income enjoyed by the poorer classes, at the expense of an equal decrease in that enjoyed by the richer classes,

---

[1] *Livelihood and Poverty*, pp. 46-7. The reason for the excess in the proportion of children in poverty is the twofold one, that poor families are apt to be larger than others, and that a large family is itself a cause of life in poverty. Cf. Bowley, *The Measurement of Social Phenomena*, p. 187.

[2] Urwick, *Luxury and the Waste of Life*, pp. 87 and 90.

is practically certain to involve an addition to economic welfare.[1]

§ 11. It should be noticed that the conclusion set out above is not exactly equivalent to the proposition that economic welfare will be increased by anything that, *ceteris paribus*, renders the national dividend less unequal. If the community consisted of two members only, it would, indeed, coincide with

[1] It should be observed, in passing, that a change in the proportions of real income received by the rich and the poor implies a change in the nature of the commodities that are purchased, and, therefore, produced. Expensive luxuries give place to more necessary articles, rare wines to meat and bread, private parks to grazing grounds or wheat fields, new machines and factories to clothes and improved dwellings. Furthermore, among the things in which the poor are likely to take out their increased income is the quasi-commodity, leisure. It is well established that the high-wage countries and industries are generally also both the short-hour countries and industries and the countries and industries in which the wage-earning work required from women and children in supplement of the family budget is the smallest. The former point is illustrated by some statistics of the wage rate and hours of labour of carpenters in the United States, Great Britain, France, Germany, and Belgium, published in No. 54 of the Bulletin of the U.S. Bureau of Labour (p. 1125). In illustration of the latter point, Professor Chapman notes the assertion that, whereas the German collier finds only 65·8 per cent of his family's earnings, the wealthier American collier finds 77·5 per cent (*Work and Wages*, i. p. 17); Mr. Rowntree's interesting table for York points, when properly analysed, in the same direction (*Poverty*, p. 171); and Miss Vessellitsky shows that low-paid home-work among women is found principally in those districts, *e.g.* East Anglia, "where the bad conditions of male labour make it almost indispensable for the wife to supplement the husband's earnings," whereas, in districts where men's wages are good, women only work at industry if they themselves can obtain well-paid jobs (*The Home-worker*, p. 4). Again, reference may be made to the familiar correlation found in recent English history between rising wages and falling hours. Yet again, a study of the rates of wages and hours of labour in different districts in England would, I suspect, reveal a correlation of the same type. It does so for the wages and hours statistics of bricklayers as given in the *Abstract of Labour Statistics for 1908* (pp. 42, etc.). Leisure, however, is not reckoned in the national dividend, when the manner of book-keeping explained in the preceding chapter is adopted. Hence, on that manner of book-keeping a transference of resources to the poor may *appear* to be accompanied by a reduction in the volume of the national dividend as a whole when in reality there is no reduction. (Cf. Chapter III. § 2.) Finally, even when the redistributed dividend is equal to the old dividend, in the sense of being the product of equal quantities of labour and capital, the money measure of it may be changed in consequence of the changes that have occurred in its constituent elements. As Dr. Bowley writes: "The values included in incomes are values in exchange, which are dependent, not only on the goods or services in question, but also on the whole complex of the income and purchases of the whole of a society. . . . The numerical measurement of total national income is thus dependent on the distribution of income and would alter with it." (*The Measurement of Social Phenomena*, pp. 207-8.) This point is also taken by Dr. Stamp, *British Incomes and Property*, pp. 420-21.

this. But, in a community consisting of more than two members, the meaning of "rendering the distribution of the dividend less unequal" is ambiguous. Professor Pareto measures inequality of distribution by dividing the logarithm of the number of incomes in excess of any amount x into the logarithm of x. This measure is very difficult to apply unless we accept Pareto's view that in any given income distribution the ratio between his two logarithms is approximately the same for all values of x; and, even so, it is a matter of dispute whether the reciprocal of his measure,—which of course would indicate less equality when the measure itself indicates greater equality,—is not to be preferred to that measure.[1] The other measures of equality in common use are all likely to be roughly accordant with the mean square deviation from the mean: With that criterion it can be proved that, assuming similarity of temperament among the members of the community, a diminution in the inequality of distribution *probably*, though not necessarily, increases the aggregate sum of satisfaction.[2]

§ 12. So far we have said nothing about possible reactions on the numbers of the population. This omission must now be remedied. To both the broad propositions set out above, relating respectively to the volume and to the distribution of the national dividend, it may be objected that an increase in the income per head enjoyed by any group causes population to increase until that income is again reduced to the old level, and, therefore, that it leads to no permanent benefit. In practice this argument is most often used about the effects

---

[1] Cf. Gini, *Variabilità e mutabilità*, p. 72.

[2] If A be the mean income, and $a_1, a_2 \ldots$ deviations from the mean, aggregate satisfaction, on our assumption,

$$= nfA + (a_1 + a_2 + \ldots)f' + \frac{1}{2!}(a_1^2 + a_2^2 + \ldots)f'' + \frac{1}{3!}(a_1^3 + a_2^3 + \ldots)f''' + \ldots$$

But we know that $\{a_1 + a_2 + \ldots\} = 0$.
We know nothing to suggest whether the sum of the terms beyond the third is positive or negative. But it is certain that $\frac{1}{2}\{a_1^2 + a_2^2 + \ldots\}f''$ is negative. If, therefore, the fourth and following terms are small relatively to the third term, it is certain, and in general it is probable, that aggregate satisfaction is larger, the smaller is $(a_1^2 + a_2^2 + \ldots)$. This latter sum, of course, varies in the same sense as the mean square deviation or standard deviation $\sqrt{\Sigma \dfrac{a^2}{n}}$.

of an increase in the income of manual workers; and it is, of course, much more plausible in this field than in any other. It will, therefore, be enough to examine this aspect of it. I shall consider it first from the point of view of the whole world, or of a single country imagined, for the purposes of the argument, to be isolated, and afterwards shall enquire how far the results achieved need to be modified for a single country constituting one among the associated family of modern nations. In the argument to be developed under these two heads it must be understood that the additions to the income of wage-earners that we have in mind do not include additions brought about by the offer, on behalf of the State, of deliberate and overt bounties upon the acquisition of large families. Under the old Poor Law in the United Kingdom bounties were, in effect, given; our present income-tax law acts in a slight degree in the same sense; and in a law passed in France[1] shortly before the war a similar policy was adopted. This class of addition to the income of the poor has, of course, a strong tendency to augment population, and, in some practical problems, the point is of importance. For the present, however, we are concerned with additions that do not offer a special differential inducement to the begetting of children.

§ 13. If we provisionally ignore the deeper-seated reactions which increased income may exert upon wants and tastes, our discussion virtually resolves itself into an enquiry into the validity of the celebrated "iron law of wages." According to this "law," expanding numbers continually press the earnings of the workpeople down "to subsistence level," thus making it impossible for their real income *per head* in any circumstances to increase. It should be noted in passing that, even if there really were such a law, the proposition that better fortune for the workers increases economic welfare would not be definitely disproved. For it might still be urged that, provided the average working family attains in the whole period of life any surplus of satisfaction over dissatisfaction, an increase of numbers

---

[1] *Economic Journal*, Dec. 1913, p. 641.

implies by itself an addition to economic welfare.[1] But, for my present purpose, there is no need to press this doubtful point. Population does not tend to expand in such a manner as to hold down income per head to a predetermined "subsistence level." It is true, no doubt, that the direct and immediate result of an increase in the dividend accruing to any group is likely to be *some* increase of population. It is well known that the English marriage rate was negatively correlated with wheat prices in the earlier part of the nineteenth century, and was positively correlated with exports, clearing-house returns and so on in the latter part:[2] and that the rate of mortality falls with growing wealth, and *vice versa*. But it is contrary to experience to assert that increased income stimulates population to so large an extent that the individual earnings of workpeople are brought down again to the level they occupied before the improvement. There are two ways in which the manual workers can use their increased claims over material things, namely, an increase in population and an increase in the standard of comfort. The distinction between these two ways is well illustrated by the following contrasted passages from Malthus's *Principles of Political Economy*. On the one hand, he found that the greater wealth resulting from the introduction of the potato into Ireland in the eighteenth century was "spent almost exclusively in the maintenance of large and frequent families." On the other hand, when the price of corn in England fell between 1660 and 1720, a considerable portion of the workpeople's "increased real wages was expended in a marked improvement of the quality of the food consumed, and a decided elevation in the standard of their comforts and conveniences."[3] It is not possible to prophesy *a priori* the precise proportion in which increased resources will be

---

[1] But cf. Sidgwick's observation: "It seems at least highly doubtful whether a mere increase in the number of human beings living as an average unskilled labourer lives in England can be regarded as involving a material increase in the quantum of human happiness" (*Principles of Political Economy*, p. 522, note).

[2] Cf. Pareto, *Cours d'économie politique*, pp. 88 *et seq.* Cf. also Marshall, *Principles of Economics*, pp. 189-90.

[3] *Principles of Political Economy*, pp. 252 and 254.

devoted to these two uses. The proportion will vary at
different times and in different places. Leroy-Beaulieu, for
example, suggests that the population use has been predominantly followed in recent times in Belgium and Germany,
and the standard-of-comfort use in other European countries.[1]
But—and this is the point—it is practically certain that
the population use will not be allowed to absorb the *whole*
fruits of increased command over nature.

§ 14. The preceding argument, as was indicated at the
outset, leaves out of account the deeper-seated reactions
that may be set up by expanded earnings. An important
school of writers, headed by Professor Brentano, admits
that the direct and immediate effect of enhanced material
prosperity in any class will, in general, be to increase the
marriage rate and, therewith, the birth rate. They maintain,
however, that the enhanced prosperity will in the long run
bring about the development of a higher spiritual and
cultural level, in which more forethought is exercised about
children, and more satisfactions rival to that of having
children come to the front. Hence, they urge, in the long
run an increase in the income of any class is likely to lead
to no increase at all, but actually to a decrease, in their
birth rate and their numbers.[2] Thus, Professor Brentano
declares that a permanent improvement in wealth and
culture, "as a comparison of different ranks, as well as
of the same ranks and the same people at different stages
of development has shown us, results in a diminution
of births. . . . As prosperity increases, so do the pleasures
which compete with marriage, while the feeling towards
children takes on a new character of refinement, and both
these facts tend to diminish the desire to beget and to bear
children."[3] Those persons, for instance, who have something
to leave to their children are more affected by the fact that,
if their family is large, what is left at their death must
be divided into a number of small parts, than those who
have nothing to leave and act apart from economic motives.

[1] *La Répartition des richesses*, p. 439.
[2] Cf. Mombert, *Archiv für Socialwissenschaft*, vol. xxxiv. p. 817. Cf. also
Aftalion, *Les Crises périodiques de surproduction*, vol. i. pp. 208-9.
[3] *Economic Journal*, 1910, p. 385.

Detailed confirmation of this view is afforded by Dr. Heron's statistical study of London. In certain selected districts he found the correlation co-efficients between the number of births per 100 wives and various indices of social status. The indices chosen were the proportion of occupied males engaged in professional occupations, the number of female domestic servants per 100 families, the number of general labourers per 1000 males, the proportion of the population living more than two in a room, and the number of paupers and of lunatics per 1000 of the population. A low index of prosperity and a high birth rate were found to go together. Against this result there had to be set the fact that a low index of prosperity was also accompanied by a high rate of infant mortality. Investigation, however, showed that the excess of mortality was not sufficient to balance the excess of births; and the conclusion emerged, that "the wives in the districts of least prosperity and culture (and of course these poor wives were married to poor husbands) have the largest families."[1] Furthermore, a comparison between the conditions of 1851 and 1901 brought out the startling fact "that the intensity of this relationship has almost doubled in the last fifty years."[2] The inferences suggested by these statistical comparisons are, indeed, less firmly based than they appear to be at first sight. The correlation between high prosperity and low birth rate may be partly due to the fact that a man with a small family is in a better position to accumulate a fortune, and that between rich districts and low birth rate may be partly due to the accumulation of domestic servants and other

[1] *The Relation of Fertility in Man to Social Status*, pp. 15 and 19. M. Bertillon has shown that, in general, a high birth rate and a high death rate are correlated (*La Dépopulation de la France*, pp. 66 *et seq.*). This correlation is partly due to the fact that the death of children induces parents to get more, and partly to the fact that a high birth rate often means many children born in poor circumstances and so likely to die. Thus, Dr. Newsholme suggests that the observed correlation "is probably due in great part to the fact that large families are common among the poorest classes, and these classes are specially exposed to influences producing excessive infant mortality" (Second Report on Infant Mortality [Cd. 6909] p. 57). A similar conclusion as regards the North of England is reached in Elderton's *Report on the English Birth-rate*, Part I.

[2] *The Relation of Fertility in Man to Social Status*, pp. 15 and 19.

dependants—a particularly infertile class—in these districts.[1] Moreover, probably a part of the correlation between wealth and small families is due to the fact that physiologically infertile stocks, having their property divided among fewer persons on inheritance, tend, on the average, to be more than ordinarily rich.[2]   But these considerations, important as they are, do not, there is reason to believe, completely account for the observed facts.   What has been said of the deeper-seated reactions of prosperity appreciably strengthens our conclusion that an improvement in the fortunes of the poor is not likely, in an isolated community, to cancel itself by causing a large expansion of population.

§ 15. When account is taken of the fact that, in the modern world, no country is isolated from the rest, the issue becomes less plain.   Of course, if the real income of the manual working class anywhere is increased because the average level of efficiency among that class has been raised, no inducement is thereby offered to immigration from elsewhere.   But, if their real income has been increased through some discovery, or invention, or stroke of policy, that improves the economic position of one country considerably more than it improves that of others, an inducement is offered.   The same thing happens if legislative or other measures bring about a transference of income from the richer to the poorer members of some one community—provided, of course, that poor persons who have immigrated are not excluded from the benefits of

---

[1] Cf. Leroy-Beaulieu's argument: "Il se trouve dans les quartiers riches une plus forte proportion de ménages âgés, de gens retraités, de domestiques, classe particulièrement stérile, et personnes qui ne passent qu'une partie de l'année à la ville ; la natalité enregistrée doit donc y être plus faible, sans qu'on puisse rien en inférer.   On qualifie le XVIᵉ arrondissement qui compte 135,000 habitants comme un arrondissement riche et le VIIIᵉ également qui, de son côte, compte 104,000 habitants.   Or, il est manifeste que les gens vraiment riches ne représentent pas la dixième partie, peut-être pas même la vingtième partie, de la population de ces arrondissements dits riches ; les gens opulents ne se comptent pas, même à Paris, par centaines de mille ; le gros de la population de ces arrondissements est composé de domestiques, de concierges, de petits boutiquiers et d'ouvriers d'élite.   Les conclusions que l'on tire de la natalité dans les quartiers dits riches de Paris sont donc sans valeur." (*La Question de la population*, p. 399.)

[2] Cf. Darwin, "Eugenics in Relation to Economics and Statistics," *Journal of the Royal Statistical Society*, 1919, p. 7.

these measures.[1] These considerations are very important; for they show that many causes tending to increase the real income per head of the wage-earners in a single country will ultimately exercise a smaller influence in that direction than they appear likely to do at first sight. It should not be forgotten, however, that that very immigration, which lessens their effect at the point of primary impact, involves indirectly an improvement in the fortunes of labour elsewhere. Hence, in any event, the beneficial influence of the changed conditions is not destroyed; but is merely spread over a wider area. In the country primarily affected *some* addition to economic welfare is necessarily secured.

§ 16. The above discussion disproves the suggestion that an increase in the real income of any group will be neutralised by an expansion of population. For the defence of our proposition about the relation between economic welfare and the average volume of the national dividend, this is all that is wanted. But the proposition about the effect on economic welfare of transferences of income from the rich to the poor is less secure. For, in order to cancel the direct benefit of these transferences, it is not necessary that the gain of economic welfare to the poor should be destroyed—only that it should be made smaller than the loss of economic welfare to the rich. It cannot be denied that this *might* happen. But, in a country where the distribution of wealth is as uneven as it is in the United Kingdom, and where, therefore, there are many high incomes which could be largely cut down with very little injury to economic welfare, the chance that it *will* happen may reasonably be regarded as small.

§ 17. We come next to the relation between economic welfare and the variability of the national dividend as a whole. Here, since it is possible by deliberate action greatly to diminish the variability of the community's consumable income, while leaving that of the national dividend unchanged, the distinction between national dividend and consumable income has much greater importance than it had in any

---

[1] The inducement to immigration offered by old-age pensions might be kept very small by a rule requiring previous residence of, say, 20 years as a condition of qualification ; for a far-off benefit affects action but slightly, the more so if, as in this case, the possibility of death makes it uncertain as well as distant.

previous portion of this discussion. This fact makes the argument a complicated one.

The first step is as follows. In § 11 it was shown that, if a given quantity of resources is consumed by two similar men, economic welfare is larger, the more evenly this quantity is shared between them. When the number of our imaginary group was increased from two similar men to many similar men, it was shown that economic welfare *is likely* to be larger, the more evenly consumption is divided among them—the degree of evenness of distribution being measured by the standard, or mean square, deviation. It is obvious that the result thus achieved is equally applicable when, for many similar men at one moment, we substitute one man at many similar moments. When the aggregate consumption of an individual, whose tastes and needs over a series of years are constant, is given, economic welfare is likely to be larger the more evenly that consumption is spread over these years.[1] From this proposition we proceed to the further proposition, that the economic welfare of a group of individuals is likely to be larger the more evenly the consumption of the representative or average member of that group is distributed through time. By an extension of the reasoning of the note to § 11 above it is readily shown that this latter proposition has equal validity with that just enunciated, when the evenness of the distribution through time of the representative member's consumption is measured by the arithmetical average of the standard, or mean square, deviations of the several members.

The second step of the argument has to do with the relation between the variability of the consumption of the representative member and the variability of the aggregate consumption of the whole community. When the variability of the community's consumption is given, the variability of the representative man's consumption will partly depend on

---

[1] Of course, if the individual's needs vary—they are likely to be greater in the period when he has a family to support than they are either before he marries or after his children become self-supporting—welfare will be greater, the more closely variations in consumption are adapted to variations in needs. For a good account of the way in which a normal working man's needs vary in different periods of his life, cf. Leroy-Beaulieu, *Répartition des richesses*, pp. 452-3.

F

how far mutual insurance arrangements provide, in effect, that those who are temporarily prosperous shall assist the temporarily unfortunate. Let us suppose, however, that the state of these arrangements is given. Then, if people were perfectly mobile between different places and occupations, anything that made the whole community's consumption less variable would necessarily also make the representative man's less variable. When perfect mobility does not exist, this need not happen; for the consumption of the community as an aggregate *might* be made steadier by a cause which made less steady the consumption of each several part of it. It is plain, however, that the generality of economic causes affecting the variability of consumption will not act in this way. One reason is that they are blind causes, "random in the technical sense" from the present point of view; and a cause which diminishes variability in one part of a group is most unlikely, unless it is specially selected for that end, so to react on variability in other parts that it increases the variability of the whole. A second reason is that by far the most important of these causes, those, namely, that act through the bounty of Nature or through business confidence, impinge directly upon the whole, without being specialised to any part. When these causes are at work, the variability of the representative man's consumption necessarily rises and falls with that of consumption in the community as a whole.

The third step concerns the relation between the variability of the aggregate *consumption* of the community and the variability of the *income of consumable goods*—or consumable income—accruing to it. These two variabilities will be different if people in good times store up consumable goods in warehouses and shops against the bad times that may follow. But, though they may be different, it is obvious that the two are correlated. Other things being equal, the variability of consumption is certain to be greater the greater is the variability of the consumable income.

The fourth and final step in the argument concerns the relation between the variability of the consumable income of the community and that of the aggregate dividend accruing to it. It is plain that the former variability will, in general, be considerably smaller than the latter, because many people invest in producers' goods, not a constant proportion of their income, but the surplus that is left to them after living up to their normal standard of life. This means that the quantity of resources invested in producers' goods will in bad times be diminished much more than the national dividend, and in good times expanded much more than the national dividend. Hence, the part of the dividend that constitutes consumable income must vary less than the whole dividend varies. This is certain. But it is also certain that, other things being equal, the variability of the consumable income of the community will be greater the greater is the variability of the aggregate dividend accruing to it.

There results from the above analysis my third main proposition: *Any cause which diminishes the variability of the national dividend, provided that it neither diminishes its volume nor injures its distribution, will, in general, increase economic welfare.*

§ 18. There remains the last of the four attributes of the national dividend that were distinguished in § 1, namely the variability of that part of it which accrues to the poorer members of the community. Here, as in the preceding section, we must study first the relation between economic welfare and the variability of consumption. Experience shows that the rate, at which the "desiredness" of consumable income to an individual diminishes, itself diminishes as the magnitude of his consumption increases.[1] It follows that the difference between the economic satisfaction yielded by a constant consumption x and a consumption the average volume of which is x, but which oscillates from $(x+h)$ to $(x-h)$, is greater the smaller is x. Hence, other things being equal, a given absolute variability in the consumption of a poor man, or a group of poor men, is more detrimental to economic welfare than an equal absolute variability in the consumption of a rich man or a rich group. This conclusion is emphasised by the reflection that, among poor persons, variability of consumption often involves,

[1] That is to say, in geometrical terms, the curve representing the desiredness of successive increments of consumable income to an individual is convex when looked at from the origin. Cf. my *Principles and Methods of Industrial Peace*, p. 70.

not merely loss of satisfaction at the moment, but also physical, and perhaps moral, damage injurious to their productive power in the future; while among rich people there are not likely to be any significant reactions of this kind. It follows that the economic welfare of rich and poor jointly will be increased by any system of transferences which, while leaving the average consumption of each group unaltered, makes the consumption of the poor less variable at the cost of making that of the rich in a corresponding degree more variable. It is, of course, conceivable that, by means of elaborate systems of borrowing, poor persons might establish for themselves a perfectly stable consumption in spite of their income being unstable; so that no advantage could be got by stabilising their income at the cost of rendering unstable the income of better-to-do persons. In practice, however, it is quite certain that they will not succeed in doing this. Consequently, from what has been said it is legitimate to infer a fourth main proposition: *Any cause which diminishes the variability of the part of the national dividend accruing to the poor, even though it increases in corresponding measure the variability of the part accruing to the rich, will, other things being equal, increase economic welfare.* For analytic completeness, it is worth while to set out this proposition. But, when we come in Part VI. to discuss variability in detail, it will be found that practical interest is confined to causes which affect in the same sense the variability of the aggregate national dividend and of the part of it accruing to the poor; and that nothing will need to be said of the type of cause contemplated in this section.

CHAPTER V

THE MEASUREMENT OF CHANGES IN THE MAGNITUDE OF THE
NATIONAL DIVIDEND AND ITS PARTS

§ 1. IN the preceding chapter it was tacitly assumed that
the conception of an increase or decrease in the national
dividend as a whole, or in the share of it accruing to any
group of persons, is definite and unambiguous. If the
dividend consisted of a single sort of commodity only, such
as wheat, this condition would, of course, be fulfilled. In
fact, however, what the community as a whole, or any group
within the community, receives from time to time as dividend
is not one large parcel of one single thing, but a number
of small parcels of different things. The sizes of these
different parcels vary independently, so that their increases
or decreases are generally in different proportions, and not
infrequently some are growing larger at the same time that
others are growing smaller. In these circumstances the
conception of an increase or decrease in the quantity of
dividend or real income accruing to any group is not
unambiguous. On the contrary, it can be defined in any
one of several different ways. Between these it is impossible
to make a choice on grounds of absolute rightness. The
only sort of rightness that is relevant is suitability for
the purpose in hand. That purpose is as follows. It has
been shown that, if the dividend was homogeneous, any cause
(operating otherwise than through compulsion to work or
through certain exceptional obstacles to movement) which
increases the productive efficiency, and, therewith, the real
earnings of any group, would, in general, increase the economic
welfare or satisfaction enjoyed by that group. The object

69

of a large part of this volume being to develop the practical implications of that proposition, it is obviously desirable so to define our terms that the above proposition shall also hold good of the *heterogeneous* dividend which emerges in actual life. Therefore, I *define a change in the dividend, or real income, of a group as follows. Apart from the introduction of compulsion to work or of the exceptional obstacles to movement referred to in the last chapter, this quantity is larger or smaller in period A than in period B, according as the amount of economic satisfaction derived from it (including the discounted future yield due to the machinery included in it), by a representative member of the group—in so far as the tastes and temperament of the group have not been changed by external causes (i.e. otherwise than as an indirect effect of their changed purchases)—is larger or smaller.*[1] The qualification set out in the last part of this sentence is obviously necessary; for, unless it was made, we should have to say that the dividend necessarily increases if people come to get more enjoyment out of it, even though its actual material content has remained unaltered. This is paradoxical and is not required in order to make our definition fit in with the main propositions of the preceding chapter.[2] It will be noticed that the definition does *not* rule out of account changes in tastes that come about as a result

---

[1] In this definition and the discussion that follows it the distinction between the measure of desire for a thing and the measure of satisfaction obtained from the possession of a desired thing, to which attention was drawn in Chapter II., is left out of account as not being of great practical importance. For theoretical completeness, of course, allowance would need to be made for it.

[2] The autonomous changes in tastes and temperament, whose effects on satisfaction are thus ruled out as irrelevant to the magnitude of the national dividend, may be distinguished into two groups: (1) changes in the intensity of desire generally, and (2) changes in the desire for some things as compared with others. This distinction can be illustrated most easily from different places instead of different times. Thus, if we contrast social classes, we may sometimes be able to say that the more cultured class A has a keener appreciation of, and derives more satisfaction from, practically all objects than the less cultured class B does. On the other hand, if we contrast the same social class in different countries, say English and German workmen, we may expect to find *general* temperaments to be much the same, but particular tastes to be different. To put the point more precisely, in case (1) we should expect £100 to yield more satisfaction in either environment to the more cultured class than to other classes; whereas in case (2) we should expect the aggregate satisfaction obtained by a German workman, from spending £100 this year in Germany and £100 next year in England, to be about the same as that

of changes in purchases. This is an important point. If certain commodities become scarce and others abundant, people, though at first perhaps getting less satisfaction out of the new purchases than out of the old, may after a time get accustomed to them and prefer them to the old. It might, therefore, happen that an enforced change from, say, a meat diet to a fish diet would lessen satisfaction for the moment, *and* that, if, after a year or so, there were an enforced return to the original meat diet, this change also would lessen satisfaction for the moment. This fluidity and adaptability of tastes cannot rightly be left out of account in a definition of the national dividend framed for the purpose here indicated. That purpose being avowedly selected in an arbitrary manner, it would be idle to canvas the *general* merits of the definition. Its merit here is that it, and it alone, is fitted for the purpose which I wish to carry out.

§ 2. So far as the main thesis of my book is concerned, it would be legitimate to stop at this point, and those who are not interested in technical problems would do well to adopt that course. I propose, however, to go a step further. Given the above definition of a change in the volume of the dividend enjoyed by a group, it is desirable to devise a *measure* of change that shall conform to that definition. The search for that measure comprises three parts: first,

---

derived by an English workman from a like proceeding, but the £100 spent in Germany to yield more to the German, and the £100 spent in England more to the English workman. Differences of the first type, *i.e.* in the general level of tastes, can never be revealed by statistics. But differences in the relative level of various tastes can sometimes be revealed by them. For example, Germans before the war would not eat mutton though it was a penny cheaper than pork, while Englishmen eat it readily (Cd. 4032, pp. xlviii and xlix). Again Germans eat rye bread, whereas English people eat white bread. We know that this is not due merely to the fact that rye bread is relatively cheap in Germany and that Germans are poorer than Englishmen, because, if it were cheapness alone that was responsible for the consumption of rye in Germany, there would presumably be a higher consumption of white bread among better-to-do Germans. This, however, is not found. Hence, we may legitimately infer that Germans have a taste for rye bread, as against wheaten bread, different from the English taste. When either of the two types of difference, or change, of taste thus distinguished is present, the measure constructed in the text cannot safely be used as an index of changes or differences in economic welfare.

a general enquiry as to what measure would satisfy the condition if all relevant information were accessible ; secondly, a mathematical enquiry as to what practicable measure built up from the sample information that we can in fact obtain would approximate most closely to this ideal measure ; thirdly, a mixed general and mathematical enquiry as to *how reliable* the practicable measure is likely to be.

§ 3. The root fact confronting us is that in the first period our group expends its purchasing power upon one collection of commodities, and in the second period it expends it on a second and different collection. Each collection must, of course, be so estimated that the same thing is not counted twice over, that is to say, it must be taken to include direct services rendered to consumers— *e.g.* the services of doctors, finished consumable articles, and a portion of the finished durable machines produced during the year,[1] but not the raw materials or the services of labour that are embodied in these things, and not, of course, "securities." Let us ignore the fact that in one of the collections there may be some newly invented kinds of commodity which are not represented at all in the other. The first collection, which we may call C_1, then embraces x_1, y_1, z_1 . . . units of various commodities; and the second collection, C_2, embraces x_2, y_2, z_2 . . . units of the same commodities. Let the prices per unit of these several commodities be, in the first period, a_1, b_1, c_1, . . .; and in the second period, a_2, b_2, c_2, . . . Let the aggregate money income of our group, in the first period, be I_1, in the second I_2. The following propositions result :

1. If our group in the second period purchased the several commodities in the same proportion in which it purchased them in the first period, that is to say, if it purchased in both periods a collection of the general form C_1, its purchase of

---

[1] This is necessary in order to conform to the definition of the national dividend given in Chap. III. Had we defined the dividend so that it included only what is actually consumed during the year, no machines would come into it. On our definition we ought strictly to include all new machinery and plant over and above what is required to maintain capital intact, *minus* an allowance for that part of the value of this machinery and plant that is used up in producing consumable goods during the year itself. In practice, of course, these subtleties must be ignored.

each commodity in the second period would be equal to its purchase of each commodity in the first period multiplied by the fraction

$$\frac{I_2}{I_1} \cdot \frac{x_1 a_1 + y_1 b_1 + z_1 c_1 +}{x_1 a_2 + y_1 b_2 + x_1 c_2 +}$$

2. If our group in the first period purchased the several commodities in the same proportion in which it purchased them in the second period, that is to say, if it purchased in both periods a collection of the general form C_2, its purchase of each commodity in the second period would be equal to its purchase of each commodity in the first period multiplied by the fraction

$$\frac{I_2}{I_1} \cdot \frac{x_2 a_1 + y_2 b_1 + z_2 c_1 + \ldots}{x_2 a_2 + y_2 b_2 + z_2 c_2 + \ldots}$$

On the basis of these propositions the problem which we have set ourselves can be solved.

§ 4. First, it sometimes happens that both the fractions distinguished above lie upon the same side of unity; they are either both greater than unity or both less than unity. If they are both greater than unity, this means that our group, if it wishes, can buy more commodities in the second period than in the first, whether its purchases are arranged in the form of collection C_1 or in that of collection C_2. Hence, the fact that in the second period it chooses the form C_2 proves that what it purchases in this form yields it more satisfaction than it could get from a collection of the form C_1 larger than the collection of that form which it purchased in the first period.[1] A fortiori, therefore, its purchase in the second period yields it more satisfaction than it did get from the actual collection of the form C_1 which it did purchase in the first period. Hence, if both our fractions are greater than unity, it necessarily follows—provided that the tastes and temperament of the representative man are not changed through external causes—that the economic satisfaction enjoyed by the

---

[1] This proposition and the results based upon it depend on the condition that our group is *able* to buy at the ruling price the quantity of any commodity which it wishes to buy at that price. When official maximum prices have been fixed, and people's purchases at those prices are restricted, either by a process of rationing or by the fact that at those prices there is not enough of the commodity to satisfy the demand, this condition is, of course, not satisfied.

group in the second period is greater than it was in the first period. By analogous reasoning—again provided that the tastes and temperament of the representative man are not changed through external causes—it can be shown that, if both fractions are less than unity, the economic satisfaction enjoyed by the group in the first period is greater than it is in the second period. In these circumstances, therefore, either of the two fractions

$$\frac{I_2}{I_1} \cdot \frac{x_1 a_1 + y_1 b_1 + z_1 c_1 \ldots}{x_1 a_2 + y_1 b_2 + z_1 c_2 \ldots} \quad \text{or} \quad \frac{I_2}{I_1} \cdot \frac{x_2 a_1 + y_2 b_1 + z_2 c_1 + \ldots}{x_2 a_2 + y_2 b_2 + z_2 c_2 + \ldots},$$

or any mean between them, will satisfy the condition that our measure is required to fulfil as a criterion of changes in the volume of the dividend.

§ 5. In the above circumstances, therefore, the condition we have laid down does not determine the choice of a measure, but merely fixes the limits within which that choice must lie. The width of these limits depends upon the extent to which the two fractions differ from one another. In some conditions there exists between them a relation of approximate equality. In recent years, as regards the United Kingdom, this relation seems to have prevailed. Half a century ago, no doubt, man's power in different directions was increasing very unevenly. Of late, however, the dominant factor in the Englishman's increased capacity to obtain almost every important commodity is one and the same, namely, improved transport; for a main part of what improvements in manufacture now accomplish is to cheapen means of transport. In other conditions the difference between the two fractions is considerable. Illustrations that would be directly applicable could easily be found. I prefer, however, to make use of one drawn, not from an inter-temporary comparison of two states of the same group, but from a contemporary comparison of the states of two groups. This illustration is provided in the Board of Trade's Report on the *Cost of Living in German Towns*. The Report shows that, at the time when it was made, what an English workman customarily consumed cost about one-fifth more in Germany than in England, while what a German workman customarily consumed cost about

one-tenth more in Germany than in England.[1] If we assume
—*what is, of course, not true*—that English and German
workmen's incomes and tastes are equivalent, and that their
consumption differs only on account of price differences, and,
if the collection x_1, etc., is the German consumption and the
collection x_2, etc., the English consumption, this result can
be expressed in the form :

$$\frac{x_1 a_1 + y_1 b_1 + z_1 c_1}{x_1 a_2 + y_1 b_2 + z_1 c_2} = \frac{100}{120}, \text{ and } \frac{x_2 a_1 + y_2 b_1 + z_2 c_1}{x_2 a_2 + y_2 b_2 + z_2 c_2} = \frac{100}{110}.$$

§ 6. Though our condition, in the class of problem so far considered, only fixes these two limits within which the measure
of dividend changes should lie, considerations of convenience
suggest even here the wisdom of selecting, though it be in an
arbitrary manner, some one among the indefinite number of
possible measures. When we proceed from this class of
problem to another more difficult class, the need for purely
arbitrary choice is narrower in range. It sometimes happens
that one of the above two fractions is greater than unity and
the other less than unity. Then it is clear that both of them
cannot indicate the direction in which the economic satisfaction
enjoyed by the group has changed. In the second period, let
us suppose, the representative man's later money income
commands a larger amount of the collection of form C_2 than
his earlier income commanded ; but it commands a smaller
amount of the collection of form C_1 than his earlier income
commanded. In these circumstances common sense suggests
that, if the fraction

$$\frac{I_2}{I_1} \cdot \frac{x_1 a_1 + y_1 b_1 + z_1 c_1 + \ldots}{x_1 a_2 + y_1 b_2 + z_1 c_2 + \ldots}$$

falls short of unity by a large proportion, while the fraction

$$\frac{I_2}{I_1} \cdot \frac{x_2 a_1 + y_2 b_1 + z_2 c_1 + \ldots}{x_2 a_2 + y_2 b_2 + z_2 c_2 + \ldots}$$

exceeds unity only by a small proportion, the economic
satisfaction enjoyed by the representative member of our
group has *probably* diminished ; and that, if conditions of an
opposite character are realised, it has probably increased.

[1] [Cd. 4032], pp. vii and xlv.

This *prima facie* conclusion can be confirmed by direct analysis as follows. If

$$\frac{I_2}{I_1} \cdot \frac{x_1 a_1 + y_1 b_1 + z_1 c_1 + \dots}{x_1 a_2 + y_1 b_2 + z_1 c_2 + \dots}$$

is less than unity by a large fraction, this means that, were our representative man to purchase in the second year a collection of the form C_1, his purchases of each item would be less by a large percentage than they were in the first year, and therefore—tastes and temperament being unchanged—he would probably enjoy an amount of satisfaction less than in the first year by a large amount, say by K_1. Therefore, the fact that, instead of doing this, he purchases in the second year a collection of the form C_2 proves only that the satisfaction yielded by his purchase of this collection in the second year does not fall short of that yielded by his purchase of the other collection in the first year by more than K_1. In like manner if

$$\frac{I_2}{I_1} \cdot \frac{x_2 a_1 + y_2 b_1 + z_2 c_1 + \dots}{x_2 a_2 + y_2 b_2 + z_2 c_2 + \dots}$$

is greater than unity by only a small fraction, this means that, were our representative man to purchase a collection of the forms C_2 in the first year, his purchases of each item would be less by only a small percentage than they are in the second year, and—tastes and temperament being unchanged—he would probably enjoy an amount of satisfaction less than in the second year by only a small amount, say K_2. Hence, we know that the satisfaction yielded by the collection actually purchased in the second year does not exceed that of the collection actually purchased in the first year by more than K_2. Since, therefore, in view of the largeness of K_1 relatively to K_2, there are more ways in which the satisfaction from the second year's purchase can be less, than there are ways in which it can be more, than the satisfaction from the first year's purchase, and since, further, the probability of any one of these different ways is *prima facie* equal to that of any other, it is *probable* that the satisfaction from the second year's purchase is less than that from the first. This argument, as stated thus far, depends on the assumption that temperament and tastes are unchanged. When account is taken of the fact, referred to at the end of § 1, that tastes tend to adapt themselves to what they feed on, it must be recognised that both K_1 and K_2 will prove in fact to be smaller than they would have been on the assumption of fixed tastes. But this gives no reason to suppose that their relative magnitude will be significantly affected; and all that our argument essentially needs is that K_1 shall be large relatively to K_2. Hence the argument remains valid; and we may conclude that the satisfaction obtained by the representative man in our group *probably* decreases or increases in the second period according as either

$$\frac{I_2}{I_1} \cdot \frac{x_1 a_1 + y_1 b_1 + z_1 c_1 \quad \cdots}{x_1 a_2 + y_1 b_2 + z_1 c_2 + \cdots} \times \frac{I_2}{I_1} \cdot \frac{x_2 a_1 + y_2 b_1 + z_2 c_1 + \cdots}{x_2 a_2 + y_2 b_2 + z_2 c_2 + \cdots}$$

or

$$\frac{I_2}{I_1} \cdot \frac{x_1 a_1 + y_1 b_1 + z_1 c_1 +}{x_1 a_2 + y_1 b_2 + z_1 c_2 +} - \frac{I_1}{I_2} \cdot \frac{x_2 a_2 + y_2 b_2 + z_2 c_2 +}{x_2 a_1 + y_2 b_1 + z_2 c_1 +},$$

or any power of either of these expressions, is greater or less than unity. Any fraction constructed on any of the above plans will, therefore, *probably* satisfy the conditions required of our measure.[1]

---

[1] It may be thought at first sight that the formulae of the text will often fail to yield a correct indication of changes in economic welfare, because they pay no attention to the fact that, of two commodities costing equal amounts of money, one may, nevertheless, carry a much greater quantity of "satisfaction" than the other. Thus Pierson writes: "The price of an article, though it expresses the utility of the last increment of that article, affords no indication whatever of each of the preceding increments. With respect to this two things are possible; the value attached to them may be only slightly greater than that attached to the last increment, or the difference in value may be very great" (*Principles of Economics*, vol. ii. pp. 33-4). It follows from this that, if we start with two articles, equal alike in quantity and in price, a halving of the supply of the one may affect economic welfare very much more than a halving of the supply of the other. That is, of course, perfectly true. But it is an error to suppose that this fact is not taken into account by our formulae. It is taken into account, because a given contraction in the supply of a commodity of inelastic demand is necessarily associated with a much larger rise of price than an equal contraction in the supply of a commodity of elastic demand. Thus, if the commodity of which x_1 units is purchased in the first period and x_2 (say half of x_1) in the second is of inelastic demand, this *implies* that a_2 will be very large relatively to a_1 and, therefore, that our formulae are much more likely to work out at a figure less than unity, thus indicating diminished economic welfare, than they would have been if the demand for this commodity had been elastic.

§ 7. The results thus obtained fix these limits within which the choice of an appropriate measure must lie. Since, however, they still exhibit an indefinite number of possible measures, any one of which would satisfy the fundamental condition that has been laid down, they do not *determine* the choice of that measure. We have, therefore, to take a further step and to choose among many eligible forms the one we deem *most* eligible. In this matter our procedure must necessarily be more or less arbitrary. Simplicity and convenience, on the whole, point to the square root of the product of the proportionate change in the purchasable amount of a collection of the form C_1 and of the proportionate change in the purchasable amount of a collection of the form C_1. In other words, they point to the formula

$$\frac{I_2}{I_1}\sqrt{\frac{x_1a_1 + y_1b_1 + z_1c_1 + \ldots}{x_1a_2 + y_1b_2 + z_1c_2 + \ldots} \times \frac{x_2a_1 + y_2b_1 + z_2c_1 + \ldots}{x_2a_2 + y_2b_2 + z_2c_2 + \ldots}}$$

as the measure of change most satisfactory for our purpose. Obviously the portion of this expression to the right of $\frac{I_2}{I_1}$ is the reciprocal of an index of the change that has taken place in general prices.

§ 8. The successful employment of the above formula depends, it will be observed, upon the assumption that no commodities are included in either of the collections C_1 and C_2 which are not included in both. If, therefore, a commodity is available for purchase in one of the two years but not in the other, the satisfaction yielded by this commodity in the year in which it is purchased is wholly ignored by our measure. So far then as "new commodities" are introduced between two periods which are being compared, that measure is imperfect. This matter is important, because new commodities, in the sense here relevant, embrace, not merely commodities that are new physically, but also old commodities that have become obtainable at new times or places, such as strawberries in December, or the wheat which railways have introduced into parts of India where it was formerly unknown. Obviously, we must not count December strawberries along with ordinary strawberries, and so make inventions for strawberry forcing raise the price of strawberries, but must reckon December strawberries as a new and distinct commodity. Since, however, new commodities seldom play an important part in the consumption of any group till some little while after they are first introduced, the imperfection due to this is much less serious for comparisons between two successive years than for comparisons between years separated by a long interval.[1] This consideration suggests that comparisons between distant years are best made, not directly, but by year to year steps. This can be done by means of the chain method devised by Dr. Marshall.[2] On this method direct comparisons are made only between each year and its immediate predecessor and successor, and the year 1860 is compared with 1890, not directly, but through a chain of successive comparisons. Thus, we may suppose prices in 1861 to be 95 per cent of what they were in 1860 : those in 1862 to be 82 per cent of those in 1861, and so on. Then prices in 1890 will be $100 \left\{ \dfrac{95}{100} \times \dfrac{82}{100} \times \cdots \right.$

per cent of prices in 1860.

§ 9. We now turn to the second main problem of this chapter. The formula set out above is accepted as the ideally best measure for our purpose. But it cannot be employed in practice because, in order to construct it, a great deal of information would be necessary which is never in fact available. It is therefore necessary to construct, from such information as we can obtain, a model, or representative, measure that shall approximate to it as closely as possible. Our ideal measure, apart from its multiplier $\dfrac{I_2}{I_1}$ representing change of income, is built up of two parts: the reciprocal of the price change of the collection C_1 (containing quantities of different commodities equal to $x_1, y_1, z_1, \ldots$), and the reciprocal of the price change of the collection C_2 (containing quantities equal to $x_2, y_2, z_2, \ldots$). Our approximate measure

---

[1] Similar considerations suggest that the existence of "new commodities," or rather, in this case, different commodities, is a more serious obstacle in the way of comparing two distant than two neighbouring places, because it is much more likely that one of the two distant places, than it is that one of the two neighbouring places, will purchase commodities that are not known in the other.

[2] Cf. Marshall, *Contemporary Review*, March 1887, p. 371 *et seq.*

will, therefore, also be built up of two parts constituting approximations to the price change of C_1 and of C_2 respectively. By what use of the method of sampling can these approximations best be made?

§ 10. With whatever collection of commodities we are concerned, whether it be that purchased at any time by people in general, or by the manual workers, or by any other body of persons, it is likely to contain commodities drawn from several different groups, the broad characteristics of whose price movements are different. It is obvious that a good sample collection should contain representatives of all the groups with different characteristics that enter into the national dividend, or that part of it which we are trying to measure.[1] Unfortunately, however, practical considerations make it impossible that this requirement should be satisfied, and even make it necessary that resort should be had to commodities that do not themselves enter into the purchases of ordinary people, but are, like wheat and barley, raw materials of commodities that do. For the range of things whose prices we are able to observe and bring into our collection of samples is limited in two directions.

First, except for certain articles of large popular consumption, the retail prices charged to consumers are difficult to ascertain. Giffen once went so far as to say: "Practically it is found that only the prices of leading commodities capable of being dealt with in large wholesale markets can be made use of." This statement must now be qualified, in view of recent studies of retail prices of food that have been made by the Board of Trade and Ministry of Food, but it still holds good over a considerable field. Even, however, when the difficulty of ascertaining retail prices can be overcome, these prices are unsuitable for comparison over a series of years, because the thing priced

---

[1] Professor Mitchell writes: "The sluggish movement of manufactured goods and of consumers' commodities in particular, the capricious jumping of farm products, the rapidly increasing dearness of lumber, etc., are all part and parcel of the fluctuations which the price level is actually undergoing. . . . Every restriction in the scope of the data implies a limitation in the significance of the results" (*Bulletin of the U.S.A. Bureau of Labour Statistics*, No. 173, pp. 66-7). This is quite correct as it stands, but it must not be interpreted to imply that both finished products and the raw materials embodied *in those same* finished products should be included.

is apt to contain a different proportion of the services of the retailer and of the transporter, and, therefore, to be a different thing at one time from what it is at another. "When fresh sea fish could be had only at the seaside, its average price was low. Now that railways enable it to be sold inland, its average retail price includes much higher charges for distribution than it used to do. The simplest plan for dealing with this difficulty is to take, as a rule, the wholesale price of a thing at its place of production, and to allow full weight to the cheapening of the transport of goods, of persons, and of news as separate and most weighty items."[1]

Secondly, it is very difficult to take account even of the wholesale prices of manufactured articles, because, while still called by the same name, they are continually undergoing changes in character and quality. Stilton cheese, once a double-cream, is now a single-cream cheese. Clarets of different vintages are not equivalent. A third-class seat in a railway carriage is not the same thing now as it was twenty years ago. "An average ten-roomed house is, perhaps, twice as large in volume as it used to be; and a great part of its cost goes for water, gas, and other appliances which were not in the older house."[2] "During the past twelve years, owing to more scientific methods of thawing and freezing, the quality of the foreign mutton sold in this country has steadily improved; on the other hand, that of foreign beef has gone down, owing to the fact that the supply from North America has practically ceased, and its place has been taken by a poorer quality coming from the Argentine."[3] The same class of difficulty is met with in attempts to evaluate many direct services—the services of doctors, for example, which, as Pareto pointedly observes, absorb more expenditure than the cotton industry[4]— for these, while retaining their name, often vary their nature.

It would thus seem that the principal things available for observation—though it must be admitted that the official Canadian Index Number and more than one index number employed in the United States have attempted a wider survey

[1] Cf. Marshall, *Contemporary Review*, March 1887, p. 374.
[2] *Ibid.* p. 375.
[3] Mrs. Wood, *Economic Journal*, 1913, pp. 622-3.
[4] *Cours d'économie politique*, p. 281.

—are raw materials in the wholesale. markets, particularly in the large world markets. These things—apart, of course, from the war—have probably of late years fallen in price relatively. to minor articles, in which the cost of transport generally plays a smaller part; they have certainly fallen relatively to personal services; and they have probably risen relatively to manufactured articles, because the actual processes of manufacture have been improving. The probable tendency to mutual compensation in the movements of items omitted from our samples makes the omission a less serious evil than it would otherwise be. But, of course, the approximation to a true measure is *pro tanto* worsened; and it is almost certain, since the value of raw materials is often only a small proportion of the value of finished products, so that a 50 per cent change in the former might involve only a 5 per cent change in the latter, that it will give an exaggerated impression of the fluctuations, that occur.

Nor does what has just been said exhaust the list of our disabilities. For the samples wanted to represent the several "collections" is a list, not merely of prices, but of prices multiplied by quantities purchased: and our information about quantities is in general even more limited than our information about prices. There are very few records of annual output—still less of annual purchases—of commodities produced at home. Quantities of imports are, indeed, recorded, but there are not very many important things that are wholly obtained by importation. The difficulty can, indeed, be turned, for some purposes, by resort to typical budgets of expenditure. These make it possible to get a rough idea of the average purchases of certain principal articles that are made by particular classes of people. But this method can scarcely as yet provide more than rough averages. It will seldom enable us to distinguish between the quantities of various things that are embodied in the collections representative of different years fairly close together.

§ 11. Let us next suppose that these difficulties have been so far overcome that a sample embracing both prices and quantities at all relevant periods is available. The next problem is to determine the way in which the prices ought

to be "weighted." At first sight it seems natural that the
weights should be proportioned to the quantities of the several
commodities that are contained in the collection from which
the sample is drawn. But, in theory at all events, it is
possible to improve upon this arrangement. For some of
the commodities about which we have information may be
connected with some excluded commodities in such a way
that their prices generally vary in the same sense. These
commodities, being representative of the others as well as of
themselves, may properly be given weights in excess of what
they are entitled to in their own right. Thus, ideally, if we
had statistics for a few commodities, each drawn from a different
broad group of commodities with similar characteristics, it
would be proper to "weight" the prices of our several
sample commodities in proportion, not to their own importance,
but to that of the groups which they represent. This, however,
is scarcely practicable. There may be certain commodities
whose representative character is so obvious that exceptional
weight may rightly be given to them, but we shall seldom have
enough knowledge to attempt this kind of discrimination.
A system of weighting based on the quantities of the several
commodities that are contained in our sample is, in general,
the best that is practically available.[1] Hence, the ideal
measure of the price change of the collection C_1 being

$$\frac{x_1 a_2 + y_1 b_2 + z_1 c_2 + \ldots}{x_1 a_1 + y_1 b_1 + z_1 c_1 + \ldots},$$

the best available approximation to this will be

$$\frac{x_1 a_2 + y_1 b_2 + \ldots}{x_1 a_1 + y_1 b_1 + \ldots},$$

[1] This proposition can be proved by means of the principle of inverse
probability. There are more ways in which a sample that will change in a
given degree can be drawn from a complete collection which changes in that
degree than there are ways in which such a sample could be drawn from a
collection that changed in a different degree. Therefore any given sample
that has been taken without bias from any collection is more likely to represent
that collection correctly as it stands than it would do after being subjected to
any kind of doctoring. It must be confessed, however, that the question,
whether a commodity whose price has moved very differently from the main
part of our sample ought to be included, is a delicate one. The omission of
"extreme observations" is sometimes deemed desirable in the calculation of
physical measurements. What should be done in this matter depends on

where the terms are limited to the number of sample articles available. It follows that the best approximation to the full ideal measure of dividend change set out at the end of § 7 is

$$\frac{I_2}{I_1}\sqrt{\frac{x_1a_1 + y_1b_1 +}{x_1a_2 + y_1b_2 +} \times \frac{x_2a_1 + y_2b_1 +}{x_2a_2 + y_2b_2 +}}$$

When the available statistics do not make it possible to distinguish the quantities purchased by our group in the two periods that are being compared, and we have to put up with mere rough quantities representing the average purchases of the group in the two periods taken together—quantities that may be symbolised by x_r, y_r, etc.—this formula necessarily yields place to the much inferior expression

$$\frac{I_2}{I_1} \quad \frac{x_ra_1 + y_rb_1 + \ldots}{x_ra_2 + y_rb_2 + \ldots}$$

But this is a *pis aller*. The other formula is the one that must be aimed at.[1]

§ 12. There remains the third portion of our inquiry, namely, a study of the circumstances upon which the *reliability*

---

whether or not *a priori* expectations, coupled with the general form of our sample, show that the original distribution, from which the sample is taken, obeys some ascertained law of error. Whether they do this or not will often be hard to decide. It should be added that the practical effect of omitting extreme observations is only likely to be important when the number of commodities included in our sample is small; and that it is just when this number is small that adequate grounds for exclusion are most difficult to come by.

[1] In the majority of index numbers purporting to provide an approximate measure of the price change of a collection, some year or average of years is taken as base; for this base year, or base period, each of the prices included in the index number is represented by 100; for all other years by a number bearing the same ratio to 100 that the price then bears to the price in the base period. It is often supposed that this process gives the same result as the last formula given in the text and differs from it merely in being arithmetically more convenient. That is a mistake. If p_1 and p_2 represent "the general price level" in the first and second period respectively, the text formula implies

$$\frac{p_2}{p_1} = \frac{x_ra_2 + y_rb_2 + \ldots}{x_ra_1 + y_rb_1 + \ldots}$$

The formula of the ordinary weighted index number, which purports to be identical with this, is, if the first year is taken as base,

$$\frac{p_2}{p_1} = \frac{x_r\left(100\frac{a_2}{a_1}\right) + y_r\left(100\frac{b_2}{b_1}\right)}{x_r(100) + y_r(100)} = \frac{(x_rb_1)a_2 + (y_ra_1)b_2}{(x_rb_1)a_1 + (y_ra_1)b_1}$$

If the second year is taken as base, it is

$$\frac{p_2}{p_1} = \frac{(x_rb_2)a_2 + (y_ra_2)b_2}{(x_rb_2)a_1 + (y_ra_2)b_1}$$

of the above measure, as an index of changes (in the sense defined in § 1) in the volume of the dividend or real income of any group, depends. This reliability is a complex of

---

If the average of the two years is taken as base, it is

$$\frac{p_2}{p_1} = \frac{\{x_r(b_1+b_2)\}a_2 + \{y_r(a_1+a_2)\}b_2}{\{x_r(b_1+b_2)\}a_1 + \{y_r(a_1+a_2)\}b_1}.$$

It is evident from these formulae that the ordinary weighted index number surreptitiously assigns different weights to the various commodities included in it according to the period that is chosen as base. Consequently, the same facts represented in the formula appropriate to one base may indicate a rise in price, and represented in that appropriate to another base they may indicate a fall. An excellent practical illustration of this discrepancy is afforded by certain tables in the Board of Trade publications concerning the cost of living in English and German towns respectively. In the Blue-book dealing with England the real wages of London, the Midlands, and Ireland are calculated by means of index numbers, in which London (corresponding in our time index, say, to the year 1890) is taken as base, and the price of consumables and the rents prevailing there are both represented by 100. On this plan, prices of consumables and rents being given weights of 4 and 1 respectively, the Board of Trade found real wages in London to be equal to those of the Midlands, and 3 per cent higher than those of Ireland. If, however, Ireland had been taken as base, real wages would have appeared—in London 98, in the Midlands 104, in Ireland 100. A similar difficulty emerges in the Blue-book on German towns. The Board of Trade, taking Berlin as base, found real wages higher in that city than in any place save one on their list (Cd. 4032, p. xxxiv). "If the North Sea ports, instead of Berlin, had been taken as base, Berlin would have appeared fourth on the list instead of second, and the order of the other districts would have been changed; and, by taking Central Germany as base, even greater changes in the order would have been effected" (J. M. Keynes, *Economic Journal*, 1908, p. 473). It is true, no doubt, that *large* discrepancies of this sort are not likely to occur, except when there are large differences, or, as between different times, large fluctuations in the prices of commodities that are heavily weighted. But it is practically certain that there will be *some* discrepancy. Since the choice between different base periods is obviously a matter of more or less arbitrary choice, this circumstance is in itself sufficiently disturbing. It is not, however, the main objection to the method of percentages. This is that, whatever base period is chosen, the weights employed are almost necessarily different from those set out in our text formula and are, therefore, almost necessarily *wrong*. A formula built up on the percentage plan, though it purports to be identical with the text formula, is only in fact identical with it if our units of quantity are so selected that the weights applied to all the several prices in the period chosen as base are equal. In general, the a's and b's being absolute quantities and the percentage numbers ratios, the latter cannot be substituted for the former without substantially altering the result. It follows that, in the construction of an approximate measure for the purpose contemplated in this discussion, price statistics should be employed in their raw form and not in the form of percentages. It may be added that, if expenditures, instead of quantities, are employed as weights, the resultant formula

$$\frac{p_2}{p_1} = \frac{(xa_1)a_2 + (yb_1)b_2 + \ldots}{xa_1 + yb_1 + \ldots}$$

is again equivalent to the text formula only if the base year weights are made equal.

two elements, the reliability of our ideal measure as an
index of dividend changes and the reliability of our approximate measure as a representative of the ideal measure.
The reliability of the approximate measure as an index of
dividend changes will evidently be diminished (or increased)
by anything that diminishes (or increases) either of these
subordinate reliabilities.   These two subordinate reliabilities
depend, however, on quite different sets of circumstances, and
must, therefore, be examined separately.

§ 13. In § 6 it was shown that our ideal measure will,
on certain conditions, *probably* vary in the same sense as
the satisfaction derived from his purchases by the representative man of our group.   This probability may, however, be
of a high degree or of a low degree.   In other words, the
ideal measure may be very much more likely than not to
speak the truth, or it may be only a little more likely
than not to do this.   Evidently it is more likely to indicate
rightly the direction in which the national dividend has
changed when it shows a large movement in either direction
than when it shows a small movement, because then a
larger error is needed to make it point wrongly.   The following more special considerations may be added.

First, it will be remembered that, on our definition, the
national dividend is not altered when people's tastes change
otherwise than as a result of changed purchases.   But, when
this happens, our measure *may* be changed.   Suppose, for
instance, that people come to have a greater affection for
some commodity which is being produced under conditions
of diminishing returns.   The price of that commodity will
go up, and our measure of the national dividend may, in
consequence, go down, though the dividend itself is by definition unchanged.   If the measure employed had been simply
the price of the collection consumed in either of the two
periods, it would be *necessary* that this misrepresentation
of the facts should occur.   The failure of *our* measure does
not, however, go so far as this.   Whether the misrepresentation will in fact occur depends, among other things, upon
the elasticity of the supply of the commodity for which
taste has changed.   The more elastic the supply is, or, in

other words, the less sharply diminishing returns act, the smaller is the probability of misrepresentation.[1] Still, a considerable chance of this form of error in the measure exists. No doubt, it could be obviated analytically, if a_2, b_2, etc., were taken to represent, not the actual prices prevailing in the second period, but the supply prices of the nth unit (n being the number of units consumed in the first period). In practice, however, the available statistics do not permit of this device, and our measure cannot be thus emended. Here, therefore, is a source of error, the seriousness of which it is not feasible accurately to gauge.

Secondly, a high degree of confidence in our measure cannot be warranted unless our group is more or less homogeneous, and is not made up of two parts containing, respectively, very rich people and very poor people, whose standards of living are widely divergent. For in groups made up in that way the relation between the amount of aggregate satisfaction purchasable with the representative man's sovereign at two different times—and it is in reference to this that the dividend is here defined—will be largely determined by the distribution of the price movements which have taken place among things chiefly consumed by the rich or by the poor; and no account of this distribution is, or could be, taken in our analysis.[2] Furthermore, the proportion in which the income of the group as a whole is shared among differently constituted parts of it may change. This

[1] This can be proved as follows. If the representative man's money income is supposed to be constant, $x_1a_1 + y_1b_1 = x_2a_2 + y_2b_2$, and our measure, as given in § 7, reduces to $\sqrt{\dfrac{x_1a_2 + y_1b_2 + \cdots}{x_2a_1 + y_2b_1 + \cdots}}$ where the a's and b's represent prices and the x's and y's quantities.

Suppose that, under the influence of enhanced taste, x_2 becomes equal to $(x_1 + h)$ and a_2 to $(a_1 + k)$.

Then our measure becomes $\sqrt[2]{\dfrac{x_1a_1 + y_1b_2 + kx_1}{x_1a_1 + y_2b_1 + ha_1}}$.

When the values of x_1a_1 and $(x_1 + h)(a_1 + k)$ are given, it is plain that this fraction is more likely to be less than unity, in which case the representation given is a true one, the smaller k is relatively to h: that is to say, the smaller is the change in the position of the demand curve that calls out a given change in production; that is to say, the more elastic is the supply of the commodity.

[2] The importance of this point is made apparent by Pareto's observation: "Il convient à un riche anglais de venir vivre en Italie; il convient également à un ouvrier italien de s'établir à Londres."

will involve a change in the collection of things purchased, the meaning of which, from the standpoint of economic welfare and the national dividend, will be entirely different according as the gain of income has accrued to the richer or to the poorer part of the group. For this reason the large transference of money available for immediate expenditure, which took place from the middle class to the artisan class during the course of the great war, practically destroys the value of general index numbers for making comparisons in the volume of the national dividend, as defined above, between different parts of that period either with one another or with any other period.

§ 14. In conclusion, we have to consider the reliability of our approximate measure as a representative of the ideal measure. Upon this matter four general observations may be made. First, when the sample is drawn from most of the principal sets of commodities, included in the collection, which have characteristic price movements, the probable error of our measure will be less than it is when a less representative field is covered. Secondly, when the sample is large, in the sense that the expenditure upon the items included in it comprises a large part of the aggregate expenditure of the group upon the whole collection, the probable error is less than it is when the sample is small. With random sampling in the strict technical sense, the reliability increases as the square root of the number of items contained in the sample. Thirdly, when each of the items constituting the total collection absorbs individually a small part of the aggregate expenditure upon that collection, the probable error is less than when some of the items absorb individually a large part of the total expenditure. The mathematical considerations upon which the two latter of these propositions rest have been worked out by Professor Edgeworth in his Report to the British Association in 1889. On the strength of them it has sometimes been argued that any reasonably constructed index number—and, of course, our measure is only an elaborated index number [1]—is fairly certain to have only

---

[1] It is a question of convenience whether the term index number should be applied to all tables exhibiting variations of price, or should be confined to

a small probable error. Attempts to confute these arguments by citing particular years for which index numbers framed on different principles have given widely different results are not really to the point. For, as Professor Edgeworth has pointed out, it may be very improbable that a given series of index numbers will seriously misrepresent the price movement of *any specified year*, and yet not at all improbable that it will seriously misrepresent the movement of *some unspecified year*.[1] None the less, the confidence generated by a purely abstract treatment of this matter should never be more than a restricted confidence. For it would be difficult to prove that the assumptions, upon which the mathematical defence of such existing index numbers as those of Sauerbeck and the *Economist* rest, are realised in fact as fully as theoretical statisticians are some-times inclined to assume.[2] Lastly, the magnitude of the error to which our index numbers are liable is greater—apart altogether from the difficulty of "new commodities" referred to in § 8—as between distant years than as between years that are close together. The reason for this is that, as Professor Mitchell, on the basis of a wide survey of facts, has shown, the distribution of the variations in whole-sale prices as between one year and the next is highly con-

---

those which *indicate* changes in respect of one object by recording changes in respect of some other related object. On the whole, it seems linguistically fitter, as well as more consonant with authority, to reserve the term for the latter meaning only (cf. Bowley, *Elements of Statistics*, p. 217). I do not, therefore, speak of a list of wheat prices, worked out as percentages of the price at some given point, as an index number of the price of wheat; whereas I might speak of it as an index number, though a very bad one, of the price of a bushel of wheat, *plus* a pound of beef, *plus* a pound and a half of bacon. In like manner, I might regard a table of wholesale price changes as an index number of retail price changes, and the index would be a good one, if I had reason to believe that the relation between wholesale and retail prices had remained fairly constant. Or, finally, I might regard a table giving the output of coal or iron, or, in this age of electricity, of copper (cf. Watkins's *The Growth of Large Fortunes*, p. 91), as an index number of the output of business in general.

[1] *Journal of Royal Statistical Society*, Jan. 1913, p. 175.

[2] Thus it may be noted that, unless we know both (1) that the collection from which samples are taken is distributed in accordance with the normal law of error, and (2) that the sampling is not subject to any bias or "systematic error," it is impossible to calculate the absolute magnitude of the probable error (cf. Poincaré, *Science and Hypothesis*, p. 209).

centrated—more concentrated than the distribution proper
to the normal law of error; but the distribution of variations
as between one year and a somewhat distant year is
highly scattered. "With some commodities the trend of
successive price changes continues distinctly upwards for years
at a time; with other commodities there is a constant
downward trend; with still others no definite long period
trend appears."[1] This proves the statement made above:
sampling will provide a much more reliable approximation
to our ideal measure when the comparison attempted is
between successive years than when it is between widely
separated years. This is true whether the comparison
between the distant years is made directly or by means
of a chain index number.[2]

[1] *U.S. Bulletin of Labour*, No. 173, p. 23.

[2] As Professor Edgeworth has pointed out, the further inference which
Professor Mitchell seeks to draw from his data, that—apart altogether from new
commodities—comparisons made by the chain method between years a given
distance apart are more reliable than comparisons made by the direct method
between these same years, does not seem to be justified. Cf. "The Doctrine
of Index Numbers," *Economic Journal*, 1918, p. 181 *et seq.*

CHAPTER VI

§ 1. THE general conclusions of the fourth chapter might, until quite recently, have been stated as they are there stated, without evoking quarrel or dispute. But of late years a great advance has occurred in biological knowledge. In former times economists had, indeed, to take some account of the reactions of economic causes upon the quantity of the population, and upon its quality so far as that was determined by environment : but questions about the reaction of economic causes upon the quality of the population as determined by fundamental biological attributes were not raised. Now, the situation is different. Biometricians and Mendelians alike have turned their attention to sociology, and are insisting upon the fundamental importance for our science of a proper understanding of the laws of heredity. Economists, it is said, in discussing, as I have done, the direct effect of the state of the national dividend upon welfare, are wasting their energies. The direct effect is of no significance; it is only the indirect effect on the size of the families of good and bad stocks respectively that really matters. For, every form of welfare depends ultimately on something much more fundamental than economic arrangements, namely, the general forces governing biological selection. I have intentionally stated these claims in a somewhat indefinite form, because I am anxious to investigate the problem thus raised in a constructive rather than in a critical spirit. I shall endeavour, in the following sections, to indicate, as precisely as possible, how far the recent advance in biological knowledge really affects our science.

To this end, I shall distinguish, first, certain results of that knowledge, which, though of great value, are not strictly relevant to economics; secondly, the general claim that the method of economic study indicated in the preceding chapters is rendered by the new knowledge trivial and unimportant; and, thirdly, certain points, in respect of which the new knowledge comes directly into contact with the problems I have undertaken to investigate, and makes it necessary to qualify the conclusions that have been reached.

§ 2. By far the most important contribution of modern biological study to sociology is the assurance, which it affords, of the definite heritable character of certain inborn defects. Whatever view be taken of the physiological mechanism of inheritance, the practical result is the same. We know that persons with congenital defects are likely, if they marry, to hand down a defective organisation to some of their children. We do not possess this definite knowledge with regard to general desirable qualities, particularly on the mental side. Professor Bateson issues a wise caution when he writes: " Whereas our experience of what constitutes the extremes of unfitness is fairly reliable and definite, we have little to guide us in estimating the qualities for which society has or may have a use, or the numerical proportions in which they may be required. . . . There is as yet nothing in the descent of the higher mental qualities to suggest that they follow any simple system of transmission. It is likely that both they and the more marked developments of physical powers result rather from the coincidence of numerous factors than from the possession of any one genetic element." [1]   Again, Mr. and Mrs. Whetham rightly observe that desirable qualities, such as ability, moral character, good health, physical strength and grace, beauty and charm, " are, from the point of view of heredity, essentially different from some of the bad qualities hitherto considered, in that they depend on the conjunction of a great many factors. Such a conjunction must be very hard to trace in the hereditary process, where possibly each character may descend independently, or different characters

---

[1] *Mendel's Principles of Heredity*, p. 305.

may be linked together, or be incompatible, in far more
complicated ways than we have traced in the qualities of
plants and animals. Our present knowledge is quite insufficient to enable us to predict how a complex combination
of factors, making up the personality of an able or charming
man or woman, will reappear in their offspring."[1] We are,
in fact, in this region, surrounded by so much ignorance
that the utmost caution is essential.   Dr. Doncaster has
well observed: " In this direction empirical rules and common
sense must still be followed, until the time shall come when
science can speak with no uncertain voice."[2]   More recently,
the late Sir Francis Galton lent the weight of his authority
to this opinion: "Enough is already known to those who
have studied the question to leave no doubt in their minds
about the general results, but not enough is quantitatively
known to justify legislation or other action, except in extreme
cases."[3]   It is well not to forget that Beethoven's father was
an habitual drunkard and that his mother died of consumption.[4]   About definite defects our ignorance is much
less profound.   These *are* the extreme cases of which Galton
was thinking.   Not a few medical men have long been
urging that authoritatively to prevent propagation among
those afflicted with imbecility, idiocy, syphilis, or tuberculosis
would mean the cutting off at its source of a long stream
of defective humanity.   This matter is especially urgent
among the mentally defective, on account of the exceptionally
high rate at which, if left to themselves, they tend to produce
children.   Thus, before the Royal Commission on the Feeble-
Minded, " Dr. Tredgold, an especially experienced witness,
pointed out that the average number of children in the
families which now use the public elementary schools is about
four; whereas, in the degenerate families, whose children are
passed over to the special schools, there is an average of
7·3 children, not including those still-born."[5]   Further-

[1] *The Family and the Nation*, p. 74.
[2] *Independent Review*, May 1906, p. 183.
[3] *Probability the Basis of Eugenics*, p. 29.
[4] Cf. Bateson, Presidential Address to the British Association, *Nature*,
Aug. 1914, p. 677.
[5] *The Family and the Nation*, p. 71.

more, feeble-minded women often begin child-bearing at
an exceptionally early age; and it must be remembered that,
even if the size of families is unaffected, early marriage is
not a matter of indifference; for, when the normal age
of marriage in any group is reduced, "generations succeed
one another with greater rapidity," so that the proportion
of the whole population embraced among the descendants
of the original members of that group is increased.[1] The
mentally defective are not, however, the only class among
which propagation might with advantage be restrained.
Some writers suggest that certain forms of criminality and
certain qualities conducive to pauperism might be eradicated
from the race in the same way. Professor Karl Pearson
makes a suggestion, which, if correct, strengthens considerably
the probability that this sort of policy would reach its goal.
He thinks that imperfections of quite different kinds are
correlated, and that "there is something akin to germinal
degeneracy, which may show itself in different defects of
the same organ or in defects of different organs."[2] Professor
Bateson, to the same practical, though not to the same
theoretical, effect, speaks of the existence of "indications that,
in the extreme cases, unfitness is comparatively definite in its
genetic causation, and can, not unfrequently, be recognised
as due to the presence of a simple genetic factor."[3] In sum,
as the last quoted writer states, there is little doubt that
"some serious physical and mental defects, almost certainly
also some morbid diatheses, and some of the forms of vice
and criminality could be eradicated if society so determined."[4]
This is a conclusion of extreme importance. It is one, too,
that seems *prima facie* susceptible, without great difficulty,
of some measure of practical application. Occasions frequently
arise when tainted persons, whether on account of crime
or dementia, are compulsorily passed into governmental
institutions. When this happens, propagation might be
prevented, after careful inquiry had been made, either by
permanent segregation, or possibly, as is authorised by law

---

[1] Haycraft, *Darwinism and Race Progress*, p. 144.
[2] *The Scope and Importance of National Eugenics*, p. 38.
[3] *Mendel's Principles of Heredity*, p. 305.
[4] *Ibid.* p. 305.

in certain American States, by surgical means.[1] The knowledge we possess seems clearly sufficient to warrant us in taking some cautious steps in this direction. There can be no doubt that such a policy would redound both to the general, and to the economic, welfare of the community. For this conclusion, and for the great step forward which it is hoped may follow from it, we are indebted to modern biology. The conclusion, however, is outside the sphere of economics, and does not in any way disturb the results that were attained in our fourth chapter.

§ 3. I pass therefore, to something of whose relevance at all events there can be no doubt, the view, namely, that biological science proves all such inquiries as we are pursuing here to be trivial and misdirected. Put broadly, the charge is this. Economic changes, such as alterations in the size, the distribution, or the steadiness of the national dividend, affect environment only; and environment is of no importance, because improvements in it cannot react on the quality of the children born to those who enjoy the improvements. This view was crystallised by Professor Punnett, when he declared that hygiene, education and so on are but "fleeting palliatives at best, which, in postponing, but augment the difficulties they profess to solve. . . . Permanent progress is a question of breeding rather than of pedagogics; a matter of gametes, not of training."[2] Mr. Lock[3] is even more emphatic in the same sense. The opinions of these writers on the practical side are substantially in agreement with those of Professor Karl Pearson.

The scientific foundation on which all such views rest is, of course, the thesis that acquired characters, which arise

---

[1] According to Dr. Rentoul, sterilisation can be effected in either sex by a simple operation that carries few incidental ill-effects (*Race Culture and Race Suicide*, chap. xx.). Sterilisation by this or some other method has been legalised to prevent the procreation of the imbecile, insane, and criminal in eight of the American States, including Indiana (1907), California (1909), Connecticut (1909), New Jersey (1911), and New York (1912) (*Quarterly Journal of Economics*, November 1911, p. 46). It would seem, however, that the constitutionality of these laws is somewhat in doubt, and scarcely any practical application of them has hitherto been made (Report of the American Breeders' Association, *Problems in Eugenics*, pp. 460 et seq.).

[2] *Mendelism* (second edition), pp. 80-81.

[3] Cf. *Recent Progress in the Study of Variation, Heredity and Evolution*, by R. H. Lock.

out of the influence of environment, are not inherited.   It is
held, at least as regards the more complicated multicellular
organisms, that the germ-cells, which will ultimately form the
offspring of a living being, are distinct at the outset from
those which will form the body of that being.   Thus, Mr.
Wilson writes: "It is a reversal of the true point of view to
regard inheritance as taking place from the body of the
parent to that of the child.   The child inherits from the
parent *germ-cell*, not from the parent body, and the germ-cell
owes its characteristics, not to the body which bears it, but
to its descent from a pre-existing germ-cell of the same kind.
Thus, the body is, as it were, an offshoot from the germ-cell.
As far as inheritance is concerned, the body is merely the
carrier of the germ-cells, which are held in trust for coming
generations."[1]   Dr. Doncaster takes up substantially the
same position: "In the earlier theories of heredity it was
assumed that the germ-cells were produced by the body, and
that they must, therefore, be supposed either to contain
samples of all parts of it, or at least some kind of units
derived from those parts and able to cause their development
in the next generation.   Gradually, as the study of heredity
and of the actual origin of the germ-cells has progressed,
biologists have given up this view in favour of a belief in
germinal continuity, that is, that the germ-substance is
derived from previous germ-substance, the body being a kind
of offshoot from it.   The child is, thus, like its parent, not
because it is produced from the parent, but because both
child and parent are produced from the same stock of germ-
plasm."[2]   If this view be sound, it follows that those definite
characteristics of an organism, whose appearance is determined
by the presence of definite structures or substances in the
germ-cells, cannot be directly affected by any quality "acquired"
by an ancestor.   It is only characteristics of an indefinite
quantitative kind, such as may be supposed to arise from the
intercommunication of the germ-cells with the other cells of
the body and the reception of fluid or easily soluble substances

---

[1] Wilson, *The Cell in Development and Inheritance*, p. 13; quoted by
R. H. Lock, *Variation, Heredity and Evolution*, p. 68.
[2] *Heredity*, p. 124.

from them, that can be affected in this way. The character-istics thus reserved are not, of course, wholly without significance. The question whether the submission of germ-cells to a poisonous environment reacts permanently upon the descendants of those cells does not seem to be a closed one. Professor J. A. Thomson writes: "There is a great difference between a poisoning of the germ-cells along with the body, and the influencing them in a manner so specific that they can, when they develop, reproduce the particular parental modification."[1] The germ-cells do not lead "a charmed life, uninfluenced by any of the accidents or incidents of the daily life of the body which is their bearer."[2] On the contrary, there is some evidence that, not only direct poisons like alcohol, but even injuries to the parent, may, by reacting on the nutrition of the germ-cells, cause general weakness and resultant bad properties in the offspring, though how far *the offspring of their offspring* would be affected is doubtful. But the general opinion among biologists appears to be that the effect of the acquired characteristics of one generation upon the quality of the succeeding generation is, at all events, very small compared with the effect of the inborn character-istics of the one generation.[3] "Education is to man what manure is to the pea. The educated are in themselves the better for it, but their experience will alter not one jot the irrevocable nature of their offspring."[4] And "neglect, poverty, and parental ignorance, serious as their results are, (do not) possess any marked hereditary effect."[5]

This biological thesis, which, since it is dominant among experts, an outsider has no title to dispute, is, as I have said, the scientific foundation of the view that economic circumstances, because they are environmental, are not, from a long-period standpoint, of any real importance. The biological premise I accept. To the sociological conclusion,

---

[1] J. A. Thomson, *Heredity*, p. 198.
[2] *Ibid.* p. 204.
[3] Lock, *Variation and Heredity*, pp. 69-71.
[4] Punnett, *Mendelism*, p. 81.
[5] Eichholz, "Evidence to the Committee on Physical Deterioration," Report, p. 14. Dr. Eichholz's view appears to be formed *a posteriori*, and not to be an inference from general biological principles.

H

however, I demur. Mr. Sidney Webb has uttered a genial
protest against a too exclusive attention to the biological
aspect of social problems. "After all," he writes, "it would
not be of much use to have all babies born from good stocks,
if, generation after generation, they were made to grow up
into bad men and women. A world of well-born, but
physically and morally perverted adults is not attractive."[1]
My criticism, however, goes deeper than this. Professor
Punnett and his fellow-workers would accept Mr. Webb's
plea. They freely grant that environing circumstances can
affect the persons immediately subjected to them, but they,
nevertheless, hold that these circumstances are unimportant,
because, not being able to influence the inborn quality of
succeeding generations, they cannot produce any lasting
result. My reply is that the environment of one generation *can* produce a lasting result, because it can affect the
environment of future generations. Environments, in short,
as well as people, have children. Though education and so
forth cannot influence new births in the physical world, they can
influence them in the world of ideas;[2] and ideas, once produced or once accepted by a particular generation, whether

---

[1] *Eugenics Review*, November 1910, p. 236.

[2] An interesting comparison can be made between the process of evolution
in these two worlds. In both we find three elements, the *occurrence of, propagation of,* and *conflict between,* mutations.

In both worlds the *kind* of mutations that occur appear to be fortuitous,
and cannot be controlled, though in both it is sometimes suggested that the
tendency to mutate is encouraged by large changes in, and particular kinds of,
environment. For example, Rae suggested, as conditions favourable to the
emergence of inventions, general upheavals, such as wars or migrations, and the
adoption in any art of a new material—such as steel in building—either for
lack of the old material or through the possession of a specially effective
new one, and he maintained that the stable agricultural districts rarely
yield inventions. (*The Sociological Theory of Capital,* pp. 172-3). In both
worlds again, with every increase of *variability,* the chance that a "good"
mutation will occur is increased. Hence, *ceteris paribus,* environments that
make for variability are a means to good. Thus, of local governments, Dr.
Marshall writes: "All power of variation that is consistent with order and
economy of administration is an almost unmixed good. The prospects of progress are increased by the multiplicity of parallel experiments and the inter-
communion of ideas between many people, each of whom has some opportunity
of testing practically the value of his own suggestions." (*Memorandum to the
Royal Commission on Local Taxation,* p. 123 ; cf. also Booth, *Industry,* v. p.
86 ; and Hobhouse, *Democracy and Reaction,* pp. 121-3.)

The *propagation* of mutations, on the other hand, does not proceed in the
same way among ideas as among organisms. Among the latter the fertility of

or not they can be materialised into mechanical inventions, may remodel from its very base the environment which succeeding generations enjoy.[1] In this way a permanent change of environment is brought about, and, since environment is admitted to have an important influence on persons actually subjected to it, such a change may obviously produce enduring consequences. Among animals, indeed, and among the primitive races of men this point is not important. For, there what the members of one generation have wrought in the field of ideas is not easily communicated to their successors. "The human race, when widely scattered and incapable of intercommunication, makes the same discovery a hundred times. Its efforts and its triumphs are annihilated with the death of the individual, or of the last member of the family in which the invention has been passed on by oral tradition."[2] But among civilised men the arts of writing and of printing have rendered thought mobile through time, and have, thus, extended to each generation power to mould and remodel the ideal environment of its successors. M. Tarde grasps this point when he writes: "To facilitate further production is the principal virtue of capital, as that term ought to be understood. But, in what is it inherent? In commodities or in particular kinds of commodities? Nay, rather in those fortunate experiments of which the memory has been preserved. Capital is tradition or social memory.

the mutated members that survive is not, but among the former it is, affected by their adaptation or otherwise to successful struggle. Animals that are failures and those that are successes are equally likely, if they survive, to have offspring. But, among ideas, those that fail are likely to be barren and those that succeed to be prolific.

Still more marked is the difference between the character of the *struggle* that takes place between mutated members in the two groups. In the physical world the process is negative—the failures are cut off. In the world of ideas it is positive—successful ideas are adopted and imitated. One consequence of this is that, in general, a successful experiment diffuses itself much more rapidly than a successful "sport."

[1] This consideration affords a powerful argument for the expenditure of State funds upon training the girls of the present generation to become competent mothers and housewives, because, if only one generation were so taught, a family tradition would very probably become established, and the knowledge given in the first instance at public cost would propagate itself through successive generations without any further cost to anybody. (Cf. Report of the Inter-departmental Committee on Physical Deterioration, p. 42.)

[2] Majewski, *La Science de la civilisation*, p. 228.

It is to societies what heredity or vital memory,—enigmatical term,—is to living beings. As for the products that have been saved and stored up to facilitate the construction of new copies of the models conceived by inventors, they are to these models, which are the true social germs, what the cotyledon, a mere store of food, is to the embryo."[1] Bacon had already exclaimed: "The introduction of new inventions seemeth to be the very chief of all human actions. The benefits of new inventions may extend to all mankind universally, but the good of political activities can respect but some particular country of men: these latter do not perdure above a few ages, the former for ever." Dr. Marshall writes in the same spirit: "The world's material wealth would quickly be replaced if it were destroyed, but the ideas by which it was made were retained. If, however, the ideas were lost, but not the material wealth, then that would dwindle and the world would go back to poverty. And most of our knowledge of mere facts could quickly be recovered if it were lost, but the constructive ideas of thought remained; while, if the ideas perished, the world would enter again on the Dark Ages."[2] Nor is even this a full account of the matter. As Dr. Marshall observes in another place: "Any change that awards to the workers of one generation better earnings, together with better opportunities of developing their best qualities, will increase the material and moral advantages which they have the power to offer to their children; while, by increasing their own intelligence, wisdom and forethought, such a change will also, to some extent, increase their willingness to sacrifice their own pleasures for the well-being of their children."[3] Those children, in turn, being themselves rendered stronger and more intelligent, will be able, when they grow up, to offer a better environment—and under the term environment I include the physical circumstances of the mother before, and immediately after, child-birth[4]—to their

---

[1] *La Logique sociale*, p. 352.
[2] *Principles of Economics*, p. 780.
[3] *Ibid.* p. 563.
[4] The importance of this point is illustrated by the observation of the London Education Committee of 1905, that the children born in a year when infant mortality is low show an improved physique, and *vice versa*. (Cf. Wells, *New Worlds for Old*, p. 216.)

children, and so on. The effect goes on piling itself up. Changes in ancestral environment start forces, which modify continuously and cumulatively the conditions of succeeding environments, and, through them, the human qualities for which current environment is in part responsible. Hence, Professor Punnett's assertion is unduly sweeping.[1] Progress, not merely permanent but growing, *can* be brought about by causes with which breeding and gametes have nothing to do. There is no fundamental difference of the kind supposed between causes operating on acquired, and causes operating on inborn, qualities. The two are of co-ordinate importance; and the students of neither have a right to belittle the work of those who study the other.

§ 4. I proceed now to the third of the topics indicated for discussion in the first section of this chapter, namely, the extent to which new biological knowledge makes it necessary for us to qualify the conclusions laid down in the preceding chapter. These conclusions, it will be remembered, were to the effect that, other things being equal, a general increase in the national dividend—provided that it is not brought about by the exercise of undue pressure upon workpeople,—a change in the distribution of the dividend favourable to the poor, and a "steadying" of the dividend, particularly of that part of it which goes to the poor, would all be likely to increase economic welfare and, through economic welfare, general welfare. The last of these conclusions may, perhaps, in the present connection, pass without challenge. But against the other two the biologically trained critic urges an important caution. May it not be, he asks, that advance along the first of these lines, by checking the free play of natural selection and enabling feeble children to survive, will set up a cumulative influence making for national weakness; and that advance along the second line, by differentiating in favour of inferior stocks, will have a similar evil effect? Is there not ground for fear that the brightness of the stream of progress is deceptive,

---

[1] In later editions of his book Professor Punnett's argument is stated in a less sweeping form and does not conflict with what has been said above. (Cf. *Mendelism*, third edition, p. 167.)

that it bears along, as it flows, seeds of disaster, and that
the changes we have pronounced to be productive of welfare
are, at the best, of doubtful import? The two parts of this
thesis must now be examined in turn.

§ 5. The danger, to national strength, that results from
a growth of wealth in general, has been emphasised by many
writers. In a softened environment children of feeble constitution, who, in harder circumstances, would have died, are
enabled to survive and themselves to have children.[1] It has
even been suggested that in this fact may lie the secret of
the eventual decay of nations and of aristocracies which
have attained great wealth. There are, indeed, mitigating
circumstances which may be urged in extenuation of this
view. First, according to the most recent biological opinion,
the survival of weakly children, if their weakness is, as it
were, accidental, and not due to inherited defect, is not
ultimately harmful to the stock, because the children of the
weakly children are quite likely to be strong. Secondly,
weakness in infancy is not necessarily a good index of
essential inborn weakness: and Mr. Yule, after reviewing
the available statistics by mathematical methods, is led to
suggest that, perhaps, "the mortality of infancy is selective
only as regards the special dangers of infancy, and its
influence scarcely extends beyond the second year of life,
whilst the weakening effect of a sickly infancy is of greater
duration."[2] These mitigating circumstances somewhat limit,
though they may well fail to overthrow, the thesis that
growth in wealth, unaccompanied by any safeguard, is likely
to deteriorate the inherent quality of the race. There is
also available a further mitigating circumstance, which is
less fundamental though not less important. For, even if
the inherent quality of the race is somewhat injured, it does
not follow that the finished products which contain, of
course, at once inherent and environmental qualities, are so
injured. If increased wealth removes influences that make
for the elimination of the unfit, it also removes influences
that make for the weakening of the fit. The total effect

---

[1] Cf. Haycraft, *Darwinism and Race Progress*, p. 58.
[2] [Cd. 5263], p. 82, (1909-10).

of this twofold. action may well be beneficial rather than
injurious.   That this is in fact so is suggested by a recent
important report published by the Local Government Board
on the relation of infantile mortality to general mortality.
In that report Dr. Newsholme directly combats the view
that improvements making for a reduction of infant mortality,
by enabling more weaklings to survive, must be inimical
to the average health of the population.   He finds, on the
contrary, "that the counties having high infant mortalities
continue, in general, to suffer somewhat excessively throughout
the first twenty years of. human life, and that counties
having low infantile mortalities continue to have relatively
low. death-rates in the first twenty years of life, though the
superiority is not so great at the later as at the earlier
ages. . . . It is fair to assume, in accordance with general
experience, that the amount of sickness varies approximately
with the number of deaths; and there can be no reasonable
doubt that, in the counties having a high infant death-rate,
there is—apart from migration—more sickness and a lower
standard of health in youth and in adult life than in counties
in which the toll of infant mortality is less."[1]   Dr.
Newsholme's argument is, indeed, open to the reply that
ascertained differences between the several counties in
infantile death-rate and later death-rate may *both* be due
to differences in the quality of the inhabitants of the several
counties.   The argument, therefore, fails to prove that the
direct beneficial effect of better environments due to greater
wealth outweighs the indirect. injurious effect of the impedi-
ment they place in the way of natural selection.   It may
be that the injurious effect is really the stronger, but that
it. is masked in the statistics because it is exercised upon
persons who are *ab initio* of better physique—as is, indeed,
suggested by their ability to earn more and so to live in
better conditions—than. the average.   This criticism lessens
the force of Dr. Newsholme's statistical argument.[2]   Still

---

[1] Report for 1909-10 [Cd. 5263], p. 17.
[2] Dr. Newsholme's argument was severely criticised—partly under a
misapprehension of its purpose—by Professor Karl Pearson in his Cavendish
lecture, 1912, p. 13.   Dr. Newsholme replied in his second (1913) report
[Cd. 6909], pp. 46-52.

the directly observed fact that good environment removes influences tending to weaken the fit remains. In company with the considerations set out earlier in this section, that fact militates against the view that a growing dividend, and the improvements that naturally accompany it, carry seeds of future weakness, and so ultimately make against, rather than in favour of, economic welfare. In any event, the danger that they may have this effect can be readily and completely counteracted, if the policy of segregating the unfit, advocated in the second section, is adopted. As Professor Thomson points out, no biological evil can result from the preservation of weaklings, provided that they are not allowed to have children.[1] There is, therefore, no need to surrender our conclusion that causes, which make for an expansion of the dividend, in general make for economic and, through economic, for aggregate, welfare.

§ 6. The danger to national strength and efficiency through an improvement in the distribution of the dividend might seem *a priori* to be very important. For, improved distribution is likely to modify the proportion in which future generations are born from the richer and poorer classes respectively. If, therefore, the poorer classes comprise less efficient stocks than the richer classes—if, in fact, economic status is anything of an index of inborn quality—improved distribution must modify the general level of inborn quality, and so, in the long run, must react with cumulative force upon the magnitude of the national dividend. Now, I do not agree with those who hold that poverty and inborn inefficiency are obviously and certainly correlated. Extreme poverty is, no doubt, often the result of feckless character, physical infirmity, and other "bad" qualities of finished persons. But these themselves are generally correlated with bad environment; and it is ridiculous to treat as unworthy of argument the suggestion that the "bad" qualities are mainly the result, not of bad original properties, but of bad original environment.[2] Nevertheless, though I do not regard

---

[1] *Heredity*, p. 528.
[2] This class of difficulty is experienced in many statistical investigations of social problems. For example, an interesting inquiry into the inheritance

it as self-evident, I do regard it as probable, that a considerable measure of correlation exists between poverty and "bad" original properties. For it is apparent that among the relatively rich are many persons who have risen from a poor environment, which their fellows, who have remained poor, shared with them in childhood; and this sort of movement is probably becoming more marked, as opportunities of education and so forth are being brought more within the reach of the poorer classes. In like manner, of course, among the poor are some persons who have fallen from a superior environment. Among the original properties of *these* relatively rich there are presumably qualities making for efficiency, which account for their rise; while, among the original properties of *these* relatively poor, there are, presumably, qualities of an opposite kind.[1] Hence, it is probably true that causes affecting the comparative rate of child-bearing among the relatively rich and the relatively poor respectively affect the comparative rate among those with "better" and "worse" original properties (from the point of view of efficiency) in the same direction. If it were true that increased prosperity in a poor class involved a higher rate of reproduction, it would follow that an improved distribution of the dividend would increase the number and,

---

of ability, as indicated by the Oxford class lists and the school lists of Harrow and Charterhouse, was published some years ago by Mr. Schuster. But, the value of his results is in some measure—it is not possible to say in *what* measure—impaired by the fact that the possession of able parents is apt to be correlated with the reception of a good formal, and, still more, informal, education. Mr. Schuster argues (p. 23) that the error due to this circumstance is not likely to be large. (Cf. also Karl Pearson, *Biometrika*, vol. iii. p. 156.) M. Nicefero, on the other hand, in his study of *Les Classes pauvres*, lays stress on the effects of environment in promoting the physical and psychical inferiority of these classes; but he does not seem to justify by evidence his conclusion that "tous les facteurs—en dernière analyse—plongent leur racine bien plus dans le milieu économique de la société moderne, que dans la structure même de l'individu" (p. 332).

[1] Professor Pareto ignores these considerations when he argues (*Systèmes socialistes*, p. 13 *et seq.*) that an increase in the relative number of children born to the rich must make for national deterioration because, since the children of the rich are subjected to a less severe struggle than those of the poor, feeble children, who would die if born to the poor, will, if born to the rich, survive and, in turn, have feeble children. In view of the facts noted in the text, this circumstance should be regarded merely as a counteracting force, mitigating, but not destroying, the beneficial consequences likely to result from a relative increase in the fertility of the rich.

therewith, the proportion, of children born from parents of stock other than the best. Since, however, it is notorious that propagation among the lowest class of all is practically untrammelled by economic considerations, an incréase in fortune to the poor as a whole could only increase the number of children born to sections of the poorer classes other than the worst. It would not, therefore, necessarily follow that the average quality of the population as a whole would be lowered. It is not, however, necessary to stop at this point. Professor Brentano's investigations, which were previously noticed, have suggested that increased prosperity in a class tends, on the whole, to diminish rather than to increase the reproduction rate of that class, and reason has been shown for believing that this tendency is not fully offset by accompanying improvements in the mortality rate.[1] Hence, it would seem, an improvement in the distribution of the dividend may be expected actually to diminish the proportion of children born from inferior stocks. In short, this biological consideration, so far from reversing the conclusion of the fourth chapter, that improved distribution makes for economic and general welfare, lends, in present conditions, some support to that conclusion. None of the main results of that chapter are, therefore, reversed by biological considerations.

[1] Cf. *ante*, Chapter IV. § 14.

CHAPTER VII

THE METHOD OF DISCUSSION TO BE FOLLOWED

THE conclusions we have reached may now be repeated. They are to the effect that: (1) other things being equal, an increase in the size of the national dividend will probably increase economic welfare; (2) other things being equal, an increase in the proportion of the national dividend accruing to the poor will probably increase economic welfare; (3) other things being equal, a diminution in the variability of the national dividend will probably increase economic welfare; and (4) other things being equal, a diminution in the variability of the part of the national dividend accruing to the poor at the cost of correspondingly increased variability of the part accruing to the rich will probably increase economic welfare. If causes affecting the size of the dividend had no influence on the absolute share of the poor or on the variability of the dividend, and causes affecting the absolute share of the poor and the variability of the dividend respectively were similarly self-contained, the remaining stages of our inquiry would be simple. Each of these groups of causes could be examined in turn separately. As a fact, however, the same cause will often affect at once the size, the distribution and the variability of the dividend, and, *prima facie*, it is not necessary that it should affect them all harmoniously. That this circumstance must greatly complicate our exposition is obvious. No method of treatment that is wholly satisfactory seems to me to be possible. After some hesitation I have decided to proceed as follows. The entirely obvious general causes affecting the magnitude of the national dividend, such as inventions and discoveries,—including inventions in organisation, such as the

banking system, limited liability and shift systems that allow
machinery to operate continuously,—the opening up of extensive sources of foreign demand, and the accumulation of
capital, I shall scarcely discuss at all. Leaving these things
aside, I shall examine in Parts II., III. and IV. the way in
which three important groups of influences affect the
magnitude of the national dividend. These influences are,
respectively, those associated with the distribution of the productive resources of the community among various uses or
occupations, those associated with the organisation of Labour,
and those associated with the collection of revenue. In Part
V. I shall inquire in what circumstances it is possible for
causes which affect the volume of the national dividend favourably or unfavourably to affect the absolute share of the dividend
enjoyed by the poor in the opposite sense; and, when ambiguous
causes are discovered, I shall study their net effect upon
economic welfare. Part VI. will be devoted to an investigation
of the principal causes which affect the variability of the
dividend as a whole and of the share of it accruing to the
poor. This arrangement is, of course, open to numerous
objections. But, on the whole, it is more convenient than
any other that I have been able to devise.

PART II

THE MAGNITUDE OF THE NATIONAL DIVIDEND AND THE DISTRIBUTION OF RESOURCES AMONG DIFFERENT USES

CHAPTER I

§ 1. THE first of the three groups of causes, whose influence upon the average volume of the national dividend we have agreed to investigate, consists of those that affect the distribution of the nation's productive resources among different uses or occupations. Throughout this inquiry—indeed throughout the whole of the present Part—it is assumed that no resources of any kind are unemployed contrary to the will of their owners. This reservation will need to be withdrawn in later Parts, but for the general analysis of this Part it conforms closely enough to the facts. In this introductory chapter the general scope of the problem before us will be indicated.

§ 2. Certain optimistic followers of the classical economists have sometimes suggested that the "free play of self-interest," if only Government refrains from interference, will automatically cause the land, capital and labour of any country to be so distributed as to yield a larger output than could be attained by any arrangement other than that which comes about "naturally." And Adam Smith himself, while making an exception in favour of State action in "erecting and maintaining certain public works and certain public institutions which it can never be for the interests of any individual, or small number of individuals, to erect and maintain," lays it down that "any system which endeavours, either by extraordinary encouragements to draw towards a particular species of industry a greater share of the capital of the society than what would naturally go to it; or, by extraordinary restraints, to force from a particular species of industry some share of the capital which would otherwise be employed in it . . . . retards, instead

111

of accelerating, the progress of the society towards real wealth and greatness, and diminishes, instead of increasing, the real value of the annual produce of its land and labour."[1] It would, of course, be unreasonable to interpret this passage in any abstract or universal sense. Adam Smith had in mind the actual world as he knew it, with an organised system of civilised government and contract law. He would not have quarrelled with the dictum of a later economist that "the activities of man are expended along two routes, the first being directed to the production or transformation of economic goods, the second to the appropriation of goods produced by others."[2] Activities devoted to appropriation obviously do not promote production, and production would be promoted if they were diverted into the channels of industry. We must, therefore, understand him to assume the existence of laws designed, and, in the main, competent, to prevent acts of *mere* appropriation such as those perpetrated by highwaymen and card-sharpers. The free play of self-interest is conceived by him to be "confined to certain directions by our general social institutions, especially the Family, Property, and the territorial State."[3] More generally, when one man obtains goods from another man, he is conceived to obtain them by the process, not of seizure, but of exchange in an open market, where the bargainers on both sides are reasonably competent and reasonably cognisant of the conditions. There is ground, however, for believing that even Adam Smith had not realised fully the extent to which the System of Natural Liberty needs to be qualified and guarded by special laws, before it will promote the most productive employment of a country's resources. It has been said by a recent writer that "the working of self-interest is generally beneficent, not because of some natural coincidence between the self-interest of each and the good of all, but because human institutions are arranged so as to compel self-interest to work in directions in which it will be beneficent."[4] The correctness of this standpoint is

---

[1] *Wealth of Nations*, book iv. chapter iv., third paragraph from the end.

[2] Pareto, *Manuale di economia politica*, pp. 444-5.

[3] Cannan, *The History of Local Rates*, p. 176. Cf. also Carver, *Essays in Social Justice*, p. 109.

[4] Cannan, *Economic Review*, July 1913, p. 333.

well illustrated by the limitations which the laws of civilised States impose upon the absolute powers of owners of property—such limitations as the Bavarian rule forbidding owners of forests to exclude pedestrians from their land, the French and American rules restraining a man from setting fire to his own ' house, and the practice prevalent in all countries of expropriating private owners where their expropriation is obviously required in the general interest.[1] It is further illustrated by the attitude of the law of modern nations towards types of contract—gambling debts, contracts in restraint of trade, agreements for contracting-out of certain legal obligations—which are deemed contrary to public policy and are, therefore, treated by the courts as void.[2] This adjustment of institutions to the end of directing self-interest into beneficial channels has been carried out in considerable detail. But even in the most advanced States there are failures and imperfections. We are not here concerned with those deficiencies of organisation which sometimes cause higher non-economic interests to be sacrificed to less important economic interests. Over and above these, there are many obstacles that interfere with production by withholding some of the nation's resources from uses in which they might make a larger contribution than they actually do towards the national dividend. The study of these constitutes our present problem. That study involves some difficult analysis. But its purpose is essentially practical. It seeks to bring into clearer light some of the ways in which it now is, or eventually may become, feasible for governments to control the play of economic forces in such wise as to promote the economic welfare, and through that the total welfare, of their citizens as a whole.[3]

[1] Cf. Ely, *Property and Contract*, pp. 61 and 150.
[2] *Ibid.* pp. 616 and 731.
[3] Cf. Marshall's observation: "Much remains to be done, by a careful collection of the statistics of demand and supply and a scientific interpretation of their results, in order to discover what are the limits of the work that society can with advantage do towards turning the economic actions of individuals into those channels in which they will add the most to the sum total of happiness" (*Principles of Economics*, p. 475).

CHAPTER II

THE NATIONAL DIVIDEND AND EQUALITY OF MARGINAL
SOCIAL NET PRODUCTS

§ 1. CONCERNED as we are with the *average volume* of the national dividend as a continuing flow, we naturally understand by the resources directed to making it, not a stock of resources, but a similarly continuing flow; and we conceive the distribution of these resources among different occupations on the analogy, not of a stagnant pond divided into a number of sections, but rather of a river divided into a number of streams. This conception involves, no doubt, many minor difficulties in connection both with the varying durability of the equipment employed in different industries and with the dynamic, or changing, tendencies of industry as a whole. In spite of these difficulties, however, the general idea is exact enough for the present purpose. That purpose is to provide a suitable definition for the concept which is fundamental throughout this Part, namely, *the value of marginal social net product*. The essential point is that this too must be conceived as a flow—as the result *per year* of the employment *per year* of the marginal increment of some given quantity of resources. On this basis we may proceed to work out our definition.

§ 2. The most obvious element in the marginal social net product of any flow of resources employed in any occupation is the direct physical net product. This is equal to the difference between the aggregate flow of physical product for which that flow of resources, *when appropriately organised,* is responsible and the aggregate flow of physical product for which a flow of resources differing from that flow by a

114

small (marginal) increment, *when appropriately organised,* would be responsible. In this statement the phrase *when appropriately organised* is essential. If we were thinking of marginal physical net product in the sense of the difference between the products of two adjacent *quantities* of resources, we should normally imagine the resources to be organised suitably to one of these quantities and, therefore, not to the other. Since, however, our interest is in the difference between the products of two adjacent *flows* of resources, it is natural to conceive each of the two flows as organised in the manner most appropriate to itself. This is the conception we need. It is excellently illustrated by Professor J. B. Clark. The marginal increment of capital invested in a railway corporation is in reality, he writes, "a difference between two kinds of plant for carrying goods and passengers. One of these is the railroad as it stands, with all its equipment brought up to the highest pitch of perfection that is possible with the present resources. The other is the road built and equipped as it would have been if the resources had been by one degree less. A difference in all-round quality between an actual and a possible railroad is in reality the final increment of capital now used by the actual corporation. The product of that last unit of capital is the difference between what the road actually produces and what it would have produced if it had been made one degree poorer."[1]

§ 3. So much being understood, it must next be observed that the marginal social net product of any given flow of resources in any occupation may include, over and above the direct physical net product just described, indirect physical effects outside the occupation in which the resources we are contemplating are invested. It might happen, for example, as will be explained more fully in a later chapter, that costs are thrown upon other people not directly concerned, through, say, uncompensated damage done to surrounding woods by sparks from railway engines. All such effects must be included—some of them will be positive, others negative

---

[1] *The Distribution of Wealth,* p. 250. I have substituted "produced" for "earned" in the sentence quoted above. For a further account of the distinction here emphasised cf. Appendix III. footnote to § 2.

elements—in reckoning up the full physical net product
of the marginal increment of any volume of resources turned
into any occupation. Further, it may happen that, besides
the physical product, there will also be effects that are
not physical—modifications, for example, in people's tastes,
that cause them to get more or less satisfaction than before
from some of their possessions or purchases. When there
is any product of this kind we must add it to the physical
product already described. The result is the full marginal
social net product of the given volume of resources.

§ 4. The *value* of this marginal social net product is
the money value of the economic satisfaction due to it.
When there is no element present other than the direct
physical addition made to output in the industry directly
concerned, this money value is identical with the marginal
increment of product multiplied by the price per unit at
which the product is sold when the given volume of resources
is being employed in producing it.[1] For example, the
value of the marginal net product per year of a million units
of resources invested in weaving is equal to the number
of bales of cloth by which the output of a million *plus* a
small increment, say a million and one, exceeds the output
of a million units, multiplied by the money value of a bale
of cloth when this output is being produced.[2] This, it should
be observed, in passing, is different from, and must by no
means be confused with, the excess of the money value
of the whole product when a million and one units of
resources are being employed over the money value of the

[1] This definition tacitly assumes that the realised price is equal to the
(marginal) demand price. If government limitation of price causes it to be
temporarily less than this, the value of the marginal net product will need
to be interpreted, as will be shown in Chap. IX., as the marginal (physical)
net product multiplied by the marginal demand price, and the marginal
demand price in these conditions will not be equal to the actual selling price.

[2] Cf. Marshall, *Principles of Economics*, p. 847. It might be thought
at first sight, on the basis of this definition, that the marginal net product
of labour in any industry is equal to the product, allowance being made for
the cost of material, which a typical workman hands over as the fruit of
his work to his employer. In fact, however, it is smaller than this, because,
when the $(n+1)$th workman is removed, there is available more capital to assist
the work of each of the remaining workmen, and the product handed over by
them to the employer is, therefore, larger than before.

whole product when a million units are being employed.
When there are in the marginal social net product other
elements besides the direct physical product, our statement
must assume a more general form.   The value of the marginal
social net product of any volume of resources in any occupation is defined as, and is measured by, the money value
of the difference made by the marginal increment of those
resources so employed to the sum total of economic welfare.

§ 5. On the basis of this definition it can be shown that,
provided there are no costs of movement between different
occupations, and provided conditions are such that only one
arrangement of resources will make the values of the marginal
net products in all occupations equal, that arrangement must
make the national dividend larger than it would be under any
other arrangement.   If the national dividend consisted of one
sort of commodity only, manufactured by means of a number of
different occupations, this conclusion would be obvious; for, if
the value of the marginal net product of resources in one of
the occupations was smaller than in another, the aggregate
quantity of this single commodity could be directly increased by
a transference.   To obtain a proof in the conditions that rule in
actual life, we need to recall the *definition* of a change in the
volume of a dividend made up of a number of diverse commodities that was given in Chapter V. § 1 of the preceding Part.
The national dividend, it was there said, is larger or smaller in
period A than in period B according as, apart from compulsion to
work or certain exceptional obstacles to movement, the amount of
economic satisfaction derived from it by a representative member
of the group to which it accrues is larger or smaller.   Now,
the value of the marginal net product of resources in any use
is the money measure of the satisfaction which the marginal
increment of resources in that use is yielding to the representative man.   Plainly, therefore, whenever the value of the marginal
net product of resources is less in any one use than it is in
any other, the money measure of satisfaction in the aggregate,
and, therefore, the national dividend as here defined, can be
increased by transferring resources from the use where the
value of the marginal net product is smaller to the use where
it is larger.   It follows from this that, since, *ex hypothesi*,

there is only one arrangement of resources that will make the values of the marginal net products equal in all uses, this arrangement is necessarily the one that makes the national dividend, as here defined, a maximum.[1]

§ 6. So far we have premised that there are no costs involved in moving resources from one occupation (or place) to another. But it is obvious that in fact there are costs—sometimes serious costs—in the way of movement. We have, therefore, to inquire in what, if any, respects this fact makes it necessary to modify the conclusions set out above. The kernel of the matter can be displayed as follows. Suppose that between two points A and B the movement of a unit of resources can be effected at a capital cost which is equivalent to an annual charge of n shillings for every year during which a unit that is moved continues in productive work in its new home. In these circumstances the national dividend will be increased by the movement of resources from A to B, so long as the annual value of the marginal net product at B exceeds that at A by more than n shillings; and it will be injured by any movement of resources which occurs after the excess of the value of the marginal net product at B has been reduced below n shillings. If the initial distribution of resources between A and B is such that the value of the marginal net product at B exceeds (or falls short of) the value of the marginal net product at A by any number of shillings less than n, say by $(n-h)$ shillings, the existing arrangement—that under which the values of the marginal net products at the two points differ by $(n-h)$ shillings—is the best arrangement from the standpoint of the national dividend, not indeed absolutely, but *relatively to the fact of the initial distribution and the existing costs of movement.* It is not, be it noted,

----

[1] A minor point should be noticed in passing. In occupations in which *no* resources are employed, the value of the marginal net product of resources will, in general, be smaller than it is in occupations where *some* resources are employed. This circumstance clearly does not imply the existence of inequality among the values of marginal net products in any sense incompatible with the maximisation of the national dividend. But, if it should anywhere happen that the value of the marginal net product of resources in an occupation where no resources are employed is larger than it is in occupations where some resources are employed, —*e.g.* a profitable venture which for some reason people have failed to exploit— *that* inequality would be an effective inequality and would be incompatible with the maximisation of the dividend.

the best arrangement relatively to the existing costs of movement alone. We cannot say that, when the costs of movement
are equivalent to n shillings, the national dividend is best
served by a distribution under which the values of the marginal
net products at A and B differ by such and such a defined
number of shillings. The only accurate statement is: when
the costs of movement between A and B are equivalent to n
shillings, the national dividend is best served by the maintenance of the existing distribution, whatever that may be, provided
that this distribution does not involve a divergence in the
values of marginal net products greater than n shillings; and,
if the existing distribution does involve a divergence greater
than n shillings, by a new distribution brought about by the
transference of sufficient resources to bring the divergence
down to n shillings.

§ 7. We have thus inquired what is the best distribution of resources from the standpoint of the national
dividend (a) where there are not, and (b) where there are, costs
of movement. For completeness we must compare with one
another the two arrangements that are respectively best in
these two sets of conditions. In this connection it is well
to recall the possibility, explained in Chapter IV. of Part I.,
that certain special obstacles to movement (and cost is, of
course, one form of obstacle) may, though injuring economic
welfare, at the same time increase the national dividend.
This, however, is an exceptional possibility of little relevance
to practice. Apart from this, it is obvious that, since the
scheme, which is best for the dividend (and economic welfare)
when there are costs, is only best because the additional
advantage to be got from an arrangement yielding equal values
of marginal net products would be less than the costs of
getting it, the dividend will be larger if no costs exist and
the distribution of resources is adjusted to no costs, than
it will be if costs exist and the distribution is adjusted to
that fact. Similarly, the dividend will be increased if costs
of movement are lessened, though not destroyed, and the
distribution of resources is adjusted accordingly.

§ 8. The foregoing analysis rests upon the assumption
that there is only one arrangement of resources which makes

the values of marginal social net products everywhere equal —or as nearly equal as, in view of costs of movement, it is to the interest of the national dividend that they should be made. This assumption would be justified if the value of the marginal social net product of resources employed in each several use was always smaller the greater the volume of resources employed there. That condition, it will be noticed, is not equivalent to the condition that what economists call "the law of diminishing returns" prevails in each several use. Diminishing returns in this sense rule when the increment of product due to the increase by a unit in the quantity of resources occupied in producing some commodity is smaller, the greater is the quantity of resources so employed.[1] The law of diminishing returns thus refers to (marginal) physical output, and our condition to (marginal) physical output multiplied by value per unit; and it may easily happen that the expansion of an industry involves a diminution in this complex quantity, even though actual physical production obeys the law of increasing returns. But, when the law of increasing returns is acting strongly, it is evident that even our condition may very well *not* be fulfilled. Hence, the conclusions set out above require to be restated in a modified form. Allowance being made for costs of movement, it is true that the dividend cannot reach the maximum attainable amount *unless* the values of the marginal social net products of resources in all uses are equal. For, if they are not equal, the dividend can always be increased by a transference of resources from the margin of some uses to the margin of others. But, when the values of the marginal social net products in all uses are equal, the dividend *need not* attain an unequivocal maximum. For, if several arrangements are possible, all

[1] Dr. Cannan has objected to the use of the term "law" in connection with diminishing and increasing returns as defined above on the ground that, whereas in some industries diminishing, and in others increasing, returns prevail, a scientific law is a statement that holds true in all, and not only in some, circumstances (*Wealth*, p. 70). It might be answered that in fact this is only true of the most general laws of physics. Biologists, for example, regularly speak of Mendel's law of inheritance, without any implication that all inheritance obeys this law. But in any event the point is a verbal one.

of which make the values of the marginal social net products
equal, each of these arrangements does, indeed, imply what
may be called a *relative maximum* for the dividend; but
only one of these maxima is the unequivocal, or absolute,
maximum. All of the relative maxima are, as it were, the
tops of hills higher than the surrounding country, but only
one of them is the highest hill-top of all. Furthermore, it
is not necessary that all positions of relative maximum should
represent larger dividends than all positions which are not
maxima. On the contrary, a scheme of distribution approximating to that which yields the absolute maximum, but
not itself fulfilling the condition of equal marginal yields,
would probably imply a larger dividend than most of the
schemes which do fulfil this condition and so constitute
relative maxima of a minor character. A point near the
summit of the highest hill may be higher than any summit
except the highest itself. It is, therefore, very important to
inquire in what conditions, in any industry or use, different
quantities of investment may yield equal values of marginal
social net products.

§ 9. The answer is as follows. In an industry in which
production obeys the law of diminishing returns and
demand is not capable of being developed by acquaintance
with the commodity supplied, this state of things is
impossible. But there are two sets of conditions in
which it is not impossible. First, the employment of
additional resources in the production of a commodity may,
after a time, enable improved methods of organisation to
be developed. This means that conditions of increasing
return prevail, in such wise that the marginal (physical)
net product of a greater quantity of resources exceeds the
marginal (physical) net product of a smaller quantity: and,
whenever this happens, it is *possible*, though, of course, it
is not *necessary*, that the value of the marginal (physical)
net product of several different quantities of resources will
be the same. Secondly, the employment of additional
resources in the production of a commodity may, after a
time, lead to an increase in the price per unit offered by
consumers of any given quantity of it. For their taste

for it may be lastingly enhanced—obvious examples are afforded by the taste for music and tobacco—through experience of it. When this happens the value per unit of a larger product will (after an appropriate interval of time) be greater than the value per unit of a smaller product. It follows that, even for commodities whose production obeys the law of diminishing returns, there *may* be, though, of course, there need not be, several different quantities of invested resources the values of whose marginal social net products are the same.

§ 10. The practical outcome of this analysis is plain. Even though the values of marginal social net products were equal in all occupations, it would not follow that the national dividend was incapable of increase. On the contrary, in any industry where the conditions are such that there is not only one, but more than one, volume of investment which would yield a marginal social net product equal in value to that obtainable elsewhere, unless it so happens that the volume actually hit upon is that one of these which is the most favourable to the national dividend, an opening for improvement must exist. Benefit could be secured by a *temporary* bounty (or temporary protection) so arranged as to jerk the industrial system out of its present poise at a position of relative maximum, and induce it to settle down again at the position of absolute maximum—the highest hill-top of all. This is the analytical basis of the argument for the protection, or other encouragement, of infant industries; and, if the right infants are selected, the right amount of protection accorded, and this protection removed again at the right time, the argument is perfectly valid. Benefit could also be secured by a *permanent* bounty so arranged as to force the industrial system from the summit of the hill-top on which it is found to any position, that overtops its present site, on the slope of a higher hill. The conditions in which interference may be expected to have this effect, rather than that of shifting the economic system to a different position on the hill that it is on already, are somewhat special. But it can be shown that, in certain states of demand and supply, *some* rates of bounty *must* have this effect.[1] These possibilities have considerable practical importance. It must be clearly understood, however, that the possible advantage of particular disturbances of, and departures from, existing arrangements that involve equality in the values of marginal social net products affords no argument in favour of disturbances or departures in general. It is true that, when the values of the marginal social net products of resources in all uses are equal, *some* disturbances and departures would augment the national dividend. But the *majority* of possible movements would not do this. Any change from a distribution of resources involving equality in the values of marginal net products in all uses, which was not specially arranged with a view to increasing the national dividend, would probably in fact diminish it.

§ 11. This general conclusion may, moreover, be extended in an important way. Just as the national dividend is likely to be damaged by a change in the distribution of resources that brings about inequality, instead of equality, in the values of marginal social net products, so also, subject to the same conditions as above, it is likely to be damaged by a change that brings about greater inequality instead of less inequality. This conclusion cannot, however, be laid down without explanation. If the uses in which resources are employed were only two in number, its meaning would be perfectly clear and its validity undoubted. In fact, however, these uses are very numerous. This circumstance gives rise to a difficulty, which has already been referred to in another connection.[2] The meaning of the concept of greater or less equality among a large number of values is ambiguous. Are we to measure the degree of equality by the mean deviation from the average value, or by the standard deviation, or by the "probable error," or by some other statistical measure? If we use the standard deviation as our criterion, the reasoning of the footnote on p. 58 shows that an increase in the degree of inequality

---

[1] The shapes of the demand and supply curves and the size of the bounty must be such that, when the demand curve is raised by the bounty, it does not cut the supply curve at any point corresponding to its former point of intersection, but does cut it at a point corresponding to a point of stable equilibrium further to the right than this. This condition can readily be depicted in a diagram.

[2] Cf. *ante*, Part I. Chapter IV. § 11.

subsisting among the values of marginal net products in different uses will *probably* lead to a decrease in the national dividend. But the probability is of a lower order than the probability that an increase in the degree of inequality when there are only two uses, and, therefore, no ambiguity about the meaning of this increase, will have that effect. A probability of the same order as that probability arises only where the increase of inequality is brought about by a group of (one or more) changes of individual values, *each one of which taken by itself* tends to increase inequality. Thus, if the distribution of resources is so altered that a number of values of marginal net products which are below the average are all reduced, or if a number which are above the average are all increased, the probability that the dividend will be decreased is of a fairly high order. But, if a cause comes into play, which, while increasing the degree of inequality among the values of marginal net products on the whole, yet diminishes *some* values that are above the average and increases *some* that are below it, the probability may be of a much lower order. This type of difficulty is not, however, of great practical importance, because the obstacles to equality with which we have to deal are, for the most part, general obstacles, and operate in the same sense at nearly all points where they operate at all.

CHAPTER III

§ 1. IT is widely believed that the return per unit obtained
from the use of any kind of resource in any occupation tends
to be equal to the value of the whole marginal net product, or,
in the language of the preceding chapter, to the value of the
marginal social net product, of the resources employed in that
occupation. Let us provisionally accept this thesis. On the
basis of it is easily shown that the free play of self-interest tends
so to distribute resources among different occupations as to
render the values of marginal social net products everywhere
equal. For there are a number of different uses into which
resources may flow. Any person considering how to employ
those over which he has control will naturally prefer that use
which promises the largest return. But, after a while, each
several use tends to become satiated, so that the devotion of
further resources to it yields a less than proportionate return.
So long as the addition of a further pound to investment in any
one use would yield a larger return than, allowing for cost of
movement, could be obtained elsewhere, it will be to everybody's interest to pour his resources into that use. When
this process has gone on for some time, the addition of a
further pound to that use will no longer yield a larger return
than it would yield elsewhere ; and it will, therefore, no longer
pay to divert resources away from other uses into that one.
But, until equality of returns, which, on our hypothesis, means
equality in the values of marginal social net products, in all
uses has been established, it will pay to do this, and, on
the reasoning of the preceding chapter, the national dividend

will probably benefit thereby.   Of course, this does not imply
that self-interest will suffice at every, or indeed at any, moment
to secure that distribution of resources which is best adapted to
the interest of the national dividend.   Mill's illustration from
wave movements on the ocean is wholly apposite.   Under the
influence of gravity there is a constant tendency to equality
of level in all parts; but, since, after any disturbance, this
tendency takes time to assert itself, and since, before the
necessary time has elapsed, some fresh disturbance is always
introduced, equality of level does not in fact ever occur.   It
is, in short, with a tendency, and not with a fact, that we have
to do.   This, however, does not affect the practical conclusion
of the argument.   Provided that the conditions contemplated
above are satisfied, obstacles in the way of that distribution of
resources which self-interest tends to bring about will render
the values of the marginal social net products of resources in
different uses more unequal, and so will probably damage the
national dividend.

§ 2. It would seem at first sight to follow from this that
the removal or lessening of any obstruction to free movement
must make these values less unequal and should, therefore, make
the dividend larger.   This, however, is not really so.   The
situation is made complex by the fact that obstructions to free
movement comprise both costs of movement and imperfections of
knowledge.   If they consisted of costs alone, or of imperfect
knowledge alone, it would be obvious that a removal or lessening
of them would make the values of marginal net products more
equal and thus, in general, increase the dividend.   But in
actual life we have to contemplate reduction of costs while
knowledge is still imperfect and improvement of knowledge
while costs remain.   The resulting complications need careful
study.

§ 3. It is plain that, if people wrongly think that a larger
return can be obtained by sending resources away from A for
investment at B, a diminution in costs will cause resources to
be sent which, as a matter of fact, would have been more
productive if left where they were.   It is thus certainly
possible that a reduction of costs in actual life may render the
values of marginal net products more unequal and so lessen

the national dividend. In the appended footnote, however, it is shown by a technical argument that this is, on the whole, unlikely. Thus, our main proposition, stated as it was in a probable form, remains so far intact.[1]

§ 4. There is a different kind of complication when costs of movement remain unchanged but knowledge is improved.

[1] The proof is as follows. Let people's judgment concerning the value of the marginal net product of resources invested at B be correct, but let their estimate of the corresponding value at A differ from fact by a defined quantity k. Let the costs of movement between A and B be equated to an annual sum spread over the period during which the unit of resources that has moved may be expected to find profit in staying in its new place. This annual sum is not necessarily the same in respect of movements from A to B and movements from B to A. Transport, for example, "acts more easily down than up hill or stream [and] . . . the barrier of language acts more strongly from England to Germany than *vice versa*" (Macgregor, *Industrial Combination*, p. 24). For the present purpose, however, we may ignore this complication and represent costs in either direction by an annual sum equal to n. Construct a figure in which positive values are marked off to the right of O and negative values to the left. Mark off OM equal to k; and MQ, MP on either side of M each equal to n. It is then evident that the excess of the value of the marginal net product of resources at B over that at A—let this excess be known as h—is indeterminate and may lie anywhere between a value OQ, which may be either positive or negative, and a value OP which may also be either positive or negative. A diminution in the value of n is represented by movements on the part of the two points P and Q towards M. So long as the values

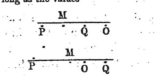

of k and n are such that P and Q lie on opposite sides of O, it is obvious that these movements make impossible the largest positive and the largest negative values of h that were possible before, and have no other effect. When, however, P and Q lie on the same side of O—in which case, of course, all possible values of h are of the same sign—they make impossible both the largest values of h that were possible before and also the smallest values. This double change seems equally likely to increase or to diminish the value of h. Hence, if it were the fact that the points P and Q always lay on the same side of O, we could not infer that diminutions of the value of n would be likely to affect the value of h either way. In fact, however, it must often happen that P and Q lie on opposite sides of O. When account is taken of these cases as well as of the others, we can infer that, over the mass of many cases, diminutions in the value of n are likely to reduce the value of h. In other words, diminutions in the costs of movement are likely, in general, to make the values of the marginal net products of resources at A and B less unequal. Furthermore, it is evident that, when the distances MP and MQ are given, the probability that P and Q will both lie on the same side of O and, therefore, the probability that a diminution in the distances MP and MQ will be associated with an increase in the value of h, is smaller the smaller is the value of k.

This improvement need not lead to an increase in equality among the values of marginal net products. For suppose the conditions to be such that, if perfect knowledge prevailed, the value of the marginal net product of resources at one point A would exceed the corresponding value at another point B by one shilling, and that the cost of moving a unit of resources from B to A would just balance this advantage. But, in fact, let us further suppose, knowledge is imperfect; people believe the value of the marginal net product at A to be higher than it really is; they therefore send more resources from B to A than they would do if better informed; and, therefore, the excess of the value of the marginal net product at A over that at B stands at less than n shillings. In these circumstances the growth of a more correct judgment would evidently *increase* the degree of inequality prevailing between the values of the marginal net products of resources at A and B. This is an awkward result. Any one holding in a loose general way that anything which has this effect must injure the national dividend would be forced to the paradox that an increase in knowledge about productive opportunities would actually do harm. But the analysis of Chapter IV. § 3 of the preceding Part disposes of this difficulty. It enables us to conclude that, in the example chosen above, an improvement in knowledge *both* makes the values of marginal net products less equal than they would have been in a régime of greater ignorance, *and* increases the national dividend.

§ 5. This last line of thought, pushed a little further, enables us to clear up yet another difficulty. This has to do with the effect of State bounties designed to lessen ignorance or reduce the costs of movement. If it was in all circumstances beneficial to the national dividend that equality among the values of marginal net products should be promoted, it must follow that the effect of a cheapening of knowledge or of movement to persons who control resources is the same whether that cheapening results from a real reduction of costs or from a transference of costs to the shoulders of other people. In either case, movements will be stimulated which diminish inequality among the values of marginal net products and, therefore, it would seem, which also increase the national dividend. The analysis cited above enables us to see that this conclusion is incorrect. A cheapening of knowledge and movement to individuals, brought about by the transference of a part of the cost of these things to the State, does, indeed, involve increased equality among the values of marginal net products at different points. But the increase of equality is an increase beyond what, *relatively to existing conditions*, is most advantageous. *Prima facie*, this sort of cheapening, despite the fact that it makes the values of marginal net products more equal, is likely to injure the national dividend.[1]

§ 6. The foregoing somewhat complicated analysis leaves intact the main thesis of our first section. Private self-interest, so far as it is not obstructed, tends to direct resources into various competing channels in such a way that the returns obtainable from further increments of investment are approximately equal in all of them. It must be remembered, indeed, that this tendency has only been proved favourable to the national dividend upon the assumption that the rate of returns to resources in any occupation is equivalent to the value of the marginal social net product there. In later chapters it will be shown that this assumption is often not warranted. When it fails, an arrangement involving equality of returns must differ in certain definite ways from the most advantageous arrangement; and there is a *prima facie* case for State, or other, interference designed to correct the error.

---

[1] To obviate misunderstanding two modifying considerations should be added. First, the presumption just established against the grant of a bounty to the industry of promoting mobility is merely a special case of the general presumption against the grant of a bounty to any industry. It may, therefore, be overthrown if there is special reason to believe that, in the absence of a bounty, investment in the industry in question would not be carried so far as is desirable. Secondly, when the State takes over the work of providing either information or the means of movement, and elects for any reason to sell the result of its efforts either for nothing or below cost price, we have, in general, to do, not merely with the grant of a bounty on these things, but at the same time with a real cheapening due to the introduction of large-scale methods. Even, therefore, though the bounty element in the new arrangement were proved to be injurious, it might still happen that that arrangement as a whole was beneficial.

K

A recognition of this fact, however, is quite consistent
with the view that obstructions which check equality, introduced otherwise than with deliberate curative design, are
likely to prove injurious.   It is true, as was implicitly
argued in § 10 of the last chapter, that particular drugs
consumed in particular quantities at particular times may
cure diseases; but it is equally true that the consumption
of drugs in general in a casual and miscellaneous manner
will damage a person's health.

CHAPTER IV

§ 1. AMONG the casual obstructions to equality of returns a high place, as has already been hinted, is held by ignorance. A flowing stream of resources is continually coming into being and struggling, so far as unavoidable costs of movement allow of this, to distribute itself away from points of relatively low returns towards points of relatively high returns. Success in this struggle is interfered with by imperfect knowledge on the part of those in whose hands the power to direct the various branches of the stream resides. To obtain an idea of the scale of the damage which results from this cause, it is desirable to study briefly certain aspects of modern business finance.

§ 2. The first thing that calls for comment is the general character of business accounts. In businesses conducted by private firms no statement of profits is made public. In businesses conducted by joint stock companies a certain amount of publicity is enforced by law. But the device of stock-watering and other devices for concealing from outsiders the real rate of return that is obtained on the capital actually invested make it exceedingly difficult, even here, for anybody other than a specialist to form a good judgment of the comparative prospects of different occupations. The difficulty is still further enhanced by the fact that the prospects which it is necessary to forecast refer, not to immediate returns only, but to returns spread over a considerable period; for it is evident that, as regards these returns, even correct knowledge of the immediate past gives but imperfect guidance. In view of these facts, it might seem that, in existing conditions, ignorance will almost entirely inhibit the tendency towards equality among the returns to resources in different uses. Such a view, however, would be unduly pessimistic. "Though it may be difficult," Dr. Marshall writes, "to read the lessons of an individual trader's experience, those of a whole trade can never be completely hidden, and cannot be hidden at all for long. Although one cannot tell whether the tide is rising or falling by merely watching half-a-dozen waves breaking on the seashore, yet a very little patience settles the question; and there is a general agreement among business men that the average rate of profits in a trade cannot rise or fall much without general attention being attracted to the change before long. And though it may sometimes be a more difficult task for a business man than for a skilled labourer to find out whether he could improve his prospects by changing his trade, yet the business man has great opportunities for discovering whatever can be found out about the present and future of other trades; and, if he should wish to change his trade, he will generally be able to do so more easily than the skilled workman could."[1]   Ignorance, in short, as to the relative profitableness of different occupations taken as a whole, though it may be complete enough among the general public, is probably much less important than it appears to be at first sight among those persons by whose agency the flow of resources into different occupations is, in the main, directed. Nevertheless, there is clearly room for improvement in the matter of business publicity,[2] and, if such improvement were made, ignorance would be lessened, equality in the values of marginal net products promoted, and the volume of the national dividend consequently increased.

§ 3. I turn next to the relation between ignorance and the quality of the persons by whom the investment of resources is controlled. In a primitive community investment is carried on almost exclusively by entrepreneurs actually engaged in the various industries and devoting to the conduct of them resources belonging to themselves. Their quality

---

[1] *Principles of Economics*, p. 608.
[2] Cf. Layton, *Capital and Labour*, ch. iv.

alone is relevant to our problem; and it is obvious that the range of error in the forecasts that are made is likely to be smaller or larger according as able men are or are not content to adopt business as a career. In the modern world, however, most forms of industry are financed from resources belonging to a great number of other people, besides those who actually manage businesses. These other people include, on the one hand, professional financiers, company promoters or promoting syndicates, and, on the other hand, moneyed people among the general public whom these promoters induce to invest in their ventures. "The promoter's special province," writes Professor Mitchell, "is to find and bring to the attention of investors new opportunities for making money, new natural resources to be exploited, new processes to be developed, new products to be manufactured, new organisations of existing business enterprises to be arranged, etc. But the promoter is seldom more than an explorer who points out the way for fresh advances of the army of industry. . . . There are always being launched more schemes than can be financed with the available funds. In rejecting some and accepting others of these schemes, the men of money are taking a very influential, though not a very conspicuous, part in determining how labour shall be employed, what products shall be used, and what localities built up."[1] In modern industry then the direction of a large part of the community's investment is in the joint control of professional financiers interested in company pro- moting and of the moneyed part of the general public. What is to be said about the capacity and business judgment of this complex directing agency?

§ 4. The comparative capacity for detecting good new openings for enterprise of the professional financier and of the ordinary business man—the entrepreneur investor of former days—is not difficult to determine. First, the professional financier is a specialist in this particular work, whereas to the ordinary business man an opportunity for undertaking it would come, if at all, only at rare intervals. Clearly, the specialist is likely to make better forecasts than the general practitioner. Secondly, the international character, which the development

---

[1] Mitchell, *Business Cycles*, pp. 34-5.

of the means of communication has in recent times given to
many industries, has made the advantage enjoyed by the
specialist much greater than it used to be when a knowledge
of *local* conditions, such as an intelligent business man would
naturally possess, afforded a sufficient basis for a good forecast.
Lastly, the fact of specialisation gives freer play to the selective
agency of bankruptcy, in eliminating persons who undertake
to choose openings for new enterprises and cannot choose well.
When the functions of financier and manufacturer are rolled
together in one man, the man may flourish through his manufacturing skill — good business tactics — despite of incompetent business "strategy."   When the two functions are
separated, anybody who undertakes the one in which he is
incompetent relatively to other people is apt to lose his
money and be driven from the field. Furthermore, the
efficiency of this natural selection is augmented by the fact
that a professional financier undertakes a great number of
transactions, and that, therefore, the element of chance plays
a small part, and the element of efficiency a large part, in the
result.   Hence, there can be no doubt that the advent into any
industry of professional financiers means the advent of persons
better able than those immediately concerned in the industry
to forecast future conditions. Against this has to be set the
fact that the great bulk of those members of the general
public, who ultimately supply the funds for the enterprises
that professional financiers have organised, are much less
capable than ordinary business men of forecasting future
conditions.   If promoters always looked for the openings
most profitable on the whole, as distinguished from those
that can be so manipulated as to become most profitable to
themselves, this ignorance on the part of people who follow
their lead would not, perhaps, greatly matter.   Unfortunately,
however, it is often to the interest, and it is usually in the
power, of the professionals, by the spread of false information
and in other ways, deliberately to pervert the forecasts of
their untutored colleagues. It is this fact that makes the net
effect of the modern system upon the distribution of the
community's investments among openings of varying merit
somewhat doubtful.   The prospect of advantage is probably

increased when, as in Germany, the flotation of new companies on the basis of shares of extremely low nominal value is forbidden by law; for then a certain number of the poorer and, perhaps, more ignorant persons, who might be most easily tricked, are driven away.[1] Again, any legislative enactment, capable of being enforced, that checks the fraudulent exploitation of incompetent investors by dishonest professionals, tends *pro tanto* to diminish the range of error to which the general mass of operative forecasts made in the community are liable. " The public regulation of the prospectuses of new companies, legislation supported by efficient administration against fraudulent promotion, more rigid requirements on the part of the stock exchanges regarding the securities admitted to official lists, and more efficient agencies for giving information to investors fall under this head."[2]

§ 5. A more fundamental remedy is introduced when the work of promotion itself is kept in the hands of bankers— whose reputation, of course, depends upon the *permanent* success of the business undertakings that they have founded. This is done in Germany. Big German banks retain a staff of technical experts to investigate and report upon any industrial ventures that may be proposed, decide after elaborate inquiries which ventures to promote and, in short, constitute themselves a financial general staff to industry. The contrast with the English system is well pointed out in the following passage: "The English joint stock companies (banks), conforming to the theory, have abstained in a *direct* way from flotations and the underwriting business, as well as from bourse speculation. But this very fact causes another great evil, namely, that the banks have never shown any interest in the newly founded companies or in the securities issued by these companies, while it is a distinct advantage of the German system that the German banks, even if only in the interest of their own issue credit, have been keeping a continuous watch over the development of

---

[1] In Germany shares are, in no case, permitted of a lower face value than £10, and they are not usually permitted of a lower face value than £50. (Schuster, *The Principles of German Civil Law*, p. 44.)

[2] Cf. Mitchell, *Business Cycles*, p. 585.

the companies which they founded.".[1] No doubt, this practice of banks acting as promoters involves. great risks and absolutely requires that their capital resources · shall be, as · they are in: Germany,[2] very much larger relatively .to their ' liabilities than is usual among English banks; for otherwise losses sustained in the promotion business, or even the temporary "solidification" of funds locked up in .this business, might render the banks unable to meet their obligations to their depositors. Moreover, it must be remembered that the position of this country as the banking centre · of the world, and, until recently, the principal free market for gold, would make the locking up of bank resources in long ventures more dangerous than in other countries. I make no suggestion, therefore, that the general policy hitherto pursued by British banks has been other than well advised. Nevertheless, there can· be no doubt that, when conditions are · such as to allow banks safely to undertake the work of promotion, a real advantage results. They are more likely than are certain types of private financiers to look out for openings which really are sound, as distinguished from openings. which can be made for a short time to look sound. It is, indeed, possible that, in some circumstances, where the rival interests of different nationalities are affected, powerful banking institutions operating· along these lines may· be

[1] Riesser, *The German Great Banks*, p. 555.

[2] The general practice of the English banks is to supply "banking facilities," that is to say advances, whether by discount of bills or otherwise, that have a short currency only, and not "financial facilities," *i.e.* advances with a long currency. It is sometimes claimed that this practice handicaps those British industries in· which opportunities may arise for the profitable expansion of plant at short notice,—to make possible, for example, their acceptance of some large order which might throw open for them the entry into some new market; for the raising of fresh capital by an issue of shares or debentures necessarily takes time. It is also sometimes claimed that our banking practice makes it difficult for British traders to make their way in those foreign markets where purchasers are accustomed to expect very long credits. It was with a view to meeting these complaints that Lord Farringdon's Committee on Financial Facilities' (1916) recommended that an .institution should be established with a large capital, not undertaking ordinary deposit banking, but prepared to provide financial facilities both for the development of industries at home and, where necessary, for the conduct of foreign trade. This recommendation was acted upon, and an institution of the kind contemplated—the British Trade Corporation—was granted a Charter in April 1917.

made the instruments of a *political* movement, and may allow their conduct to be swayed by other than economic considerations. But this aspect of the matter is unsuited for discussion here.

§ 6. It is not, however, only by acting as promoting agents that bankers can help to direct resources into productive channels. It is true that ordinary bankers in their loans to traders, whether made directly or through bill-brokers, are concerned only with the safety of the debt. The judgment that they make about the capacity of would-be borrowers to meet their obligations involves, when acceptable security is offered, no judgment as to the comparative profitableness of the undertakings into which different would-be borrowers will put the money they succeed in raising. But, when bankers are required to make loans to persons who are not in a position to offer full banking security, they are compelled to assume a more important rôle. They cannot lend on a mere promise to pay, but are bound, in their own interest, to make elaborate inquiry, both as to the trustworthiness of the borrower, and also as to the purpose to which he proposes to devote the proceeds of the loan. Speaking of the peasant borrowers of India, Sir Theodore Morison writes: "It is useless, however amiable, to believe that the ryot is only thirsting for capital in order to invest it at once in the improvement and development of his estate." [1] Again, in the Report on the working of the Co-operative Credit Societies Act in Burma, issued in 1907, it is urged that "in Burma borrowing is mostly due to habit and want of forethought and not to necessity; that the capital really required to finance cultivation (apart from luxury) is very much less than what is generally supposed, and that mere provision of cheap money, through co-operative societies or otherwise, tends, owing to the existing state of public feeling, to induce waste of income rather than thrift; and, lastly, that in Burma very special care will be necessary to see that the societies are managed in such a way that the prevention of waste and inculcation of thrift

---

[1] *The Industrial Organisation of an Indian Province*, p. 110.

are effectively impressed on the members' minds."[1] The recognised machinery for exercising this type of control and supervision is provided by People's Banks, such as the Raiffeisen Banks in Germany and their Italian counterparts. These banks evoke the necessary knowledge by a double process. First, the persons brought together as members of the Bank and, therefore, as potential borrowers, are gathered from a small area only, in such wise that the controlling committee can easily obtain intimate personal information concerning all of them. Only those persons are allowed to become members, of whose probity and general good character the committee have satisfied themselves. In some banks—in the Italian Banchi Popolari, for instance— the committee draw up, *ab initio* and independently of any particular application, a list of the sums which in their opinion may safely be lent to the various members.[2] This list is afterwards used as a basis for loans, just as the lists of the communal *bureaux de bienfaisance* in France are used as a basis for the grant of Poor Relief. Secondly, the grant of a loan is often made conditional on its being employed for a specified purpose, and subject to certain rights of supervision reserved for the lender. Thus, whereas in most land-banks (where material security is taken) "the proceeds of mortgages may be used as the borrower pleases, *e.g.* in paying off loans, in portioning younger sons, etc.," in the Raiffeisen Banks careful inquiry is undertaken into the purpose for which the loan is required, and provision is made for its recall should the borrower divert it from that purpose.[3] The general tendency of this arrangement is to lessen the number of investments made under the impulse of ignorance in undertakings that yield an abnormally low return, and so indirectly to augment the national dividend.

---

[1] Report, p. 15.
[2] Cf. Wolf, *People's Banks*, p. 154.
[3] For an account of Raiffeisen and kindred Banks, cf. Fay, *Co-operation at Home and Abroad*, Part I.

CHAPTER V

HINDRANCES TO EQUALITY OF RETURNS DUE TO IMPERFECT
DIVISIBILITY OF THE UNITS IN TERMS OF WHICH
TRANSACTIONS ARE CONDUCTED

§ 1. ALONGSIDE of imperfect knowledge, as discussed in the preceding chapter, there is a further influence hindering the tendency to a distribution involving equality of returns in different occupations. This is a peculiar kind of cost of movement. A pure mathematical treatment of economic problems always assumes that, when there is opportunity at any point for the profitable employment of given quantities of the several factors of production, each factor can be received there in units that are indefinitely small and are capable of being separated completely from units of any other factor. In so far as this assumption is not warranted, it is readily seen that the tendency to equality of returns will be imperfectly realised. For, on the one hand, if an enterprise is only financed, in respect of any one factor, by means of units, each of which has the value of £1000, it is obvious that, though the transference of £1000 worth of the factor to or from elsewhere could not, when equilibrium is established, bring about an increased aggregate return, the transference of any sum less than £1000 might have this effect. In short, when the units, in terms of which transactions are made, are not indefinitely small, the tendency to equality of returns in all uses degrades into a tendency to limitation of inequality—a limitation the extent of which is diminished with every increase in the size of the units. On the other hand, if an enterprise is only financed, in respect of any two factors, by means of units which combine factor A and factor B in a definite proportion, it is obvious that, though the transference of one of those complex combined units to or from elsewhere could not, when equilibrium is established, bring about an increased aggregate return, the transference in isolation of some quantity of either of the two factors might have this effect. Hence, when the units, in terms of which transactions are made, are compounded of fixed proportions of two or more factors, the tendency to equality of returns in all uses again degrades into a tendency to limitation of inequality. It follows that largeness or complexity in the units, in terms of which transactions are made, act in the same way as obstacles to movement. In general they obstruct the tendency of self-interest to make the return obtainable by each several factor of production equal in all uses.

§ 2. At one time it may have been true that the units in which capital transactions were made were noticeably large. Of recent years, however, the size of those units has been greatly reduced in two ways. Of these one is obvious, the other relatively obscure. The obvious way is the diminution in the value of individual deposits which banks will accept—the Savings Bank, for example, allows pennies to be deposited separately—and a similar, though less extensive, diminution in the value of the individual shares issued by companies.[1] The more obscure way depends upon the fact that a unit of capital is, as it were, two-dimensional. A man can reduce the quantity of capital which he provides, not only by altering the number of pounds that he lends over a defined time, but also by altering the time over which he lends a defined number of pounds. Reduction in the time-extension of the units in which capital is borrowed is of great importance in practice, because, whereas most enterprises require funds for a long period, many borrowers are only willing to cut themselves off inexorably from their resources for a short period. There have been evolved in the modern world two devices, through which the required reduction in time-extension has been

---

[1] It must be remembered, as was indicated in § 5 of the preceding chapter, that this tendency is not without incidental disadvantages.

effected. The first of these is the actual acceptance of loans
for short terms by entrepreneurs, in dependence partly on the
elasticity of the wants of their enterprise, and partly on the
chance of opportunities for reborrowing elsewhere. The
second is the organisation of the Stock Exchange, by resort
to which the funded debts of enterprises can be transferred,
—a device which is, from the lender's point of view, the
next stage to permission to recall his loan from the enterprise
itself. These two devices have fairly distinct spheres. To
rely too largely on short loans is felt to be dangerous. "In
proportion as enterprises depend upon short-time credits
rather than upon paid-up capital or · permanent loans
are they in danger of failure in times of stress" [1]—through
inability to renew the credits. There has, therefore, grown
up a rough general understanding that , short-time paper
is an unsuitable means of raising money for things like new
equipment, from which the turn-over is necessarily slow; it
should be used only . to finance expenditure on materials
and labour employed in making commodities that are likely
to be sold before the maturity of the paper.[2] This distinction
between the two devices is not, however, important for the
present purpose. Both of the devices are essentially similar;
for both depend on the general probability that the willingness of the aggregate community to lend will be less variable
than that of an average individual. In consequence of this,
on the one hand, a company, by discounting bills through
banks, borrows part of its capital for a series of short terms
from different people, thus enabling any one of them to lend
for a few months. On the other hand, a man, who makes
savings for a "treat" or to meet an accident, instead of
storing what he expects to want, invests it in long-time
securities, in reliance on the organisation of the Stock
Exchange to enable him to realise his capital at need. These
devices are not perfect. In times of stress the discounting
of new bills may. prove very difficult and costly, and the
realisation of capital by the sale of shares may not be
possible except at heavy loss. They have availed, however,

---

[1] Burton, *Financial Crisis*, p. 263.
[2] Cf. Meade, *Corporation Finance*, p. 231.

to bring about a large and important reduction in the time-extension of the units in terms of which capital transactions are conducted. As regards labour transactions, it is plain enough that the units are fairly small. Hence, in the modern world, apart from certain special problems of land transfer that cannot conveniently be discussed here, the only department in which largeness in the units of transactions obstructs the tendency of self-interest to bring about equality of returns in different occupations would seem to be that of employing power. The average wielder of employing power cannot be regarded as indefinitely small, as compared with the aggregate quantity of employing power that is in action in any use. This fact brings it about that the returns to employing power in different uses are checked from approaching very closely towards equality; and, hence, that the national dividend is rendered smaller than it would be if employing power were more fully divisible.

§ 3. Let us next consider complexity, or compound character, in the units in terms of which transactions are made. Here, as before, it is capital which calls for the greatest amount of discussion. For, capital, as ordinarily conceived in business, is not a pure elementary factor of production. In the concrete, of course, it appears in the form either of plant and equipment or of a system of connections called goodwill. But this concrete capital is always made up of a combination, in varying proportions, of two factors, namely, waiting and uncertainty-bearing.[1] Under primitive conditions, if an enterprise was undertaken by more than one

---

[1] The nature of the service of "waiting" has been much misunderstood. Sometimes it has been supposed to consist in the provision of money, sometimes in the provision of time, and, on both suppositions, it has been argued that no contribution whatever is made by it to the dividend. Neither supposition is correct. "Waiting" simply means postponing consumption which a person has power to enjoy immediately, thus allowing resources, which might have been destroyed, to assume the form of productive instruments and to act as "harness, by which natural powers are guided so as to assist mankind in his efforts" (Flux, *Principles of Economics*, p. 89). The unit of "waiting" is, therefore, the use of a given quantity of resources—for example, labour or machinery—for a given time. Thus, to take Professor Carver's example, if a manufacturer buys one ton of coal a day on each day of the year and buys each day's supply one day ahead, the waiting he supplies during that year is one ton of coal for one year—a year-ton of coal (*Distribution of Wealth*, p. 253). In more general terms, we may say that the unit of waiting is a

person, it was practically necessary for *each* of the several contributors to furnish waiting and uncertainty-bearing in the proportions in which these factors were required in the aggregate. They would, in-effect, pool their capital, taking upon each £ lent an equal measure of uncertainty-bearing. They would be partners, or, if we wish to suppose them in the enjoyment of limited liability, joint shareholders in a company whose capital consisted entirely of ordinary shares. In modern times, however, this is no longer necessary. An enterprise that requires, say, x units of waiting *plus* y units of uncertainty-bearing, need no longer obtain from each subscriber of one unit of waiting $\frac{y}{x}$ units of uncertainty-bearing also. By the device of guarantees its demand can be separated into two streams, in such wise that waiting alone is drawn from one set of people and uncertainty-bearing alone from another set. Guarantees may assume a great variety of forms. They are given to industrialists by insurance companies, which undertake, for a consideration, that the industrialists' earnings shall be unaffected by fire or accident. They are given by Exchange Banks, such as those which, in India before 1893, bought importers' and exporters' bills at the time of their bargain, and so, for a price, insured them against loss (or gain) from any fluctuations in the exchange which might occur in the interval between the bargain and the realisation of the bills. Where industrialists have to do with staple goods, for which grading permits the establishment of future markets, they are given, for the more general risks of business, by speculators. For a miller or cotton merchant, undertaking an order to supply flour or cotton goods, can buy the speculator's promise to

---

year-value-unit, or, in the simpler, if less accurate, language of Dr. Cassel, a year-pound. The graver difficulties involved in the conception of uncertainty-bearing are discussed in Appendix I. A caution may be added against the common view that the amount of capital accumulated in any year is necessarily equal to the amount of "savings" made in it. This is not so even when savings are interpreted to mean net savings, thus eliminating the savings of one man that are lent to increase the consumption of another, and when temporary accumulations of *unused* claims upon services in the form of bank-money are ignored; for many savings which are meant to become capital in fact fail of their purpose through misdirection into wasteful uses.

provide him with his raw material in the future for a
stipulated sum, irrespective of the price which may then
prevail in the market; and, in like manner, a farmer whose
crop has not yet been harvested, can buy the speculator's
promise to take it off his hands in the future for a stipulated
sum, irrespective of the price then ruling.[1] Like guarantees
are given to a banker preparing to discount a bill for an
industrial enterprise, when a second banker, or a bill-broker,
or some independent person, consents to accept, or endorse,
the bill, or, as is usual with "cash credits" in Scotland, to
stand surety for the original borrower.[2] They are given
to a Central Bank, when a People's Bank, working, either
on unlimited liability or with a subscribed capital of guarantee,
in effect borrows money on behalf of its local clients.[3] They

[1] In actual practice the method usually pursued of transferring uncertainty-
bearing to the speculative market is somewhat more complicated than the
above. The miller protects himself by "buying a future" in wheat when he
makes a contract for future delivery of flour, and then selling the future *pari
passu* with purchases of spot wheat of various grades as he needs them for his
milling. In like manner, the farmer protects himself by selling a future at an
early stage, and then buying to cover it in the speculative market and selling
his actual wheat in the spot market at the same time. The detailed methods
that may be adopted—and there are many varieties of them—do not, however,
affect the essential nature of these transactions. One further point should be
added. It must not be supposed that all the transactions that occur on the
produce exchange consist in purchases from producers or sales to ultimate
consumers. There are many transactions between traders neither of whom
will ever come in contact with the commodity traded in. These transactions
act upon price in the same way as the others, and constitute, in fact, the
machinery through which a number of persons, who make it their business to
forecast market conditions, are enabled to make their influence felt. Mr.
Emery's remark that "speculation consists in assuming the inevitable economic
risks of changes in value" (*Stock and Produce Exchanges*, p. 101) is thus somewhat misleading. Speculation as ordinarily understood does, indeed, only
assume uncertainties which arise *in connection with* inevitable changes of value,
but the mass of uncertainties which it assumes is considerably larger than the
mass that would exist if there were no speculation.

[2] The essence of the guarantee given by the acceptor's signature is the
same whether the bill is drawn in respect of goods received, or is an accommodation bill endorsed by an accepting-house, which lends its name for a
consideration. The variety of accommodation bills known as "pig-on-bacon,"
where the acceptor is a branch of the drawing house under an *alias*, is, of
course, different, because these bills, in effect, bear only one name; and the
same thing is substantially true when the fortunes of the endorsing house and
the original borrower are so closely interwoven that the failure of the one would
almost certainly involve the failure of the other.

[3] The controversy between the advocates of limited and unlimited liability
has sometimes been keen. In the ordinary banks and in the Schulze-Delitzsch

are given finally to a banker or other lender when a borrower obtains a loan from him by a deposit of "collateral" security. By far the most effective form of security consists in the stock and share certificates of industrial enterprises. For the deposit of these, unlike the deposit of chattel security, involves no present loss to the depositor, while their ultimate assumption, unlike the foreclosure of a mortgage, threatens no difficulty to the person in whose favour the deposit has been made. Furthermore, the "continuous market" provided for securities by the Stock Exchanges of the world safeguards the holders of them against the danger of slumps in value so sudden and large as those to which persons holding, as collateral, the title-deeds of parcels of real estate are liable.[1] In recent times, partly in consequence of· the supersession of partnerships by joint stock companies,[2] the proportion of national wealth represented by stocks and shares, and, therefore, available as collateral security, has enormously increased. According to Schmoller's estimate of a few years before the war, whereas 100 years ago only a very small proportion of any country's wealth was in this form, to-day in Germany 17 per cent—Riesser says 33 per cent—and in England 40 per cent, of it is covered by paper counterparts.[3] According to Mr. Watkins's investigations, 77 per cent of the capital value owned by residents in the United Kingdom, on which estate duty was levied in 1902–3, was "personalty," and, out of personalty, 70 per cent was paper property.[4] As a natural consequence, the area over which the device of guarantees can be employed, and, therefore, the segregation of waiting from uncertainty-bearing brought about, has been greatly extended.

§ 4. This device is not, however, the only method by

People's Banks limited liability is the universal rule. On the other hand, in the People's Banks of Italy and originally, before their absorption by the Imperial Federation, in the Raiffeisen Banks of Germany (except that the law insists on some' *small* shares) the method of unlimited liability was adopted, for the reason that the poor people, for whom the banks were designed, would find difficulty in becoming shareholders to any substantial extent.

[1] Cf. Brace, *The Value of Organized Speculation*, p. 142.
[2] Cf. Fisher, *The Rate of Interest*, p. 208.
[3] Quoted by Watkins, *The Growth of Large Fortunes*, p. 42.
[4] *Ibid.* pp. 48-9.

L

which modern ingenuity has broken up the complex unit of capital into its component parts. It enables waiting to be separated from "uncertainty-bearing." But uncertainty-bearing is itself not a single simple thing. To expose a £ to an even chance of becoming 21s. or 19s. is a different thing from exposing it to an even chance of becoming 39s. 10d. or 2d. There are, in short, a great number of different schemes of uncertainty which different people are ready to shoulder. Over against these there are a great number of different schemes of uncertainty which the undertaking of various business enterprises involves. It is evident that what is offered can be adjusted to what is wanted more satisfactorily when any given demand of industry can be met by combining together a number of different schemes that individually do not fit with it. This can now be done. When enterprises, for which capital had to be provided by several people, were worked on the partnership plan, all those concerned submitted the resources invested by them to the same scheme of uncertainty. Consequently, unless a sufficient number of people could be found ready to undertake that particular scheme of uncertainty, profitable industries were liable to be hung up. In the modern world this difficulty has been, in great part, overcome by the device, which joint stock companies now invariably adopt, of raising capital by means of different grades of security. Instead of an arrangement, under which every pound invested in an enterprise is submitted to the same scheme of uncertainty, we have systems of capitalisation combining debentures, cumulative preference shares, non-cumulative preference shares, ordinary shares, and sometimes further special sub-varieties. Each of these classes of security represents a different scheme, or sort, of uncertainty-bearing. This specialisation of shares into a number of different classes has the same kind of effect in facilitating the distribution of resources in the way most advantageous to the national dividend as the simpler specialisation into two grades, one involving some uncertainty and the other involving none.

§ 5. There is yet one more form of specialisation. Hitherto we have tacitly assumed that a given type of holding

in a company will always remain what it was when it was first
taken up. In fact, however, this is obviously not so: as a
company becomes established, holdings that at first involved
much uncertainty-bearing often cease to do so. The modern
system of industrial finance enables adjustment to be made to
this fact, so that shares of companies are in general held by one
set of people while the companies are new, and by a different
set of people when they become established. Thus, when an
important "proposition" is floated, the funds are provided
in the first instance by a contributing syndicate—or are
guaranteed by an underwriting syndicate—consisting of
persons who are willing to risk large losses in the hope of
large gains but are not prepared to lock up their capital for
long. The syndicate in its early stages may succeed in
disposing of many shares to speculators on margins and
others who are similarly willing to provide uncertainty-
bearing but not waiting;[1] and these, in turn, after a short
"flutter," may sell again to others like unto themselves. At
a later stage, when trial has shown what the concern is
really like, and so has greatly reduced the element of
uncertainty-bearing involved in taking up its shares,
the "investing public," those who are anxious to furnish
waiting alone, come into the field and purchase the shares.
In this way providers of uncertainty-bearing and providers
of waiting are both afforded an opportunity of playing the
parts for which they are respectively fitted.

§ 6. The broad result of these modern developments
has been to break up into simple and convenient parts the
compound units in terms of which it was formerly necessary
for capital transactions to be conducted. In transactions
affecting labour and land—apart from the fact, to be examined
in Part III., that the family must sometimes be taken as
the unit of migration—there has never been any great
complexity in the units. In the field of "enterprise" complexity still rules, in so far as employing power can only
find an engagement if it brings with it a certain amount of
capital. But the advent of salaried managers, working on
behalf of joint stock companies, has done much to break down

[1] For details cf. Meade, *Corporation Finance*, pp. 153-7.

the complex unit here also. In general, therefore, we may conclude that, in the modern world, complexity in the structure of the units in which transactions are conducted is not an important hindrance to adjustments making for equality of returns in different occupations.

CHAPTER VI

§ 1. WE now return to the caution set out in the last
section of Chapter III. The returns per unit to resources in
certain uses may differ from the value of their marginal social
net product. When this happens, an arrangement which makes
returns equal may make the values of marginal social net
products unequal, and, consequently, certain specific acts of
interference with normal economic processes may be expected,
not to diminish, but to increase the national dividend. In
developing this thesis the first step is to distinguish between
the social net product of any unit ·of investment and the
trade net product. By the "social net product" is meant the
aggregate contribution made to the national dividend ; by the
"trade net product," the contribution (which may be either
greater or less than the above) that is capable of being sold
and the proceeds added to the earnings of those responsible
for the industry under review. It is evident that, in general,
industrialists are interested, not in the social, but only in
the trade, net product of their operations. Clearly, therefore,
there is no reason to expect that self-interest will tend to
bring about equality 'between the values of the marginal
social net products of investment in different industries,
when the values of social net product and of trade net
product in those industries diverge. But there does seem
reason to expect that self-interest will tend to bring about
equality in the values of marginal trade net products,
because *prima facie* the value of the marginal trade net product of resources in any occupation must be equal to the

returns per unit yielded there. In the present chapter I shall provisionally assume that this is in fact so. On this assumption we may lay it down that the value of the marginal social net product, in any selected industry, will exceed or fall short of the value of the marginal social net product yielded in the generality of industries, by the amount by which it exceeds or falls short of the value of the marginal trade net product in the selected industry. I shall proceed, therefore, to examine the various circumstances in which the values of the social net product and the trade net product of any given (r^{th}) increment of investment in an industry diverge from one another in either direction. There are certain general sorts of divergence that are liable to occur even under conditions of simple competition, certain additional sorts that may be introduced under conditions of monopolistic competition, and yet others that may be introduced under conditions of bilateral monopoly.

§ 2. The source of the general divergences that occur under simple competition is that, in some occupations, a part of the effects of employing a unit of resources fails to be reflected in the remuneration of the person responsible for the investment. Such failure, when it occurs, is usually the result of practical and technical difficulties impeding complete adjustment; and these difficulties are, of course, various. We may consider first resources that are invested to build up, or to improve, a durable instrument of production by persons who do not own the instrument but only hold a lease of it for a limited period of time. The extent to which the actual owners of durable instruments leave the work of maintaining and improving them to temporary occupiers varies, of course, in different industries and is largely determined by considerations of technical convenience. It also depends in part upon tradition and custom, and is further liable to vary in different places with the comparative wealth of the owners and the occupiers. It appears, for example, that in Ireland, owing to the poverty of many landlords, the kinds of expenditure on land which they leave wholly to their tenants are more numerous than in England.[1] Details thus vary, but

---

[1] Cf. Bonn, *Modern Ireland*, p. 63.

there can be no doubt that over a wide field some part of the investment designed to improve durable instruments of production is often made by persons other than their owners. Whenever this happens, some divergence between the trade and the social net product of this investment is liable to occur, and is larger or smaller in extent according to the terms of the contract between lessor and lessee. These terms we have now to consider.

§ 3. The social net product of an assigned dose of investment being given, the trade net product will fall short of it by an especially large amount under a system which merely provides for the return of the instrument to the owner, at the end of the lease, in the condition in which the instrument then happens to be. Under this arrangement, the trade net product of any r^{th} increment of investment falls short of the social net product by nearly the whole of the deferred benefit which would be conferred upon the instrument. It need not fall short of it by quite the whole of this deferred benefit, because a tenant, who is known to leave hired instruments in good condition, is likely to obtain them more easily and on better terms than one who is known not to do this. So far, careful tenancy yields an element of trade, as well as of social, net product. Since, however, separate contracts are often made at considerable intervals of time, this qualification is not especially important. Passing it over, therefore, we notice that, since the effects of investment in improving and maintaining instruments generally exhaust themselves after a while, the contraction of trade net product below social net product, which the form of tenancy just described brings about, is not likely to be considerable in the earlier years of a long lease. In the later years of such a lease, however, and during the whole period of a short lease, it may be very considerable. Indeed, it is often found that, towards the close of his tenancy, a farmer, in the natural and undisguised endeavour to get back as much of his capital as possible, takes so much out of the land that, for some years afterwards, the yield is markedly reduced.[1]

[1] Cf. Nicholson, *Principles of Economics*, vol. i. p. 418.

§ 4. The form of tenancy just described is obviously illustrated by that primitive type of contract between landlord and tenant, in which nothing is said about the condition of the land at the end of the lease. But it is by no means confined to this type of contract. Another very important field in which it is present is that of "concessions" to gas companies, electric lighting companies and so forth. An arrangement under which the plant of a concessionaire company passes ultimately, without compensation, into the hands of the town chartering it, corresponds exactly to the system of land leases without provision for compensation for tenants' improvements. Such an arrangement governs the Berlin Tramways. The Company's charter provides that, "at the end of the contract, all property of the road located in the city streets, including poles, wires, any waiting-rooms built on city property, and patents, come into the possession of the city without charge."[1] From the present point of view, this system is similar to that of the British Tramways Act of 1870 and Electric Lighting Act of 1881, which provide for the taking over of the company's plant "upon terms of paying the then value (exclusive of any allowance for past or future profits of the undertaking, or any compensation for compulsory sale or other consideration whatever)." For the "reproduction cost," which value in this sense seems to represent, of a concern established many years back bears very little relation to the quantity of investment originally made in it. On the one hand, the physical cost of replacing the plant is likely, through the progress of industry, to be quite different from the cost of setting it up; and, on the other hand, the expenses of advertisement, including the supply of service at a loss with a view to establishing a connection and building up goodwill, are not counted in reproduction cost at all. It follows that, under the German and English plans alike, the terminating franchise system must, unless some plan is adopted to obviate that result,[2] reduce the trade net product

[1] Beamish, *Municipal Problems*, p. 565.
[2] Of course, the English plan is not so severe as the German in respect of investments in plant made near to the close of the lease; for, presumably, for a short time the cost of manufacturing such plant will remain fairly constant. But for investments designed to create goodwill, and, through this, future

of investments in extensions and so forth considerably below
their social net product, thus causing them to be carried less
far than the best interests of the national dividend
require. Furthermore, it is obvious that the restrictive
influence will be most marked towards the close of the concession period. In view of this fact, M. Colson recommends a
policy, under which negotiations for the renewal of concession
charters would be taken up some 15 or 20 years before these
charters are due to expire.[1]

§ 5. The deficiency of the trade, as compared with the
social, net product of any r^{th} increment of investment, which
arises in connection with what I have called the primitive type
of tenancy contracts, can be mitigated in various degrees
by compensation schemes. These may conveniently be
illustrated from the recent history of land tenure. Arrangements can be made for "compensating" tenants when they
leave their holdings for whatever injury or benefit they may
have caused to the land. Negative compensation for injury
is practically everywhere provided for in the terms of the

---

business, it is exactly similar. Thus, after the agreement of 1905, by
which the Post Office undertook to buy up in 1911 such part of the National
Telephone Company's plant as proved suitable, at the cost of replacement, the
Chairman of the Company stated that "the Company would not attempt to
build up business that would require nursing as well as time to develop;
it would confine itself to operations that from the start would pay interest and
all other proper charges" (H. Meyer, *Public Ownership and the Telephones*, p.
309). A device for getting over the difficulty considered in the text was embodied
in the contract extending the franchise of the Berlin Tramway Company to 1919.
This contract provided, *inter alia*: "If, during the life of the contract, the city
authorities require extensions within the city limits, which are not specified in
the contract, the company must build as much as 93 miles, double track being
counted as single. But the company should receive from the city one-third of
the cost of construction of all lines ordered between Jan. 1, 1902, and Jan. 1,
1907; and one-half of the cost on all lines ordered between Jan. 1, 1908, and Jan.
1, 1914. For all lines ordered after that the city must pay the full costs of construction, or a full allowance towards the cost of operation, as determined by
later agreement. The overhead trolley was to be employed at first, except where
the city demanded storage batteries; but, if any other motor system should
later prove practicable and in the judgment of the city authorities should appear
more suitable, the company may introduce it; and, if the city authorities
request, the company must introduce it. If increased cost accrue to the
company thereby, due allowance being made for benefits obtained from the new
system, the city must indemnify the company" (Beamish, *Municipal Problems*,
p. 563).

[1] Cf. Colson, *Cours d'économie politique*, vol. vi. p. 419.

leases.   In its simplest form it consists in monetary
penalties for failure on the part of tenants to return their
land to the owner in "tenantable repair." These penalties
may be made operative directly, through an explicit legal
contract; or they may be made operative indirectly, by a
rule forbidding the tenant to depart from the local customs
of husbandry; or, again, they may be made operative through
a modification in this rule concerning local customs, so
arranged as to free enterprising tenants from the burden
which the rule in its simple form imposes, without sacrificing
the purpose of the rule. . Thus, under the Agricultural
Holdings Act, 1906, a tenant may depart from local custom,
or even from a contract, as to cropping arable land, provided
that he shall make "suitable and adequate provision to
protect the holding from injury or deterioration"—except
in the year before the expiration of the contract of tenancy.
If the tenant's action under this section does injure the
holding, the landlord is entitled to recover damages and
to obtain, if necessary, an injunction against the continuance
of the tenant's conduct. Positive compensation was of somewhat later growth.   Rules about it were at first a matter of
voluntary arrangement in the yearly leases made by landlords.
Mr. Taylor quotes a Yorkshire lease, in which the landlord
covenants to allow the tenant "what two different persons
shall deem reasonable," in payment for the capital put into
the land in the course of ordinary farming operations during
the last two years of the lease.[1]   Gradually, compensation
schemes have been given a legal status.   Something in this
direction was done in Ireland under the Act of 1870—the
need for it being specially great in a country where the English
custom, under which the landlord provides the buildings
and permanent improvements, seldom applied.[2] In 1875 an
Act laying down conditions for compensating the outgoing
tenant in England and Wales was passed, but contracting-
out was permitted.   In 1883 a new Act, the Agricultural
Holdings Act, was passed, in which contracting-out was
forbidden.   This Act distinguished between improvements

---

[1] Cf. Taylor, *Agricultural Economics*, p. 305.
[2] Cf. Smith-Gordon and Staples, *Rural Reconstruction in Ireland*, p. 20.

for which the landlord's consent was necessary and those for which it was not necessary.[1] Scotland is now under a similar Act. It has largely superseded the old long leases, and these are now practically being modified out of existence.[2] In the detailed drafting of all Acts of this class difficulty is caused by the fact that some "improvements" do not add to the enduring value of the estate the equivalent of their cost of production. If the compensation for these improvements is based upon their cost, the trade net product is raised above the social net product. In practice, this danger is largely overcome by the rejection of initial cost as a basis of compensation value, coupled with the requirement of the landlord's consent to some kinds of improvement. Under the Town Tenants (Ireland) Act, 1906, for example, when a tenant proposes to make an improvement, he must give notice to the landlord, and, if the latter objects, the question whether the improvement is reasonable, and will add to the letting value of the holding, is determined by the County Court. But even on this plan the trade net product may be slightly in excess. In order that trade and social net product may coalesce, the value of an improvement, for compensation purposes, should in strictness be estimated subject to the fact that, at interchanges of tenants, the land may stand for a time unlet, and that during this time the improvement is not likely to yield its full annual value. If this is not done, it will pay a tenant to press investment slightly—very slightly—further than it will pay either the landlord or society to have it pressed; and hence, where, as in market-gardening, improvements can be made without the landlord's consent, it will check landlords from letting land. It is, thus, theoretically an error in the Agricultural Holdings Act of 1906, that it defines the compensation, which an outgoing tenant may claim for improvements, as "such sum as fairly represents the value of the improvements to an incoming tenant." The standard ought to be "the value to the landlord." But when, as is usual, improvements exhaust themselves in a few years, the practical effect of

---

[1] Cf. Taylor, *Agricultural Economics*, pp. 313 *et seq.*
[2] *Ibid.* p. 320.

this slight error is negligible, and does not cause the trade and social net products of any r^{th} increment of investment to diverge appreciably.

§ 6. These compensation arrangements, as so far considered, possess one obvious weakness, which generally impedes the adjustment they are designed to effect between trade and social net product. It is true that a tenant can claim compensation for improvements on quitting. But he knows that the rent may be raised against him on the strength of his improvements, and his compensation claim does not come into force unless he takes the extreme step of giving up his farm. Hence, the trade net product of investment is still contracted below the social net product. This result is partially mitigated under the Agricultural Holdings Act of 1906; where it is provided that: "When the landlord, without good and sufficient cause, and for reasons inconsistent with good estate management, terminates a tenancy by notice to quit," or when the tenant leaves in consequence of a proved demand for increased rent consequent upon tenants' improvements, the tenant may claim, not merely compensation for the improvements, but also "compensation for the loss or expense directly attributable to his quitting the holding," in connection with the sale or removal of household goods, implements of husbandry, and so forth. The above remedy is, however, defective in several respects. In the first place, since a tenant quitting his holding under the conditions contemplated obtains no compensation for the loss of "good-will" or the non-monetary inconveniences of a change of home, he will still be very unwilling to leave, and the landlord will still possess a powerful weapon with which to force him to consent to an increase of rent. And, in the second place, notice to quit on account of sale is not held to be "incompatible with good estate management." Consequently, when the land farmed by a sitting tenant is sold by one landlord to another, the tenant, if he leaves, obtains no secondary compensation of the kind just described. He will, therefore, be even more unwilling to leave. Should he elect, however, to rent the farm under the new landlord, he "is liable to the rent on any improvement which he has executed, without receiving any

compensation."[1] It is probably a recognition of this danger
that has given rise to the growing demand among farmers for
legislation permitting them, when the landlord wishes to sell,
to purchase their holdings on the basis of the old rent. A
provision for secondary compensation on disturbance similar
to that of the Agricultural Holdings Act is contained in the
Town Tenants (Ireland) Act, 1906. Here, under the circumstances specified, compensation may also be claimed for "good-
will."[2] But even with this provision it is apparent that the
adjustment secured cannot be more than partial.

§ 7. In view of these imperfections in compensation
arrangements, it is often contended, in effect, that for a really
adequate adjustment, not merely compensation for tenants
vacating their holdings, but legal security of tenure coupled
with the legal prohibition of renting tenants' improvements, is
required. Of course, in some circumstances the state of things
which this policy is designed to bring about is attained without any legislative intervention. In Belgium, for example,
it is substantially established everywhere by the force of
custom:[3] and, no doubt, many English landlords conduct the
management of their estates in a like spirit. It is plain,
however, that the willingness of landlords to refrain from
using economic power for their own advantage, when the use
of this power is permitted by law, cannot always be assumed;
indeed, if it could be assumed, the whole elaborate development of compensation laws, which we have been discussing,

---

[1] *Report of the Committee on Tenant Farmers* [Cd. 6030], p. 6. Notice given
to a sitting tenant on the ground that his land is wanted for building is also
"not incompatible with good husbandry " and carries no secondary compensation.
There would plainly be danger in the grant of such compensation here, since it
would encourage the investment of resources in agricultural improvements at
the cost of a *more than equivalent* social injury in postponing the use for
building of land that has become ripe for it.

[2] The argument for compensation, it should be noted, is not that it would
benefit the tenant. Professor Nicholson is right when he observes "that
compensation for improvements will not benefit the tenant so much as is
generally supposed, because the privilege itself will have a pecuniary value ; .
that is to say, a landlord will demand, and, the tenant can afford to give, a
higher rent in proportion. Under the old improving leases, as they were
called, the rent was low because ultimately the permanent improvements were
to go to the landlord " (*Principles of Economics*, vol. i. p. 322). Cf. Morison's
account of Indian arrangements (*The Industrial Organisation of an Indian
Province*, pp. 154-5).

[3] Cf. Rowntree, *Land and Labour*, p. 129.

would have been unnecessary. We are thus led forward to a consideration of the policy of legally enforced security of tenure *plus* "fair rents." In the way of this policy there are two principal difficulties. In the first place, the security of tenure that is granted cannot be absolute; for, if it were, considerable economic waste might sometimes result. It would appear, therefore, that security must be conditional upon reasonably good farming. Furthermore, it must be "conditional upon the land not being required in the public interest, whether for small holdings, allotments, labourers' cottages, urban development, the working of minerals, or the making of water-courses, roads, and sanitary works. When it is required for any of these purposes the Land Court should have the power to terminate the tenancy, while ensuring adequate compensation to the tenant."[1] The precise drafting of appropriate conditions is not likely to prove altogether easy. In the second place, security of tenure being plainly illusory if the landlord can force the tenant to give notice by arbitrary increases of rent, it is necessary that fair rents be somehow enforced. This cannot be done by a mere prohibition of any increases of rent, for in some circumstances an increase would be fair. There would be no justice, for example, in taking from the landlord and giving to the tenant the benefit of an addition to the value of the land brought about by some general change in agricultural prices wholly independent of the tenant's action. Hence, this policy seems to involve the setting up of a tribunal to fix rents, or, at all events, to settle disputes about rents when invoked for that purpose. Were the Land Court, or whatever the body set up may be, omniscient and all-wise there would, indeed, be no objection to this. But, in view of the necessary imperfection of all human institutions, there is some danger that a tenant may be tempted deliberately to let down the value of his holding, in the hope of obtaining a reduced rent. Under the Irish system of judicial rents, a defence against this abuse is nominally provided in the form of permission to the Courts to refuse revision. But this remedy is not utilised in practice. Very often, "not pro--ductivity, but production, and more especially the evidences of

[1] *Land Enquiry Report*, p. 378.

production in the fifteenth year, were the determining factors." in rent revision.[1]   Professor Bonn illustrates the result thus: "Two brothers divided a farm into two shares of equal values —the good husbandman got a rent reduction from the Courts of $7\frac{1}{2}$ per cent, the bad got one of $17\frac{1}{2}$ per cent."[2]   It is not, therefore, by any means obvious that the policy of fixity of tenure and judicial rents will really bring marginal trade net product and marginal social net product more closely together than they are brought by simple compensation laws.   The gap between the two marginal net products can only be completely closed if the person who owns the land and the person who makes investments in it are the same.   But this arrangement is frequently uneconomic in other ways.   For, especially when the farmers are small men, they are likely, as owners, to find much difficulty in raising the capital required for those larger improvements which, under the English land-system, it is now usual for the landlord to undertake.   It is beyond the scope of this volume to attempt a detailed discussion of the controversial topics thus opened up.   What has been said, however, will suffice to illustrate one type of discrepancy between marginal trade net product and marginal social net product, that is liable to arise in occupations where resources have to be invested in durable instruments by persons who do not own the instruments.

§ 8. I now turn to a group of causes of divergence between social and trade net product which are not dependent on this peculiar condition.   Here the essence of the matter is that one person A, in the course of rendering some service, for which payment is made, to a second person B, incidentally also renders services or disservices to other persons C, D and E, of such a sort that technical considerations prevent payment being exacted from the benefited parties or compensation being enforced on behalf of the injured parties. If we were to be pedantically loyal to the definition of the national dividend given in Chapter III. of Part I., it would be necessary to distinguish further between industries in which the uncompensated benefit or burden respectively is and is

[1] Smith-Gordon and Staples, *Rural Reconstruction in Ireland*, p. 24.
[2] Bonn, *Modern Ireland*, p. 113.

not one that can be readily brought into relation with the measuring rod of money. This distinction, however, would be of formal rather than of real importance, and would obscure rather than illuminate the main issues. I shall, therefore, in the examples I am about to give, deliberately pass it over.

Among these examples we may set out first a number of instances in which marginal trade net product falls short of marginal social net product, because incidental services are performed to third parties from whom it is technically difficult to exact payment. Thus, as Sidgwick observes, "it may easily happen that the benefits of a well-placed lighthouse must be largely enjoyed by ships on which no toll could be conveniently levied."[1] Again, uncompensated services are rendered when resources are invested in private parks in cities; for these, even though the public is not admitted to them, improve the air of the neighbourhood. The same thing is true—though here allowance should be made for a detriment elsewhere—of resources invested in roads and tramways that increase the value of the adjoining land—except, indeed, where a special betterment rate, corresponding to the improvements they enjoy, is levied on the owners of this land. It is true, in like manner, of resources devoted to afforestation, since the beneficial effect on climate often extends beyond the borders of the estates owned by the person responsible for the forest. It is true also of resources invested in lamps erected at the doors of private houses, for these necessarily throw light also on the streets.[2] It is true of resources devoted to the prevention of smoke from factory chimneys:[3] for this smoke in large

[1] *Principles of Political Economy*, p. 406.
[2] Cf. Smart, *Studies in Economics*, p. 314.
[3] It has been said that in London, owing to the smoke, there is only 12 per cent as much sunlight as is astronomically possible, and that one fog in five is directly caused by smoke alone, while all the fogs are befouled and prolonged by it (J. W. Graham, *The Destruction of Daylight*, pp. 6 and 24). It would seem that mere ignorance and inertia prevent the adoption of smoke-preventing appliances in many instances where, through the addition they would make to the efficiency of fuel, they would be directly profitable to the users. The general interest, however, requires that these devices should be employed beyond the point at which they "pay." There seems no doubt that, by means of mechanical stokers, hot-air blasts and other arrangements, factory chimneys can be made practically smokeless. Noxious fumes from alkali works are suppressed by the law more vigorously than smoke (*ibid.* p. 126).

towns inflicts a heavy uncharged loss on the community, in
injury to buildings and vegetables, expenses for washing
clothes and cleaning rooms, expenses for the provision of
extra artificial light, and in many other ways. Lastly and
most important of all, it is true of resources and activities.
devoted alike to the fundamental problems of scientific
research, out of which in unexpected ways discoveries of high
practical utility often grow, and also to the perfecting of
inventions and improvements in industrial processes. These
latter are often of such a nature that they can neither be
patented nor kept secret, and, therefore, the whole of the
extra reward which they at first bring to their inventor is very
quickly transferred from him to the general public in the form
of reduced prices. The patent laws aim, in effect, at bringing
marginal trade net product and marginal social net product
more closely together. By offering the prospect of reward for
certain types of invention they do not, indeed, appreciably stimulate inventive activity, which is, for the most part, spontaneous,
but they do direct it into channels of general usefulness.[1]

—— Corresponding to the above investments in which marginal
trade net product falls short of marginal social net product,
there are a number of others in which, owing to the
technical difficulty of enforcing compensation for incidental
disservices, marginal trade net product is greater than marginal
social net product. Thus, incidental uncharged disservices are
rendered to third parties when the game-preserving activities
of one occupier involve the overrunning of a neighbouring
occupier's land by rabbits—unless, indeed, the two occupiers
stand in the relation of landlord and tenant, so that compensation is given in an adjustment of the rent. They are
rendered, again, when the owner of a site in a residential
quarter of a city builds a factory there and so destroys a great
part of the amenities of the neighbouring sites; or, in a less
degree, when he uses his site in such a way as to spoil
the lighting of the houses opposite:[2] or when he invests

---

[1] Cf. Taussig, *Inventors and Money Makers*, p. 51.
[2] In Germany the town-planning schemes of most cities render anti-social
action of this kind impossible; but in America individual site-owners appear to
be entirely free, and in England to be largely free, to do what they will with
their land. (Cf. Howe, *European Cities at Work*, pp. 46, 95, and 346.)

resources in erecting buildings in a crowded centre, which,
by contracting the air space and the playing-room of the
neighbourhood, tend to injure the health and efficiency of the
families living there.   Yet again, third parties—this time
the public in general—suffer incidental uncharged disservices
from resources invested in the running of motor cars that wear
out the surface of the roads.   The case is similar—the
conditions of public taste being assumed—with resources
devoted to the production and sale of intoxicants.   To enable
the social net product to be inferred from the trade net
product of a sovereign invested in this form of production,
the industry should, as Mr. Bernard Shaw observes, be
debited with the extra costs in policemen and prisons which
it indirectly makes necessary.[1] Exactly similar considerations
hold good of certain sorts of foreign enterprise.   When the
indirect effect of an investment made abroad, or of the
diplomatic manœuvres employed in securing the concession
for it, is an actual war or preparations to guard against
war, the cost of these things ought to be deducted from
any interest that the investment yields before its net contribution to the national dividend is calculated.   When this
is done, the net contribution even of investments which,
as may often happen in countries where highly profitable
openings are still unworked and hard bargains can be driven
with corrupt officials, yield a very high return to the
investors, may easily turn out to be negative.   Yet again,
when the investment consists in a loan to a foreign government and makes it possible for that government to engage
in a war which otherwise would not have taken place, the
indirect loss we shall suffer in consequence of the impoverish-
ment caused by the war to the rest of the world should be
debited against the interest we receive.   Here, too, there may
well be a net loss to the country as a whole.   Perhaps,
however, the crowning illustration of this order of excess of trade
over social net product is afforded by the work done by women
in factories, particularly during the periods immediately
preceding and succeeding confinement; for there can be no
doubt that this work often carries with it, besides the earnings

[1] *The Common Sense of Municipal Trading*, pp. 19-20.

of the women themselves, grave injury to the health of their children.[1] The reality of this evil is not disproved by the low, even negative, correlation which sometimes is found to exist between the factory work of mothers and the rate of infantile mortality. For in districts where women's work of this kind prevails there is presumably—and this is the cause of the women's work—great poverty. This poverty, which is obviously injurious to children's health, is likely, other things being equal, to be greater than elsewhere in families where the mother declines factory work, and it may be that the evil of the extra poverty is greater than that of the factory work.[2] This consideration explains the statistical facts that are known. They, therefore, militate in no way against the view that, *other things equal*, the factory work of mothers is injurious. All that they tend to show is that prohibition of such work should be accompanied by relief to those families whom the prohibition renders necessitous.[3]

§ 9. At this point it is desirable to call attention to a somewhat specious fallacy. Some writers unaccustomed to mathematical analysis have imagined that, when improved

---

[1] Cf. Hutchins, *Economic Journal*, 1908, p. 227.

[2] Cf. Newsholme, *Second Report on Infant and Child Mortality* [Cd. 6909], p. 56. Similar considerations to the above hold good of night work by boys. The recent *Departmental Committee on Night Employment* did not, indeed, obtain any strong evidence that this work injures the boys' health. But they found that it reacts injuriously on their efficiency in another way, *i.e.* by practically precluding them from continuing their education in continuation classes and so forth. The *theory* of our factory laws appears to be that boys between 14 and 18 should only be permitted to work at night upon continuous processes of such a kind that great loss would result if they did not do so. The *practice* of these laws, however, permits them to be employed at night on unnecessary non-continuous processes which are carried out in the same factory as continuous processes. Consequently, the Committee recommend that in future "such permits should be granted in terms of processes, and not of premises, factories, or parts of factories without reference to processes" ([Cd. 6503], p. 17).

[3] Cf. *Annual Report of the Local Government Board*, 1909-10, p. 57. The suggestion that the injurious consequences of the factory work of mothers can be done away with, if the factory worker gets some unmarried woman to look after her home in factory hours, is mistaken, because it ignores the fact that a woman's work has a special personal value in respect of her own children. In Birmingham this fact seems to be recognised, for, after a little experience of the bad results of putting their children out to "mind," married women are apt, it was said before the war, to leave the factory and take to home work.— Cadbury, *Women's Work*, p. 175.

methods of producing some commodities are introduced, the
value of the marginal social net product of the resources
invested in developing these methods is less than the value of
the marginal trade net product, because there is not included
in the latter any allowance for the depreciation which the
improvement causes in the value of existing plant; and, as
they hold, in order to arrive at the value of the marginal
social net product, such allowance ought to be included.[1] If
this view were correct, reason would be shown for attempts
to make the authorisation of railways dependent on the railway
companies compensating existing canals, for refusals to license
motor omnibuses in the interests of municipal tramways, and for
the placing of hindrances in the way of electric lighting enterprises in order to conserve the contribution made to the rates
by municipal gas companies.   But in fact the view is not
correct.   The marginal social net product of resources devoted
to *improved methods of producing a given commodity* is not, in
general, different from the marginal trade net product; for
whatever loss the old producers suffer through a reduction in the
price of their products is balanced by the gain which the reduction confers upon the purchasers of these products. This is
obvious if, after the new investment has been made, the old
machines continue to produce the same output as before at
reduced prices.   If the production of the old machines is
diminished on account of the change, it seems at first sight
doubtful.   Reflection, however, makes it plain that no unit
formerly produced by the old machinery will be supplanted by
one produced by the new machinery, except when the new
machinery can produce it at a *total cost* smaller than the *prime
cost* that would have been involved in its production with the
old machinery : except, that is to say, when it can produce it
at a price so low that the old machinery would have earned
nothing by producing it at that price.   This implies that every

---

[1] For example, J. A. Hobson, *Sociological Review*, July 1911, p. 197, and *Gold,
Prices and Wages*, pp. 107-8. Even Sidgwick might be suspected of countenan-
cing the argument set out in the text (cf. *Principles of Political Economy*, p. 408).
It does not seem to have been noticed that this argument, if valid, would
justify the State in prohibiting the use of new machinery that dispenses with
the services of skilled mechanics until the generation of mechanics possessing
that skill has been depleted by death.

unit taken over by the new machinery from the old is sold to the public at a price *reduced* by as much as the whole of the net receipts, after discharging prime costs, which the old machinery would have obtained from it if it had produced that unit. It is thus proved that there is no loss to the owners of the old machines in respect of any unit of their former output that is not offset by an equivalent gain to consumers. It follows that to count the loss to these owners, in respect of any unit taken over from them by the new machinery, as a part of the social cost of producing that unit would be incorrect.

An attempt to avoid this conclusion may, indeed, still be made. It may be granted that, so far as direct effects are concerned, ordinary commercial policy, under which investment in improved processes is not restrained by consideration for the earnings of other people's established plant, stands vindicated from the standpoint of social advantage. There remain, however, indirect effects. If elaborate and costly plant is liable to have its earnings reduced at short notice by new inventions, will not the building of such plant be hindered? Would not the introduction of improved processes on the whole be stimulated, if they were in some way guaranteed against too rapid obsolescence through the competition of processes yet further improved? The direct answer to this question is, undoubtedly, yes. On the other side, however, has to be set the fact that the policy proposed would retain inferior methods in use when superior methods were available. Whether gain or loss on the whole would result from these two influences in combination, is a question to which it seems difficult to give any confident answer. But this impotent conclusion is not the last word. The argument so far has assumed that the rapidity with which improvements are invented is independent of the rapidity of their practical adoption; and it is on the basis of that assumption that our comparison of rival policies fails to attain a definite result. As a matter of fact, however, improvements are much more likely to be made at any time, if the best methods previously discovered are being employed and, therefore, watched in actual operation, than if they are being held up in the interest of established plant. Hence, the holding-up policy indirectly delays, not merely the adoption of improvements that have been invented, but also the invention of new improvements. This circumstance almost certainly turns the balance. The policy proper to ordinary competitive industry is, therefore, in general and on the whole, of greater social advantage than the rival policy. It is not to the interest of the community that business men, contemplating the introduction of improved methods, should take account of the loss which forward action on their part threatens to other business men. The example of some municipalities in postponing the erection of electric-lighting plant till their gas plant is worn out is not one that should be imitated, nor one that can be successfully defended by reference to the distinction between social and trade net products. The danger that beneficial advances may be checked by unwise resistance on the part of interested municipal councils is recognised in this country in the rules empowering the central authority to override attempts at local vetoes against private electrical enterprise. The policy followed by the Board of Trade is illustrated by the following extract from their report on the Ardrossan, Saltcoats and District Electric Lighting Order of 1910: "As the policy of the Board has been to hold that objection on the grounds of competition with a gas undertaking, even when belonging to a local authority, is not sufficient reason to justify them in refusing to grant an Electric Lighting Order, the Board decided to dispense with the consent of the Corporation of Ardrossan." [1]

§ 10. So far we have considered only those divergences between trade and social net products that come about through the existence of uncompensated services and uncharged disservices, the general conditions of popular taste being tacitly assumed to remain unchanged. It remains to observe that a further element of divergence may emerge in the form of uncompensated or uncharged effects upon the *satisfaction that consumers derive from the consumption of things other than the one directly affected.* For the fact that some people are now able to consume the new commodity may set up a psychological reaction in other people, directly changing the amount

[1] Cf. Knoop, *Principles and Methods of Municipal Trading*, p. 35.

of satisfaction that they get from their consumption of the old commodity. It is conceivable that the reaction may lead to an *increase* in the satisfaction they obtain from this commodity, since it may please them to make use of a thing just because it is superseded and more or less archaic. But, in general, the reaction will be in the other direction. For, in some measure, people's affection for the best quality of anything is due simply to the fact that it is the best quality; and, when a new best, superior to the old best, is created, that element of value in the old best is destroyed. Thus, if an improved form of motor car is invented, an enthusiast who desires above all "the very latest thing" will, for the future, derive scarcely any satisfaction from a car, the possession of which, before this new invention, afforded him intense pleasure. In these circumstances the marginal social net product of resources invested in producing the improved type is somewhat smaller than the marginal trade net product.[1] It is *possible* that the introduction of electric lighting into a town may, in some very slight degree, bring about this sort of psychological reaction in regard to gas: and this possibility may provide a real defence, supplementary to the fallacious defence described in the preceding section, for the policy of municipalities in delaying the introduction of electricity. This valid defence, however, is almost certainly inadequate. The arguments actually employed in support of the view that municipalities should not permit competition with their gas plant are those described in the preceding section. They are, in general, independent of any reference to psychological reactions, and are, therefore, like

---

[1] It should be noticed that the argument of the text may be applicable even where the product formerly consumed is wholly superseded by the new rival, and where, therefore, nobody is actually deriving diminished satisfaction from the old product: for it may be that complete supersession would not have come about unless people's desire for the old product had been reduced by the psychological reaction we have been contemplating. Furthermore, the preceding argument shows that inventions *may* actually diminish aggregate economic welfare; for they may cause labour to be withdrawn from other forms of productive service to make a new variety of some article to supersede an old one, whereas, if there had been no invention, the old one would have continued in use and would have yielded as much economic satisfaction as the new one yields now. This is true, broadly speaking, of inventions of new weapons of war, so far as these are known to all nations, because it is no advantage to one country to have improved armaments if its rivals have them also.

the arguments which persons interested in canals brought against the authorisation of the early railways, wholly fallacious.

§ 11. It is plain that divergences between trade and social net product of the kinds we have so far been considering cannot, like divergences due to tenancy laws, be mitigated by a modification of the contractual relation between any two contracting parties, because the divergence arises out of a service or disservice rendered to persons other than the contracting parties. It is, however, possible for the State, if it so chooses, to remove the divergence in any field by " extraordinary encouragements " or " extraordinary restraints " upon investments in that field. The most obvious forms, which these encouragements and restraints may assume, are, of course, those of bounties and taxes. Broad illustrations of the policy of intervention in both its negative and positive aspects are easily provided.

The trade net product of any unit of investment is unduly large relatively to the social net product in the businesses of producing and distributing alcoholic drinks. Consequently, in nearly all countries, special taxes are placed upon these businesses. Dr. Marshall has proposed to treat in the same way resources devoted to the erection of buildings in crowded areas. He suggested, to a witness before the Royal Commission on Labour, " that every person putting up a house in a district that has got as closely populated as is good, should be compelled to contribute towards providing free playgrounds." [1] The principle is susceptible of general application. It was employed, though in a very incomplete and partial manner, in the British enactment of a special petrol tax and motor car licence upon the users of motor cars, the proceeds of which were to be devoted to the service of the roads.[2] It is employed again in an ingenious manner

---

[1] *Royal Commission on Labour*, Q. 8665.

[2] The application of the principle is incomplete, because the revenue from these taxes, administered through the Road Board, must be devoted, "not to the ordinary road maintenance at all, however onerous it might be, but exclusively to the execution of new and specific road improvements" (Webb, *The King's Highway*, p. 250) Thus, in the main, the motorist does not pay for the damage he does to the ordinary roads, but obtains in return for his payment an additional service useful to him rather than to the general public.

in the National Insurance Act. When the sickness rate in any district is exceptionally high, provision is made for throwing the consequent abnormal expenses upon employers, local authorities or water companies, if the high rate can be shown to be due to neglect or carelessness on the part of any of these bodies. Some writers have thought that it might be employed in the form of a discriminating tax upon income derived from foreign investments. But, since the element of disadvantage described in § 8 only belongs to some of these investments and not to others, this arrangement would not be a satisfactory one. Moreover, foreign investment is already penalised to a considerable extent both by general ignorance of foreign conditions and by the fact that income earned abroad is frequently subjected to foreign income tax as well as to British income tax.

The trade net product of any unit of investment is unduly small in industries, such as agriculture, which are supposed to yield the indirect service of developing citizens suitable for military training. Partly for this reason agriculture in Germany was accorded the indirect bounty of protection. In like manner, uses promising a distant return, the trade net product of which is made by the fact of death unduly small, may sometimes claim the encouragement of a State loan free of charge, or, as with Indian railways, of a Government guarantee of interest.[1] Finally, an extreme form of bounty, in which a governmental authority provides all the funds required, is given upon such services as the planning of towns, police administration, and, sometimes, the clearing of slum areas. This type of bounty is also not infrequently given upon the work of spreading information about improved processes of production in occupations where, owing to lack of appreciation on the part of potential beneficiaries, it would be difficult to collect a fee for undertaking that task. Thus the Canadian Government has established a system, " by means of which any farmer can make inquiry, without even the cost of postage, about any matter relating to his business " ;[2] and the Department of the Interior also sometimes provides, for a time, actual

---

[1] Cf. Part I. Chap. II. § 5.
[2] Mavor *Report on the Canadian North-West*, p. 36.

instruction in farming.[1] Many Governments adopt this same principle in respect of information about Labour, by providing the services of Exchanges free of charge. In the United Kingdom the various Agricultural Organisation Societies are voluntary organisations, providing a kindred type of bounty at their subscribers' expense. An important part of their purpose is, in Sir Horace Plunkett's words, to bring freely " to the help of those whose life is passed in the quiet of the field the experience, which belongs to wider opportunities of observation and a larger acquaintance with commercial and industrial affairs."[2] The Development Act of 1909, with its provision for grants towards scientific research, instruction, and experiment in agricultural science, follows the same lines.

It should be added that sometimes, when the inter-relations of the various private persons affected are highly complex, the Government may find it necessary to exercise some means of authoritative control in addition to providing a bounty. Thus it is coming to be recognised as an axiom of government that, in every town, power must be held by some authority to limit the quantity of building permitted to a given area, to restrict the height to which houses may be carried,—for the erection of barrack dwellings may cause great overcrowding of area even though there is no overcrowding of rooms,[3]—and generally to control the building activities of individuals. It is as idle to expect a well-planned town to result from the independent activities of isolated speculators as it would be to expect a satisfactory picture to result if each separate square inch were painted by an independent artist. No " invisible hand " can be relied on to produce a good arrangement of the whole from a combination of separate treatments of the parts. It is, therefore,

---

[1] Mavor, *Report on the Canadian North-West*, p. 78.

[2] O. Webb, *Industrial Co-operation*, p. 149.

[3] Mr. Dawson believes that this type of overcrowding prevails to a considerable extent in German towns. He writes: " The excessive width of the streets, insisted on by cast-iron regulations, adds greatly to the cost of house-building, and, in order to recoup himself, and make the most of his profits, the builder begins to extend his house vertically instead of horizontally " (*Municipal Life and Government in Germany*, pp. 163-4). Hence, German municipalities now often control the height of buildings, providing a scale of permitted heights which decreases on passing from the centre to the outlying parts of a town.

necessary that an authority of wider reach should intervene
and should tackle the collective problems of beauty, of air,
and of light, as those other collective problems of gas and
water have been already tackled.   Hence, shortly before the
war, there came into being, on the pattern of long previous
German practice, Mr. Burns's extremely important town-
planning Act.   In this Act, for the first time, control over
individual buildings, from the standpoint, not of individual
structure, but of the structure of the town as a whole, is
definitely conferred upon those town councils that are willing
to accept the powers offered to them.   Part II. of the Act
begins: "A town-planning scheme may be made in accordance with the provisions of this Part of the Act as respects
any land which is in course of development, or appears likely
to be used for building purposes, with the general object
of securing proper sanitary conditions, amenity, and convenience in connection with the laying out and use of the
land, and of any neighbouring lands."   The scheme may
be worked out, as is the custom in Germany, many years
in advance of actual building, thus laying down beforehand
the lines of future development.   Furthermore, it may, if
desired, be extended to include land on which buildings have
already been put up, and may provide "for the demolition
or alteration of any buildings thereon, so far as may be
necessary for carrying the scheme into effect."   Finally,
where local authorities are remiss in preparing a plan on
their own initiative, power is given to the Local Government
Board to order them to take action.   There is ground for
hope, however, that, so soon as people become thoroughly
familiarised with town-planning, local patriotism and inter-
local emulation will make resort to external pressure from
the central Government no longer necessary.

§ 12. So far we have been concerned with forms of
divergence between social and trade net product that are liable
to occur even under conditions of simple competition.   Where
conditions of monopolistic competition [1]—competition, that is
to say, between several sellers each producing a considerable
proportion of the aggregate output—are present, the way is

[1] Cf. *post*, Ch. XII.

opened up' for a new kind of·investment. This consists in
competitive· advertisement : directed to the sole purpose ' of
transferring the ·demand for a given· commodity from one
source · of .supply, to ''another.[1] ' There · is, indeed, little
opportunity. for·this as regards goods of a .kind'·whose quality
is uniform and;·as with salt, lumber. or grain; can be easily
tested ; but, where quality cannot be easily tested, and especially
where goods ·are sold in. small quantities, which can readily be
put into distinctive packages for the use of retail customers,
there is plenty of opportunity.[2] ·· Not· all· advertisement is, of
course,· strictly competitive. Some advertisement,· on ' the
contrary, fulfils a social · purpose, in informing people · of the
existence of articles adapted to their tastes. Indeed; it has
been said " that advertising is a necessary consequence of sale
by ·,description," and· represents merely a · segregated· part of
the complex· work formerly· done· by those ·middlemen who
exhibited, as well as sold, their: goods.[3] ' Without it many
useful articles,·such as new machines, or useful services, such
as that· of life·,insurance,· might not be brought at all ·to the
notice of potential purchasers who have a' real ·need for them.
Furthermore, some advertisement serves to develop an entirely
new, set of wants on the part of consumers, the satisfaction of
which involves a real ,addition to·social: well-being; and ·the
development of which on a large scale : at the same time
enables the commodity that satisfies them to be 'produced on
a large scale and, therefore, cheaply.[4] Under this head it· is
possible to make out a case in .favour of; the peculiar· system
of advertisement arranged on behalf of the general body of its
currant growers (without the mention of individual names) by
the Greek Government :[5] though; of course, the development
of· a taste for.currants is probably in. part at the expense of
the taste for something else. · It is not;'however, necessary to

---

[1] Under simple competition, there .is no purpose in this advertisement,
because, *ex hypothesi*, the market will take, at the market price, as much as any
one small seller wants to sell.'' Practically monopolistic competition comprises
all forms of imperfect competition.
[2] Cf. Jenks and Clark, *The Trust Problem*, pp. 26-7.
[3] Cf. Shaw, *Quarterly Journal of Economics*, 1912, p. 743.
[4] Cf. the discussion of "constructive," and "combative" advertisements in
Marshall's *Industry and Trade*, pp. 304-7.
[5] Cf. Goodall, *Advertizing*, p. 49.

my purpose to attempt an estimate of the proportion which strictly competitive advertisement bears to advertisement in the aggregate—an aggregate the cost of which has been put, for the United Kingdom, at eighty million pounds, and, for the world, at six hundred million pounds per annum.[1] That a considerable part of the advertisement of the modern world is strictly competitive is plain.[2] This is true alike of the more obvious forms, such as pictorial displays, newspaper paragraphs,[3] travellers, salesmen, and so on; and of the more subtle forms, such as a large exhibit of jewellery in the shop window, the according of credit, with the consequential expenditure on book-keeping and on the collection of recalcitrant debts, expenditure in keeping shops open at hours inconvenient and costly to the sellers, and other such forms. It is plain that, up to a point, investment of this type, in so far as it retains, or gains, for the investor "a place in the sun," yields, like expenditure upon national armaments, a considerable trade net product. A curve, representing the trade net products yielded by successive increments of it, would indicate positive values for a long distance. What relation does this curve bear to the corresponding curve representing the social net products of successive increments?

First, it may happen that the net result of the expenditures made by the various rivals in conflict with each other is to bring about an alliance between them. If this happens, the expenditures induced by a state of monopolistic competition are responsible for the evolution of simple monopoly. It does not seem possible to determine in a general way the comparative effects on the volume of national dividend of simple mono-

---

[1] Cf. Goodall, *Advertizing*, p. 2.

[2] It should be observed that this type of advertisement, which aims in effect at diverting custom from a rival to oneself, may be pressed to lengths that the law of modern States will not tolerate. Thus in some European States certain definite false statements about awards alleged to have been won at exhibitions or about an exceptional offer of bankrupt stock, direct disparagement of a rival's character or produce, and attempts to pass off one's own goods as the goods of a well-known house are punishable offences (cf. Davies, *Trust Laws and Unfair Competition*, Ch. x.).

[3] Of course the "resources" invested in these things are measured by the actual capital and labour involved in the production of the paragraphs, not by a monopoly charge—if such is made—exacted for them by the newspaper concerned.

poly and of monopolistic competition. Consequently, no general statement can be made as to whether the curve representing the social net products of successive increments of investment will indicate positive values over any part of its course.

Secondly, it may happen that the expenditures on advertisement made by competing monopolists will simply neutralise one another, and leave the industrial position exactly as it would have been if neither had expended anything. For, clearly, if each of two rivals makes equal efforts to attract the favour of the public away from the other, the total result is the same as it would have been if neither had made any effort at all. This point was set in a very clear light in Mr. Butterworth's Memorandum to the Board of Trade Railway Conference in 1908. He points out that, under competitive arrangements, the officers of rival companies spend a great part of their time and energy in " scheming how to secure traffic for their own line, instead of in devising how best to combine economy with efficiency of working. At present much of the time and energy of the more highly-paid officials of a railway company is taken up with work in which the trading community has no interest, and which is only rendered necessary in the interest of the shareholders whom they serve by the keen competition which exists between companies."[1] In these circumstances, the curve representing the social net products of successive increments of investment will indicate negative values throughout.

Thirdly, it may happen that the expenditures lead simply to the substitution in a market of goods made by one firm for the same quantity of equivalent goods made by another firm. If we suppose production, both under A's auspices and under B's, to obey the law of constant return, and to involve equal cost per unit, it is clearly a matter of indifference to the national dividend from which of these two producers the public buys. In other words, all units of resources expended by either producer in building up goodwill as against the other have a social net product equal to zero. If conditions are such that a diminution in the aggregate cost of production

[1] [Cd. 4677], p. 27.

of the commodity would be brought about by the transference of some of the orders from B to A, some units of resources employed by A to abstract orders from B would yield a positive social net product, while all units of resources employed by B to abstract orders from A would yield a negative social net product. If we suppose the more efficient and the less efficient firms to expend resources in these hostilities in about equal measure, in such wise that their efforts cancel one another and leave things much as they would have been had the efforts of both been removed, it is obvious that the social net product of any compound unit of these efforts taken as a whole is, again, zero. There is, however, some slight ground for believing that firms of low productive efficiency tend to indulge in advertisement to a greater extent than their productively more efficient rivals. For, clearly, they have greater inducements to expenditure on devices, such as special packages, designed to obviate comparison of the bulk of commodity offered by them and by other producers at a given price. This consideration suggests that the curve representing the social net products of successive increments of investment is likely to indicate negative values throughout.

The discussion of the preceding paragraphs makes it plain that, speaking generally, the social net product of any r^{th} increment of resources invested in competitive advertisement is exceedingly unlikely to be as large as the trade net product. The consequent waste might be diminished by special undertakings among competitors not to advertise, such as hold good among barristers, doctors and members of the London Stock Exchange. Failing this, the evil might be attacked by the State through the taxation, or prohibition, of competitive advertisements — if these could be distinguished from advertisements which are not strictly competitive. It could be removed altogether if conditions of monopolistic competition were destroyed.

§ 13. We now turn to conditions of bilateral monopoly, that is to say, conditions under which the relations between individual buyers and sellers are not rigidly fixed by a surrounding market. The presence of bilateral monopoly in this sense implies an element of theoretical indeterminateness, and, therefore, opens up the way for the employment of activities and resources in efforts to modify the ratio of exchange in favour of one or other of the "monopolists." The nature of the indeterminateness present is different according as the monopolists are, as it were, solidified units, such as single individuals and joint-stock companies, or representative units, such as Trade Unions or Employers' Federations, whose officials negotiate to establish a rate of pay, but whose individual members, when this rate is established, are still free at will to continue or to abandon business. This distinction is, for some purposes, important and ought not to be ignored.[1] It does not, however, bear directly upon our present inquiry. For, whatever the nature of the indeterminateness, it is plain that activities and resources devoted to manipulating the ratio of exchange may yield a positive trade net product; but they cannot—even the earliest dose of them cannot—yield a positive social net product, and they may, in some conditions, yield a negative social net product.[2] The activities here contemplated consist chiefly—for physical force exercised in direct plunder does not operate through exchange—in the brain work of "bargaining" proper and in the practice of one or other of two sorts of deception. These latter are, first, deception as to the physical nature of a thing offered for sale, and, secondly, deception as to the future yield that it is "reasonable to expect" from a thing offered for sale, when the physical nature of that thing has been correctly described.

§ 14. Of bargaining proper there is little that need be said. It is obvious that intelligence and resources devoted to this purpose, whether on one side or on the other, and whether successful or unsuccessful, yield no net product to the com-

---

[1] With solidified units the *settlement locus—i.e.* the range of possible bargains—lies along the contract curve, and with representative units along portions of the two reciprocal demand (or supply) curves. For a technical discussion of this and connected points cf. my paper "Equilibrium under Bilateral Monopoly" (*Economic Journal*, Jan. 1908, pp. 205 *et seq.*); also my *Principles and Methods of Industrial Peace*, Appendix A.

[2] It will be understood that net product here means net product of dividend. It is not, of course, denied that, if a poor man outbargains a rich one, there is a positive net product of economic satisfaction, and, if a rich man outbargains a poor one, a corresponding negative net product of satisfaction.

munity as a whole. According to Professor Carver, a considerable part of the energies of business men is devoted to, and a considerable part of their earnings arise out of, activities of this kind.[1] These activities are wasted. They contribute to trade, but not to a social, net product. But this conclusion does not exhaust the subject. It is often pointed out that, where their clients, be they customers or workpeople, can be squeezed, employers tend to expend their energy in accomplishing this, rather than in improving the organisation of their factories. When they act thus, the social net product even of the earliest dose of resources devoted to bargaining may be, not merely zero, but negative. Whenever that happens, no tax that yields a revenue, though it may affect an improvement, can provide a complete remedy. For that absolute prohibition is required. But absolute prohibition of bargaining is hardly feasible except where prices and conditions of sale are imposed upon private industry by some organ of State authority.[2]

§ 15. Deception as to the physical nature of a thing offered for sale is practised through false weights and measures, adulteration and misnaming of goods, and dishonest advertisement. Before the days of co-operation, "the back streets of the manufacturing towns swarmed with small shops, in which the worst of everything was sold, with unchecked measures and unproved weights."[3] To a less degree similar practices still prevail. There is little temptation to adopt them in marketing "production goods," where the buyers are large industrial concerns, like railway companies, which possess elaborately organised "testing" departments. But, in selling "consumption goods"—particularly semi-mysterious consumption goods like patent medicines—to poor and ignorant buyers, and even in selling production goods to less skilled buyers, such as farmers, there is still some temptation. It is always profitable for sellers to "offer commodities which seem rather than are useful, if the difference between seeming

---

[1] Cf. *American Economic Association*, 1909, p. 51.
[2] The legislation of many States concerning private labour bureaux is relevant here. For an account of this legislation, cf. Becker and Bernhardt *Gesetzliche Regelung der Arbeitsvermittelung.*
[3] Aves, *Co-operative Industry*, p. 16.

N

and reality is likely to escape notice."[1] Deception as to
the future yield, which it is reasonable to expect from a thing
offered for sale, is practised, in the main, by unscrupulous
financiers selling stocks and shares. Among the methods
employed, are the manipulation of dividend payments,
"matched orders," the deliberate publication of false
information,[2] and — a practice less clearly over the border
line of fairness—the deliberate withholding of relevant
information.[3] It is evident that, up to a point, activities
devoted to either of these forms of deception bring about a
positive trade net product, but not a positive social net
product. Furthermore, they often lead to enhanced purchases
and, therefore, enhanced production of the thing about which
deception has been practised. Hence, they divert to the
production of this thing resources that would otherwise have
been devoted to investments yielding the normal marginal
return. Therefore, when this indirect consequence is taken
into account, the social net product, even of the earliest dose
of resources devoted to deception, is, in general, not zero but
negative. If the thing in question is something the production of which involves no expenditure of resources, like

[1] Sidgwick, *Principles of Political Economy*, p. 416.

[2] For a lurid account of some of these methods *vide* Lawson, *Frenzied Finance*,
passim, and for an analysis of the protective devices embodied in the celebrated
German law of 1884, *vide* Schuster, "The Promotion of Companies and the Valuation of their Assets according to German Law," *Economic Journal*, 1900, p. 1
et seq. It should be observed that the device of "matched orders" may
be made difficult by a rule forbidding offers and bids for large amounts
of stock on the terms "all or none." For, when such a rule exists, there is
more chance that a seller or buyer operating a matched order may be forced
unwillingly to make a deal with some one other than his confidant (cf. Brace,
The Value of Organised Speculation, p. 241).

[3] It is interesting to observe that, whereas the law often, and public opinion
generally, condemns a seller who withholds relevant information, a buyer who
acts in this way is generally commended for his "good bargain." Thus, to pick
up a piece of valuable oak furniture in an out-of-the-way cottage for much less
than it is worth is thought by some to be creditable; and nobody maintains that
the Rothschild, who founded the fortunes of his house by buying government
stock on the strength of his early knowledge of the battle of Waterloo, was
honourably bound to make that information public before acting on it. The
reason for this distinction probably is that the possessor of an article is
presumed to have full opportunity of knowing its real value, and, if he fails to
do this, becomes, for his carelessness, "legitimate prey." A director of a
company who bought up shares in that company on the strength of knowledge
gained in the Board room, and so obviously not available to the shareholders
generally, would be universally condemned.

the fictitious situations created by fraudulent registry offices, the social net product does not, indeed, sink below zero, for extra production of these imaginary entities involves no withdrawal of resources from elsewhere. As a rule, however, the social net product of any dose of resources invested in a deceptive activity is negative. Consequently, as with bargaining, no tax that yields a revenue, though it may affect an improvement, can provide a complete remedy, and absolute prohibition of the activity is required. Attempts to establish such prohibition have been made, on the one side, in various laws concerning false weights and measures and the adulteration of foods, and, on the other side, in various laws—laws, which to be effective, must be enforcible at the instance, not of the damaged party, but of public inspectors or commissioners [1]—designed to control and regulate the practice of company promotion. In other fields the evil can be met in a more direct way by the establishment of Purchasers' Associations, in which the interests of the sellers and the buyers are unified.[2]

[1] Cf. Van Hise, *Concentration and Control*, pp. 76-8.
[2] Cf. *post*, Part II. Ch. XVI.

CHAPTER VII

MARGINAL TRADE AND SOCIAL NET PRODUCTS IN RELATION
TO INDUSTRIAL FORMS

§ 1. In the preceding chapter we were engaged in a study of
the differences between the marginal social net product and
the marginal trade net product of resources devoted to various
occupations or industries. It is now necessary to conduct an
analogous inquiry about resources devoted to various forms of
economic organisation within the several occupations or industries. Dr. Marshall has observed that "as a general rule
the law of substitution—which is nothing more than a special
and limited application of the law of the survival of the fittest—
tends to make one method of industrial organisation supplant
another when it offers a direct and immediate service at a
lower price. The indirect and ultimate services, which either
will render, have, as a general rule, little or no weight in the
balance."[1] These indirect services constitute the difference
between the social net product and the trade net product of
a unit of resources invested in any form of economic organisation. Our present task is to distinguish the principal fields
in which they play an important part.

§ 2. One very important indirect service is rendered by
the general economic organisation of a country in so far as, in
addition to fulfilling its function as an instrument of production,
it also acts, in greater or less degree, as a training ground of
business capacities. In order that it may do this effectively,
the size of business units must be so graded that persons
possessed of good native endowments can learn the principles
of enterprise in some small and simple concern, and thereafter

[1] *Principles of Economics*, p. 597.

180

can gradually move upwards, as their capacity improves with practice, to larger and more difficult posts. The point may be put in this way. When the separate steps in the agricultural or industrial ladder are large, it is difficult for a man adapted, if adequate practice is obtained, for life at one stage, but standing by some accident at another stage, to move to his proper place. Thus—to take a hypothetical example—if agriculture or industry were worked exclusively in large units consisting of one or two large entrepreneurs assisted by a number of mere labourers, any capacity for management and direction that might be born among people in the labouring class would have no opportunity for use or development. Many persons endowed with native capacity would thus be compelled to be watchers only and not doers. But, as Jevons has well taught, it is doing, and not watching, that trains. "A few specimens probed thoroughly," he writes, "teach more than thousands glanced at through a glass case. The whole British Museum accordingly will not teach a youth as much as he will learn by collecting a few fossils or a few minerals, *in situ* if possible, and taking them home to examine and read and think about."[1] The point was put even more forcibly by Dr. Marshall in his address to the Co-operative Society in 1885 : "It is a better training in seamanship to sail a fishing-boat than to watch a three-masted ship, the tops of whose masts alone appear above the horizon."[2] Thus it would seem that, in the absence of a proper ladder, a great deal of the business capacity born among the working classes must run to waste. If, however, industry or agriculture is organised by way of units of many different sizes, a workman possessing mental power beyond what is normal to his class can, without great difficulty, himself become the entrepreneur of a small establishment, and gradually advance, educating his powers the while, higher up the ladder that is provided for him.

§ 3. This train of thought suggests that, in a community organised on the general lines of a modern industrial State, associations of workers combined together in small co-partner-

[1] *Methods of Social Reform*, p. 61.
[2] *Loc. cit.* p. 17.

ship workshops constitute an industrial form, investment
in which is likely to yield a marginal social net product
considerably in excess of the marginal trade net product.
For such workshops provide the first stage of the ladder
that is needed to lift upwards the great fund of capacity
for management that is almost certainly lying latent among
the manual labouring classes. They furnish, as it were, a
first school in which this capacity can be developed, and, in
so doing, contribute for the service of the community, not
merely boots and shoes, but well-trained, competent men.
Much the same thing holds good of the analogous workers'
businesses in agriculture. Gardens and small allotments
near their cottages for workmen in regular employment
elsewhere, large allotments for workmen occasionally taking
odd jobs elsewhere, and small holdings for those who devote
themselves entirely to work on these holdings, provide in
combination a complete ladder from the status of labourer
to that of independent farmer. This ladder yields a product
of human capacity over and above its immediate product of
crops. That element of social net product, however, does
not accrue to those persons by whom the size of agricultural
holdings is regulated, and is not included in the marginal
trade net product of the resources invested in them. This
is enough to establish a *prima facie* case for the "artificial
encouragement," by State action or by private philanthropy,
of Workers' Associations and of various grades of allotments
and small holdings. Such encouragement is given to
Workers' Associations, in England by the support of Retail
Co-operative Societies, and in France and Italy by the grant
of special facilities for tendering on Government work. The
movement for developing allotments and small holdings
has also, in this country, received governmental help.

§ 4. The same line of thought, looked at from the other
side, suggests that the marginal social net product of activities
devoted to bringing about any widespread "trustification" of
industry is likely to be smaller than the marginal trade net
product. For large combinations—this does not apply to
those Kartels whose members remain separate and independent on the productive side—by lessening the oppor-

tunities for training in the entrepreneur function, tend to prevent the level of business ability from rising as high as it might otherwise do. "The development of a high order of undertaking genius in the few seems to depend upon a wide range of undertaking experience in the many." With the main part of industry organised into million dollar combines, the ladder connecting different stages of managing ability would be gravely damaged. Nor would the opportunity for obtaining positions as managers of departments in a giant concern go far to make up for this; for, apart from the limited degree of independent initiative which the management of a department, as compared with the control of a business, necessarily involves, departments will not vary in size so widely, or reach so low down in the scale, as private businesses may do. In his address to the Royal Economic Society in 1908, Dr. Marshall called attention to the educative possibilities of small businesses, illustrating his thesis from the present organisation of the milk trade. He pointed out that, so far as the working of industries by the State—and the same thing, of course, applies to the working of them by large commercial combinations—does away with this sort of educative ladder, the mere proof that it was *immediately* more economical than private management would not suffice to show that it was more economical on the whole.[1] This is the same thing as saying that the marginal social net product is less than the marginal trade net product. The practical inference, so far as the present argument goes, is plain. Though in the special emergency of the great war, when immediate output was absolutely essential and had to be won even though the future suffered, the State might rightly intervene to *enforce* various forms of combination that would not have come about without it, yet in normal times of peace it should always hesitate before encouraging, and should perhaps in some instances impede, any threatened excess in the growth of giant businesses, whether these are publicly or

---

[1] We may notice that, when, as in such a country as India, the narrowness of the markets and other causes prevent the development of any large scale industries, the top end of the industrial ladder is cut off, and there is a difficulty, analogous to the difficulty discussed in the text, about the provision of an adequate training-ground for the higher forms of business ability. (Cf. Morison. *The Industrial Organisation of an Indian Province,* p. 186.)

privately ,owned. ; What has been. said above, however,
obviously does ·not exhaust the considerations relevant to this
problem. 'Further discussion of it will be found in 'Chapters
XI. and XVIII.

 · § 5. Considerations of the same general character as the
above are relevant to certain developments in the method and
practice of standardised production.[1] It has long been known
that, by specialisation to a limited number of standard forms,
great economy of cost and increase of production can be
achieved. This economy, furthermore, is not confined to the
point at which standardisation is first applied; for, if one
industry agrees to standardise its product, the industries which
make machines and tools for making that product are in turn
enabled to standardise theirs. The Standards Committee of
the Engineering Trade of this country has done much work in
drawing up, for screws, nuts, certain motor parts and various
other things, standard specifications which have been adopted
throughout the engineering industry of the country generally.
The experience of the great war, in which military equipment
and munitions had necessarily to be of uniform patterns,
brought out more clearly than before the enormous scope for
direct economies which, partly by making possible the employment of relatively unskilled labour, standardisation of
product is able, in favourable circumstances, to create. The
urgent need for immediate large output at a minimum of
cost even led to standardisation, under Government authority,
of such things as ships and boots. The essence of the matter
is that the standardisation of certain products over the whole of
an industry, by enabling the firms that make them, and the
other firms that make tools for making them, to specialise more
closely than would otherwise be possible, leads immediately to
an enormously increased output of these products. This increased output we may call, if we will, the trade net product of
the method of standardisation. If, however, attention is concentrated exclusively upon this, the net advantages of the method
will sometimes be greatly exaggerated. For standardisation

[1] In *Industry and Trade*, bk. ii., chapters ii. and iii., Dr. Marshall, after
distinguishing between standards *particular* to an individual producer and
standards that are *general* to the greater part of an industry, has much interesting discussion of modern developments in standardisation.

almost inevitably checks the development of new patterns, new processes and new ideas. It is all very well to make rules for revising periodically the standard specifications. This is not an adequate remedy, because the real danger of standardisation is, not so much that it will prevent the adoption of new things when their superiority has been recognised, but that it will greatly lessen the inducement to manufacturers to devise and try new things. For in normal industry the profit which a man gets out of an improvement is chiefly won in the period when he is ahead of his competitors, before the improvement is adopted generally. With a rigid system of standardisation nobody would be able to be ahead of anybody else or to introduce a new pattern till the whole trade did so. The whole line, in short, must advance together; and this means that no part of it has any great inducement to advance at all. The marginal social net product of effort devoted towards standardising processes falls short of the marginal trade net product to an extent measured by its indirect consequences in checking inventions and improvements and so lessening productive powers in the future. Obviously the gap thus indicated is not equally wide for all commodities. It is difficult to believe, for example, that the establishment of standard sizes and standard forms for such things as screws and nuts is likely to prevent the development of any important improvement. In these simple things there is little or no room for improvement. But with complex manufactures the position is altogether different. Even in the course of the great war, when large output was of overwhelming importance, it would have been madness to standardise the production of aeroplanes; the opening for discovery and for the development of better types was so wide. And plainly, in many other finished manufactures, it is impossible to feel any confidence that the final form has already been evolved. There is, therefore, always the danger that, by standardisation, we shall augment enormously the production of the good at the cost of never attaining to the better. In any action that the State may take to foster standardisation for the sake of the immediate and direct stimulus which it gives to output this danger must be carefully borne in mind.

§ 6. Yet again the analysis here developed is applicable to certain aspects of that method of business organisation that has come to be known as "scientific management." The general characteristics of that system are well known. Elaborate study of the various operations to be performed is undertaken by trained experts, who analyse these operations into their separate elements, and, on the basis of this analysis, coupled with careful observation of the methods actually followed by a number of good workmen, construct, by combination, an ideal method superior to any yet in vogue. The kind of improvement to which this process leads is illustrated by the results of Mr. Gilbraith's investigation of the problem of laying bricks. He "studied the best height for the mortar box and brick pile, and then designed a scaffold, with a table on it, upon which all of the materials are placed, so as to keep the bricks, the mortar, the man, and the wall in their proper relative positions. These scaffolds are adjusted, as the wall grows in height, for all of the bricklayers, by a labourer especially detailed for this purpose, and by this means the bricklayer is saved the exertion of stooping down to the level of his feet for each brick and each trowelful of mortar and then straightening up again. Think of the waste of effort that has gone on through all these years, with each bricklayer lowering his body, weighing, say, 150 pounds, down two feet and raising it up again every time a brick (weighing about 5 pounds) is laid in the wall! And this each bricklayer did about one thousand times a day."[1] This device is, however, merely one example of what scientific management endeavours to achieve in general. The central conception involved in it is that of handing over the task of planning methods to trained experts, and then explaining to the workmen in elaborate detail what it is they have to do, including even the pauses and rest periods that they should take between successive operations and movements. "The work of every workman is fully planned out by the management at least one day in advance, and each man receives in most cases complete written instructions, describing in detail the task which he is to accomplish, as well as the means to be used in doing the work. And the work planned in advance

[1] Taylor, *The Principles of Scientific Management*, p. 78.

in this way constitutes a task which is to be solved, as explained
above, not by the workman alone, but in almost all cases by
the joint effort of the workman and the management. This
task specifies, not only what is to be done, but how it is to be
done and the exact time allowed for doing it." [1] The work of
teaching the workmen how to do it, and of seeing that they
properly understand and carry out their instructions, is entrusted to a new class of officials known as "functional foremen." These officials, working in conjunction with the
accounting officer, can ascertain at once how far the costs of
any particular workman's output exceed the proper costs laid
down beforehand, and can then concentrate attention and
instruction at any point where there is *prima facie* reason to
hope for improvement.[2] Now it is perfectly plain that this
type of industrial organisation is likely to yield large immediate
economies, and that the careful teaching involved in it must
up to a point yield much permanent good. It is a paradox that,
"though in the athletic world instructors exist to teach boxers
how to balance themselves and use their arms, and cricket
professionals are constantly at work improving the efficiency of
batsmen and bowlers, and coaches are a necessity to teach a
boat's crew collectively and individually how and when to
move their bodies and hands, yet in the industrial world the
value of teaching operatives how to earn their livelihood is
hardly yet recognised."[3] Nevertheless, there is real danger
lest this new-found science should be pushed too far. Carried
to excessive lengths it *may*, from a long period point of view,
defeat its own ends. First, it is plain that, so far as the
operations of the individual workman are reduced to a
mechanical plan, the original source from which the directing
authority derived its standard methods—namely, a combination of the best points in the *varied* individual methods of
different workmen—would be dried up. Overt suggestions
from workpeople for improvements in method would also,
perhaps, be rendered less probable. No doubt, this loss could

---

[1] Taylor, *The Principles of Scientific Management*, p. 39.
[2] Cf. Emerson, *Efficiency*, ch. vii. Mr. Dicksee draws some instructive
comparisons between these methods and the various forms of drill practised
among soldiers. (*Business Methods and the War*, Lecture 2.)
[3] Health of Munition Workers Committee, *Interim Report*, p. 77.

be partly atoned for by the employment of scientific experts specially charged with the task of experimenting in new methods. But, after all, these are available under ordinary systems of works' management and cannot, therefore, be regarded as a peculiar asset of the Taylor system to be set against its peculiar failings. Nor is it only in respect of specific suggestions and devices that injury may be indirectly wrought by this system. There is grave reason to fear lest the *general* initiative and independent activity of workpeople may be injured by their complete subordination to the detailed control of functional foremen, much as the *general* initiative of soldiers is injured by the grinding of an over-rigid and mechanical military system. By the removal of opportunities for the exercise of initiative, capacity for initiative may be destroyed; and the quality of the labouring force may in this way be subtly lowered. In so far as this happens, the marginal social net product of resources invested in the development and application of scientific management falls short of the marginal trade net product. Unless the State or philanthropy intervenes, there is a danger that this method of industrial organisation may be carried further and applied more widely than the interest of the national dividend—not to speak of the more general interest of society—when viewed as a whole, demands.

CHAPTER VIII

DIVERGENCES BETWEEN MARGINAL TRADE NET PRODUCT AND MARGINAL INDIVIDUAL NET PRODUCT [1]

§ 1. IN the preceding chapters it was provisionally assumed that the rate of return to investment in any industry is equivalent to the value of the marginal trade net product there, and, therefore, that the tendency of self-interest to equalise returns in all industries is in effect a tendency to equalise the values of marginal trade net products. From this assumption it followed that self-interest fails to equalise the values of marginal social net products only in so far as trade and social net products diverge. We have now to inquire how far the provisional assumption thus made is correct. Is it the fact that the free play of self-interest tends to equate the values of marginal trade net products in different industries? To simplify this inquiry I shall imagine a central level of value of marginal trade net products in industries in general, and shall concentrate attention upon the influences which determine whether or not the value of the marginal trade net product of resources in some single occupation selected for review will tend to stand at that central level.[2] In future chapters I shall investigate this problem as it presents itself under conditions of monopolistic competition, simple monopoly and discriminating monopoly respectively. But the present

[1] A diagrammatic version of the argument of this chapter will be found in Appendix III.

[2] It is not necessary to suppose that this central level is actually attained in any industry; it is rather to be conceived as the level which would be attained in any industry operating under conditions of constant return, or, as the average of the levels which would be attained in all industries if their departures from constant return in both directions balanced each other.

189

chapter will be concerned exclusively with "simple competition," that is to say, with conditions under which it is to the interest of each seller to produce as much as he can at the ruling market price, and not to restrict his output in the hope of causing that price to rise.

§ 2. The broad general solution of this problem can be reached without great difficulty. Let us place ourselves in imagination in a country where the flow of resources coming annually into being has to be distributed regularly among a variety of occupations. It is assumed that, when any given quantity of resources is devoted to a given occupation, the concrete form assumed by these resources—their distribution, for example, into many or few individual firms and so forth—is the most economical form available (from the standpoint of the period of time relevant to our problem) for that quantity of new resources; and that, when a slightly greater quantity is devoted to the occupation, the concrete form assumed is the most economical form available (from the same standpoint) for that quantity.[1] When this assumption is made, it is plain that, if one unit is added to the resources that normally flow into any one occupation, that unit will yield the same net product as each of the other units in the flow. All the units are interchangeable in this sense. But, in consequence of the addition of the extra unit, the general organisation of the industry may be modified in such wise that each unit of the flow directed towards it yields a different net product from what it would have done had the addition not been made. Thus, the net product of the (marginal) 10,000th unit consists of two parts, a direct net product equal to the net product which every unit would have yielded had the organisation of the industry remained unchanged, i.e. which every unit did yield when 9999 units were employed, and an indirect net product, equal to the increase or decrease in the net product of all the units employed, which is due to the changed organisation of the industry. These two things together constitute the marginal trade net product of the resources devoted to the industry when 10,000 units of resources are devoted to it. But

[1] Cf. the definition of marginal net product given in Chap. II. § 1.

the assumption that the value of this marginal trade net product is equal to the returns obtained by the investor is not correct. The owner of the marginal unit of the flow of resources will not reap for himself the whole of this net product. He will only reap the direct net product of this unit, together with a fraction of the indirect net product equal to the fraction which his private investment bears to the aggregate investment. Under simple competition, however, since that condition of things implies that each individual seller is only responsible for a very small share of the aggregate output, this fraction is necessarily very small. It follows that the marginal trade net product in any industry differs from the net product reaped by the individual investor—the marginal individual net product as we may say—by very nearly the whole amount of the indirect net product due to changes brought about in the general organisation of the industry. In an industry working under conditions of constant returns, an increment of resources yields no indirect net product; hence marginal trade net product is equal to marginal individual net product. In an industry working under conditions of diminishing returns, an increment of resources yields a negative indirect net product; hence marginal trade net product is less than marginal individual net product. In an industry working under conditions of increasing returns, an increment of resources yields a positive indirect net product; hence marginal trade net product is greater than marginal individual net product. These results are, of course, equally valid, whether the product of the industry in question is a single commodity or a number of different commodities produced by it under conditions of joint supply. An important practical conclusion immediately follows. Clearly it is the value of the marginal individual net product in any industry that self-interest tends to make equal to the value of the marginal net product of resources in general. Hence, in an industry where marginal trade net product differs from marginal individual net product, the value of marginal trade net product does not tend to coincide with that general level. Rather, in industries of increasing returns the value of the marginal trade net product of investment tends to exceed, and in industries of diminishing returns to fall short of the value of the marginal trade net product yielded in industries in general. Furthermore, the "error" in either case is greater, the more sharply diminishing or increasing returns, as the case may be, are acting.[1]

§ 3. The argument of the preceding sections is complete, if we suppose that all the various sources or regions of supply, from which the aggregate supply is contributed, are precisely similar. *Prima facie,* indeed, it might seem that, in industries subject to increasing returns, we need to suppose further—a supposition incompatible with our assumption of simple competition—that only a single producer is at work; for, with more than one supplier in the market, it is difficult to understand how stable equilibrium can exist. But the difficulty is apparent rather than real. Provided that certain external economies are common to all the suppliers jointly, the presence of increasing returns in all together is compatible with the presence of diminishing returns in the special work of each severally; and this is sufficient to permit of stable equilibrium. Hence, no second supposition is required to validate our argument. It remains, however, to consider what results will follow if the first supposition mentioned above, that, namely, of precise similarity of all the various sources or regions of supply, is withdrawn. In conditions of simple competition, equilibrium will be established, when the marginal individual net products of new resources in all the sources of supply are equal. But equality of marginal individual net products between two sources only implies equality of marginal trade net products, provided that the difference between marginal trade net product and marginal individual net product is the same in the two sources; and this implies that the circumstances of the two sources are exactly alike. But, when the various sources of supply are not exactly alike, it is by no means obvious that the difference between the marginal trade net product and the marginal individual net product in

---

[1] Cf. Marshall, *Principles of Economics,* bk. v. chapter xiii., for the whole of the preceding argument.

any one of them will be the same as it is in any other. It can, indeed, be shown that, in general, this will not be so.[1] Hence, simple competition involves a further element of maladjustment, additional to that which has so far been discussed. The values of the marginal trade net products of resources invested in different sources of supply will diverge from the value of the marginal trade net product of resources in general, not in a uniform manner, but some to a greater, and others to a smaller, extent.

§ 4. The results we have obtained lead directly to the following conclusions. When there is only one source of supply, or when all the sources are similar, it is possible to conceive, for every industry obeying the law of diminishing returns, some uniform rate of tax, the levy of which on the industry would make the value of the marginal trade net product of resources in that industry more nearly equal to the value of the marginal trade net product of resources in general than it would otherwise have been. In like manner, it is possible to conceive, for every industry obeying the law of increasing returns, some uniform rate of bounty, the grant of which would have this effect. When two or more of the sources of supply are not precisely similar to one another, it is still possible to conceive under diminishing returns some uniform rate of tax, and under increasing returns some uniform rate of bounty, which would make the values of the marginal trade net products of resources in the different centres of our industry more nearly similar to the value of the marginal trade net product of resources in general than they would have been under a regime of complete laissez-faire. But it is not possible, in general, to conceive any uniform rate of tax (or of bounty) which would make the values of the marginal trade net products of resources in all the centres of our industry equal to the value of the marginal trade net product of resources in general. To achieve this latter purpose a system of differential taxes (or bounties) is necessary, under which, in general, a heavier impost is laid on those sources of supply where the law of diminishing returns acts with the greatest force, and a lighter one on

[1] Cf. Appendix III. § 12.

the other sources.[1] This result is of considerable theoretical importance, because it is in direct conflict with the widespread opinion that, apart from certain possible indirect effects, differential taxes are necessarily wasteful and necessarily cause people to obtain what they want by a more costly, instead of by a less costly, route. This opinion is incorrect, and the nature of the error can be easily illustrated. Suppose there are two roads ABD and ACD both leading from A to D. If left to itself, traffic would be so distributed that the trouble involved in driving a "representative" cart along each of the two roads would be equal. But, in some circumstances, it would be possible, by shifting a few carts from route B to route C, greatly to lessen the trouble of driving those still left on B, while only slightly increasing the trouble of driving along C. In these circumstances a rightly chosen measure of differential taxation against road B would create an "artificial" situation superior to the "natural" one. But the measure of differentiation must be rightly chosen.

§ 5. What has been said in the preceding paragraphs exhausts the topic, which, if the logical scheme of this work is strictly adhered to, is proper to the present place. For the relation between the magnitude of the national dividend and economic welfare was examined in a general way in Part I., and Part II. has been reserved for a discussion of certain influences by which the magnitude of the national dividend is affected. After all, however, logical arrangement is a servant, not a master, and may be disregarded for sufficient cause. In the present instance such cause exists. The fact that individual producers, in determining their investments under simple competition, disregard an element in the marginal trade net product, namely, the indirect effect exercised upon the costs of other producers, is interesting to us *primarily* because it makes the national

---

[1] The whole of the above remarks apply to joint products as well as to commodities produced in isolation. But a peculiar effect is possible when a tax in kind—not an ordinary tax in money—is levied on one of two joint products. If the elasticity of demand for one of them is less than unity, a tax in kind on that product will increase the output of both products, thus positively benefiting the consumers of the other product and, in some conditions, adding to the aggregate sum of consumers' surplus.

dividend smaller than it might be. But this fact itself is only interesting to us *ultimately* for the reason that, generally speaking, anything that affects the national dividend injuriously also affects injuriously the sum of economic welfare. If, therefore, there exists a fact precisely analogous to the one we have been discussing, which exercises an influence upon national welfare directly, and not through the national dividend, it would be mere pedantry to refuse to discuss it here. A precisely analogous fact of the kind described does exist. Just as the investment of an increment of resources sometimes yields an indirect product, not taken account of by the investor, through its effect on the productive efficiency of other people's resources, so also it sometimes yields an indirect product by affecting the *amount of satisfaction which other people derive* from the consumption of a given quantity of commodity. This form of indirect product may be either positive or negative. Among commodities, the desire for which is partly a desire to possess what other people possess, the creation of the 1000th unit adds more to the aggregate satisfaction than it actually carries itself, because it makes every unit of the commodity more common. Top-hats are examples. Among commodities, the desire for which is partly a desire to possess what other people do not possess, the creation of the 1000th unit adds less to aggregate satisfaction than it actually carries itself, because it makes every unit of the commodity more common. Diamonds are examples.[1] Among industries whose products are desired for their own sake, and not as means to any form of distinction, the creation of the 1000th unit adds to aggregate satisfaction exactly as much satisfaction as it carries itself. On the basis of this analysis, practical inferences analogous to those set out in § 4 are easily obtained. In every industry, the desire for whose products is enhanced

---

[1] It should be added that, when commonness or rareness is an element in the esteem in which a person holds a thing, it is often not general commonness or general rareness alone, but, in many instances, both commonness among one set of people and also rareness among another set. As Mr. McDougall writes of the followers of fashion: "Each victim is moved not only by the prestige of those whom he imitates but also by the desire to be different from the mass who have not yet adopted the fashion" (*Social Psychology*, p. 336). This aspect of the matter cannot, however, be pursued here.

if they become less common, it is possible to conceive some uniform rate of tax, the levy of which on the industry would increase economic welfare; and in every industry the desire for whose products is enhanced if they become more common, it is possible to conceive some uniform rate of bounty, the imposition of which would produce a like effect. But there is reason to believe that the great bulk of common commodities consumed by the mass of the population are desired almost entirely for their own sake, and not as a means to any form of distinction. The sphere of usefulness that could belong, even under a perfectly wise and perfectly virtuous Government, to these fiscal devices is, therefore, probably smaller than it might appear to be at first sight.

CHAPTER IX

§ 1. The preceding discussion seems at first sight to prove that, apart from divergences between individual, trade and social net product, State interference, designed to modify in any way the working of free competition, is bound to injure the national dividend; for this competition left to itself will continually push resources from points of lower productivity to points of higher productivity, thus tending always away from less favourable, and towards more favourable, arrangements of the community's resources. We have now to confront this general presumption with the extensive policy of price regulation which was followed by the British, as by most other Governments, during the course of the great European War. I propose first to give a general account of that policy and then to inquire how far, if at all, the experience gained should modify the conclusions reached in preceding chapters.

✓ § 2. Broadly put, the position was as follows. The war caused in two ways a great shortage in certain things. On the one hand, for munition articles, army clothes and so forth, there was an enormous new Government demand much in excess of normal supplies. On the other hand, for various articles of ordinary civilian use, the contraction of available tonnage and the withdrawal of labour for the army and munition work caused supplies to fall much below the normal. The shortage brought about in one or other of these ways put it in the power of persons who happened to hold stocks of short commodities, or to be able to produce them quickly, to charge for them prices very much higher than usual. When the shortage was due to increased Government demand, the

scale of business done by these persons being as large as, or
larger than, before, the high prices that they were enabled to
charge necessarily yielded them abnormally large profits.
When it was due to contraction of supply (*e.g.* through the
withdrawal of labour or other obstacles to output), the gain
from high prices *might* be cancelled by loss due to lessened
sales; so that abnormally large profits were not obtained.
For a great number of things, however, the conditions of
demand are such that a shortage of, say, 10 per cent in the
supply causes the price offered by purchasers to rise by much
more than 10 per cent. For the sellers of articles of this
class the shortage, even when it was due to a supply contraction, often meant abnormal profits. Of course, some of these
abnormal profits were more apparent than real, for, if prices
all round are doubled, a doubling of money profits will only
enable a man to get the same amount of things as before.
Very often, however, the money profits were enhanced very
much more than in proportion to the rise in general prices.
Wherever this happened, certain specially favoured persons
were benefiting greatly as a direct consequence of the war.
This state of things naturally caused resentment, and suggested
State interference.

§ 3. This interference might follow either of two principal
lines. On the one hand, fortunately situated sellers might be
allowed to charge such prices as the market would bear, thus
collecting abnormal profits in the first instance; but, thereafter, be deprived of the bulk of these for the benefit of the
Exchequer by a high excess profits tax. On the other hand,
the prices they were allowed to charge might be limited by
authority to rates at which it was estimated that abnormal
profits would not accrue to them. Apart from points of
technique and administration, the choice between these two
plans makes no difference to the fortunately situated seller.
But it does make a difference to the people who happen to
need the particular goods or services that he sells. For,
whereas under the maximum price plan they are left untouched, under the excess profits plan a special levy is, in
effect, placed upon them for the benefit of the general taxpayers.
It follows that, where the taxpayers themselves, through the

Government, are the principal buyers, or where the public are buyers more or less in the proportion in which they are tax-payers, it does not greatly matter which of the two plans is chosen.   But where, as in practically all articles of food, poor people play a much larger part, compared with rich people, as buyers of an article which is short than they play as tax-payers, it does greatly matter.   For, if the State were to adopt the excess profits plan in preference to the maximum prices plan, it would be relieving the well-to-do of a large block of taxation, and throwing it, by a roundabout and semi-secret process, upon the shoulders of the poor.   Whatever might be thought of the desirability of exacting a larger contribution to the expenses of the war from relatively poor persons, it was obvious that a device of that kind would never be tolerated.   Consequently, over a large part of the field, the excess profits plan could not practically be made the *main* engine for preventing fortunately situated sellers from making fortunes out of the war.   Resort had of necessity to be had to the plan of maximum prices.

§ 4. In the actual working out of that plan, a great number of difficulties emerged, which it will be well to set out in order.   The first of these was the difficulty of definition. The same name often covers a great variety of different qualities of article, which it may be extremely hard to disentangle in any formal schedule.   When this condition prevails it is impossible to exercise control over prices by general rules, and it becomes necessary to fall back upon the cumbrous device of individual appraisement.   Thus, under the Raw Cocoa Order of March 1918, it was laid down that no raw cocoa might be sold except at "a fair value," this fair value being determined by a person authorised by the Food Controller to determine the grade of the various lots of cocoa.   A similar plan was adopted at the end of 1917 for controlling the prices of cattle and sheep sold by live weight at market.   Obviously, how-ever, this plan could not be employed on a large scale, owing to the vast amount of labour that it involves.   Consequently, in general, some modification of it was essential, and some general classification of grades had, in spite of the openings for evasion that this permits, to be, in one way or another, relied upon.

A second difficulty, when the problem of *defining* grades of quality was overcome, resulted from the mere fact that grades were often very numerous. The task of fixing prices directly for a great variety of these might well be more than any authority, at all events in the earlier stages of its operation, was prepared to enter upon. When there were only a few grades, it was comparatively easy, with the help of advice from experts, to do this; but, when there were a great many, it was thought better to rely, not on a schedule of maximum prices, but on a general Order determining the relations between the prices that might be charged in the future and those that had been charged in the past. An example of this plan was the Order of the Ministry of Munitions, issued in August 1916, by which sellers of machine tools were forbidden, except with the sanction of the Minister, henceforward to charge prices higher than they were charging in July 1915.

An analogous difficulty had to be faced when a commodity, about the grading of which, perhaps, there was no need to trouble, was produced under different conditions in a number of different localities, in such wise that a single maximum price would not treat different producers fairly. Here, too, inability to construct a schedule as varied as the circumstances required forced the controlling authority to fall back on the plan of fixing, not future prices themselves, but the relation between future prices and past prices. Thus, in May 1917, an Order was issued that no imported soft wood should be sold at prices above those that ruled *in each several locality* in the week ending 31st January 1917. This Order was subsequently modified as regards imports from Scandinavia; but with that we are not concerned.

So far it has been tacitly assumed that the maximum price aimed at for any one commodity of a given grade is a single price. For some commodities, however, no one uniform price ruling throughout the year is adapted to the conditions of their production and sale, and a series of maxima is needed. Plainly, a series is more difficult to determine correctly than a single price. Consequently, here again the controlling authority was driven to the method of regulating

the *relation* between future and past prices. Thus, in July
1917, it was ordered that the wholesale price of milk per
imperial gallon should not henceforward anywhere exceed
by more than 6½d. the price charged in the corresponding
month a year before, and that the retail price per imperial
quart should not exceed this corresponding price by more
than 2d. The same plan was followed in the Price of Coal
(Limitation) Act of 1915, which decreed that no colliery
company should charge a price exceeding by more than 4s.
(afterwards raised to 6s. 6d.) the price charged on a similar
sale at a similar date in 1913–14.

Plainly, all these indirect and roundabout methods of
control left the way open for evasion and were likely
to prove difficult to enforce. Consequently, controlling
authorities, as they got a better grip and better knowledge
of the conditions of various industries, tried to step forward
to the more precise method of maximum price schedules.
More and more this became the predominant plan. The
producers' and wholesalers' prices of most of the more
important articles of food came to be fixed directly by
schedule, as were also the prices of most of the commodities
controlled by the Ministry of Munitions. For most things
it was found sufficient to set up a single schedule. But
sometimes different producers' prices were fixed for different
parts of the country. For hay, for example, Scotland was
given one price, England another. Sometimes, too, a series
of schedules were set up to apply to different parts of the
year. For potatoes the Order of February 1917 fixed one
price up till March 31st, and another higher price after that
date ; and for peas and beans an Order of May 1917 fixed
three prices, diminishing in amount, for sales in June, July,
and later months. Similarly for wheat, oats and barley, to
be harvested in the United Kingdom, the Food Controller,
in August 1917, fixed a series of prices rising gradually
in each successive two months from November 1917 on to
June 1918. A later Order fixing maximum milk prices
made a similar differentiation between different parts of the
year. It is plain that the direct establishment of maximum
prices is, if the appropriate prices can once be worked out

satisfactorily, likely to prove much more effective than any roundabout plan.

So far we have only taken account of industries so simply organised that the producers sell a finished product direct, without any intermediary, to ultimate consumers. In most industries, however, there are several stages between the original material or service and the finished product in consumers' hands. This fact gives rise to further problems. The conditions of demand for any finished product being given, when an artificial price is fixed for any material or service used in the course of making and selling it, the price of the finished product need not be lowered correspondingly, but it is in the power of other persons in a line between the provider of this material or service and the finished product to add on to their charges the equivalent of whatever has been knocked off the charges of the regulated sellers. Thus, if the price of coal at the pit-mouth were reduced by State action and nothing else were done, the only effect might be that dealers in coal could buy more cheaply while retaining the old price of sale. Again, if the price of cattle were forced down, and nothing else were done, retail prices might remain unaltered, while butchers and meat dealers gained enormously. Yet again, if freight-rates on imported materials were kept artificially low by Government action, the various people who use these materials in their industries might get the whole benefit. Nor is it merely *possible* that this *might* happen. In general it *would* happen, except in so far as the people, on whom a power of exaction was thus conferred, deliberately from patriotic motives, or from fear of popular resentment, decided to forgo their advantage. In order to prevent this, the fixing of maximum prices at the earlier stages of production had to be coupled with control over the profits which manufacturers or dealers at a later stage may make by adding further charges on to these prices. One way in which this control was exercised was by limiting the *percentage* addition that might be made by any seller in the line. In May 1917, for example, it was decreed that no timber from Russia should be sold at an advance of more than 10 per cent on the purchase price; and in September

1917 a schedule of prices for fish was fixed as between fish-curers and wholesale dealers, and other sellers (with the exception of retailers) were prohibited from adding more than 10 per cent on to the scheduled prices. More usually it was not the *percentage*, but the *amount*, of addition that was limited. Thus, under the Cheese Order of August 1917, first-hand prices of various sorts of British-made cheese were fixed as from the maker, and it was provided that no dealer other than the maker should add on to them more than the actual charge for transport *plus*, in general, 6s. per cwt. In October it was provided further that retailers should not add on to the prices actually paid by them more than 2½d. per lb. In the same month the prices of the various sorts of leather were regulated on the same general plan. In like manner the price of horse and poultry mixture was controlled, in November 1917, by an Order forbidding the maker to charge a price exceeding the cost to him of his ingredients by more than £1 : 10s. per ton ; and the amount that other sellers might add on was limited to 1s. per cwt. on sales of 6 cwt. and more, 3s. per cwt. on sales of from 3 to 6 cwt.; and so on. In meat a variant on this plan was adopted, in the first instance, on account of difficulties due to the custom among retailers of obtaining different proportions of their profit from the sale of different joints. In an Order of September 1917 it was laid down that no person shall in any fortnight sell meat by retail at such prices as cause the aggregate price received by him to exceed actual costs to him by more than a prescribed percentage (20 per cent or 2½d. per lb., whichever shall be less). In August 1917 a rule on similar lines was laid down for retailers of bacon and hams.

It is evident that plans of this kind for controlling the charges to be made at the later stages of a commodity's progress to the consumer suffer from the same sort of disadvantage that roundabout attempts to control producers' charges suffer from. They are liable to evasion. Consequently, the controlling authorities sought, as they became more masters of their work, to evolve some more satisfactory arrangement. One stage in this evolution is illustrated by

the Butter Prices Order of August 1917. In that Order
it was laid down that retailers may not add to the price of
butter sold by them more than 2½d. per lb. above the actual
cost of it to them; but it was provided further that local
Food Control Committees *might* prescribe a scale of maximum
retail prices in accordance with the general directions of the
Order (which includes rules about maker's, importer's, and
wholesaler's prices), although conformity with that scale
should not relieve any retailer from the obligation not to
add on more than 2½d. per lb. A slightly more advanced
stage is illustrated by the plan adopted for regulating the
retail prices of coal. The general principle was laid down
that retailers should not add on to their own purchase price
more than 1s. per ton over and above the costs of actual
handling and dealing with the coal (including office expenses
apart from the trader's own salary). But this principle was
not left, as it were, in the air. It was provided that local
authorities, after consultation and inquiry, should work it out
and apply it in the form of a definite list of retail prices
applicable to their district. Yet a further stage is reached
when the controlling authority itself fixes lists of maximum
prices at more than one point on the way from production
to consumption. The Potato Order of September 1917
was of this type. Maximum prices were fixed for growers;
wholesale dealers were forbidden to sell in any week at prices
that yielded them more than 7s. 6d. a ton beyond their
total costs on all purchases of potatoes—costs which varied
with the transport conditions of different districts; and an
elaborate scale of retail prices was fixed, which related the
permitted price per lb. to the price per cwt., including price
of transport, that the retailer had actually paid for different
classes of potatoes. The final stage is reached when definite
schedules are fixed throughout—for producer, wholesaler, and
retailer equally—by the controlling authority itself. This was
the arrangement to which the Ministry of Food steadily
progressed. It was definitely attained in regard to British
onions, most sorts of fish, beef and mutton, fruit for jam and
jam, peas and beans, and hay, oats and wheat straw. Lest,
through imperfect knowledge, the special circumstances of

particular districts should have been neglected in the construction of these scales, a safeguard was sometimes provided in the form of a rule empowering local Food Committees, with the sanction of the Food Controller, to vary the maxima in their district. This provision was introduced into the Order of January 1918, fixing maximum prices for rabbits. In like manner it was provided in an Order of September 1917, that, where the Food Controller or a local Food Committee was satisfied that, by reason of some exceptional circumstance, flour or bread could not be sold by *retail* at the official maximum price "so as to yield a reasonable profit," a licence might be issued, either for the whole or for a part of any Committee's area, permitting higher prices to be charged. The Order of January 1918, fixing -a schedule of maximum prices for most kinds of fish, was made subject, as regards *retail* prices, to similar local revision, as was also the Milk Prices Order of March 1918. A like power of varying local retail prices, with the sanction of the Food Controller, was accorded to the local Food Committees under the Potato Prices Order of September 1917.

Hitherto attention has been confined to commodities that come into the consumer's hands in much the same form as that in which they leave the hands of producers. Further complications are introduced when we have to do with raw materials that are worked up into elaborately finished articles. Here, owing to the various parts which the raw material plays in different types and grades of finished goods, it is not generally possible to fix schedules of price beyond the raw material. Consequently, for two important articles, boots and clothes, an ingenious roundabout plan was adopted. An attempt was made to induce or compel manufacturers to devote a considerable part of their plant to making "standard articles" to be sold at prices calculated on a basis of conversion costs, in the hope that the competition of these articles in the market would indirectly keep down the price that it is profitable to charge for similar articles that are not standardised. In boots, manufacturers were ordered to devote one-third of that part of their plant which was engaged on civilian work to making "standard boots." In clothes, no fixed proportion of plant was forced into making standard goods, but manufacturers were tempted to take up this kind of work by relatively favourable treatment in the matter of the quota of raw wool allowed to them. In cotton goods, though the price of raw cotton was artificially controlled, no corresponding control of the finished commodity was attempted, the argument being that cotton manufacturers were sufficiently burdened by having to provide a special levy to pay benefit to workpeople thrown out of work by the reduction in the number of spindles and looms that might be operated.

The foregoing account of the difficulties encountered and the expedients employed in the exercise of price control suggests a question of some theoretical interest. It is plain enough that, in the earlier stages of control, practical considerations make it necessary to begin at the producer's, rather than the retailer's, end; for the local differentiations needed in a retail schedule are generally much more serious and require much more knowledge to allow of their being fairly made. As has been shown, however, as the controlling authority became more expert and got a better grip on its industries, it tended to make price schedules all along the line from the producer to the final seller. Thus, in the end, retail maximum prices often were fixed. The point in doubt is whether, when this has all been arranged, there is any real need to continue the earlier stages of control. Will not maximum retail prices be reflected back all along the line, and so automatically stop " profiteering " at earlier stages ? The view that this will be so seems to have guided the work of some of the Ministry of Food's controls. For example, the prices of turnips and swedes were regulated by a rule that *nobody* might sell them for more than 1½d. per lb., and the price of chocolates and sweets by a rule that *nobody* might sell them for more than 3d. per oz. and 2d. per oz. respectively. In general, however, it was thought better to maintain price schedules at the earlier stages, separate from, and adjusted to, the retail maxima. In a world of pure competition it does not appear that this would really have been necessary. If the retail maxima were rightly arranged, everybody in line would automatically be forced to charge prices that yielded them about the ordinary

rate of profits. The artificial restriction upon retail price
would act in exactly the same way as a fall in the public
demand for the commodity sufficient to counteract the shortage
of supply. It is probable, however, that this adjustment
would not, in real life, be made without a certain amount of
friction, and that some of the traders affected might be in a
position to exercise quasi-monopolistic pressure against particular
shopkeepers or others who happened to be mainly dependent
on them. Consequently, when schedules of maximum prices
for the earlier stages had already been worked out, to drop
them, in the hope that the retailers' schedules subsequently
superimposed would by themselves achieve the whole of the
ends desired, would probably have been unwise.

§ 5. We have now to consider the broad analytical problem
which these expedients of war time suggest. What *exactly* is
to be said of the relation between the kind of price regulation
that was then attempted and the volume of the national dividend?
The great upheaval of the war had caused the existing distribution of resources to be uneconomic, in the sense that the
value of the marginal net product of those employed in making
certain specially scarce articles was abnormally high. Apart
from outside interference abnormal values of marginal net
products mean abnormal returns to the investor; and these
abnormal returns tend to draw resources from occupations of
relatively low productivity to those occupations of greater
productivity in which they rule. When prices are cut down
by law, the value of the marginal net product of any given
quantity of resources in any occupation is, indeed, necessarily
cut down also, because we have defined this value as the
marginal physical net product multiplied by the realised
price. Plainly, however, this definition tacitly assumes the
realised price to be identical with the demand price. When
these two are artificially divorced, our definition must be
changed. The values of the marginal net products of resources,
which it is to the interest of the national dividend to make
equal everywhere, consist in the marginal physical net products
multiplied by the demand prices. When this is understood, it
is evident that an artificial reduction of price, while lowering
returns in the industry affected by it, leaves the true value of

the marginal net product of any quantity of resources invested there unchanged. The desirability, from the standpoint of the national dividend, of a transference of resources is thus un-altered, while the principal influence tending to bring it about is weakened. To put the same point in more general terms, any external limitation imposed on the price of an article produced under competitive conditions (*i.e.* otherwise than by a monopolist) must lessen the inducement that people have to make that article. Normally it is just through high prices and high profits that a shortage of anything corrects itself. The prospect of exceptional gain directs free resources into the industry which makes the thing that is short. Cut off this prospect, and that increase of supply, which the interest of the national dividend demands, will be checked, and checked more severely the greater is the cut made from the "natural" price.

§ 6. In the special circumstances of the Great War this injurious tendency of price limitation was largely counteracted by other influences. For the State itself, in many departments of industry, took over the task of allocating resources among different occupations. It built up munition works, controlled shipbuilding, and urged on agricultural production by the promise of land, tractors, and labour drawn from the Army. Thus, though price regulation might weaken the directive force normally exercised by economic motives, the task of direction was taken over by another and more powerful agency. No doubt, had prices in any occupation been artificially pushed down so low that profits to the "representative" firm fell actually below the ordinary money level, capital and labour would have gone elsewhere in spite of government pressure. But, of course, prices were not artificially pushed down to this extent in any occupation. On the contrary, complaint was often made that they were left high enough to yield abnormally large profits, not merely to firms that could fairly be regarded as "representative," but even to those very weak and inefficient firms which, in the ordinary course, would have been making losses and decaying out of business.[1] On the

---

[1] It has been suggested that maximum prices could have been fixed at a considerably lower level if the good and bad firms had been formed into a kind

whole, therefore, we may conclude that, as things were, in view of the abnormal activity of the State, and, it should be added, of the effectiveness of appeals to patriotism, price control in the peculiar circumstances of the war probably caused very little damage to the volume of the national output.

§ 7. It would, however, be a great error to infer from this that a general permanent policy of control, designed to prevent groups of producers from reaping abnormal profit on occasions when the conditions of the market give them power to do so, would be equally innocuous. People, in making choice of investment, take account of these ups and downs, and, so far as their judgment is correct, place their resources in such a way that, on the average and on the whole, the marginal yield works out about equally in different occupations. In these circumstances it is obvious that any general State policy of cutting down prices in any industry below the competitive level, on occasions when the conditions of demand and supply would enable that industry to obtain exceptional profits, must, in effect, penalise it as compared with stable industries. For if, in a hilly district where the average level of peaks and valleys is the same as it is on a plateau, the tops of the peaks are removed, the average level there will, of course, be reduced below that of the plateau. The discouraging effect of this differential action cannot be made good by any direct manipulation of production by the State. For here we have to do, not merely with a tendency for free resources to go elsewhere *at the time* when the

---

of pool, the war profits in the better firms being used to cancel any excess of cost above selling price that there might be in the worst firms. Professor Taussig has pointed out that, before an arrangement of this kind could be worked, very serious administrative difficulties would have to be overcome and an elaborate system of detailed costings set up (*Quarterly Journal of Economics*, Feb. 1919). But, besides this technical objection, and the obvious further objection that efficient management would be very greatly discouraged since it would reap no reward, there is also an objection of principle. Some of the consumers of an article treated in this way would be getting their stuff at actually less than it cost to produce it. The abnormal profit which the war accorded to more favourably situated or better managed concerns would be used, not for the service of the State in general, as under the excess profits tax, but to provide this exceptional and peculiar privilege. At a time when the State has need of all possible resources, very special reasons are required to justify it in using them up in this way.

P

regime of price control is at work, but with a tendency that operates continually and checks the general flow of resources that would otherwise seek investment in building up the permanent equipment of the threatened industry. If, for example, the State adopted a general policy of forbidding farmers to charge high prices when they have power to do so on account of a bad world harvest, this would check investment in agriculture; because people expect bad world harvests from time to time and look to high prices then to set against low prices in bumper years. While, therefore, on the one hand, our analysis does not imply that the policy of price control adopted in the abnormal circumstances of the war worked injury to the national dividend, on the other hand, the experience of the war gives no ground for doubting that a general permanent policy of price limitation, in non-monopolised industries, would produce this effect. This conclusion is, of course, subject to the special considerations set out in Chapter VIII., and also to the qualification that, if maximum prices are fixed so high as to leave all ordinary sales unaffected and merely to protect an occasional weak purchaser from exploitation by unscrupulous dealers, they will not hurt the dividend.

CHAPTER X

STATE REGULATION OF SUPPLIES

§ 1. It is not only in the matter of prices that the war afforded examples of Government interference with competitive industry. Extensive interference also took place with the free distribution of commodities among different industries, different firms within the same industry, and different ultimate consumers. This interference had to be undertaken in order to get over difficulties to which the price regulations described in the preceding chapter gave rise. For, when prices in competitive industries are artificially reduced below the level that they tend naturally to assume, the ordinary market influences regulating the distribution of commodities between different purchasers are thrown out of gear. When there are no price restrictions, at any price everybody buys for every purpose as much of a thing as, at that price, he wants, and this process exhausts the whole supply. But, when, *in competitive industries*, prices are artificially kept down, the sum of the demands of all purchasers for all purposes is greater, and may be much greater, than the supply. In the United States, where the wheat for the whole year comes from the national harvest, the result of price limitation unaccompanied by rationing was that everybody got all they wanted in the earlier part of the harvest year and had to fall back on substitutes in the later part.[1] There was, in short, a bad distribution through time. For most commodities, however, production as well as consumption is continuous. Thus, at no time can everybody get all they want, but there is a

[1] Cf. Supplement to *American Economic Review*, March 1919, p. 244.

continuous shortage. Distribution becomes, if nothing is done, the sport of accident, influence, and ability to stand for a long time without fainting in a queue. There is no reason to expect that the result reached through these agencies will be, in any sense, a good distribution. Consequently, when, during the course of the war, the policy of controlling prices was adopted, it was, in general, found necessary to control distribution also, and, with that object, to establish some criterion for fixing the shares available for different purchasers.

§ 2. When the commodity dealt with was a material that could be employed for several alternative purposes, the obvious criterion was relative urgency, from the point of view of national war service, of these several purposes. The simplest method of applying this criterion was to make rules cutting off the supply of material from the least urgent uses either in part or altogether, thus leaving more available for more urgent uses. Examples of this method were :

(1) The imposition of Treasury restrictions upon the investment of new capital abroad and, in a less degree, in civilian home industries.

(2) The enunciation of a rule that no building costing more than £500, and no building whatever containing structural steel, should be put up without a licence.

(3) The reduction of railway service for all forms of civilian, as distinguished from military, use.

(4) The prohibition of the use of petrol for pleasure.

(5) The withdrawal of materials, etc., from the less important tramways and light railways to others of greater national importance.

(6) The regulation of the use of horses in towns and on farms and the control of road transport generally.

(7) The prohibition of the use of paper for newspaper contents bills, and, under certain conditions, traders' circulars, and the abolition of "Returns."

(8) The prohibition by the Timber Supplies Department against packing various articles in wooden cases and crates.

(9) The prohibition of the use of electricity for lighting shop fronts, and the order restricting the hours during which

hotel and restaurant dining-rooms might use artificial light or theatres might remain open. This method is entirely negative: the least urgent uses are definitely ruled out, either by a general order, or by making a licence—which, of course, is refused to the least urgent uses—a necessary condition of action.

§ 3. Obviously, devices of this character are of limited application. They take no account of the fact that uses other than the least urgent are not all of equal urgency. Consequently, if the material or labour available is insufficient for all the uses that are left when the least urgent uses have been cut off, it becomes necessary to arrange for some system of priority among those that are left. The simplest way in which this was attempted was as follows. The material was left in private hands, but a system of Priority Certificates was instituted, which only permitted sales to would-be buyers with certificates of lower urgency after those with certificates of higher urgency had been satisfied. Government work had the first grade of certificate, work of special national importance (e.g. export work deemed valuable for protecting the foreign exchanges) the next, and so on in successive stages. Iron and steel products were dealt with on this plan, and quarry stone and other road material on less elaborate, but substantially equivalent, lines. When the proportion of the available commodity that is needed for Government war work or other especially urgent need is very large, the plan of priority certificates by itself is not always safe. The Government may get less than it needs. To meet this risk it is tempted itself, either by purchase or requisition, to become an owner (or hirer) of so much of the commodity as is of specially urgent need. It may then hand over to firms engaged on Government work, or other specially urgent work, the supplies that are required for that work; but, even so, it will need to distribute the surplus on some system of priority to other firms. This plan was followed in a rough general way with imported leather and flax and with a number of metals.

§ 4. The application in these different forms of the criterion of comparative urgency among competing uses presented very considerable difficulties during the war. These difficulties, however, were necessarily much less than those which would have to be overcome if a similar criterion had to be applied to normal conditions of peace. For the comparative urgency of different uses in war time depends on the contribution which they severally make to national war efficiency. This provides a definite standard to which to work. It is obvious that food and munitions and the support of the armed forces must take precedence over everything else; and, though, as the rivalry between the demands of munitions and of ships for steel made plain, it is difficult, still it is not impossible, by conferences between representatives of the various Ministries, to work out a fairly satisfactory scheme of priorities. The reason for this is that everything is subordinated to a single relatively simple end. Under a regime of established peace—apart, of course, from possible " key " industries, for which the obvious method of assistance is bounties or a tariff, and not the allocation of material—there is no single end of this kind. We have no longer to deal with the Government's wants for war service, but with the wants of an immense and varied population for necessaries, comforts and luxuries. In war time it is obviously more important to bring steel into the country than it is to bring paper, and to manufacture army baking ovens than private kitchen ranges. But in peace time none of these simple propositions can be laid down. Those things ought to be made which are most wanted and will yield the greatest sum of satisfaction. But the Government cannot possibly decide what these things are; and, even if it could decide what they are at one moment, before its decision had been put into effect conditions would very probably be changed, and they would have become something entirely different. It is not easy to see how this obstacle to a permanent policy of rationing materials among the several industries of the country could be satisfactorily overcome.

§ 5. To allocate materials to different uses according to the comparative national urgency of these uses was not a complete solution of the war problem. Within each grade of use purchases are sought by a number of rival firms anxious to work up the material into the finished product. Normally price would hàve established itself at such a level that each firm obtained the quantity of material which, at that price, it desired. With restricted prices it is necessary to provide an alternative basis for distribution among these firms as well as among the different categories of urgency. The basis adopted by the British Government was that of comparative pre-war purchases. It is illustrated by—

(a) The regulation of the Cotton Control Board (1918), limiting the proportion of machinery that any firm might keep at work on American cotton;

(b) The condition imposed on importers by the Paper Control that they should supply their customers (i.e. manufacturers) in the same proportion as in 1916–17.

In highly organised trades, like the cotton industry, there was no technical difficulty in applying regulations on these lines. But in many of the metal trades a special organisation had to be created for the purpose. It is clear that this basis of allocation could not be employed in connection with any policy designed to last for more than a short period. For an arrangement, which tended to maintain the various firms engaged in an industry always in the same relative position as they occupied in an arbitrarily chosen year, would constitute a quite intolerable obstacle to efficiency and progress.

§ 6. When the prices of finished products as well as of their raw materials were limited by regulation, a problem exactly analogous to the above had to be faced as regards distribution among ultimate consumers. To organise a basis for this is obviously only practicable in connection with commodities in wide, regular and continuous consumption. The basis aimed at here was, not comparative pre-war purchases, but an estimate of comparative current need. For coal, gas and electricity an objective measure of this was sought in the number and size of rooms and the number of inhabitants in different people's houses. For food products, while some differentiation was attempted by means of supplementary rations to soldiers, sailors, heavy workers, invalids

and children, in the main the knot was cut by assuming
the needs of the general body of all the civil population
to be equal, and rationing all alike.   This sort of distributional arrangement is fundamentally different from the
other two kinds.   The passage from war to peace does not
destroy or render violently unsuitable the criterion adopted
for it.   Plainly, however, in peace, as indeed in war also,
its necessarily rough and arbitrary character constitutes
a very serious objection to it.   "The proportion in which
families of equal means use the different 'necessaries of
life' are very different.   In ordinary times they distribute
their expenditure among the different necessaries in the manner
which seems best, some getting more bread, some more meal
and milk, and so on.   By equal rationing all this variety
is done away with; each household is given the same amount
per head of each commodity; allowance for age, sex, occupation and other things can only be introduced with difficulty."[1]
There can be little doubt that British Food Rationing during
the war, in spite of this disability, led to a much more satisfactory result than would have been attained from the
scramble—a scramble in which rich people would have been
able to exercise various sorts of pull upon tradesmen—that
must have resulted had food prices been limited but distribution left to take care of itself.   In peace, however,
where presumably the alternative to rationing would be less
intolerable, the inconvenience and inequalities attaching to it
have correspondingly greater weight.

§ 7. If we are content to regard the various arrangements
which I have been describing as merely supplementary to
price restrictions already decided upon, it is plain that, though
they may affect the volume of the national dividend, as it
were, at the second remove—if, for example, they grant
priority to steel for making machinery rather than motor-
cars—they cannot affect it directly or fundamentally.   They
modify the use to which the dividend is put, not the production of it.   This is modified by the price regulations
in the way that was explained in the preceding chapter.   It
is not modified further by any distributional supplements

[1] Cannan, *Economic Journal*, Dec. 1917, p. 468.

to those regulations.   Consequently, from the standpoint of the present Part, no further analysis is required; though in Part V., where the distributional relations of rich and poor are examined, something more will have to be said about the rationing of food.

CHAPTER XI

THE CONDITIONS OF MONOPOLISATION

§ 1. WE may now return to the main argument. In Chapter VIII. we supposed self-interest to act along the route of simple competition, and we inquired into its tendency to equalise the values of marginal trade net products in all uses upon the basis of this supposition. The supposition, however, is not always warranted. As has already been observed, an essential note of "simple competition" is that the supply of each seller constitutes so small a part of the aggregate supply that his advantage is best consulted if he "accepts market prices without trying, of set purpose, to modify them."[1] When any seller's output constitutes a substantial part of the whole, there is scope for various sorts of monopolistic action; and, when any sort of monopolistic action is present, self-interest does not tend to evolve an output such that the value of the marginal net product of resources devoted to its production is equal to that yielded by resources employed elsewhere. In future chapters I shall examine monopolistic action in detail. Before that is done, however, convenience suggests that some study should be made of the conditions which determine the appearance of monopolistic power.

§ 2. First, other things being equal, circumstances which, when the aggregate scale of an industry is given, make it structurally economical for the typical individual establishment to be large, pro tanto increase the likelihood that a single seller will market a considerable part of the aggregate output of his industry; for such circumstances neces-

[1] Pareto, Cours d'économie politique, i. p. 20.

sarily increase the probability that a single *establishment* will market a considerable part of that output. Whether any single establishment will, in fact, become big enough, relatively to the whole of an industry, to procure an element of monopolistic power, depends on the general characteristics of the various industries concerned. Such an event is more than usually likely in industries that produce fancy goods liable to become "specialities." For, in these industries, there often exist, within the broad general market, minor markets, to a certain extent non-competitive among themselves; and, when this is so, an individual seller may supply a considerable proportion of his own minor market, without himself being of very great size absolutely. In a few peculiar industries, among those concerned with staple goods and services, it may also well be that the prospect of internal economies will lead to the evolution of single establishments large enough to control a predominant part of the whole output of the industry. One of the most notable instances of this is afforded by the industry of railway transportation along any assigned route. In view of the great engineering cost of preparing a suitable way, it will, obviously, be much less expensive to have one or, at most, a few railways providing the whole of the transport service between any two assigned points than to have this service undertaken by a great number of railways, each performing an insignificant proportion of the whole service. Similar remarks hold good of the industries of furnishing water, gas, electricity, or tramway service to a town. The existence of many separate establishments involves a large number of main pipes, wires and rails. But the whole business of any ordinary district can be worked with a very small number of these mains. Therefore, the existence of many separate establishments implies the investment of a great quantity of capital in mains that are only employed up to a very small proportion of their capacity. There is an obvious economy in avoiding such investment. This economy is the *ultimate* reason for the tendency, which appears strongly in the class of industry just discussed, for individual establishments to furnish a large proportion of the total supply. The truth is partly veiled by the fact that the *immediate* reason is, in general, unwillingness, on the part of national and local governmental authorities, to allow the right of eminent domain to be invoked, or the streets to be disturbed, on more occasions, or by more people, than is absolutely necessary. It is, however, the extra expense of such procedure that lies behind this unwillingness on the part of the authorities. In the general body of industries concerned with staple goods and services, the conditions peculiar to railways and their allied industries are not reproduced. Internal economies reach the limit at different points in different kinds of industry, at one point in the cotton industry, at another in the iron and steel industry; generally at a less advanced stage where the part played by labour relatively to capital is large and at a more advanced stage where it is small; but always long before the individual establishment has grown to any appreciable fraction of the whole industry of which it is a part.[1] When this happens, internal economies evidently cannot be responsible for monopolistic power.

§ 3. Secondly, other things being equal, circumstances which, when the aggregate scale of an industry and the size of the typical individual firm are given, make it structurally economical for the typical individual unit of business management—a number of establishments, for example, controlled by one authority—to be large, *pro tanto* increase the likelihood that a single seller will market a considerable part of the aggregate output of his industry. This proposition has, in recent times, become of predominant importance, and it is, therefore, necessary to examine carefully the various structural economies, for which large scale control may, in different situations, be responsible.

Much has been made by some writers of the fact that, when a number of parallel establishments are grouped under a single head, the different plants can be thoroughly specialised to particular grades of work; and of the other kindred fact

[1] Cf. Van Hise's account of the development of various important industries in the United States (*Concentration and Control*, pp. 42 et seq.) and Prof. Chapman's discussion of the normal size of individual factories in the cotton industry (*Journal of the Royal Statistical Society*, April 1914, p. 513).

that the orders in any place can be met from the plant nearest to that place, and that, thus, cross freights are saved. That the economies resulting from close specialisation upon particular articles or even particular processes may, in some circumstances, be very great has been abundantly proved in the British engineering industry during the war.   But it does not appear that a single control over many separate establishments is essential in order to secure these economies. Even though the different establishments were to remain separate, it might be expected, when once their great importance is realised, that the industrial organism would tend, under the sway of ordinary economic motives, to evolve them. In the paper industry of the United States, for example, each mill confines itself as a rule to the manufacture of some one quality of paper;[1] and in the Lancashire cotton industry, not only was fine spinning, coarse spinning, and weaving localised separately, but individual firms frequently specialise on a narrow range of counts for spinning.[2]   The same thing is true of the economies obtainable from the utilisation of by-products.   Nor does it appear that those economies in respect of marketing, which some writers ascribe to large-scale control, are a dominating factor making for combination.   For, "if a manufacturer is purchasing raw material, there is generally a market price for it which all must pay, and which any one can obtain it for, so long as he buys the customary minimum quantity; while, if what he requires is a partly manufactured article, purchases amounting in value to hundreds of pounds per annum, accompanied by prompt payment, can generally be made at the cheapest possible rate.   The sole advantage enjoyed by the largest concerns in the purchase of raw materials seems to me to lie in the possibility of occasionally clearing the market of raw materials or of a surplus output of partly manufactured stuff, by some purchase quite out of the power of a smaller concern to compass.   Such an operation, however, partakes of the nature of a speculation, and the profit, when gained, is hardly to be called a cheapening of the cost of production, if only for the reason that

---

[1] Cf. Chapman, *Work and Wages*, vol. i. p. 237.
[2] Cf. Marshall, *Industry and Trade*, p. 601.

the opportunity for such a special purchase cannot be relied upon to occur very often, and, when it does occur, is perhaps as likely to result in a loss as in a gain."[1]   Nor, again, should much importance be attached to those advantages of large-scale management, which have been summarised as "concentration of office work, provision of central warehouse for goods, centralisation of insurance and banking, establishment of a uniform system of accounts, enabling easy comparison to be made of the working of branches, institution of a uniform system of costing and of a central sales agency,"[2] and so forth.   For these economies are scarcely practicable under the lower types of price-fixing kartel, which are common in Germany, and, even in fusions and holding companies,[3] they are very soon outweighed by the immense difficulty of finding people competent properly to manage very large businesses.

There are, however, certain structural economies of large-scale management, which are of a different order and have a wider reach.   First, greater size, implying, as it does, greater wealth, makes it possible and profitable to spend more money on experiment.   The Committee on Scientific and Industrial Research report: "Our experience up to the present leads us, indeed, to think that the small scale on which most British industrial firms have been planned is one of the principal impediments in the way of the organisation of research with a view to the conduct of those long and complicated investigations which are necessary for the solution of the fundamental problems lying at the basis of our staple industries."[4]   This is obviously a very important matter; though it is not clear why

[1] Hobson, The Industrial System, p. 187, quoted from W. R. Hamilton, The Cost of Production in Relation to Increasing Output.

[2] McCrosty, Economic Journal, Sept. 1902, p. 359.

[3] Dr. Liefmann writes: "Einige Trusts, so der Zucker- und Spiritustrust, bildeten sich zu einer einzigen Gesellschaft um, also im Wege der vollstandigen Verschmelzung, der Fusion, d.h. die betreffenden Unternehmungen gehen alle in einer einzigen derart auf, dass sie als besondere wirtschaftliche Organisation aufhoren zu existieren.   Die meisten aber nahmen in neuester Zeit nach verschiedenen Versuchen die Form der sogenannten Holding Company, einer Kontrollgesellschaft, wie wir es nennen konnen, an, d.h. die Gesellschaft erwarb alle oder doch die Mehrheit der Aktien samtlicher zum Trust gehorender Einzelgesellschaften" (Kartelle und Trusts, p. 114).

[4] Report, p. 25.

a number of small firms should not, while retaining full independence in other respects, agree to collaborate in promoting research. Secondly, the union into one of what would have been many firms means that, instead of each wielding only the secret processes discovered by itself, each can wield the secrets of all; and in some circumstances this may involve large savings. Thirdly, a business combining many establishments is, in general, in contact with a number of different markets, in which the fluctuations of demand are, in some measure, independent. It follows that the operation of such a business involves in the aggregate less uncertainty-bearing than the operation of its parts would involve if they were separated. The general economy resulting from this fact may manifest itself in the greater facility with which loans can be obtained, or in the lower price that has to be paid for them, or in the smaller proportionate reserve fund that the concern needs to keep for equalising dividends, or in other ways. The essential point is that the general economy, however it manifests itself, is necessarily there. The larger the unit of individual control, the larger is this economy. After a point, indeed, its growth, as the unit grows, becomes exceedingly slow. But, until the unit has reached a very large size, it grows rapidly, and constitutes a powerful force making for larger units—except, indeed, among commodities suitable for grading, for which a general speculative market may be developed, enabling small manufacturers, through the practice of hedging, to put themselves in this respect on a level with large manufacturers.[1] Further, even if the actual volume of fluctuations were not lessened, amalgamation might still lead to economies, by enabling the bulk of the plant to be run steadily, and reserving, after the pattern of the Sugar Trust, one specially adapted plant to adjust its output to the fluctuations in aggregate demand.[2] One further point may be mentioned. In certain special industries large-scale control not only achieves a direct economy by lessening the uncertainty-bearing that is involved in given fluctuations in the individual fortunes of different firms; it

[1] Cf. Brace, *The Value of Organised Speculation*, p. 210.
[2] Cf. Jenks and Clark, *The Trust Problem*, p. 43.

also achieves an indirect economy by reducing the probability that fluctuations will occur. It does this in occupations where public confidence is important, and where largeness of capital resource is calculated to create confidence. This condition is fulfilled in banking—the more so since publicity of bankers' accounts has become common. The reason that banks differ in this respect from other concerns is, of course, that their customers are their creditors, and not, as in most trades, their debtors.[1]

§ 4. So far, we have considered exclusively what I have called *structural* economies. There is also another sort of economy that, in certain circumstances, favours the growth of large-scale management. So long as an industry is occupied by a number of establishments separately controlled, expenditure is likely to be incurred by all in defending their market against the others. A large part of the expenditure upon advertisements and travellers is, as was indicated in Chapter VI., of this character. But, when, instead of a number of competing firms, there appear, in any section of an industry, a number of firms under a single authority, a great part of this expenditure can, as was also indicated in that chapter, be dispensed with. A and B being united, it is no longer to the interest of either to spend money in persuading people, whether through travelling salesmen or in other ways, to prefer the one to the other. It was stated, in regard to railways, before the Board of Trade Conference of 1908: "It is well known that railway companies find it necessary to spend large sums of money in canvassing against one another, and, if competition were removed by judicious amalgamation, the greater part of this money could be saved."[2] This economy is, of course, liable to be largest where, apart from unification, "competitive" expenditure would be largest, namely, not in staple industries providing easily recognised standard articles, but in various sorts of "fancy" trades.[3]

---

[1] For a very full study of the subject-matter of §§ 2-3, cf. Marshall, *Industry and Trade*, bk. ii. chaps. iii.-iv.

[2] *Railway Conference*, p. 26.

[3] The suggestion, that combination enables savings to be made in respect of the number or quality of travelling salesmen and so on, is not upset by the

§ 5. Let us next suppose that the size of the individual firm and the size of the individual unit of management in an industry have been adjusted to the structural and other economies obtainable, and that the units evolved in this way are not large enough to exercise any element of monopolistic power. It is then clear that monopolistic power will not be called into being incidentally, as a by-product of developments that take place without reference to it. But there still remains, as an influence tending to produce it, the direct expectation of the gains to which it may lead. When promoters have reason to believe that the speculative community will expect a particular monopoly to prove more profitable than it really will do, this fact promises extra gains to those who form amalgamated companies, because it enables them to unload their shares at inflated values. Apart from this special consideration, however, we may lay it down that the magnitude of the gains obtainable from monopolisation depends, the conditions of supply being given, on the elasticity of the demand—*i.e.* the fraction obtained by dividing a (*small*) percentage change in price into the associated percentage change in quantity purchased—for the commodity concerned.[1] The less elastic the demand, the greater, *ceteris paribus*, are the probable gains. The principal conditions of highly inelastic demand, as given in Dr. Marshall's authoritative exposition, must, therefore, be set out here.

The first condition is that the commodity shall be of a kind for which it is not easy to find convenient substitutes.

---

fact that, in some instances, after the formation of a combination, the aggregate annual wages paid to salesmen increased. For the increase was probably due to attempts on the part of the combination to extend its market into fields which were not formerly occupied by any of its constituent members, or in which the business accessible to *single* firms was not enough to make it worth while for any of them to have salesmen there.

[1] If x is the quantity purchased and $\phi(x)$ the demand price per unit, the elasticity of demand is represented by $\dfrac{\phi(x)}{x \cdot \phi'(x)}$. If this is equal to unity for all values of x, the demand curve is a rectangular hyperbola. The verbal definition of the text is an approximate translation of the above technical definition so long as the term *small* contained in it is emphasised. But, of course, a 50 per cent fall in price must be accompanied, if the elasticity of demand is to be equal to unity, by a 100 per cent rise in consumption.

Q

The demand for mutton is made comparatively elastic by the existence of beef, the demand for oil by the existence of gas, and the demand for the service of trams by the existence of omnibuses. In like manner, the demand for the service of transport by rail is relatively more elastic in England than in continental America, because "the long broken coast-line of England and the great number of ports" render the competition of water carriage exceedingly powerful;[1] and the demand for the services of any particular line of railway is, in general, fairly elastic, even where no water competition exists, in consequence of the indirect competition of lines running to other markets.[2] From another field a good example of the point I am now considering is furnished by Jevons, in his book on the *Coal Question* : "When the Government of the Two Sicilies placed an exorbitant tax on sulphur, Italy having, as it was thought, a monopoly of native sulphur, our manufacturers soon had resort to the distillation of iron pyrites or sulphide of iron."[3] As regards the kinds of commodity, for which it is likely that substitutes can be employed, little of general interest can be said. It should be observed, however, that the products of a district, or a country, whose efforts are directed to leadership in quality, as distinguished from quantity, are less exposed to the competition of substitutes than other products. For example, the prime qualities of beef and mutton in Great Britain have not been affected by the development of the American and Australian trade to nearly the same extent as the inferior qualities.[4] It is, therefore, a commercially important fact that English manufacturers enjoy a very marked leadership of quality in wall-papers, fine textiles and cables, whereas in the electrical and chemical industries they are in a decidedly inferior position.[5] Obviously, from the present point of view, we must include among the substitutes for any commodity produced by a seller exercising monopolistic power the same commodity produced by other

---

[1] Cf. Macpherson, *Transportation in Europe*, p. 231.
[2] Cf. Johnson, *American Railway Transportation*, pp. 267-68.
[3] *The Coal Question*, p. 135.
[4] Cf. Besse, *L'Agriculture en Angleterre*, pp. 45 and 85.
[5] Cf. Levy, *Monopole, Kartelle und Trusts*, pp. 227, 229, 237.

sellers. The larger, therefore, is the proportion of the total output of product that a seller exercising monopolistic power provides in any market, the less elastic the demand for his services will be. Inelasticity of demand for monopoly goods is, therefore, promoted in industries where importation from rival sources is hindered by high transport charges, high tariffs, or international agreements providing for the division of the field between the combined producers of different countries.[1] Furthermore, in order that the elasticity of demand may be affected by substitutes, it is not necessary that the rival source of supply should be actually existing. In some industries manufacture by people who are normally purchasers is itself a possible rival source of supply. Thus, the Committee on Home Work observe: "Unless the price, at which these articles (baby linen and ladies' blouses and underclothing) are sold to the wives and daughters of the better-paid working men and small middle-class people, is low, those who would otherwise be purchasers will buy the materials and make the articles at home." The same remark seems to apply to laundry-work and charing. The poor housewife has the power, if reason offers, to do these things for herself. Consequently, the demand for the services of specialists at such tasks is exceptionally elastic.[2] For example, it has been remarked of Birmingham: "The washerwomen are among the first to suffer in any period of trade depression, for, as the first economy in bad times is to do your own washing, the tiny laundry with a very local connection is soon emptied."[3]

The second condition, making for inelasticity of demand, is that a commodity shall give rise to only a small proportion of the total cost of any further commodities in the production of which it may be employed. The reason, of course, is that,

[1] Since 1905 an international agreement of this kind seems to have existed in regard to steel rails (Levy, *Monopole, Kartelle und Trusts*, p. 250). There is a similar agreement in the tobacco industry (*ibid.* p. 254).

[2] Cf. Chapman, *Unemployment in Lancashire*, p. 87.

[3] Cadbury, *Women's Work*, p. 172. It may be added that, from a short-period point of view, the elasticity of the demand for new production of certain durable goods is made greater than it would otherwise be by the fact that half-worn-out garments and other such things are possible substitutes for new ones. (Cf. Chapman, *The Lancashire Cotton Industry*, p. 120.)

when the proportion is small, a large percentage rise in the price of the commodity, with which we are concerned, involves only a small percentage rise in the price of these further commodities, and, therefore, only a small percentage contraction of consumption. Dr. Levy suggests that this condition makes the demand for the ordinary raw materials of industry highly inelastic.[1] A similar line of thought brings out the fact that the elasticity of the demand for commodities at wholesale will be smaller, the larger is the proportionate part played by retailing and transport expenses in the cost of the commodities to consumers.

The third condition is that the further commodities, if any, in whose production our commodity is employed, shall be such that substitutes cannot easily be found for them. Thus, the raw materials of the building trade should be subject, other things being equal, to a less elastic demand than those of the engineering trade, because foreign machines can compete with English machines much more easily than foreign houses can compete with English houses.[2]

The last condition is that the other commodities or services, which co-operate with our commodity in the making of a finished product, shall be easily "squeezable," or, in technical language, shall have an inelastic supply schedule.

§ 6. The preceding considerations suggest that units of control adequate to exercise monopolistic power will often be found, even though neither structural economies nor advertisement economies dictate their formation. The tendency towards this result is opposed by the difficulty and cost involved in bringing about agreements among competing sellers. This difficulty and cost depend upon the following general circumstances. First, combination is easier when the number of sellers is small than when it is large; for small numbers both facilitate the actual process of negotiation, and diminish the chance that some party to an agreement will subsequently

---

[1] *Monopole, Kartelle und Trusts*, p. 280.
[2] It should be noticed, however, that, though houses as wholes cannot be imported, it is becoming always easier to import *parts* of them. The imports of wrought stone, marble, and joinery doubled between 1890 and 1902; whereas, from the provinces to London the "imports" of these things have increased still more largely (Dearle, *The London Building Trades*, p. 52).

violate it. An attempt to form a Kartel in the German match trade in 1883 is reported by Liefmann to have failed, because no less than 245 separate producers had to be consulted.[1] Secondly, combination is easier when the various producers live fairly close to one another, and so can come together easily, than when they are widely scattered. The reason why combination prevails in the German coal industry, and not in the English, is partly that, in Germany, the production of coal is localised, and not spread over a number of different districts, as it is in this country.[2] A similar reason probably accounts, in great measure, for the excess of combination that appears among sellers in general, as compared with buyers in general; for, it may be observed, at auctions, where buyers also are closely assembled, combination among them is not infrequent. Thirdly, combination is easier when there is a certain uniformity about the product of the various firms. There is great difficulty in arranging any form of Kartel agreement in respect of goods that have to be adapted to individual tastes, or are subject to the influence of changes of fashion. One writer suggests that a reason why English firms are combined to a less extent than foreign firms is that they concern themselves, as a rule, with the higher qualities, and the more specialised kinds, of commodities, rather than with "mass goods";[3] and another, in like manner, attributes the greater ease with which Coke Kartels are formed in Germany, as against Coal Kartels, to the greater uniformity of quality generally found in coke.[4] Fourthly, combination is easier when the tradition and habit of the country is favourable, than when it is unfavourable, to joint action in general. When employers have been accustomed to act together in Chambers of Commerce, in agreements as to discounts and rebates, or in negotiations with unions of workpeople, the friction to be overcome in making a price agreement is evidently less than it would be if they came together for the first time for that purpose. Thus: "The Association—such as the Merchants' Association of New York—has, indeed, no monopoly power,

---

[1] *Unternehmeverbände*, p. 57.

[2] Cf. Levy, *Monopole, Kartelle und Trusts*, p. 172.

[3] Levy, *Monopole, Kartelle und Trusts*, p. 187.

[4] Walker, *Combinations in the German Coal Industry*, p. 43.

but it is, nevertheless, of very great importance, owing to its socialising effects and its tendency to prepare the way for a stronger organisation, the combination or. pool."[1]   In like manner, the New Zealand arbitration law "forces employers into unions, for only thus can they defend themselves under the Act, and these naturally evolve into organisations for restricting competition."[2]   Yet again, there can be no doubt that the various forms of joint action which British engineering firms, for example, were compelled to take during the Great War, must have done much to smooth the way for future combination.   Perhaps, the opposing friction is also somewhat smaller when the producers concerned are companies than it is when they are private firms, in whose operations the sense of personal importance plays a larger part.

§ 7. The preceding section has tacitly implied that, where the gain from unification exceeds the cost and trouble involved, unification will, in fact, occur.   This implication, however, is not warranted.   It does not necessarily follow that, because an opportunity for agreement advantageous to all parties exists, an agreement will in fact be made.   The reason is that mutual jealousy may cause A and B to leave the melon of common gain uncut, rather than that either should allow the other to obtain what he considers a share unduly large relatively to his own.   Shall "participation" be proportional to the capacity of the several combining firms, or to their average product during recent years, or to the amount of the investment that has to be made in plant and goodwill, or to some other quantity ?   "One manufacturer has patents and special machinery, which have cost him a great deal of money, and by which he sets much store.   He will not enter the proposed combination unless these costs are made up to him.   Another manufacturer may have a large productive capacity, fifty nail machines, for example.   He may have been unable to find a market for the output of more than half his machines, but in the combination, he contends, all his capacity will become available.   He, therefore, insists that productive capacity should be the basis on which the allotment

[1] Robinson, *American Economic Association*, 1904, p. 126.
[2] V. S. Clark, *United States Bulletin of Labour*, No. 43 p. 1251.

of shares in the trust should be made. A third man, by the excellence of his equipment and the energy of his methods, has been able to run his plant at its full capacity, while his competitor, with a larger productive capacity but a less favourable location or a less capable body of subordinates, has operated only half time. The successful manufacturer contends that average sales should be the basis of allotment."[1] Disputes on these lines may easily prevent agreement if direct negotiation between the different firms is attempted. It should, however, be noticed that they can, in great part, be obviated, and that the difficulty of combination can be correspondingly reduced, when an amalgamation is effected gradually by the process of absorption (exemplified among English banks), or when a company promoter, undertaking to buy up and consolidate a number of competing concerns, negotiates terms separately with each of them, without stating into what arrangements he has entered with the others.

---

[1] Meade, *Corporation Finance*, p. 36.

CHAPTER XII

MONOPOLISTIC COMPETITION

§ 1. A CONDITION of monopolistic competition exists when each of two or more sellers supplies a considerable part of the market with which they are connected. In these circumstances it can be shown that there is no tendency for either of them to devote to production such an amount of resources as will render the value of their marginal trade net products equal to that yielded by resources employed in industries in general. A demonstration of this proposition can be given in ordinary language as follows.

§ 2. Let us first ignore all forms of action which aim, by sacrifice in the present, at obtaining an advantage against rivals in the future. We have, then, to do with the pure problem of "multiple monopoly." This problem assumes its simplest form when two monopolists only are supposed to be present; and, in this form, it has been much discussed among mathematical economists. Cournot decided, as is well known, that the resources devoted to production under duopoly are a determinate quantity, lying somewhere between the quantity that would have been so devoted under simple competition and under simple monopoly respectively. Professor Edgeworth, on the other hand, in an elaborate critique, maintains that the quantity is indeterminate. This latter view is now accepted by all mathematical economists. The quantity of resources which at any moment it will be most profitable to A to employ in his business depends on the output which B is employing, and *vice versa*. The quantity employed by each, therefore, depends on his judgment of the policy which the other will pursue, and this judgment may be anything accord-

ing to the mood of each and his expectation of success from a
policy of bluff. As in a game of chess, each player's move is
related to his reading of the psychology of his opponent and
his guess as to that opponent's reply. Hence, the investment
of each separately and of the two jointly is indeterminate.
There are, however, limits outside of which it cannot travel.
At the one extreme, it cannot, in any circumstances, pay either
seller to invest less than nothing. At the other extreme, it
cannot, in general, pay either to invest more than it would
pay him to invest if the other seller were investing nothing.
Hence, the range of indeterminateness of aggregate investment
stretches from nothing at the one extreme, up to the sum of
the investment that would maximise A's monopoly revenue in
the absence of B and the investment that would maximise B's
monopoly revenue in the absence of A. It can be shown by
a technical argument, developed in Appendix III. § 15, that
this sum is likely to be smaller than the quantity of resources
that would have been invested by A and B jointly under
conditions of simple competition. Now, we have learned from
Chapter VIII. that, under conditions of constant return, this
last quantity would be such as to make the value of the
marginal trade net product in our industry equal to the value
of marginal trade net products in general; under conditions of
increasing return greater than this; and under conditions of
diminishing return less than this. It follows that, where
conditions of constant or increasing return prevail, the quantity
of resources invested in an industry subject to monopolistic
competition will, in general, be such that the value of the
marginal trade net product there exceeds the value of marginal
trade net products in general, the extent of the excess being
indeterminate; and that in conditions of diminishing return,
the value of the marginal trade net product in an industry
subject to monopolistic competition is not likely to be equal
to, but may be either greater or less than, the corresponding
general value.

§ 3. So far, we have specifically excluded the effects of
price warfare designed to secure future gains by driving a
rival from the field or exacting favourable terms of agreement
from him. The indeterminateness just described exists under

monopolistic competition, even though neither of the monopolists
" hopes to ruin the other by cut-throat prices." [1] In many
instances of monopolistic competition, however, price warfare
—or cut-throat competition—does, in fact, take place. It
consists in the practice of selling at a loss in order to inflict
injury on a rival. It must be distinguished carefully from
the practice of reducing prices down to, or towards, prime cost,
which frequently occurs in periods of depression. This latter
practice may involve large reductions of price below the
" normal," and it is certain to do this when demand is variable
and prime cost is small relatively to supplementary cost; but
it does not involve " selling at a loss " in the strict sense.
Cut-throat competition proper occurs only when the sale price
of any quantity of commodity stands below the short-period
supply price of that quantity. When it occurs, the quantity
of investment is no longer indeterminate between nothing and
some quantity smaller than the quantity proper to simple
competition, but is liable to exceed this quantity to an extent
determined by the opinion entertained by each of the combatants
about the staying power of his opponent, and by other strategical
considerations. There is, obviously, no tendency for it to
approximate to the quantity that will make the value of the
marginal trade net product of the resources employed equal to
that which is yielded by resources in general; but it is not
possible to say anything further than this.

§ 4. The broad result of this discussion is that, in industries
under monopolistic competition *minus* the " cut-throat " element,
the value of the marginal trade net product of investment is
indeterminate, but is likely, except under conditions of
diminishing returns, to exceed the value of marginal trade
net products in general; and that, in industries under monopolistic competition *plus* the cut-throat element, it is uncon-
ditionally indeterminate.

[1] Edgeworth, *Giornale degli economisti*, November 1897, p. 405.

CHAPTER XIII

§ 1. A CONDITION of simple monopoly exists when a single seller only is exercising monopolistic power—whether or not there are other sellers in the market who accept the price fixed by this seller—and when, allowance being made for cost of carriage and so forth, the same price rules throughout the whole of his market. This condition of things works out in two different ways, according as, on the one hand, the entry to the industry is so far restricted that no resources are drawn into it other than those actually finding employment in it, or, on the other hand, entry to the industry is free. I shall study first industries of restricted entry.

§ 2. In Chapter VIII. it was shown that, when simple competition prevails, the value of the marginal trade net product of resources invested in an industry is equal to the value of the marginal trade net products of resources in general if production obeys the law of constant returns, greater than this central level if it obeys increasing returns, and less than this central level if it obeys diminishing returns. When simple monopoly prevails, it is to the interest of the monopolist to restrict his investment of resources in order to raise the price of the product; and he will so regulate its amount as to make the excess of his aggregate receipts over his aggregate costs (including earnings of management and so forth) as large as possible. It follows that under simple monopoly the value of the marginal trade net product will always be larger than that which would emerge under conditions of simple competition. Hence, in any industry working under conditions of constant returns or of increasing returns, the

235

substitution of simple monopoly for simple competition necessarily, other things being equal, causes the value of the marginal trade net product to diverge from (in the sense of exceeding) the central level more widely than it did before; and, when the conditions are such that several positions of equilibrium exist, the divergence may be very large indeed. In an industry working under conditions of diminishing returns this result is not certain; for in such an industry simple competition causes the value of the marginal trade net product to fall short of the central level. In these circumstances that contraction of investment, to which simple monopoly leads, *may* evolve a value of marginal trade net product that diverges from the central level to a smaller extent than the value of marginal trade net product associated with simple competition. In Appendix III. the conditions in which output under monopoly will diverge less than output under simple competition from the ideal output—which are substantially equivalent to the conditions in which monopoly will be less injurious to the national dividend—are displayed. It does not seem possible to say generally whether these conditions are likely or unlikely to be realised in an industry obeying diminishing returns that is selected at random. But in practice simple monopoly is much more likely to be introduced into industries of increasing returns than into industries of diminishing returns; and here, as indicated above, there is no uncertainty about the result.

§ 3. When monopolistic power is exercised by a combination of sellers through the agency of a price-agreement, the restrictive influence upon investment may be enhanced in an indirect way by a further circumstance. It is not practicable to make an agreement touching more than one or two roughly defined grades of service. Consequently, since an adapted charge cannot be made for them, the intermediate grades tend to disappear, even though numerous purchasers—some of whom, as things are, buy nothing—would have bought these grades, if they had been obtainable at a proportionate charge. Therefore, resources, which, under a perfectly constructed monopoly agreement, would have been devoted to the production of these grades, are excluded by the imperfect character of actual agreements. This effect is chiefly found among railway and shipping companies, which are bound by freight-rate conventions but compete in the frequency, speed, and comfort of their trains or ships.[1] Thus, there may be a demand for slow delivery of goods at a cheap rate, but no such delivery may be available. "Vans are sent out with light loads in order to secure the earliest delivery, and, in many cases, and particularly in the suburbs of larger towns, two or three vans will be engaged in delivering light loads which could easily be conveyed in one";[2] first-class rapid vessels are employed to carry things for which they are quite unnecessary, because agreements preclude the offer of lower rates if slower and cheaper vessels are used;[3] and so forth. The misdirection of resources that arises in this way is additional to the misdirection due to a simple exercise of monopolistic power.

√ § 4. Some qualification of the above results is necessary in industries where temporary low prices may lead to the development of new demands. For, when a prospect of this kind exists, particularly if conditions of increasing return prevail and if the ruling rate of interest on investments is low, it may pay a monopolist to accept low prices for a time, even though to do so involves production at a loss, for the sake of the future gain; whereas it would not pay any one among a large number of competing sellers to do this, since only a very small proportion of the future gain resulting from his action would accrue to himself. It is important, however, to observe that the creation of a new demand, which may thus sometimes be credited to monopoly, is only a social gain when the demand is really new, and not when it is merely a substitute for some other demand which is at the same time destroyed. It is not, for example, a social gain if a railway company, by temporary

---

[1] The agreements, short of pooling, between railways sometimes embrace agreements as to speed; those between the members of some, but not all, shipping conferences, agreements as to the relative number of sailings permitted to the various members (*Royal Commission on Shipping Rings, Report*, p. 23).

[2] *Report of the Board of Trade Railway Conference*, p. 39.

[3] *Royal Commission on Shipping Rings, Report*, p. 108.

low prices, "develops the traffic" from one district at the expense of destroying the traffic from another equally well situated district; and it is not a social gain if, by a like policy, some ring of traders causes people, who used to obtain a given measure of satisfaction from crinolines and no satisfaction from hobble-skirts, to obtain the like given measure of satisfaction from hobble-skirts and no satisfaction from crinolines. This consideration suggests that the transitional advantage of simple monopoly, that has just been set out, is not generally very important in comparison with the long-period disadvantages previously explained.

§ 5. In the discussion so far we have assumed the entry to industries, in which simple monopoly prevails, to be so far obstructed or restricted that no resources are drawn into them other than those actually finding employment there. As a rule this condition is fulfilled, because, when it is not fulfilled, the trouble of forming monopolistic agreements will seldom be worth undertaking. Still, monopolistic agreements without restriction of entry are sometimes made. It is easy to show, that, under these agreements, the national dividend suffers more than it would do, if the same monopolistic price policy prevailed in conjunction with restriction of entry to the industry. For, broadly speaking, what happens is this. The marginal net product of resources actually finding employment in the monopolised industry is the same as it would be under a system of restricted entry. But, besides these resources, other resources have been drawn away from employment elsewhere and have become attached to the industry. These extra resources will either be all idle themselves, or will make a corresponding quantity of resources already in the industry idle. The dividend, therefore, will be reduced below what it would have been under a system of restricted entry, by the difference between the productivity of that quantity of resources which it pays to set to work in the monopolised industry and the productivity of that quantity for which the receipts of the industry would suffice to provide normal earnings. This consideration does not, of course, prove that restriction of entry to an industry, in which monopoly prevails, is socially desirable ; for it may well happen that free entry would compel the monopolist to change. his policy, and to adopt one approximately equivalent to that dictated by competition. It only proves that restriction is advantageous in those— probably exceptional — monopolies where the removal of restriction cannot affect price policy.[1]

[1] Attention may be called here to a peculiar case. Suppose the same process to yield two joint products, one of which is controlled monopolistically but the other is not. Then, as shown above, if entry to the industry can be restricted, simple monopoly will make the outputs of both products less than they would be under simple competition. The whole of the non-monopolised joint product that is produced will be sold, but a part of the other product will probably be thrown away. If, however, entry to the industry is not restricted, more resources will flow into it than would so flow under simple competition. This will mean that the output and sale of the non-monopolised joint product is larger than it would have been under simple competition. It is *possible*, though improbable, that, as a net result, there may be evolved a larger sum of consumers' surplus than simple competition would allow. (Cf. *ante*, Ch. VIII. footnote to p. 194.)

CHAPTER XIV

DISCRIMINATING MONOPOLY [1]

§ 1. UP to this point we have supposed that monopolisation, when it occurs, will be of the simple form which does not involve discrimination of prices as between different customers. We have now to observe that this variety of monopolisation is not the only possible sort. Discriminating power will sometimes exist alongside of monopolistic power, and, when it does, the results are affected. It is, therefore, important to determine the circumstances in which, and the degree to which, monopolists are able to exercise, and find advantage in exercising, this power.

§ 2. The conditions are most favourable to discrimination, that is to say, discrimination will yield most advantage to the monopolist when the demand price for any unit of a commodity is independent of the price of sale of every other unit. This implies that it is impossible for any one unit to take the place of any other unit, and this, in turn, implies two things. The first of these is that no unit of the commodity sold in one market can be transferred to another market. The second is, that no unit of demand, proper to one market, can be transferred to another market. The former sort of transference needs no description, but the latter is somewhat subtle. It would occur if the promulgation of different rates for transporting coal originating in A and coal originating in B enabled the more favoured district to

---

[1] In this chapter some of the results, depending, as they do, on mathematical reasoning that cannot readily be translated into ordinary language, are necessarily stated in a somewhat dogmatic form. For proof of these results reference must be made to Appendix III.

increase its production of coal and, therefore, its demand for carriage, at the expense of the less favoured district. In order that the conditions most favourable to discrimination may prevail, this sort of transferability, as well as the other, must be excluded. Under the monopolistic arrangements practicable in real life the above kinds of transferability are absent or present in varying degrees. I propose to set out a series of examples under each of the heads just distinguished.

§ 3. Units of commodity are entirely non-transferable when the commodity in question consists of services-applied directly by the sellers to the persons of their customers, such as the services of medical men, barristers, teachers, dentists, hotelkeepers and so forth. A medical man's offer to charge any one set of persons less than any other set cannot lead to the one set becoming middlemen for the services which the other set desire. Services applied directly by the seller to commodities handed to them for treatment, such as the service of transporting different articles, are also entirely non-transferable. A railway's offer to charge one price for a ton-mile of transport service to copper merchants and a lower price to coal merchants cannot lead to any middleman device, because it is physically impossible to convert copper into coal for the purpose of transport and afterwards to reconvert it. A slightly, but only slightly, lower degree of non-transferability exists among services that are normally rendered in physical connection with the private dwellings of purchasers. Gas and water supplied to private houses are instances in point. Here transference is not entirely excluded, because it is *possible*, at sufficient cost of money and trouble, to detach the commodities from the distributing plant along which they are brought and to carry them elsewhere. Lesser degrees of non-transferability exist among commodities whose transference is obstructed merely by high costs of transportation or by tariff charges. The degree of non-transferability in these circumstances may, evidently, be large or small, according as the distance, or the rate of customs duty, that separates two markets between which discrimination is attempted is large or small. In like manner, various degrees of non-transferability can

R

be brought about artificially by enforcing upon purchasers contracts that penalise re-sales. For example, in the Ruhr coal district, the agreement made by the syndicate with industrial purchasers provides "that re-sale to railways, gas works, brick works or lime-kilns, or any reshipment from the original point of destination, shall be penalised by an addition of 3 marks per ton to the selling price."[1] If no agreement of this kind, no cost of carriage, and no tariff exist, complete transferability will prevail.

§ 4. Units of demand are almost completely non-transferable from one market to another, when the commodity concerned is something ready for final consumption, and when the markets, between which discrimination is to be made, are distinguished according to the wealth of the purchasers. It is clear, for instance, that the willingness of doctors to charge less to poor people than to rich people does not lead to any rich people, for the sake of cheap doctoring, becoming poor. In like manner, the provision of the service of transport at different rates to coal merchants and to copper merchants does not lead to any copper merchants, for the sake of the cheap transportation, becoming coal merchants. No doubt, in both these examples some slight transference *may* be achieved through successful fraud, such as a pretence on the part of rich people that they belong to the poorer group, and the smuggling of copper in the guise of coal; but this kind of thing is of no practical importance. It is interesting to note that sellers often attempt artificially to create the above type of non-transferability by attaching to different grades of their product trade marks, special brands, special types of packing and so on—all incidents designed to prevent possible purchasers of the grades that are highly priced relatively to the cost of production from becoming instead purchasers of the grades that are sold at a lower rate of profit.[2]

---

[1] Walker, *Combination in the German Coal Industry*, p. 274.

[2] It must be added, however, that, though trade marks are sometimes mere devices for creating monopoly power, there is, nevertheless, a valid reason for protecting them against infringement by legal enactments, because "an inducement is thereby given to make satisfactory articles and to continue making them." (Cf. Taussig, *American Economic Review Supplement*, vol. vi., 1916, p. 177.)

A smaller degree of non-transferability exists between the markets for hotel accommodation in the season and out of the season; for heavy discrimination might cause a considerable number of people to change the time of their holiday. A still smaller degree of non-transferability exists between the markets for railway transport from A to B, which are provided respectively by traders in A wishing to send a given commodity direct to B, and by traders in C wishing to send this commodity to B through A. For a large difference in the rates charged would cause production, that would normally occur at the less favoured, to take place instead at the more favoured, point. Perfect transferability exists when the markets are distinguished by some badge, the attachment of which involves no cost, as, for example, if railways charged one fare to passengers carrying pencils and another fare to passengers without pencils. The immediate effect of this discrimination would be to transfer *all* demands from the less to the more favoured market, and discrimination would yield *no* advantage to the monopolists.

§ 5. When a degree of non-transferability, of commodity units on the one hand, and of demand units on the other hand, sufficient to make discrimination profitable, is present, the relation between the monopolistic seller and each buyer is, strictly, one of bilateral monopoly. The terms of the contract that will emerge between them is, therefore, theoretically indeterminate and subject to the play of that "bargaining" whose social effects were analysed at the end of Chapter VI. When a railway company is arranging terms with a few large shippers, the indeterminate element may have considerable importance. Usually, however, where discrimination is of practical interest, the opposed parties are, not a single large seller and a few large buyers, but a single large seller and a great number of relatively small buyers. The loss of an individual customer's purchase means so much less to the monopolistic seller than to any one of the many monopolistic purchasers, that, apart from combination among purchasers, all of them will almost certainly accept the monopolistic seller's price. They will recognise that it is useless to stand out in the hope of bluffing a concession, and

will buy what is offered, so long as the terms demanded
from them leave to them *any* consumers' surplus. In what
follows I assume that the customers act in this way. So
assuming, we may distinguish three degrees of discriminating
power, which a monopolist may conceivably wield. The
ideal degree would involve the charge of a different price
against all the different units of commodity, in such wise
that the price exacted for each was equal to the demand
price for it, and no consumers' surplus was left to the buyers.
A second degree would obtain if a monopolist were able to
make n separate prices, in such wise that all units with
a demand price greater than x were sold at a price x, all with
a demand price less than x and greater than y at a price
y, and so on. A third degree would obtain if the monopolist
were able to distinguish among his customers n different
groups, separated from one another more or less by some
practicable mark, and could charge a separate monopoly price
to the members of each group. This degree, it will be
noticed, differs fundamentally from either of the preceding
degrees, in that it may involve the refusal to satisfy, in one
market, demands represented by demand prices in excess of
some of those which, in another market, are satisfied.

§ 6. These three degrees of discriminating power, though
all theoretically possible, are not, from a practical point of
view, of equal importance. On the contrary, in real life the
third degree only is found. No doubt, we can imagine
conditions in which discrimination even of the first degree
could be achieved. If all consumers had exactly similar
demand schedules,[1] it could be achieved by the simple device
of refusing to sell in packets of less than the quantity which
each consumer required per unit of time, and fixing the
price per packet at such a rate as to make it worth the
consumer's while, but only just worth his while, to purchase
the packet. Thus, if every demander would give for a
hundredth physical unit of commodity, when he already has
ninety-nine units, the sum of one shilling, but would prefer

---

[1] A person's demand schedule for any commodity is the list of different
quantities of that commodity that he would purchase at different price levels.
Cf. Marshall, *Principles of Economics*, p. 96.

to give 300 shillings for a hundred units, rather than have
no units at all, the monopolist may make his unit of sale
one hundred physical units and charge for this unit of
sale a price of 300 shillings. If there is no combination
among the buyers, the number of units sold will then
be the same as would have been sold at a price of
one shilling per physical unit, and, in effect, the physical
units satisfying demands of different keenness will have
been sold at different prices. But this method of discrimination, whether in a complete or a partial form, is
scarcely ever practicable, because the individual demand
schedules, of which the market demand schedule is made
up, are, as a rule, very far indeed from being similar. For
this reason an analysis of the method is of academic interest
only.[1] Apart from this method, ideal discrimination might
still conceivably be established by detailed separate bargaining with every separate customer. But it is obvious that
that method involves enormous cost and trouble. Furthermore, since it implies separate bargains with individuals,
it opens the way, not only to error, but also to the perversion
of agents through bribery. These considerations are, in
general, sufficient to make monopolists themselves unwilling
to adopt the method; and, even if they were not thus
unwilling, it would be hardly possible for the State, in view
of the large opportunities for "unfair" competition which
the method affords, to leave their hands free. "Whatever
financial advantage there may be in charging against each
act of transport a rate adapted to its individual circumstances,
the arbitrary nature of a system of rates arranged on this
plan implies so much uncertainty and lends itself to such
serious abuses, that we are compelled to condemn it."[2]   Thus,

---

[1] For such an analysis, cf. my paper "Monopoly and Consumers' Surplus,"
Economic Journal, September 1904.

[2] Colson, *Cours d'économie politique*, vol. vi. p. 211. Special opportunities
for injurious discrimination of this sort exist when a railway company is also
itself a large producer of some commodity, say coal, which it also transports
for rival producers. To prevent the obvious abuses to which this state of things
may lead, the "commodity clause" of the Hepburn Act passed in 1906 in the
United States made it unlawful for any railway to engage in interstate
transport of any commodity which had been mined or manufactured by itself.
The law does not, however, prevent a railway from transporting a commodity

a powerful influence is always at work persuading or compelling monopolists to act on general rules, with published tariffs, guarded, as effectively as may be, against the undermining influence of unpublished rebates. This means that they cannot, except in extraordinary circumstances, introduce either the first or the second degree of discrimination, and that the third degree is of chief practical importance.

§ 7. Monopoly *plus* discrimination of the third degree is not a determinate conception. It is theoretically possible to divide any market in an indefinitely large number of different ways, of which some would be more, and others less, advantageous to the monopolist. If the monopolist had an absolutely free hand in the matter, the division he would choose would be such that the lowest demand price in sub-market A exceeded the highest demand price in sub-market B, and so on throughout. If the aggregate demand of the markets collectively had an elasticity greater than unity throughout, the resulting system would be identical with that proper to the second degree of discrimination, for the lowest demand price in each group would also be the price calculated to yield maximum monopoly revenue from that group. If the aggregate demand had not an elasticity greater than unity throughout, the maximising price in some groups would be greater than the lowest demand price in those groups, and the system would, therefore, be different from the above. In any event, the separation of markets, in such wise that the lowest demand price in the first exceeds the highest demand price in the second, and so on, would obviously be better, from the monopolist's point of view, than any other kind of separation. But in practice the monopolist's freedom of action is limited by the need, already referred to, of acting on general rules. This consideration makes it necessary that he shall choose, for his sub-markets, groups that are distinguishable from one another by some readily recognisable mark. Moreover, since a hostile public opinion might lead to legislative intervention, his choice must not be such as to outrage the

produced by a company in which it holds a majority of the shares, and it can, therefore, be evaded without great difficulty. (Cf. Jones, *The Anthracite Coal Combination*, pp. 190 *et seq.*)

popular sense of justice. Thus, he will not distinguish and bring together entirely new groups, but will make use of distinctions already given in nature. Nor is this all. For in some circumstances the condition of non-transferability holds good, not generally, but only as between certain markets which are constituted independently of the monopolist's volition. Thus, the existence of an import tariff or of high transport charges on imports to all parts of his country's frontier—a condition easiest to realise when that country is an island— may make it possible for a seller to charge a lower price for his goods abroad than at home without the risk of inviting the return and resale of his exports. Clearly, therefore, a monopolist cannot hope to find a series of sub-markets that conforms to his ideal altogether, but he may find one in which only a comparatively small number of the demand prices embraced in the first sub-market are lower than the highest demand price of the second sub-market, and so on throughout all the sub-markets.

§ 8. I now pass to an analysis of consequences, and, as in the preceding chapter, I shall begin with monopolised industries to which entry can be restricted. The analysis, to be complete, would need to take account of the fact that, in real life, the demand of one purchaser for any r^{th} unit of a commodity is sometimes, in part, dependent upon the price at which this commodity is being sold to other purchasers.[1] When markets are interdependent in this way, the issue is complicated, but the broad results, though rendered less certain, are not, it would appear, substantially altered. Consequently, in the following pages I shall assume that the quantity demanded in each sub-market depends only on the price ruling in that sub-market. This procedure enables resort to be had to the same general method that has been pursued hitherto.

§ 9. As already explained, practical interest centres upon monopoly *plus* discrimination of the third degree. But, before studying this, we may, with advantage, glance at the simpler problem presented by the two higher forms of discrimination. It is easily seen that under monopoly *plus* ideal discrimination, since, with a monopolist, individual net product and trade

---

[1] Cf. Appendix III. §§ 9-10.

net product are necessarily identical, it is to the advantage
of the monopolist to push forward investment in his industry
to the point at which the value of the marginal trade net
product of resources there is exactly equal to the value of the
marginal trade net product of resources in general. In general,
this result is more advantageous to the national dividend
than anything that can be hoped for under simple monopoly.
It is, indeed, equally advantageous with that yielded by simple
competition, provided that conditions of constant returns prevail.
But, when conditions of diminishing returns prevail, it is more
advantageous, because, in these conditions, simple competition,
as was shown in Chapter VIII., would cause investment in the
industry to be pushed unduly, so that the value of the marginal
trade net product there would be less than that attainable
elsewhere. When conditions of increasing returns prevail, it
is also more advantageous, because, in these conditions, simple
competition would cause investment in the industry to be pushed
inadequately, so that the value of the marginal net product there
would be greater than that obtainable elsewhere. It appears
further that the advantage involved in monopoly *plus* ideal
discrimination is greater, the more elastic is the demand for
the commodity produced by the industry, and the more markedly
the conditions of supply depart from constant returns, either
on the side of diminishing or on the side of increasing returns.[1]
Finally, it should be observed that, when conditions of increasing returns prevail, monopoly *plus* ideal discrimination
may be associated with a considerable amount of investment
in, and output from, an industry in which, under a regime of
simple competition, it would not have been to anybody's interest
to make any investment at all. It is shown in Appendix III.
that this result is most likely to be realised (1) if, other
things being equal, increasing returns are acting strongly, in
such wise that a small increase of output involves a large fall
in the cost of production per unit, and (2) if, other things
being equal, the demand for the commodity or service is
elastic till fairly low price levels have been reached.[2]

§ 10. It is readily seen that the effects of monopoly

---

[1] Appendix III. § 20.
[2] Cf. *ibid.* § 21.

plus discrimination of the second degree approximate towards those of monopoly *plus* discrimination of the first degree, as the number of different prices, which it is possible for the monopolist to charge, increases; just as the area of a polygon inscribed in a circle approximates to the area of the circle as the number of its sides increases. Let us call the output proper to ideal discrimination *a*. Then monopoly of the second degree would lead to an output less than *a*, but approaching more nearly towards it the larger is the number of the different price groups which the monopolist is able to distinguish; and the value of the marginal trade net product of resources invested in our industry would, in like manner, approach more nearly towards equality with the value of the marginal trade net product elsewhere, the larger is this number.

§ 11. The study of monopoly *plus* discrimination of the third degree is more complicated than that of either of the two higher forms. In the discussion of these we were able to make use of a simple relation between the aggregate output which comes about in various circumstances, and the output which I have called the ideal output. According as actual output exceeds, falls short of, or is equal to the ideal output, we could conclude that the value of the marginal trade net product of resources invested in our industry falls short of, exceeds, or is equal to the value of the marginal trade net product in industries in general. But, under monopoly *plus* discrimination of the third degree, the relation between actual output and ideal output no longer suffices for a criterion. The reason is that, when a demand represented by a demand price *p* is satisfied, it is not necessary, as it has been necessary so far, that all the demands represented by demand prices greater than *p* shall have been satisfied. On the contrary, the monopolist may, in one market, be satisfying all demands represented by demand prices higher than *p*, while, in another market, he is refusing to satisfy any demands whose demand prices fall short of $(p+h)$. It follows that the resources invested in the industry fall into a number of different parts, in each of which the value of the marginal trade net product is different. Consequently, we

have no longer to ask how the value of the marginal trade
net product of resources invested *in the industry* is related
to the value of the marginal trade net product of resources
in industries in general, but how the various values of marginal
trade net products of resources invested *in each of the several
markets of the industry* are related to that standard. Our
ideal output ceases to be a single output of the whole
industry, and becomes a number of separate outputs sold
in separate markets. A given output of the whole industry
may be broken up in different ways among these markets,
and the system of values of marginal trade net products will
be different according to the way in which it is, in fact,
broken up. Hence, a study of the effect which monopoly *plus*
discrimination of the third degree produces upon output,
is only a first step to a study of the effect which it produces,
as compared with that which simple monopoly and simple
competition respectively produce, upon the relation between
the values of marginal trade net products in different parts
of the industrial field. Nevertheless, it is well that such
a study should be made. To facilitate it, let us suppose that
the demands for the product of an industry can be broken
up into two markets A and B, between which price
discrimination is feasible; and let us ask first whether
output under discriminating monopoly of the third degree
will be absolutely greater or smaller than output under
simple monopoly and simple competition respectively.

§ 12. To compare the output proper to discriminating
monopoly with that proper to simple monopoly, we may
conveniently distinguish three principal cases. First, let
the conditions be such that, under simple monopoly, some
of the commodity, in which we are interested, would be
consumed in both A and B. In these conditions there is
no adequate ground for holding either that output under
discriminating monopoly is likely to exceed, or that it is
likely to fall short of, output under simple monopoly.
Mathematical analysis shows that the result is quite
uncertain.[1] Secondly, let the conditions be such that, under
simple monopoly, some of the commodity would have been

---

[1] Cf. Appendix III. § 23.

consumed in A, but none in B. In these conditions it is
impossible that the introduction of discriminating power
should lead to diminished output. On the contrary, if there
is any substantial demand in B, it must lead to increased
output. The amount of the increase will be specially great
if the demand in B is elastic, and if the supply of the
commodity obeys the law of increasing returns. These
conditions are often fulfilled among Kartels selling regularly
at specially low rates in markets, foreign and other, where
they are exposed to competition. An interesting practical inference is that, if a commodity whose production obeys the law
of increasing returns is monopolised, it is to the interest of
the consumers in the producing country that the Government should allow the monopolist to make sales abroad at
lower prices than at home, rather than that, while still permitting monopoly, it should forbid this discrimination. This
inference cannot be upset by reference to the more advanced
industries that use the commodity as a raw material,
because the sales abroad, being at market prices there,
do not enable foreign users to get it more cheaply than
they could before. Finally, let the conditions be such
that, under simple monopoly, none of the commodity would
have been consumed in either A or B. In these conditions it is obviously impossible that the introduction of
discriminating power should lead to diminished output. It
is possible that it may lead to increased output. The
condition for this is the same as the condition, mentioned
in the next paragraph, that enables discriminating monopoly
of the third degree to yield some output, though simple
competition would yield none.

§ 13. We have now to compare the output proper to
discriminating monopoly with that proper to simple
competition. Under conditions of constant returns and
diminishing returns it is, obviously, impossible for discriminating monopoly of any sort to make output greater
than it would be under simple competition. Discriminating
monopoly of the third degree must make it smaller than it
would be under that system. When, however, increasing
returns prevail, the question is more complex. It has been

proved in an earlier section that, in that event, monopoly *plus* ideal discrimination must raise output above the quantity proper to simple competition. Furthermore, it is evident that discrimination of the third degree approximates towards ideal discrimination, as the number of markets into which demands can be divided approximate towards the number of units for which any demand exists. Hence, it follows that, under increasing returns, monopoly *plus* discrimination of the third degree *may* raise output above the competitive amount, and is more likely to do this the more numerous are the markets between which discrimination can be made. Sometimes, but not, of course, so frequently as with ideal discrimination, discriminating monopoly of the third degree will evolve some output where simple competition would have evolved none. In view, however, of the limitation, which practical considerations impose, alike upon the number of markets that can be formed, and upon the monopolist's freedom to make up the several markets in the way most advantageous to him, it appears, on the whole, exceedingly improbable that, in an industry selected at random, monopoly *plus* discrimination of the third degree will yield an output as large as would be yielded by simple competition.

§ 14. In the preceding paragraphs we have compared *the absolute amount* of output under discriminating monopoly of the third degree with the absolute amount under simple monopoly and simple competition respectively. The next step is to compare the degree of approximation towards the ideal output that is attained under these different systems. Under diminishing returns, an output less than that proper to simple monopoly is likely to diverge more from the ideal output than either the output of simple monopoly or the output of simple competition; and an output intermediate between that of simple monopoly and that of simple competition may or may not be nearer to the ideal output than either the one or the other of these. Under increasing returns, an output less than that proper to simple monopoly is certain to diverge further from the ideal output than either the output of simple monopoly or that of simple competition : an output intermediate between these two will be nearer to the ideal than that of simple monopoly, and further from it than that of simple competition; and an output greater than that of simple competition will be nearer to the ideal than either of the rival outputs. Combining these results with those set out in the two preceding sections, we conclude that, both under diminishing and under increasing returns, discriminating monopoly of the third degree will not improbably yield an output closer to the ideal output than simple monopoly yields; that, under diminishing returns, it may, but is unlikely to, yield one closer to the ideal output than simple competition yields; and that, under increasing returns, it may, but is *very* unlikely to, yield one closer than this.

§ 15. I now return to the considerations suggested in § 11. It was there pointed out that the measure of correspondence between the actual aggregate output of an industry and the ideal output does not, when discriminating monopoly of the third degree is in question, carry the same implication as in other circumstances. Suppose, for example, that discriminating monopoly of this degree brings about an output closer to the ideal output than either simple monopoly or simple competition would bring about. The value of the marginal trade net product of resources invested in those parts of the industry, that satisfy the demand of markets to which discriminating monopoly accords a lower price than simple monopoly or simple competition would do, exceeds the value of the marginal trade net product of resources in industries in general by less than it would do under either of the rival systems. But, *per contra*, the value of the marginal trade net product of resources invested in those parts of the industry, if there are any such, that satisfy the demands of markets, to which discriminating monopoly accords a higher price than simple monopoly or simple competition would do, exceeds the value of the marginal trade net product of resources in industries in general by more than it would do under these systems. Hence, even where discriminating monopoly makes aggregate output more nearly conformable to the ideal than simple monopoly or simple competition would do, it does not follow that it will involve greater equality between the

values of marginal trade net products in our industry and
elsewhere. Nor need we stop at this negative result. It can
be shown, further, that the establishment in any industry of a
given output associated with discriminating prices is likely to
conduce less towards equalisation among the values of marginal
trade net products as a whole than the establishment of the
same output associated with uniform prices. For let the
value of the marginal trade net product of resources in general
be P; and let the quantity of resources invested in our industry be such that, if the product is sold at the same price in
all markets, the value of the marginal trade net product of the
resources employed to supply each of them will be equal to
p. Then, if this same quantity of resources is invested
in the industry, but the product is sold at a higher price in
some markets than in others, the value of the marginal trade
net product of the resources utilised for the higher priced
markets will be greater than p, and that of the resources
utilised for the lower priced markets will be less than p. This
implies that the mean square deviation (our measure of
inequality) of these various values from P is likely to be
greater than it would have been if all of them had stood at p.
Hence, the probability, that discriminating monopoly of the
third degree will be more favourable to equality among the
values of marginal trade net products than simple monopoly
or simple competition, is less than the probability that it will
be more favourable than they are to the production of the
ideal output. When this result is added to those achieved in
previous sections, we may summarise the situation as follows.
First, there will sometimes be some, but there will generally
not be much, advantage to the national dividend in discriminating monopoly of the third degree as against simple monopoly;
but, when discriminating monopoly makes it profitable to sell
in a market, in which under simple monopoly no sales would
occur, some advantage *must* result. Secondly, as between dis-.
criminating monopoly of the third degree and simple competition,
it is, in general, very unlikely that discriminating monopoly will
prove superior. It *must* prove superior, however, when the
conditions are such that simple competition would yield no
output, but discriminating monopoly does yield some output.

§ 16. So far we have supposed that discriminating monopoly is coupled with power to restrict the entry to the monopolised industry. When this condition is not satisfied, reasoning analogous to that employed at the close of the preceding chapter is applicable. Resources tend to be attracted into the industry till the point is reached at which the expectation of earnings there is equal to that ruling elsewhere. So long as monopoly prices are maintained, this means that a considerable part of the resources so attracted are standing idle and are yielding no net product whatever. It is evident, therefore, that the national dividend suffers more from discriminating monopoly without restriction of entry than it does from discriminating monopoly *plus* restriction of entry. But, as with simple monopoly, so also here, it may, nevertheless, be desirable that restriction should be forbidden, because, when it is absent, there is a better chance that the entrenchments of monopolistic power will ultimately be broken down.

CHAPTER XV

§ 1. THE discussion of the preceding chapter has necessarily been somewhat abstract. It has, however, practical applications of very great importance in connection with the charges that should be made for such things as water, gas and electricity, when these commodities are supplied to different groups of consumers or for different purposes. Still greater interest, however, attaches to it in connection with the rates chargeable by railway companies. Considerable controversy has taken place between those who hold that these rates should be based on "the cost of service principle," and those who would base them on the "value of service principle."[1] The "cost of service principle" is, in effect, the simple competition discussed in Chapter VIII.: "the value of service principle" is discriminating monopoly of the third degree. In the light of what has been said, the issue between them can be clearly set out; and it will, in the present chapter, be examined. We have no concern with the circumstance, explained in Chapter XIII., that, in certain conditions, a railway with power to discriminate may find it profitable, *as a temporary measure*, to charge exceptionally low rates for transport between certain places or for certain selected commodities, with a view to building up a new demand; nor yet with the related circumstance that this policy, if the demand is really a new one, and not merely a

---

[1] It is interesting to note that the problem of how retail shops should distribute their charges for the act of retailing over the various commodities that they sell is very closely analogous to the problem of railway charges. Among retail shops, however, there is the additional complication that a retailer is sometimes able to obtain a general advertisement for his shop by selling particular well-known goods practically free of retailer's profit.

substitute for another that has been supplanted, may be more advantageous to the national dividend than anything which simple competition—unless it were modified by a system of State bounties—could evolve. These matters call for no further investigation here. Leaving them aside, I propose to exhibit the meaning, in concrete form, of the cost of service principle—or simple competition—and of the value of service principle—or discriminating monopoly of the third degree,—and to compare their respective consequences.

§ 2. It is generally agreed that, except in so far as the transport services sold to one set of purchasers are "supplied jointly" with those sold to another set, simple competition would tend to bring about a system of uniform rates per ton-mile for similar services.[1] For these services the level of the uniform rate would be such that the demand price and the supply price would coincide; and, when the service of railway transport was sold in conjunction with some other service, such as cartage or packing, an appropriate addition would be made to the charge. This general analysis can be briefly developed as follows.

First, the actual level of the uniform mileage rate, to which simple competition would lead on any particular railway, will depend on the circumstances and position of the railway. *Ceteris paribus,* a specially high rate would be appropriate if the route lay through districts, where, as with mountain railways, the engineering costs of making a line are specially great, or where the traffic is very irregular from

---

[1] It is, indeed, sometimes maintained that this will only happen if "simple competition" is defined to include complete transferability of the things that are sold among customers, and it is pointed out that competition, apart from this condition, has proved compatible with discriminating charges for services sold to different sets of persons by shipping companies and by retailers; different sorts of cargoes are carried at different rates, and the absolute charge for retailing work is different in regard to different articles. (Cf. G. P. Watkins, "The Theory of Differential Rates," *Quarterly Journal of Economics,* 1916, pp. 693-5.) Reflection, however, shows that, when competition really prevails, seller A must always endeavour to undersell seller B by offering to serve B's better-paying customers at a rate slightly less than B is charging, and that this process must eventually level all rates. The explanation of the discriminations cited above is, not the absence of complete transferability, but the fact that custom and tacit understandings introduce an element of monopolistic action.

one time to another;[1] because, in these conditions, the supply prices of all quantities of transportation along the route is specially high. In like manner, *ceteris paribus*, a specially high rate would·be appropriate if the route lay through sparsely populated regions where little traffic can be obtained, or through regions where the configuration·of the country renders water transport a readily available substitute for land transport for certain classes of commodities between the terminals; because, in these conditions, the demand schedule is specially low, and the supply schedule indicates increasing returns; the expenses involved in building and working a railway adapted for a small amount of traffic being proportionately greater than those involved·in the·production of transport service on a large scale. It is, no doubt, in recognition of these considerations that the *maxima*, imposed in the British Parliamentary freight classification, are made different for different lines,··though the classification itself is, of course, the same for all of them.

Secondly, departures from the uniform mileage rate would occur under simple competition, in so far as buyers of a ton-mile of transportation require,·along··with this, other incidental services involving·expense. The·adjustments needed are exactly analogous to the adjustments made in the price of plain cotton cloth delivered c.i.f. to buyers who live at different distances from the seat of manufacture. Thus, rates should be comparatively low for the transport of any class of goods, when the method of packing adopted is convenient to the railway. It is more costly, other things being equal, to carry small consignments than large. "Small consignments mean to a railway three distinct sources of· serious additional expense: separate collection and delivery, separate handling, invoicing, accounting, etc., at the terminal stations; and bad loading in the railway waggons."[2] It is, therefore, proper that, in the English parliamentary classification, goods, which are placed in class A—the cheapest class—when loaded in lots of 4 tons, are raised to class B when despatched in loads between 2 and 4

[1] Cf. Williams, *Economics of Railway Transport*, p. 212.
[2] Acworth, *Elements of Railway Economics*, p. 120.

tons, and to class C when despatched in loads of less than 2 tons. On a like principle, it is proper that English railway companies should voluntarily make arrangements, under which certain goods are put into a class lower than the parliamentary classification requires, on condition that they are loaded in certain quantities or packed in certain ways. Further, when the method of packing is given, it is proper that rates per ton should vary with conditions that affect the cost of handling, such as bulk, fragility, liquidity, explosiveness, structure and so on; and also with the speed and regularity of the service required.[1] This point is clearly brought out in one of the decisions of the United States Railway Commissioners. They declared: "Relatively higher rates on strawberries appear to be justified by the exceptional character of the service connected with their transportation. This exceptional service is necessitated by the highly perishable character of the traffic, requiring refrigeration *en route*, rapid transit, specially provided trains, and prompt delivery at destination. There is also involved in this service extra trouble in handling at receiving and delivering points, the "drilling" of cars in a train, reduction of length of trains to secure celerity of movement, partially loaded cars, the return of cars empty, and perhaps other similar incidentals."[2] Finally, it is proper that the rate for carrying from A to B goods that are to go forward to C on the same line should, in general, be less than the rate for so carrying goods destined for consumption at B. In so far as terminal charges are paid for in the rate, this is obvious, because, on the former class of goods, terminal charges at B are saved altogether. Even apart from terminals, however, the journey from A to B, as a part of a longer journey, is less costly than the same journey undertaken as an isolated whole. The reason is that, roughly speaking, the interval of idleness for engines and plant, following upon any journey, involves a cost properly attributable to that journey, and the length of the interval does not vary with the length of the journey which it follows. Thus, "long hauls get more mileage out of

---

[1] Cf. Haines, *Restrictive Railway Legislation*, p. 148.
[2] *Quarterly Journal of Economics*, November 1910, p. 47.

engines, waggons, train-staff, etc., than a number of short hauls, necessarily with waits between; engines and waggons are better loaded, and the line is more continuously utilised."[1] This consideration points to some form of tapering rate for the actual service of carriage, apart from terminal charges. The English classification of merchandise rates accepts this. It provides for one maximum ton-mile rate for the first 20 miles, a lower maximum for the next 30 miles, a still lower one for the next 50 miles, and the lowest of all for further distances. This scale does not include terminal charges, which are fixed independently of distance.[2]

Thirdly, attention must be called to the fact that services, though physically similar, are not necessarily similar in respect of cost, when they are rendered at different times or seasons of the year. This consideration is in practice chiefly important as regards the supply of electricity. In order that it may be possible to provide the current required at "the peak of the load," a large quantity of equipment must be erected additional to what would be required if there were no hours or seasons of exceptional demand. Let us suppose that during one-fifth of the time 2 million units per hour are wanted and during the rest of the time $1\frac{1}{2}$ million units, and that, in consequence, the equipment costs $\frac{4}{3}$ times what it would have done had $1\frac{1}{2}$ million units been required always. Then the real cost of the peak-load current, so far as it depends on cost of equipment, can be calculated as follows: the equipment cost of producing the units needed in the aggregate of off-peak times is $\frac{4}{5}$ times $\frac{3}{4}$ths (i.e. $\frac{3}{5}$ths) of the total equipment cost, and the equipment cost of producing the units needed in peak times is $\frac{1}{5}$ times $\frac{3}{4}$ths of the total equipment cost, plus the whole of $\frac{1}{4}$ of that cost, i.e. $\frac{2}{5}$ths of the whole. That is, the cost of providing 2 million units at the peak is equal to $\frac{2}{3}$rds that of providing 6 million units off the peak: or, in other words, the equipment cost (apart from prime cost) of peak load service is twice as much per unit as the equipment cost of normal service. This shows that simple competition, or the cost of service principle, involves

---

[1] Acworth, *Elements of Railway Economics*, footnote, pp. 122-3.
[2] Cf. Marriott, *The Fixing of Rates and Fares*, p. 21.

different charges for electricity supplied at different times. The same thing obviously holds good of telephone service and cable service—not to speak of hotel and lodging-house service in places that cater specially for seasonal visitors. In industries the product of which can be stored in slack times, and where, therefore, the equipment can be adjusted to produce continuously the average output demanded, these differences should not exceed the cost and the loss of interest involved in storage. Railways, however, at least in the matter of passenger transport, are directly akin to electricity concerns, in that they provide a service which must be produced at the time that it is supplied. Consequently, the cost of service principle would seem to warrant higher fares for travel at busy seasons and at busy hours of the day than are charged at other times. Differential charges of this character are not, of course, exactly adjusted. Indeed, as a matter of fact it so happens that, for other reasons, it is just for the most crowded parts of the day and week that the cheapest tickets (workmen's tickets and week-end tickets) are issued. In a concealed form, however, differential charges of this type do exist: for, when a man travelling as a straphanger in the London Tube at 5 o'clock in the evening pays the same absolute price as he does when travelling in comfort at 3 o'clock, it is obvious that the service which he buys is a very much inferior one. There is just as real a differentiation as there would be if he travelled in equal comfort on both journeys and paid a considerably higher fare at the crowded time.

Lastly, the cost of service principle in some conditions leads logically to lower charges to people whose purchases are continuous than to those who buy intermittently. One reason for this is that a man taking continuous service cannot contribute to the existence of a peak load, whereas one taking intermittent service is likely, in some degree, to do so. Hence, if it is impracticable to charge differential rates directly as between peak and off-peak service, this may sometimes be attempted indirectly by differentiation between continuous and intermittent services. The defence of the practice of issuing season tickets at less than ordinary rates

rests in part on this ground. In the main, however, the cost
of service principle will lead to this type of differentiation
only in industries where special equipment has to be laid down
to enable the service to be supplied to the various customers
severally. Obviously, if this equipment is used rarely, a
greater sum will have to be charged for each act of service
than if it is used frequently. If desired, adjustment can, of
course, be made by exacting a lump charge, or an annual rent,
for the installation of the equipment and, thereafter, charging
the same rate to everybody per unit of service obtained
through it. This is, broadly, the plan in vogue with telephones.
When, however, for any reason this plan is not followed, and
the whole charge is levied through the price of the service,
the cost of service principle necessarily leads to differentiation against customers whose individual load factor is small.
But this consideration has no direct application to railway
rates, since, apart from special sidings for which direct charges
are made, railways do not provide equipment specialised to
the service of particular customers.

§ 3. The results so far obtained are only valid in so far
as transport services sold to different groups of purchasers
are not jointly supplied. If they are jointly supplied, simple
competition, or the cost of service principle, would no longer
imply that, subject to the reservations of the preceding
section, all ton-miles of transportation must be sold at the
same price. It would not imply this any more than it
implies that a pound of beef and a pound of hides must be
sold at the same price. For, when two or more commodities
or services are the joint result of a single process, in such
wise that one of them cannot be provided without facilitating the provision of the other, simple competition evolves,
not identical prices per pound (or other unit) of the
various products, but prices so adjusted to demand that
the whole output of all of them is carried off. Thus, if
the transport of two commodities A and B, or the transport
of commodity A for two purposes X and Y, were joint
products, simple competition might well evolve for them
different rates per ton-mile. It is, therefore, of great importance to determine how far the various services provided

by railway companies are in fact joint products in the sense defined above.

§ 4. Many writers of authority maintain that joint costs play a dominant part in the industry of railway transportation. They believe that the transport of coal and the transport of copper along a railway from any point A to any point B are essentially and fundamentally joint products; and that the same thing is true of the transport from A to B of commodities to be consumed at B and the transport from A to B of commodities to be carried forward to C. This argument is developed by Professor Taussig as follows. First, he observes: "Whenever a very large fixed plant is used, not for a single purpose, but for varied purposes, the influence of joint cost asserts itself."[1] Further: "The labour which built the railway—or, to put the same thing in other words, the capital which is sunk in it—seems equally to aid in carrying on every item of traffic. . . . Not only the fixed capital of a railway, but a very large part, in fact much the largest part, of the operating expenses, represents outlay, not separate for each item of traffic, but common to the whole of it or to great groups of it."[2] The existence of a large mass of common supplementary costs is not, in Professor Taussig's view, by itself sufficient to bring joint supply into action. For that it is essential that the plant be used for *varied purposes*. Thus, he writes: "Where a large plant is used for producing one homogeneous commodity—say steel rails or plain cotton cloth—the peculiar effects of joint cost cannot, of course, appear."[3] Further, he is willing to admit that the transport of tons of different things and the transport of the same thing for different purposes from A to B do constitute, *in one sense*, a single homogeneous commodity, on precisely the same footing as plain cotton cloth. The fact that some "carrying of tons" is sold to copper merchants and some to coal merchants does not imply that two different services are being provided, any more than the fact that some plain cotton cloth is sold to one purchaser

---

[1] *Principles of Economics*, vol. i. p. 221. Cf. also vol. ii. p. 369.
[2] Taussig, "Theory of Railway Rates," in Ripley's *Railway Problems*, pp. 128-9.
[3] *Principles of Economics*, vol. i. p. 221.

and some is sold to another implies that two different commodities are being provided. He holds, however, that these different transports, though homogeneous in one sense, are not homogeneous "in the sense important for the purpose in hand—namely as regards *the conditions of demand*." [1] Thus, his essential contention is that, when a commodity, in the production of which supplementary general costs play a large part, is supplied, not to different people in a single unified market, but in a number of separated markets, the provision to one market is supplied jointly with the provision to the other markets, in such wise that simple competition might be expected to evolve a system of divergent prices.

Now, whether or not the term joint products should be used of services related in the way that Professor Taussig is contemplating is, of course, a verbal question: but whether these services are joint products *in such wise that simple competition might be expected to evolve a system of divergent prices* is a real question. In my view, the conjunction of large common supplementary costs with separation between the markets to which they are supplied does *not* make railway services joint products in this—the only significant—sense. In order that they may be joint products, it is further necessary, not merely that additional investment in plant and so on may be used alternatively to facilitate the supply to either market, but that such additional investment cannot be used to facilitate the supply to one market without facilitating the supply to the other. The point may be illustrated as follows. When cotton goods are provided for two distinct and isolated markets, the costs of furnishing these different markets are, in great part, *common*: for they consist, to a large extent, of the supplementary expenses of the cotton industry, which cannot be allocated specifically to the goods destined for the different markets. A given addition to these costs does not, however, necessarily add anything to the output available for *each* of the two markets. If, before it occurred, the first market received x units of cotton and the second y units, after it has occurred the extra cotton may be divided between them, or it may go wholly to the first, or wholly to the

[1] *Quarterly Journal of Economics*, 1913, p. 381.

second. When, however, cotton fibre and cotton seed are provided for two distinct and isolated markets by one and the same process, a given addition to these costs does necessarily add something to the output available for each of the two markets. In the latter case it is easily seen that simple competition will, in general, lead to divergent prices. In the former case, however, it will not do this. For, if there are a number of competing sellers supplying transportation, or anything else, to several markets with separate demand schedules, and if the price in one of these markets is higher than in another, it is necessarily to the interest of each individual seller to transfer his offer of service from the lower-priced market to the higher-priced market; and this process must tend ultimately to bring the prices in the different markets to a uniform level. This result, *when conditions of simple competition prevail*, obviously holds good independently of the question whether or not the commodity or service under discussion is one in the production of which supplementary costs are large relatively to prime costs. Hence, Professor Taussig's argument cannot be accepted. Joint supply, in the sense in which we are here using the term, does not prevail in the industry of railway transport in that fundamental and general way that he supposes it to do.[1]

---

[1] On the general subject of the relation of the concept of joint costs to railway service, cf. a discussion between Professor Taussig and the present writer in the *Quarterly Journal of Economics* for May and August 1913. One further point should be added. It is sometimes maintained that the concept of joint costs, in the sense assigned to it in the text, is applicable where only one sort of commodity is produced, provided that the units of process, by which the commodity is made, are large relatively to the units of commodity. When, for instance, the marginal unit of process produces 100 units of product, it may be argued that 100 units must yield a price sufficient to remunerate one unit of process, but that it is immaterial to the suppliers by what combination of individual prices the aggregate price of 100 units is made up. This suggestion, however, *when stated in the above general form*, ignores the fact that 100 units of product can be removed, not only by abstracting one unit from the fruit of each of a hundred units of process, but also by abolishing one unit of process, and that, under free competition, if any units of product were refused a price as high as $\frac{1}{100}$th part of the supply price of a unit of process, this latter method of abstraction would naturally be employed. This shows that physically identical products, yielded by the same process at the same time, are not, *in general*, joint products in every sense, even though the marginal unit of the process of production is large. But this reply is not relevant, and the concept of joint supply cannot be ruled out, when the number of units of process that are actually being provided

§ 5. At the same time it should be clearly recognised that, in the services rendered by railway companies, joint supply does play *some* part. This is conspicuously true as between transportation from A to B and transportation in the reverse direction from B to A. The organisation of a railway, like that of a steamship company, requires that vehicles running from A to B shall subsequently return from B to A. The addition of a million pounds to the expenditure on moving vehicles necessarily increases both the number of movements of vehicles from A to B and the number of movements from B to A. This implies true jointness. It follows that a competitive system of railway or shipping rates would not, in general, make the vehicle charges the same for journeys from A to B and from B to A, but the direction, for which the demand was higher, would be charged a higher rate. This is, of course, the reason why outward freights from England are generally low, relatively to inward freights, for commodities of similar value. Our imports being largely food and raw materials, and our exports, apart from coal, mainly finished manufactures, the former naturally make a greater demand for shipping accommodation. If it were not for our coal exports, the disparity would be much greater than it is. There is a similar relation in the transport of goods—though not of passengers—between eastward and westward travel in the United States; because "those who supply the world with food and raw materials dispose of much more tonnage than they purchase." [1] This element

is the minimum number that it is practicable to provide so long as any are provided. In these circumstances there is nothing incompatible with the analysis of the text in regarding the resultant units of product as jointly supplied. The costs of constructing through any region the least expensive railway that it is possible to construct at all are joint costs of all the various items of service rendered by the railway. It is possible by following this line of analysis to reach the results obtained by the different line of analysis to be followed in § 8. In the special problem of the least expensive railway that it is possible to contract at all, the two lines are equally admissible. (Cf. *Quarterly Journal of Economics*, August 1913, p. 688.) Since, however, analysis by way of joint supply is only applicable in a single and peculiar type of problem, whereas analysis by way of discriminating monopoly, to be adopted in the text, is applicable to all problems, the latter method should be given preference.

[1] Cf. Johnson, *American Railway Transportation*, p. 138. It should be noticed that, whereas there is little jointness as between first and third class passenger service on railways, there is probably a considerable element of such

of jointness is, however, of comparatively small importance. Contrary to the general opinion of writers on railway economics, the services provided by railway companies are, in the main, not jointly supplied. Hence, the conclusion emerges that, subject to the reservations set out in § 2, simple competition would, in general, evolve a system of equal ton-mileage rates for all commodities, whatever their character, and whether they are to be consumed at B or sent on from B for some further part of a "long haul."

§ 6. The meaning in concrete form of "the value of service principle," or monopoly *plus* discrimination of the third degree, is more complicated. It was shown in the last chapter that a monopolist adopting this principle will divide the total market served by him into a number of minor markets, by discriminating between which he may make his aggregate advantage as large as possible. It was shown, further, that the kind of division best calculated to promote this end is one under which the separate markets are arranged, so far as practical considerations allow, in such a way that each higher priced market contains as few demands as possible with a demand price lower than the highest demand price contained in the next market. When once the minor markets have been separated, the determination of the rates to be charged in them presents no analytical difficulty, and can be expressed in a simple mathematical formula.[1] It is not, indeed, true, as is sometimes supposed, that the relative rates charged to different markets will depend, if this plan is adopted, simply upon the comparative elasticities (in respect of some unspecified amount of output) of the demands of these markets, nor yet that they will depend simply upon the comparative

---

jointness as between first and third class service on ships : because the structure of a ship necessarily involves the provision at the same time of more and of less comfortable parts of the vessel.

[1] Thus, let $\phi_1(x_1)$, $(\phi_2)x_2$ . . . represent the demand prices in n separate markets and $f(x)$ the supply price.

The prices proper to the separate markets under monopoly *plus* discrimination of the third degree are given by the values of $\phi_1(x_1)$, $\phi_2(x_2)$ . . . that satisfy n equations of the form :

$$\frac{d}{dx_r}[x_r\{\phi_r(x_r)-f(x_1+x_2+ . . .)\}]=0.$$

These n equations are sufficient to determine the n unknowns.

demand prices (also in respect of some unspecified amount
of output) ruling in these markets. The true determinant
is the whole body of conditions represented in the complete
demand schedules of the different markets.[1] Still, though the
determinant is, in general, complex, when once the constitution of the different markets has been settled, it is
precise. The real difficulty lies in the choice, limited, as it is,
by practical conditions, which a railway company has to
make between various possible systems of minor markets.
The search for the most advantageous system—from the
company's point of view—has evolved, in practice, elaborate
schemes of classification both for passenger traffic and for goods
traffic. To show the application of the value of service principle
in practice, some description of these schemes is required.

In passenger traffic, railway companies find the value
of service principle most nearly satisfied by a classification
based, in the main, on the relative wealth of different groups
of persons, the presumption being that most of the demands
for the transport of richer people yield demand prices higher
than most of the demands for the transport of poorer people.
Since it is impracticable to make a classification founded
directly on differences of wealth, various indices or badges,
generally associated with varying degrees of wealth, are
employed. Thus, in the United States, certain railways
make specially low rates for immigrants—lower than those
required from native Americans,—even though the latter are
willing to travel in immigrant cars.[2] In certain colonies
there is a discriminating rate according to the *colour* of the
traveller, black men, who are supposed, in general, to be less
well-to-do, being charged lower fares than white men.[3]
Again, in England, and still more markedly in Belgium,[4]

---

[1] Where the curves representing the demand schedules are straight lines,
this complex determinant dissolves into a simple one, namely, the comparative
demand prices of those units which are most keenly demanded in each of the
several markets. Under these conditions, if constant returns prevail, the
monopoly price proper to each market can be shown to be equal to one half
of the difference between the supply price and the demand price of the unit
that is most keenly demanded there.

[2] *Quarterly Journal of Economics,* November 1910, p. 38.

[3] Cf. Colson, *Cours d'économie politique,* vol. vi. p. 230.

[4] Cf. Rowntree, *Land and Labour,* p. 289.

railway companies charge specially low rates for workmen's tickets. This procedure is exactly analogous to that of those London shopkeepers, who charge to customers with "good addresses" prices different from those charged to others, and of the Cambridge boatmen who used to charge a collective customer of five persons 5s. for the hire of a boat for an afternoon, while to a single person they would let the same boat for one shilling. A classification based on indices of wealth alone is, however, somewhat crude, since people of the same wealth will desire a given journey with very different intensities on different occasions. In recognition of this fact, railway companies have constructed a variety of cross-groupings, based on such incidents as the degree of comfort or of speed with which, or the hour at which, journeys are undertaken, or the presumed purpose which these journeys serve. Thus, the fares for first-class accommodation, or for conveyance by certain express trains, are made to exceed those for inferior accommodation or lower speed by more than the difference in the cost of providing these different sorts of service;[1] and specially low fares are sometimes charged for journeys made in the early morning.[2] In like manner, attempts are made to separate holiday journeys, of presumed low demand, from necessary business journeys, by the supply, on special terms, of tourist, week-end and excursion tickets.

In goods traffic, railway companies find the value of service principle most nearly satisfied by a classification based, in the main, upon the relative value of the different commodities claiming transport, the presumption being that most of the demands for the transport of a more valuable group of goods yield demand prices higher than most of the demands for the transport of a less valuable group. The reason for this presumption is as follows. The demand price for the transport of any n^{th} unit of any commodity from A to B is measured by the excess of the price of that commodity in B over its price in A, which would prevail

---

[1] M. Colson suggests that a plan, under which all trains should take third-class passengers, the fast trains charging a supplement, would be superior to the present continental plan, under which a passenger, who wishes to travel fast, has to pay the whole difference between third and second class fare.

[2] Cf. Mahaim, *Les Abonnements d'ouvriers*, p. 12.

if the said n^{th} unit were not transported. But, on any law of distribution, the probable difference between the prices of any article in A and B respectively, which would arise if these two places were not connected by the assigned act of transport, is greater, the greater is the absolute price that would prevail in either of them; just as the probable difference in the heights of poplars in A and B is greater than the probable difference in the heights of cabbages. There is no reason to expect that the percentage difference will be greater for valuable than for cheap commodities, but there is reason to expect that the absolute difference will be greater. A study of the details of the classification adopted for British railways under the Railway Rates and Charges Act shows that, in the main, the value of the commodities concerned has been taken as a basis. Broadly speaking, the lower the position of any class in the list, the cheaper are the goods that it contains.[1] In like manner, several of the decisions of the United States Railway Commissioners have been founded on the proposition that less expensive articles ought not to be put in a higher class than more expensive articles—chair materials than finished chairs, raisins than dried fruits, and so on.[2]

Sometimes it is practically inconvenient for a company or a regulating authority to group goods directly in accordance with their value. When this is so, a like result can be obtained indirectly by grouping them according to indices, whose differences are likely to correspond to differences of value. Thus, since the valuable qualities of any commodity are generally packed better than the cheap qualities, rates are sometimes made to vary with the elaboration of the packing employed. For example, in France, where good wines are generally packed " en barriques de 220 à 230 litres " and common wines " en demi-muids de 650 à 700 litres ou en wagons-réservoirs," [3] wines in " barriques " are charged on a higher scale.

It must be added that, as with passenger service, so also

---

[1] Cf. Marriott, *The Fixing of Rates and Fares*, p. 27 *et seq.* for these lists.
[2] Cf. *Quarterly Journal of Economics*, November 1910, pp. 13, 15, and 29.
[3] Colson, *Cours d'économie politique*, vol. vi. p. 227.

with goods service, a classification based exclusively on the value of the commodities transported is necessarily somewhat crude. In consequence of this, cross-groupings based upon other incidents have also been employed. Thus, within each group of commodities of given value transported from A to B, a subdivision may be made between those which B can easily make for itself or obtain elsewhere than from A, and those which it cannot so make or obtain; and a higher rate may be charged to the latter group. Again, within a homogeneous group made up of units of the same commodity, sub-groups are constructed. For example, vegetables imported from Germany to England during the weeks before the English crop is ready used to be charged more than vegetables imported from Germany to England after this crop had appeared; and the same thing is true of vegetables sent from the south to the north of France.[1] Sometimes, again, an attempt is made to charge different rates for the transport of the same thing according to the use to which it is to be put—bricks for building, paving bricks and fire bricks being put in different classes. It should be observed, however, that the United States Interstate Commerce Commission has declined to recognise the validity of a classification on this basis.[2] More important is the subdivision according to ultimate place of destination. Thus, commodities sent from A to B, to be consumed at B, are placed in a different group, and charged, for that act of transport, a different rate, from commodities sent from A to B to be forwarded from B to C. The reason is that different parts of the world do not differ in nature in proportion as they differ in distance. There is not much ground for expecting *a priori* that the costs of producing a given commodity in B will differ from the cost in A to a greater extent if A is 500, than if it is 100, miles away. Consequently, the demand for any r^{th} mile's worth of carriage is probably less in long transports of goods than in short transports. This consideration applies with especial force to articles of food and raw material, which are physically adapted to growth over a wide range of

---

[1] Cf. Colson, *Cours d'économie politique*, p. 227.
[2] Ripley, *Railroads, Rates and Regulation*, p. 318.

temperature and climate. But it has some relation to all sorts of goods and is, no doubt, partly responsible for the systems of tapering rates for goods,—but not for passengers,— that prevail in England, France and Germany.[1] The case for discriminating rates is, however, much stronger, when A is connected with C by direct water transport, as well as by a railway from A to B *plus* either more railway or water from B to C. In these circumstances, the demand price of *many* units of transportation from A to B, of any commodity to be consumed at B, is likely to be much higher than the demand price of *any* unit of transportation from A to B, of the same commodity to be carried on from B to C. Grouping in accordance with this fact is responsible for the occurrence of rates from Cheshire to London, for goods imported through Liverpool, much below the rates for corresponding goods originating in Cheshire. On the same principle, "special rates have been granted by the Prussian State Railways for the conveyance of grain traffic from Russia to oversea countries (Sweden, Norway, England, etc.), and the rate per ton per kilometre from the frontier to the German harbours, Königsberg, Danzig, etc., is lower than the charge for German grain between the same points. .... It was pointed out that this specially low rate was granted with the object of securing the traffic to the Prussian railways, as it need not necessarily pass over the Prussian lines, but could go via Riga, Reval, and Libau, and would have done so without this reduction in the rates."[2]

§ 7. We are now in a position to compare the principle of cost of service and the principle of value of service from the point of view of the national dividend. It is well known that, in common opinion, the determination of railway rates by the value of service principle, or, in the alternative phrase, by what the traffic will bear, is unquestionably superior to its rival. The popular view, however, as I understand it, rests, in the main, upon two confusions. The first of these starts from the assumption that the transport of copper and the transport of coal, and the transport from

---

[1] Cf. Marriott, *The Fixing of Rates and Fares*, p. 43.
[2] *Report of the Railway Conference*, 1909, p. 99.

A to B when further transport respectively is, and is not, required, are joint products. . This assumption was proved to be unwarranted in . § 4. It proceeds by means of the further assumption that to charge for joint products rates adapted to comparative marginal demands is to charge in accordance with the value of service principle. This assumption is no less unwarranted than the other. A moment's reflection shows that to charge for joint products in this way would be to follow the guidance of the cost of service principle or— what is another name for the same thing—of simple competition. The second confusion is an *ignoratio elenchi.* Arguments are advanced to prove that the value of service principle, in the proper sense of discriminating monopoly, is superior to simple monopoly. Thus, it is pointed out that, when the conditions are such that the rate most advantageous to himself which the monopolist can make, subject to the condition that equal rates shall be charged for the transport of copper and of coal, will cause him to stop transporting coal altogether while continuing to transport copper at a high rate, the national dividend could be increased by permission to discriminate between the two rates.[1] Such an argument, it is obvious, though valid in its own field, is wholly irrelevant to the question whether discriminating monopoly of the third degree is superior, not to simple monopoly, but to simple competition. When these confusions are swept away, the issue between the value of service principle and the cost of service principle in railway rates is seen to constitute a special case of the general issue, set out in the preceding chapter, between the said discriminating monopoly of the third degree and the said simple competition.

§ 8. The result of the discussion on that issue was that simple competition is, in general, more advantageous. There emerged, however, one set of conditions, in which the advantage lies with its rival. These conditions are that, while no uniform price can be found, which will cover the expenses of producing *any* quantity of output, a system of discriminating prices is practicable, which will make *some* output profitable. They have been illustrated by Principal Hadley,

---

[1] Cf. Ch. XIV. § 12.

T

with special reference to discriminations between the charges for
carriage from A to B, that are made for goods going to B
for consumption at B, and for goods going to B for further
transport to C. "Suppose," he writes, "it is a question
whether a road can be built through a country district, lying
between two large cities, which have the benefit of water
communication, while the intervening district has not." To
meet water competition, the charge for carriage from one
extreme A to an intermediate point B must be low for goods
to be carried forward to the other extreme C; so low that,
if it were applied to all carriage from A to B, it would make
the working of this part of the road unprofitable. But, the
demand for carriage from A to B, in respect of goods to
be retained at B, is so small that this alone cannot support
the road, no matter how low or how high the rates are made.
"In other words, in order to live at all, the road must secure
two different things—the high rates for its local traffic, and
the large traffic of the through points, which can only be
attracted by low rates. If they are to have the road, they must
have discrimination."[1] It is obvious that an exactly analogous
argument can be constructed in favour of discriminations in the
ton-mile rate that is charged on different commodities, when
the conditions are such that, apart from discrimination, there
would be no quantity of transportation units, the proceeds
of whose sale would cover their expenses of production. On
the same principle, it may happen that a roundabout line
ought to be permitted to charge abnormally low rates
between its terminal points, with the effect of preventing the
development of a direct line between these points; for conditions may be such that, apart from this arrangement, no
roundabout line could be profitably built, and so centres
which it might serve would suffer. I have no quarrel with
the proposition that these conditions *may* occur in practice.
Principal Hadley and his followers, however, not content with
demonstrating that they are possible, implicitly add, without

---

[1] *Railroad Transportation*, p. 115. It may conceivably be objected to the
construction of a railway in these circumstances that it will injure the rival
industry of water carriage to an extent that will offset the advantages to which
it leads. This objection can, however, be shown to be inapplicable, so long
as the railway as a whole pays its way. Cf. *ante*, Part II. Ch. VI. § 9.

argument, that they are typical of the whole railway world, and, suppose themselves, therefore, to have proved that the value of service principle ought to be followed in the determination of all railway rates. Such an unargued inference is, plainly, illegitimate. A careful inquiry is necessary concerning the range over which conditions, justifying the value of service principle, are likely to extend in practice.

§ 9. From an analytical point of view, the situation is simple. As explained in the preceding chapter, in order that monopoly *plus* ideal discrimination may create an output where simple competition fails to do so—I take the simplest case, in which the demand in one market is independent of the price in the other—certain relations which were there described between the general conditions of demand and of supply must exist. The conditions enabling monopoly *plus* discrimination of the third degree to lead to this result are less precise. Circumstances, in which ideal discrimination would only just succeed, will not, in general, enable discrimination of the third degree to succeed. We may conclude, roughly, however, that discrimination of the third degree will have a good chance of succeeding—a chance that is better, the more numerous are the markets between which discrimination is made, and the more satisfactory, from the monopolist's standpoint, is their constitution—when the conditions are such that ideal discrimination would succeed with a wide margin. Our problem is to determine how far this state of things is likely to occur in practice.

First: it has been shown that the likelihood of this is greatest in forms of investment in which the law of increasing returns acts strongly. Among railways there is ground for believing that, at all events until considerable development has been reached, this condition is generally satisfied. The reason is that the fixed plant of a railway cannot, in practice, be so made as to be capable of effecting less than a certain considerable minimum of transportation. The aggregate costs of arranging for rail transport for one ounce per week are very nearly as great as those of arranging for the transport of many thousand tons. For the same heavy expenditure must be undertaken for surveying and legal charges, bridging valleys and torrents, tunnelling through rock, erecting stations and platforms, and so on. This implies increasing returns acting strongly till a large investment has been made, and afterwards less strongly. So far, therefore, conditions in which discriminating monopoly would prove superior to simple competition are more likely to occur in railway service than in some other industries.

Secondly, it has been shown that the likelihood of discriminating monopoly yielding some output when simple competition yields none is greatest in forms of investment where the demand for the product is elastic. In railway service, when once rates have been brought down to a moderate level, there is reason to believe that a small reduction of rates would call out a large increase of demand, not only from commodities that might otherwise have been transported by some other machinery, but also from commodities that otherwise would not have been transported at all. In other words, there is reason to believe that the condition of elastic demand is, in general, satisfied. Here, too, then, it may be said that railway service is more apt to yield conditions suitable for discriminating monopoly than some other industries.

Granted, however, both that increasing returns act strongly until considerable density of traffic has been attained, and that the demand for the service of railway transport is elastic, these conditions alone are by no means sufficient to ensure that discriminating monopoly would evolve some output, while simple competition would fail to do this. It is necessary, further, that the actual levels of demand price and supply price for a small quantity of service—more generally, the demand schedule and the supply schedule as a whole—shall be related in a particular way. Clearly, if the demand price for a small quantity is greater than the supply price, some output will be evolved under simple competition, and, therefore, the conditions we have in view do not arise. Clearly, again, if the demand price for a small quantity is very much less than the supply price, it is unlikely that any output will be evolved either under simple competition or under discriminating monopoly, and, therefore, again these conditions do not arise. In order that they may arise, a sort of intermediate position must, it would seem, be established. Thus, on the one hand, the district affected must not be too busy and thickly populated; on the other hand, it must not be too little busy and sparsely populated. There is a certain intermediate range of activity and population that is needed. This range, compared with the total range of possibility, is naturally not extensive. Hence, the probability that the conditions necessary to make discriminating monopoly more advantageous to the national dividend than simple competition will be present in any railway selected at random at any time seems *a priori* to be very small. There are, indeed, many *dicta* of practical experts which suggest that they have in fact a wide range. But, as Professor Edgeworth, who lays stress upon this point, recognises, " the testimony of high authorities would, no doubt, carry even greater weight if it should be repeated with a full recognition of the *a priori* improbability" to which it is opposed.[1]

§ 10. It must be observed, however, that, as population and aggregate wealth in any country expand, the demand schedule for railway service, along any assigned route, gradually rises. Hence, though, at any moment selected at random, it is improbable that the conditions affecting any route, selected at random, are such that a railway rate system, based on the value of service principle, would be more advantageous to the dividend than one based on the "cost of service principle," it is not improbable that any route, selected at random, will *pass through a period* during which the conditions are of this kind. Such conditions tend to emerge when one point in the growth of wealth and population has been reached, and to disappear when another somewhat later point has been reached. If the cost of service principle ruled universally, and if no State bounties were given, certain lines would not be built till the arrival of the latter point—when there is hope of "building up" a demand by experience of supply, this point need not, of course, be such that the railway pays at the moment—

---

[1] *Economic Journal*, 1913, p. 223.

despite the fact that they could have been built, with
advantage to the community, on the arrival of the earlier
point. The inference is that discrimination, or the value
of service principle, should be adopted when any route is
in the intermediate stage between these two stages, and that
this principle should give place to simple competition, or the
cost of service principle, as soon as population has grown
and demand has risen sufficiently to lift it out of that stage.[1]
The period proper to the value of service principle would
seem, in most ordinary lines, to be a comparatively brief one.[2]

§ 11. Even this limited application of the principle is
only warranted on the assumption that there is no third way
between the pure value of service principle and the pure cost
of service principle. In fact, however, there is a third way.
The cost of service principle may be maintained and the State
may give a bounty. Plainly, with the help of a bounty exactly
the same effect in speeding up the building of a railroad could
be accomplished under the cost of service principle as would
be accomplished under the value of service principle without
a bounty. The community as a whole would be providing
out of taxes the necessary profit for the railway, which, on
the other plan, would come from the charges made to the
people who buy the most highly-charged freight service.

[1] Mr. Bickerdike (*Economic Journal*, March 1911, p. 148) and Mr. Clark
(*Bulletin of American Economic Association*, September 1911, p. 479) argue, in
effect, that the transition from the one system to the other should occur, not
when rising demand lifts the railway in question out of the stage just described,
but when, if ever, it rises so high as to impinge on that point of the supply
curve, at which a negative slope passes into a positive one. There is not, in
my opinion, any adequate ground for this view.

[2] It is possible to maintain, on lines similar to the above, that, after a
railway has been built, and has reached the stage of profitable working on the
cost of service principle, another stage will presently arrive, at which a return
to the value of service principle would enable a second track to be laid down
with advantage to the community, though, under a rate system based on the
cost of service principle, such an extension would not as yet be profitable to
the company. This argument justifies the establishment of a system of
discriminating rates, *to be applied to traffic carried on the new track only*; and
a modification of it justifies the establishment of such a system, to be applied
exclusively to traffic carried in any *additional* train or truck which, apart from
discrimination, it is just not worth while to run. In practice, however, it is
impossible to apply the value of service principle in this limited way. If it is
introduced for the traffic proper to the second track or the extra truck, it must,
in real life, be introduced for all the traffic carried on the line. The argument
set out above does not justify this.

Since the building of the railway is in the general interest, it would seem, on the whole, to be fairer that the taxpayers, and not a special class of traders—or rather, in the end, the consumers of these traders' products—should provide these funds. In view of the obvious awkwardness of changing from a discriminating to a non-discriminating system of rates when the intermediate stage described in the preceding paragraph is passed, the plan of giving a bounty for a time and withdrawing it when it is no longer needed, is also superior from the side of administrative convenience. If, on account of the indirect advantages of cheap railway transport in facilitating the division of labour between different parts of the country, making possible the development of large-scale localised industries, and, through the improved communication of markets, lessening local price fluctuations—all changes which in one way or another benefit production—it is held that the railway industry is one to which a general bounty should be accorded permanently, it is obvious that a second instrument for doing what bounties can do by themselves is not required, and that no place is left for the value of service principle.

§ 12. Of the relative advantages of the cost of service principle, or prices proper to simple competition, and the value of service principle, or prices proper to discriminating monopoly, this is all that need be said. There is, however, yet another possible arrangement. Control might be exercised in such a way that a railway company should only secure competitive or normal profits on the whole, but these profits might be obtained by a combination of some charges below cost with others above cost, just as a doctor's profits are obtained by a combination of low prices to poor patients and high prices to rich patients. In one field of railway service there is a plain *prima facie* case for an arrangement of this kind. Great social advantage can be derived from the provision of cheap workmen's tickets: for in favourable circumstances this makes it possible for workpeople to live in the country, though working in towns, and thus to bring up their children in healthy surroundings.[1] Such provision can be

---

[1] In Belgium the system of cheap workmen's tickets, which has been carried to great perfection, seems to act in this way. (Cf. Rowntree, *Land and Labour,*

ensured if railway companies (whose earnings are supposed to
be kept down by regulation to a normal competitive level) are
compelled to make it, and are allowed to recoup themselves
by "monopolistic" charges upon other traffic.   Plainly, however, exactly the same result can be achieved if the reimburse-
ment required for the railway companies is provided out of the
national revenue.   There seems to be no good reason for
throwing this burden upon persons who make use of the
service of railways rather than upon the general body of tax-
payers.   For, though it may well be that railway service is a
suitable object through which to impose a tax on these persons,
we can hardly suppose that the extent to which they ought
to be taxed through this object exactly corresponds to the
amount of funds required for the bounty to poor purchasers of
railway service.   There is still less reason for allowing discriminated rates, determined not in the purchasers' interest,
but at the choice of the railway companies themselves.   Hence,
this system of discriminated charges coupled with regulated
profits cannot, on the whole, be justified.   We are thus left
with the cost of service principle modified at need, sometimes by general bounties, sometimes by bounties on particular
services deliberately sold for less than cost price.

§ 13. One last point remains.   To apply this cost of
service principle accurately involves, as was shown in § 2, a
number of delicate adjustments.   For the principle leads, not
to a single price for everybody, but to prices that vary with
the incidental costs attaching to each service and with the time
at which it is provided in relation to the peak of the load.
To provide for these adjustments in practice is often a very
difficult matter involving costly technique and account-keeping.
It is, therefore, always a question how near to the ideal it is
desirable to approach ; at what point the advantage of getting

---

p. 108.)   Dr. Mahaim offers some confirmation of the view that it acts so in the
fact that Belgium is a land of "large towns" rather than of "great cities," a
much larger proportion of the population living in communes of from 5000 to
20,000 inhabitants in that country than in France or Germany (*Les Abonnements
d'ouvriers*, p. 149).   At the same time, Dr. Mahaim admits that the cheap
tickets have also an adverse effect.   "On commence par aller à la ville ou à
l'usine en revenant tous les soirs ou tous les samedis chez soi ; puis on s'habitue
peu à peu au nouveau milieu, et l'on finit par s'y implanter" (*ibid.* p. 143).   In
fact the cheap tickets "apprennent le chemin de l'émigration."

closer is outweighed by the complications, inconveniences, and expense involved in doing so. In the early days of the telegraph service, the desire for simplicity and ease in rate making led to a system in which flat rates were charged for the use of instruments, without any reference whatever to the number of calls made; and water rates are even yet often based, not on any measurement of the supply that is actually taken, but on an estimate of what is likely to be taken, derived from the rental of the houses served. For electricity, while ingenious meters have been devised, which not only record the supply taken, but also weight more heavily the part of it which is taken in the peak hours, nevertheless the high cost of any sort of meter still causes the service of small houses to be charged in many districts on a flat unmetred rate. In like manner, though for the transport of parcels it has been thought worth while to take account, in the charges made, of those differences in the cost of service which arise out of differences of weight, for the transport of letters this is not done : and for neither parcels nor letters are charges adjusted to the distance (within the British Empire) over which they have to be conveyed. On similar grounds of simplicity and cheapness, a railway administration, which had decided to base its rating system upon the cost of service principle, must, nevertheless, ignore, within considerable limits, differences in the weight of luggage which different passengers carry. This class of consideration shows that there is not necessarily any departure from the spirit of the cost of service principle when a railway administration elects to utilise a system of zone tariffs. A street railway system obviously must do this; for the mere fact that there is no coin smaller than a farthing makes it physically impossible to fix different fares for every different distance of journey. So long as the zones are narrow, zone tariffs on ordinary railways have an equally good defence. If, however, the zones are made broad, the cost of service principle is deliberately violated. A system under which the rates are the same for all places in broad zones involves substantial differentiation in favour of firms situated far from their markets, as against firms situated nearer to them. In effect, it confers upon them a kind of bounty at the expense of their rivals. It was, indeed, shown in Chapter VIII. that differentiation in favour of one source of supply as against another source may, in certain circumstances and if introduced in a certain manner, be advantageous to the national dividend. The sort of differentiation that results from the zone system is, however, random differentiation, not specially designed to favour a carefully chosen list of selected firms. It is, thus, on the average, like differentiation in favour of one set against another set of *similar* firms. This sort of differentiation can easily be shown to imply the production (including transport) of some part of the commodity concerned at greater real cost than is necessary; for the marginal real costs of producing anything in the distant source and bringing it to the market must necessarily be greater than the marginal real costs of producing it in the nearer source and bringing it to the market.[1] It is possible to maintain that the direct loss resulting from this may be balanced by the effect of the zone system in scattering the producing firms belonging to an industry, and so making combination, with the opportunity this gives for anti-social monopolistic action, more difficult.[2] But this argument does not appear to have great force. It is not, in itself, desirable to check the formation of large productive units, since such units introduce economies. As will be argued presently, it would seem a better policy to attack the evil consequences of monopolistic action, which combination threatens, directly, rather than indirectly by attempts to discourage unification.[3]

[1] Cf. *Quarterly Journal of Economics*, February 1911, pp. 292-3, 297-8 and 300; also *Departmental Committee on Railway Rates*, p. 10.
[2] Cf. *Quarterly Journal of Economics*, May 1911, pp. 493-5.
[3] Cf. *post*, Chap. XVIII. § 2.

CHAPTER XVI

§ 1. The results of the preceding chapters make it plain that, in many industries, neither simple competition, nor monopolistic competition, nor simple monopoly, nor discriminating monopoly will lead to equality in the values of marginal trade net products in different fields, and, hence, through a consequent equality in the values of marginal social net products, to the maximisation of the national dividend. It will have been noticed, however, that the systems so far investigated have all been systems under which goods are produced by one set of people and sold to another set. The failures of adjustment, to which they lead, have, therefore, all been dependent on this fact. Hence, the question naturally arises; Could not these failures be eliminated by the device of voluntary groups of purchasers undertaking for themselves the supply of the goods and services they need ?

§ 2. Now, the essence of a Purchasers' Association, whether it is formed of the consumers of finished goods or of producers who will utilise their purchases in further production, is that its policy is directed to maximise aggregate purchaser's benefit *minus* aggregate costs. It must, therefore, tend to produce just that quantity of output which equates demand price and marginal supply price, and so, except where others besides the purchasers of any commodity are affected by its production, it must make the value of the marginal social net product of investment in the occupation covered by it equal to the value of the marginal social net product of resources in general. Consequently, other things being equal, it must eliminate, in great measure, the disharmonies belonging alike to monopoly and to simple competition. This preliminary abstract statement does not, however, solve our problem. It is not enough to know that, *if other things are equal*, Purchasers' Associations will advantage the national dividend. Before we can infer anything from this about the effect of these Associations in actual life, we need to inquire how they compare with ordinary commercial businesses in crude economic efficiency; for it is clear that any advantages, which a Purchasers' Association may possess in price policy, are liable to be outweighed if it is inefficient on the productive side.

§ 3. As a prelude to this task, it is desirable to guard against certain confusions. First and most obviously, we need to rule out all appeals to the superior efficiency, in certain fields, of Purchasers' Associations, as compared with the members of these Associations operating as isolated individuals. It is easy to point to services, which many persons need in small individual lots, but which can be produced much more economically in large lots. An obvious example is the service of marketing agricultural products of variable quality produced in small quantities by small farmers. For economical selling requires careful grading of qualities and a fairly continuous supply of each grade; and small farmers, who attempt individually to market their butter or their eggs, are not operating on a large enough scale to meet these requirements satisfactorily. Thus, Mr. Rider Haggard writes of Denmark: "In 1882 what was called 'peasant butter' fetched 33 per cent less than first-class butter made on the big farms, but in 1894 the co-operative butter, which, of course, for the most part comes from the peasant farms, took more medals and prizes than that from the great farms, and what used to be called second and third class butter ceased to exist as a Danish commodity of commerce."[1] The fact, however, that, for this kind of reason, the manufacture of butter, the curing of bacon, and the marketing of eggs "afford a splendid opening for the application of co-operative principles," is irrelevant to the present issue, since these things also afford a splendid opening for the

[1] *Rural Denmark*, pp. 195-6.

application of commercial principles.[1] It is true that a Purchasers' Association can work in this field much more cheaply than a single small farmer; but, exactly the same thing is true of an ordinary commercial firm, undertaking to sell the service of marketing to these farmers. Two examples are given by Sir R. H. Rew. "One is the French butter trade. This has been built up by the merchants in Normandy and Brittany—some of whom are Englishmen—who purchase the butter at the local markets from the individual farmers, and work it up in their blending houses. Another instance is the poultry trade in the Heathfield district of Sussex. There the system is that the fatteners, or 'higglers' as they are termed, purchase and collect the chickens from those who rear them; they are then duly fattened, killed and prepared for market, and again collected by the carrier or railway agent by whom they are forwarded to London and other markets. Both these are instances of complete organisation without co-operation."[2] Secondly, we must refrain from stressing unduly the history of English Co-operative Stores. The reason is that, when the device of Purchasers' Associations was introduced into the field of retail trading, it is very doubtful if the rival method was fairly represented.[3] Partly in consequence of the imperfect competition between different shops, not all the economies that were available had been taken up. Even from their own point of view, "retailers

---

[1] In like manner, the charge that the development of Purchasers' Associations on the part of groups of persons other than ultimate consumers may make possible monopolistic action against these consumers is irrelevant; for, so also may the development of commercial firms.

[2] Rew, *An Agricultural Faggot*, p. 120.

[3] Care must be taken, however, not to treat as waste in the work of retailing those costs that are necessarily involved in the kind of retailing that the public chooses to ask for. "Imagine that every one intending to buy a pair of shoes or a suit of clothes was called on to send notice of his proposed purchase a week or two in advance, to give a preliminary account of the thing wanted, and then to accept an appointment for a stated place or time at which the purchases must be made. It is easy to see how the work of retailing could be systematised, how the selling force would be kept constantly employed, how stocks would be kept to the minimum. As things now stand, we pay heavily for the privilege of freedom in the use of our time, for vacillation and choice, for the maintenance of a stock and a staff adequate for all tastes and all emergencies. It is common to speak of the waste of competition; much of it is in reality the waste necessarily involved in liberty" (Taussig, *American Economic Review*, vol. vi. No. 1 Supplement, 1916, p. 182).

as a body kept far more shops than was necessary, spent far too much trouble and money in attracting a few customers, and then in taking care that those few customers paid them in the long run—the very long run—for those goods which they had bought on credit, or, in other words, had borrowed; and for all this they had to charge. . . . Retail trade was the one accessible business—Dr. Marshall was probably not thinking of house-keeping and domestic cooking as a business —in which there were great economies to be effected." [1] This view of the matter is fortified by Professor Pareto's observation, that retail shops were easily ousted by the competition, not only of *sociétés co-opératives*, but also of *les grands magasins.*[2] A comparison between retail trading, as it stood when our consumers' stores came into being, and these stores cannot, therefore, be accepted with confidence as a conclusive test of the relative merits of the industrial forms they represent. It is like a comparison between a member of one race whom there is some reason to suspect of being less healthy than the average of his compatriots and a thoroughly sound member of another. No great weight, therefore, can reasonably be attached to historical examples, and we are driven forward to an analytical study.[3]

§ 4. In attempting, from this point of view, to estimate the economic efficiency of Purchasers' Associations, we may observe, first, that these Associations are, in structure, a form of Joint Stock Company. Like any other Joint Stock Company, a Purchasers' Association is owned by share-holders, and is controlled by a manager under the supervision of a committee elected from among the shareholders. The alternatives to it are the private business and the ordinary commercial company. In attempting to compare its economic efficiency with theirs, we naturally look to the organisation of the management. Under this head the Purchasers'

---

[1] Marshall, *Inaugural Address to the Co-operative Congress*, 1889, p. 8.

[2] Cf. *Cours d'économie politique*, p. 274.

[3] It should be added that, *even if other things were equal*, the payment of a dividend by a co-operative society trading at the same price as another concern would not prove greater efficiency of management; for, if, as is common, the society proceeded to a greater extent on a system of cash sales, the dividend would *pro tanto* be simply payment to purchasers of interest on their earlier discharge of indebtedness.

Association and the commercial company alike are inferior to the private business, just in so far as Boards of officials lack the opportunities for quick action and the stimulus of personal possession belonging to the private business.[1] But the Purchasers' Association is likely, in some degree, to make up for this deficiency through the ardour instilled into the manager and the committee by the fact that they are engaged in a service suited to evoke public spirit. The Purchasers' Association may, in fact, utilise the altruistic motives, alongside of the egoistic, as a spur to industrial efficiency. Against this consideration, however, there has to be set a second. In so far as Purchasers' Associations consist of poor persons, unaccustomed to large business, there is a danger that they may grudge adequate salaries to managers, and so may be forced to employ less able men than commercial companies. Furthermore, their committee-men are drawn from a more limited area, and are apt to possess less business experience than the directors of commercial companies. These conflicting influences will, of course, have different weights in different circumstances.

Secondly, when any section of a country's industry is given over to monopolistic competition, ordinary commercial businesses are bound to engage in much wasteful expenditure on advertising in the manner described in Chapter VI. § 12. In this respect Purchasers' Associations are in a much more favourable position. When the services they provide consist of such things as the purchase of agricultural feeding stuffs or manures, or the work of wholesale trading, they are practically assured, without any direct effort on their part, of the whole demand of their members. When they provide the service of packing eggs, or curing bacon, or converting milk and cream into cheese and butter, their members may, indeed, sometimes be tempted by an offer of better terms to go elsewhere, but it is

---

[1] In the United States, where the President of a company often holds a very large individual interest, it appears that he sometimes acts on behalf of the company, just as a private owner would do. "Generally speaking, the President of an American Corporation acts just as freely and energetically on behalf of his company as he would on his own behalf" (Knoop, *American Business Enterprise*, p. 26). He only consults the directors when he wishes to do so.

possible for the Societies, by making "loyalty" within limits a condition of membership, in great measure to restrain such action without resort to advertisement. When they provide the service of retailing or of granting credit, the enforcement of loyalty by rule is, indeed, impracticable, and is not attempted; but even here loyalty will in fact be largely maintained through the members' sense of proprietary interest in their own shop. Among non-members, no doubt, when it is desired to extend the range of any Association's business, advertisement of one sort or another may be necessary. The Purchasers' Association, however, has a considerable advantage over an ordinary Joint Stock Company, because it is able to offer to those who join it, not only cheap goods, but also a certain sense of part ownership in an important corporate institution. Such advertisement as it does undertake, therefore, is likely to prove more effective, and less of it is needed to achieve a given result. By so much its efficiency is, *ceteris paribus*, greater than that of its rivals.

Thirdly, there is another way, besides the saving of advertisement costs, in which the "loyalty" referred to in the preceding paragraph makes for economy. It enables the work of a co-operative concern to be conducted steadily without those large fluctuations, to which private concerns are often subject and the presence of which inevitably involves cost. Thus, the rule insisting upon loyalty as a condition of membership of co-operative bacon factories and creameries enables these establishments to count on a constant supply of raw material with greater confidence than private firms can do;[1] and, in like manner, the practice of the English and Scotch

---

[1] In the Danish co-operative bacon factories loyalty is generally enforced by a provision to the effect that members shall deliver all their saleable pigs (with certain specified exceptions) to the factory for a period of seven years, unless in the meantime they remove from the district (Rew, *An Agricultural Faggot*, pp. 123-4). In like manner many Irish dairying societies provide that "any member who shall supply milk to any creamery other than that owned by the society for the space of three years from the date of his admission to membership, without the consent in writing of the Committee, shall forfeit his shares together with all the money credited thereon" (*Report on Co-operative Societies* [Cd. 6045], 1912, p. xxxix). It will be noticed that in these classes of societies—and it is only in them that loyalty is enforced in the rules—the use of a considerable plant makes the maintenance of a steady demand a more important influence in eliminating cost than it would be in, say, an agricultural purchasing society.

Wholesale Societies and of local Retail Associations, in concentrating the constant part of their demand upon their own productive departments and throwing the variable part upon outside traders, greatly lessens the fluctuations to which these productive departments are exposed. No doubt, the economies which co-operative concerns secure in this way have, from a national point of view, to be balanced against any diseconomies that may be caused to outside concerns by increased fluctuations thrown upon them; and so are not a net gain to the nation. To the co-operative concerns themselves, however, they are a net gain. Moreover, in so far as the aggregate demand or supply of a market is constant, and fluctuations in the parts are due to other causes than fluctuations in the whole, the introduction of steadiness in one part cannot increase, but necessarily diminishes, the fluctuations of other parts. Hence it is probable that a considerable part of the economies which co-operative concerns derive from loyalty represent a net increase in efficiency for the community as a whole as well as for themselves.

Fourthly, the relation that is set up between the various members of a Co-operative Society greatly facilitates the dissemination among them of knowledge about the best methods of production. Thus, Sir Horace Plunkett observes of the work of the Irish Department of Agriculture : "It was only where the farmers were organised in properly representative societies that many of the lessons the Department had to teach could effectually reach the farming classes, or that many of the agricultural experiments intended for their guidance could be profitably carried out."[1] And the root of the matter is reached by Mr. Fay when he writes : "Both the co-operative society and the firm are trading bodies, and they will not pay the farmers more than their milk is worth. But, whereas the firm's remedy is to punish the farmer by the payment of low prices, the society's remedy is to educate him so that he may command high ones."[2]

Fifthly, when in any field of industry there is an element of bilateral monopoly, ordinary commercial businesses and their customers, respectively, are driven to expend energy, if

---

[1] *Ireland in the New Century*, p. 241.
[2] *Co-operation at Home and Abroad*, p. 164.

U

not money, after the manner described in Chapter VI. §§ 13-15, in attempts to get the better of one another. When a Purchasers' Association exists, this class of expenditure is likely to be reduced. In co-operative retail stores, as Dr. Marshall has observed, the proprietors, since they are also the customers, have no inducement to adulterate their goods, and costly precautions to prevent such adulteration are therefore unnecessary.[1] The gain is no less clear in societies providing for their members the services of insurance and the retailing of loans. The insurance contract is conditional on some event happening to the buyer; the loan contract is conditional on the buyer's promise to repay. In the one case, the buyer may gain at the seller's expense by simulating, or even by voluntarily bringing about, the event provided against; in the other, he may gain by deliberately breaking, or by so acting as to render himself unable to perform, his promise. Now, it is, of course, true that individual buyers are able to gain by this class of conduct, not only when the relation of identity between buyers and sellers collectively does not exist, but also when it does exist. The point, however, is this. Under the Joint Stock form of industrial organisation the fraudulent or quasi-fraudulent conduct of one buyer does not matter to the other buyers, and can, therefore, only be guarded against by an elaborate and continuous system of inspection. Under the Purchasers' Association form, however, the other buyers are directly injured by such conduct, and are, therefore, interested to prevent it. If, then, the Purchasers' Association consists of neighbours, all will, incidentally and in the course of the ordinary conduct of life, constitute themselves voluntary and unpaid inspectors of each. In this way small local Purchasers' Associations for the supply of insurance or the retailing of loans are, in effect, free from a substantial part, not merely of the nominal, but also of the real, costs that Joint-Stock Companies, attempting to furnish these services, would be compelled to bear. In so far as people are less willing—apart altogether from the prospect of success—to try to defraud a Mutual Association than a commercial company, the gain under this head is increased.

§ 5. The various advantages that have been enumerated above

---

[1] Cf. Inaugural Address to the Co-operative Congress, 1889, p. 7.

suggest that there is a wide field over which Purchasers' Associations are likely to prove at least as efficient as any other form of business organisation. And in many important departments of industry they have proved their fitness by prosperous survival. This is, true of the so-called supply associations often formed by farmers—associations, that is to say, which supply to their members the service of marketing from manufacturing firms such things as manure, seeds and agricultural machinery. It is true of the agricultural selling societies which provide such services as the sorting, grading, selling and packing of eggs or of butter. It is true of the Co-operative Creameries, which play so important a part in Denmark and in Ireland, and whose services include a manufacturing as well as a marketing operation. And, last but not least, it is true of the general organisation based on consumers' stores, which provides for the retailing, wholesaling, and sometimes even the manufacturing of staple household goods (including houses themselves) for large agglomerations of working people with fixed homes.

§ 6. Even, however, in departments of work where experience gives good hope of efficiency and success, it does not follow that Purchasers' Associations will always come into being. Very poor people may lack the initiative and understanding needed to form one. When the population is migratory, attempts are especially unlikely to be made — a circumstance which explains why co-operative stores "have seemed to shun capital and seafaring towns." Better-to-do persons, while fully competent to develop Purchasers' Associations, if they had the wish, may, in fact, not have the wish. With commodities on which they only spend a very small part of their income at rare intervals—commodities that are luxuries to the main body of purchasers—the possible savings may be too small to be worth while. Or again, even when they are worth while, it may be possible to get an equivalent advantage in some other less troublesome way. British tenant farmers, for example, with their traditional right to appeal to the squire in times of difficulty for a reduction of rent, are slow to overcome their, native individualism for the (to them) relatively small advantages of co-operation with their neighbours. No doubt, encouragement may be given to them

by State action. Thus, in Canada "in 1897 the Dominion
Department of Agriculture established a system by means of
which loans were made to farmers who undertook to organise
themselves into Butter and Cheese Manufacturing Associations
and to send their produce to Co-operative Creameries equipped
by means of the loans. The Department undertook to
organise the management of these creameries, and to manufacture and sell the butter for a fixed charge of four cents
(2d.) per lb., an additional charge of one cent per lb. being
made for the amortisation of the loans."[1] But this device is
obviously of limited scope. Moreover, there are a number of
very important sorts of work to which the Purchasers'
Association form of organisation is plainly unsuited. Whenever a large speculative element is present, whenever, in other
words, much uncertainty has to be borne, this factor of production will not be readily forthcoming from organised
purchasers. For, if capital has to be ventured at a hazard, the
people who venture it will expect to exercise control and to
harvest the profits more or less in proportion to their venture.
Associations that raise capital at fixed interest and distribute
surplus in accordance, not with investment, but with purchases,
do not enable them to do this. The graded machinery of
debentures, preference shares and ordinary shares furnished by
joint-stock companies is much more satisfactory. In risky
undertakings, therefore, Purchasers' Associations will not work.
Nor will they work as regards commodities and services for
which economy demands centralised production, but of which
the purchasers are spread over wide areas. The idea, for
instance, that the services now rendered by the cotton industry
could be provided satisfactorily by any arrangement of
Purchasers' Associations is plainly fantastic. We conclude,
therefore, that, though the Purchasers' Association, as a means
of overcoming the evils of ordinary competitive and ordinary
monopolistic industry, has, undoubtedly, an important part to
play, the field open to it is limited in extent, and the study
of further remedies is, therefore, still required.[2]

---

[1] Mavor, Report on the Canadian North-West, p. 44.
[2] For a full discussion of the various forms of co-operative activity, *vide* Fay,
Co-operation at Home and Abroad. I am also indebted to Mr. Fay for useful
criticism and suggestion in connection with the revision of this chapter.

CHAPTER XVII

§ 1. OVER the large field of industry, where voluntary Purchasers' Associations are not an adequate means of overcoming those failures in industrial adjustment which occur under the more ordinary business forms, the question arises whether the magnitude of the national dividend might not be increased by some kind of governmental intervention, either by the exercise of control over concerns left in private hands or by direct public management. In the present chapter we are concerned, not with the comparative merits of these two sorts of intervention, but with the broadest aspects of intervention generally.

§ 2. It is natural at first sight to look for light on this question from the experience of the war. The urgent national need for enlarged supplies of munitions, home - grown food, ships, and certain other articles, led to extensive State intervention in production. National productive establishments were set up, and private establishments were controlled and sometimes accorded special grants to enable them to expand their operations; while the Board of Agriculture took powers to encourage, and, if need be, to compel, increased cultivation of land, and also provided a number of facilities in the way of soldiers' and prisoners' labour and specially imported machinery to assist farmers. A study of what was accomplished under these and other heads would, indeed, be of great interest. But it would not really do much to help our present inquiry. The difference between war and peace conditions is too great. In those four years of strain the underlying motive of the main part of the Government's industrial action was to force capital, enterprise and labour forthwith, and at no matter what cost, into the production of particular urgently needed things. Nobody denies that, when there is a shortage of anything relatively to the demand for it, this fact by itself always tends to stimulate people to direct their efforts towards producing that thing rather than other things. But this reaction is usually a slow one; and in the Great War the essential requirement was always speed. The principal purpose of government assistance and coercion was to secure this; to surmount at once by direct attack obstacles that, in the ordinary course, could only be turned by a slow and gradual movement. And the need for such action was, of course, intensified in industries where the Government itself, by artificially keeping down prices, had removed what would normally have been the main stimulus to private efforts after increased production. With the end of the war all this has been changed. The problem of national economy is no longer to effect an instantaneous transformation, but to maintain a steady stream of production at the smallest cost. Nor is this the only difference. On the one hand, the thing aimed at by Government during the war was fundamentally different from what it would be in normal times. Products were wanted of uniform types and in enormous quantities for the direct use of the Government itself. No evidence that governmental interference was effective for this end could demonstrate its competence for the quite different end proper to normal times, namely, to help ordinary citizens to satisfy their current needs with reasonable economy. On the other hand, the various controls set up by Government were necessarily improvised in a great hurry in a time of abnormal difficulty and pressure. No evidence that interference in these conditions was wasteful or ineffective could prove that it would display the same defects in the more favourable conditions of normal life. For these reasons war experience can afford very little real guidance, and our problem must be attacked by other means.

§ 3. For some persons the obvious approach towards it is blocked by the supposition that there are certain industries, those, namely, that make use of the right of eminent domain, such as railway service (national and street), gas-lighting, electric supply, water supply and so forth, with which governmental authorities have a special title to interfere, over and above what they possess in connection with other industries. This supposition is erroneous. It is true that the exercise of eminent domain practically implies monopoly, since neither State nor municipal authorities are at all likely to allow double parallel interference with streets and highways. But this circumstance only puts these public utility services into the general class of monopolistic services: it does not render them different, in any essential respect, from services that have come into that class—like the oil and steel industries in America—in quite other ways. Thus, eminent domain is in no way a condition precedent, either to governmental management, or to governmental control-through a licence. Public slaughter-houses, licensed premises for the sale of intoxicants and the system of licensed cabs in London are practical illustrations of this fact. The broad question of policy is different, according as we are concerned with monopolistic or with non-monopolistic industries; it is different again, within monopolistic industries, according as discriminating prices are, or are not, practicable; but it is the same, *ceteris paribus*, whether the industry concerned does or does not require to exercise the right of eminent domain. No doubt, as will appear presently, undertakings at the start of which this right has to be exercised, since they necessarily come into contact with the public authorities in their first beginnings, and therefore can be brought under control at once before any vested interests have grown up, can be subjected to State intervention much more easily than others. This distinction of practice is very important, but it is not, and should not be treated as, a distinction of principle.

§ 4. It is clear that there has already emerged a *prima facie* case for governmental intervention in regard to industries of a monopolistic character. The case, however, cannot become more than a *prima facie* one, until we have considered the qualifications, which governmental agencies may be expected to possess for intervening advantageously in this

class of matter. It is not sufficient to contrast the imperfect
adjustments of unfettered private enterprise, with the best
adjustment that economists in their studies can imagine.
For we cannot expect that any State authority will attain,
or will even whole-heartedly seek, that ideal. Such authorities
are liable alike to ignorance, to sectional pressure, and to
personal corruption by private interest. A loud-voiced part
of their constituents, if organised for votes, may easily
outweigh the whole. This objection to public intervention
in industry applies both to intervention through control of
private companies, and to intervention through direct public
operation. On the one side, companies, particularly when
there is continuing regulation, may employ corruption, not
only in the getting of their franchise, but also in the execution
of it. "Regulation does not end with the formulation and
adoption of a satisfactory contract, itself a considerable task.
. . . As with a constitution, a statute, or a charter, so with
a franchise. It has been proved that such an agreement
is not self-enforcing, but must be fought for, through a term
of years, as vigorously as at the time of formulation and
adoption. A hostile, lax, or ignorant city council, or even
a State legislature, may vary the terms of the agreement
in such a manner as totally to destroy or seriously to impair
its value."[1] For this, the companies maintain a *continuing
lobby*. "It is from them that the politicians get their
campaign funds."[2] This evil has a cumulative effect; for
it checks the entry of upright men into government, and
so makes the corrupting influence more free. On the other
side, when municipalities themselves work enterprises, the
possibilities of corruption are changed only in form. "The
new undertakings proposed by the municipalisers would lead
to dealings to the extent of many million dollars with tradesmen, builders, architects, etc., to the increase, by hundreds, of
important offices, and to the employment of tens of thousands
of additional public servants. Party leaders would have their
proportion of increased patronage. Every public official is a

---

[1] *Municipal and Private Operation of Public Utilities* (Report to the National
Civic Federation, U.S.A.), vol. i. p. 39.
[2] Bemis, *Municipal Monopolies*, p. 174.

potential opportunity for some form of self-interest arrayed against the common interest."[1]

§ 5. The force of this argument for non-interference by public authorities, is, clearly, not the same at all times and places; for any given kind of public authority will vary, alike in efficiency and in sense of public duty, with the general tone of the time. Thus, during the past century in England, there has been "a vast increase in the probity, the strength, the unselfishness, and the resources of government. . . . And the people are now able to rule their rulers, and to check class abuse of power and privilege, in a way which was impossible before the days of general education and a general surplus of energy over that required for earning a living."[2] This important fact implies that there is now a greater likelihood that any given piece of interference, by any given governmental authority, will prove beneficial than there was in former times. Nor is this all. Besides improvement in the working of existing forms of public authority, we have also to reckon with the invention of improved forms. This point may be put thus. The principal disadvantages of municipal and national representative assemblies, as organs for the control or the operation of business, are four in number. First, in the United Kingdom—though this statement is hardly true of Germany,—these bodies are primarily chosen for purposes quite other than that of intervention in industry. Consequently, there is little reason to expect in their members, any special competence for such a task. Secondly, the fluctuating make-up of a national government or of a town council is a serious handicap. Sir W. Preece wrote: "I have the experience of electric lighting in my mind. Large municipalities overcome the difficulty by forming small and strong committees and selecting the same chairman, and thus maintain a kind of continuity of policy. Small corporations start with very large committees; they are constantly changing, and the result is that you find, sometimes inability to agree upon the system to be used, sometimes inability to agree upon the means to be employed to

---

[1] *Municipal and Private Operation of Public Utilities*, vol. i. p. 429.
[2] Marshall, "Economic Chivalry," *Economic Journal*, pp. 18-19.

conduct the service; and it is incessant trouble and squabble."[1]   Secondly, this incident of fluctuating membership may lead to action based on short views—views bounded by the next election, instead of looking to the permanent interests of the State.   Thirdly, the areas, to which public authorities are severally allocated, are determined by non-commercial considerations, and, consequently, are often likely to prove unsuitable for any form of intervention with the working of an industry.   It is well known, for example, that attempts, on the part of some municipalities to regulate, and of others to operate, the service of street-traction and the supply of electrical power have suffered greatly from the fact that these services, since the development of modern inventions, can be organised most economically on a scale much in excess of the requirements of any one municipality. Finally, as indicated above, regular governmental agencies, in so far as they are elective bodies, are obviously liable to injurious forms of electoral pressure.   These four disadvantages are all serious.   But all of them can be, in great measure, obviated.   The first, second and fourth are practically done away with under a system of municipal government such as prevails in Germany, where the burgomasters and aldermen, corresponding to the English chairmen of committees, are whole-time paid experts with practically permanent tenure of office.   All four disadvantages can be overcome, perhaps, even more effectively by the recently developed invention of "Commissions," that is to say, bodies of men appointed by governmental authorities for the express purpose of industrial operation or control.   An example of a Commission for operation is afforded by the Railway Department of New South Wales, and one of a Commission for control by the Interstate Railway Commission of the United States.   The members of these Commissions can be specially chosen for their fitness for their task, their appointment can be for long periods, the area allotted to them can be suitably adjusted, and their terms of appointment can be such as to free them, in the main, from electoral pressure. It may be added that the system of Commissions also, in great

[1] H. Meyer, *Municipal Ownership in Great Britain*, p. 258.

part, escapes a further important objection to intervention in industry by municipal councils. This objection, as stated by Major Darwin, is that such intervention "lessens the time which these bodies can devote to their primary and essential duties, and, by increasing the unwillingness of busy men to devote their time to public affairs, it lowers the average administrative capacity of the Local Authorities."[1] When industries are operated or controlled by special public Commissions, this objection is inapplicable. The broad result is that modern developments in the structure and methods of governmental agencies have fitted these agencies for beneficial intervention in industry under conditions which would not have justified intervention in earlier times.

[1] Darwin, *Municipal Trade*, 102.

§ 1. IN the course of Chapters V.I., VII., and VIII., reference was frequently made to devices, by which the State could interfere, where self-interest, acting through simple competition, failed to make the national dividend as large as it might be made. Apart from governmental operation of the industries concerned, and apart also from penal legislation in extreme cases, these devices were fiscal in character and consisted in the concession of bounties or the imposition of taxes. Where self-interest works, not through simple competition, but through monopoly, fiscal intervention evidently ceases to be effective. A bounty might, indeed, be so contrived as to prevent restrictions of output below what is socially desirable, but only at the cost of enabling the monopolist to add to his already excessive profits a large ransom from the State. In the present chapter, therefore, I propose to consider what methods are available under conditions of monopoly. For simplicity of exposition, I shall ignore the qualifications set out in Chapter VIII. and proceed as though simple competition might still be believed, as it was believed by some of the more rigid followers of the classical economists, to make the national dividend a maximum. The State, then, contemplating a monopoly or the possibility of a monopoly, may be supposed to contrast the dividend under it with the dividend under simple competition. Its problem will be, not to make things perfect, but to make them as good as they would be if monopolistic power were not at work.

§ 2. In some departments of production, roughly those

departments where monopolistic power is liable to be introduced through the development of industrial combinations, it is open to the State, if it chooses, to aim at preventing monopoly power from arising, or, if it has arisen, at destroying it. The original Federal Anti-Trust Law (1890) of the United States, commonly known as the Sherman Act, was overtly directed against actions "in restraint of trade or commerce among the several States," but was interpreted in the earlier decisions of the Supreme Court as an Act banning all combinations large enough to possess a substantial element of monopolistic power. Thus, Justice Harlan's judgment in the Northern Securities Case, 1904, asserted that "to vitiate a combination, such as the Act of Congress condemns, it need not be shown that the combination in fact results, or will result, in a total suppression of trade or in a complete monopoly, but it is only essential to show that by its necessary operation it tends to restrain interstate or international trade or commerce, or tends to create a monopoly in such trade or commerce and to deprive the public of the advantages that flow from free competition."[1] The Clayton Law of 1914, while making no further provision as regards combinations that had already been formed, follows the line of this interpretation as regards the formation of new combinations in the future. It lays it down, not only that no person shall be a director of more than one large bank or large corporation, but also that no corporation shall acquire (acquirements already made are not affected) the whole or part of the stock of any other corporation, when the effect of such acquisition may be substantially to lessen competition, or to restrain commerce in any section of the community, or to tend to the creation of a monopoly in any line of commerce. This general policy—trust prohibition and trust breaking—seems, however, to be open to three serious objections.

First, it is a policy exceedingly difficult to enforce in an effective manner. The legislature and the courts may succeed in getting rid of certain forms of combination, but the result will often be merely the appearance of other forms—possibly of forms which, as would happen if an

[1] Jenks and Clark, *The Trust Problem*, p. 295.

informal price-fixing agreement took the place of a complete amalgamation, sacrifice the merits, without getting rid of the demerits, of those which preceded them. The declaration of the Supreme Court of the United States, that the granting of a power of attorney to common trustees by a number of companies was *ultra vires*, led, in some industries, to the purchase of a majority of stock in each of the companies by the said trustees, and, in others, to the substitution of a holding company for a Trust. Governmental attacks on holding companies can easily be met either by complete consolidation, if this is not also made illegal, or by dissolution into separate companies, each subject to the same controlling interest. The Austrian law against Kartels likely to injure the revenue abolished Kartels possessed of a central office; but only with the result of substituting informal understandings. A recent British Committee on Railway Agreements and Amalgamations sums up the situation thus: "While Parliament may enact that this must be done and that must be prohibited, past experience shows that even Parliament appears to be powerless to prevent two parties, either by agreement or without formal agreement, from abstaining from a course of action, namely, active competition, that neither party desires to take. Parliament can, of course, refuse to sanction Bills authorising the amalgamation or working union of two or more railway companies, and may provide that certain classes of agreement shall be invalid or even illegal. But it cannot prevent railway companies [and, of course, the same thing is true of industrial companies] coming to understandings with each other to adopt a common course of action, or to cease from active competition."[1] The recent policy of the United States Government and Courts, in forcing the dissolution of monopolistic companies into their constituent parts and providing at the same time various regulations to prevent these becoming subject to a common control, may, indeed, for a time be more effective, and, even though it does not succeed in stimulating real competition among men formerly colleagues, yet may, by its harassing

---

[1] *Departmental Committee on Railway Agreements and Amalgamations,* 1911, p. 18.

effect, make the task of forming new combinations less attractive. It is alleged, for example, by Professor Durand, that no new combinations have been formed since the Government began to bring suits under the Sherman Act.[1] This policy, however, is too recent to afford much scope for generalisation. It may still be claimed, as the teaching of experience ·as a· whole, that laws aimed directly at "maintaining competition" have very small prospect of succeeding in their purpose.

There is a second serious objection to this policy. The root idea lying behind it is that competition implies a condition of things, in which the value of the marginal social net product of investment in the businesses affected is about equal to the value of the marginal social net product elsewhere. But, passing by the qualifications to this view set out in Chapters VL and VIII., we have to note that the competition, from which the above good result may be expected, is "simple competition," whereas the competition, to which laws against combination lead, will very probably be monopolistic competition, namely, competition among a *few* competitors. With railway combinations this result is certain; for the number of railways plying between any two given centres is necessarily very small. With industrial combinations the issue at first sight seems more doubtful, since there is no such necessary limitation in the number of industrial concerns of any given type. When, however, we reflect that combination can rarely be organised except in industries where, as a matter of fact, the number of leading firms is small, the force of this objection is much reduced. Among industrial combinations, as well as among railway combinations, dissolution is much more likely to lead to monopolistic than to simple competition. It has been shown, however, in Chapter XII., that monopolistic competition does not tend to bring about an output of such a magnitude that the value of the marginal net product of investment in the industry affected is equal to

---

[1] *American Economic Review Supplement*, March 1914, p. 176. For a full account of American anti-Trust Laws and Cases cf. Davies, *Trust Laws and Unfair Competition.*

that prevailing elsewhere. On the contrary, the output is indeterminate. When the competitors hope to destroy or to absorb one another, we may get " cut-throat competition," under which production is carried so far as to involve absolute loss; and the chance of this is made greater by the desire of one giant business to win even a barren victory over another. In short, even if the conditions were such that laws for " maintaining competition " could really prevent combination, they would still be unable to secure the establishment of competition in that sense in which alone it can be expected to evolve the level of prices and rates which is most advantageous to the national dividend.

Even now, however, the case against the policy we are considering is not exhausted. There remains a third objection. Combination is not the parent of monopoly only, but also, very often, of incidental benefits. Thus, as was observed in Chapter XI., a combination, which is large relatively to the market in which it trades, has more inducement than a small single seller to adopt a policy of developing demand among potential customers, since it may reckon on receiving a larger proportion of the gain resulting from any investments it may make with this object. In addition to this, a large combination will often enjoy certain economies of production, which, if the Government were to adopt a policy of maintaining active competition, would fail to emerge. No doubt, some of those forms of Kartel agreement, under which a proportion of the market is guaranteed to the several members, since they tend to conserve weak firms, which competition would "naturally" destroy, not only fail to yield economies, but actually yield diseconomies.[1] It should be observed, however, that pooling agreements do not necessarily act in this way.

[1] Cf. Walker, *Combinations in the German Coal Industry*, p. 322. Mr. Walker points out, however, that this tendency, at all events in the Ruhr Kartel, is smaller than appears at first sight, since the large mines, by sinking more shafts and by buying up small mines, can increase their "participation" (*ibid.* p. 94). Morgenroth, in his *Export politik der Kartelle*, emphasises this point in regard to Kartels generally. He points out further that the anti-economic effects of Kartels are mitigated by their tendency to lead to the development of "mixed works," which refuse to admit any limitation in their output of raw stuff to be worked up in their own further products Thus, among these important mixed works the selective influence of competition is not restrained by agreements (*loc. cit.* p. 72).

The British Committee on Trusts (1919), for example, reports that in a great many associations there is an arrangement under which firms, on producing less than their quota, receive from the pool 5 per cent in value upon the amount of their deficiency. It was urged by some witnesses that this arrangement had the effect of driving weak firms out of the industry by the economical method of pensioning, instead of the more costly method of fighting them.[1] Against this, indeed, we have to set the fact that the money to provide the pensions has to be obtained by some kind of tax on firms that exceed their quota—a necessary discouragement to them. Moreover, some forms of pool, by making the profits of each severally depend on the efficiency of all collectively, may lead to relaxed energy and enterprise. But, on the other hand, in all combinations that involve any measure of common management, savings of the kind referred to in Chapter XI. are bound to accrue in greater or less degree.[2] In a peculiar industry like the telephones, where the actual thing supplied to A is improved if B draws his supply from the same quarter, the advantage is especially great. It may also be considerable in more ordinary industries. *Inter alia*, weak or badly situated plants are apt to be shut down much more quickly than they would be under competition; while, among those that remain, the purposive force of "comparative cost accounting" is apt to stimulate the energy of managers more strongly than the blind force of market rivalry could ever do.[3]

We must, indeed, be on our guard against exaggerating the importance of these economies. For, if by combina-

---

[1] Report of the Committee on Trusts, 1919, p. 3.

[2] Cf. Liefmann's statement : "Verschiedene grosse Unternehmungen erwarben nämlich diese kleinen Zechen nur um ihrer Beteiligungsziffer im Syndikat willen, legten sie aber dann still und förderten deren Absatzquote auf ihren eigenen Schächten billiger. War dies auch natürlich für die betroffenen Arbeiter und Gemeinden sehr nachteilig, so ist doch zu berücksichtigen, dass diese kleinen Zechen bei freier Konkurrenz längst zugrunde gegangen wären. Höchstens kann man sagen, dass dann die Still-legung und die Entlassung der Arbeiter sich weniger plötzlich vollzogen hätte und länger voraussehbar gewesen wäre" (*Kartelle und Trusts*, pp. 61-62).

[3] Cf. Macgregor, *Industrial Combination*, p. 34. This device rules prominently in the United States Steel Corporation (Van Hise, *Concentration and Control*, p. 136). An elaborate account of it is given by Jenks in the *U.S.A. Bulletin of Labour*, 1900, p. 675.

tion we mean existing combinations, it is necessary to recollect that, since the magnitude of the unit of control is determined by monopolistic considerations as well as by considerations of structural and other economies, this unit is often larger than the unit of maximum efficiency. If we mean only such combinations as it would be profitable to form *de novo*, were the exercise of monopolistic power wholly excluded, combination will, indeed, evolve the unit of maximum *immediate* efficiency, but that unit will very likely prove too large when ultimate indirect effects, as well as immediate effects, are taken into account. For this there are two reasons. The first is that a producer controlling the main part of any industry, in considering the wisdom of adopting any mechanical improvement, is tempted to take account, not merely of the direct positive yield to be expected from capital invested in that improvement, but also of the indirect negative yield in lessening the returns to his existing plant. But, if he does this, he will, as was shown on pp. 164-5, be holding back from improvements, which it is to the interest of the national dividend that he should adopt. A monopoly makes no proper use—at all events is under temptation to make insufficient use—of that invaluable agent of progress, the scrap heap.[1] The second reason is that indicated in Chapter VII., namely, that large combinations, by lessening the opportunities for training in the entrepreneur function, which are available when men who have done well in one company can be passed on to more responsible work in another, and by weakening the stimulus to keenness and efficiency, which is afforded by the rivalry of competing concerns, tend indirectly to prevent the average level of business ability from rising as high as it might otherwise do.

The qualifications which these considerations suggest are of great importance. They tell strongly against the claim made by Professor Clark, when he writes: "A nearly ideal condition would be that in which, in every department of industry, there should be one great corporation, working without friction and with enormous economy, and *compelled to give to the public the full benefit of that economy.*"[2] Neverthe-

---

[1] Clark, *The Control of Trusts* (revised edition), p. 14.
[2] *The Control of Trusts*, p. 29.

less, there can be little doubt that, *in some circumstances*, the combination of competing institutions into "Trusts" and consolidations that dominate the market does involve, even from a long-period point of view, considerable net economies.[1] These economies *may* be so great that the favourable effect produced by them on the dividend exceeds the unfavourable effect due to the exercise of monopolistic power. Attempts to determine, by a comparison of prices, or of "margins" between prices and the costs of material, before and after the formation of any combination, whether or not this has actually been so, are inevitably baffled by inability to allow for changes in manufacturing methods and the utilisation of by-products, or to gauge accurately the—probably abnormal—price conditions that ruled immediately before the combination was formed.[2] Analysis, however, enables us to say that, under increasing and diminishing returns alike, combination would, on the whole, increase output and lower prices, provided that the economies were so large that, had they been introduced without monopolisation, they would have raised output to about double its former amount.[3] Economies so large as this are, no doubt, improbable, and I do not, therefore, seriously claim that the abolition of combination in any department of industry would often make the dividend actually smaller than it is at present. I do claim, however, that such abolition would often be more injurious than the retention of combination *plus* the abolition of monopolistic action.

§ 3. A second line of policy which it is open to the State to pursue is as follows. Instead of endeavouring, by obstruct-

---

[1] Professor Durand argues in favour of a policy of Trust-breaking that, in general, the business units evolved apart from combination would be large enough to secure practically all the structural and other economies of production available to Trusts (*Quarterly Journal of Economics*, 1914, p. 677 *et seq.*). It should be observed, however, that, even if this were true, the policy of Trust-breaking would not be shown to be superior to one of depriving Trusts of monopolistic power: for *both* policies would then lead to the establishment of business units of a size yielding maximum efficiency. In fact, however, it is plainly not true in all industries; and, when it is not true, Trust-breaking leads to the establishment of units too small to yield maximum efficiency.

[2] For these reasons the admirable price studies in Jenks's *Trust Problems* are hardly adequate to support the favourable judgment as to the effect of combinations that he rests on them.

[3] This proposition is exactly true on the hypothesis that the curves of demand and supply are straight lines.

ing combination, to prevent industrial concerns from becoming possessed of monopolistic power, it may seek, by conserving *potential* rather than actual competition, to make it to their interest to leave that power unexercised; the idea, of course, being that, if they know new competitors will come into the field should prices become high enough to yield abnormal profits, they will have no inducement to charge more than " reasonable " prices. The policy to which this line of thought leads is that of penalising the use of "clubbing" devices, whose repute might otherwise drive potential competitors away. Among these devices the two principal are cut-throat competition, as described in Chapter XII., and various forms of boycott, namely, the exercise of pressure upon third parties not to purchase services from, or sell services to, a rival seller on terms as favourable as they would have offered to him if left to themselves.[1]

§ 4. It is obvious that the weapon of cut-throat competition, or, as it is sometimes called, " destructive dumping," when practised by a business already large enough to monopolise any department of industry, must prove overwhelmingly powerful against newcomers. The monopolist necessarily possesses immense resources, and these can be poured out, in almost unlimited quantities, for the destruction of a new, and presumably much less wealthy, intruder. This is especially clear when a monopolist, dealing in many markets or in many lines of goods, has to do with a competitor dealing only in a few; for in these conditions the competitor can be destroyed by a cut, made either openly or through a bogus independent company,[2] that affects only a small part of the

---

[1] The weapon of boycott can also be used to force upon retailers an agreement to maintain the prices of particular goods sold by them at a level dictated by the manufacturers of the goods. It would seem that manufacturers do not wish quality articles to be sold too cheap to consumers, lest they should "lose caste" with them. But probably their main motive is the knowledge that, if the goods are made into "leaders," on which the retailers make scarcely any direct profit, and which serve merely to advertise other wares, the retailers will tend not to push their sale (Taussig, *American Economic Review*, vol. vi. No. 1 Supplement, 1916, pp. 172-3).

[2] This method is alleged to have been practised by the Standard Oil Company. The object, of course, is to obviate a clamour from customers in other markets for a similar cut on their purchases. (Cf. Davies, *Trust Laws and Unfair Competition*, p. 319.)

monopolist's business. An extreme example of this kind of cut is given in the statement of certain opponents of the Standard Oil Trust, "that persons are engaged to follow the waggons of competitors to learn who their customers are, and that then they make lower offers to those customers; and it is still further asserted that at times the employés in the offices of rivals are bribed, to disclose their business to the Standard Oil Company."[1] It is needless to emphasise the immense power of this weapon. "After two or three attempts to compete with Jay Gould's telegraph line from New York to Philadelphia had been frustrated by a lowering of rates to a merely nominal price, the notoriety of this terrible weapon sufficed to check further attempts at competition."[2]

§ 5. The weapon of boycott has a narrower range than that of cut-throat competition. It is worked through a refusal to deal, except on specially onerous terms, with any one who also deals elsewhere. When the worsened terms attached by a dominating seller to dealings with himself are more injurious to the client than the loss of that client's other dealings, the monopolist can force the client to boycott his rivals. In order that he may be able to do this, the goods or services that he offers for sale must be rendered, by nature or by art, non-transferable;[3] for it is impossible to hurt a customer by refusing to sell to him, if he is able to purchase through a middleman the goods which are refused to him by the monopolist. Hence, when nature does not cause non-transferability, there must be stringent conditions about re-sales in the contracts between the monopolist and any intermediary agents, if such there are, who intervene between him and the ultimate consumers. But non-transferability is not sufficient by itself. It is necessary, further, that the rival producer's possible supply *to one recalcitrant consumer* at current prices shall be very small. Usually, of course, though any one seller's output is likely to be small relatively to the total consumption of the market,

---

[1] *U.S.A. Industrial Commission,* I. i. p. 20.

[2] Hobson, *Evolution of Modern Capitalism,* p. 219.

[3] Cf. my paper, "Monopoly and Consumers' Surplus," *Economic Journal,* September 1904, p. 392.

it is many times as large as that of any representative single consumer.   Where this is so, recalcitrant consumers can successfully counter a refusal to sell on the part of the monopolist by purchasing all that they want from outside competitors and leaving to non-recalcitrants the whole output of the monopolist.   This consideration is not, however, entirely fatal to the weapon of boycott, because, in many industries though by no means in all,[1] producers deal with their customers indirectly through wholesalers or further manufacturers or transporters, who purchase individually a considerable mass of products.   When intermediaries of this kind are present, effective boycott may become practicable.

First, a boycott can be forced when the commodities or services supplied by the monopolist consist, not in a single kind of good, but in several goods, and when, among these several goods, there are one or more for which the demand is very urgent, and of which the monopolist has, through patents or reputation (e.g. brands of tobacco) or otherwise, exclusive control.   A good example is furnished by the boot and shoe trade, in which certain firms control important patents.   The patented machines are not sold, but are let out on lease, under "conditions which debar manufacturers from employing these machines save and except in conjunction with other machines supplied by the same controlling owners . . . one of the conditions being that the latest machines must not be used for goods which have, in any other process of manufacturing, been touched by machines supplied by other makers."[2]   This kind of boycott is also illustrated by the "factors' agreement," which makers of popular proprietary goods sometimes secure from retailers.

Secondly, a boycott can be forced where it is important for purchasers—here as before, the purchasers are, in general, manufacturers—to be able to get the service that they need

---

[1] Thus, Jenks (U.S.A. Bulletin of Labour, 1900, p. 679) states that "about half the combinations reporting sell direct to consumers."

[2] Times, 8th February 1903.   Cf. Appendix to the Report of the (British) Committee on Trusts, 1919, p. 27.   Action of this kind is directly prohibited in Australia under the Patents Act of 1903. (Cf. Davies, Trust Laws and Unfair Competition, p. 247.)   The British Patents Act of 1907 permits it only provided that the lessee is given an opportunity of hiring the patented machine without the tying clauses on "reasonable," though not, of course, equal terms.

immediately the need arises, and where an ordinary supplier, though producing much more service in the aggregate than any single purchaser wants, may not be producing more than such a purchaser wants at some definite single moment. This condition is realised in the transport for goods which are so perishable, or for which the demand is so instant, that transport, to be of use, must be available at the moment when it is asked for. It is in the transport by sea of goods of this kind that the method of boycott has been most fully elaborated. The transport of goods, which are in fairly steady demand and which have no need of speedy delivery, can be arranged for by purchasers, if they wish, wholly through tramp steamers; but the transport of urgent goods cannot be so arranged for, because tramps and small lines cannot guarantee regular sailings.[1] Hence, it comes to be practicable for shipping rings to force a boycott against independent lines. They usually accomplish this through " deferred rebates." [2] Of these there are two degrees. In the West African Shipping

---

[1] Cf. *Royal Commission on Shipping Rings*, Report, p. 13. The commissioners suggest that it is for this reason that the deferred rebate system is not applied to our outward trade in coal or to the greater part of our inward trade, which consists of rough goods, but only to those cargoes for which a regular service of high-class steamers is essential. (Cf. *ibid.* p. 77.)

[2] This method has been described by the Royal Commissioners on Shipping Rings thus: "The Companies issue a notice or circular to shippers informing them that, if at the end of a certain period (usually four or six months) they have not shipped goods by any vessels other than those despatched by members of the Conference, they will be credited with a sum equivalent to a certain part (usually 10 per cent) of the aggregate freights paid on their shipments during that period, and that this sum will be paid over to them, if at the end of a further period (usually four or six months) they have continued to confine their shipments to vessels belonging to members of the Conference. The sum so paid is known as a deferred rebate. Thus in the South African trade at the present day the amount of the rebate payable is 5 per cent of the freight paid by the shipper. The rebates are calculated in respect of two six-monthly periods ending with the 30th June and 31st December respectively, but their payment to the shipper is not due until a further period of six months has elapsed, that is to say that, as to shipments made between the 1st January and the following 30th June, the rebates are payable on the 1st January following, and, as to shipments made between the 1st July and the 31st December, the rebates are payable on the following 1st July. It follows that in this instance the payment of the rebate on any particular item of cargo is withheld by the shipowners for at least six months, and that, in the case of cargo shipped on the 1st January or 1st July, it is withheld for a period of twelve months. If during any period a shipper sends any quantity of goods, however small, by a vessel other than those despatched by the Conference Lines, he becomes disentitled to rebates on any of his shipments by Conference vessels during that period and the preceding one" (Report, pp. 9-10).

Conference and in all the Conferences engaged in the trade with India and the Far East, the rebates are paid to exporting merchants only, on condition that these merchants have not been interested in any shipment by rival carriers, but there is no requirement that the forwarding agent, through whom the merchant may have acted, shall have dealt exclusively with the Conference in respect of the goods of his other clients.[1] In the South American Conferences, however, "the form of claim for rebates has, in the case of goods shipped through a forwarding agent, to be signed by such agent as well as by the principal, and, if the forwarding agent has not conformed to the conditions of the rebate circular in all his shipments for all his clients, claims to rebates are invalidated."[2]

Thirdly, a boycott can be forced when the intermediary, whom a monopolist wishes to use as his instrument, is, not a manufacturer or a wholesaler purchasing that rival's goods, but a railway company conveying them. When an alternative route for his own goods is available, the monopolist, by threatening the railway with the withdrawal of his custom, is sometimes in a position to compel it to charge differential rates against his rival. In the boycott engineered by the Oil Trust it is even asserted that the railways were compelled to hand over a part of the extra charges levied on their rivals to the executive of the Trust.[3] A boycott of this kind may also be operated through banks, pressure being exerted upon them to refuse loans to a rival producer.

§ 6. Attempts to prevent the use of cut-throat competition, *i.e.* destructive dumping, by legal enactment are confronted with the difficulty of evasion. The American Industrial Commission recommended that "cutting prices in any locality below those which prevail generally, for the purpose of

---

[1] *Royal Commission on Shipping Rings*, Report, pp. 29-30.

[2] *Ibid.* p. 30. The decision of the House of Lords in the Mogul Steamship Co. case, 1892, was to the effect that the party injured by an arrangement of this kind had no ground of action for damages, but it did not, it would seem, necessarily imply that the combination against which action was brought was itself lawful (Davies, *Trust Laws and Unfair Competition*, p. 234). In a similar case in the German Imperial Court (1901), an injunction against discrimination was granted (*ibid.* p. 262).

[3] Cf. *The Great Oil Octopus*, p. 40 ; Ripley, *Railroads, Rates and Regulation*, p. 200.

destroying local competition," should be made an offence.
Any person damaged was to have the right to sue for penalties,
and officers were required to prosecute offenders.[1] It is plain,
however, that, even when it is possible, as it is with public
service corporations, to insist that tariff rates shall be regularly
published, evasion may be practised by unpublished discounts
and rebates to particular customers; nor, since discovery is
unlikely, will the enactment of heavy penalties against
breaches of the law necessarily secure obedience thereto.[2]
Where destructive dumping is threatened, not by public
service corporations, but by industrialists engaged in the
manufacture of many commodities at different places, the
enforcement of regular published rates is impracticable.
Hence, the problem confronting the legislator demands the
unravelling of still more tangled knots. Where the form
of destructive dumping which is employed is that of price-
cutting limited to the local market of a particular competitor
or group of competitors, the offence is at least definite, though,
especially when worked through a bogus independent company,
it may be extraordinarily difficult to detect. Against destructive
dumping of this kind *operated by foreigners* the Governments
of Canada (1904) and South Africa (1914) have endeavoured
to guard their citizens by anti-dumping legislation, providing
that, when goods are imported at prices substantially below
the contemporary prices ruling at home, these goods shall be
subjected to a special import duty equivalent to the difference
between the home and foreign prices.[3] This legislation,
however, hits, not merely destructive dumping in the sense
here defined, but also (1) the clearing of surplus stock on a

---

[1] *United States Industrial Commission*, vol. xviii. p. 154.

[2] It is instructive to read in M. Colson's great work (*Cours d'économie
politique*, vol. vi. p. 398) that abusive discriminations "semblent être devenus
bien plus rares en Angleterre qu'en Amérique, bien que l'Administration y ait des
pouvoirs beaucoup moins étendus et que les pénalités y soient moins sévères,
parce que l'entente entre Compagnies y est admise par la loi; au contraire, en
Amérique, les pouvoirs publics s'efforcent d'empêcher les accords qui mettraient
fin à la concurrence, cause essentielle des inégalités de traitement, et par suite ne
sont pas arrivés, jusqu'ici, à déraciner celles-ci."

[3] For these laws cf. Davies, *Trust Laws and Unfair Competition*, pp. 550-1.
Australia (1906) has a more complicated law which condemns dumping in the
Canadian sense, along with certain other forms of importation, under the
general head of unfair competition, and meets it with a penalty, not a special
duty.

foreign market at less than home prices in periods of depression, and (2) the permanent selling abroad at the world price, by a foreign monopolistic producer, of goods for which at home he is able to charge monopoly prices. The policy of discouraging the former, of these two practices is one whose merits are open to debate, but clearly there is nothing to be said for discouraging the second—except, indeed, the least tenable of the things that can be said in favour of all-round protection. The United States Government, wishing to direct its legislative blows against destructive dumping exclusively, included in the Federal Revenue Act, of 1916, the following modified version of the Canadian anti-dumping law. In Section 801 of the Act it is enacted: "That it shall be unlawful, for any person importing or assisting in importing any articles from any foreign country into the United States, commonly and systematically to import, sell or cause to be imported or sold such articles within the United States at a price substantially less than the actual market value or wholesale price of such articles, at the time of exporting to the United States, in the principal market of the country of their production, or of other foreign countries to which they are commonly exported, after adding to such market value or wholesale price freight, duty and other charges and expenses necessarily incident to the importation and sale thereof in the United States. Provided, that such act or acts be done with the intent of destroying or injuring an industry in the United States or of preventing the establishment of an industry in the United States or of restraining or monopolising any part of the trade or commerce in such articles in the United States." Offences against this clause are penalised, not, as in Canada, by a special duty, but by fines or imprisonment. We need not concern ourselves here with the difficult problems which legislation of this kind provides for the officials charged with ascertaining the relevant facts—including, as these do under the United States law, the motive actuating foreign sellers—and for those who have to detect and prevent the evasive use of nominally independent agents, on whose account goods may be imported at full price, thereafter to be sold at less than was

paid for them. The main point for our present purpose
is that,· when, as in the conditions which this legislation
contemplates, destructive dumping is attempted by inter-
local price discriminations, the task of preventing it is *relatively*
easy, because there is something definite to go on. When,
however, as, in domestic trade, often happens, we have to do
with cuts made on *all* sales of a particular line of goods, the
offence is not definite ; for, clearly, not all cuts are destructive
dumping, and it is difficult to distinguish among them the
innocent from the guilty. One authoritative writer proposes
as a test that, "·if the price of the particular grade of goods
were first put down and then put up again, and if rivals were
crushed in the interval, this would be evidence that the
purpose of the cut was illegitimate."[1]   Such a test has been
attempted in the American Mann-Elkins Railway Law of 1910,
which provides that, "when a railway reduces rates between
competitive points, it shall not be permitted to increase the
rates on the cessation of the competition, unless it can satisfy
the Commission that the conditions are changed otherwise
than by the mere elimination of water competition."[2]   There
is a similar provision in the American Shipping Act of 1916
as regards shipping charges in interstate trade.[3]   But this
test cannot be pushed very vigorously ; for, if it were, any
firm, which lowered prices in a time of depression or for
purposes of experiment, might find itself precluded from
afterwards raising them again, if, meanwhile, any other firm
in the same line had failed.

Similar difficulties stand in the way of effective legislation
against boycotts. It is true that such legislation has been
widely attempted. The United States (under the Clayton
Law), Australia, and New Zealand all prohibit, under penalty,
any person from making the act of sale, or the terms of sale,
of anything conditional on the buyer not using or dealing in
the goods of any competitor. On similar lines the United
States Federal Revenue Law of September 1916 "imposes a
double duty upon goods imported under agreement that the

---

[1] Clark, *The Control of Trusts*, p. 69.
[2] *Economist*, 25th Jan. 1910, p. 1412.   Cf. Ripley, *Railroads, Rates and Regulation*, p. 566.
[3] Federal Revenue Act 1916, Section 502.

importer or others shall use those goods exclusively."[1] Yet again, the American Shipping Act of 1916 makes deferred rebates illegal. It is obvious, however, that, when the condition or agreement is made between a manufacturer and a dealer, both of whom profit by it, the difficulty of preventing evasion must be very great. When the boycott is worked, not through a wholesaler, but through a railway company, the difficulty is still greater. American law has long endeavoured to prevent railway discriminations favourable to the large Trusts. But: "A partisan of the Trust said to me: 'The Pennsylvania Railroad could not refuse the cars of a competitor of the Standard Oil Company, but nothing could hinder it from side-tracking them.'"[2] "A consignment note acknowledges the receipt of 70 barrels of flour; 65 only are shipped, and the railway company pays damages for the loss of the five non-existent barrels." Except when long notice of alterations is required by law, rates may be changed suddenly, secret notice being given to the favoured shipper and no information to others; and so forth. It is true that the Attorney-General of the United States declared in 1903, after the passing of the Elkins law: "The giving and taking of railroad rebates is now prohibited by a law capable of effective enforcement against corporations as well as against individuals."[3] This view, however, appears to have been unduly optimistic. The Interstate Commerce Commission reported, as to the conditions in 1908, that many shippers still enjoy illegal advantages. "Thus the rebate, as an evil in transportation, even since amendment of the law in 1906–10, while under control, is still far from being eradicated. Favouritism lurks in every covert, assuming almost every hue and form. Practices which outwardly appear to be necessary and legitimate, have been shown to conceal special favours of a substantial sort."[4] The boycott engineered through railway companies is, therefore, not yet dead, and,

---

[1] The English Patents and Designs Amendment Act of 1907 prohibits exclusive dealing contracts of this kind, unless the seller, lessor, or licensee proves that, when the contract was made, his competitors had the option of obtaining the patented goods on reasonable terms without the exclusive condition (Davies, *Trust Laws and Unfair Competition*, p. 539).

[2] Quoted by Ely, *Monopolies and Trusts*, p. 97.

[3] *Economist*, 28th Feb. 1903.

[4] Ripley, *Railroads, Rates and Regulation*, p. 209.

indeed, many authorities hold that it is likely to survive so long as competition is retained in the railway world.

These considerations make it clear that a policy of legal prohibition against the exercise of clubbing methods cannot easily be rendered proof against evasion. It should not be forgotten, however, that laws, which *could* be evaded if people took sufficient pains, as a matter of fact are often not evaded. For the mere passage of a law reacts on public opinion and throws on the side of the practice upheld by law the strong forces of " respectability " and inertia. Hence, we may reasonably expect that laws of this character, if carefully prepared, would, at all events, partially succeed in their immediate purpose. It is, therefore, of great interest to observe that Section 5 of the United States Federal Trade Commission Act of 1914 declares " that unfair methods of competitive commerce are hereby declared unlawful," and establishes a Federal Trade Commission to take proceedings to enforce this declaration whenever it appears to it to be in the public interest to do so. Section 14 of the Clayton Act provides further that, whenever a corporation violates any of the penal provisions of any of the anti-trust laws, " such violation shall be deemed to be also that of the individual directors, officers, or agents of such corporation as shall have authorized, ordered, or done any of the acts constituting in whole or in part such violation." Upon conviction any director, officer, or agent is subject to a fine not exceeding 5000 dollars, or to imprisonment not exceeding one year, or to both, in the discretion of the Court.

§ 7. Granted that clubbing methods can be, in some measure, prevented, we turn to the further question, how far their prevention would avail to maintain potential competition. Professor Clark appears to hold that it would avail completely for this purpose. " In so far," he writes, " as legitimate rivalry in production is concerned, it is safe enough to build a new mill." In reality, however, even when clubbing methods are excluded, other obstacles to the full maintenance of competition are still present. First, when the unit firm normal to any industry is very large, the heavy capital expenditure required to start a new firm will check the ardour of aspirants. Furthermore, it should be noticed, in this connection, that, in many industries, the size of the normal unit firm has recently been increasing. For example, the output of the English paper industry between 1841 and 1903 rose from 43,000 to 773,080 tons, but the number of firms fell from 500 to 282;[1] and a like development has taken place in the raw iron industry. Secondly, the ease with which new competitors can spring up is smaller, the greater are the productive economies which concentration on the part of the monopolistic seller has involved. For, if great economy has been brought about by concentration, a potential competitor will know that the monopolistic seller, by simply abandoning some of his monopoly revenue, can, without suffering any positive loss, easily undersell him. Thirdly, the obstacles in the way of new competition are further enlarged, when a policy of secrecy as to costs and profits makes it difficult for outsiders to guess at what rate the monopolistic seller *could* sell, if he were to content himself with the normal gains of competitive industry. Fourthly, a combination, by extensive advertising or a distinctive trade mark, may have established a sort of monopoly of reputation, which it would require heavy advertising expenditure on the part of any would-be rival to break down. It may, indeed, be suggested that, even so, the combination would be kept in check for fear of a rival concern being started with a view to forcing the combination to buy it out. But there is less in this than there might appear to be at first sight. For, if a rival did succeed in this policy, the increase in the combination's capital might well be so large that the rate of profit available per unit of capital would turn out too small to make the venture worth the rival's while.[2] These considerations would, of course, tend strongly to hold him back. Thus, attempts to maintain potential competition by preventing the employment of clubbing devices can at best be only partially successful, and are, therefore, very imperfect means of preventing bodies that possess monopolistic power from making use of that power. This is true even of industry proper. In some departments of production,

---

[1] Levy, *Monopole, Kartelle und Trusts*, p. 197.
[2] Cf. Jenks and Clark, *The Trust Problem*, pp. 69-70.

roughly those covered by public utility concerns, the obvious wastefulness of competition makes it practically certain that the public authorities will not permit it, and so exempts monopolists from any check which the fear of it might otherwise exercise upon them.

§ 8. The inadequacy, as a method of control, of preventing combination, which means maintaining actual competition, or of anti-clubbing legislation, which means maintaining potential competition, leads forward naturally to the suggestion of direct methods. The position, which is relevant to industrial, no less than to railway, monopolies, is well put by the Departmental Committee on Railway Agreements and Amalgamations (1911) with special reference to the latter class. They write: " To sum up, we are strongly of opinion that, in so far as protection is required from any of the consequences which may be associated with railway co-operation, such protection should, in the main, be afforded by general legislation dealing with the consequences as such, independently of whether they occur as the result of agreement or not. Such a method would afford a much more extensive protection than the regulation of agreements. It would protect the public in the case of understandings as well as agreements. . . . It would not tend to introduce a confusing distinction between what a company might reasonably do under an agreement and what it might reasonably do if no agreement existed." [1] If this method could be employed with perfect accuracy, there would, of course, be no need for *any* accompanying indirect methods of the kind we have so far been discussing. In practice, however, the policy of dealing directly with the consequences of monopolistic power is, as will presently appear, exposed to very great difficulties. Furthermore, since in most forms it must almost necessarily work on the basis of some standard of reasonable earnings, deduced from the circumstances of other industries in which competition is available, these difficulties would become enormous, if attempts to maintain potential competition were abandoned altogether and resort had universally to direct

[1] *Report of the Departmental Committee on Railway Agreements and Amalgamations*, p. 21.

methods. Consequently, it would seem that the policy of maintaining potential competition should be pursued everywhere vigorously, and that direct methods of dealing with the consequences should be employed, not instead of, but in addition to it.

§ 9. At first sight it seems obvious that direct dealing with the consequences of monopolistic power means, and can only mean, some kind of direct interference by the public authority with the terms of sale. In the main, of course, this is what it does mean. But it is of some theoretical interest to note a possible alternative line of policy, which was advocated, as regards shipping, by the Royal Commission on Shipping Rings. The Commission recommended, in effect, that the State should encourage the formation, over against a monopolistic seller, of a combination of buyers possessing also monopolistic powers. It was hoped that the combination of buyers might be able to neutralise attempts on the part of the seller to charge monopoly prices. This plan was advocated by the majority of the Royal Commission on Shipping Rings, as a partial remedy for the evils that have arisen out of the conference system. Analytically, the plan is a weak one, because what the creation of the second monopolist does is, not to bring prices to the natural, or competitive, point, but to render them indeterminate over a considerable range, within which that point lies. No doubt, the position of the purchasers is made better than it would be if combination among them were absent; and there is reason to hope that prices and output will approach more nearly to what, from the standpoint of the national dividend, is desirable than they would do under those conditions. But the chance that the bargain between the two combinations will lie in the near neighbourhood of that proper to simple competition is not very large. This difficulty would exist, even though the monopoly created to stand against the sellers were a monopoly of ultimate consumers. In practice, however, ultimate consumers are scarcely ever in a position to combine in this way. The only persons who can so combine are middlemen between the ultimate consumers and the monopolistic seller,—middlemen who are not particularly concerned to fight for the consumers' interests.[1] If they combine, the goods in which they deal will have to pass through the hands of two monopolistic combinations instead of one, before they reach the ultimate consumers. The effect upon the price which those people will then have to pay is economically indeterminate. The price may be less than it would have been if the middlemen had not combined, but it may, on the other hand, be greater. In any event, it is likely to be exceedingly unstable.[2] These considerations make it plain that there is a serious flaw in the Commissioners' policy.

§ 10. We turn, therefore, to the direct method of interference with the terms of sale—a method which *may* be necessary even in industrial enterprises, when the "remedies" considered so far prove inadequate, and which, apart from public operation, is the only possible method in public utility concerns. Analytically, the problem may be stated as follows. Assuming that the output proper to simple competition (allowing, of course, for any economies in production which a combination may have introduced) is also the output most advantageous to the national dividend, we need so to regulate things that that output will be forthcoming. In industries operating under conditions of diminishing returns, this type of regulation cannot be accomplished by the machinery of price control alone. For, if the price be fixed by the State at the level proper to competitive conditions, *i.e.* at such a level that, if competitive conditions prevailed, the output would be adjusted to yield normal profit, it will pay a monopolist to produce less than this output. By reducing output he will, under conditions of diminishing returns, also diminish the supply price, thus obtaining a monopoly gain measured by the difference between the regulated selling price multiplied by the output and the supply price multiplied by the output. It will be to his interest to control his output in such a way as to make this monopoly gain as large as possible. According to the form of the demand and supply schedules, the resultant output may be greater or less than it would have been

---

[1] Cf. Marshall, *Industry and Trade*, p. 625.
[2] Cf. Marshall, *Principles of Economics*, bk. v. ch. xiv. § 9.

under unregulated monopoly; but, in any event, it is certain
to be less than the output proper to competition, at which the
Government is aiming. This difficulty, however, is only present
in industries operating under conditions of diminishing returns.
When constant returns or increasing returns prevail, it will not
pay a monopolist, when price is fixed at the competitive level,
to reduce output below the competitive output; for he would not
secure any diminution in his costs by doing this. Consequently,
if the Government can succeed in fixing prices at the competitive level, it will also indirectly secure competitive output.
Since, therefore, as a matter of practice, concerns (whether
industrial combinations or public utility corporations) which
it is necessary to regulate are hardly ever found in industries
of diminishing returns, but almost always in industries of
increasing returns, regulation of output can be effected in the
way required by regulation of price. Control, in short, means
control over price.[1]

§ 11. When this has been said, there inevitably comes to
mind the sort of control over prices which was exercised during
the great war, and some account of which was given in Chapter
IX. It is very important, however, to realise that what we
are now concerned with is fundamentally different from that.
In controlling monopoly, it is required to prevent the monopolist from charging high prices, because, by so doing, he will
reduce output below the level at which he could put it with
normal profit to himself. As explained above, under conditions of constant returns or increasing returns, the fixing of
maximum prices at the rate corresponding to the "competitive" output will in fact cause that output to be forthcoming.
There is no question of the maximum price being associated
with an output for which the demand price that the public
are prepared to pay exceeds that price.[2] But in the war
problem, as was clearly brought out in Chapter IX., the
whole point of intervention was to fix a maximum price
below the demand price that the public would be prepared, at
need, to pay for such quantity of the commodity as was forth-

---

[1] Cf. Appendix III. § 18.

[2] In technical language, the limitation of monopoly prices moves the exchange
index along the demand curve towards the right; the limitation of competitive
prices pushes the exchange-index below the demand curve.

coming. This is the reason why, at the maximum price, there was always a greater quantity demanded than could be supplied, and why, therefore, it was necessary to prevent accidental inequalities in distribution by rationing all consumers to purchases smaller than many of them would have wished to make. This, too, is the reason why it was not sufficient to fix prices as from the producer only. Because the demand price was bigger than the price which the Government wished to allow, to have limited, *e.g.*, shipping freights, without also limiting the price of the things brought in at the limited freights, would merely have enabled the intermediaries between the ship and the consumer to take the whole benefit for themselves. It was necessary, therefore, not merely to fix maximum prices to the original producer, but also to fix maximum additions that might be put on to these prices by the various persons through whose hands (whether as further manufacturers or as retailers) the controlled commodities would afterwards pass. In the regulation of monopoly charges there is, of course, no need for any of these secondary arrangements.

§ 12. We may now proceed to investigate this form of price control directly. One way in which it may be exercised is, as it were, negative. It may take the form of general provisions against "unreasonable" conduct, leaving the definition of what is, in fact, unreasonable to the decision of a Commission or of the Courts. This way is, in substance, followed, for proposed *changes* of rates, in the work of the English and, prior to the Hepburn law, the American commissioners regulating railways. The commissioners have to decide whether any proposed increase of rates is reasonable and to permit or forbid it accordingly. Thus, their task is *comparatively* light. They have not to regulate all prices always, but only to intervene against specially unreasonable prices ; and, furthermore, the knowledge of their existence is likely to serve indirectly as a check against the setting-up of unreasonable prices.[1] The negative way is also followed in certain franchises, which permit municipalities to take over the business of a licensed corporation *at a proper price*—an ambiguous phrase—should the corporation fail to "operate and

[1] Cf. Van Hise, *Concentration and Control*, p. 261.

develop it in compliance with reasonable public requirements."[1] It is followed again: in the Canadian Industrial Combines Investigation Act (1910). Provision is made for determining whether, with regard to any article, on the subject of which complaint has been made, "there exists any combine to promote unduly the advantage of the manufacturers or dealers at the expense of the consumers by fixing the price higher than is proper."; and, if the charge is established, penalties are provided. In New Zealand the Act of 1910 applies the same test. "Any person commits an offence, who, either as principal or agent, sells or supplies, or offers for sale or supply, any goods at a price which is unreasonably high, if that price has been in any manner, directly or indirectly, determined, controlled, or influenced by any commercial trust of which that person or his principal (if any) is or has been a member." The Russian Criminal Code of 1903 had a similar proviso: "A merchant or manufacturer who increases the price of victuals or other articles of prime necessity in an extraordinary degree in accord with other merchants or manufacturers dealing in the same articles shall be punished with imprisonment."[2] In all these rules excessive prices are forbidden, but no attempt is made actually to fix prices by decree. The other, positive, way, in which control may be exercised, consists in the authoritative determination of definite maximum rates of charge or minimum provision of service. This way is illustrated by the terms of the charters usually accorded to companies operating public utility services under lease from city governments, and by the power, conferred on the Interstate Commerce Commission by the Hepburn law of 1906, to "determine and prescribe" maximum rates for railway, telephone and other services of communication.

§ 13. Whether the negative or the positive way of regulation is followed, it is obvious that some sort of sanction to the law must be provided. This can be done in a variety of ways. Sometimes the penalty for breach is a direct money fine. Sometimes, in protected countries, for example in

---

[1] National Civic Federation, *Municipal and Private Operation of Public Utilities*, vol. i. p. 41.

[2] The text of these laws is printed in Appendix G to Jenks and Clark, *The Trust Problem*.

Brazil,[1] it consists in the withdrawal of duties on competing foreign goods. The Canadian Industrial Combines Investigation Act of 1910 provides for both sorts of penalty. If a statutory Commission "finds that there is a Combine, the Government may either lower or repeal the duties, and; in addition, impose a fine of 1000 dollars a day on those who continue in their evil courses after the judgment of the Board has been officially published."[2] Another interesting form of sanction is provided, as against the owners of vessels which violate any of the American anti-trust laws, by a clause in the Panama Canal Act of 1912 forbidding the use of the canal to their ships.[3] Sometimes the sanction consists in the threat of governmental competition. Thus, in connection with the 1892 agreement, by which the Post-Office took over the National Telephone Company's trunk lines, the Chancellor of the Exchequer hinted that the State, while securing its right to compete, would not be likely to exercise that right if the Company acted reasonably.[4] Sometimes, again, the sanction consists in the threat of State purchase, on terms, either fixed beforehand or to be decided by arbitration, of the whole of the plant of the regulated business. Sometimes, finally,— and this, in effect, is what seems to be contemplated under the authoritative interpretation of the Sherman Act, as given by the United States Supreme Court in the Standard Oil Case (1911)—combinations, whose price (and other) policy is found to be reasonable, may be left undisturbed, but combinations which use their power to the injury of the public may be dissolved by order of the Court.[5]

§ 14. Though, however, many sanctions, some of them of great force, are available, when breaches of the law are detected, it is necessary to add that, whether the negative or the positive method of control is adopted, it is exceedingly difficult to prevent these sanctions being

---

[1] Cf. Davies, *Trust Laws and Unfair Competition*, p. 294.

[2] *Economist*, March 26, 1910, p. 665. Cf. *Annals of the American Academy*, July 1912, p. 152.

[3] Cf. Johnson and Huebner, *Principles of Ocean Transportation*, p. 386.

[4] H. Meyer, *Public Ownership and the Telephones*, pp. 56, 199.

[5] Cf. The judgment of Chief-Justice White, laying down in this case what has now become known as "the rule of reason" in interpreting the Act (quoted by Jenks and Clark, *The Trust Problem*, p. 299).

escaped by evasion. Thus, in the pre-war period our
railway companies, in effect, raised their rates without applying for the sanction of the railway commissioners. Charges
for rent of sidings and so forth were created; the
number of articles which the companies refuse to carry
at owner's risk, unless packed to their satisfaction, was
increased; rebates were withdrawn; and other such devices
were employed.[1] But the kind of evasion which it is hardest
to deal with is that which meets price regulation by manipulating quality. To prevent this it is essential to couple
with rules about maximum price further rules about minimum quality. But in some things, such as the comfort and
punctuality of a tramway service, or the sanitary condition of
slaughter-houses and sewers, it is difficult to *define* a minimum
of quality. When there are a number of different grades of
quality, all of which have to be distinguished from one another
and subjected to a separate maximum price—different grades,
even of simple things like tea, and still more of complicated
things like hats—the difficulty of effective definition is
enormous. It is easy to sell a lower-grade thing at a higher-
grade price. In other things, such as water supply, gas
supply, milk supply and house accommodation, where tests
of quality are available to give a basis for definition, it may
be difficult to *detect* departures from the stipulated minimum.
Something can, no doubt, be done by an elaborate system of
inspection, like that developed in support of the Adulteration
of Food and Drugs Act, but the openings for evasion are, in
any event, likely to be considerable.

§ 15. Even, however, if this difficulty could be completely overcome, the most formidable obstacle in the way of
direct control would still remain. It is necessary to determine
what prices shall be regarded as unreasonable, and, when
the positive method of fixing maxima is adopted, what the
maxima shall be. As was explained at the beginning of this
chapter, the goal aimed at is the competitive price, *i.e.* the
price which would have been arrived at had other things
been the same but the monopoly element absent. It is obviously impossible, in any enterprise, to calculate this except

[1] Cf. *Railway Conference Report*, p. 57.

by reference to the earnings of the enterprise. Competitive prices must be taken to be prices that yield competitive earnings—that is, earnings normal to the type of enterprise. It is conceivable that some reader, thinking loosely upon recent experience, may question this statement and claim that competitive prices could be determined directly from the ascertained expenses of converting the raw material used into finished goods. Plainly, however, in order to get the *full* conversion costs, we need to know how much should be added to the cost of material and labour for the share due, for the article we are studying, to the standing charges and profits of the business. This implies some prior and independent decision as to what these profits are to be. Given a decision about that, we can, indeed, then, by conversion cost accounting—the technique of which has greatly developed during the war—determine the proper price for any particular product; but to proceed in the reverse direction is impossible. The calculation of conversion costs is, of course, a necessary step towards any practical scheme of price regulation. But it is a subordinate step. The crux of our problem—to which it is altogether irrelevant,—is, as I have said, to determine what profits in any particular enterprise, the price of whose products have to be regulated, may rightly be considered normal.

§ 16. At first sight it might be thought that this could be settled fairly easily. Will not normal profit be such profit that, when allowance is made for earnings of management (as in joint-stock companies is done automatically), what is left provides interest at the ordinary rate on the capital of the concern? This plausible suggestion is, however, easily shown to be very far from adequate. Let us, to begin with, suppose that the ordinary rate of interest really does correspond in all businesses to normal profits. We have still to determine what the capital is on which this ordinary rate is to be paid. Clearly, we cannot interpret it as the market value of the concern, because, the market value of a business being simply the present value of its anticipated earnings, these earnings *must* yield the ordinary rate of interest on it, allowing for the particular risks involved, whatever sum they amount to. Indeed, if we are to take existing market value as our basis, since this depends on what people believe the system of rate regulation will be, we should come perilously near to circular reasoning. Capital value, therefore, for rate control purposes, is something quite different from capital value for, say, taxation purposes. It must mean, in some sense, that capital which has in fact been invested in the business in the past. If we were to push our analysis to the end, we should need to note that, since price levels are different in different times, the practice of estimating capital investments merely by reference to their money value at the time they were made is incorrect. A real investment of 1000 days' labour will be called £1000 if it is made in one year, while an exactly identical real investment will be called £2000 if it is made in another year. To this class of difficulty, however, if we are to hope for any result at all, we must resolutely close our eyes. Apart from it the task is complex enough. When the sums of money invested include commission paid to a promoter for accomplishing a fusion, the advantage of which is expected to consist in the power to exact monopoly charges from the public, this commission ought not, it would seem, to be counted, except in so far as the fusion has also brought about increased productive efficiency. That this is an exceedingly important point becomes apparent when we learn that, according to high officials in some of the industrial combinations of the United States, " the cost of organisation, including the pay of the promoter and financier, amounts often to from 20 to 40 per cent of the total amount of stock issued." [1] The same difficulty has to be faced as regards that part of the capital expenditure which has been employed in buying up existing concerns at a price enhanced by the hope that combination will make monopolistic action practicable. Apart from these difficult items, what we want to ascertain is the original capital expenditure, whether employed in physical construction, parliamentary costs, the purchase of patent rights or the upbuilding of a connection by advertisement, together with such later expenditure, in excess of the repairs and renewals required to keep the original capital intact, as has

---

[1] Jenks and Clark, *The Trust Problem*, p. 90.

not been taken out again in earnings, allowance being made for
the different dates of the various investments.[1] For new
businesses, to be established in the future, it would be easy
enough to secure by law that information about all these
items should be made available. But for businesses already
long established it may be impossible to get this information.
For example, similar expenditures on good-will and so
forth, which one concern may have charged to capital,
another will have treated as current expenditure, in such
a way that it cannot practically be distinguished. In view
of these difficulties some roundabout way of approximating to
the truth may have to be employed. Obviously the nominal
capital is quite useless for this purpose. It may have been
watered and manipulated in ways that completely disguise the
real facts. The market value of the capital we have already
shown to be inappropriate. It is usual, therefore, to make use
either of the estimated "cost of reproduction" of the concern's
plant—which may be very misleading if prices have changed
substantially since the original investment was made—or of a
value ascertained by direct physical valuation of the plant—
the amount of which will, of course, depend on the principles
in accordance with which the valuation is made—; and then to
make some more or less arbitrary allowance for costs of
promotion, investments to build up good-will, patent rights,
and so on. These *data* are not wanted for themselves, but
are supposed to enable a rough estimate to be made of the
actual capital investment, when this is not directly ascertainable. To develop the difficulties of this process is outside my
present purpose. What has been said will suffice to show
that to determine what the capital of a concern is, on which
"ordinary" interest is to be allowed, is not an easy task.[2]

§ 17. But this is not all. It is not true that the normal
"competitive" profits of any enterprise are the profits that
would yield the "ordinary" rate of interest on the capital
that has actually been invested in that enterprise. For the
establishment of different enterprises involves both different

---

[1] Cf. Heilman, "Principles of Public Utility Valuation," *Quarterly Journal
of Economics*, Feb. 1914, pp. 281-90.

[2] Cf. Barker, *Public Utility Rates*, Chapters v. and vi.

degrees of risk and different initial periods of development during which no return at all is likely to be obtained; and appropriate compensation under these heads must be made to those investors—the only ones with whom the State can deal —whose enterprises turn out successfully, and who, therefore, must be paid enough to balance the losses of those who have failed.[1] This circumstance need not, indeed, be responsible for large practical difficulties in industries in which production has attained more or less of a routine character, but in all industries in an experimental stage it is of dominant importance.[2] Furthermore, even if there were no risks, we could not regard as proper prices which would yield the ordinary rate of interest in all circumstances, but only prices which would yield that rate, if the management, and indeed the actual organisation of the original investment also, were conducted with "ordinary" ability; and this is a vague and difficult conception. As Professor Taussig pertinently observes: "Every one knows that fortunes are made in industries strictly competitive, and are to be ascribed to unusual business capacity. . . . When a monopoly or quasi-monopoly secures high returns, how are we to separate the part attributable to monopoly from the part attributable to excellence in management?"[3] To allow the same rate of return to companies which invest their capital wastefully as to those which invest it well plainly makes against economical production. Incidentally, if there were two competing combinations to be dealt with, it would logically require forcing the better managed one to charge lower prices than the other, an arrangement which would not only have awkward consequences at the moment but would effectively discourage good management. In this connection,

---

[1] Cf. Greene, *Corporation Finance*, p. 134.

[2] If a concern has been taken over by a company after the first stage of speculative adventure has been successfully passed, the purchase price will probably include a large sum above cost. This may be a fair remuneration for the risk taken and uncertainty borne. But clearly, after it has been paid, to allow the new company to reap profits which are both adjusted to the risks of the occupation and also calculated upon a capital which includes the above sum, would be to compel the public to reward it for risk-taking for which it has not been responsible, and recompense for which has already been made. For an excellent general discussion of good-will cf. Leake, *Good-will, its nature and how to value it.*

[3] *American Economy Review Supplement*, March 1913, p. 132.

it should be noted that to extend combination further, so long as extension involves economies, is a form of good management, and a form that would be discouraged if prices were so regulated that no advantage were allowed to accrue to those who had brought it about. In view of these complications, and of the necessary limitations of its knowledge—for, as a rule, the controllers are bound to be much behind the controlled in technical experience—a public authority is almost certain either to exact too easy terms from the concerns it is seeking to control, and so to leave them with the power of simple monopoly, or to exact too hard terms, and so, though not permitting monopoly exaction to them, nevertheless to prevent the development of their industry to the point proper to simple competition. The British Tramways Act of 1870 appears to have failed in the latter way, and to have been responsible for prolonged delay in the development of electric traction in this country.

§ 18. It is evident that the difficulties, which are involved in determining what scale of return should be regarded as normal in any particular productive enterprise, complicate alike the negative way of control, under which the Legislature simply condemns unreasonable prices, leaving the Courts to decide whether any given price scheme is in fact unreasonable, and the positive way, which lays down definite price maxima. Plainly, however, they complicate the positive way more seriously than the other. An ordinary industrial concern produces a great number of different varieties of goods, the raw materials for which are continually altering in cost, and the distinctive character of the finished product continually being modified. For any outside authority to draw up a schedule of permitted charges for a concern of this sort would be a hopeless task. On the other hand, for a trained Commission or judicial body, equipped, like the American Federal Trade Commission, to make full inquiries, it would not be impossible to decide in a broad way whether, taking one product with another and one time with another, some selected large combination—the Standard Oil Company, the United Steel Corporation, or another—was charging prices calculated to yield to it more than the return deemed in the circumstances to be reasonable.

For industrial concerns in normal times no attempt has ever
been made to go beyond this negative way, and it does not
seem, at all events in the present condition of economic
knowledge and governmental competence, that any such
attempt either can, or should be, made. Imperfect as the
results to be hoped for from the negative way are, they
are better than would be got from a blundering struggle
after the other. In public utility concerns, on the other
hand, the excess difficulty of the positive over the negative
way is slight. As a general rule, the service provided by these
concerns is single and relatively simple (gas, water, electricity, transport of passengers). Not many separate prices
—railway freight rates are, of course, a very important exception—have, therefore, to be fixed. Further, the demand
is generally unaffected by fashion, and equipment plays
so large a part in the cost that changes in the price
of raw material do not very greatly matter. Finally,
even if these things were otherwise, the nature of the
goods sold and the convenience of customers make it
very desirable that the prices charged should not undergo
frequent change. In these concerns, therefore, the positive
way of control by fixing maximum prices has generally been
adopted.

§ 19. When this is done, it becomes imperative to seek
out the best means of guarding against the two opposite
sorts of error, undue laxness and undue harshness, to which,
as was shown in § 17, all forms of regulation are in practice
inclined. For this purpose one device sometimes recommended is to put up the licence to operate certain public
utility services to a kind of auction. This plan allows
the persons most interested themselves to present estimates
of terms which they would reckon profitable. It has been
described thus: " According to the best plan now in vogue, the
City sells the franchise for constructing the works to the company, which bids to furnish water at the lowest rates under
definitely specified conditions, the franchise being sometimes
perpetual, but often granting to the City at some future date
an option for the purchase of the works." Since, however,
in many cities, the companies capable of making tenders

will be very few in number, and since, furthermore, their own estimates must be largely tentative, the adoption of this device is not incompatible with large errors. The likelihood of error is made greater by the fact that the conditions of most industries are continually changing, in such wise that the scheme of price-regulation, which is proper at one time, necessarily becomes improper at another.

§ 20. A further effort at limiting the range of error can be made through arrangements, under which the regulations imposed are submitted to periodical revision. Franchises "cannot be fixed, or justly fixed, for all time, owing to rapidly changing conditions."[1] With the general growth of improvements and so on, it may well happen that a maximum price designed to imitate competitive conditions will, after a while, stand above the price that an unrestricted monopolist would find it profitable to charge, and will, therefore, be altogether ineffective. "The public should retain in all cases an interest in the growth and profits of the future."[2] A provision for periodic revision in a franchise may, however, by creating uncertainty, restrict investment in the industry concerned to an extent that is injurious to the national dividend. Further, if the revision is to occur at fixed intervals, it may tempt companies, shortly before the close of one of these intervals, to hold back important developments till after the revision has taken place, lest a large part of their fruits should be taken away in the form of lowered prices;[3] and this difficulty cannot be wholly overcome by clauses stipulating for the introduction of such technical improvements as are, from time to time, invented elsewhere. One way of meeting these dangers is to hedge round the revising body with conditions designed to defend the company's interest. For example, the Railway Act of 1844 provided that, if dividends exceeded 10 per cent on the paid-up capital after twenty-one years from the sanctioning of the lines, the Lords of the Treasury might revise tolls, fares, etc., on the condition that they guaranteed a 10 per cent dividend for the next twenty-

[1] Bemis, *Municipal Monopolies*, p. 32.
[2] *Municipal and Private Operation of Public Utilities*, vol. i. p. 24.
[3] Cf. Whitten, *Regulation of Public Service Companies in Great Britain*, p. 224.

one years. Another way is to make the revision period
so far distant from the date at which an undertaking is
initiated that the effect upon investment due to the anticipation of it will be very small. It is evident that, just in
so far as either of these lines of defence is adopted, the
efficacy of revision, as a means of lessening the gap between
actual regulation and ideal regulation, is diminished. But
plainly, if regulation is to be attempted at all, the retention
by the State of revising powers in some form is absolutely
essential. It would seem that this could be provided for without
imposing a serious check either to investment or to enterprise,
if the principles on which the revision would proceed were
clearly laid down and understood. The revisers might be
instructed at each revision period to fix a price—or, when
they have to do with joint products, several adjusted prices—
sufficiently high to continue to the company a fair rate
on their total real investment, account being taken of the
fact that the capital turned into it in the first instance was
probably subject to great risk, while that added subsequently
needs a less reward under this head. And they might be
instructed further, in deciding what constitutes a fair return,
to consider generally the quality of management that has
been displayed, fixing prices to yield higher returns when
the management has been good than when it has been
indifferent or bad. No doubt, the technical difficulty of
this kind of revision would be exceedingly great; but it
would not be nearly so great as that of the initial regulation.
It is not unreasonable to suppose that a class of official
might eventually be evolved whose decision on such matters,
when founded on adequate comparative statistics, would at
once deserve and command the confidence of would-be
investors. Such investors would have the consolation of
knowing that, while, on the one hand, the price of their
product was liable to enforced reduction, on the other hand,
if costs of material and labour went against them, it might
be raised in their favour.

§ 21. Yet another device designed to limit the range of
error remains. In all ordinary industries many variations
of demand occur *within* the successive revision periods. If

the guidance of "simple competition" is to be followed, such variations should be accompanied by variations in the price charged. Furthermore, it is easily shown that these corresponding variations in price should be especially great, in response to given variations of demand, in industries where the part played by supplementary costs—which are not reduced proportionately when output is reduced—is large relatively to the part played by prime costs. There is reason to believe that these costs are in fact becoming more important in the generality of industries. It follows that any system of control, which endeavours to fix prices at a constant level independent of short period oscillations of demand, is liable to miss somewhat widely the mark of simple competition. No doubt, where, as in railway service, the technical inconvenience of constantly changing prices would be very great, it may be worth while to adopt such a system for fairly long periods, in spite of its tendency to reduce output both in times of depression and, unless special arrangements are made in times of boom to increase production beyond the point of maximum profit, in these times also. Obviously, however, this defence of constant prices cannot be pressed beyond a point. Where it is not applicable, and adjustment of prices to demand changes is deemed desirable, franchises sometimes lay down, not a fixed system of rates, but some form of self - adjusting scale. Such a scale might conceivably be based on the price of some commodity which the regulated industry buys, or in connection with which it renders its services. A scale on these lines appears in "the arrangement adopted on at least one railway, according to which the rates charged for the conveyance of iron-making materials rise and fall according to the price of pig-iron."[1] More frequently, however, scales based, not on any kind of price, but on the rate of dividend paid to shareholders, are utilised. These scales permit an increase in the rate of dividend during any licence period, only on condition of an accompanying defined reduction of prices. Illustrations of them are furnished in English Acts of Parliament dealing with gas companies.

[1] *Departmental Committee on Railway Agreements*, p. 23.

One Act, for example, fixes a standard price of 3s. 9d. per thousand cubic feet, and provides that, for every penny put on or off that price, the company may, when there are reductions, and must, when there are increases, move the dividend up or down a quarter per cent. Another illustration is furnished by the Act governing the Lancashire Power Company which furnishes electricity in bulk. This Act "provides for a dividend of 8 per cent and an additional 1·25 per cent reduction in price for every 0·25 per cent increase of dividend above 8 per cent, in respect of every 5 per cent charged below the maximum price allowed by the Act."[1] Sliding scales of this kind, like sliding scales of wages, are, of course, provided, not as a substitute for, but as a complement to, a system of periodic revision of the licence terms; for, if they were treated as permanent arrangements, all improvements and discoveries that reduced cost of production, whether made by the concerns themselves or by others, would steadily and continually enhance profits. They are not easily organised for new companies, because the appropriate standards of price and dividend cannot be determined till some experience has been gained of the working of a concern. But it is feasible, and is in fact the practice of the Board of Trade in dealing with gas companies, to fix a simple maximum price at first and to reserve power to substitute a sliding scale after the lapse of a certain interval.[2] An important objection to these scale arrangements is that they are liable to push prices up, not only when the costs of raw materials and labour rise, but equally when the profits of a company are reduced by incompetent management. This characteristic represents a lapse from the ideal of simple competition and *pro tanto* weakens the inducement towards enterprising management—unless, indeed, as sometimes happens, the manager's salary, or a part of it, is also made dependent on the scale. But, in spite of these difficulties, sliding scales, when carefully constructed, may be expected to make possible a nearer approach to the system of

---

[1] H. Meyer, *Municipal Ownership in Great Britain*, p. 281.
[2] Cf. Whitten, *Regulation of Public Service Companies in Great Britain*, p. 129.

prices proper to simple, competition than would be possible without them.[1]

§ 22. There remains, however, another difficulty of a different order. The main part of what has been said so far has tacitly assumed that, in forming our control policy, we start with a clear table. For industrial monopolies that come into being after the general lines of our policy have been fixed, and for public utility corporations upon which conditions are imposed at the time when the original franchise is granted, this is, of course, true. But, in so far as we have to do with monopolistic concerns over which at present control is either not exercised at all or exercised in a very imperfect manner, the case is different. To bring these concerns now under a system of price regulation of the type that we are contemplating would, in many instances, involve a large reduction in their income and in the capital value of their shares. So far as original shareholders or persons who have inherited from them are concerned, this does not greatly matter. The fact that these persons have made abnormal profits in the past is no reason why they should be allowed to do so in the future. But the position is different with recent purchasers of shares, whose purchase price has been regulated by the conditions ruling before control, or the strict form of control here contemplated, was seriously thought about. Such persons may perhaps be getting now, say 8 per cent on their money, and control may knock it down to 5 per cent, reducing the value of their capital by one-third or even one-half. To make regulations that will strike with cruel severity on arbitrarily selected groups of perfectly innocent persons is not a thing to be lightly undertaken. There are limits to the right of the State to ride rough-shod over legitimate expectations. And yet to refrain from control that ought to be imposed, because we neglected our duty in not imposing it before, is to enslave ourselves to past mistakes. Surrender to the "widows and orphans" argument means, in substance, abandonment of

---

[1] It should perhaps be mentioned that this system of sliding scales in gas companies was originally introduced, not for the purpose discussed in the text, but as a substitute for regulation by the fixing of a maximum dividend. That method, involving as it does severe discouragement to good management, is plainly much inferior to a scale system.

reform. No perfect solution of this conflict can be hoped for.
But it would seem a reasonable compromise, and one adequately
careful of vested interests, to provide that, when the sudden
introduction of a full measure of price control on the principles
indicated above would greatly depress values, this control
should only be introduced after an interval of notice, and then
by gradual steps.

§ 23. Even, however, if this somewhat special difficulty be
left out of account, the preceding general review makes it
evident that, under any form of State control over private
monopoly—and it should be noticed that, though the examples
cited have to do only with special kinds of private monopoly,
the argument refers to all kinds—a considerable gap between
the ideal and the actual is likely to remain. The method of
control, whether positive or negative, is, in short, an exceedingly
imperfect means of approximating industry towards the price
level and output proper to simple competition. Moreover,
it is apt to prove a costly method. As Professor Durand
observes: "Government regulation of prices and profits of
private concerns always involves a large element of waste,
of duplication of energy and cost. It means that two sets of
persons are concerning themselves with the same work. The
managers and employees of the corporation must study cost
accounting and conditions of demand in determining price
policy. The officers and employees of the Government must
follow and do it all over again. Moreover, the fact that
these two sets of persons have different motives in approaching
their work means friction and litigation, and these spell further
expense. To superimpose a vast governmental machinery
upon the vast machinery of private business is an extravagance which should be avoided if it is possible to do so."[1]
This consideration is one that ought not to be ignored.

[1] *Quarterly Journal of Economics*, 1914, pp. 674-5 ; and *The Trust Problem*,
p. 57.

CHAPTER XIX

PUBLIC OPERATION OF INDUSTRIES

§ 1. THE preceding chapter has shown that attempts at
public control over monopolistic industries, whether direct
or indirect, are likely to be very imperfectly successful. It is
sometimes thought that the difficulties can be got over by an
arrangement under which a government (or municipal) authority owns a concern and leases it out to a private company to
operate. This is the plan under which railways are worked in
Italy and Holland. No doubt, it provides the controlling
authority with a more powerful means of enforcing its orders
that would be available against a privately owned railway
company; for the authority could threaten to terminate the
lease, as it can now do with the leases granted to private
tramway companies. This, however, is comparatively a small
matter. When, indeed, the Government desires to regulate
an industry which is not already a monopoly, as, for example,
the coal industry, the leasing system has the advantage
of maintaining some measure of individual initiative
and competitive enterprise, which nationalisation in the full
sense would exclude. When, however, we have to do with
undertakings in which the competitive element is already
practically extinct, it would seem that, though various
compromise arrangements are possible, and sometimes,
for political or other reasons, may be desirable, the dominant
issue is between clear-cut public control of private concerns
and clear-cut public operation of public ones. It is in this
relatively simple form that I propose to study it here. In view
of the difficulties of control described in the preceding chapter,
coupled with the evident fact that it is easier to regulate

oneself than to regulate somebody else, the question arises
whether the national dividend would not be advantaged if the
public authorities themselves operated monopolistic industries,
instead of struggling to control their operation by others.   If
nothing else were involved besides the comparative precision with
which output can be adjusted under the two plans, in such wise
as to make the values of marginal net products everywhere equal,
there could be no doubt that this question should be answered
in the affirmative.   In actual practice, however, other things
besides this are involved, just as other things were involved in
our comparison between voluntary Purchasers' Associations
and ordinary commercial businesses.   We are not entitled to
assume without argument that the economies of supply will
be the same under public operation and private operation.
It may be that public operation is less economical than private
operation, even when private firms are subject to public control.
If this is so, the disadvantages of public operation on the side
of economical production have to be balanced against its advantages on the side of adjustment between supply and demand.
Hence, before any real answer to our question can be attempted,
it is necessary to undertake some comparison of public with
private operation, from the standpoint of productive efficiency.

§ 2. At the outset, it must be made clear that attempts
to conduct such a comparison by reference to statistics are
foredoomed to failure.   No doubt, if it could be shown that,
other conditions being the same, a given output was, in
general, obtained at greater, or at less, real cost under public
than under private management, genuine evidence about the
relative efficiency of the two forms of organisation would be
obtained.   But in real life this is impracticable.   In the first
place, the quality of services, which are called by the same name,
varies enormously in different places, and it is almost impossible properly to allow for these variations.   " Our street cars,"
say the Reporters of the American Civic Federation, " run
faster, carry more strap passengers, and kill and injure more
people than the street cars, public or private, of any other
country.   Our people seem to like this, but the English would
not." [1]   How can differences of this sort possibly be taken

---

[1] *Municipal and Private Operation of Public Utilities*, vol. i. p. 287.

into account? Again, the conditions of production in different places are utterly different. " In Syracuse (U.S.A.) the water flows to the city by gravity; in Indianapolis it must be pumped." [1] " To compare a private corporation within the limits of a great city, where an immense supply is furnished, and where special conditions of non-interference with adjoining property rights are to be met, with some municipal plant in a suburban town, upon a basis of the relative amount of supplies and labour required per unit of electrical energy, would obviously be unfair to both contestants. Nor is it possible to compare in this manner two lighting-stations having approximately the same yearly output, and which are similarly located with reference to adjoining interests, but are situated, the one in the North and the other in the South, for the reason that the daily period of service will vary in these two localities on account of variation in the hours of darkness. For the same reason we cannot compare the summer service of one station with the winter service of another, even though we should attempt to reduce them both to a common basis by obtaining the amount of human effort employed per unit of electrical energy." [2] In short, arguments from statistics, even apart from the pitfalls with which unwary inquirers are confronted in the interpretation of municipal accounts,[3] are, in this field, almost entirely valueless. This remark is of general application. But, in view of the exceptional psychological conditions of war-time and the temporary use by Government of a large number of able men normally engaged in private business, as well as of the fact that the commodities produced in Government factories during the war were for State use and not for the market, it has very special relevance to arguments drawn from the experiences of the war period.

§ 3. Statistical evidence being thus inadequate, it is necessary to proceed—again as in our study of voluntary Purchasers' Associations—by way of general considerations. The discussion along these lines may well be started with an observation of the Committee of the American Civic Federation:

---

[1] *Municipal and Private Operation of Public Utilities*, vol. i. p. 21.
[2] Bemis, *Municipal Monopolies*, pp. 289-90.
[3] Cf., *inter alia*, Knoop, *Principles and Methods of Municipal Trading*, chap. v.

"There are no particular reasons why the financial results from private or public operation should be different if the conditions are the same."[1] The reason for this remark, of course, is that, whether a service is provided by a private company or by a public governmental authority, the actual running of the business must be similar. An expert staff must be appointed, controlled in a general way, in the one case by a committee of directors chosen by the shareholders, in the other case by a committee appointed — perhaps by direct, perhaps by indirect, election—to represent the public. Managing power, as a whole, may be conceived as distributed among electors, directors—or committee—and staff, and Major Darwin has undertaken an elaborate inquiry into the probable comparative efficiency of these three bodies under private enterprise and that particular form of public enterprise known as municipal trading. It is obvious that the result of such an inquiry must be indefinite, and I do not propose to repeat it here. It is enough to say that, in England, a public undertaking is substantially equivalent to a voluntary Purchasers' Association, save only that its directors are less permanent and are elected for their political, rather than for their commercial, qualifications, and are, therefore, likely to prove, other things being equal, somewhat less well fitted for commercial leadership. One point, however, demands attention. So far as the electors of the committee, under the system of public management, are, at the same time, employees in the business affected, public operation is analogous to "productive co-operation," and is liable to experience, in respect of discipline and the adequate remuneration of the higher officials, the difficulties which these bodies, in a much greater degree than Consumers' Associations, have always encountered. It has even been suggested that, in some towns, city engineers have been hindered by the Council from introducing labour-saving devices, by which the employment of some of the Councillors' electors would be threatened.[2] Against this disadvantage, however, must be set a corresponding advantage also found in connection with productive co-operation, the advantage, namely, that, for

---

[1] *Municipal and Private Operation of Public Utilities*, vol. i. p. 23.
[2] *Ibid.* vol. i. pp. 342-3.

a given sum of money, a more efficient engineer or manager can be obtained than will be forthcoming under private management, for the reason that the position of a public servant is at once attractive in itself and also makes appeal to altruistic motives. This advantage, it must be clearly understood, is a real advantage, and not a kind of bounty obtained at the expense of the engineer or manager; for there is created a new value in the extra satisfaction which the said engineer or manager derives from the fact of serving the public. The difference between what a man of given ability would have been willing to work for in a private company and what he does work for in a State department is, in effect, extra product due to the adoption of the public form of industrial organisation. This difference is not, of course, equivalent to the difference between the earnings of the head of a State department and those of the head of a private business, because, in the earnings of the latter, there is generally included a return for "waiting" and "uncertainty-bearing"—services which in the public departments are provided by the taxpayer. It is, thus, fallacious to take the excess of the income of an American railway king over that of the administrator of the Prussian State railways as a measure of the comparative wastefulness of private enterprise. Still there is an advantage, and one that can reasonably be set against the preceding disadvantage. The general conclusion is that the efficiency of management in public and in joint-stock enterprise—apart, of course, from special examples of incompetent officialdom in certain small towns—is likely to be pretty much the same.

§ 4. This broad statement does not, however, exhaust the discussion. There remain three important groups of considerations, which tend to suggest that public operation is, on the whole, inferior to public control. The first of these has to do with the fact that, not only different producers within the same industry, but also different producers in apparently disconnected industries, are often, in reality, rivals. No doubt, an industry can be imagined which is monopolistic in the widest possible sense, in such wise that, not only are there no competing firms within it, but also that there are no competing industries outside it. There is some reason to believe that the service of supplying a modern city with water is monopolistic in this sense. It would be possible, by combining together a number of industries that are now separate, to create other monopolies of the same sort. For example, the various means of communication, such as omnibuses, tram-lines, motor cars and carriages might all conceivably be brought together under one hand. The same thing might conceivably be done with all the means of providing artificial light or all the means of providing power. But such arrangements are quite out of relation to actual facts. As things are at present, I should doubt if any industry, except that of water supply, can properly be regarded as monopolistic in the wide sense here taken. Now, the interest of the national dividend requires that, where a number of establishments, whether in the same industry or in different industries, are competing for the supply of some public need, that one which can supply it most efficiently shall oust the others.[1] But, when any enterprise is operated by a public authority, it is likely to be maintained by artificial support, even though it is less efficient than its rivals. The reason is that persons in control of any governmental enterprise, being naturally anxious to make that enterprise a success, tend to identify the good of the whole with the good of their own department. Hence, a governmental authority embarked on business is almost certain, if it prove commercially weak, to employ unfair weapons from its non-commercial armoury, the use of which will maintain it more or less permanently in the industry, despite the fact that its productive methods are more costly than those of its rivals. These unfair methods are of two sorts, according as they are directed primarily to defend the governmental enterprise or to obstruct its competitors.

Defensive non-commercial methods consist, in the main, in the conscious or unconscious practice of devices for securing a differential bounty from the general public. A government authority, which is engaged partly in business and partly in rendering general unremunerated services, may charge expenses that really belong to the business against the other part of

[1] Cf. ante, Chapter VI. § 9.

its' work. A very glaring example is the practice of the London County Council in writing down the value of land purchased for workmen's dwellings to the value which it has, not in the general market, but as ear-marked for this particular purpose. Again, municipal tramway accounts may be given a false appearance of prosperity by the charging of expenditure upon roads, which is properly attributable to them, to the general road account.[1] A like device is adopted in a milder form when a municipality fails to set aside a special fund to balance the advantage it possesses over private enterprise in the lower rate at which it can borrow money. "A municipality can float bonds at a lower rate of interest than a private company, since the whole assessable property of the town is generally liable for the payment of interest and principal, while the company can give security only on the works."[2] This ability on the part of a municipality is, thus, due, in the main, simply to the fact that it is able to force upon the ratepayers an obligation to pay its bondholders even if the enterprise fails, while a private company has, by the offer of higher pay, to secure debenture holders who are prepared, in the event of failure, to lose their money. Except in so far as the fear of failure, and, therefore, the extra compensation asked for by debenture holders, is due to public ignorance of facts which are more readily ascertainable in connection with municipalities than with companies[3]—to that extent municipal operation effects a small real saving—the social cost of the municipality's cheap loan is the same as that of the company's relatively dear loan. If the two enterprises are to compete fairly, the municipality ought to transfer to the rates the bulk of its gain from better credit, before balancing the accounts of its business. If it does not do this, it is, in

---

[1] *Municipal and Private Operation of Public Utilities*, vol. i. p. 469.

[2] Bemis, *Municipal Monopolies*, p. 45.

[3] The advantage available for municipal enterprise, thus hinted at, turns upon the fact that, when people invest in any undertaking through an intermediary, they necessarily assume the risk that this intermediary may prove to be unwilling or unable to fulfil his obligations. The uncertainty-bearing undertaken in this way is a real element in the cost of production. When the State is the intermediary, its honesty and financial strength are, in general, so well known that this element is practically eliminated.

effect, assisting that business by a contribution from the
general public. In so far as the lower terms on which it
can engage managers and engineers is due to the fact that
the shouldering of risks by the rate-payers safeguards them
against the possibility of their employers' going bankrupt; it
is doing the same thing a second time, unless it transfers the
gain made under this head also to the rates. Of course, if
a municipally-managed undertaking, *on account of superior
efficiency*, is less likely to make a loss than a corresponding
private concern, there is a real gain. But since, in any event,
there is the gilt-edged guarantee of the rate-payers, that gain
is not reflected in the better terms on which the municipality
can borrow.

Aggressive non-commercial methods are made possible by
the fact that public authorities, besides operating their own
enterprises, are often also endowed with powers of control
over other enterprises. When they are in this position, there
is a grave danger that the public authorities may be tempted
to use their powers of control in such a way as to obstruct
and injure rivals. It is obvious that an Education Authority,
which both runs schools of its own and makes regulations for
the running of rival schools, is under strong temptation. So
is an authority which at once builds houses and frames building bye-laws; and so also are municipalities operating gas-
lighting or tramways and controlling electric-lighting or
motor-omnibuses. Among the methods of aggression open to
them perhaps the simplest is that of making the conditions
about sinking funds, under which their own establishments
work, more favourable than the conditions about purchase at
the end of the lease, which are imposed upon private companies. A public authority which provides a sinking fund to
extinguish the capital debt of its enterprise, as well as a fund
to cover depreciation and obsolescence, is, in effect, taxing its
present citizens for the benefit of posterity.[1] In like manner,
a public authority which confers a franchise on a private
company upon condition that the company's plant shall pass

---

[1] The Board of Agriculture has made a new departure in not requiring the
County Councils to charge small holders, who hire land from them, rents high
enough to provide this kind of sinking fund.—[Cd. 4245], p. 12.

to itself at the end of the lease, either free of charge or at "cost of replacement," is imposing a similar tax. · It is readily seen that the terms of sinking funds and franchises respectively *can* be so arranged that the burden under the sinking fund is the smaller, and, therefore, that private operation suffers, as against the rival system, a differential injury.

There are, however, grosser forms of aggression than the above. It is notorious that those municipalities which operated their own gas-plant vigorously obstructed, by the exercise of their veto and in other ways, the development of electric lighting companies. Again: "Since 1898 the desire to protect the local municipal electric light plants has been permitted to impede the spread of the so-called electricity-in-bulk generating and distributing companies."[1] In like manner, the central government, in order to protect its telegraph monopoly, has placed administrative obstacles in the way of other means of electrical communication. In 1884 the Postmaster-General declined to allow the National Telephone Company to receive or deliver a written message at any of its offices, and, in defending this course, said, "It would make, I am afraid, a serious hole in the telegraph revenue, if written messages were allowed to be sent."[2] Finally, in the charter granted to the Marconi Wireless Company in 1906, permitting the transmission of wireless messages between the United Kingdom and North America, it is specially provided that permission will not be granted for messages to or from any European country except Italy, the purpose being to safeguard the interests of the cables owned by the British and Continental governments.[3]

The use of defensive and aggressive weapons of an " unfair " uncommercial character by public authorities operating industries brings it about, as already explained, that an industry run by them is often maintained in existence, despite the fact that the end served by it would be served more cheaply by a rival industry. It is necessary to note, in conclusion, that the use of these methods tends to extrude economically superior rivals even more effectively than it appears to do at

[1] H. Meyer, *Public Ownership and the Telephones*, p. 351.
[2] *Ibid.* p. 18.   [3] *Ibid.* pp. 341-2.

first sight.   For it acts, not only directly, but also indirectly
through anticipation.   It not only drives out of the · market
existing competitors, but checks the entry of new ones.   When
a man contemplating a philanthropic enterprise is given to
understand that, should his experiment succeed, a governmental authority will enter the field he has proved fruitful,
he does—or should—rejoice.   But, when a man engaged in a
business enterprise is given to understand this, the end he is
pursuing is not, like the philanthropist's, furthered.   It is, on
the contrary, thwarted, and his energies are, therefore, diverted.
from the undertaking.   An effect of this kind is claimed to
have resulted from municipal experiments in house-building.
These considerations, when they have relevance, evidently
strengthen the probability that governmental operation of
industries will be injurious to productive efficiency; and they
are bound to have some degree of relevance except in industries
that are monopolistic in the widest possible sense.

§ 5. I pass to a second consideration.   This has to do with
the fact that the working of any industrial enterprise involves
some degree of uncertainty.   As will be explained at length in
Appendix I., the exposing of money to uncertainty is a definite
factor of production, which makes output larger than it would
become without it.   In the long run, willingness to expose
£100 to an equal chance of becoming £160 or of becoming
£50 is bound to increase the national dividend.   If willingness to expose money to uncertainty on the part of people in
control of industry is "artificially" restricted, enterprise and
adventure that make for industrial progress, and, therewith,
production, will be hampered.   Furthermore, the injury thus
wrought is very much larger than appears at first sight.   For,
since any experiment with an untried process *may* fail, a
diminished willingness to expose money to uncertainty implies
a restriction of experiment, and, hence, a diminution in the
inducement to enterprising persons to make useful inventions.
No doubt, there is reason to believe that, with the growing
dependence of industry upon non-commercial science, this
consideration has become less important than it used to be.
Dr. Mertz has well observed: "The great inventions of former
ages were made in countries whose practical life, industry and

commerce were most advanced; but the great inventions of the last fifty years in chemistry, electricity and the science of heat have been made in the scientific laboratory; the former were stimulated by practical wants; the latter themselves produced new functional requirements, and created new spheres of labour, industry and commerce."[1] It still remains true, however, that, though the fundamental discoveries are often non-commercial, yet the application of them through "inventions," in the earlier stages before the inventions have been proved by experience, generally requires a commercial stimulus. Anything which restricts unduly willingness to make ventures in any industry must still, therefore, threaten heavy loss. The point I have to urge is that a public body engaged in industrial operations is *likely* to restrict unduly this willingness.

The defence of this proposition rests on the following reasons. First, public authorities recognise that hostility to government on the part of the people is an evil, and they also recognise that an unsuccessful State speculation, "if it involves repudiation or oppressive taxation for years to come, produces a popular revulsion and deep-seated distrust of government itself in all its branches." Secondly, the persons at any time in control of a public authority, when that authority is dependent on the party system, cannot but know that "failure would give their political opponents too good an opportunity to ride into power."[2] Thirdly, these persons are partly able to perceive that, if people are *compelled* to expose resources to uncertainty in proportion to the rateable value of their houses, more real sacrifice will be involved than if the same aggregate of resources to be exposed to the same scheme of uncertainty were obtained, by way of voluntary contributions, in proportion to the attractive force exercised upon the several contributors by the prospective profits. Finally, and this is really the most fundamental point, if inventors must appeal to government officials, they are confronted, as it were, with the average daring of the community, whereas, if they are free to appeal to private enterprise, they can select a group of supporters

---

[1] Mertz, *History of European Thought*, vol. i. p. 92.
[2] H. Meyer, *Public Ownership and the Telephones in Great Britain*, p. 349.

from persons above this ·average. As Leroy Beaulieu well writes : " A man of initiative will always find; among the forty million inhabitants· of a country, *some* audacious persons who will believe in him, will follow him, will make their fortunes with him or will ruin themselves with him. He would waste his time in trying to convince those hierarchical bureaus which are the heavy and necessary thought-organs and action-organs of a State." [1]   It follows that, in general, while the hope of gain operates more strongly on private enterprise than on the public authority, the fear of loss operates more strongly on ·the public authority. This *implies* that a public authority will be less willing than a private concern to take risks, or, to put it technically, to provide the factor uncertainty-bearing.· A good illustration of this tendency is afforded by the conduct of the British Government in regard to the working of the tele-phone trunk lines after they had been taken over by the Post Office in 1892. " The Treasury compelled the Post Office to adopt the policy of refusing to make any extensions of doubtful prospect, unless private persons, or the local authority interested, should guarantee ' a specific revenue per year, fixed with reference to the estimated cost of working and maintaining a given mileage of trunk-line wire.' " [2] The opinion of Sir George Gibb may be cited in evidence that this proceeding is representative of the general attitude of public authorities. He writes : " Whatever may be thought as to the respective merits of private and public ownership, it cannot be denied that private enterprise does take more risk than any government is likely to do except under pressure of military necessities." [3]   Dr. Marshall brings out very clearly the effect upon inventions implied in this unwillingness of public bodies to bear uncertainty : " It is notorious that, though departments of central and municipal governments employ many thousands of highly-paid servants in engineering and other progressive industries, very few inventions of any importance are made by them ; and nearly all of these few are the work of men like Sir W. H. Preece, who had been thoroughly trained in free

---

[1] *L'Etat moderne*, pp. 55, 208.
[2] H. Meyer, *Public Ownership and the Telephones in Great Britain*, p. 65.
[3] *Railway Nationalisation*, p. 9.

enterprise before they entered Government service. Government creates scarcely anything. . . . A Government could print a good edition of Shakespeare's works, but it could not have got them written. . . . The carcase of municipal electric works belongs to the officials, the genius belongs to free enterprise."[1] The position is summed up in the Report of the American Civic Federation, where we read: "The Assistant Secretary of the Board of Trade, Mr. Pelham, told the Committee [of the Civic Federation] that they did not encourage the trying of new inventions, or the trying of systems in any way experimental, by municipalities. They waited for these to be proven out by private companies. Progress is all with the companies."[2]

Now, it is evident that the effect of a restriction of the willingness to take risks, and, therewith, of the stimulus to invention, upon the economies of production will vary in importance in different industries, according to the extent of the speculative element involved in them. Hence, it follows that the relative inefficiency of public operation, as compared with private operation, is very large in highly speculative undertakings and dwindles to nothing in respect of those where the speculative element is practically non-existent. This idea is sometimes crystallised in an attempt to group industries into two divisions, the speculative and the non-speculative, after the manner in which trustees distinguish between speculative securities and investment securities. This grouping, it is sometimes suggested, can be adequately worked out, by setting on the one side new industries in an experimental stage, and, on the other, industries that are already tried and known. Thus, Sir George Gibb distinguishes, from this point of view, the railway industry at an early, and at a mature, age. "As regards the age of construction, at all events, England has derived incalculable benefit from the fact that the railway system has been made by private enterprise. But the problem of working the railway system after it has been constructed is, I admit,

---

[1] *Economic Journal*, 1907, pp. 21-22. Cf. also Ryan, *Distributive Justice*, p. 165.

[2] *Municipal and Private Operation of Public Utilities*, vol. i. p. 437.

essentially different from the problem of securing its construction." [1] In like manner, Professor Commons, writing in 1904,
while he approved of the establishment of city electric lighting
plants at that time, considered that "those cities which entered
upon municipal electric lighting eight or ten years ago are
open to criticism." "Private parties," he holds, "should be
encouraged to push forward in all the untrod fields." [2] The
distinction thus insisted on has, no doubt, considerable importance. Two points, however, should be noticed. First,
an industry, which is old-established at one place, may need
new construction at another, and the conditions of construction
there may be such that a large speculative element remains.
For example, though the industry of water supply is an old
one, different towns have to be supplied from sources situated
so differently, and along routes of such varying character, that
little guidance for one town can be drawn from the experience
of others. Secondly, no industry is likely to be so far established that experimentation—which involves speculation—as
to improved methods is undesirable. In some measure, all
industries, in which possibilities of development remain, demand
readiness to take risks if further inventions are to be made,
and are, therefore, liable to be hampered by anything that
obstructs this readiness. It would, therefore, be an error to
suppose that the relatively uneconomic character of public
operation, due to the circumstances discussed in this section,
is significant only for new industries. It probably has some
appreciable significance in regard to nearly all industries,
though, of course, its importance is greatest in regard to those
in an experimental stage.

§ 6. I pass to a third consideration. The relative inferiority of public operation, due to the interference which it
causes with the most economical combination of the different
factors of production—for that is, in effect, what obstacles in
the way of people's readiness to take risks, or to brave uncertainty,
implies—is paralleled, in many industries, by a further inferiority due to interference with the most economical size of
business unit. Practically speaking, public undertakings can

---

[1] *Railway Nationalisation*, p. 11.
[2] Bemis, *Municipal Monopolies*, p. 56.

only be operated by groups of people united into some form
of political organisation. But it is highly improbable that
the areas of control, most economical for the working of any
industry, will correspond in size with the areas covered by the
public authorities existing in a modern State, since these are
set up with regard to quite other considerations than the
efficient running of industries. Consequently, in general, it
must either happen that special public authorities are created
for the express purpose of running certain industries, or that
the size of the units of control in these industries is altered to
fit the scope of existing public authorities. For very large
enterprises having a scope midway between that of the central
government and that of the relevant local authority, experience
shows that special public bodies, adapted to this scope, can be,
and have been, erected. We are familiar, for example, with
the various harbour trusts and dock trusts, with the London
Water Board and the Port of London Authority. Another
device is that of joint boards of management representing two
or more local authorities. "In England and Wales, during
the year 1907-8, there were twenty-five joint boards or committees for the supply of water, two for the supply of water
and gas, and one for the supply of electricity and the management of a tramway undertaking."[1] Though, however, for very
large businesses, the creation of special public bodies is admittedly a practicable policy, it is not always likely to be
adopted. The danger that, under public operation, local
authorities inadequate in area will become the agents of that
operation, is especially great in industries originally adapted
to the area covered by these agents, but afterwards fitted, as a
result of new inventions, for larger areas. In former times the
areas of management most suitable for the industries of water
supply, gas lighting and electric power supply were approximately coincident with the several municipal areas. But, since
the advent of certain modern discoveries, the areas, which might
be expected to prove economically most efficient, are often
much larger than municipal areas. Thus, "with horse traction

[1] Knoop, *Principles and Methods of Municipal Trading*, p. 117. As Mr. Knoop
further points out, it not infrequently happens that a municipality enters into
an arrangement with smaller authorities to extend its tramway, water or gas
system beyond its own boundaries so as to include adjacent areas also.

2 A

the limit of each local authority was, roughly, the limit of commercial working. With electric traction the parish became a mere item in a comprehensive system, which might extend over a whole county."[1] Again, with the improvement in methods of distribution for electricity in bulk, the most economical area for the supply of electricity has come to extend over thousands of square miles. Even in the supply of water, now that the needs of large towns are satisfied by the tapping of distant lakes, there is obvious economy in a joint organisation for supplying a number of towns along the route that the pipes must follow. Indeed, it would seem that gas lighting is the only one of the public utility industries for which the most economical area of management at the present time does not exceed the municipal area. These changes in the area proper to management have not, however, in general, been followed by the transference of the public utility industries to new public authorities created *ad hoc*; for the task of ousting the municipalities is opposed by an immense amount of friction, and is, therefore, little likely to be successfully undertaken. Hence, in practice, public operation often implies that industries, whose most economical area of management is intermediate between those representative of the central authority and of local authorities respectively, will, in fact, be worked by local authorities; and this, of course, implies a reduction of the unit of management below what is economically best.[2] In enterprises whose most economical area of management is smaller than that covered by the smallest existing type of public authority, the creation of new authorities for the special purpose of running them cannot even be said to be

[1] Porter, *Dangers of Municipal Ownership*, p. 245.

[2] It may be objected that the alternative to municipal operation is usually municipal control, and that this control, when the area of the municipality is too small, may render private undertakings as inefficient as municipal undertakings would be. But it is easier to transfer control than it is to transfer operation to an authority of wider scope than the municipalities. The British Light Railways Act of 1906 establishes such a wider authority in the shape of the Light Railway Commissioners. (Cf. H. Meyer, *Municipal Ownership in Great Britain*, p. 69.) Again : "When, as in Massachusetts, it is not uncommon for a street railway company to operate franchises from ten, and, in one case, from nineteen different towns, independent municipal control is out of the question. The State railroad commission is the recognition in law of this condition of fact" (Rowe, *Annals of the American Academy*, 1900, p. 19).

practicable. If such industries are to be taken over by any public authority, this authority can hardly be other than one of the authorities that already exist for other purposes. Consequently, in these industries public operation, not merely in general, but practically always, implies the introduction of a scale of management larger than is economically most efficient.

§ 7. Now, if it were the fact that under private enterprise all industries would always evolve the most economical unit of management, it would follow that public operation could not, in this respect, be superior, and would, in general, be greatly inferior, to private operation. In industries normally conducted under conditions of simple competition, such as the industries of baking, milk-supply, house-building or farming, we may fairly presume that private enterprise will, for the most part, evolve the most efficient size of unit. But, where any element of monopoly is present, we may by no means presume this. The most economical unit may be prevented from realising itself through friction, or through the hindrance imposed by popular dislike of large amalgamations, or in other ways. The probability that it will be so prevented is especially great in an industry whose normal condition is, not that of simple monopoly, but that of monopolistic competition. Here, as was pointed out in Chapter VI., there are large wastes due to competitive advertisement and so forth, which centralisation under a single management might remove. Of railways, for example, Sir George Gibb wrote some years ago: "Each railway company works for its own route. The result is that unnecessary mileage is run, and train loads are lessened. . . . If those responsible for the handling and carriage of railway traffic could work with a single eye to economical results, and in all cases forward traffic by the routes which yielded the best working results, great economies could undoubtedly be effected."[1] This statement has been borne out by the experience of the joint working of British railways during the war; though it must be remembered that the character of war-time traffic, with its large trainloads of munitions and troops, has been exceptionally favourable to

[1] *Railway Nationalisation*, p. 21.

economical working. Like economies are sometimes obtainable
from the combination, not of different firms engaged in the
same occupation, but of different occupations. There is
probably an economy in the co-ordination under one hand
of the various industries that utilise the public streets.
"Water mains may be laid before streets are paved, thus
saving the damage and expense of tearing up good pavement
to lay water pipes."[1] In like manner, it may well be held
that important economies would result if the work of treating disease could be brought, by means of a State medical
service, into direct connection with the work of preventing
disease that is now undertaken by the Public Health
authorities. Though, therefore, the danger of indirect evil
consequences of the kind discussed in Chapter VI. must not be
forgotten, it is at least possible that, in enterprises of this
sort, public operation, instead of hindering, might actually
foster the growth of the most economical unit of management.

§ 8. So far of generalities. When the practical issue is
raised whether a particular class of enterprise could, with
greater advantage to the national dividend, be publicly controlled or publicly operated, it will be necessary, in order to
reach a satisfactory conclusion, to take into account both the
comparative effects which the two forms of management are
likely to have on productive efficiency, and also the comparative
ease with which whatever regulation the public interest may
require can be applied to them. In industries closely associated with the public health, where reliable quality is essential
and where inspection cannot easily be made thorough, public
operation may be desirable, even though the probable alternative
is competitive, and not monopolistic, production. Thus, there
is much to be said for the public provision of slaughter-houses,
to which, as in Germany, all butchers are compelled to resort,
and for the public provision of milk for the use of young
children. The Reporters to the American Civic Federation
are of opinion that "undertakings in which the sanitary
motive largely enters should be operated by the public."[2]
But, broadly speaking, industries which would normally

---

[1] Bemis, *Municipal Monopolies*, p. 46.
[2] *Municipal and Private Operation of Public Utilities*, vol. I. p. 23.

be operated under competitive conditions cannot usefully be managed on a large scale by public authorities. Apart from a few special exceptions, the proposal for public operation is a live one only in industries that tend towards monopoly. The case for it, as against the case for public control, is strongest in industries which have been reduced more or less to routine and in which there is comparatively little scope for daring adventure. It is relatively weak in industries which are to an important extent rival to other privately operated industries, or in which the normal unit of management is widely different from the area of existing public authorities. Whether any particular monopolistic industry should be publicly operated or publicly controlled cannot be determined in a general way. Before a decision between these alternative methods is arrived at, a detailed investigation of the industry must be made, and this should be supplemented by an impartial estimate of the quality of the particular public authority whose action is involved, as well as of the probable effect of new tasks upon its efficiency for the purpose of its primary non-industrial duties.

§ 9. If, on the strength of the foregoing or other considerations, it is decided that an industry already in existence and operated by private persons shall be taken over by public authority, it is necessary to settle the terms on which this shall be done. Let us, for simplicity, suppose the conditions to be such that under public operation the technical efficiency of production will be unaltered. Public ownership is desired ' because, without it, a monopolistic or partially monopolistic concern is able to force up prices against the public and so to check the development of the industry under its command. If, in these circumstances, a public authority buys up the concern *at its market value*, it will have either itself to charge the same price for its services as the private company was charging, or else to operate the concern at a loss. In other words, if it buys the concern at its market value, the proprietors will have made the public *buy* their right to make monopolistic exactions; for the market value will, of course, be in part the result of people's belief in their possession of that right. It is natural, therefore, to say that

the price paid ought not to be the market value as it actually
is, but the market value as it would be if this anti-social
right were eliminated. But here the considerations set
out at the end of the last chapter give us pause. Some
concession must, it would seem, be made in the interests
of recent purchasers who have acquired shares in the concern
in good faith at the high existing values. How large this
concession should be cannot, of course, be laid down in
general terms. In each separate instance a detailed review
will have to be made of all relevant circumstances, including
"legitimate expectations" that have been created, and on this
foundation common sense must be invoked to furnish a
"reasonable" compromise. When the purchase price is
settled, payment will, of course, in general be made by
an issue of government, or municipal, or "public authority"
(*e.g.* Port of London Authority) stock bearing fixed interest,
and not by an actual transfer of cash.

§ 10. This question of the purchase price leads on to
a very important consideration with which this Part may
suitably close. At first sight it might seem that, if the
public has to pay the full market value for a monopolistic
concern, which is charging exorbitant prices for its products,
no national advantage can possibly result. The monopolist
simply takes in a lump sum what otherwise he would have
got in an annual tribute. This way of looking at the
matter is, however, mistaken. The evil of monopoly is not
merely, or even mainly, that it enables one set of people to
mulct another set. It is that it causes resources to be held
back from a form of investment in which the value of the
marginal social net product is larger than it is elsewhere,
and thereby contracts the national dividend. To do away
with this monopolistic policy will increase production and so
benefit the country as a whole, in spite of the fact that,
in order to do away with it, one part of the community has
to pay a fine to another part. From the standpoint of the
national dividend, therefore, it is greatly preferable that the
Government should pay the ransom demanded by the
monopolist, write off part of the purchase price, and then
operate the concern on terms that would have yielded normal

returns if no ransom had been necessary, than that it should allow the private monopolist to continue, by exorbitant charges, to hold back production and check the flow of resources into the enterprise. This fact must not, of course, be allowed to make those who have to bargain on the public's behalf unduly pliant to the pressure of interested sellers. But it is none the less the governing and dominant fact. When the vested interests of new shareholders in monopolistic concerns make the Government unwilling to force prices down to the proper level through a policy of control, it constitutes a very powerful argument for a policy of purchase. If purchase is made, the natural consequence would be for the Government to operate the industry itself. But if, for any reason, it does not wish to do this, and prefers to sell or ·lease it to private persons on new terms, which involve a money loss to itself but provide for the establishment of a proper price level, it will still have eliminated the evil of monopolistic restriction of output and indirectly benefited the national dividend.

PART III

THE NATIONAL DIVIDEND AND LABOUR

CHAPTER I

IT is obvious that, when labour and equipment in any industry are rendered idle by a strike or lock-out, the national dividend must suffer. Furthermore, the loss of output for which these disputes are responsible often extends much beyond the industry directly affected. This is well illustrated by the fact that, during the great coal strike of March 1912, the general percentage of unemployment over the whole body of trade unionists in the United Kingdom was no less than 11 per cent, as against an average level for March during the ten years 1903–12 of $5\frac{1}{2}$ per cent. The reason for this is that a stoppage of work in an important industry checks activity in other industries in two ways. On the one hand, by impoverishing the people actually involved in the stoppage, it lessens the demand for the goods the other industries make; on the other hand, if the industry in which the stoppage has occurred is one that furnishes a commodity or service largely used in the conduct of other industries, it lessens the supply to them of raw material or equipment for their work. Naturally not all strikes and lock-outs produce this secondary effect in equal measure. The larger the range they cover and the more fundamental the commodities or services they supply, the more marked is their influence. Coal and transport service, for example, are basal goods essential to practically all industries, and a miners' or a railway servants' strike will, therefore, produce a much larger indirect effect than a cotton-workers' strike of the same extent and duration. But, in some degree, all stoppages of work inflict an indirect injury upon the national dividend by the reactions they set up

in other industries, in addition to the direct injury that they
carry in themselves. It is true, no doubt, that the net contraction of output consequent upon industrial disputes is generally
smaller than the immediate contraction; for a stoppage
of work at one place may lead both to more work at the
same time in rival establishments and to more work at a
later time (in fulfilling delayed orders) in the establishments
where the stoppage has occurred. It must be admitted also
that, on some occasions, the direct damage caused by strikes
and lock-outs is partly compensated by the stimulus indirectly
given to improvements in machinery and in the organisation
of work. Mr. Nasmyth, in his evidence before the Trades
Union Commission of 1868, laid very great stress upon this.
"I believe," he said, "that, if there were a debtor and creditor
account made up of strikes and lock-outs with the interests
of society, up to a certain point they would be found to have
been a benefit. Such has been the stimulus applied to
ingenuity by the intolerable annoyance resulting from strikes
and lock-outs, that it has developed more than anything those
wonderful improvements in automaton machinery that produce
you a window frame or the piston-rod of a steam-engine of
such an accuracy as would make Euclid's mouth water to
look at. These things are pouring in in quantities as the
result of the stimulus given to ingenuity through the annoyance of strikes. It is not being coaxed on by some grand
reward in the distance, but I think a kick from behind is
sometimes as useful as a gentle leading forward in front."[1]
These reflex effects of conflict are, no doubt, important. But
it would be paradoxical to maintain that the reaction of the
industrial organism against the evils threatening it ordinarily
outweigh those evils themselves. By adapting itself to
injurious changes of environment it can, indeed, lessen, but
it cannot altogether abolish, the damage to which it is exposed.
An excellent parallel is afforded by the effects of a blockade

---

[1] *Minutes of Evidence*, p. 71. Clifford (*Agricultural Lock-out*, p. 179)
describes the way in which farmers were stimulated by the 1874 dispute to
improve their organisation, and to do the same work as before with fewer men.
In like manner, the great anthracite coal strike in the United States in 1902
led to the invention of economical methods of utilising other fuels, which continued to be employed after normal conditions had returned.

instituted by one State against the ports of another. The immediate effect both upon the blockaded State and upon neutrals is an obvious, and sometimes a considerable, injury. By altering the direction and character of their trade they may reduce the extent of their losses. It is even conceivable that the search for new trade openings may lead to the discovery of one, *which otherwise would not have been found*, and which is possessed of advantages great enough to outweigh all the evils of the blockade period. Any such result is, however, extraordinarily improbable, and nobody, on the strength of it, would dream of suggesting that blockades in general are likely to do the world more good than harm. So with industrial disputes. It is conceivable that one of them may stir to action some otherwise mute, inglorious inventor; but it is immensely unlikely that it will, at best, do more than slightly antedate the discovery that he makes. On a broad view, the hypothetical gain is altogether outweighed by the certain loss of production in the industries directly affected and in related industries the raw material of which is cut off or the product of which cannot be worked up into its final stage. Moreover, there may be lasting injury to the workpeople in industrial careers interrupted, a load of debt contracted to meet a temporary emergency, and permanent damage to their children's health through the enforced period of insufficient nourishment. The extent of these evils varies, of course, partly with the degree to which the commodity whose production is stopped is consumed by the poorer classes, and partly with its importance for life, health, security and order. But, in any event, the aggregate damage with which industrial disputes threaten the national dividend is very grave. It has been pertinently asked: "Would any Board of Managers attempt to run a railway or start an electric-lighting plant, or operate a mill or factory, or send a liner to sea, with a mechanical equipment which was certain to break down periodically and lie in inevitable idleness until repairs could be patched up? And yet that is almost an absolute analogy to the state of labour conditions throughout nearly the whole range of such enterprises."[1] Anything that makes

[1] Goring, *Engineering Magazine*, vol. xx. p. 922.

it less likely that these break-downs will occur is bound to prove of substantial benefit to the national dividend. Hence the eagerness of social reformers to build up and fortify the machinery of industrial peace. They recognise, indeed, that in the work of pacification constitutions and agreements cannot accomplish much. In industrial, as in international negotiations, perfection of machinery counts for far less than good faith and good will. Care must, therefore, be taken not to stress unduly matters of mere technique. Nevertheless, the type of machinery employed is certain to have some effect, and may have a considerable effect, both directly and also by its reflex influence on the general attitude which employers or employees take to one another. It is, therefore, important to the present purpose to examine the principal problems which have to be faced in building up machinery, through whose aid it is hoped that industrial peace may be preserved.

CHAPTER II

§ 1. A NECESSARY preliminary to analysis is some classification of differences. The classification which naturally suggests itself in the first instance is one based upon the character of the matters in dispute. Such a classification yields two divisions, each in turn containing further subdivisions. The divisions comprise respectively differences about "the fraction of wages" and differences about "the demarcation of function." Differences about the fraction of wages may be subdivided into:

(1) Those connected with the reward of labour, generally raising an issue as to the money rate of wage, but sometimes touching such matters as workshop fines or the amount of special allowances, whether in money or in kind;

(2) Those connected with the doing and bearing of the employees, generally involving the question of hours.

Differences as to demarcation of function include, besides the well-known, but relatively unimportant, "demarcation disputes" between kindred trades, all quarrels arising out of claims by the workpeople to a larger share in the work of management. They generally relate to either:

(1) The way in which work is apportioned between different classes of workmen and machine tools; or

(2) The sources from which the employer draws his workpeople; or

(3) The voice allowed to workpeople in the settlement of working conditions.

The second of these subdivisions includes all questions concerning discrimination against, preference to, or exclusive employment of trade unionists.

§ 2. For many purposes the above classification is the most convenient to follow. But for the task of constructing machinery for preserving industrial peace it is not of serious value, because in practice the design of the machinery never turns upon distinctions between wages differences, differences about hours, or differences about the demarcation of work. We have, therefore, to seek some classification better adapted to the purpose in hand. In this search we are driven to follow two lines of thought, neither of which affords exact or sharp distinctions, but both of which, as will presently appear, somehow run together and yield a compound classification. They turn, respectively, upon the degree of self-sufficiency enjoyed by the parties to the difference and upon the extent of the theoretical ground which they have in common.

§ 3. Under the former of these two heads the determining factor is the relation between the bodies which control negotiations and those which are directly affected by their result. Both the employers and the workpeople implicated may be entirely independent, or both may be subordinate branches of larger organisations; or the employers may be independent and the workpeople a branch; or the employers a branch and the workpeople independent. This distinction is, however, somewhat blurred in practice, because to be a branch of a wider organisation is not the same thing as to have no control over negotiations affecting one's own interests. The extent to which local organisations are subordinated in this matter to national unions varies greatly in different times and places. They may be left entirely free; they may be free to make, but not to denounce, agreements; they may be offered advice or deprived of strike pay; or they may be mere branches, compelled to carry out the instructions of the central executive. Consequently, in this form of classification, no sharp dividing lines can be drawn.

§ 4. The same remark applies to the latter of the two forms distinguished above. In every industrial difference there is *some* common ground between the parties. Even when they diverge most widely, both sides agree that the decision ought to be "just." Sometimes the full limit of agreement is expressed by this phrase. A case in point is the coal strike of 1893, in which the employers understood by justice payment according to efficiency, and the work-people, in a vague way, payment according to needs. The common basis is wider when it is agreed, whether formally or informally, that justice, rightly interpreted, is the doctrine that the wage level should move in the same general direction as some accepted external index. This stage is often reached when the wages of a small group of workmen are in question; for it is generally recognised that these ought not, as a rule, to move very differently from the average wage level of other men in the neighbourhood engaged in similar employment. It is also reached with regard to the wages of larger groups, when the doctrine is accepted that, other things being equal, wages ought, in some sense, to follow prices. Thus, throughout the series of arbitra-tions in the North of England iron trade, studied by Mr. Price, "there is a general agreement that the basis of award is to be primarily the relation of wages to selling price."[1] The common ground here, however, is merely that wages shall rise when prices rise and fall when prices fall. The question of what proportion should hold between the two movements, or what change on the one side "corresponds" to a given change on the other, is left unanswered. A further stage is reached when the exact proportion that the wage change ought to bear to a given change in the index is agreed upon. This is done where employers and employed, in any locality or firm, accept, as in the spinning industry, the average efficiency wage of the trade or district as their own standard, or when wage is related to price by a definite sliding scale. Here the common ground, so far as principle is concerned, is complete, and differences between the parties can only arise upon matters of fact.

§ 5. The discussion of the two preceding sections shows that no sharp divisions are to be found along either of the lines of classification which have been discussed. This, how-ever, is not the last word upon the matter. It may still be necessary, here as elsewhere, for the student with a practical

[1] L. L. Price, *Industrial Peace,* p. 62.

2 B

end in view to depart somewhat from the majestic continuity
of Nature, and to erect an arbitrary landmark of his own.
Such a landmark may be made out of the common division
of industrial differences into " those which concern the interpretation of the existing terms of employment," and " those
which have to do with the general terms of future employment." [1] This distinction is analogous to one familiar to the
theory of jurisprudence. " The settlement of such general
questions may be likened to an act of legislation; the interpretation and application of the general contract may be
likened to a judicial act." [2] The place assigned to any particular difference is made to turn primarily upon the question
whether or not it is governed by a formal agreement between
the parties. All differences which arise when there is an
agreement are called " interpretation differences," and are
distinguished from " those which arise out of proposals for
the terms of engagement or contract of service to subsist for
a future period." [3] Furthermore, these differences are often
identical with those which superior organisations undertake
to settle on behalf of their local branches; they " are for the
most part limited to particular establishments, of little
importance and often purely personal"; [4] dealing, it may
be, with controversies of fact concerning quantity or quality,
or the more precise definition of the mutually accepted pattern
of quality itself. " General questions," on the other hand, are,
for the most part, equivalent to those in which independent
organisations are directly concerned; they are "frequently
of wide interest, affect large bodies of men, and are the
most general cause of strikes and lock-outs on a large scale." [5]
Of course, it is not maintained that interpretation differences
in the above sense are *necessarily* of minor importance. Not
only, as with judge-made law, may the act of interpretation
slide insensibly into that of alteration, but also what is called
interpretation may cover as wide a field, and raise questions
quite as fundamental, as those treated in the general agreement. For example, there is no difference in this respect

---

[1] *U.S.A. Industrial Commission*, xvii. p. lxxv.   [2] *Ibid* p. lxxvi.
[3] *Royal Commission on Labour, Report*, p. 49.
[4] *Ibid*. p. 49.   [5] *Ibid*. p. 49.

between the question how many pounds a ton of coal is to be taken to contain, or how much "topping" the men must put upon a car-load, and the question what the wage per ton or car-load ought to be. Moreover, it sometimes happens that general questions are deliberately submitted for discussion on what are apparently interpretation references. For example, in the pottery boom of 1871, it was arranged that, for each branch of the trade, an individual case should be selected for arbitration, and that the whole branch should act in accordance with the award.[1] On subsequent occasions exactly the same result was achieved by general arbitrations of the ordinary type. Similarly, it is not maintained that differences as to the terms of a future contract, to be made otherwise than by the interpretation of some overshadowing agreement, must *necessarily* affect large bodies of men. Where the local branches of ill-organised trades have to negotiate new contracts for themselves without reference to such an agreement, the number of men affected by any difference which may arise must be small. Nevertheless, the sentences quoted above from the American Industrial Commission and the British Royal Commission on Labour represent the facts sufficiently well to provide the basis of a rough practical classification.

[1] Cf. Owen, *Potteries*, p. 142.

CHAPTER III

VOLUNTARY ARRANGEMENTS FOR CONCILIATION
AND ARBITRATION

§ 1. It is well known that, as industries become better
organised and the associations of employers and employed
grow more powerful, differences about matters other than
general questions are more and more likely to be adjusted. It
is not in the interest of powerful organisations to fight about
a little thing, and it is generally, though not, of course, always,
in their power to control small bodies of their members.
Various arrangements—the most perfect, perhaps, is the
famous system of "professional experts" in the Lancashire
cotton industry—are made for the prompt and effective solution of minor difficulties. We need not pause to examine
them. The real problems to be faced are found in connection
with those broad general questions, of the successful treatment
of which by purely voluntary means the United Kingdom
may fairly claim to provide the classical example.

§ 2. In any study of the comparative advantages of
different types of machinery devoted to this end, the first
question to decide is whether it is better to rest content with
a simple agreement—which must, of course, be subject to
renewal or denunciation from time to time—to employ defined conciliatory processes when a conflict is threatened, or
to set up and maintain permanently in being some regularly
constituted organ of negotiation. Upon the right answer to
this question there is a fairly general consensus of opinion.
Unless there is some machinery already established, it will be
necessary to appoint negotiators at a moment of heated controversy, and the attempt to do this may not only involve delay

but also afford opportunity for obstruction and friction. More generally, as Professor Foxwell observed many years ago: " The fact is that, where human beings are concerned, where personal relations should be formed, and where moral forces are at work, a certain permanence of conditions seems to be essential. The altruistic and social feelings, which are the very cement of the social fabric, and enormously lessen the irksomeness of effort and the friction of industry, seem to require time for their development, and frequently cannot exert their full strength unless they are embodied in the symbol of an organisation." [1] No doubt, when the Associations upon both sides are exceptionally strong and the relations between them exceptionally satisfactory, this consideration loses much of its importance. In general, however, there can be no doubt that the prospects of peace will be substantially improved by the establishment of permanent Boards containing representatives of employers and employed meeting together regularly. They will be still further improved if these Boards are entrusted, as is contemplated under the Whitley Scheme for national, district, and local industrial councils in each principal industry, not merely with the settlement of differences, but with general collaboration in determining conditions of work, methods of remuneration, technical education, industrial research, improvement of processes, and so forth. For, working jointly at these broad problems, the representatives of employers and employed will come to regard themselves more as partners and less as hostile bargainers, and, consequently, when differences between them do arise, not only will the general atmosphere of discussion be a good one, but also both sides will have at the back of their minds a feeling that extreme action must at all costs be avoided, lest it destroy an organisation proved capable of much valuable work in their common interest.

§ 3. The constitution of the Boards or Councils has next to be considered. The essential point is that the representatives of either side, and particularly of the workmen, should have the confidence of their clients. The mechanism by which this can best be secured varies somewhat according

---

[1] *The Claims of Labour*, p. 190.

to the character of the two organisations. In some of the Boards in the Iron and Steel industry, and in the Railway Conciliation Board under the agreement of 1914, representatives are appointed by a vote of the employers and employed connected with separate firms or districts. When, however, the Associations are strong, this device is not necessary. The confidence of the rank and file in the Board can be obtained without it. The important thing is that the chief Association officials should have confidence in it. If they are convinced, the loyalty of the rest is as well assured as it can be ; if they are not convinced, the authority of the Board is worthless. Consequently, though delegates from different works may still attend to supply information, the Board ought, essentially, to represent the Associations themselves. The old forms, where they exist, may be retained, and new Boards may be started, whose forms are copied from the old. But the representatives must always be controlled by the officials of the Associations, and, in many instances, may also, with advantage, be appointed by them.

§ 4. The next point has reference to procedure. The fact that " general questions " are important, and bear directly upon the permanent interests of all concerned, makes the discussion of them, both on the Board itself and among those who will be bound by its decisions, peculiarly delicate. Consequently, even when the relations between the parties are good, it is important that everything which might engender irritation should be excluded from the machinery of industrial peace.

From this principle the most obvious inference is that technicalities and lawyers should not be admitted before the Board. Such a policy—apart altogether from the saving in cost and time—tends to reduce to a minimum the appearance, and hence, indirectly, the reality, of the opposition between the parties. There is less of a struggle for victory, and, therefore, less fear of the introduction of " matters of sentiment." In the practice of the chief English Boards and in the report of the Labour Commission, the policy of excluding legal representatives, and the legal forms which may be expected to accompany them, is fully recognised. Finally, the conciliatory, as distinguished from the litigious, character of negotiations, is often still further emphasised by an arrangement, in accordance with which the chairman (a representative employer) and vice-chairman (a representative workman) sit side by side at the Board, thus securing opportunities for conference at critical points in the discussion.[1]

A second inference is that the Board should not be allowed to pronounce upon any matter by the vote of a bare majority. When the solidarity of both of the two sides is complete, there is, of course, little prospect that any vote will be given, which is not either unanimous or equally divided. But, when organisation is less perfect, there is always the possibility of defection on the part of one or two representatives of either party. To allow the result of the discussion to be determined by such an incident is to court grave danger. So much dissatisfaction might be aroused that the whole conciliatory machinery would be immediately overturned. It is true that these difficulties do not seem to have been experienced in this country, and that, in a number of instances, the rules provide for a bare majority vote, subject, of course, to the condition that, if equal numbers of employers and employed happen to be present, only equal numbers shall have the opportunity of voting. In the United States, however, where, owing to the weakness of the Unions, there is a greater probability of cross-voting, things have worked out differently. Thus, Mr. Durand, Secretary of the Industrial Commission, asserts, both that the bare majority method will not work, and also that decision by unanimous agreement has become the ordinary practice.[2]

Thirdly and lastly, it will not, as a rule, be desirable for the meetings of the Board to be conducted, like those of the American interstate bituminous coal conferences, in public. It may, indeed, be held that such a system has educative advantages; but, on the other hand, the policy of deliberation *in camera*, which is usual in England, may be expected to

---

[1] As in the Midland Iron and Steel Board (Ashley, *British Industries*, p. 57).

[2] *Industrial Conciliation Conference*, p. 43. It may, perhaps, be suggested that a decision by a large majority, *e.g.* seven-eighths of those present, would be a still better plan, as it would eliminate the possibility of obstructive tactics on the part of a single faddist.

conduce better both to frankness in the discussion itself and also to uncomplaining acceptance of the decision reached.

§ 5. We have next to compare mere agreements to submit differences to conciliation with those under which provision is also made for arbitration in the last resort. The relative merits of the two plans have long been the subject of vigorous controversy. A number of authorities argue in favour of the former, and the Lancashire cotton trade, the British engineering industry, and most of "the important systems of collective bargaining in the United States"[1] follow their views in practice. Other authorities, on the contrary, agree with Mr. Crompton that all conciliation agreements should contain a clause providing for "some power in reserve by which recurrence to strikes may be avoided,"[2] and are, in turn, followed by certain of the best-developed English industries. Thus, in important conciliation schemes in the coal-mining, iron-mining, and boot and shoe industries provision has been made in one way or another for reference to arbitration.

Before entering upon the merits of the controversy between the two methods, we may note a preliminary matter upon which the champions of both views are agreed. Everybody admits that, in differences so important as "general questions," a settlement by arbitration will almost always stir up *considerably* more irritation and bad feeling than a settlement by mutual agreement on a Conciliation Board. Consequently, resort to it should never take place except when it is absolutely necessary. Conciliation should be developed and arbitration reduced to a minimum. In the United Kingdom it may safely be said that there is no trade in which the relations between employers and employed are so good that this proposition fails. In the United States the right line of policy is still clearer; for there, as was strongly urged twenty years ago, to allow the conditions under which they shall work to be determined by an outsider is "peculiarly obnoxious to the workmen," and they will never agree to it till conferences have failed and no other resort

---

[1] *Industrial Commission*, xvii. p. c.
[2] *Industrial Conciliation*, p. 134.

is left.[1]   Hence, in general questions, even when there
is an arbitration agreement in reserve, it is well to enforce
delay, in the hope that the greater coolness of an adjourned
discussion may bring about a settlement.   The Federated
Districts Coal Board realises this so fully that, when they
fail to agree, a second meeting is held of which twenty-one
days' notice must be given.   At this meeting the neutral
chairman is present, but he only exercises his casting vote
after another effort has been made to bring about a settlement acceptable to both sides.

Granted, however, that arbitration is a *pis aller*, the
question still remains whether provision should be made
for resort to it in the last instance.   The argument in
favour of incorporating a clause to this effect in industrial
agreements is drawn from the obvious direct advantages
derivable therefrom.   In the absence of such a provision,
differences may entail strikes and lock-outs, with all the
material loss and mutual irritation which these involve.
And, even if a *modus vivendi* upon the immediate issue be
found, we can never be certain that the controversy will
pass away without incidentally destroying the established
conciliatory system.[2]   If, however, the means of securing
an arbitrator are provided beforehand, both sides have
guarded themselves, in a calm moment, against a possible
future access of passion and excitement.   Their policy is
similar to that of a person who, unable to trust his will
to be sober, goes voluntarily into an inebriate home.   The
vis inertiae is thrown upon the side of peace, since there
is no escape from an amicable solution except the strong
step of withdrawal from the Board.

The opposing argument depends upon certain indirect
disadvantages, to which the inclusion of an arbitration
clause is said to lead.   In the first place, the representatives
of the two sides will not make so serious an effort to agree.
They may hesitate to offer concessions lest, in the subsequent arbitration, their suggestions should be used against

---

[1] Cf. Aldrich, *U.S. Federation of Labour*, 1898, p. 253.
[2] This result came about in the federated coal district in 1896 (MacPherson,
U.S. Bulletin of Labour, 1900, p. 478).

them;[1] or, in loyalty to their constituents, they may "feel obliged to win, if possible, through the odd man." In the second place, the possibility of gain, unbalanced by the danger of a stoppage of work, will tend to breed speculative differences. If these things happen, though one or two strikes will be prevented, the number of differences, which reach the stage of arbitration, will be so far increased that a large amount of friction is generated, and, as a result, before very long the whole arrangement breaks down. This danger is, indeed, comparatively slight, when the parties are on good terms with one another and are educated up to a proper appreciation of their own ultimate interests. It can also be obviated, in some degree, by a rule enabling the arbitrators, at their discretion, to order the defeated side to pay the whole cost of an arbitration, thus checking speculative appeals. It is evident, however, that it cannot be eliminated altogether.

Between these two conflicting sets of arguments no general *a priori* decision can be made. Until we know the temper of the parties in each particular industry, their affection or otherwise for a "policy of pin-pricks," the strength of their organisations, the power of the leaders over the men, and the probability that an award will be obeyed, it is impossible to judge whether a provision for arbitration in the event of conciliation failing can safely be put into an industrial agreement. In some circumstances a third way may be the best. A number of conciliation agreements among, for example, the iron-founders of the north-east coast, the Leicester dyeing trade and the Scotch coal trade, while not containing a regular arbitration clause, have, nevertheless, provided for arbitration by "mutual consent," if, when the time arrives, both parties desire it. Of course, an intractable difference is more likely to end in a strike under this system than under one backed by an arbitration clause. But this result is indecisive so long as we are unable to gauge the chances, under the two systems respectively, that the stage

---

[1] Cf. the discussion in the boot and shoe trade conference previous to arbitration in 1893. The employers were careful to insist that the concessions they proposed were not to be taken as prejudicing their case in the event of arbitration becoming necessary. Cf. also Mr. V. S. Clark's Report on Labour Conditions in New Zealand, U.S.A. Bulletin of Labour, No. 49, pp. 1192-3.

of intractability will be reached. Plainly, however, when the conditions are such that the arbitration clause can be inserted without danger of indirect ill-consequences, the direct advantages that follow from it leave no doubt that it ought to be adopted.

§ 6. When it is adopted, the constitution of the arbitrating authority has to be determined. We have to inquire into the qualities of the persons of whom it should be composed, the number of these persons and the best method of appointing them. These points may conveniently be examined in the order in which they have just been stated.

The qualities most needed for a successful panel are obviously a reputation for impartiality and a reputation for competence. These requirements in combination are, however, not easily satisfied. Persons, whether employers or workpeople, who have been brought up in a trade are inclined to believe that nobody without a "practical knowledge" of it can possibly form an intelligent judgment upon its problems. The natural inference is that the rule of the Midland Iron and Steel Board,[1] which required the independent chairman to be personally connected with the industry, should be followed. Since, however, practical knowledge is scarcely found except among employers or workpeople who have been, or are, actually engaged in the calling, it will rarely happen that a practical expert is available whom *both* sides believe to be unbiassed. It would seem, therefore, that the demand for "practical knowledge" will, in general, have to be abandoned. This can be done the more readily because, as a matter of fact, the decision of broad disputes on such matters as wages and hours calls chiefly "for a *general* economic knowledge of the industry concerned, and, inasmuch as all industries are connected, an acquaintance with the condition of the whole national trade."[2] When technical knowledge is needed, this can be provided by associating with the arbitrator assessors representing both sides, whose business it is to give him whatever help he requires, and not to take part in the decision. Even so, however, the field of selection for the arbitrator will

[1] *Industrial Commission*, xvii. p. 500.
[2] Schultze-Gaevernitz, *Social Peace*, p. 165.

be limited. Employers, for example, will not be enthusiastic over a politician in the House of Commons, because workpeople's votes are worth winning, while workpeople are apt to think that any member of the professional classes must, from the very nature of his life and upbringing, be unconsciously biassed in favour of capital. Hence, though a judge or a member of the House of Lords may satisfy the employers, the workpeople's ideal arbitrator can hardly be other than one of themselves. Unless, therefore, there happens to be available some one like Sir David Dale or Lord Askwith, personally known to, and trusted by, both sides, the choice can hardly be other than a compromise.[1] In these circumstances, the best way out of the difficulty may often lie in the selection of some man of outstanding eminence, whose conscious motives, at all events, whatever may be said of his subconscious ones, are above suspicion. Such a man, moreover, if, like the late Lord James of Hereford or Sir Edward Fry, he serves in the same way without payment frequently, may gradually win for himself a large measure of respect and confidence throughout the industrial community. Another solution may be found in the governmental manufacture of professional arbitrators. Something in this direction was attempted when an official panel of arbitrators was set up by the Board of Trade. The establishment of a standing Industrial Court under the Act of 1919 is a further step on the same lines.

What has just been said implicitly determines the number of persons by whom the arbitration panel should be constituted. Eminent outsiders are not likely to be obtained in groups. If their services are to be secured at all, it is practically necessary that the panel shall consist of a single man— very likely the man who also serves as neutral chairman to the Conciliation Board. This, however, is not the only argument against a compound tribunal. Reasoning of a general character shows that, even when practicable, such an arrangement is to be deprecated. The compound body in its most

---

[1] Even Sir David Dale, though entirely trusted by the men's representatives, seems on one occasion to have been suspected by some of the rank and file, who know him less well (cf. Price, *Industrial Peace*, p. 50).

attractive form comprises one representative of each side together
with an umpire, selected either by these representatives or by
their principals, to be referred to in the event of disagreement.
The argument in favour of it is that the two representatives may
possibly agree. On one occasion Messrs. Mundella and Williams
succeeded in doing this, and, in a miners' strike on the Loire,
M. Jaurès and the employers' representative followed their
example. A decision reached in this way is likely to command
a higher degree of confidence than one imposed upon the parties
by a single arbitrator. On the other hand, agreement between
the representatives is improbable, and the real decision will
generally rest with the umpire. When that happens, a compound tribunal resembles an elaborate machine, two-thirds of
which is ornament. Nor is this all. So often as a division
of opinion emerges in this type of tribunal the authority of
its decisions is weakened. It is true that the division can be
concealed by devices like that once adopted in a Staffordshire
potteries' agreement. "The award when given in such general
arbitration shall be signed by the umpire and the arbitrators,
and shall be issued as their joint award, signified by their
individual signatures thereto, and nothing shall be divulged
by any of them, or appear on the face of such award, to
signify whether the umpire and arbitrators are unanimous in
their decision, or whether it is only the award of the majority
of them."[1] It may, however, be questioned whether make-
shifts of this kind are really of much avail. For it is highly
probable that, in spite of, or, perhaps, partly because of, them,
the Board will be *thought* to have disagreed, and this is the
important point. Except, therefore, when the opinion of the
parties tends strongly in favour of multiplicity, it seems clear
that the panel had best be a single man.

Thirdly, we have to consider the method of an arbitrator's appointment. There are several different ways in
which he may be chosen.[2] Perhaps the most satisfactory is

---

[1] *Strikes and Lock-outs*, 1892, p. 217. There was the same rule for the
National Arbitration Board, agreed upon in 1901 between the American
Newspaper Publishers' Association and the International Typographical Union
(*Industrial Commission*, xvii. p. 367).

[2] The Window Glass Cutters' League of North America has the following
interesting method of selection : "If the arbitrators cannot agree on the referee,

that of the Durham Wages' Board, where he is elected at the first Board meeting of each year. Annual election of this kind, while not incompatible with prolonged tenure of office, avoids some of the dangers involved in a permanent or very long appointment. For great friction might arise if one side came to consider the arbitrator at once irremovable and biassed in favour of their opponents. Furthermore, election at fixed periods is superior to election *ad hoc*, because an arbitrator is most likely to command confidence if he is chosen by agreement of both sides, and he will seldom be so chosen if his election is deferred until after a difference has arisen. When, in spite of these considerations, an *ad hoc* appointment is preferred, the most obvious arrangement is that the parties should first try to agree on an arbitrator, and, if unsuccessful, should accept one nominated by an impartial outsider. There is, however, a danger that they may try, *and fail*, to agree on the very man who is afterwards imposed on them from without, or that they may have urged against some other suggested name reasons which hold equally against him. It is, therefore, more satisfactory for them to nominate an impartial person, such as the Speaker of the House of Commons, whose duty it shall be to appoint an arbitrator when requested to do so, no name having previously been discussed by the Conciliation Board.

§ 7. The next point to notice is relevant both to arrangements in which there is, and to arrangements in which there is not, provision for arbitration in the last resort. On the whole it seems unwise, *if it can be helped*, to allow anything in the nature of a referendum from the appointed negotiators to the main body of either employers or employed. The ill-informed popular discussion, which would necessarily follow, could hardly fail to stir up irritation and water the seeds of conflict. When the Conciliation Board cannot agree, and when there is not provision for arbitration, it might, indeed, appear at first sight as though an appeal from the

---

then each arbitrator shall write two names of disinterested parties, not in any way connected with the glass business, on slips of paper, and all names put into a bag, and the first name drawn out shall be the person selected as the referee" (Rule 18, *ibid.* p. 365).

representatives to their constituents is worth trying as a forlorn hope to prevent war. Practically, however, such a provision will often do more harm than good. If the men's representatives—it is on the men's side only. that the question of a referendum has any practical importance—think a point worth fighting for, their constituents are perfectly certain to be at least as bellicose as they. If the representatives do not think it worth fighting for, were there no referendum, they would arrange it; if there is a referendum, they may be weak enough to shift the responsibility, and the men may elect to fight. Moreover, the employers will probably limit their attempts at conciliation when failure to agree means to them, not the absolute certainty of a strike, but only a probability, the extreme greatness of which optimism may lead them to minimise.[1] Hence, the chance of an agreement being reached, so far from being augmented, is actually reduced. When there is provision for arbitration, an intermediate reference to the Board's constituents after the failure of conciliation is at least equally dangerous. For, again, the men are practically certain to support their leaders when these are bellicose, and it will hardly conduce to calmness or good feeling should they vote in a body against the very terms which an arbitrator afterwards finds it his duty to award. The off-chance of avoiding arbitration is a worse argument for the referendum than the off-chance of avoiding a strike.

What has been said against this policy in controversies about which the Conciliation Board has failed to agree has, of course, still greater force in those where it has succeeded. If there is no arbitration clause, a referendum, in these circumstances, might not improbably substitute war for peace. If, on the other hand, there is such a clause, the referendum would be futile, since an arbitrator, called in through the refusal of either side to endorse the Board's decision, is

---

[1] This argument is more strong, but the preceding one is considerably less so, when the referendum is on the plan of that provided for in the rules of the American Amalgamated Association of Iron, Steel and Tin Workers. Here, when a conference between employers and employed fails to agree, "it requires two-thirds of all the members of the organisation voting to insist upon the demands which have given rise to the disagreement" (*Industrial Commission,* xvii. p. 340).

practically bound to reiterate that decision, if not still further to stiffen it in opposition to the dissatisfied party.

These results are, of course, subject to the general caution that what appears to be ideally best is not always practically possible. When the men's organisation is weak or the authority of their leaders slight, acceptance by referendum may sometimes be the only form in which acceptance for a decision can be secured at all. In a Grimsby fishing dispute in 1902 the officials of the Gasworkers' Union even found it necessary to take a ballot as to whether a decision promulgated, not by a conciliation committee, but by a regularly appointed Board of Trade arbitrator applied for by both sides, should or should not be accepted. These difficulties must be clearly recognised. They do not, however, interfere with our conclusion that a referendum from negotiators to their constituents should be avoided whenever this is possible.

§ 8. Finally there is the question of guarantees—whether for the observance of agreements entered into directly by the parties, or for the acceptance of the award of an arbitrator, to whom they have agreed to submit the dispute. In some agreements each party gives a guarantee in the form of a money deposit subject to forfeit. Thus, after the great strike of 1895, the National Associations in the English boot and shoe trade agreed to place £1000 each with trustees, part of which would be forfeited should either be "deemed to have broken an agreement, award or decision"; while, "if any provision of this agreement, or if an award, agreement or decision is broken by any manufacturer or body of workmen belonging to the Federation or National Union, and the Federation or National Union fail within ten days either to induce such members to comply with the agreement, decision or award, or to expel them from the organisation, the Federation or the National Union shall be deemed to have broken the agreement, award or decision,"[1] and shall thereupon become

---

[1] Provision 9 of the Agreement, *Report on Collective Agreements*, Cd. 5366, 1910, p. 231. When the Union failed to expel the London strikers in 1899, Lord James of Hereford awarded £300 damages from the Union's deposit to the employers (*ibid.* p. 505). Evasion of the fine by refusal to replace money withdrawn under it can be met by a rule that, in this event, the whole of the deposit shall be forfeited. When the agreement was renewed in 1909, the phrase providing for expulsion from the organisation was deleted.

liable to forfeit some or all of their deposit. No doubt, when there is uncertainty as to the power of an association to maintain discipline among its members, its ability to show recalcitrant members that their conduct is causing it to be fined would do something to strengthen its position against them. Apart, however, from this condition—and in strong Unions it is not an important one—the value of monetary guarantees is doubtful. The Report of the Industrial Council (1912) on the advantages and disadvantages involved is as follows: " Considerable diversity of opinion appears to exist in regard to the efficacy of a monetary guarantee. If the fund is intended to be one out of which a penalty is payable equivalent to the amount of damage suffered, it is clear that, in order to provide for a case involving a large number of persons, the sum of money which it would be necessary to deposit would be such that many of the smaller organisations would be unable to set aside so large a proportion of their funds, or to obtain money for such a purpose. If, on the other hand, the penalty to be paid is merely in the nature of a fine, it does not appear that the adoption of the principle adds much to the restraining influence which is already exercised by the moral obligation to observe agreements. . . . We are of opinion, therefore, that the general adoption of the system of monetary guarantees, in the form of a deposit of money, cannot be regarded as constituting a practicable and efficient means of ensuring the fulfilment of agreements. At the same time, when monetary guarantees are voluntarily offered, we see no objection to their adoption." [1] This conclusion will probably command general assent.

<hr>

[1] *Loc. cit.* p. 11.

CHAPTER IV

MEDIATION

§ 1. THE experience of the United Kingdom and of the United States affords abundant proof that purely voluntary arrangements entered into by employers and workpeople, when worked in a friendly spirit, can do a great deal towards promoting industrial peace. But these arrangements are not adequate to prevent strikes or lock-outs in all circumstances. Purely conciliatory schemes may be broken into by war even during the period of their currency; and schemes in which provision is made for arbitration may fail to be renewed when this period comes to an end. On occasions of this kind, when voluntary machinery within an industry is lacking or threatens to prove inadequate, something further is necessary if industrial war is to be averted. The solution which naturally suggests itself is that of friendly mediation. In behalf of this the general argument is strong and straightforward. When once a difference has become accentuated, and, still more, when it has developed into an open conflict, both sides are apt to be striving for the "mastery," as well as for the particular object in dispute. They stand to lose dignity as well as money, and, consequently, their obstinacy will be much greater than the material point alone can justify. Not only is this, as a matter of fact, so, but it is frequently known to be so by the parties themselves. They will often have considered some matter worth the *chance* of a rupture, but not worth the certainty of one. Hence, when the rupture actually arrives, all that may be needed is some device for facilitating withdrawal, without undue loss of dignity, from a position assumed for purposes of bluff. Even if, in the earlier stages of a conflict, no way out seems acceptable, a point is sure to be reached sooner or later when one party will be willing to yield, if it can " save its face " in doing so. Hence the opportunity for the " good offices " of a mediator. His appearance on the scene makes prominent the fact, apt to be lost sight of in the heat of controversy, that the general public, as well as the parties directly concerned, have an interest in peace. The mere suggestion from him that a conference should be held may, in some circumstances, of itself suffice to bring about a settlement; and, where it falls short of this large measure of success, tact and a genial luncheon party may still indirectly advance the prospects of peace.[1] For, in the presence of a mediator, the element of " proper pride " and " courage never to submit or yield " is eliminated by the suggestion that reconciliation is made as a favour to a friend and not as a concession to an adversary. Furthermore, even when good offices do not effect an actual settlement, they may secure that a difference shall be resolved by arbitration instead of by industrial war. Perhaps the most effective way in which a mediator can forward this result is by helping the disputants in the difficult task of finding some mutually acceptable person to decide between them. In this matter the assistance of the British Board of Trade, before its duties were taken over by the Ministry of Labour, used frequently to be invoked.

§ 2. Since there is, thus, scope for mediatorial intervention, it becomes important to examine the different institutions through which it may be made to work. There are three kinds of mediators—the eminent outsider, the non-governmental Board, and the Board connected with some part of the governmental system of the country. These are not mutually incompatible, but can advantageously be used to supplement one another. The great advantage of the first is that the intervention of men like Bishop Westcott,[2] Lord Rosebery,[3] Lord James,[4] Mr. Asquith,[5] or the Prime Minister

---

[1] Cf. Mr. and Mrs. Webb's opinion of the efficacy of Lord Rosebery's luncheon party in conciliating the parties in the coal dispute of 1893 (*Industrial Democracy*, p. 242).

[2] The Durham Coal Strike, 1892.   [3] The Federation Coal Strike, 1893.

[4] The Clyde and Belfast Engineering Dispute, 1895.

[5] The London Cab Strike.

of the day, of itself tends somewhat to smooth the course of events by flattering the disputants with a sense of their own importance. The ordinary Board of Mediation, whether voluntary or official, has not, as a rule, such distinguished names to conjure with, and is, so far, inferior. Hence, for a certain class of disputes the eminent outsider cannot be dispensed with.

§ 3. The usefulness of the non-governmental Board is less generally admitted. It has, indeed, the advantage over the eminent outsider that, not being constituted *ad hoc*, it is more readily brought into play, and has a better chance of making its voice heard in that breathing space before a strike or lock-out actually begins, when mediation is most likely to succeed. It has been urged, however, that whereas in this country a great number of mediatorial Boards have been set up by the Chambers of Commerce and Trades Councils of different towns, none of them, except the London Board, has produced the slightest effect. In short, according to this argument, the system of non-governmental Boards has been tried and found by experience to be worthless. The evidence adduced, how-ever, is inadequate to support so sweeping a conclusion. The Boards which have failed are exclusively *municipal* Boards, and, with labour organised as it is in England, the conduct even of purely local differences is not likely to be left altogether to the men on the spot. May it not, then, be fairly urged that the failure of these Boards was due, not to their non-governmental character, but to the narrowness of the area which they covered, and does not the comparative success of the London Board add weight to this suggestion? If, however, the facts can be thus explained, they do not warrant us in supposing that local non-governmental Boards would fail if tried on the less completely unionised soil of the Continent. Still less do they prove that a non-governmental *national* Board is doomed to failure. Indeed, a Board of this kind, under the name of the Industrial Department of the National Civic Federation, has had considerable success in the United States.

§ 4. Nevertheless, though it would be a mistake to ignore the possibilities of non-governmental Boards, it is plain that there are certain advantages inaccessible to them, but readily available to Boards attached to the governmental machinery of the country. In the first place, the latter possess exceptional facilities—facilities second only to those enjoyed by voluntary Conciliation Boards in particular industries—for ascertaining the existence of differences at the earliest possible moment. For administrative officials can be required to supply them with immediate information whenever a strike or lock-out occurs or is seriously threatened. In the second place, they have greater intellectual and financial resources, and are likely to be more liberal in the use of them. Thus, it is probable that the trained ability which the Board of Trade (now Ministry of Labour) can command has a good deal to do with the preference displayed for it, as against local Boards, by the parties to disputes covering a small area. Lastly, when, as on the plan adopted in England, the emissaries employed are sent out directly from a central State department, instead of being, as in France, mere local officials endowed with mediatorial powers, they are likely to wield a modicum of reputation which may help them considerably in their work. Consequently, it is not surprising to find that in recent times the work of mediation in industrial disputes has been taken over in great part by machinery attached to some organ of government. In some countries the offer of mediation may only be made on the request of one or other of the parties to a difference. Thus, a Belgian law of 1887 authorises the establishment locally of councils of industry and labour with sections representing different industries, and provides; "Whenever circumstances appear to demand it, at the request of either party, the governor of the province, the mayor of the commune, or the president of the section for the industry in which the dispute occurs must convene that section, which is to endeavour, by conciliation, to arrange a settlement."[1] More frequently, however, mediation is authorised at the discretion of the public authority, whether it is asked for by a party to the difference or not. This is the arrangement under the French law of 1892 and under the English Conciliation Act of 1896. The latter Act provides: "When a difference exists, or is apprehended,

[1] *Bulletin of U.S.A. Bureau of Labour*, No. 60, p. 421.

between an employer or any class of employers and workmen, the Board of Trade may, if they think fit, exercise all or any of the following powers, namely : (1) inquire into the causes and circumstances of the difference ; (2) take such steps as to the Board may seem expedient for the purpose of enabling the parties to the difference to meet together, by themselves or their. representatives, under the presidency of a chairman mutually agreed upon or nominated by the Board of Trade or by some other person or body, with a view to the amicable settlement of differences ; (3) on the application of employers or workmen interested, and after taking into consideration the existence and adequacy of means available for conciliation in the district or trade and the circumstances of the case, appoint a person or persons to act as conciliator or as a board of conciliators." The Ministry of Labour, fortified with the Industrial Courts Act of 1919, has inherited these powers from the Board of Trade. Experience shows that mediation, skilfully and sympathetically conducted along these lines, can often bring about the adjustment of differences that might otherwise very probably have led to a stoppage of work.

§ 5. Thus, we may conclude generally that eminent outsiders, non-governmental Boards and official agencies of mediation are all valuable in their spheres. It must not, however, be forgotten that they are also dangerous. As an indirect consequence of their presence, the development of peace-promoting machinery within separate industries—a more effective solvent of differences than "good offices" are ever likely to be—may be checked. To prevent this result, discretion on the part of the intervening body is essential. It should never arrogate to itself the claim to more than a transitory usefulness, and should carefully encourage—as the British Board of Trade, under the Act of 1896, has always aimed at doing—the formation of mutual Boards in the industries with which it is brought into contact.

CHAPTER V

COERCIVE INTERVENTION

§ 1. Just as differences may prove too hard for voluntary conciliation schemes, so too they may defy the efforts of mediators. The possibility, or rather, except in the developed industries of countries which have reached a high stage of industrial peace, the frequent occurrence of these intractable controversies makes it necessary to inquire whether, and how far, resort should be had to the coercive powers of the State. Intervention of this kind may take place in four principal ways. Of these the simplest and mildest merely makes provision for disputants to enter the net of compulsory adjudication whenever both of them wish to do so. Examples are fairly numerous. In New South Wales the Industrial Arbitration Act of 1901 empowered any industrial union to make an agreement relatively to any industrial matter with another union or with an employer, which, "if made for a specified term not exceeding three years, and, if a copy be filed with the registrar, will be binding on the parties thereto and on every person while he is a member of any union which is a party to the agreement"; and declares "that any such agreement, as between the parties bound by the same, shall have the same effect, and may be enforced in the same way, as an award of the Court of Arbitration."[1] The New Zealand law makes industrial agreements enforceable in the same way as awards of the national Court of Arbitration. Mr. Mundella's abortive English Act of 1872, the Massachusetts provision that, when both parties refer a difference to the State Board, the decision automatically becomes binding,

---

[1] *Labour Gazette*, Feb. 1902, p. 39.

and the Federal Railway Act of 1898, enabling interstate
carriers voluntarily to establish Arbitration Boards with compulsory powers,[1] were similar in character and intention.
The English law has proved a dead letter, and was repealed
in 1896, but those of Massachusetts and New Zealand have
had a considerable measure of success.

In opposition to this arrangement it may be urged, first,
that, when once arbitration has been agreed upon, a sense of
what is fair and a wholesome respect for public opinion
already afford an adequate guarantee that awards will be
obeyed; secondly, that the introduction of a legal sanction
would so far destroy the honourable one—the payment of the
penalty being felt to condone the offence [2]—that the *net*
sanction would be no stronger than before; and thirdly, that,
through the association in the popular mind of the idea of
compulsion with that of arbitration, "resort to [Conciliation
Boards] for their various purposes would be made less freely
than at present." [3] It may be replied, however, that, at the
worst, since non-coercive arbitration would still be open to
those who preferred it, there is little reason to believe that
differences which, save for the change, would have been
settled peaceably, will now involve a conflict. Furthermore, the effect of coercive sanctions, in checking resort even
to those Courts which wield them, is much slighter than is
generally supposed. In some circumstances their influence
would actually tend in the opposite direction. In differences
where each party considered itself, and knew that the other
party considered itself, the stronger, there might be no settlement procurable under a system of weak sanctions, from
which one or other of them would not think it worth while
to break away. Consequently, arbitration might be declined
from dislike to the risk of these ineffective sanctions. If,
however, the sanctions offered were strong, the position would
be different. A series of possible settlements would be

[1] *U.S.A. Industrial Commission*, vol. xvii. p. 423.
[2] Cf. *The Report of the Industrial Council on Industrial Agreements*,
1912, p. 7.
[3] *Royal Commission on Labour*, Report, p. 99. Of course, universal compulsion to accept awards, unaccompanied by universal compulsion of reference,
would have this effect in a far more marked degree.

opened up, which, when awarded, could not be profitably violated by either side, and the risk of which both would be willing to incur, since the extra loss involved in failure would be balanced by an extra gain in success. Finally, the power to invoke legal sanctions may strengthen the hands of the leaders of either organisation against their discontented followers. This consideration is especially important when, as in the United States, the direct control of Union executives over individual members is comparatively slight. It is not, however, to be ignored even in this country, for, though, in our greater Unions, breaches of award in defiance of the central authority are rare, among the low-skilled industries they are fairly common. On the whole, therefore, the case seems to be made out for some system under which opportunities for referring differences to a Court with coercive powers is given to those who desire to avail themselves of it.

§ 2. The second way in which the State may intervene is by enabling organisations of employers and employed to invoke Government aid in extending to the whole of a trade in a district or country an agreement that has been entered into by associations representing the main body of employers and workpeople engaged in it. In South Australia an Act of 1910 provides that, in trades where there are no Wages Boards, three-fifths of the employers and of the employed may make an agreement and require the Government to promulgate it, so that it becomes binding upon the whole trade. The English Munitions Act of 1917 contained a substantially similar provision. The principal argument in favour of legislation of this kind is that, in the absence of it, agreements entered into by the great majority of those engaged in an industry are liable to be disrupted by the competition of a few "bad" employers. It has been stated, for example, that "one of the provoking causes of the second and disastrous transport strike in London was the withdrawal of a firm of carters from an agreement which it had signed, in order to compete with the other firms by paying a lower scale of wages than they did."[1]   On the other side, however, several

---

[1] Ramsay MacDonald, *The Social Unrest*, p. 109.

considerations of weight may be advanced. In the first place, State action of the kind contemplated would dangerously facilitate the formation of rings and alliances to the detriment of consumers. Secondly, there would sometimes be very great practical difficulty in determining the lengths to which extension should be carried. For the similarity between the products of different districts in an industry is often more apparent than real, and, when this is so, the maintenance of a parallel movement between the rates prevailing in them might work against peace rather than in favour of it. This difficulty may be illustrated from certain voluntary arrangements which have prevailed at one time or another in this country. Thus, in 1874 a combined scale was constructed for the iron trade of the Midlands and the north of England. In the north, however, iron rails were still the chief product, while in the Midlands manufacturers were already engaged in producing bars, plates and angles. For the former the market was falling, but it was rising for the latter, with the result that the employers of the north were compelled, at the first adjustment under the scale, to raise wages 3d., although the price of their own chief ware was falling. Consequently, the scale collapsed within the year. Similarly, there existed for some time in many parts of Lancashire an understanding that the wages of cotton-spinners should rise and fall with advances and reductions in the Oldham district. But "the increasing specialisation of districts, with respect to the yarns produced in them, was instrumental in rendering unworkable an arrangement which had at least been possible, if not desirable, some time before. What had been one market for yarns, roughly speaking, became many markets; and the prices for different ranges and qualities of yarn beginning to move more independently, rendered any sliding arrangements between the lists unsatisfactory."[1] It is true, no doubt, that a policy of extension does not absolutely exclude adjustment to the varying conditions of different districts. But it can hardly be doubted that the task of making these adjustments would often demand greater elasticity in the extensions than the patience and wisdom of the officials concerned are

[1] Chapman, *Economic Journal*, 1899, p. 598.

competent to provide.   Thirdly, it may be urged that, where
the workpeople's organisation is powerful, extension by
authority is superfluous, because private enterprise is
sufficient to ensure it.   The employers are anxious to have
recalcitrant competitors brought into line, and the workpeople
are no less anxious to help them.   Hence, "Trade Unions
assist employers' associations to coerce employers into submission to an agreement which they have not signed," and
"collective bargaining thus extends over a much larger field
than Trade Unionism." [1]   The United States Industrial Commission found, for example, that in Illinois the United
Mine Workers' Society is expected to strike or threaten to
strike in order to bring recalcitrant employers to terms and
that in practice it is generally successful in securing this
result.[2]   This last consideration, however, is obviously not
relevant to industries in which the workpeople's organisation
is weak.   On the whole, in spite of the possible risks to
consumers and of the practical difficulties set out above, and in
spite also of the danger that "the extension of the benefits of
organisation to the unorganised may tend to perpetuate the
class of non-union hangers-on of labour, and unfederated
hangers-on of capitalists, men who reap the benefit of
organisation but refuse to pay their share," [3] it would seem
that opinion in this country is moving in favour of this
strictly limited form of coercive State intervention.   Definite
support was given to it in the Report of the Industrial
Council (1912), subject to the condition that the Board of
Trade should not entertain any application for the extension
of an agreement, unless such application was received from
both the parties to the agreement.

    § 3. The third way of State intervention is by laws com-
pelling industrial differences to be referred to some tribunal
before any strike or lock-out in the industries covered by the
law is permitted.   This system is best illustrated by the
Canadian Industrial Disputes Investigation Act of 1907.
This Act is not of general application; but refers exclusively

---

[1] Gilman, *Methods of Industrial Peace*, pp. 116-17.
[2] Cf. *Industrial Commission*, vol. xvii. p. 329.
[3] Cole, *The World of Labour*, p. 314.

to certain industries in which there is reason to believe that a stoppage of work would prove exceptionally injurious to the community as a whole. The industries covered are mining, transportation, all forms of railway service, the supply of electricity and other motive power, the working of steamships, the telegraph and telephone services, gas supply and water supply. Practically speaking, the Act comes into play in these industries whenever a stoppage of work is seriously threatened, and 'it cannot be successfully evaded by a joint refusal of both parties to invoke it. The principal provisions are as follows. Thirty days' notice must be given of any proposed change in the terms of contract between employers and employed. If the proposed change is resisted by the other side, a strike or lock-out in reference to it is prohibited, under penalties, until the dispute has been investigated by a Board appointed by public authority, and until this Board has made a report, together with recommendations as to the proper terms of settlement, for publication by the Minister of Labour. When the report has been published; there is no obligation upon either party to accept its recommendations, and a stoppage of work may legally take place. But, until the report is published, a stoppage is prohibited by law and renders any individual taking part in it liable to a fine, for employers engaging in a lock-out, of from 100 to 1000 dollars per day; for workpeople engaging in a strike, of from 10 to 50 dollars per day.

This law, it will be noticed, has three distinct aspects. First, it goes a long way towards ensuring serious discussion between the parties—this is practically involved in the Board's investigations—and an attempt to settle their differences under the guidance, and with the help, of an impartial authority. Secondly, it gives full power to a tribunal appointed by the Government " to investigate the matter in dispute, with similar powers in regard to witnesses, production of documents and inspection as are vested in a court of record in civil cases, with a view, if conciliation fails, to recommendations being made as to what are believed to be fair terms." [1] Thirdly, it makes a stoppage of work unlawful until the investigation of the

[1] Report by Sir George Askwith [Cd. 6603], p. 17.

difference has been completed and a report presented. It has been held by competent authorities who have studied the working of the law that the first of these aspects is, in practice, the most valuable. The Reporter to the United States Bureau of Labour writes: "The principal service of the Board is in bringing the parties to the controversy together for an amicable discussion and in guiding the negotiations to a voluntary settlement."[1] And again: "The Government in appointing Boards, and the most successful Boards in conducting proceedings, have interpreted the Act as a statute for conciliation by informal methods, looking towards a voluntary agreement between the parties as its object."[2] In like manner, Sir George Askwith, in his Report to the British Board of Trade in 1913, expressed the opinion "that the forwarding of the spirit and intent of conciliation is the more valuable portion of the Canadian Act."[3] None the less, the provision for the promulgation at need of an authoritative report and recommendations may also, on occasions, yield good results. It is true that in trifling disputes, in which the general public takes small interest, little pressure from public opinion can be evoked, and that in all disputes, when once the passion of conflict has been aroused, even strong pressure may be ignored. But, when the issue is one which seriously affects the whole community, by threatening to disorganise, e.g.. the railway service or the coal supply, public opinion is a force which must at least be reckoned with; and it is interesting to observe that, on a number of occasions, when one or another of the parties at first refused to accept the recommendations of the Board and a strike or lock-out took place, the dispute was ultimately settled substantially on the basis of the Board's proposals. The third aspect of the law, that which makes a strike or lock-out unlawful until after the Board has reported, is the one about which the most serious doubts have been expressed. There is the objection that, given determined opposition, it may prove impracticable to enforce the law; and the objection that the success of a strike often depends upon its suddenness, so that any enforced delay necessarily

[1] *United States Bulletin of Labour*, No. 86, 1910, p. 17.
[2] *Ibid.* No. 76, p. 666.   [3] [Cd. 6603], p. 17.

handicaps the workpeople. These objections are undoubtedly substantial, though there are some industries, *e.g.* the transport industries, in which the strike weapon is not appreciably weakened by delay in resort to it. On the other side, stress is laid upon the fact that, when once industrial war has broken out, the issue chiefly in dispute is apt to be lost in a fight for mastery, which only exhaustion can end, and that, therefore, even though the law should often fail to prevent an outbreak, the chance that it will sometimes succeed, and so obviate grave injury to the community, constitutes for it an adequate defence. Plainly, on this issue no decision of a general kind is possible. What ought, in fact, to be done depends chiefly on what workpeople and employers think ought to be done and are, therefore, prepared to support. There can, however, be little doubt that an Act on the Canadian model, without penal clauses against strikes and lock-outs prior to the promulgation of the Board's recommendations, and accompanied, so far as possible, by safeguards to prevent injurious reactions upon the development of voluntary schemes of conciliation and arbitration, would, in Lord Askwith's words, be "suitable and practicable for this country." Part II. of the Industrial Courts Act of 1919 in effect constitutes such an Act. At present it could not safely include the critical penal clause. But there is much to be said for that clause; and if, through the establishment of a League of Nations, delay in political war comes really to be enforced by an overriding authority, public opinion may be ready to accept a similar restraint upon the outbreak of industrial war.

§ 4. The fourth and last way of State intervention is what is commonly and loosely known as compulsory arbitration. Under the Canadian Act, if the parties remain intractable alike to efforts at conciliation and to the suasion of opinion, strikes and lock-outs can ultimately take place without any infringement of the law. It has been left to the Australasian colonies to introduce a type of legislation under which, not only does a publicly appointed Board recommend terms for the settlement of differences, but the terms so recommended are legally binding and a strike or lock-out against them is a punishable offence. This type of legislation, when fully

developed, closes that loop-hole for a stoppage of work which
the Canadian law leaves open. Generally speaking, some
effort is made not unduly to discourage settlement by discussion and conciliation, but the principal stress is laid on
preventing resort to a strike or lock-out in those difficult
conflicts where less heroic expedients have failed. In New
Zealand, indeed, contrary to common opinion, a small loop-hole
is still left. For the compulsory arbitration law of that
colony applies only to unions of workpeople registered under
the arbitration law. In the corresponding laws of New South
Wales and Western Australia, however, there is no such
reservation, and the same remark holds true of the Commonwealth law relating to differences that extend over more than
one State. In all these laws the arbitration awards are
"sanctioned" by a money fine. In New Zealand individual
employers and unions of workpeople who break the law are
liable to a penalty of £500, and, if a union of workpeople
fails to pay, its individual members are each held liable to a
fine of £10, which may be collected through a writ of attachment of wages. Western Australia, like New Zealand, relies
wholly on money penalties, but the New South Wales law
provides also for the imprisonment of persons who fail to pay
their fines, and the Commonwealth law awards imprisonment,
without the option of a fine, for a second offence. It is
obvious, of course, that no legal prohibition and no provision
of penalties can ensure that the prohibited action will *never*
be performed. No surprise need, therefore, be caused by the
circumstance that, in the Australasian colonies, in spite of
their coercive laws, stoppages of work on account of industrial
disputes have, in fact, occurred. This is only to be expected.
The advocates of compulsory arbitration do not deny it. Nor
are they blind to the practical difficulties that may be presented by collusive evasions of the law or by independent
refusals to pay fines. Their claim is, not that these laws
can create a "country without strikes," but that, by invoking
a pressure more direct and potent than that of unorganised
opinion, upon which alone the Canadian law in the last resort
relies, they can render stoppages of work less frequent than
they would otherwise be. How far this claim has been made

good in the experience of New Zealand and the Australian States is a controversial question, which could only be answered satisfactorily after prolonged study on the spot. But, from the practical standpoint of English statesmen at the present time, that study is not necessary. It is common ground that legislation, to which the opinion of large masses of the population is strongly opposed, is likely to prove at once difficult to enforce and injurious to that general respect for law which it is to the interest of every community to maintain. Mr. Pember Reeves, the author of the New Zealand law, has himself declared that "to attempt to force such a statute upon an unwilling people would be foredoomed to disaster." [1] In England—and the same thing would seem to be true of the United States—anything in the nature of compulsory arbitration is at present looked upon by employers and employed alike with very great distrust. To introduce it at a single stride in the face of this general sentiment would be both impracticable and unwise. Public opinion may, no doubt, change, and at a future time welcome what it now rejects, but at present, whatever may be thought of its abstract merits, compulsory arbitration in the United Kingdom is not practical politics in any department of industry. The partial resort that was had to it during the war does not suggest that it affords a satisfactory method of avoiding strikes, and in normal times, when the pressure of the national need is slighter, it would probably meet with still less acceptance and, therefore, with still less success. [2]

[1] *State Experiments in Australia*, p. 168.
[2] Cf. *The Report on Conciliation and Arbitration*, to the Ministry of Reconstruction [Cd. 9099], 1918, Par. 2.

CHAPTER VI

AN ANALYTICAL VIEW OF INDUSTRIAL PEACE

§ 1. WHAT has been said in the preceding chapters will serve well enough for the rough purposes of practice. But it is interesting to the economist to probe somewhat deeper and to set out some of the broader issues that have been raised in a different guise. From an analytical point of view disputes between a workmen's union and a employers' association are closely analogous to disputes between two nations. When the disputes concern such things as the general conditions of work, the methods of wage payment, the hours of labour and the demarcation of work, the analogy is complete. But, when they concern wages, there is an important difference. Disputes between nations relate to a *thing*, disputes about wages to a *rate*. In bargains about a thing it is obvious that, the more either side can push the terms up against the other, the greater the advantage it will gain for itself. But in bargains about a rate, when the amount to be sold is not included in the terms of the bargain, this is not so. For, after a point, any further raising of the rate against one's opponent will bring about such a reduction in the quantity of the thing which he is prepared to buy that, to put it paradoxically, one is made actually worse off by getting better terms. Thus, when the bargain is about a rate, there will be certain upper and lower limits outside of which it will not pay either party to go, whereas, when the bargain is about a thing, there are no such limits.

§ 2. When, both on the side of workpeople and on that of employers, competition works with perfect freedom, the result of a bargain about the rate of wages is determinate at a single definite rate, which is settled by the conditions of reciprocal demand. If any worker asks for more than this from any employer, that employer will refuse to engage him and take somebody else, and, if any employer offers any less than this to any workman, that workman will refuse to work for him and go to somebody else. Where, however, wage rates are settled, not by the action of free competition, but by bargaining between a workmen's association on one side and an employers' association on the other, the rate of wage is no longer determinate at a single point. There is, on the contrary, a *range of indeterminateness*. The workmen's association will prefer to the competitive rate something higher than that rate, and the employers' association something lower. In view of the fact that a rise in the rate will lessen the amount of employment obtainable, there will be a certain maximum rate above which the workpeople's association will not wish to go, and, in view of the fact that a reduction in the rate will lessen the amount of labour obtainable, there will be a certain minimum rate below which the employers' association will not wish to go. *The range of indeterminateness* is constituted by all the rates enclosed within these two limits. Let us suppose that they are 40s. and 30s. respectively. From any rate lying outside this range it is to the interest of both sides to depart in the same direction. It is, therefore, impossible for a settlement to be reached with any wage rate outside that range. If there is any settlement it must fall at some point within it. The extent of the range will be larger the less elastic is the demand for labour by the employers, and the less elastic is the demand for jobs with these employers by the workpeople.

§ 3. In considering their policy, the workpeople's association will reflect that, if they elect to fight a battle about wages, the fight will cost them so much and the terms obtained at the end of the fight are likely to be such and such. Weighing up these things, they will determine on a certain minimum wage which it is worth while, if necessary, to accept rather than fight. This will be, as it were, their *sticking point*. If they think that a fight would cost them a great deal and that they would get bad terms at the end, this sticking point will be low. It may be a good deal lower than the 30s., which we have supposed to be the lower limit of the range of indeterminateness. On the other hand, if they think that a fight would cost them very little (or, still more, if they think that the actual process of it would benefit them), and that they would get good terms at the end, their sticking point will be high. It may be as high as, but cannot be higher than, the 40s., which is the upper end of the range of indeterminateness. Thus, the workpeople's sticking point may, according to circumstances, be any wage less than 40s. By similar reasoning it can be shown that the employers' sticking point may, according to circumstances, be any wage greater than 30s. When the workpeople's sticking point is lower than the employers' sticking point, the range of wages between the two sticking points constitutes, subject to a qualification to be introduced presently, the *range of practicable bargains*. Thus, if the workpeople would take 32s. rather than fight and the employers would pay 37s. rather than fight, this range is made up of all rates between 32s. and 37s. When, however, the workpeople's sticking point is above the employers' sticking point, when, for example, the workpeople would go as low as 35s., but no lower, rather than fight, and the employers would go as high as 33s., but no higher, rather than fight, there is no range of practicable bargains; and it is impossible for the issue between the two sides to be settled without a fight.

§ 4. If both sides have the same expectations as to the way in which a fight would end and as to the wage-rate that would be established in consequence of it, and if each side believes that the process of the fight would involve some positive cost to it, the workpeople's sticking point *must* be below the employer's sticking point, and there must, therefore, be some range of practicable bargains. If, however, the workpeople expect a fight to yield a higher wage rate than the employers do, this is not necessary, even though each side expects the conflict to involve some positive cost. And, if one side expects the conflict to be actually of benefit to it,—to involve, as it were, negative cost—it is not necessary, even though workpeople and employers both anticipate the same result to the fight.

§ 5. It should be added in this connection that negative cost is by no means, as might perhaps be thought at first sight, a mere mathematical figment. On the side of the employers it may easily be looked for if their commodity is one the demand for which is highly inelastic, and if, at the time of the conflict, they have large accumulated stocks in hand. Thus, it is sometimes alleged that coalowners are enabled by a conflict "to clear their stocks at famine prices, while postponing the fulfilment of their contracts under strike clauses." [1] They may also anticipate negative costs if they have reason to believe that, by precipitating a conflict in times of bad trade, they can insure themselves against being hampered by one when trade improves.[2] On the side of the workpeople, negative cost is, in the early stages of industrial organisation, fairly common. For in that period what the men are really aiming at is, not the concession of a higher wage, but respect for their Trade Union and consequent increased readiness to deal fairly with them in the future. Or again, the real purpose of the conflict may be to solidify the trade union itself and to attract non-unionists to its ranks. So far as conflicts are undertaken for objects of this kind, the advantage anticipated from the acquisition of those objects needs to be subtracted from the anticipated material losses of the dispute, and, when so subtracted, may leave a net negative result. In these circumstances the men may elect to fight, even though they expect both to be beaten and to be subjected to great suffering in the process. Negative costs are, however, obviously exceptional; as a general rule both sides are sure to expect that the actual conduct of a conflict will involve them in loss.

§ 6. The qualification forecasted in § 3 has now to be introduced. Since the workpeople's sticking point may be anything below the highest point in the range of indeterminateness, it may be below the lowest point in that range. In like manner, the employers' sticking point may be above the highest point in that range. Thus, with a range of indeter-

---

[1] *Political Science Quarterly*, vol. xii. p. 426.
[2] Cf. Chapman, *The Lancashire Cotton Industry*, p. 211.

minateness between 30s. or 40s. we might have the work-people's sticking point at 25s. and the employer's sticking point at 48s. In these circumstances the range of practicable bargains will not extend to the two sticking points: for no bargain is practicable that lies outside the range of inde-terminateness. Though one side may be willing to concede such a wage rather than fight, the other side will not be willing to accept it. Consequently, any wage rate above the workpeople's sticking point and any wage rate below the employer's sticking point, which lies outside the range of indeterminateness, is wholly ineffective. *The range of practic-able bargains*, that is the series of wage rates which both parties would prefer to a fight, is constituted by the wage rates (if any) which both lie above the workpeople's sticking point and below the employers' sticking point and also fall within the range of indeterminateness. This explanation is essential to the practical inferences to which we now pass.

§ 7. The extent of the range of indeterminateness is de-termined, as was pointed out in § 2, by the elasticities of the reciprocal demands of the two parties. From the present point of view, therefore, it may be taken as fixed. The range of practicable bargains cannot, in any circumstances, be extended beyond the limits so determined. *Within these limits* it is in-creased by anything that moves the workpeople's sticking point downwards or the employers' sticking point upwards. The workpeople's sticking point is moved down by anything that increases the cost which they look to suffer in a conflict; and the employers' sticking point is moved up by anything that increases the cost which they look to suffer in it. An increase in the strength of the workpeople's associa-tion alone will probably both lower the anticipated cost to them and increase it to employers. Hence, it will probably raise both sticking points, but it is impossible to say whether it will widen the gap between them. An increase in the strength of the employers' association alone will, in like manner, lower both sticking points. In practice, since the development of one rival association is almost certain to lead to the development of the other also, the most likely form of increase of strength is an increase on both

sides, leading to an increase in the cost anticipated by both.
This will mean a lowering of the workpeople's sticking point
accompanied by a rise of the employers'. Within the limits
set by the range of indeterminateness it will, therefore,
extend the range of practicable bargains in both directions,
provided that such range already exists, and it may bring
such a range into being if none exists. This tendency is
exhibited in international, as well as in industrial, negotiations.
If the adjustment of some political difference by war means
adjustment by a world war embracing powerful alliances on
both sides, the enormous probable cost of a fight makes it
certain that, unless the stake at issue is of almost inconceivable importance, some range of practicable bargains will
be available. In like manner, when the organisations of
workpeople and employers in some industry are extended to
embrace the whole country instead of being merely local, so
that a strike or lock-out, if it occurred, would be national in
its scope, an issue affecting, say, the wages payable in some small
district, for which, before, it may be, no range of practicable
bargains was available, is likely no longer to prove intractable.
Broadly speaking, as things are to-day, with the great strength
which nations and industrial associations alike possess, we
may safely conclude that, for nearly all minor matters and
interpretation differences, a wide range of practicable bargains
will be available. To both parties there will be an enormous
number of ways of settling, say, the political status of an
obscure African village, or the exact application to a particular
pit of a general wage agreement between coal-owners and coal-
miners, any one of which would be very much more advantageous to both parties than a conflict could possibly be. When the
matter in dispute is an important one, such as the possession
of a large and rich territory or the determination of the
general standard of wages in an industry, it is not, of course,
equally certain that a range of practicable bargains will exist.

§ 8. When two nations, or two associations, representing
employers and employed respectively, have entered into an
agreement not to fight but to settle differences by arbitration,
there is created a real cost, partly moral and partly material
(through the probable loss of outside support), to either of

them if it breaks the agreement. This is additional to the direct cost which conflict would involve whether there had been an arbitration agreement or· not. Thus, the setting up of such an agreement increases the cost of war to both parties, and so, within the limits set.by the range of indeterminateness, tends to bring into being, and, if it is already in being, to widen, a range of practicable bargains. Workers, who, apart from the·agreement, would have fought rather than accept 32s., may, in view of the agreement, keep at work though only 31s. is awarded; and employers, who would have locked out against a 35s. demand, may now go to 36s.

§ 9. When arbitration is voluntary, entrance into it means to each party, in the circumstances contemplated above, the risk of having to accept a rate less favourable to itself than the worst rate it would have accepted without fighting if it had not entered into arbitration. This consideration will not prevent the parties entering into it if each thinks that the risk of loss, which it assumes by doing so, will be roughly balanced by a corresponding chance of gain. But it is not certain that there will be a balance of this kind. If, for instance, the lower end of the range of practicable bargains is already lying at the lower end of the range of indeterminateness, the introduction of an arbitration agreement cannot extend the range of practicable bargains in a sense favourable to employers, while it may extend it in a sense adverse to them. In these circumstances they will be disinclined for arbitration agreements. The same thing is true of workpeople in the converse case. When, however, conditions are such that entrance into an arbitration agreement leaves both ends of the range of practicable bargains within the range of indeterminateness, the chances of gain and loss resulting from it are likely to balance for both sides, and, consequently, both sides will often be willing to enter into it in spite of the danger of losing more by it than they would look to have lost by war.

§ 10. But this does not exhaust the matter. If it were feasible to construct a voluntary arbitration agreement in such a way as to preclude the arbitrator from making an award outside that range of practicable bargains, which is established by general conditions coupled with the fact of the agreement,

there would, indeed, be nothing more to be said. But it is
very hard to include a provision of this kind in any workable
scheme. Even when arbitration is proposed in respect of a
single existing dispute, the parties can hardly give their case
away so far as to reveal to the arbitrator beforehand what
their respective sticking points are, and bind him not to go
outside them. When it is a question of a general arbitration
treaty to cover future disputes not yet in being, the difficulty
is still greater. If, however, no provision of this kind is
included, each side will fear that the arbitrator may award
terms so unfavourable to him that, in spite of the agreement,
he will feel compelled to fight against them, and so make a
net loss of his honour. For this danger the knowledge that
his opponent may be placed in a similar position by an award
of an opposite character is no compensation. Consequently,
both sides will tend to confine arbitration agreements to types
of dispute, in which, in their judgment, it is practically certain
that arbitrators will not give awards falling beyond their respective sticking points. Thus, in international treaties, States
have often reserved from arbitration "vital interests" and
"questions of national honour"; and in several plans for the
League of Nations a distinction was drawn between "justiciable"
disputes, to be submitted to a Court whose awards the League
would enforce, and non-justiciable disputes, which should go to
a Council empowered only to make non-binding recommendations. Similarly in industrial affairs, while employers and
workpeople are generally ready to arbitrate minor matters or
interpretation differences, they often hesitate to deal in this way
with the general question of wage rates.

§ 11. This unwillingness of the parties to enter voluntarily
into far-reaching arbitration agreements has been an important
factor in determining State authorities to intervene. Compulsory reference of disputes to a body entitled to recommend,
but not to enforce, an award, as under the Canadian Industrial
Disputes Investigation Act, tends, subject to the conditions
which have been enumerated, to widen the range of practicable
bargains, because a hostile public opinion adds to the cost of
fighting against any settlement which has been recommended
by an impartial public authority. It *may*, therefore, in some

instances create a range where none would otherwise exist. The Canadian system is exactly parallel to the arrangement under which international disputes are to be submitted to a Conciliation Council·before,war about them is permitted by the League of Nations. Laws which provide, not only that disputes must be submitted to arbitration, but also that the arbitrator's award must be accepted on pain of legal penalties, since they make battle more costly and success in it less probable to a recalcitrant party, will act still more forcibly to create and to extend in both directions the range of practicable bargains.

§ 12. We have now to make clear the bearing of these results upon the prospects of industrial peace. It has already been shown that, when there is no range of practicable bargains, a settlement without conflict is impossible. But it would be wrong to infer that, when there is such a range, a peaceful settlement *must* occur. This is by no means so. The existence of a range of practicable bargains implies that there are a number of possible adjustments, whether it be of territory or of wages or of anything else, any one of which both disputants would prefer to accept rather than engage in conflict. Each of them, however, naturally wishes to obtain the best terms that he can, and is also, though this is not necessary to the analysis, almost certainly ignorant of how far the other would yield rather than fight. Thus, we may suppose that a Trade Union has decided to fight rather than to accept a wage below 30s., and the corresponding employers' Association to fight rather than pay more than 35s. There is then a range of practicable bargains including all rates between 30s. and 35s. But, even though the workmen know that 35s. is the sticking point of the employers, and the employers know that 30s. is the sticking point of the workmen, there is still a conflict of will as to the precise point within the range, 30s. to 35s., at which the wage shall be put. Each side tries to push the other to his limit. The employers may think that, if they say firmly enough, "not a penny more than 31s.," the workmen will give way; the workmen may think that, if they insist unfalteringly on 34s., the employers will give way. In the result, both sides, equally the victims of unsuccessful bluff,

may find themselves in a fight over an issue which both know
is not worth it.   In the circumstances the chance that conflict
will be avoided is clearly greater the more cordial are the general
relations between workpeople and employers and the better
is the machinery available for bringing about friendly negotiations.   Thus, when a regular Conciliation Board is ready to
hand or, failing that, when a mutually acceptable mediator is
prepared to intervene, the prospect of a peaceful settlement is,
so far, improved.   When an arbitrator is available in the last
resort, it is improved still further.   For, when once an
award is given that falls within the range of practicable
bargains, it will not pay either side to fight rather than accept
this award.   One or other of them may, indeed, think it worth
while to bluff in the hope of modifying the award by later
negotiation.   But the award having, as it will have, particularly when the arbitration has been entered upon voluntarily,
a certain moral force behind it, is not likely to be disputed
unless one side thinks it bad enough to fight against—unless,
in fact, it lies outside the range of practicable bargains.   But
the wider the range of practicable bargains is, the greater is
the chance that an arbitrator will succeed in placing his
award somewhere upon it.   It follows that, when settlements
are arbitrated, the chances of a peaceful adjustment are greater
when the range of practicable bargains is wide than when it
is narrow.   This conclusion, however, does not follow when
settlements are negotiated.   On the contrary, since, the wider
the range of practicable bargains, the greater are the opportunities for bluff by both sides, the opposite conclusion seems
more easily defensible.

   § 13. From the general course of this discussion it is
easily seen that the need for arbitrators does not, as is sometimes supposed, arise solely out of the ignorance of the parties
to a dispute, and that their function is not "simply to find
out what the price would naturally have tended to become."[1]
Dr. Schultze-Gaevernitz, who enunciates this view, suggests
that "the determination of relative strength, which is the
function of a contest, could be equally well performed by an
exercise of the intelligence, just as we test the pressure of

[1] Schultze-Gaevernitz, *Social Peace*, p. 192.

steam by a special gauge instead of finding it out by the bursting of the boiler."[1] The implication of this argument is that, when all the facts are known to both sides, the range of practicable bargains is necessarily a single point, representing a wage equal to the one which battle would have established. This, as we have seen, is not so. It is true that an arbitrator, if he is to be successful, must act as an interpreter and not as a controller of economic tendencies, in the sense that he must place his award within the range of practicable bargains—a range, be it remembered, which the appointment of the arbitrator has probably somewhat widened. It is also true that, if all the facts are known to both parties, the wage rate which battle would have established will necessarily be represented by a point within this range. But it is not true that this wage rate is the only award open to the arbitrator which the litigants would be prepared to obey. The range of practicable bargains is not limited to that point unless, not only are all facts known to both sides, *but also* the costs which a fight is expected to involve is, for both of them, nothing at all.[2]

[1] Schultze-Gaevernitz, *Social Peace*, p. 136.
[2] For a mathematical treatment of the problems discussed in this chapter, cf. Appendix A of my *Principles and Methods of Industrial Peace*.

CHAPTER VII

§ 1. Our next problem has to do with the relation between the volume of the national dividend and workpeople's hours of labour. The effect of improved shift systems, under which, with any given hours for workpeople, the hours for the employers' machinery are prolonged, and, therefore, the quantity of machinery required to maintain a given output correspondingly reduced, will not be discussed here. It is evident that, after a point, an addition to the hours of labour normally worked in any industry would, by wearing out the workpeople, ultimately lessen rather than increase the national dividend. Physiology teaches that, after a certain period of work of given intensity, the body requires a certain interval of rest in order to return to its initial state, and that this interval grows more rapidly than the period of work. Failing adequate intervals, our faculties become progressively blunted. The extra nourishment that enlarged earnings afford cannot be properly digested and yields little benefit. "Fatigue so closes the avenues of approach within that education does not educate, amusement does not amuse nor recreation recreate."[1] Furthermore, besides this direct injury to efficiency, indirect injury also comes about, in so far as recourse to stimulants or unhealthy forms of excitement is induced by the fact of exhaustion.[2] As a result, output suffers both from lost time due to slacker attendance and unpunctuality and from diminished vigour and application throughout the working spell. Of course, the exact length of working day beyond

---

[1] Goldmark, *Fatigue and Efficiency*, p. 284.
[2] Cf. Chapman, "Hours of Labour," *Economic Journal*, 1909, p. 360.

which an increase would contract the national dividend varies
with the class of workpeople affected. Children and women,
particularly women who, besides industrial work, have also
the burden of looking after their homes, can, in general, stand
less than adult men. Further leisure for them yields a
bigger return—for children in opportunities for healthy sleep
and play, for women in opportunities for better care of their
homes.[1] An important factor, too, is the kind of work that is
done. Long hours of heavy muscular exertion and mental or
nervous strain are obviously much more injurious to efficiency
than long hours of mere mild attention. Again, workers earning good money will be better nourished, and so likely to be
able to stand more, than very poor workers. Yet again, the
effects will vary according to the way in which the workpeople spend their leisure, whether in mere dissipation or in
hard work on gardens of their own or in true recreation. It
will also vary according as the shortened hours do or do not
lead to greater intensity of effort and consequent strain
during the hours that are worked—a matter which depends
partly on whether wages are paid by piece or by time, partly
on whether the work is of a sort that can be speeded up by
improved ways of working or only by greater exertion, and
partly upon whether or not the intervals of rest and the
hour of starting work are based on careful tests of what best
promotes efficient working.[2] In view of these considerations
it is clear that no general statement as to the relation
between hours of labour and the national dividend can be
made. The relation will be different for different types of
workpeople and different kinds of work. "Where output is
controlled mainly by machinery the loss [due to long hours]
may be small. Where it depends more especially upon the
worker it will be great. Purely mechanical work can sometimes be performed sufficiently well by tired men. Skilled
work calling for judgement and discretion demands freshness
and vigour."[3] It must be remembered, indeed, that even the

---

[1] Cf. Marshall, *Royal Commission on Labour*, Q. 4253.
[2] On the effects upon output of a pre-breakfast start, cf. [Cd. 8511], p. 58
et seq. This Report concludes that in certain types of munition work the start
before breakfast may be abolished with advantage to the output (p. 66).
[3] *Second Interim Report on Industrial Fatigue* [Cd. 8335], p. 50.

feeding of a purely automatic machine can be done with greater
or less regularity and completeness, and that the *number* of
machines which can be entrusted to the control of an un-
fatigued worker is larger than can be entrusted to a fatigued
one.[1] The essential point, however, is that, in each several
industry, for each class of workers there is *some* length
of working day the overstepping of which will be disadvantageous to the national dividend. A detailed official investigation into the condition of munition workers in 1916 led the
investigators to conclude that the hours of work yielding
maximum output were, for men on "very heavy work" about
56 hours a week, for men on "heavy work" about 60 hours,
for men on "light work" about 70 hours, for women on
"moderately heavy" work 56 hours, and for women on "light
work" 60 hours.[2] It must be remembered, however, that, as
the investigators point out, their *data* relate to those fittest
persons among would-be munition workers, who did not drop
out from the strain. "Hence, the *best* hours for work, suited
for peace-time, are in every case considerably shorter than
those mentioned."[3]

§ 2. *Prima facie* it might be thought that this conclusion
is of academic rather than of practical importance, because the
self-interest of employers and workpeople must prevent unduly
long hours from being worked. There is, however, a large
volume of experience, which contradicts this optimistic view
and suggests that private self-interest has often seriously failed
in this matter. It is not necessary to invoke the terrible
history of the early days of the factory system. In quite
recent times Dr. Abbe, of Zeiss's works maintained, on the
strength of experiments conducted by himself, that, among at
least three-quarters of all industrial workers, a greater absolute
product—not merely a greater product per hour—may be
expected from regular work of between 8 and 9 hours a day
than from regular work of any longer period.[4] In his own
works, "in 253 different kinds of work, he found that a 4 per
cent larger output was obtained in nine hours [than in ten],

---

[1] Cf. Leverhulme, *The Six Hours Day*, p. 21.
[2] *Health of Munition Workers*, Memorandum, No. 12 [Cd. 8344], p. 9.
[3] *Ibid.* p. 10.
[4] Conrad, *Handwörterbuch der Staatswischenschaften*, vol. i. p. 1214.

using exactly the same machinery,"[1] and a number of similar
instances are on record from elsewhere both before and during
the period of the war.[2] It is, indeed, very difficult to draw
confident conclusions from even the most careful experiments
in this field. For the results will be misleading; (1) if the
extra output per hour that is obtained is due to a mere spurt
by men temporarily on their mettle, and not to a real increase
of efficiency; (2) if the reduction of hours has been introduced
in company with improvements in the general organisation of
the business—especially if it has been introduced in conjunction with the substitution of a three-shift for a two-shift
system, involving an increase of from, say, a 15-hour to a
24-hour day for the machinery employed; or (3) if the reduction
of hours has attracted to the experimenting works a grade of
workmen superior to those formerly employed there. In spite,
however, of these and other difficulties,[3] the evidence is fairly
conclusive that hours of labour in excess of what the best
interests of the national dividend require have often in fact
been worked. This inference is strengthened when we reflect
that any distant effect, which shorter hours may have in
prolonging the working life of the persons concerned, cannot
be displayed in these experiments.

§ 3. The question *how* such a state of affairs can come
about can be elucidated by the following considerations. In
ordinary economic discussion we are accustomed to speak of
the demand for, and supply of, labour in any industry, as
though both these things represented simply a series of relations between wage rates and quantities of labour. But this
conception is only exact if it is assumed that the number of
hours embraced in the normal day's work is already fixed. If
that is not assumed, the demand price or the supply price of,
say, a million hours' work of a particular kind in a year is not
a single thing. There are, rather, a series of demand prices
for this aggregate quantity of hours, which are greater or less

---

[1] Report of the Labour Association, *Special Committee on Hours of Labour in
Continuous Industries*, p. 10.

[2] *Ibid.* pp. 10, 11.

[3] For a good discussion of the pitfalls to be avoided in a concrete study of
the relation between hours of labour and efficiency, cf. Sargent Florence, *Use of
Factory Statistics in the Investigation of Industrial Fatigue*.

according as the work is to be done in longer or shorter day spells. Thus, employers might be willing to offer 10d. an hour for this aggregate amount of work, if it were to be done in 16-hour days, 9d. if it were to be done in 12-hour days, 8d. if it were to be done in 9-hour days, and so on. The reason for their preference for long days is, of course, that, other things, including the number of shifts, being equal, the longer the daily hours, the sooner the whole million hours is accomplished, and the plant, therefore, set free for further profitable employment. In like manner, there are a series of supply prices for this same aggregate quantity of hours, which are also greater or less according as the work is to be done in longer or shorter day spells; for naturally, after a point, work-people prefer a shorter day to a longer one, and require, other things being equal, a greater inducement to provide a million hours' work in 20-hour days than in 12-hour days. The general form of the schedules embodying these demand and supply prices would, of course, be different in different industries. The employers' preference for long days over short days—except, of course, when shifts can be so arranged that there is a full day for the plant irrespective of the length of day for the representative workman—would be greater the more important is the part played in his business by plant and equipment as compared with that played by labour; and the workpeople's aversion to long days would be greater the greater the amount of muscular or nervous strain involved in the occupation. But, whatever the forms of the schedules might be, in conditions of perfect competition the length of the working day would be determined in such a way as to establish equilibrium between them.

§ 4. Now, it seems at first sight that, in occupations where this competitive adjustment is in fact brought about, the resultant working day cannot be longer than the interests of the national dividend require. This, however, is not so; for the reason that, in general, both the employers' demand schedule and the workpeople's supply schedule are built up without adequate reference to the injurious effect which unduly long hours exercise—despite their accompaniment of larger immediate earnings—upon the efficiency and conse-

quent productivity of the workpeople subjected to them.
That the workpeople should lack forethought in this matter
is on a par with the general inability of all classes adequately to
foresee future happenings *in* themselves as distinguished from
future happenings *to* themselves; while, even if they foresaw
correctly, their poverty must cause them to discount the
future at an abnormally high rate. Furthermore, in making
choice between leisure and the payment to be got by sacrificing
leisure, they are apt to reckon the satisfaction from extra payment on the basis of the present length of their daily leisure,
and to ignore the fact that, if a part of this leisure is sacrificed,
they will have less opportunity of enjoying whatever purchases
their extra earnings enable them to make. The position of
employers is somewhat different. Frequently, no doubt, they
too fail to realise that shorter hours would promote efficiency
among their workpeople, and so would redound to their own
interest. But this is not the principal thing. Except in
firms which possess a practical monopoly in some department of
industry, and so expect to retain the same hands permanently,
the lack of durable connection between individual employers
and their workpeople makes it to the employers' interest to
work longer hours than are in the long run to the interest of
the national dividend as a whole. This point was well brought
out in some remarks of an employer who has successfully
undertaken many schemes for the welfare of those whom he
employs. "The employer as such," he said, "is not primarily
interested in keeping labour in excellent condition. What he
wants is a sufficient supply of efficient labour to meet his
immediate demands; and, though ultimately this supply will
be curtailed unless the whole nation allows a margin for wear-
and-tear and for the stimulation of progressive efficiency, he
cannot afford, under our present competitive system, to take a
very long view. He can act with others, but not much in
advance of them. In so far then as he represents immediate
and limited, rather than ultimate and general, interests, his
economic outlook must stand in marked contrast to that of
the nation as a whole."[1] From the state of things thus
depicted it follows that, even if competitive forces acted quite

[1] Cf. Proud, *Welfare Work*, pp. 50-1.

2 E

freely; the length of the working day would often be substantially longer than the real interests of the national dividend demand. This is naturally most likely to happen with the hours worked by children and young persons, whose aggregate efficiency throughout life, is especially liable to suffer injury from overstrain in youth.

§ 5. What has been said does not, however, exhaust the subject. In real life it may well be that hours of labour are established in excess of those which conditions of perfect competition would bring about. For, where mobility is imperfect, and where, therefore, as will be shown when we come to discuss "unfair wages," there is some range of indeterminateness in the bargain between an employer and his workpeople, the employer's bargaining power, as against unorganised workpeople, is greater in the matter of hours of labour than it is in the matter of wages. For, whereas a workman striving to get better wages has only, as it were, to lift his own weight, it is, as a rule, impossible for technical reasons, that any concession about the hours of labour should be made to him that is not general in character, and, therefore, less willingly granted. Moreover, if an employer succeeds in exploiting his workpeople in the matter of wages, the poverty which he thus induces in them will often make them *willing* to work for longer hours. It follows, that, when exploitation is present at all, it is extremely likely to make itself felt in hours of labour too long for the best interests of the national dividend.

§ 6. To have shown that the play of economic forces, if left to itself, is liable to bring about a longer working day than the true interests of the national dividend require is to have made out a *prima facie* case for State intervention. This case, however, cannot be regarded as established until the possibility of evasions of the law has been considered. In laws about wages, as will appear presently, this point is of great practical importance. For example, when it is proposed to force up wage rates on the ground that an increase of pay would soon produce a corresponding increase of efficiency, it can be objected that, since the reaction on efficiency will not be immediate, employers will be tempted by an enforced increase in the wage rate to dismiss those workpeople who are not already worth what they are called upon to pay. But against proposals to reduce hours of labour this class of objection does not hold good. Provided that the hourly rate of wages is not raised, a shortening of the hours of labour does not, at all events until there has been time for it to bring about a reduction in the mechanical equipment of factories, make it to the interest of employers to employ fewer workpeople than before. It follows that a sufficient interval will be allowed, as it will not always be allowed when wage rates are increased, for the improvements in efficiency which they tend to produce to work themselves out. This means that, by the time the danger of dismissals has become real, efficiency will often be so far improved as to neutralise and abolish it. This consideration is important, but it is not, of course, decisive. It is still necessary to consider how far governmental authorities are competent to frame the delicately adjusted regulations which analysis shows to be desirable. Hitherto, the basis of systematic knowledge upon which policy should be built up has been small, and there is wide scope for further study. Meanwhile, it may be agreed that the general principle underlying legislation to limit the hours of work in industry is sound. The movement, which has advanced with remarkable rapidity in many countries since the beginning of 1919, to fix a general maximum of eight hours a day in all industries, subject to certain special exceptions, may well be justified on broad social grounds. But it is very important that the different needs of different classes of workers should be recognised, and that the general maximum should not tend to become a general minimum also.

§ 7. One further aspect of this matter has to be considered. It is plain that, whatever limitation is imposed, it cannot be made absolutely rigid; because, if this were done, work would be prevented on some occasions when the immediate need for it was so urgent as to outweigh any indirect consequences. Certain materials, for example, become fit for use for a brief space only, and, if they are not worked upon then, are absolutely wasted. An obvious example is the fruit used in the fruit-canning industry. To refuse permission for occasional excessive hours of work in this industry might mean, from time to time, the total loss of very valuable crops.[1] Certain forms of repair work are in a similar position. They are urgent in the sense that they must be executed *at once* on pain of very serious loss. It is evident that, when conditions of this kind prevail, some relaxation from rigid rules should be made. In other words, some amount of overtime beyond the hours normally permitted should *sometimes* be permitted. But it is very important that this concession should not be abused. It must be clearly understood that overtime is injurious, even though it be followed by an equivalent period of slack time. "During overtime leisure and rest are cut down at the very same time that heavier and longer demands are made upon the human organism. It is practically inevitable that the metabolic balance should be thrown out of gear. . . . There is no rebound, or an infinitely slow one, when our elastic capacities have been too tensely stretched. It takes much more time, rest, repair than the working-girl can possibly afford to make good such metabolic losses. Compensation—off-time—comes too late. . . . After a doubled task muscle requires, not double, but four times, as long a rest for recuperation, and a similar need for more than proportionally increased rest after excessive work is true also of our other tissues and of our organism in its totality."[2] "When once an individual has, through labour during ordinary hours, reached a certain degree of fatigue, and proceeds to further labour (overtime) without taking the repose necessary to dissipate the fatigue already produced, this further labour has a greater physiological effect and exhausts the organism more than would a similar amount of labour performed when fatigue was absent."[3] These injurious effects follow from overtime work, however cogent the excuses for it may be. The excuses offered should always, therefore, be scrutinised with very

---

[1] As Miss Goldmark points out, however, this consideration affords no excuse for the overtime that in fact often prevails in the United States Canneries among the workpeople who label and stamp the cans after they have been sealed (*Fatigue and Efficiency*, p. 187).

[2] Goldmark, *Fatigue and Efficiency*, p. 88.

[3] Second Interim Report on Industrial Fatigue [Cd. 8335], 1916, p. 16.

great care. In the conduct of this scrutiny it is essential
to bear in mind that the immediate damage, which the
prohibition of overtime would bring about, is often in fact
much smaller than it appears to be at first sight. For,
first, in so far as pressure upon one set of firms in an
industry occurs when other firms are slack, the prohibition
need not kill the work they would have done, but may
lead to its being given out, either on commission or by
direct order, to other firms. Secondly, in industries that
manufacture goods capable of being made for stock, prohibition of overtime in periods of general boom will, indeed,
directly lessen the hours of work done in these periods, but
it will also indirectly increase the hours of work done
in antecedent periods of depression. Furthermore, in this
connection, the notion "making for stock" should be given
a significance more extended than usual. Articles which
have to be manufactured to individual order are not
capable of being made for stock in the ordinary sense. But,
in so far as they are capable of being stored prior to need
by their purchasers, they ought to be so regarded from
the present point of view. It is this class of commodity
that the Minority of the Poor Law Commissioners had
in view when they wrote: "The variations in the consumers'
pressure can be made much less extreme by means of a legal
limitation of the hours of labour. When the hours of cotton
operatives were settled by the individual mill-owner, cotton-
spinning and weaving were extreme instances of seasonal
trades; and the manufacturer was unable to resist the
customers' insistence on instant delivery. Now that the
maximum hours are legally fixed, the buyer has learnt
to be more regular in his demands. The extreme seasonal
irregularity of the London dressmaking trade would undoubtedly be mitigated, if dressmakers were absolutely prevented from working more than a fixed maximum day.
Customers would simply not be able to insist on delivery
in an unreasonably short time."[1] As a result, the output produced in *antecedent* times would be increased, thus
partly offsetting the diminution of output directly consequent

[1] *Report of the Royal Commission on the Poor Laws*, p. 1185, footnote.

upon the diminution of overtime in periods of boom. Thirdly, there are certain things, whether or not they are capable of being made for stock in any sense, the demand for which can be *postponed* for a substantial period. Commodities and services that are consumed in a single use do not as a rule fall into this class. If a desire for bread or beer or doctor's services or railway travel existing now is not satisfied, that fact does not cause any greater desire for these things to exist in the future than would have existed if it had been satisfied. *Some* goods and services, indeed, even of an immediately consumable kind, are subject to demands which can be postponed. For example, a man may wish to do the Grand Tour once in his lifetime; if he cannot do it this year, he will desire to do it next year. But much the most important things for which the demand can be postponed are durable goods, such as boots, clothes, pianos, machinery and houses. The desire for these things is based upon an expectation of services to be rendered by them through a considerable period. Suppose, for example, that a bicycle has a normal life of seven years and that I desire to purchase one now. If I succeed in doing this, I shall have no desire to repeat my purchase next year; but, if I fail, the effect of failure will be to carry over to next year a demand at least six-sevenths as intense as my present demand. In all industries which make commodities of this class, the check, which the prohibition of overtime puts upon work in boom periods, is partially cancelled by a stimulus to work in *subsequent* periods of depression. Against these considerations it is, indeed, necessary to set one upon the other side. If overtime is prohibited, employers may find it to their interest to attach to themselves, through the offer of higher wages, a larger reserve of workpeople than they would otherwise have thought necessary. For, the more extensive this reserve is, the less likely it is that inability to work overtime will prevent them from fulfilling orders that they would like to fulfil[1] When, however, the reserve is large, the workmen comprising the fringe of it are only actually em-

---

[1] This point is illustrated indirectly by the small amount of overtime found among women workers, as compared with men workers, in the bespoke tailoring trade. The men are skilled hands whose number cannot easily be supple-

ployed during boom periods; in moderate and bad times they
are attached in idleness to the industry which commands their
services, instead of being employed, as they might otherwise have
been, in some different industry.   In so far as this happens,
restriction of overtime leaves the amount of work done in the
industry directly affected substantially unaltered both in boom
periods and in depression periods, but makes the amount of
work done throughout the whole body of industries smaller
than it would otherwise have been in both sorts of period.   This
form of reaction is specially liable to be set up in industries
where casual methods of engaging workpeople prevail.   When
it is threatened and cannot be, or is not, successfully resisted,
the case in favour of close restrictions upon overtime is so
far weakened.

mented.   But the women are unskilled hands, and "the readily available
reserve of semi-skilled wives and daughters, who may at any time be pressed
into work, tends to relieve the seasonal pressure upon the less skilled, or women's
section of the trade" (Webb, *Seasonal Trades*, p. 87).

CHAPTER VIII

THE METHODS OF INDUSTRIAL REMUNERATION

§ 1. AN influence, less important, indeed, than the hours of labour, but still very important, is exercised upon the national dividend by the methods of industrial remuneration. Whatever methods are adopted in any industry, the general tendency of economic forces will be to cause the wages offered for each class of workpeople to approximate, on the whole and on the average, to the value of the marginal trade net product of that class. At first sight it might seem that, if this be so, things must work out the same whatever method of remuneration is in vogue. But the truth is otherwise. For, though under all systems a man will be paid over a year the worth of his work during the year, under some systems it will be to his interest to do more work, and so to have a larger worth, than under others. Thus, payment may be made independently of the results achieved by the worker at any moment, being adjusted only to what experience shows he may be expected under that method of remuneration to achieve on the average; or it may be adjusted to results, not merely on the average, but continuously and in detail; or some compromise between these plans may be adopted. Broadly speaking, the worker's output will be larger and the national dividend more advantaged the more nearly the method of remuneration in vogue approximates to complete adjustment. This, no doubt, is not true invariably. There are certain sorts of work where interest in the work itself, or interest in the result to which it ultimately leads, induces people to work as hard as they can without reference to the mode in which payment for their services is made. This is probably true of most work of original artistic creation, of the higher administrative work of the civil service and even of some kinds of private business. In these occupations the national dividend will be none the worse if a fixed salary by the year, or a fixed wage by the hour, is paid without any reference to what the worker actually accomplishes in any particular period. There is even an opening, if the jobs are sufficiently stable to make a high degree of mobility unnecessary, for payment by a life salary with yearly increments, adjusted not so much to presumed changes in the value of the employee's work as to presumed changes in his domestic status, and, therefore, in his "needs." Most of the tasks, however, that ordinary manual workers have to perform, are routine tasks, and—owing to the division of labour—are so remotely connected with any finished product that interest in them sufficient to evoke continuous, spontaneous and disinterested effort can hardly be expected. Even here, no doubt, some men will be found whom an ardour for excellence for its own sake or a stern sense of public duty will cause to exert themselves to the utmost without reference to expectations of reward; and the prospect that this will happen is specially favourable where systems of Labour Copartnership have succeeded in evoking in the workpeople a feeling of proprietorship in, and patriotism towards, the concern in which they are employed. From the main body of ordinary workpeople engaged in manual occupations this, however, is not at present to be looked for. The amount of work they will do in any hour, week or year will be greater if the payment made to them does, than it will be if it does not, vary as this amount varies. The national dividend will be larger the more nearly each increment of effort on the part of any individual worker is rewarded by a payment equal to the value of the difference which that increment of effort makes to the total product. This does not, of course, imply that the pay should be equal to the value of a man's output as ordinarily understood; for this output is in part due to machinery and equipment, which, if not engaged in assisting him, would have helped to increase the output of other workpeople. But it does imply that the pay should be *proportioned* (in a ratio

calculable and different in different occupations) to output as
ordinarily understood. In other words, it should *correspond*
for any worker with the results, conditions remaining constant,
actually achieved by him.

§ 2. In order to construct a wage system of this kind,
under which a man's pay is based directly and immediately
on his output, we must have some means of ascertaining, with
greater or less accuracy, how large that output from time to
time actually is. In the way of this there are a number of
obstacles, the importance of which varies in different occupations. The first, though not the principal, of these is that
a workman's output, when strictly interpreted, may include
other elements in addition to the physical product that his
labour, in conjunction with the machinery entrusted to him,
brings to birth. For, as Jevons long ago observed, "In every
work there are a thousand opportunities where the workman
can either benefit or injure the establishment, and, could he
really be made to feel his interests identical with those of
his employers, there can be no doubt that the profits of the
trade could be greatly increased in many cases." [1] Among
these additional elements perhaps the most important are
the suggestions which a workman may be able to offer for
more effective or more economical methods of work, and the
contribution which he may make by his influence towards a
spirit of harmony and good-fellowship in the shop. These
elements can, indeed, be taken account of in a rough general
way, and money rewards designed to induce workpeople
to provide them can be offered; but anything in the nature
of approximate measurement of their value is obviously
impossible. [2]

---

[1] Jevons, *Essays*, p. 123.

[2] Arrangements are frequently made by progressive firms both in America
and in this country for enabling workmen to submit suggestions that occur to
them to the higher officials of the business without the intervention of overseers
and foremen who might be actuated by motives of jealousy towards them; and
for rewarding with prizes and premiums such suggestions as it is decided to
adopt. (Cf. Gilman, *A Dividend to Labour*, p. 230; Rowntree, *Industrial
Betterment*, p. 31, and Meakin, *Model Factories and Villages*, p. 322.) And
in Van Marken's establishment a premium is given for "evidences of good-
fellowship and co-operation, thus encouraging those whose behaviour conduces
to the smooth working of the concern" (Meakin, *Model Factories and Villages*,
p. 315).

§ 3. The second difficulty is that the physical output for which an individual workman is responsible is liable to vary, not only in quantity, but also in quality. Ability to measure its quantity is, therefore, not sufficient, unless workmen can be prevented from making output larger at the expense of making it worse. In some circumstances this can be done by means of carefully thought-out schemes of inspection and supervision. Mechanical "gauges" can also be made use of in certain types of work. It has been said that "in the munition industry, where accuracy is of such vital importance, quite as many employees are engaged in gauging the output as will be actually producing it, and every single unit of output—not merely samples—will be subjected to the process."[1] These devices, however, cannot be effectively applied either to work that has to be done by workmen acting in scattered places or to work the results of which— as in plumbing and sewer-making—are speedily covered up. In these types of work, since defects of quality threaten serious injury to health, it is generally thought better to refrain from any attempt at making the wage-payment depend on the quantity of output.

§ 4. Even where a proper standard of quality can be enforced and the danger of injurious reactions on quality eliminated, to measure the quantity of output by itself is often difficult. It is especially so when the work consists of general surveillance and attention rather than of specific mechanical operations. The work done by seamen, telegraph and telephone operators, carmen and railway signalmen, is of this kind. So also is much agricultural work. Thus, M. Besse writes: "The essence of measurable things is their homogeneity, their identity with themselves. Harvesting and the weeding of roots, for example, allow of piece-wages, because the work remains the same for days and weeks, and, in order to measure its efficiency, all that is needed is to count the sheaves amassed or to calculate the surface weeded. The greater part of the work of cultivation is similar. But, on the other hand, the task of men who look after and

---

[1] Sargent Florence, *Use of Factory Statistics in the Investigation of Industrial Fatigue*, p. 72.

manage animals varies from hour to hour of the day and begins again every morning in such wise that no summary or addition of it is possible. It consists of watching the pasture lands, grooming the animals, cleaning the stables, and so on, all operations complex in themselves, admitting of no common measure, needing to be done in a limited time and at a fixed hour, and often of such a kind that nothing would be gained by any extra stimulus to exertion. This is why piece-wages, very widespread in arable districts like the east and south-east of England, are so rare in the districts devoted to stock-raising."[1] In mechanical work the total product of *a body of men* is, in general, fairly definite and measurable. But even here it is sometimes very difficult to distinguish and measure separately the contribution that is made to it by separate individuals. This difficulty is prominent in the work done by gangs of harvesters or navvies. It is also of some slight importance in that of shop-assistants, for it is the business of these people, not merely to serve customers, but also, when they are themselves engaged, to hand them over tactfully to some other assistant.

§ 5. Let us now suppose that we have to deal with occupations in which this difficulty has been, in some degree, overcome, so that some rough measure, or estimate, of the individual worker's contribution, as he works from day to day or week to week, can be made. It is required so to arrange things that pay is adjusted to this measure. To some extent—a more considerable extent than is often supposed —this can be, and is, done under ordinary systems of time-wages. By means of careful records and corresponding adjustments, time-wages can be arranged at differing rates adapted to the different efficiencies of individual workpeople.[2] It is frequently urged, indeed, that, where standard rates for average workpeople are established, either by bargaining between associations of employers and employed or by authoritative intervention on the part of the State, adjustment is exceedingly difficult, alike for workpeople below the average of

---

[1] *La Crise et l'Évolution de l'Agriculture en Angleterre*, pp. 99-100.
[2] Cf. for an elaborate attempt on these lines, Gannt, *Work, Wages, and Profits*, ch. iv.

efficiency and for workpeople above it. Experience, however, does not bear out this view.

As regards workpeople below the average; when their relative inferiority arises out of some definite physical cause, such as old age, adjustments are made very freely. Trade unions often have special arrangements permitting men over sixty to accept less than the standard (time) rate. Such arrangements, Mr. Beveridge states, " occur, for instance, in the rules of several furnishing trade unions, and of others in the printing, leather, and building trades. In one union, indeed, members over fifty-six years of age may not only be allowed, but be compelled, by their branches to accept less than the standard rate (so as to clear the unemployed fund)."[1] " It is," he adds, " of course, possible that, in some of these cases, the formal rule of exception is seldom put in force, or that the branch refuses its consent to a lower rate. On the other hand, it is quite certain that many unions in fact make exceptions for their aged members without possessing any formal rules on the subject. This is done by the Amalgamated Society of Carpenters and Joiners, and, to a less extent, by the Amalgamated Society of Engineers. The question is, indeed, very largely one of the strength and feeling of the particular branch concerned. If the standard rate is firmly established, it may appear safe to make exceptions for the older men."[2] There are, however, many relatively inefficient men in industry, even among the membership of trade unions with fairly stringent capacity

---

[1] *Unemployment,* p. 124, footnote.

[2] *Ibid.* p. 124. The peculiarity and uncertainty of these arrangements is brought out in Mr. Barnes' evidence to the Poor Law Commissioners: " In the Amalgamated Society of Engineers we do not require a man to shift from one town to another after he is fifty years of age, and, putting it generally, we do not require him to get the standard rate of wages—according to the discretion of the committees who may deal with the matter—after about fifty-five years of age." But the percentage of men who take advantage of this is very small. " In fact, although we allow men to work under the rate at fifty-five years of age, it is rather the case that the men at fifty-five, or even sixty, do not avail themselves of the opportunity. So strong is the sense of discipline in the trade unions, and their sense of loyalty to their fellows, that in most cases a man would rather give up work altogether than accept work at the lower rate. So that, instead of trade unions standing in the way of the men accepting lower rates, the opposite is the fact, and the trade unions rather encourage it" (Evidence of Mr. G. N. Barnes, M.P., quoted in the Report of the Commission, p. 313, footnote).

tests at the time of admission, whose inefficiency is not associated with a definite objective thing, such as old age or infirmity. For these men adjustment is more difficult. The nature of the difficulties involved may be illustrated from the much discussed case of the "slow workers" under the New Zealand Arbitration Law. In connection with its award of "minimum" wages, it is usual for the Arbitration Court to provide for a tribunal to fix an "under-rate" for slow workers.[1] In the earlier years of the Act, permits to claim the under-rate used to be obtainable from the president or secretary of the trade union concerned. But it was found that, for slow workers, as distinct from those who are more obviously afflicted by age, accident, or infirmity, these officials hesitated to issue permits. Under the revised Act, therefore, the power of issue is entrusted to the chairmen of local Conciliation Boards, after hearing the representatives of the unions. In Victoria the issue is in the hands of the Chief Inspector of Factories, subject to the condition that the persons working with licences in any factory must not exceed one-fifth of the adult workers who are employed there at the full minimum rate.[2] The unwillingness of the unions to sanction permits is due to the fear that, through them, the standard required of the ordinary grade of workmen in the industry may be raised, and the minimum thus insidiously lowered.[3] This unwillingness tends, of course, to be checked, when the unions are under obligation to pay large out-of-work benefit to unemployed members.

[1] Cf. Broadhead, *State Regulation of Labour in New Zealand*, p. 66.

[2] Cf. Aves, *Report on Wages Boards*, p. 61, and Raynaud, *Vers le salaire minimum*, p. 96.

[3] The danger of allowing under-rating to become a means of evasion of awards is clearly seen by those in charge of the Acts. "In granting permits, the Chief Inspector is guided by claims based on personal disability of some kind, and not by the exigencies either of an industry or of a particular business. If conditions have changed, making the applications for permits more urgent on that account, the view is held, very consistently, that the occasion would then have arisen for the reconsideration of its determination by the Board concerned. While the determinations are in force, wages conditions, it is held, should conform to them, and in their power to arrest or postpone a fall some consider that they will in the future prove their greatest value. Such is the hope, but to that form of testing they have not yet been subjected. The point, which it is necessary to emphasise here, is that at such a period the permit is not regarded as the appropriate instrument on which to fall back " (Aves, *Report on Wages Boards*, p. 63).

In all circumstances, however, it is likely to operate to some extent, and it is, furthermore, backed by the reluctance of border-line workpeople to ask for permits, and of employers to obtain a reputation for employing under-rate workers. Thus, it would be idle to pretend that for these under-rate workers adjustment is a perfectly smooth and simple matter. Even for them, however, a good deal is done.

As regards workpeople above the average of capacity, there is, of course, never any formal rule precluding payment to them of more than the standard rate. But, it is often asserted, employers as a matter of fact refuse to pay more than the standard rate for efficiency in excess of the standard, for fear that trade unions should make this action an excuse for demanding a rise in the standard itself.[1] And it is, no doubt, true that, especially among large employers, the convenience of a uniform rate acts strongly to prevent adjustment to individual differences. "The secretary of the Composition Roofers estimates that not more than two per cent of the members in New York City receive more than the minimum. An official of the Steam Filterers estimates that for his union in New York City the proportion is not less than five nor more than ten per cent."[2] On the whole, however, the tendency for the minimum rate to become the maximum does not appear to be nearly as strong as is generally supposed. Thus, the Inspector of Factories in Victoria in 1902 stated that, in the clothing trade, while the minima for men and women workers respectively were 45s. and 20s., the average wages were 53s. 6d. and 22s. 3d.[3] Furthermore, in the Report of the Bureau of Labour for 1909, it is stated that " out of 2451 employees in factories in Auckland City, excluding under-rate workers and young persons, 949 received the minimum rate, and 1504, or 61 per cent of the whole, received more than the minimum. In Wellington the percentage receiving more than

---

[1] It should be noted that, when it is a question of an excess of wage sought by particular men above the standard time-wage, the unions under a time-wage system are not in a position to resort to collective bargaining; and that, therefore, the employers' bargaining power is more likely to be superior to the workpeople's than it is as regards the standard itself. (Cf. McCabe, *The Standard Rate in American Trade Unions*, p. 114.)

[2] McCabe, *ibid.* p. 118 *n.*

[3] Cf. Webb, *Socialism and the National Minimum*, p. 73.

the minimum was 57, in Christchurch 47, and in Dunedin
46."[1] The same point is illustrated in a rough way by the
policy of certain American unions, which enter into agreements with employers concerning both a standard and a
minimum wage. In the Norfolk and Western Railway shops
in Roanoke the minimum wage was 20 cents, while the
standard rate was that received by the largest number of men
in the shop, namely, 24 cents per hour. Again, in an agreement made in 1903 between the "Soo" Railway and the
International Association of Machinists, "it is stipulated that
in the machine shops of the railway company the minimum
rate shall be 30 cents per hour, and the standard rate $34\frac{1}{2}$
cents per hour."[2] The whole matter is well summed up by
the Reporter to the United States Bureau of Labour in 1915:
"Employers have frequently said to me that they believed
there was a tendency in that direction—*i.e.* for the minimum
to become the maximum—but they have seldom been able
to furnish evidence to that effect from their own establishments. At times I have found on enquiry that not a single
man in their own plants was receiving the minimum wage.
The employers' opinion seems to be more the result of
a priori reasoning than the result of experience. Nor on reflection is it easy to see why the minimum should become the
maximum. . . . There seems to be no reason why under this
system there should not be the same competition among employers as under the old system to secure the most efficient
and highly skilled workmen, and there is no reason why such
men should not get wages based on their superior efficiency.
Victorian statistics on this point are lacking, but in New
Zealand, where minimum wages are fixed by the arbitration
court, statistics as to wages tabulated in 1909 by the Labour

[1] *Quarterly Journal of Economics*, 1910, p. 678. The tendency of the
minimum to become the maximum is, of course, stronger in some circumstances
than in others. Thus, Mr. Broadhead writes of New Zealand : "In those
trades, in which there is no competition with the outside world, many of the
workers, according to their degree of skill, are paid more than the minimum
wage fixed by the court, but, in others, in which there is competition with the
imported article, the practice of making the minimum the maximum wage is, I
believe, pretty general. In the latter case the employers contend that they
cannot afford to pay to any worker any more than is fixed by law" (*State
Regulation of Labour in New Zealand*, p. 72).

[2] Holland and Barnett, *Studies in American Trade Unionism*, p. 118.

Department showed that, in the four leading industrial centres
of the Dominion, the percentages of workers in trades where
a legal minimum wage was fixed, who received more than the
minimum, varied from 51 per cent in Dunedin to 61 per cent
in Auckland. There is no reason to think that a dissimilar
situation would be revealed by a statistical investigation in
Victoria."[1] Even where the open payment of increased time-
wages as a reward of increased efficiency is prevented by
friction and jealousy, the result aimed at may sometimes be
attained by secret payments.[2] It should be remembered, too,
that, when time wages are fixed rigorously and there is
no machinery for payments in excess of the standard rate,
the standard rate is usually fixed at different levels in different
centres, and men of more or less similar quality tend to be
concentrated at each several centre. Thus, even when a
specially efficient workman cannot increase his earnings by
working harder at the place where he is, he can do so by
migrating to one where higher wages and larger output are
the rule, and working harder there.

Yet again, even when extra efficiency is not rewarded by
any addition to the wage rate, it may be rewarded by selection
for continued employment in bad times and, in businesses where,
as in railway service, there are a number of grades of employees
receiving different rates of pay, for promotion when opportunity
offers. The former of these processes is particularly important.
Its working is well illustrated from the records of the Amalgamated Society of Engineers made in the days when the trade
worked predominantly upon time-wages. The " vacant books "

---

[1] "Minimum Wage Legislation," *U.S. Bulletin of Labour Statistics*, 1915,
p. 136, No. 167.
[2] For example, a New Zealand employer told Mr. Aves that "he was alive
to the danger of a rigid scale of remuneration, and that to some of his men he
was paying 'something extra' a day. But this was done ' on the quiet.' The
men are paid in paper and metal currency, the loose coinage being folded in the
notes. The array of little packages was shown me. All are paid with great
rapidity, and 'no one can tell what any one else receives'" (*Report on Wages
Boards* [Cd. 4167], p. 109). In like manner, an English employer told the
Charity Organisation Society's Committee on Unskilled Labour : " If one man
is better than another, we give him 1s. or 2s. extra at the end of the week. We
have to be careful that other men do not know that, or they want to know why.
They cannot understand that it is because the man has served us better. You
cannot say openly, ' I will give you 2s. more.' The man would be considered
a favourite, and he would have a warm time in the stable at night" (*Report*, p. 109).

of the Society, after the results of a number of years, some good and some bad, had been averaged, yielded the following table of days lost through want of work:

Loss less than 3 days per annum	70·4 % of the Union.
„ between 3 days and 4 weeks	13 %	„
„ from 4 to 8 weeks	4·6 %	„
„ from 8 to 12 weeks	2·8 %	„
„ over 12 weeks	9 %	„

Thus, the greater part of the unemployment that occurred was concentrated upon a comparatively small number of men. That its distribution was associated with inefficiency is suggested by the annexed table showing the age-distribution of the men who drew unemployment benefit in 1895 (a medium year). [1]

		Average number of days lost in a year.
Members between 15-25 years old		8·8
„ 25-35 „		13·1
„ 35-45 „		12·3
„ 45-55 „		20·1
„ 55-65 „		33·1
„ 65 and over (excluding superannuated)		26·9

These tables take no account of time lost through "short time," sickness, unpunctuality or trade disputes, or of time gained through overtime. It is apparent that the older, and presumably less efficient, men suffer most. Moreover, "a comparison of 1890 with 1893 yields the rather striking result that almost as large a proportion of members (21·4 per cent) were unemployed during one of the best years as during the worst (26·4 per cent)." [2] The implication of these figures is emphasised in the blunt statement of the Transvaal Indigency Commission. "The really efficient man is rarely unemployed except for short periods between jobs, because, being competent, he is the last to be thrown out of employment, and has generally sufficient money to enable him to migrate to some place where his services are wanted." [3]

The general result of this discussion, therefore, is that under time-wages some considerable degree of adjustment of payment to immediate output can be achieved.

[1] Cf. *British and Foreign Trade and Industry*, Second Series, p. 99.
[2] Beveridge, *Unemployment*, p. 72.
[3] *Report of the Transvaal Indigency Commission*, p. 121.

§ 6. Plainly, however, a very much closer adjustment can be made by resort to the method of piece-wages. Under this plan workmen, working in given conditions and with given machinery, are paid exactly in proportion to their physical output. Of course, the piece-rate offered to a man on a new machine in a factory or in a good place in a mine is lower than that offered to a man on an old machine or in a bad place; and, of course, it is recognised "that, if a manufacturer contributes anything directly toward reduction in the time by supplying an improved machine, or improved jigs or fixtures, or high-speed steel cutting tools, where previously carbon steel tools had been used at the original setting of the time, that then it would be perfectly proper and fair to lower the time set,"—which means, in effect to lower the piece-rate. If this were not done, the benefit of improvements made in any industry would be seized by the particular workers engaged there—and they, in order to keep it, would have to form themselves into a close ring and exclude new-comers—instead of being spread, as normally it would be, over the general body of the purchasing public. In given conditions, however, under simple piece-wages a workman is paid, *from the standpoint of the moment*, in direct proportion to his output, the actual amount of the pay per unit of service being approximately equal to the (marginal) value of his services in assisting the machinery to make this output.[1] It is true that the adjustment is not exact. In a factory—though not, of course, among home workers—the worker, who is inferior because he is slow, "occupies" the employer's machine or workspace for a longer period than the fast worker in producing the same quantity of commodity; and the worker, who is inferior because he is careless, is more likely to have an accident, and so to mulct the employer under the Workmen's Compensation Act, than the careful worker. For these reasons, in order to obtain equality of efficiency wages, we should, in strictness, need a piece-rate wage, varying, not proportionately, but progressively, with the number of pieces accomplished; and this

---

[1] Of course, this statement does not hold good of "collective piece-wages," where each man's pay depends upon the output of the whole group of which he forms a part. When the group is very small, some inducement to exertion is offered by this form of piece-wage, but, when the group is large, practically none.

point becomes more important the greater is the value of the
plant in a factory relatively to its wages-bill.[1] Even under
piece-wages, therefore, superior efficiency is not rewarded
directly in full proportion to its superiority. Nevertheless,
when account is taken of the fact that, on this system as well as
on the time-wage system, the better worker is more secure of
regular employment, while unemployment is concentrated on
the worse worker,[2] it may fairly be said that adjustment is
nearly exact. Consequently, it would seem at first sight
that this is the system under which, apart from possible
overstrain to the workpeople, to be referred to presently, and
provided that the level of the rate is properly adjusted, the
largest practicable output is bound to be obtained.[3] The
system has been for a long time established and has operated with great success in this country in coal-mining, the
textile industries, the boot and shoe industry and a number
of others.

§ 7. Experience has shown, however, that over a wide
range of industries piece-wages have been a failure. When
a piece-rate has been introduced, and, under its influence, the
workers have increased their output, employers, thinking that
some men were now earning too much money, have sometimes

---

[1] This consideration is sometimes used as an argument against paying equal
piece-rates to women engaged in the same operations as men. In certain
engineering operations, for example, employers have claimed that women, being
slower workers than men, involve much higher proportionate overhead charges
(*Report of the War Cabinet Committee on Women in Industry*, p. 84). Plainly,
however, reasoning of this type points to a lower piece-rate to all slow workers,
whether male or female, than to fast workers, not for a lower piece-rate to
women as such than to men as such.

[2] Thus in the London Compositors' Society, where work is mainly on piece-
wages, Mr. Beveridge has shown that "about seven-eighths of the total payment
(of unemployed benefit) in 1904 went to men who had to claim again in 1905"
(*Unemployment*, p. 140).

[3] It may be noted that, if piece-wages were substituted for time-wages
throughout industry generally, with the result that a large increase of effort was
put out by workpeople, the value per unit of workpeople's effort would by that
fact be slightly depreciated, and, therefore, the payment for a given effort and
output would have to be slightly less than before. Thus, if under time-wages
at 1s. an hour two pieces had normally been produced, so that 6d. was paid for
each, under a general system of piece-wages the basis of adjustment would have
to be slightly less than 6d. per piece. When, however, a change from time to
piece-wages is accomplished in one industry only, the effect in this direction
(after the distribution of workpeople among different industries has been
adjusted) will, in general, be very small.

"cut" or "nibbled" the rate. The workers, perceiving this, realise that extra effort on their part is likely to involve, not only an immediate increase of earnings, but also a subsequent reduction of the piece-rate, the effect of which will be to make it impossible for them to earn their original wage without working harder than before. To prevent this they tend, whether by formal agreement or otherwise, deliberately to limit their output, so that very little, if any, advantage is secured for the national dividend as against the output under time-wages.

§ 8. The apparently obvious solution of this difficulty, namely that employers should rigidly abstain from rate-cutting in any circumstances, has occasionally been adopted. Thus, in the United States, "in the spring of 1902, the Moulders officially agreed with the Employers' Defence Association that no limit (of output) should be observed in the stone-moulding branch, in view of the agreement that the earnings of the individual moulders should not be considered in adjusting prices of work."[1] Apart, however, from the fear of indirect cutting by slight alterations in the nature of a job and large accompanying alterations in the rate, which would enable unscrupulous employers to get round this kind of guarantee in a dishonourable way, the extreme difficulty of ensuring that rates are fixed reasonably in the first instance will make even the best employers hesitate to give such a guarantee. For, as a result of it, they might find themselves bound for a long time to pay four or five times as much for a piece of work as they could get the work done for in a free market. Some of them have, therefore, taken the line that, if there is to be an effective guarantee against "nibbling," they must be insured against the guarantee costing them too much. This is the origin of the various methods of remuneration embraced under the general title of *premium plans.* The essential characteristic of these is that the increases of wage, which correspond to increases of output above the standard, are proportionately smaller than these increases of output, but that, in compensation for this, the workpeople—in theory at least—are guaranteed against any cutting or nibbling of the rate, so

[1] McCabe, *The Standard Rate in American Trade Unions*, pp. 224-5.

long as the existing methods of production are maintained.
The precise relation between the amount of the premium and
the amount of increases of output above the standard varies
with different systems.   Under the plan known as the Halsey
plan, for every 1 per cent increase of output above the
standard output the wage rises above the standard wage by
a constant fraction of 1 per cent : under the equally well-
known Rowan plan, it rises by a constantly diminishing
fraction of 1 per cent.[1]   The advocates of these plans maintain that the low rate of the premium, as compared with that
ruling under simple piece-wages, which is offered under them,
and the consequent limitation of the employers' liability,
make it possible for a really effective guarantee to be given
against any nibbling of the rate, and that, therefore, on the
whole, the adjustment of remuneration to output is closer
than it would be under simple piece-wages.   There is, indeed,
considerable difficulty in the employment of premium plans
except in workshops where all the workpeople are of more or
less similar capacity.   For, if their capacities are widely
different, a strong man who produces half as much again as
a weak man is paid much less than half as much again in
wages ; and, in these circumstances, friction can hardly fail to
result.   But, when, for technical reasons, the differences

---

[1] These plans can conveniently be represented by the following formulae,
which are convertible into those printed by Mr. Schloss in the *Journal of the
Royal Economic Association* for December 1915.
Let W be the standard wage, P the standard output, w the actual wage
earned by a workman, and p the actual output of that workman :
Then the general formula for the Halsey plan is

$$w = W\left\{1 + \frac{1}{n}\,\frac{p-P}{P}\right\}$$

when n is any integer.   In the particular variety of this plan employed in Mr.
Halsey's works, n has the numerical value 2.   The general formula of the
Rowan plan is

$$w = W\left\{1 + \frac{p-P}{P}\,f(p)\right\} \text{ when } f'(p) \text{ is negative.}$$

In the particular variety of this plan employed in the Rowan works $f(p)$ is
given the value $\frac{P}{p}$.   The resulting equation is that of a parabola, and the
maximum value to which w can attain is 2W.   In England, but not in
Germany, plans of this type are usually associated with the guarantee of
a minimum time-wage irrespective of output ; that is to say, when p is < P, the
formula is not applied, but the standard wage W is paid.

of output between individuals cannot be great, this difficulty does not arise, and it is claimed that premium plans should prove an effective means of stimulating production.[1]

§ 9. Now, it is quite possible that, if workpeople can be got to regard them as fair, and to trust the guarantee against cutting, these plans will be more effective than piece-wages under which cuts are feared. As a matter of fact, however, they are not fair. When a workman, other things being equal, doubles his output, he contributes, owing to his shorter occupation of machinery for a given product, rather more than twice as much as before to his employer's service. For the employer to give him, as under all premium plans he will do, considerably less than twice his former pay, is, and, when the position is realised, is felt to be, exploitation. Nor is it an adequate reply that the prospect of retaining a part of the resulting gain stimulates the employer to provide a number of conveniences and aids—"additional facilities, small tools, more power, improved lighting, better organisation, etc." [2]— which are themselves partly responsible for the worker's extra output. These things may or may not be provided. If they are provided, the rate should be adjusted to allow for them. But premium plans do not give any pledge that this will be done ; they ensure that, even when conditions are absolutely unchanged and the whole additional output is due to the worker's effort, a doubled output shall mean much less than a doubled wage. This unfairness is bound sooner or later to be perceived, and, when it is perceived, the resentment which the worker will naturally feel at it is likely to drive down the output and nullify any good effect the plan may at first have had upon the national dividend. In any event, the only advantage that premium plans can claim over piece-wages is that they make possible effective guarantees against cuts. Clearly, therefore, they must be inferior to a piece-rate system so organised that the cut difficulty is overcome. The real problem is, not to evade the task of devising such a system, as premium plans substantially do, but to confront that task in those industries in which it is still formidable, and to overcome it

---

[1] Cf. Chapman, *Work and Wages*, vol. ii. pp. 184-5.
[2] Rowan Thompson, *The Rowan Premium Bonus System*, p. 12.

there, as it has already been overcome in the textile industries
and in coal-mining.

§ 10. The cutting or nibbling of rates may be attempted
by an employer either quite honestly, when experience has
shown that a particular rate was fixed too high relatively
to rates generally, or dishonestly in pure exploitation. It is
plain that the first sort of cutting ought, in any satisfactory
system, to be provided for, just as provision should also be
made for raising rates which have accidentally been set too
low. Elaborate precautions should be taken to ensure that
both these sorts of error occur very rarely, but, when they do
occur, machinery for correcting them should be available. If
the machinery is regarded with confidence by the workpeople,
the fear of this class of cut will do little harm. Exploitation
cuts, on the other hand, must be absolutely prevented. With
piece-wages settled by individual bargaining between separate
wage-earners and their employers, neither of these things can
be done. Furthermore, when a bad employer, under this
arrangement, succeeds in "nibbling" the rate, his success
makes it difficult for his competitors to refrain from following
his example, and is apt, therefore, to start a cumulative
movement. But it is not necessary that piece-rates should
be fixed by individual bargaining. In this fact the solution
of the problem may be found. For collective bargaining
furnishes a guarantee against the kind of nibbling which
is really exploitation and also makes it easy to provide
machinery — whether joint-committees or jointly appointed
rate-fixers — to adjust particular rates, in the original fixing
of which a mistake has been made. In this connection it is
interesting to note that the rapid extension of piece-work in
the engineering trade, which took place during the war—it
was no doubt facilitated by the greater uniformity of products
which was required—"led to a great variety of forms of
collective bargaining. In some establishments a new piece-
price is submitted to the Works Committee before it is
discussed with the individual workman. In others an
Appeals Committee has been instituted to consider and bring
forward complaints against piece-prices or premium bonus
times fixed by the management. In others again . . .

prices have been discussed, not with the individual workman, but with the workman and two or three of his mates on similar work." [1]   These collective bargains within particular works are, of course, not made in the air.   They aim at such an adjustment of rates to the peculiar conditions of the works as will bring them into line with the standard conditions established for the industry as a whole by collective bargaining between representative associations of employers and employed.[2] In industries such as textiles, coal-mining and the boot and shoe industry, where piece-wages have been successful and willingly accepted by the workpeople, they have always been associated with collective bargaining.   Where there has been difficulty and opposition, as in engineering, woodworking and building, the real reason has been that subtle differences of quality and detail and great differences in the amount and kind of machinery in use in different shops have made anything like uniform piece-rates unsuitable, and so have stood in the way of successful collective bargaining.   In these circumstances the supersession of time-wages by piece-wages would often have meant the surrender of collective bargaining in favour of rates really fixed by the arbitrary decision of employers or their representatives dealing with isolated workmen. In order that the piece-wage system, and the benefit to production which it carries with it, may win further ground, what is required is to develop in these more difficult industries an adequate machinery for subordinating piece-wages, as they are subordinated in the textile industry, to the full control of collective bargaining.[3]

§ 11. A word must here be said about a method of wage payment, different from both time-wages and piece-wages, which has been associated with some developments of " scientific management" under the name of task-wages. The essence of this method, of which there are several different forms, is as follows.   Experiments are set on foot to ascertain how large an output a first-class workman, working under given conditions and exerting himself to his full capacity without

[1] *Report on Works Committees*, 1918, p. 11.   [2] Cf. *ibid.* pp. 37-8.
[3] For an excellent discussion of this subject cf. Webb, *The Works Manager To-day*, chap. vi. ; also D. H. Cole, *The Payment of Wages, passim.*

overstrain, can produce in a given time. The output thus
ascertained then becomes the standard task. . The workpeople
are so selected and trained that all those employed in establishments operating the system are first-class workmen (it would
serve equally well if they were of any other class provided all
were similar) from the standpoint of the operations to be performed there ; and the wage system is adjusted in such a way
that they earn very much better pay if they succeed in
accomplishing the standard task than if they fail to do
this.[1] The method has been described thus: "Under
this system each man has his work assigned to him in the
form of a task to be done by a prescribed method, with
definite appliances, and to be completed within a certain time.
The task is based on a detailed investigation by a trained
expert of the best method of doing the work; and the task
setter, or his assistant, acts as an instructor to teach the
workmen to do the work in the manner and time specified.
If the work is done within the time allowed by the expert
and is up to the standard for quality, the workman receives
extra compensation (usually 20 to 50 per cent of the time
allowed) in addition to his day's pay. If it is not done in the
time set, or is not up to the standard for quality, the
workman receives his day's pay only."[2] Under the Gannt
variety of the method ordinary time-wages are paid *plus* a
large bonus to those who perform the standard task: under
the Taylor variety ordinary piece-wages are paid, but the rate
of piece-wages is abruptly raised by a large amount when the
standard task is attained.

§ 12. Hitherto, when this plan has been employed in the
United States, the standard has been fixed by the employers
without resort to collective bargaining. When workpeople
are prepared to allow this, and when employers are reasonable

---

[1] It should be noted that, in effect, a very stringent form of this method
is employed as regards the number of hours during which workpeople work per
day ; for, if a man is not willing to work the regular factory day, he will not be
employed at all and will get no wages. The reason for this is, of course, to be
found in technical considerations of factory management. To have different
men working in a factory different numbers of hours per day would be a much
more serious inconvenience than to have them working with different intensities
of effort.

[2] Going, *Principles of Industrial Engineering*, p. 135.

and liberal, there may, no doubt, be good results. But there is an obvious danger that unscrupulous employers may use their power to fix the standard as a means of exploitation;[1] and it is certain that in this country, where trade unions are strong, the workpeople would never consent to place this power in their hands. If the standard was fixed by collective bargaining, so that the workpeople were prepared to accept it, *and was fixed right*, the best result possible would be only equal to that given by a smoothly-working piece-wage system; and, for that result to be achieved, it would be necessary that all the workpeople to whom any standard was applied should be *exactly* equal in capacity and temperament. Unless this impossible condition is fulfilled, adjustment under the task-wage system is bound to be less perfect than under a properly arranged piece-wage plan. On the whole, therefore, since it is difficult to imagine circumstances in which it would be practicable to set tasks rightly but not practicable to arrange simple piece-wages, there is little to be said for introducing the task-wage system into this country.[2]

---

[1] Certain investigations into the effect of the Taylor system upon some women employed under it do not suggest that this evil possibility has been realised in fact. (*Quarterly Journal of Economics*, 1914, p. 549). But Mr. Hoxie (*Scientific Management and Labour*, pp. 44 *et seq.*) is less optimistic upon this point. He writes: "As a matter of fact, time study for task setting is found in scientific management shops in all its possible variations, both with reference to methods and results. In some the highest standards are maintained in regard to all the factors enumerated—all or a large proportion of the workers are timed, the largest practicable number of readings is made, cordial relations are established between the time study man and the workers, and the latter are cautioned against speeding up when being timed, and, if doubt remains, the allowances are purposely made large to cover all possible errors. Liberality of the task is the keynote. In other shops the maximum task is just as surely sought, and the method is warped to this end. The swiftest men are selected for timing, they work under special inducements or fear, two or three readings suffice, allowances are disregarded or cut to a minimum. The task of 100 per cent efficiency is to all intents and purposes arbitrarily fixed, sometimes practically before the time study, at what it is judged the workers can be forced to do. The main use of the time study is to prove to the workers that the task can be done in the time allowed." (*loc. cit.* p. 53).

[2] The central argument of this chapter can be brought into clear light by means of a simple diagram. Let us suppose the number of workpeople employed in any industry and the length of the working day to be given. It is then possible to construct a demand curve representing the employers' demand prices (in terms of product) for different amounts of exertion per unit time from a typical workman, and a supply curve representing the workman's supply prices (in terms of product) for different amounts of exertion. Units of exertion are

§ 13. The practical conclusion to which the reasoning of this chapter has tended is that the interest of the national dividend will be best promoted when immediate reward is adjusted as closely as possible to immediate results, and that this can, in general, be done most effectively by piece-wage scales controlled by collective bargaining. This conclusion, it has now to be remarked, depends on the tacit assumption that the marginal trade net product of labour is not appreciably in excess of the marginal social net product. It is possible to argue that under a piece-wage system this condition is not satisfied, but that workpeople produce a large material output at the cost of exertions that wear them out prematurely and so damage their efficiency and output in the long run. If these charges were true, the advantage I have claimed for

---

marked off along Ox, and the demand and supply prices (in terms of product) of different amounts of it along Oy.

Since every increase of exertion on the part of workpeople enables employers to finish any given job more quickly, and so to start their machinery upon some

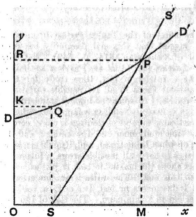

other job, the demand curve DD' will slope upwards towards the right. Since, if a man is at work at all, neither public opinion nor his own comfort will allow him to do absolutely nothing, the supply curve SS' will start at a point some distance along Ox, and, thereafter, will slope upward somewhat steeply. Let it cut DD' in P. Through P draw PM perpendicular to Ox, and PR perpendicular to Oy. Then, apart from possible injurious reactions on efficiency that are not here considered, the amount of exertion by a typical workman, which is most advantageous to the national dividend and economic welfare, is measured by OM, and the corresponding amount of his output by the rectangle OMPR. If the wage paid to him is wholly independent of his exertions and consequent output, the amount of his exertions will approximate to OS, and his output to OSQK. An amount of exertion OM, and consequent output OMPR, can be obtained *either* by the offer of a rate (in product) PM for each unit of exertion (which means each PM units of output); *or* by the offer of an aggregate wage (in product)—per day or whatever the time-unit may be—equal to OMPR, conditional upon the man producing OMPR units of output, any failure to reach this standard involving the payment of a considerably lower wage.

piece-wages would be proved to be, in part at least, illusory. It must be admitted that, when a piece-wage system is first introduced among workpeople not hitherto accustomed to it, it sometimes leads to a spurt of energy that could not be maintained for long without bad results. But experience does not show that it promotes overstrain, when once the men who have been brought under it have become, as it were, acclimatised to the new conditions. Moreover, it has to be remembered that greater intensity of work often means more thought, care and interest—which do not imply extra wear and tear—rather than greater muscular or nervous effort.[1] Little weight, therefore, need be assigned to this objection, and the conclusions set out above may be taken to hold good.

[1] Thus Mr. Cadbury writes of piece-wages: "If properly trained, the worker will try to find the quickest method of work, and the one involving the least strain; and it has been found that, when a piece-rate has been fixed where previously there had been a time-basis, the output has doubled without any undue strain on the part of the worker, largely as the result of adopting better methods. This especially applies to hand processes" (*Experiments in Industrial Organisation*, p. 142).

CHAPTER IX

THE DISTRIBUTION OF LABOUR AMONG OCCUPATIONS AND PLACES

§ 1. THE subject matter of this Chapter is the distribution of labour among different occupations and places. The analysis of the preceding Part showed that, if the national dividend is to stand absolutely at its maximum, the values of the marginal social net products of every form of resource in all uses must be equal. It showed, further, that in many occupations marginal social net product differs from marginal trade net product, and that in yet other occupations this again differs from marginal individual net product. Hence, the maximisation of the national dividend does not require that the values of marginal individual net products shall be equal in all uses. On the contrary, such a condition of universal equality is incompatible with maximisation. In spite of this, however, our argument showed that any departure from equality at any point, brought about otherwise than with the deliberate design of improving the dividend, *is likely* to indicate a lapse on the part of the dividend below the level at which it might have stood. This general result is applicable to labour. Any failure from equality in the values of the marginal individual net products of labour—values that are always equivalent to the demand prices, and generally equivalent to the wages paid per efficiency unit at different points—*probably* indicates a distribution of labour between different points other than the distribution most favourable to the national dividend. In general, therefore, causes of failure from equality in the demand prices and wage-rates of labour of given quality at different points are also causes of injury to the national

446

dividend. These causes may be divided into three broad groups—ignorance or imperfect knowledge, costs of movement, and restrictions imposed upon movement from outside.

§ 2. The most fundamental way in which the first of these causes, ignorance, operates is by impairing the initial distribution of new generations of workpeople as they flow into industry. Those persons who direct the choice of avocations made by young men and women are ignorant of the level at which the demand price for labour of any particular grade will stand in different occupations at a later period of those young persons' lives. A great part of this ignorance is, of course, inevitable in a world of change. Even though opinions were continually modified in the light of the most recent experience, yet newer experience would necessarily belie the best-based forecasts. But, besides the ignorance that is inevitable, there is also ignorance due to the frailty of individual minds and the poverty of organised information. About occupations for people this ignorance is likely to be more extensive than it is about occupations for capital; for the same reason that ignorance about the relative advantages of different forms of spending is more extensive than ignorance about the choice of investments. Those persons who have to direct their children's choice of a career are not rendered efficient by the selective influence of competition. Fathers who invest their sons' activities unremuneratively are not expelled by bankruptcy from the profession of fatherhood, but continue, however incapable they may be, to exercise in this matter the functions of entrepreneurs. The grave errors that result are well known. "Many parents let their boys go into offices or as telegraph messengers, because they seem respectable jobs, but they have never considered, and, perhaps, have no means of knowing, whether there are any future prospects." This aspect is dwelt upon in the reports of many of the skilled employment committees. If the father is not himself in a position to get a boy into a good trade, he does not know in many cases how to manage it."[1] The point is well illustrated by Sir H. Llewellyn Smith's observation, some

[1] Jackson, Report on Boy Labour, *Royal Commission on the Poor Laws*, Appendix, vol. xx. pp. 9-10.

years back, that, among the Cradley Heath hand nailmakers, "although the trade has been decaying for more than half a century, children are still going into, and are further crowding, their parents' trade." Again: "A very large number of parents are ignorant of the relative advantages of different occupations. . . . The boys tend always to follow their older companions into the same factory or yard, or at any rate into the same kind of occupation; and, where the prevailing trades are of a poor grade . . . the boys will generally follow the line of least resistance."[1] This sort of ignorance may, of course, be overcome in part through the spread of accessible information about the prospects of different trades, together with improved education enabling parents to make better use of the information that is open to them. And it may be overcome still further if those parents, who are not themselves in a position to make any good study of the labour market, have access to the advice of persons who are in a position to do this. At the best, however, since the prospects that are relevant are the prospects that will prevail in future years when the children and youths now selecting an occupation are grown up, this type of ignorance must always be extensive.

§ 3. But this type of ignorance is not the only one that prevents labour of any particular grade from being initially distributed among different uses in such a way as to make the demand-prices — or values of marginal net products — equal. The same effect is produced by ignorance as *to what the grade is* to which any individual boy or girl, whose fate is being decided, belongs. For different children are born with different capacities and aptitudes. So far as some of those belonging to one grade drift into occupations more fitted to those of another grade, the value of their marginal net product there will be less than that of children of the same grade who have been turned into occupations more suitable to that grade. Hence the immense importance

---

[1] Jackson, Report on Boy Labour, *Royal Commission on the Poor Laws*, Appendix, vol. xx. p. 161. The general tendency of children to enter their parents' trades is illustrated by a very interesting special inquiry undertaken by Prof. Chapman and Mr. Abbot in the neighbourhood of Manchester (*Statistical Journal*, May 1913, pp. 599 *et seq.*).

of a rational sorting of children of different intellectual qualities, and their guidance into lines of work for· which their several qualities are fitted.   " It is probable that labour exchanges for boys leaving school would be of very great value in securing . that , all the, more intelligent and able boys had a chance of securing good openings.   It is the ignorance of the boy which so often leads him into employment which is not suited to him."[1]   There is—or was—an excellent example of the organisation required in Strasburg, where the Labour Exchange works in definite association with the teachers of the municipal schools.   Our own Education (Choice of Employment) Act, 1910, endeavours to foster an alliance of this kind.   But, if this type of organisation is to be made thoroughly effective, the fitness of different boys for different occupations must not be judged by mere rough general impressions.   There is required a scientific analysis, on the one hand of the qualities for which various occupations call, and, on the other hand, of the qualities which different individual boys possess.   The practical problems thus suggested have been discussed in a very interesting manner by Professor Munsterberg.   He cites a bicycle factory in which the reaction times of different individuals were scientifically measured, and the results used as a test of fitness for the work of inspecting the balls of bicycle-bearings;[2] and he describes certain devices which he himself has invented for testing fitness for the work of motor-men. Tests with the same general purpose have recently been used by the military authorities to assist them in the selection of recruits for the Royal Air Force.   Such methods can often guide the individual's choice of employment when he first steps into industry—or first moves from a boy's occupation to a man's occupation [3]—more effectively, and much less blindly,

---

[1] Jackson, Report on Boy Labour, *Royal Commission on the Poor Laws*, Appendix, vol. xx. p. 31.

[2] *Psychology and Industrial Efficiency*, pp. 54-5.

[3] Cf. Professor Chapman's observation : "Certain occupations cannot be entered by any adequate number of people until they have nearly attained their full strength ; for instance, the occupations of manual workers on the railways, navvies, and dock labourers, and certain occupations in the building trades. This means that other callings must employ more young people than they can permanently find room for, unless some young people in search of work are to

than the ordinary rough and tumble of trial and error. They would be made still more effective if a device could be invented for testing, not merely capacity at the moment, but also capacity to attain capacity through training. It is, therefore, of interest to learn that experiments " have been actually started to determine the plasticity of the psychological apparatus as an independent inborn trait of the individual." [1]

§ 4. The ignorance so far considered has been mere ignorance. But the initial distribution of new generations of workpeople among different occupations is also injured by a more special kind of ignorance, which may be called biassed ignorance. By this is meant definite false judgments tending to direct the new generation's labour into certain

---

be left standing idle in the market-place. But to seek to obviate this tendency by making each industry more self-contained would not be a very wise proceeding, because it is poor economy to have a man doing a lad's work, or a lad doing a man's work, and from the operation of a certain amount of selection among the labour forces of the community productive efficiency results. . . . It may be that the partial *cul-de-sac* employment is a necessary part of a highly developed industrial system. If this is so, the establishment of labour-training institutes becomes doubly necessary, and an added importance attaches to Labour Exchanges with special reference to the claims of the rejected of certain trades whom it is essential to deal with before they become demoralised or suffer in vigour or spirit " ("Industrial Recruiting and the Displacement of Labour,"*Proceedings of the Manchester Statistical Society*, 1913-14, pp. 122-3).

[1] Munsterberg, *Psychology of Industrial Efficiency*, p. 126. Initial testing of capacity is, perhaps, not very important among workpeople who begin their career in large and varied establishments, where employees found unsuitable for the job they first select can be rapidly transferred to other jobs. Of firms which follow Mr. Taylor's doctrine of scientific management it is said that, "by a careful study of each individual of a group of men in any department, it may be found that many are not physically or temperamentally adapted to performing the particular functions required in that department and that they are adapted to the performing of functions in some other department. There follows a redistribution of men between departments, with the result that, without an increase in aggregate energy expended, there is an increase in aggregate productivity. It is the scientific method of adapting instrument to purpose " (Tuck School Conference, *Scientific Management*, p. 6). But in comparatively small and homogeneous establishments—and these employ a very large proportion of the world's workers —"the working man who is a failure in the work which he undertook would usually have no opportunity to show his strong sides in the same factory, or at least to be protected against the consequences of his weak points. If his achievement is deficient in quality or quantity, he generally loses his place and makes a new trial in another factory under the same accidental conditions, without any deeper insight into his particular psychical traits and their relation to special industrial activities " (Munsterberg, *Psychology of Industrial Efficiency*, p. 121).

specified occupations to a greater extent than is required to
make the value of the marginal net product there equal
to what it is in other occupations. In the industrial world
of to-day two principal forms of such false judgments are
prominent. On the one hand, as it seems, workpeople over-
estimate the advantages of dangerous, unhealthy and fluctuating trades, as against safe, wholesome and steady trades;
on the other hand, they overestimate the advantages of trades
which yield a large immediate wage with little training of
capacities, as against trades which yield a smaller immediate
wage and more training. Both these forms of over-estimate
arise, in the main, out of a common cause, namely, the fact
that people can grasp more easily the obvious, which forces
itself into the field of vision, than the more remote, which
has to be dragged there. The wage rate that is paid
anywhere is obvious in this sense; but the chances of
accident or unemployment, and the prospect of future gains
through enhanced industrial capacity, cannot be fully realised
without inquiry and a deliberate act of attention. Furthermore, the exaggerated view which workmen hold of the
advantages of dangerous, unhealthy and fluctuating industries—
the problem of training *versus* non-training occupations is
deferred for separate treatment in Part V.—is enhanced by
the subconscious sentiment inherent in most men that they
personally are somehow superior to the "average" man
situated similarly to themselves. *They* do not need that
machinery should be fenced; *their* constitution is not so
feeble that deficiencies of light, air and sanitation in their
place of work will injure them; *they* are not the sort of
men who will lose their job in bad times. In short, workpeople
are endowed, in Adam Smith's phrase, with "that natural
confidence which every man has, more or less, not only in
his own abilities, but in his own good fortune." This personal
optimism towards the facts on the part of the persons directly
concerned intensifies the maladjustment due to the difficulty,
which they and their parents alike experience, in learning
fully what the facts are. So far as false judgments in these
matters prevail, labour is pressed into dangerous, unhealthy
and fluctuating trades, till the value of its marginal net

product there falls short of the value of its marginal net
product elsewhere by the excess of the imagined advantage,
which the false judgments attribute to these trades over their
actual advantage; and, so far as the false judgments are
corrected, the inequality in the values of marginal net products
is correspondingly reduced. Against these definite false
judgments more direct and specific measures of correction can
be applied than are practicable against mere general ignorance.
Such specific measures are provided in Workmen's Compensation Acts and in State coercion towards insurance
against industrial accidents, industrial diseases (including the
premature general wearing out of a man's strength by
continued overstrain) and unemployment, in dangerous,
unwholesome and fluctuating trades — trades, that is to
say, which are *more* dangerous, unwholesome and fluctuating
than the trade least unfavourably situated in these respects.
In one form or another, these devices exhibit the remote
and inobvious chances of injury, illness, or unemployment
in the obvious shape of reductions in wages or immediate
payments out of wages.[1] They thus tend to lessen the
proportion of people who enter dangerous, unwholesome and
fluctuating trades, and so to bring the value of the marginal

---

[1] Whether the funds required to meet compensation or insurance claims
are collected from the employers in proportion to the wages they pay, or
whether workpeople pay a part and employers another part, is, from a long-
period point of view, a matter of small importance, just as it is a matter of
small importance whether local rates are collected from landlords or from
tenants. The employers' demand for labour varies in accordance with the
proportion of the burden that is thrown on them, in such wise that, when
they provide the compensation fund, wages are less by the amount of that
fund than they would have been if the workpeople had provided it. The
Austrian law requires one-tenth of the necessary funds to be raised by workpeople and nine-tenths by employers; the British Workman's Compensation
Law (1897) and the German Accident Insurance Law require the whole funds
to be raised by the employers. Of course, it is not a matter of indifference
whether the arrangements are or are not such that the employer stands to gain
by improving his mechanical arrangements so as to reduce the probability of
accident. In Germany each mutual association "determines for itself the
danger class to which each of the contributory establishments belongs, and is
authorised to levy a premium according to hazard. It is also empowered to
enforce rules and regulations" (Frankel and Dawson, *Working Men's Insurance
in Europe*, p. 96). Employers neglecting the rules may be put into a higher
hazard class (*ibid.* p. 115). In Austria "it is to the interest of each employer
to cut down the number of accidents in his establishment, as his annual contribution may then be apportioned on the basis of a lower danger coefficient.

net product of labour in these trades more nearly to equality with the value of the marginal net product of labour in general. State bounties, so arranged as to *persuade* people to expend more money on insurance, serve, though less effectively, to promote the same object. On the other hand, State provision of insurance against accidents, industrial diseases and unemployment, in so far as it relieves people from the need of providing against these things, whether the provision be of the *whole* cost or of a *proportion* of it, differentiates in favour of dangerous, unhealthy and fluctuating trades, and causes an excess of people to enter them.[1] It is plain, for example, that to follow the practice of the old relief works and "to give regularly to a casual labourer 13s. a week employment relief for four weeks in each year is arithmetically equivalent to subsidising his weekly wages by a shilling throughout the year"[2] and must operate as a direct bounty to casual trades.

§ 5. So far attention has been concentrated upon the initial distribution of new generations of workpeople among the various occupations open to them. Plainly, however, this initial distribution is not the only thing to be considered;

This is the chief factor in the campaign of accident prevention in Austria, insurance institutions not being permitted to make prevention regulations, as is the case in the trade associations of Germany " (*ibid.* p. 120). A device on the same lines, designed to encourage preventive measures against unemployment, is found in the English National Insurance Act. This Act, in effect, imposes a reduced rate on employers, so far as they engage men for long terms and so far as they meet periods of depression by working "short time:"

[1] For a further discussion of Insurance, cf. Part VI. Chapter XIII. It should be added that, since there is evil in uncertainty as such, the invention of insurance and compensation devices incidentally renders to dangerous, unhealthy, and fluctuating trades a greater benefit than it renders to other trades. The effect is similar to that of the invention of a machine applicable in one department of industry and not elsewhere. By altering general conditions, the invention brings it about that a different distribution of workpeople among industries is fitted to maximise the national dividend from the distribution which would have been fitted to do this apart from the invention. This effect is obviously *additional* to the effect, discussed in the text, of approximating the actual distribution towards the most favourable distribution that is possible under existing general conditions. We have to deal, in practice, with a change which both alters the position of a target and alters the mean deviation of shots from the bull's eye. In the text attention is paid to the latter effect only.

[2] *Report of the Royal Commission on the Poor Laws*, p. 395.

for mistakes made at the start may be rectified by subsequent movement. This may happen even for certain forms of capital. Thus, Dr. Clapham writes of the worsted weaving industry: "The light women's dress goods have very generally a cotton warp and a worsted weft. They often approach cotton goods in character; and the quite narrow looms on which they are mostly made can readily be used for the weaving of pure cotton fabrics, linings, and so forth, and constantly are so used when wool is dear, or when, for any other reason, fashion turns towards cotton."[1] In like manner, certain kinds of machinery can be readily removed, not merely from one factory to another, but from one occupation to another. For labour there are, *prima facie* at least, equal facilities for correcting mistakes by movement. Nor is this all. The distribution of labour, not only between occupations but also between places, may be made wrong from time to time by temporary fluctuations in the demand for and supply of different things, even though we suppose the initial direction given to new generations of workpeople to have been guided by perfect wisdom. Here, too, there is, in rightly directed movement, a means of making the distribution of labour better. The point we have now to consider is that ignorance, over and above the injury described already, inflicts a further injury on the national dividend by impeding and deflecting movement.

§ 6. Beyond doubt a great deal of ignorance prevails among workpeople in one place or occupation as to the comparative demand prices—by which the values of their marginal net products are represented—for their services prevailing there and elsewhere. The discussion of this matter is complicated by the fact that, since, from seasonal and other causes, work is less regular in some occupations than in others, wage rates per day or per week do not by themselves afford an adequate measure of comparative demand prices as a whole. Such a measure can only be obtained when both the wage rate for full employment and the prospect of unemployment have been taken into account. Clearly, workpeople can less easily gather information about the comparative liability of different occupations to unemployment

---

[1] *The Woollen and Worsted Industries*, p. 144.

than about comparative wage rates. This point, however, need not be enlarged upon here, and attention may be confined to wages. The extent of people's ignorance about the level of wage rates in any place or occupation depends, in great part, upon the form in which wage contracts are made. Some forms make the real prospect of earnings offered to work-people much more difficult to calculate than other forms. In nearly all forms, indeed, there is a good deal of obscurity. For real wages, in the widest sense, embrace the conditions of a man's work in respect to sanitary arrangements, safety appliances, and so forth; and these cannot be fully known to any workman before he is actually working under them. But the obscurity is much enhanced when fines are charged for damaged work and information about this is suppressed, and when wages are paid partly in commodities on which some fictitious value may be set. It is, therefore, an important fact that wage contracts embracing these elements are restricted in most modern States. To meet direct suppression of relevant information, the law has intervened in this country through the Particulars Clause inserted in the Factory and Workshops Act, 1901. "That section provides that, in industries to which it is applied by Order of the Secretary of State, persons, to whom work is given out to be done, shall receive from the employer sufficient particulars of the rate of wages applicable to the work to be done and of the work to which that rate is to be applied to enable the worker to compute the total amount of wages payable in respect of the work. This provision, the enforcement of which is placed upon the Inspectors of Factories, is intended to secure to the outworker information beforehand as to the price he· is to get for the work, and to protect him against arbitrary alterations or reductions when the work is brought in. The provision has been extended by Orders of the Secretary of State to the outworkers in a number of trades."[1] To meet indirect suppression of information through part payment in objects of ambiguous value, the law in this country has adopted the broad policy of prohibiting such part-payment, despite the risk that in so doing it might incidentally suppress

---

[1] *Select Committee on Home Work Report*, 1908, p. viii.

some useful institutions.[1] The fundamental provision of the Truck Act of 1831 was that "wages are to be made payable in current coin of the realm only," and that no condition should be made as to where or with whom any part of the wages should be expended.[2] This provision was made to apply by the Act of 1887 to any one engaged in manual labour who has entered into or works under an expressed or implied contract with an employer; it did not include outworkers who contract in terms of product, not of work. It was decided by the Courts that to make deductions for rent of machines, standing-room, etc., was not incompatible with the Act, because wages meant what was left after such payments had been made. Fines were also held to be no contravention. By the Act of 1896, however, "deductions in respect of fines, in respect of loss to the employer by bad or spoiled work or materials, etc., and in respect of the supply of materials, tools and other conveniences to the worker were made subject to conditions intended to protect the worker against harsh or unfair charges on the part of the employer."[3] Some practical problems under this head still demand solution and were discussed at length by the Committee of 1908.[4]

§ 7. In what has just been said, a very important problem was left on one side. It was tacitly assumed that a worker, if he chose, could always continue at full work where he was,

---

[1] Cf. C. D. Wright's account of some American systems of company stores in regions remote from ordinary shops (*The Industrial Evolution of the U.S.A.*, pp. 282 et seq.).

[2] *Report of the Select Committee on the Truck Acts*, p. 6. This provision can be evaded by a company establishing a provision store and informally putting pressure on its workpeople to buy there. The French law of 1910 meets this danger by forbidding any employer to "connect with his establishment any store at which he shall sell directly or indirectly to his employees or to their families provisions or goods of any description whatever" (*Labour Gazette*, May 1910, p. 156).

[3] *Report of the Select Committee on the Truck Acts*, p. 9.

[4] Thus, the Committee find that some deductions in respect of fines may be useful to secure discipline, and suggest that abuse be guarded against by a statutory provision that "the maximum fine or accumulation of fines in any one week permissible by law shall not exceed 5 per cent of the wages of the worker" (p. 29). Deductions for damage to materials and so on they hold may be usefully employed to prevent waste, under an arrangement, say, for charging for the material as given out and *adding* the value of it to the wage for the work in which it is afterwards incorporated (p. 41). Still, they conclude that, in view of the liability of such charges to become fraudulent, they should be pro-

his wages being adjusted to the value of his product and any movement that he might make to another place or occupation being entirely voluntary. In actual life, however, though, no doubt, many workpeople are always free agents in this sense, there are also great numbers who, in the face of short-period variations of demand, have not the choice between staying at work where they are and going elsewhere. They are definitely thrown out of work, and, if they are to be employed at all, have to go elsewhere. So long as they are out of work, the national dividend is damaged, not because they are working at less productive jobs that they might have been engaged on, but because they are not working at all. What is needed is that they shall, as speedily as possible, move from where they are not wanted to where they are wanted. So long as in one place or occupation men are out of work, while in another place or occupation there are vacancies which they are capable of filling, the national dividend suffers loss. Ignorance delays the required corrective movement. If it was complete and if, in spite of this, workpeople who had lost their jobs were to set out to look for work elsewhere—a step which their ignorance would make them hesitate long to undertake—they would wander aimlessly round to the firms that have not, as well as to those that have, vacancies, engaging themselves in a weary " tramp from one firm to another, in the attempt to discover, by actual application to one after another, which of them wants another hand." [1]

As a rule, ignorance is somewhat less complete than this. Some sort of general information is available about the comparative state of the demands for labour in various places and occupations. This can be obtained through newspaper advertisements, the talk of friends and the reports about local conditions collected by trade unions. Mr. Dearle has an interesting

---

hibited, subject to a power of the Home Secretary to relax the prohibitions in special cases (*e.g.* of costly material). The Committee further hold that the general provisions of the Truck Acts should be extended to outworkers (p. 78). They discuss, but do not definitely recommend, rules prohibiting employers from making it compulsory for their hands to live in houses provided by them (p. 53). The real objection to such compulsion is, not so much possible deception through it as regards real wages, as the power it carries with it of putting undue pressure on employees in times of strike.

[1] *Royal Commission on the Poor Laws*, Minority Report, p. 1125.

account of the development of these methods in the London building trades : " That system of mutual assistance in getting jobs, which a man and his mates render to one another, is extended and carried out in a more systematic manner by means of the vacant books of the trade unions. Each man, as he becomes unemployed, writes his name in the vacant book at the local branch office or meeting-place; and then every other member of the branch—and branches ordinarily number from 20 up to 400 or 500—is looking for a job for him, or, to be more exact, all members of the branch are on the look-out for vacancies to clear the vacant book. Obligations are imposed on all members to inform the branch secretary when men are wanted anywhere; and, whilst in some unions—for instance, the Amalgamated Carpenters and Joiners—a small sum, generally 6d. per member, is given to any one who will take unemployed men off the books, a heavy fine is imposed on any one known to be giving preference to non-union men. The usual thing is to inform the secretary where men are, or are likely to be, wanted, and the latter is bound to inform out-of-work members where best to look for jobs." [1] In England since 1893 still further information of this kind, in a more widely accessible form, has been furnished officially through the *Labour Gazette*. At the present time the Employment Exchanges also act as powerful informing agencies. They extend the inquiry work carried on by trade unions, and "enable the workman to ascertain, by calling at an office in his own neighbourhood, what enquiries have been made for his own kind of labour all over London." [2] When the Exchanges of different towns are inter-connected, the workman is brought into contact with a still wider range of information. Thus, in Germany : " In order to ensure the mobility of labour, it is considered to be of importance that the agencies for obtaining employment in the different parts of the German Empire should be linked up by a system of inter-communication. This system is provided by the Federations of Labour Registries. . . . In the Grand Duchy of Baden all are telephonically in communication, and want or superfluity of

[1] *Unemployment in the London Building Trades*, p. 133.
[2] *Royal Commission on the Poor Laws*, Minority Report, p. 1125.

labour in one place is immediately known in all the others."[1] In Bavaria the system is extended by the publication of lists of vacancies in villages in which no Exchange exists.[2] In England the development from the isolated to the connected form was consummated in the Labour Exchanges Act. It is evident that an organised system of this character may serve as a powerful instrument for facilitating the movement of workpeople out of jobs to vacancies having need of them.

It might seem at first sight that, when once this system has been set up, nothing further can be required. That, however, is a mistake. Information that at the present moment there are two vacancies open in the works of a particular firm is not equivalent to information that the vacancies will be open when the men, to whom this fact has been narrated, arrive there in search of work. The ignorance that obstructs mobility may, therefore, be still further reduced if, in place of centres of information as to the vacancies there and then available in different establishments or departments of establishments, there are instituted centres at which hands can be definitely engaged for these different establishments or departments. When that is done, workmen are informed, not merely that there are so many vacancies now in certain places, but also that these vacancies will still be available when they arrive in quest of them. The probability that this kind of unification will be brought about is, naturally, different in different circumstances. The obstacles in the way of it are least when separate establishments belong to the same company —this is, *pro tanto*, an argument in favour of Trusts,—when they are fixed in position, and when they are physically close together. Thus, in the London and India Docks unification came about many years ago.[3] The obstacles are somewhat

---

[1] [Cd. 2304], p. 65. [2] *Ibid.* p. 93.

[3] For an account of the introduction of the new policy at the Docks after the strike of 1889, cf. *Report of the Royal Commission on the Poor Laws*, p. 356. Mr. Beveridge summarises the changes introduced as follows: " Formerly each of the forty-seven departments of the Company's work was a separate unit for the engagement of men ; each department had its insignificant nucleus of regular hands and its attendant crowd of more or less loosely attached casuals ; 80 per cent of the work was done by irregular labour. Now the whole Dock system is, so far as the Company's work goes, the unit for the engagement of men ; 80 per cent of the work is done by a unified staff of weekly servants directed from on spot to another by a central office" (Beveridge, *Economic Journal*, 1907, p. 73

more serious when the different establishments, though still belonging to the same company or person, are scattered and moving, as in the London building trade. No doubt, even here unification is sometimes introduced. Before the Committee on Distress from Want of Employment, a witness, referring to the building trade, observed : " In the case of one employer, he said he did not hand over, as was the common practice, the responsibility of taking on men to his foremen, but did it himself, with this special object of having men permanently, and being able, as the foreman is not able to do, to move them on from job to job, the foreman being unable to pass them on to another job of which another foreman would be in charge. Although one understands why the other practice is adopted, it seems a very desirable thing that the practice of this individual employer should be more widely followed."[1] In general, however, builders' workmen in London are engaged independently by the different foremen of the firm employing them. The obstacles to unification are still more serious, when the separate establishments belong, not to one company or person, but to several ; for then, in order that unification may come about, a definite organisation for engaging workpeople has to be set up, either by the companies themselves or by some outside body, and, having been set up, has to be used for this purpose. This evidently involves the overcoming of considerable friction.

§ 8. If and when this friction has been overcome, it is evident that the range over which ignorance is dissipated and mobility improved will be greater, the larger is the proportion of the vacancies occurring in any locality that are filled by engagements negotiated through the local Employment Exchange acting as an engagement agency. This proportion, under a voluntary arrangement, will be larger, the more attractive Exchanges are made to employers. Experience seems to show that, if they are to win an extensive clientèle, they should be public—not run as a private speculation by possibly fraudulent private persons ; that they should be managed jointly by representatives of employers and employed; that they should take no notice of strikes and lock-outs, but

---

[1] Report of the Committee on Distress from Want of Employment, Evidence by Aves, Q. 10,917.

simply allow each side to post up in the Exchange a statement
that a stoppage of work exists in such and such an establishment; that they should be wholly separated from charitable
relief—association with such relief both keeps away the best
men from fear of injuring their reputation as workers and
makes employers unwilling to apply to the Exchanges; that
they should be given prestige by municipal or State authorisation, and should be advertised further, so far as practicable,
by being made the exclusive agency for the engagement of
workpeople employed by public authorities. The question
whether fees should be charged to the workpeople making
use of them is debatable. The French law of 1904 forbids
even private Exchanges to make such a charge. But the
Transvaal Indigency Commission points out that " the charging
of fees is by far the most effective method of keeping away
those who are not really in search of work ";[1] and, if such
persons are driven off, the Exchanges will undoubtedly prove
more attractive to employers. It is, further, open to the
State, if it chooses, to increase the proportion of vacancies
that are filled through Exchanges by some form of legal
suasion. A step in this direction would be taken if the
registration at an Exchange of all workpeople out of employment were made obligatory; for, if that were done, the
inducement to employers to resort to these centres of engagement would be increased. Such a step is suggested by the
Poor Law Commissioners in these terms: " We think that,
if, as will be proposed subsequently, the State contributes
to the unemployed benefit paid to each trade unionist, the
State might well make it a condition of such payment that
the trade unionist, when out of work, should register his
name and report himself to the local Labour Exchange, in
addition (if it is so desired) to entering his name in the
vacant book of his union. If the State supports and
encourages the trade unions, it seems only reasonable that
the trade unions should assist the State by supporting the
national and nationally needed Labour Exchanges."[2]   A
more drastic arrangement would be to provide by law that

---

[1] *Report of the Transvaal Indigency Commission*, p. 135.
[2] *Royal Commission on the Poor Laws*, Majority Report, p. 403.

employers and workmen should never enter into a contract of work without reference to an Exchange. This plan, which already rules in England for sailors in the mercantile marine, was at one time recommended for general adoption by Mr. Beveridge. Fearing that the effectiveness of the Exchanges might be weakened by lack of support from employers, he boldly claimed complete compulsion. "If the thing cannot be done voluntarily, it will have to be done, and will be done, compulsorily. A new clause in the Factory Code, *e.g.* that no man should be engaged for less than a week or a month, unless he were taken from a recognised Labour Exchange, would be a legitimate and unobjectionable extension of the accepted principle that the State may and must proscribe conditions of employment which are disastrous to the souls and bodies of its citizens."[1] The British National Insurance Act, without going so far as this, offers the inducement of what is, in effect, a slightly reduced charge for the insurance of their workmen both against sickness and, where this form of insurance is provided, against unemployment, to those employers who engage their workpeople through Employment Exchanges.[2] All these devices, in so far as they foster a more extended use of the Exchanges, tend, other things being equal, to break down ignorance of the conditions of the demand for labour, hence to lessen unemployment, and hence to increase the national dividend. It must be observed, however, that the extent to which they do this, and, therefore, the benefit to be expected from their introduction, is likely to be smaller in a country already provided with a widely-extended system of trade unions than in one where unionism is comparatively little developed. This point is brought out by the fact that, while in Germany, before the war, the Employment Exchanges were as effective in finding places for skilled men as for unskilled men, in the United Kingdom their success was confined in the main, at all events as regards the finding of work in the immediate neighbourhood, to the latter class, among whom no strong union organisation existed.[3]

---

[1] Beveridge, *Contemporary Review*, April 1908, p. 392.

[2] Cf. *National Insurance Act*, § 99 (1).

[3] Cf. Schloss, *Economic Journal*, 1907, p. 78 ; also *Bulletin de l'Association pour la lutte contre la chômage*, Sept. 1913, p. 839.

§ 9. Our study of ignorance as a cause of errors in the distribution of labour is now complete. We turn, therefore, to the second cause distinguished in § 1, namely, " costs of movement." But, before these costs can be examined in detail, certain matters of a general character require elucidation. As was indicated in the footnote to p. 127, the cost of movement may most conveniently be regarded as equivalent to an annual sum spread over the period during which the workman who has moved may expect to find profit in staying in his new place or occupation. The task of calculating this annual sum presents some difficulty. First, the costs of movement are not the same for all persons liable to move. Old workmen with families are, for example, rooted more firmly to their homes than young unmarried men. At first sight it might seem, indeed, that this fact does not greatly concern us, since the movement in which we are interested is the movement of those persons whose movement costs least—not fluidity in general, but fluidity at the edges. But the costs of movement of those persons whose movement costs least are themselves dependent upon the number of persons who are moving. Hence, for complete accuracy, we should need to treat these costs, not as a constant, but as a function of the volume of movement. For purposes of approximation, however, it is generally sufficient to take rough *discontinuous* groups, for which different fixed costs of movement can be set out. Thus, whether A and B represent different places or different occupations, and whether movement means movement in space or the acquisition of a new trade, we can in ordinary times—the position in the later period of the Great War was, of course, different —take for our costs those proper to the movement of young men without family encumbrances. It should, indeed, be noted that, as a trade or place decays and the young men gradually leave, the relevant costs of movement will tend to rise, because the age distribution of the population will be modified. Statistical inquiry shows that in decaying trades the proportion of old men is above the normal, and becomes greater and greater as the decay proceeds.[1] But this complication is

---

[1] Cf. Booth, *Life and Labour, Industry*, vol. v. pp. 43 and 49. In like manner, Lord Dunraven observes that " Ireland has a larger population of aged

one of detail rather than of principle. Secondly, when the
capital cost of movement is given, the annual sum, to which
we have to equate it, is not fixed, but is larger, the shorter is
the period during which a workman who has moved expects
to find profit in staying in his new place. For example, in
the eyes of a man considering whether or not to move
away from a point of slack demand, this annual sum will
be larger if the depression is, say, a seasonal depression and
likely to pass away rapidly, than if it is likely to continue
for a long time. Thirdly, from the present point of view, the
costs of movement between any two places or occupations A
and B are not necessarily the actual costs, but may be a lesser
amount, which we may call the "virtual" costs, and which
consist of the sum of the costs of movement along each of the
separate stages that lie between A and B. When the costs in
view are merely costs of physical transport, this point is not,
indeed, likely to be important. For, in general, long-distance
journeys are cheaper per mile than short-distance journeys,
and, therefore, there will not exist any virtual cost smaller
than the actual cost. If, however, the costs in view are those
arising out of the need of learning particular accomplishments,
it is very important. The costs of transport, in this sense,
between the occupation of agricultural labourer and that of
master manufacturer may be infinite; but those between
agricultural labourer and petty shopkeeper, between petty
shopkeeper and large shopkeeper, between large shopkeeper
and departmental manager, between departmental manager
and general manager, between general manager and master
manufacturer, may all be small. The same class of consideration is applicable to those costs which consist in the
subjective burden of leaving one's home and settling elsewhere.
Probably these costs, in respect of one movement of a thousand
miles, greatly exceed those involved in two hundred move-

---

than any other country in the king's dominions " (*The Outlook in Ireland*, p. 21).
It must be noted, however, that we cannot *infer* decay or expansion unreservedly
from such considerations, because, in some industries, the *normal* age distribution differs widely from the average. Messengers are young men who expect to
become something else, and lightermen are generally retired sailors. Furthermore, some industries have an abnormal proportion of old, simply because they
are abnormally healthy or attract abnormally healthy people.

ments of five miles each. A good illustration of this point is afforded by the following account of mediaeval France: "If Lyons had need of workmen, it called upon Chalon-sur-Saône, which supplied them. The void made at Chalon was filled by men drawn from Auxerre. Auxerre, finding that less work was offered than was required, called to its aid Sens, which, at need, fell back upon Paris. . . . Thus, all the different places were stirred at once by a demand for labour, however distant that might be, just as a regiment in column, marching in one piece and only advancing a few paces, would be."[1] This class of consideration is important.

§ 10. We may now look at the costs of movement somewhat more in detail. As between two given places, we perceive at once that they include, not only the sheer money cost of travel to a workman who contemplates moving, but also the sacrifice of the goodwill of shopkeepers to whom the workman is known, and the wrench involved in leaving his friends and the district with which he is familiar. The money cost, of course, becomes less in any country, as the means of communication are developed and transport, therefore, becomes cheaper. The other element of cost, in like manner, becomes less as the speed of travel is increased, because, as this happens, it becomes easier for workpeople to change the seat of their work without having at the same time to change their homes.[2] As between two given occupations, the costs of movement become less, the more closely industrial progress causes the operations required in one occupation to resemble those required in another. Assimilation of this sort tends to come about more and more markedly the further the division of labour is carried. For division of labour means the splitting up of complex operations, formerly executed as wholes, into their elementary parts, and it so happens that a comparatively

---

[1] De Foville, *Transformation des moyens de transport*, p. 396. There is an exactly analogous phenomenon in the movement of capital between countries. People in the United States can move a given capital to Central or South America, and at the same time people in England move an equal capital to the United States at a less aggregate cost in uncertainty—because of differences of local knowledge—than that at which Englishmen could move that capital to Central or South America direct. Hence, this roundabout method of investment in fact occurs. Cf. C. K. Hobson, *The Export of Capital*, pp. 29-32.

[2] Cf. Mahaim, *Les Abonnements d'ouvriers*, p. 170.

2 H

small number of elementary parts, when combined in different ways, make up nearly all the wholes. Consequently, the range of movements open to workmen helping to produce any given article, while " narrowed as regards the power of interchange among themselves is, as a rule, widened as regards the power of interchange with those performing corresponding processes of other trades.".[1] As M. de Rousiers well observes : "More and more the constantly developing applications of machinery are approximating the type of the mechanic to that of the shop assistant. The shop assistant passes readily from one kind of commerce to another, from drapery to provisions, from fancy goods to furniture, so much so that, at the present time, retail shopkeeping, in the hands of men of superior ability, is no longer confined to one or another single branch, but takes on the form of the large general store. Manufacture cannot yet pretend to so large a range, but, just as an assistant passes easily from one counter to another, so the workman passes easily from the supervision of one machine to the supervision of another machine, from the loom to bootmaking, from paper-making to spinning, and so forth.".[2] In like manner, the same persons, at different times, may be found at match-box making, hopping, step-cleaning and hawking; and the Poor Law Commissioners' investigators "found a tailoress working at bookbinding, a jam girl at screws, and a machinist giving pianoforte lessons at 1s. an hour.".[3] In these developments there is evidence of great versatility. Specialised technical skill is coming to play a smaller part in industrial operations, relatively to general capacity, than it used to do; and this means that the costs of the new training required to enable a workman to move from one occupation to another are becoming smaller. It should be added that, in so far as people's estimate of the cost of new training is greater than the actual cost, it is the estimated cost that is relevant to mobility; and, therefore, if they come to realise that the estimate has been excessive, mobility is

---

[1] Llewellyn Smith, *The Mobility of Labour*, p. 19.
[2] *La Question ouvrière en Angleterre*, p. 334. Cf. also Marshall, *Principles of Economics*, pp. 207 and 258.
[3] *Report of the Royal Commission on the Poor Laws*, p. 406.

increased. There is reason to suppose that the experience of
the war has taught people that specialised skill can be gained
more easily and quickly than used to be supposed.[1]

So far, we have spoken of movement between places
and movement between occupations separately. But, of
course, in the concrete, movement from one occupation to
another may well necessitate, at the same time, movement
from one place to another. Hence, the aggregate costs of
movement from one occupation to another are kept low,
when kindred occupations, in which the fluctuations of
demand for labour more or less compensate one another,
are carried on in the same neighbourhood. This is one
of the advantages of the cottage industries of the country
districts of India, where for three months of the year agriculture is almost at a standstill;[2] and also of recent extensions
of small holdings and allotments, to which workpeople
can resort during temporary unemployment in their main
industry. The reduction of costs is still greater when the
complementary occupations are conducted in the same establishment. It is, therefore, especially interesting to read in
a Board of Trade Report issued shortly before the war:
"The more competent and thoughtful employers endeavour
to overcome the natural fluctuations of the seasons by
superior organisation. With the manufacture of jam and
marmalade they combine the making of sweets and the potting
of meats. They thus occupy the time of the majority of their
employees. An artificial florist, employing over two hundred
girls and women in a trade which occupies six months of the
year, has introduced a second trade, the preparing of quills for
hat-trimming, and now the workers are employed all the year
round. In Luton, where the staple trade is straw-hat making,
and where work is always slack during six months of the year,
felt-hat making has been introduced; and it is now very usual
to find the two trades carried on by the same firm, employing
the same workpeople at different periods of the year."[3] Some-

---

[1] Cf. Cannan, *The Reorganisation of Industry* (Ruskin College), Series iii.
p. 11.
[2] Cf. Muckerjee, *The Foundations of Indian Economics*, p. 323.
[3] *Cost of Living of the Working Classes* [Cd. 3864], p. 284.

times, no doubt, arrangements of this kind are introduced
from philanthropic motives. But there is also a powerful
motive of a purely self-regarding character at work in the
same direction. It is clearly cheaper for one factory to work
all the year round than for two to be built to work, one in
one part and the other in another part of the year ; and the
gain in cheapness is particularly great when the plant and
equipment are elaborate and costly. Hence, whenever it is
practicable, it is to the interest of employers to adapt their
factories—if they are engaged in seasonal production—to the
manufacture of a series of different things so arranged that
there is work to do at some of them in every part of the year.
Anything that facilitates the adoption among employers of
this policy necessarily reduces the effective costs of movement
to labour.

§ 11. In the preceding sections we have permitted ourselves certain refinements of analysis. Turning back to coarser
matters, we may conclude generally that workpeople's movements away from their present occupation to other occupations
offering a higher wage, and, therefore, presumably yielding a
larger value of marginal net product, are often impeded by
considerable costs ; and that workpeople's movements from
their present locality to other and distant countries, particularly
if these are separated off by strong barriers of race, religion and
language, may often be similarly impeded. But, so far as the
forms of cost hitherto discussed are concerned, workpeople's
movements to other parts of their native land, at all events in a
small country such as England, will, in general, only be impeded
by small costs. There remains, however, a peculiar form of
cost obstructing movements from certain places to certain other
places, which may be large even in a country like England.
This cost arises out of the fact that husband, wife and young
children generally live together. Because of this the movement
of one member of the family implies the movement of the others,
and the movement of the others may carry with it a large loss
by cutting off the wages that they have hitherto been able to
earn. This loss is really a part of the cost of movement of
the member of the family who is tempted by higher wages
to move elsewhere. For example, the men workers in a

district where there are opportunities for their women folk to earn wages might know that they themselves could earn more in other districts where these opportunities do not exist. But, in reckoning up the advantages and disadvantages of movement, they would need to count as a true cost the prospective loss of their women folk's contribution. This cost may be very large and, consequently, may make possible wide differences in the values of the marginal net products, and therefore in the wages, of labour of a given grade in two districts of the same small country. As Dr. Marshall has well observed: "The family is, in the main, a single unit as regards geographical migration; and, therefore, the wages of men are relatively high, and those of women and children low, where heavy iron or other industries preponderate, while in some other districts less than half the money income of the family is earned by the father, and men's wages are relatively low."[1] It is evident that all improvements in the speed and all cheapening in the cost of passenger transport, to which reference was made in an earlier section, because they make it possible for different members of a family, while living together, to work in places more widely separated from one another, will mitigate the injury to the distribution of labour for which this kind of cause is responsible.

§ 12. In addition to ignorance and costs there remains the third cause of error in the distribution of labour which was distinguished in § 1, namely, artificial restrictions upon movement imposed from without. These restrictions may assume any number of different forms. For example, until the end of the eighteenth century "place mobility" was seriously obstructed by the law of settlement, which, in order to prevent workpeople born in one part of the country from becoming "chargeable" on the rates of another part, greatly limited their right to move. "It was often more difficult," Adam Smith wrote, "for a poor man to pass the artificial boundary of a parish than an arm of the sea or a ridge of high mountains." Again, at the present day, mobility between occupations is, in some industries, considerably impeded by the demarcation rules of Trade Unions—rules which attempt to reserve particular jobs to

---

[1] *Principles of Economics,* footnote to p. 715.

workers at a particular trade, and forbid, under threat of a
strike, their being undertaken by other tradesmen. A
bricklayer, for example, is not allowed by his union to do
stone-mason's work, or a pattern-maker to do joiner's work.
Nor can a man easily escape this kind of obstacle by
changing his union. For, apart from affiliation arrangements
among kindred unions, if he tries to do this, "and is not
blocked by rules about apprenticeship, he will be penalised by
the immediate loss of unemployed and other benefit, and he is
not for some time qualified for the trade union benefit of the
trade into which he transfers his labour."[1] This difficulty is
of real importance, and it is one which, whether by the
development of industrial unionism, as exemplified by the
National Union of Railway Workers, alongside of craft unionism, or by some system of affiliation, both among the craft
unions themselves and between the craft unions and unions
of unskilled workers, the leaders of the Labour movement will
need before long to face. Probably, however, the most serious
artificial restrictions that are current in modern times are
certain traditions and customs, which obstruct and practically
prevent labour power, when embodied in a particular type of
person, from flowing to channels where similar labour power,
embodied in other types of persons, is yielding a more valuable
marginal net product than is obtainable in the channels to
which all labour has free access. In some countries traditions
and customs of this sort relate to industrial occupations open
to workpeople of different race and colour. But their most
important action—at all events, so far as Europe is concerned—
is in the sphere of women's work. There are a number of
occupations in which the value of the marginal net product,
and, therefore, the wage, of women's work would, if women were
admitted to them, be larger than it is in occupations where
they are in fact engaged; but they are excluded from these
occupations by tradition and custom. When new occupations
such as the working of typewriters and telephones are introduced, or when old occupations are transformed by the
introduction of new types of machinery, women are, indeed,
generally offered a free field. But in occupations which men

[1] *Report of the Royal Commission on the Poor Laws*, p. 398.

have for a long time been accustomed to regard as their own, even though under present conditions women could adequately pursue them, tradition and custom frequently exercise a powerful excluding influence. The best known occupations in which such exclusion still prevails in fact, if not in form, are the two branches of the legal profession. Waiting in restaurants and railway clerical work were also, until a year or two ago, notable instances. The entrance of women into these occupations, prior to 1914, was hindered, as Mr. Cannan observes, "not so much by law as by the inertia of employers and their fear of inconvenience from the active resistance of the men employed at present."[1] This kind of resistance may be broken down by a world-shattering event like the Great War, but the difficulty with which it was overcome in 1915–16, even in munition-making trades, is witness to its strength. It is probable that employers do not battle with it so strongly as they otherwise might do, because women workers are liable to leave after a little while on getting married. As one employer put it: "There are many jobs one might teach women to do, but it does not seem worth while to risk a quarrel with the men when you know that the brighter a girl is, the more likely she is to go off and get married just as she is beginning to be of some use."[2] The men's opposition can, indeed, be modified by a stringent rule that women shall be paid equal wages with men of equal efficiency; for, when this rule exists, the men are less afraid of losing their jobs. But, on the other hand, when this rule is insisted upon, either by the State, or, as in ordinary times is more likely to happen, by the men, and when it means that women in the industry affected must be paid more than similar women earn in the generality of industries, a strong motive, which employers would otherwise have, for fighting against the tradition that excludes them, is removed. The rule of equal pay for equal efficiency is, in these circumstances, though not, of course, in all circumstances, itself an artificial barrier—a second line of defence set up by the men when attempts at direct exclusion are overcome—to save them from being ousted by women from occupations in which it is to the general

---

[1] Cannan, *Wealth*, p. 206.
[2] *The Round Table*, March 1916, p. 275.

interest that women should be employed exclusively instead of them. Women who support the claim for equal pay for equal efficiency in industries where this rate of pay affords them more than normal women's earnings, are really fighting at once against the general advantage and against their own cause. A better understanding by women workers of what their proper interest is, no less than a diminution of sex jealousy on the part of men workers, is wanted, if the most advantageous distribution of women workers among the industrial occupations which they are qualified to undertake is to be secured.[1]

§ 13. We have now studied in some detail the principal causes that make the distribution of labour diverge from the most advantageous distribution. All these causes alike work against the maximising of the national dividend, and it might, therefore, seem at first sight that, if the deflection of labour distribution for which they are responsible were overcome, the national dividend would necessarily be increased. This conclusion, however, ignores the fact that there are three distinct and different methods by which this deflection can be overcome. The obstacles in the way of a nearer approach to what may be called the ideal distribution may *crumble from within*, or they may be *pulled down at public cost*, or they may be left as they are and *leapt over*. The effects of these three methods of overcoming them are not the same, but require separate investigation.

§ 14. When it is said that obstacles to ideal distribution *crumble from within*, it is meant that information and the means of movement are supplied more cheaply to workpeople, or that traditions hostile to movement are weakened, through the general progress of ideas, the introduction of large scale organisation into the machinery of mobility, or in other such ways. The essence of the matter is that the real costs to the community as a whole of providing information and transport, and not merely the expenses charged to particular workpeople purchasing these facilities, are lessened. When this happens, the actual distribution of labour will, *generally speaking*, be brought closer to the ideal distribution. It is true that, if the obstacle whose magnitude is diminished is

---

[1] Cf. *post*, Chapter XIII. § 9.

costs of movement or tradition, this does not *necessarily* happen. For, as was pointed out in Part II. Chapter III., increased freedom to move may, when knowledge is imperfect, lead to movement in the wrong direction. Thus, it is sometimes an open question whether a *mere* cheapening of the costs of travel to workpeople, unaccompanied by any other change, will have a beneficial effect; though, of course, it is never an open question whether cheapening, coupled with intelligent direction to specific vacancies, will have such an effect. That this point is now winning general recognition is suggested by the fact that, in England, travelling benefit, originally paid out by Trade Unions indiscriminately to all members in search of work, is now mainly used to enable selected members to reach places in which work has actually been found for them; by the fact that the British Labour Exchanges Act contains a clause permitting the Exchanges, subject to the approval of the Treasury, to authorise advances, by way of loan, towards the expenses of workpeople travelling to definite situations; and finally, by the fact that, in Germany, the Exchanges provide cheap railway tickets, not to work-seekers in general, but to those only for whom they have found definite situations.[1] The difficulty thus exemplified is an important one. There would, however, be no dispute among economists that, with the organisation of knowledge concerning industrial conditions developed to the point at which it stands in modern civilised States, a reduction in the costs of movement, or a breach in traditions of exclusion, would, on the whole and in general, cause the distribution of labour to approach more closely towards the ideal. In so far as it has this effect, it must also increase the national dividend.[2]

---

[1] *Report of the Royal Commission on the Poor Laws*, p. 401.

[2] To make our discussion complete, it is desirable to add here that the increase in the national dividend *may*, if information about vacancies is provided, not merely to the workpeople who are *unemployed* at one place, but to *all* the workpeople there, be accompanied, not by a decrease, but by an increase in the volume of unemployment. Mr. Jackson has observed, in his discussion of boy labour, that the very fact that boys can secure a new job with ease makes them abandon jobs light-heartedly (*Report on Boy Labour*, p. 14), and Mr. Heath has suggested that the development of Employment Exchanges in Germany increased the extent to which men were employed for

§ 15. When it is said that obstacles to ideal distribution are *pulled down at public expense*, it is meant that information or the means of movement are supplied more cheaply to workpeople, not because the real costs have been reduced, but because a part of these costs has been transferred to the shoulders of the tax-payers. This form of cheapening and that discussed in the preceding section do not react

---

short periods (*Economic Journal*, 1910, p. 345). Plainly, the greater number of people who fall out of old jobs *may* have more effect in increasing unemployment than the greater speed with which new jobs are found has in diminishing it.

Let us suppose there is no conventional element in wage rates anywhere, so that anybody, by staying where he is, *could* get employment at *some* wage; and that some new arrangement is introduced which shortens the average time required to move from one job to another.

Let the loss of earnings resulting from the time occupied in movement from A to B be equivalent, before that time is lessened, to a diminution of the wage by C.

After the time is lessened, let it be equivalent to a diminution by $C(1-h)$. Then the actual quantity of unemployment that takes place is, before the improvement, mC times the number of men displaced from A, and, after the improvement, $mC(1-h)$ times the number displaced.

Let the wage in both A and B stand originally at W; and let the wage in B be raised somehow to a level $W+q$.

In these circumstances, before the time required for movement is shortened, the wage in A will be raised to $(W+q-C)$; after the time is shortened, to $\{W+q-C(1-h)\}$.

Let η be the elasticity of the demand for labour at A, and k a constant. Then the number displaced at A, before the time is shortened

$$= \eta\left\{\frac{q-C}{W}\right\}k;$$

after the time is shortened

$$= \eta\left\{\frac{q-C(1-h)}{W}\right\}k.$$

∴ the *unemployment involved* before the time is shortened

$$= mC\eta\left\{\frac{q-C}{W}\right\}k;$$

after the time is shortened

$$= mC(1-h)\eta\frac{\{q-C(1-h)\}}{W}k.$$

∴ the excess of unemployment after the improvement, over that before the improvement,

$$= \frac{mC\eta}{W}[(1-h)\ \{q-C(1-h)\} - \{(q-C)\}]k.$$

This is positive or negative, according as $\{C(2-h)-q\}$ is positive or negative. That is to say, an improvement in mobility is more likely to diminish unemployment, (1) the larger are the fluctuations that start movement, (2) the smaller was the cost of movement before the improvement, and (3) the larger is the reduction of this cost consequent on the improvement.

in the same way upon the relative values of marginal net products at different·points and, therewith, upon the magnitude of the national dividend.   For this kind of cheapening implies that a greater quantity of resources is invested in the work of securing knowledge and effecting movement than would normally be devoted to that work.   It implies, in fact, that a particular form of investment is being stimulated by means of a bounty.   Economic analysis, however, warns us that, as a general rule, bounties lead to economic waste. There is reason to suspect that such waste actually occurs, to some·extent, as a result of the system of artificially cheapened workmen's tickets operated by the Belgian railways. The following passage from Dr. Mahaim's interesting monograph is strongly suggestive of this conclusion: "A villa had to be built in the suburbs of Liège, where, assuredly, there was no lack of labour.   The contract was secured by a builder from Nivelles.   He employed exclusively Brabant workpeople, who came in, some every day and some every Monday. Not one iota of the general labour required was executed by Liège men."[1]   There are other passages of like effect, suggesting that the bounty—for such in substance it is—which the State pays upon workmen's tickets tempts employers in one place, when they are given work to do in another, to have workmen transported there, despite the fact that suitable labour could be. found for the job in the place where it has to be done.   This leads to something very like a double transference of gold, instead of the use of bills of exchange, in the settlement of the·accounts of international trade—a process that is necessarily wasteful to the community as a whole, whether or no the fiscal arrangements in vogue make it wasteful to the individuals undertaking it.   As was shown, however, in Chapters VI. and VIII. of Part II., the presumption thus established against the grant of a bounty to any industry may be overthrown, if there is reason to believe that, in the absence of a bounty, investment in that industry would not be carried far enough to bring the value of the marginal net product of resources employed in it down to the general level.   Partly because

[1] *Les Abonnements d'ouvriers*, p. 157.

the industry of promoting the mobility of workpeople yields a product difficult to sell satisfactorily for fees, it is one about which there is reason to believe this. Consequently, up to a point, it is probable that the expenditure of public money in improving mobility would make the values of the marginal net products of resources in different occupations more equal, and so would increase the national dividend. It is necessary, however, for the State to watch this expenditure carefully; for, if it is carried too far, though it will yield a benefit in the matter of unemployment, that benefit will be at the expense of more than equivalent injury to the aggregate output of the nation's industry.

§ 16. When it is said that obstacles to ideal distribution are *leapt over*, it is meant that ignorance, costs of movement and tradition remain unaltered, but that, in spite of their existence, the distribution of labour is somehow forced towards what it would have been if they did not exist. This may be done by the compulsory removal of workpeople, or more probably, as will be explained in Chapter XIII. § 5, by certain forms of authoritative interference with wage rates. The way in which it is done is not, however, important for our present problem. What we wish to ascertain is the effect on the national dividend of an " improvement " in the distribution of labour brought about *in spite of* the continued existence of obstacles. This effect is different with different obstacles. A redistribution of labour more conformable to ideal distribution, which is brought about in spite of opposing ignorance or tradition, necessarily augments the national dividend. For the defiance of these obstacles involves no expense, and so leads to exactly the same consequences as would be produced by their crumbling from within. But the result is different with a redistribution brought about in spite of opposing " costs of movement." For, when the obstacles to movement which these costs present are overborne, the costs themselves are by that very process incurred. Thus, defiance does involve expense, and leads to the same consequences as would be produced if the obstacle were *pulled down at public cost*. That is to say, there is a general presumption that it will injure the national dividend, but there are grounds for believing that this presumption is, within certain limits, reversed.[1]

[1] This conclusion involves the verbally inconvenient result that the *ideal* distribution of labour, when brought about in certain ways, is not the *best possible* distribution. Confusion will be avoided, however, if we recollect that the distribution we have called ideal, namely, that which makes the values of the marginal net products of labour everywhere equal, is only ideal in an absolute sense. It is the best distribution accessible to a man who has unlimited power over all relevant circumstances, and can, therefore, at will abolish costs of movement. But it is not the best distribution accessible to one who must accept the costs of movement as brute fact, and has, therefore, to aim at maximising the national dividend subject to that limiting condition.

CHAPTER X

§ 1. THE general analysis of the preceding chapter has an important bearing upon a problem from which it seems at first sight to be remote. This problem is to determine the comparative effects on the national dividend of the principal ways which are open to employers for meeting periods of depression. When, in consequence of lessened demand for his product, an employer finds that a continuance of output on his former scale will involve him in loss, he can accomplish the necessary reduction in any one of three ways; (1) by working full time and dismissing a part of his staff; (2) by working full time and retaining his whole staff, but rotating employment so that only a proportion (say 2/3rds) is actually at work at any one time; or (3) by working short time and putting the whole of his staff to work during the whole of the working period.

§ 2. As between the short time plan and both the others the relevant influences are primarily technical. Resort to the short time plan is easiest when the conditions are such that an appreciable advantage can be gained by cutting down the most expensive *hours* of work, those, for example, that involve extra charges for lighting and heating. But one or other of the rival plans is favoured when much expensive machinery is employed and it is practicable, by spreading labour more sparsely, to keep the whole of this going with a reduced staff.

§ 3. As between the dismissal plan and both the others the issue depends to a large extent upon how important it is to an employer to maintain a lien upon

the services of the people who have so far been working for
him. When the work to be done is skilled and specialised,
it is often very important for him to do this. Workpeople
possessed of special aptitudes practically always acquire special
value to the particular firms which have employed them for any
length of time. This is partly because the detailed methods
of different factories are different, and, therefore, workmen
who have become accustomed to any given factory, particularly
if the work they have to do in it is of an all-round kind, are
more useful there than other similar workmen would be. It
is partly also because skilled workmen often handle expensive
materials or delicate machinery, and employers naturally
prefer to entrust these things to men of whose qualities they
have had continuing experience. And finally, among firms
making certain proprietary articles, it is partly because workmen may be expected after a time to get an inkling of their
firm's manufacturing secrets, and the firm is, therefore, unwilling to let them enter the service of its rivals.[1] Thus, "among
goldsmiths and jewellers the masters share work among a
permanent staff, since there are many secret and special
patterns, and adjust production by overtime for short periods." [2]
In like manner, employers are keenly anxious to retain a lien
on the services of engine-drivers, domestic servants and
specialised agricultural labourers.[3] Even when the work to
be done is of such a sort that a man who has been employed
before with a particular firm is not appreciably more valuable
to that firm than one who has not, an employer in bad
times, who knows, or hopes, that things will improve, will like
to keep in touch with more men than he needs at the moment,
so as to make sure that enough will be available later on.
This consideration is especially likely to influence employers
in industries where the fluctuations are known to be seasonal;
for in these industries there is practical certainty that a full
staff will be needed again shortly. It has been suggested
that seasonality of this kind is partly responsible for the
prevalence of the short time method in coal-mining and in
agriculture. Moreover, even when employers, if left to

---

[1] Cf. Fay, *Co-partnership in Industry*, p. 90.
[2] Webb, *Seasonal Trades*, p. 43.   [3] *Ibid.* p. 23.

themselves, would tend to the dismissal method, trade unions, which naturally dislike that method because it involves them in a larger burden of unemployment benefit, sometimes sway them in favour of one or other of the rival plans.

§ 4. In this choice between the dismissal plan and the other two, another very important factor is the degree of accuracy with which wages are adjusted to efficiency. When the payment normally made to inferior workers is higher relatively to their efficiency than that made to better workers, there is a strong inducement to employers to meet bad times by dispensing with the least profitable part of their staff. It is, thus, natural to find that the dismissal method is relatively dominant in time-wage industries as compared with piece-wage industries. Discussing the principal ways in which a slackness of demand is met in this country, Sir H. Llewellyn Smith once wrote: "Looking at the question broadly, we may distinguish two main methods. The first general method is by short time, or short work, for all or the majority of those employed. A good example of that is mining, in which, for the most part, the contractions do not result so much in throwing out a certain number of colliers altogether, but in the colliery working a smaller number of days per week. Another example would be the boot and shoe trade (I mean apart, for the moment, from the great factories where machinery is used, but where it is carried on on the ordinary piece-work system), in which in slack times there are not many people entirely unemployed, but a very large number of people will have a short amount of work. The second method, which applies in other industries, is not by working short time, but by throwing out of work a certain proportion of the workers, who form a fluctuating margin of unemployed. Examples of such trades are the building, engineering and shipbuilding trades. I do not mean to say there is not short time known in any of those trades, or that overtime is not worked in times of inflation; but, the main method by which they adjust themselves to a change in demand is by throwing out workers or taking on more workers."[1]

---

[1] *Third Report of the Committee on Distress from Want of Employment,* Evidence, Q. 4540.

An examination of the industries mentioned in this passage, shows that those, ¡which Sir H. Llewellyn Smith classes among the short-time industries, are just those in which piece-wages predominate, while those, which he classes as dismissal industries, employ time-wages. It may, indeed, be thought at first glance that the engineering trade belies this rule. Though, however, this trade contains a good deal of piece-work, it was until recently *mainly* a time-work trade, and so is no exception.[1] In like manner, it is natural to find that in Germany where, before the war, trade unions were relatively weak, and where, partly as a consequence of this, a rigid standard rate in time-wage industries was much less effectively enforced than it was in this country, the practice of meeting slack periods by working short time, rather than by a reduction of staff, was considerably more general. "Some of the German authorities declare that the practice of short time in some industries reduces earnings by as much as one-fourth or one-third in the course of a year. It is certain that, though certain British industries, notably coal-mining and the cotton industry, resort to the system of short time, the extent to which this system operates to lower the figure of unemployed workmen in the United Kingdom is much less than in the German Empire."[2] I do not wish to stress these facts unduly. They seem, however, to illustrate the general tendency set out at the beginning of this section.

§ 5. As between rotation of hands and the two other plans the dominant fact is that the rotation method is troublesome to arrange and involves a good deal of organisation and collaboration with the workpeople. It appears to prevail among "the riverside corn porters working regularly at the Surrey docks;"[3] it has been practised to some extent among the iron-workers of the north of England; and it was tried, alongside of the short time plan, in the cotton industry during a part of 1918. Yet again, as a result of negotiations with the Tailors' Trade Union, the Master Tailors' Association announced: "We fully recognise that the work ought to be fairly shared

[1] *Third Report of the Committee on Distress from Want of Employment*, Evidence, Q. 4541, *et seq.*
[2] *Report on the Cost of Living in German Towns* [Cd. 4032], p. 522.
[3] *Report of the Royal Commission on the Poor Law*, p. 1156, footnote.

2 I

during the slack seasons (subject to certain explanations), and we urge upon our members throughout the country to carry these principles into effect."[1] But, broadly speaking, the inconvenience of this method has not permitted it to be adopted at all widely.

§ 6. The general result is that, in the main part of industry, depressions are met by either the short time method or the dismissal method, or a mixture of the two. Professor Chapman gives some interesting figures to illustrate the varying degrees in which different textile industries, all employing the same (namely the piece wage) form of wage payment, have adopted the two methods respectively. Between November 1907 and November 1908 it appears that, in the cotton industry, among the firms investigated, a 13·3 contraction of output was met, to the extent of 5 per cent by reduction of staff, and to the extent of 8·3 per cent by short time; whereas, in the silk industry, an 8·1 per cent contraction of output led to a 6·2 per cent reduction of staff and 2·1 per cent short time.[2] As is well known, the method of short time is dominant in coal-mining, where it is carried out by a reduction, in times of depression, in the number of shifts worked per week; and the method of dismissal in the building, shipbuilding and engineering trades.[3]

§ 7. *Prima facie* it would seem that, from the standpoint

[1] *Report on Collective Agreements*, 1910, p. xxviii.

[2] Cf. Chapman, *Unemployment in Lancashire*, p. 51. When a firm employs both factory workers and home workers, it is, of course, to its interest in bad times to withdraw work from home workers rather than to reduce factory work and home work equally, because it is thus enabled to keep its machinery going. It may be added that the power to treat home workers in this way indirectly checks employers from superseding home work altogether by factory work, because it enables them to face the prospect of periodic expansions without the need of erecting factories too large for the demand of ordinary times. (Cf. Vessilitsky, *The Home Worker*, p. 3.)

[3] Of course, it is not meant that in these trades no short time is known. On the contrary, even when the dismissal method is adopted for contractions of work from below the normal, what is, in effect, the short time method is always adopted to some extent for contractions from above the normal. Thus, in the engineering trade, whereas the average amount of formal short time is very small, overtime adds on the average 3¾ per cent to the normal man's working time (Cd. 2337, p. 100), and, as against overtime working, normal hours are, of course, really short time. All that is meant is that "the main method by which these industries adjust themselves to a change in demand is by throwing out workers or taking on more workers" (Llewellyn Smith, *Third Report of the Committee on Distress from Unemployment*, Evidence, Q. 4540).

of the national dividend, the dismissal, or reduction of staff,
method is certain to be more injurious than the short time
method, because it reacts injuriously on the quality of those
men whom it condemns to longer or shorter periods of unemployment. The most obvious way in which it does this is
through the larger and more concentrated loss of individual
earnings, which unemployment, as compared with short time,
involves. This threatens severe privation in food, clothing
and firing, not only to the men directly affected, but also to
their wives and children. If pushed far enough, this privation
may easily lead to a lasting *physical* deterioration. Nor is
this all. It may also cause those who suffer from it to supply
their needs by means which threaten a permanent weakening
of moral fibre. . *Inter alia*, it may lead to resort to the
Poor Law; for, as is well known, the curve of pauperism in
this country follows about a year behind the curve of unemployment.[1] Resort to the Poor Law, however, or to
vagrancy, marks, according to some, a definite stage of descent.
There is a definite line between poverty, where struggle and
independence prevail, and pauperism. "Paupers are not, as
a rule, unhappy. They are not ashamed; they are not keen
to become independent; they are not bitter or discontented.
They have passed over the line which separates poverty from
pauperism."[2] Again: "the men who enter the workhouse or
go on tramp, leaving their families to the Poor Law, are, as
a rule, those whom adversity, combined, no doubt, with their
own weaknesses, has made no longer able-bodied or respectable.
Having once entered, they seldom return to industry again."[3]
Sir H. Llewellyn Smith sums the matter up thus: "It is, I
think, a definite induction from history and observation that,
when risk falls outside certain limits as regards magnitude
and calculability, when, in short, it becomes what I may call
a gamblers' risk, exposure thereto not only ceases to act as
a bracing tonic, but produces evil effects of a very serious

---

[1] The interval is probably partly due to resistance made possible by savings,
the pawning of household goods, children's earnings, etc. ; partly to the fact that
a check to the *inflow of pauperism* will not involve a diminution of pauperism
until the inflow falls below the outflow brought about by death and other causes.
(Cf. Beveridge, *Unemployment*, p. 49.)

[2] Hunter, *Poverty*, p. 3.　　　[3] Beveridge, *Unemployment*, p. 50.

kind."[1] Leroy-Beaulieu in like manner declares, and is surely
right in declaring : " It is not the insufficiency of pay which
constitutes, in general and apart from exceptional cases, the
social evil of to-day, but the precariousness of employment."[2]
Nor is it only through the sense of insecurity that harm is
done. The mere fact of idleness, apart altogether from the
privation by which it is normally accompanied, is likely, unless,
indeed, it is mitigated by opportunities for work on land
belonging to, or rented by themselves,[3] to exercise a seriously
deteriorating influence—an influence, too, which grows rapidly
as the amount of the idleness grows—upon the economic and
general efficiency of those affected by it. It is well known,
for instance, that drunkenness is often worst in times of slack
employment.[4] The Royal Commissioners on the Poor Laws
have in evidence: "The enforced idleness on completion of
a job naturally throws the men upon their own resources,
which is, in nine cases out of ten, the nearest public-house.
The frequent change from strenuous hard work to absolute
indolence to men of this character naturally tends to gradual
moral and physical degeneration, and ultimately the individuals become unfit for work, even when opportunity offers."[5]
A large employer of labour is reported to have said: "Between
5 and 6 per cent of my skilled men are out of work just now.
During the long spell of idleness any one of these men invariably deteriorates. In some cases the deterioration is very
marked. The man becomes less proficient and less capable,
and the universal experience of us all who have to do with

---

[1] *Economic Journal*, 1910, p. 518.

[2] *Répartition des richesses*, p. 612.

[3] In Belgium the cheapness of workmen's tickets on the railways enables
many workers to live in cottages with gardens attached to them, to the cultivation of which they turn when out of ordinary work (cf. Rowntree, *Unemployment*, p. 267).

[4] Cf. Charity Organisation Committee's *Report on Unskilled Labour*, p. 56.

[5] Quoted in the *Minority Report*, p. 1138. It should be noted, however,
as observed by Mr. Beveridge (p. 47), that unemployment is correlated negatively
with both the consumption of alcohol and the convictions for drunkenness.
The reason, no doubt, is that periods of high unemployment mean reduced
wages also to the employed and so less drink. That this is, in fact, so is
well shown by Mr. A. D. Webb in an article on "The Consumption of
Alcoholic Liquors in the United Kingdom" (*Statistical Journal*, Jan. 1913).
These statistics do not prove, however, that those *who are actually unemployed*
drink less.

large numbers of working men is that nothing has a worse effect upon the calibre of such men than long spells of idleness."[1] The Transvaal Indigency Commission report: "Unemployment is one of the most fruitful causes of indigency of a permanent and hopeless . kind.   However skilled a man may be, he is bound to deteriorate during a long period of unemployment. His hand loses some of its cunning and he acquires the habit of idleness.   The tendency is for the unemployed to sink to the level of the unemployable."[2]   There is evidence that the men who have once become casuals are not readily reconciled again to regular work.[3]   Reference may also be made to the results of a recent American inquiry: "If a period of enforced idleness were a season of recuperation and rest, there would be a good side to lack of employment.   But enforced idleness does not bring recuperation and rest.   The search for labour is much more fatiguing than labour itself.   An applicant, sitting in one of the charity offices waiting for the arrival of the agent, related his experiences while trying to get work. He would rise at 5 o'clock in the morning and walk 3 or 4 miles to some distant point, where he had heard work could be had.   He went early so as to be ahead of others, and he walked because he could not afford to pay car fare.   Disappointed in securing a job at the first place, he would tramp to another place miles away, only to meet with disappointment again. . . . As the man told his story, he drove home the, truth that lack of employment means far more than simply a loss in dollars and cents; it means a drain upon the vital forces that cannot be measured in terms of money."[4]   Moreover, the evil consequences of lean months are not balanced by good consequences in fat months.   Indeed, it may well be that, when, as often happens, the fat months imply long hours of overtime, they will not yield any good effects to set against the evil effects of the lean months, but will themselves add further evil effects.

[1] Alden, *The Unemployed, a National Question*, p. 6.
[2] *Report of the Transvaal Indigency Commission*, p. 120.
[3] Some evidence before the Unskilled Labour Committee of the C.O.S. relates how an attempt to convert casual dockers into permanent hands failed through the men refusing to turn up regularly (*Report*, p. 183).
[4] *United States Bulletin of the Bureau of Labour*, No. 79, pp. 906-7.

§ 8. It is at this point that the analysis of the preceding chapter becomes relevant. The inference that the short time method of meeting depressions is always more advantageous to the national dividend than the dismissal method, to which the preceding observations seem to lead, must not be accepted out of hand. There is an important consideration to be set on the other side. When, in the analysis just referred to, costs of movement were discussed, it was tacitly assumed that the gains from movement to be set against them were definitely determined by the economic situation, and needed no special investigation. In fact, however, this assumption is not wholly warranted. If in a factory (or industry) employing 100 men the demand so falls that, at the current rate of wages —which we assume to be maintained—$\frac{1}{100}$th part less work than before is required, this state of things may be met either by short time all round to the extent of $\frac{1}{100}$th part of normal time or by the dismissal of one man. It is plainly in the interest of the national dividend that one man should move elsewhere if the cost of movement, translated into terms of daily payment in the way described on p. 463, is less than the whole of the daily wage. If the method of dismissal rules, one man—the one who has been dismissed—will, in fact, given that he has the necessary knowledge, move elsewhere when this condition is fulfilled. But, if the method of short time (or rotation of work) rules, nobody will move unless the cost of moving, translated as above, is less than $\frac{1}{100}$th part of the daily wage. On this side, therefore, the method of short time—and it may be remarked in passing that the method of engaging employees at an annual salary operates even more strongly against movement—must be more injurious to the national dividend than the method of dismissal. When the costs of movement are so large (e.g. when it is a question of moving from one skilled industry to another), or when the depression of demand is only expected to last for so short a time, that movement would not take place on either plan, there is, indeed, nothing to set against the direct and immediate advantages of short time. But, when the conditions are such that movement would have taken place on the dismissal plan, but does not take place on the short time plan, the national

dividend so far suffers.   This objection to the short time plan
is often not decisive; for it has to be balanced against the
greater damage the dismissal method may do to workpeople's
efficiency.   But it deserves more attention than is usually paid
to it.   It is interesting to observe that an objection on exactly
the same lines lies against the cotton industry's war policy of
a special levy on employers to provide an unemployment fund
for workpeople out of work, and, in a lesser degree, against all
plans of unemployment insurance; for these plans lessen the
gain that a man will get if he moves to a new trade where
work might be obtained.   This objection also, it need hardly
be said, is not decisive.[1]   The difference made to movement
will generally be small, while, on the other hand, many men
will be saved from the grave injury which unemployment,
if no provision has been made against it, may inflict.   Still,
the fact that the objection exists ought not to be ignored.

[1] The Jute Control in March 1918 introduced a scheme for compensating
workers dismissed owing to a decision to stop certain machinery with a view to
reducing jute consumption by 10 per cent.   But the compensation was specifically confined to workpeople who were not able to find other employment, and
any workman who refused suitable employment without reasonable cause was to
receive no further benefit (cf. *Labour Gazette*, 1918, p. 135).   A similar condition
was made in a plan adopted in Germany at about the same time for compensating workpeople whose work was stopped through shortage of coal
(*Labour Gazette*, 1918, p. 141).

CHAPTER XI

§ 1. THE purpose of the remainder of this Part is to inquire whether, and if so in what circumstances, the magnitude of the national dividend can be increased by interference designed to raise the rate of wages in any industry or part of an industry above the "natural rate." The natural rate is here taken to mean the rate that would prevail apart from interference by some person or body of persons external to the workmen and employers directly concerned. Monopolistic action, whether by employers or by employed, is thus included in the "natural course of things"; and the only interference that we have to consider is interference by consumers and interference by public authorities, acting, not as consumers, but as governors.

§ 2. Interference by consumers consists in attempts by customers to compel employers to grant better conditions to their workpeople by agreeing to confine their custom to those whose treatment of their workpeople comes up to a standard that is considered fair. The scope of this method varies greatly in different industries. It can be applied more readily, for example, to the hours of labour of assistants in retail shops, whom the customers actually see, than to those imposed on factory or domestic workers, whom they do not see.[1] It is always much restricted by the imperfections of customers' knowledge, and by the fact that many articles pass through a number of stages of manufacture before they reach the man who ultimately sells them to the consumer. Associations of private persons have, nevertheless, sought to employ this method through the devices of the White List and the Trade Union

[1] Cf. Mény, *Le Travail à domicile*, p. 173.

Label.[1] It has been employed with greater effect by public bodies which have extensive contracts to offer. The Fair Wages Resolution of the British House of Commons in 1893 endeavoured to secure that Government Departments should use it by demanding that, on Government contracts, not less than " the rate of wages current (in the district) should be paid to employés." The London County Council furnish a schedule of wages, which all firms tendering on their contracts must agree to pay to the workpeople they employ on them. Some municipal authorities insist, further, that no contract shall be given to a firm that fails to pay " fair " rates, not merely on the town's contract, but regularly on all its work. Thus, " Belfast and Manchester have standing orders, under which contractors tendering for, or executing, work must be paying all their workpeople the rate of wages, and observing the hours of labour, agreed upon by the organisations of employers and workpeople, and must not prohibit their workpeople from joining trade unions; while at Bradford the contractor gives an assurance that, for three months immediately preceding his tender, he has paid all his workmen the rate agreed upon between the employers' association and the trade union." [2] Interference by public authorities—acting in their capacity, not as consumers, but as governors—has been made familiar by Australasian experience, and now plays a considerable part in this country also. To determine the way in which these different sorts of interference are likely to affect the national dividend is a complicated problem, which it is necessary to approach by stages. In this chapter I shall ask the preliminary question whether it can in practice be made operative, and whether, therefore, it can really affect the magnitude of the national dividend at all.

---

[1] The Australian Trade Marks Act of 1905, which directed that all goods sold should be marked with a label, showing whether or not their makers employed Union labour exclusively, was ruled by the High Court to be unconstitutional, on the ground that the Federal title to legislate about trade marks did not permit legislation in respect of marks not designed for the benefit of the manufacturer using them (*Economist*, Sept. 19, 1908, p. 532).

[2] *Report of the Fair Wages Committee*, p. 50. Unless the requisition that contractors shall pay standard wages is made to apply to all their work, and not merely to their work on particular contracts, unscrupulous contractors can evade it by employing the same men for part of their time on contract work at full wages and for another part of their time on other work at exceptionally low wages.

§ 3. The answer to this question depends in part on the further question whether it is possible for employers and workpeople to evade the recommendations or decrees of the intervening body without being detected. Detection is made difficult by the fact that the contract which an employer makes with his workpeople for their services is complex, including, besides the money wage, explicit or implicit conditions as to speed of work, arrangements for the workers' comfort during the work, and also, sometimes provision for certain payments in kind. By operating on one or other of these items it may be possible for an employer, if he wishes to do so, to neutralise apparent additions to the money wage.[1] It is not, however, only in this way that undetected evasion can come about. Since a poor man will often prefer to accept a low wage rather than lose his job, collusion may take place between employer and employed, and, as is well known to happen in the Chinese factories of Victoria, a lower wage may be paid actually than is paid nominally. When workpeople are unorganised—and they are specially likely to be unorganised if they are very poor or if they work apart from one another in their own homes [2]—even a strong Government, not to speak of a Consumers' Association, must have immense difficulty in enforcing its will. This fact may be illustrated from the experience of our own laws about sanitation, safety and hours of labour for women and children. It has always been found very difficult to bring the smaller and less obvious units of a trade under effective control—especially as to hours of labour—since, in " domestic workshops " and among solitary workers, household and workshop labour can so easily be intermingled.[3] In England at present any place where employers,

---

[1] In this connection it is interesting to observe that the State Wages Boards of California, Oregon, Washington and Wisconsin are given power to regulate, not merely wage-rates but also hours of work and " conditions of labour " for the women whom they cover (*The World's Labour Laws*, Feb. 1914, p. 78).

[2] Mr. Lloyd writes: "The chief reason why the grinders both in Sheffield and Solingen have been better organised than the cutlers is that they are more congregated at their work " (*Economic Journal*, 1908, p. 379).

[3] It is sometimes suggested that they could be enforced more easily if the giver-out-of-work, or even the landlord, as well as the employer, in a domestic workshop, were made legally responsible for breaches of the law. (Cf. Webb, Evidence before the Royal Commission on Labour [C. 7063-1], Q. 3740.) In Massachusetts responsibility is sometimes thrown on the giver-out-of-work.

working in their own houses, employ persons from outside, is a "workshop," and is subject to the ordinary provisions of the factory law. Any place where employers, working in their own houses, employ only members of their own family, is a "domestic workshop," and its sanitary arrangements, and also, though in a less degree than ordinary workshops, the hours of young persons and children working in it are regulated. But, when a home-worker works alone in her house for an outside firm, these things are not regulated. Even in workshops and domestic workshops, it is doubtful whether, with the existing staff of inspectors, the rules are satisfactorily enforced.[1] Throughout, the inspectors' task is exceedingly heavy; so much so that, in England, the demand for a larger staff is continually being made. If, however, the kind of regulation we have just been discussing is thus difficult, wage-regulation is more difficult still. As has been well observed, wage rates are not, like sanitary arrangements, hours and so forth, things easily detected by the watch or nose of an inspector.[2] Hence, the violation of rules about them can scarcely be discovered except through overt action by the workers; and, when they are not organised, individual workers will often fail to act for fear a worse thing should befall them. The administration of the English Trades Boards Act has been much hampered by this difficulty, especially in its relation to home-workers.[3] Where, however, an effective workers' association exists, this difficulty can be overcome. For the workers, having unemployed benefit to fall back upon, will not be terrorised into accepting less than the union rate by fear of losing their job, but will complain to the union officials; and, even when individual workmen do not do this, their officials will play the part of a body of lynx-eyed unpaid inspectors. It is, therefore, encouraging to learn that State action designed to raise wages in depressed industries (*e.g.* the

---

[1] Cf. the difficulties experienced in New Zealand and Victoria in enforcing the law limiting the hours of shop assistants. In New South Wales these difficulties are partly avoided by means of a general law regulating the hours for all shops, whether employing assistants or not. (Cf. Aves, *Report on Hours of Employment in Shops*, p. 12).

[2] Mrs. Macdonald, *Economic Journal*, 1908, p. 142.

[3] Cf. Vessilitsky, *The Home Worker*, chap. vii.

chain-making industry) has several times led to an improvement in the workpeople's organisation. "One especially hopeful feature in the situation (connected with the establishment of Trade Boards) is' that women in the industries affected are taking heart to join their trade unions, some of which have received large accessions of members. A frequent objection to wages regulation has been that it would be useless for unorganised trades, which are the very ones that need it most. The actual fact seems to be that the prospect of wages regulation is encouraging organisation by giving these poor workers the sense of some public support at their back."[1] At the same time, of course, by giving them more money, it makes it easier for them to pay trade union subscriptions. These considerations seem to show that interference, though it may *sometimes* be baffled by undetected evasion, cannot be thus baffled generally.

§ 4. This general statement, however, does not do full justice to the difficulty involved in setting up a really watertight system of regulation. When it is practicable for the regulating authority itself to construct and impose a complete scale of piece-rates, there is, indeed, no additional difficulty... But this procedure can only be resorted to over a limited field, because in many industries differences of machinery, factory arrangements, quality of work required (*e.g.* in making button-holes) and so on, make a different piece-rate "appropriate" to different firms ; and it is seldom practicable for a Trade Board or other official authority to have the knowledge needed to deal with these differences. Consequently, as the Boards appointed under the British Trades Board Act have often found, the best they can do is to lay down a so-called minimum day-wage as a standard, at the same time authorising employers to draw up a piece-list, subject to the condition that the piece-rate shall allow an "ordinary" worker in their industry to earn the equivalent of this day-wage. On this plan, unless some further provision is made, there is a subtle opportunity for evasion on account of the

---

[1] Hutchings and Harrison, *History of Factory Legislation*, p. 269. For evidence as to the favourable reaction of Trade Boards upon organisation in the tailoring trade, cf. Tawney, *Minimum Rates in the Tailoring Industry*, pp. 90-94.

ambiguity attaching to the term "ordinary." To shut this loop-hole some definition of the term must be furnished. In the wage-determination given by the Trade Board controlling |the paper-box-making trade, this is done by providing that any piece-work operation must yield not less than the minimum day-wage to 85 per cent of any group of piece-workers. Thus, the 85th worker (out of a hundred) from the top of the scale of capacity was taken to represent the worst " ordinary " worker. But even a numerical definition of this kind will not make evasion impossible. It is still in the power of employers in effect to force down the general standard of pay by dismissing their worst workmen, engaging better men instead of them, and then fixing a piece-rate below what would have been necessary to enable 85 per cent of their original workpeople to earn the standard day-wages. To escape this danger the Trade Board in the tailoring trade fixes a minimum time-wage for " ordinary " workers, and lays it down that, if 85 per cent of a firm's employees are earning this minimum, there is *prima facie* evidence that the piece-rates established there are adequate. But it permits this *prima facie* evidence to be rebutted by information that the number of slow workers employed by a firm at a particular rate has been substantially reduced. The 85th man in a hundred is only to be regarded as the lowest " ordinary " worker when the firm has not specially selected its workpeople.[1] The rule established by the Trade Board in the box-making industry is similar.[2] Such a rule obviously leads to delicate questions of detail, which must be referred in the last resort to some form of joint Board. Thus, under the Minimum Wage (Coal Mines) Act, the question whether any workman, whom an employer wishes to treat as below the ordinary, can rightly be so regarded, is adjudicated upon by a joint Committee of employers and employed. Under an arrangement of this kind, evasion, if not stopped altogether, can at all events be effectively checked.

§ 5. Granted, however, that evasion cannot take place without an overt breach of law that is capable of being detected, this does not by itself make interference with the

---

[1] Cf. Tawney, *Minimum Rates in the Tailoring Industry*, pp. 50-1.
[2] Cf. Bulkley, *Minimum Rates in the Box-making Industry*, pp. 21-2.

natural course of wages really operative. For it might happen
that no sanction was available to restrain evasion even when
it was detected. But in fact sanctions are available. Even a
Consumers' Association commands the weapon of the boycott,
and, when it is backed by a trade union, can also call upon
that body to exercise in its behalf the weapon of the strike.
And a public authority controls a large armoury of sanctions.
Of these the least stringent is a simple appeal to informed
public opinion, like that relied upon in the Canadian Industrial
Disputes Investigation Act. On this model, a law recently
passed in the State of Massachusetts sets up a Commission
with authority to investigate—through a Wages Board—any
trade in which there is good reason to believe that the wages
paid to women workers are " inadequate to supply the necessary
cost of living and to maintain the worker in health." After a
public hearing, the Commission recommends rates of wages, and
" issues a decree of its award together with a list of the
employers who fail or refuse to accept it. This list is thereupon published in at least four newspapers, but no further
penalty is imposed." [1] It would be an error to belittle the
power of this form of sanction. There can be little doubt that
the rates of pay of our low-grade workers " would be lower
than they actually are but for the effective force of conventional or customary standards." [2] It is probable, too, that the
frequency with which the wage of women workers used before
the war to approximate to 10s. a week was, in some measure,
due to the sanction of public opinion. A somewhat more
stringent sanction is made use of, for a special and limited
purpose, in the English Trade Boards Act of 1909. This Act
provides that, in the preliminary period before the determinations of Boards are made obligatory, Government contracts
shall only be given to firms which pay the wage-rates they
have recommended. A more stringent sanction still was
proposed by the Australian Excise Tariff Act of 1906, which
was afterwards declared by the Supreme Court to be uncon-

[1] *The World's Labour Laws,* Feb. 1913, p. 49. A summary of this law and
of the similar laws of other American States is given in Marconcini's *Industria
domestica salariata,* p. 546 *et seq.*
[2] *Report of the Royal Commission on the Poor Laws,* Appendix, vol. xvii.
p. 377.

stitutional.[1] A differential excise duty was to be imposed upon native manufacturers who pay less than "fair and reasonable rates" to their workpeople. If these lesser sanctions fail, resort may be had to fines, a sanction which is embodied, not only in the well-known laws of Victoria and other Australian colonies and in the British Trades Boards Act, but also in more recent laws—applicable only to women and minors—which have been passed by the States of Oregon and Washington.[2] In some of these laws there is added also the sanction of imprisonment. Nor has the last word even yet been said. There is a sanction more powerful than fines and imprisonment. For there is always a margin between rates of wages which employers resent and would elect to resist by a temporary stoppage of work, and rates which would drive them to abandon their industry altogether. Of this margin the State or other public authority can make use in two distinct ways. First, in certain specially situated industries, it can threaten to expel employers from their occupation unless they consent to pay the wage-rate which it decrees. When, for instance, as in ordinary or street railways, a business depends upon franchises granted by authority, the terms of the concession may provide that any refusal to accept the authority's decision about wage-rates shall cause it to lapse.[3] Secondly, in industries in general, if obdurate employers try to pay less than the decreed wage, the State can subsidise workpeople who strike against them, or can even close their works by force. By these devices it can deprive them of any third way between surrender and a permanent change of occupation. Nor is resort to such measures rendered impracticable by the chaotic character of the procedure which they would involve. They cannot be laughed out of court as meaning a ceaseless conflict between the Executive and rebellious associations of employers. For their success is so certain that, if once the Government was understood to be determined upon them, resistance would never take place. At the worst, a single exhibition of force would be sufficient:

---

[1] Mr. St. Leger, in his book, *Australian Socialism*, pp. 394 *et seq.*, prints the judgment of the Supreme Court.

[2] Cf. *Labour Gazette*, Jan. 1913, p. 204.

[3] Cf. Mitchell, *Organised Labour*, p. 345.

> That great two-handed engine at the door
> Stands ready to strike once and strike no more.

This form of sanction is the most powerful of all that are available.[1]   Of course, neither it nor any of the other sanctions is absolute and compelling in all circumstances.   Critics can easily show that, when employers are extraordinarily obstinate, interference to raise wages cannot be successfully carried out. But this fact is not relevant to the practical issue.   When it is asked how people can be compelled to continue in a particular industry at a loss, the answer is that they cannot be so compelled.   But, as was indicated in the chapter dealing with compulsory arbitration, to prove that a law will *sometimes* fail in its purpose is a very different thing from proving that it is futile.   It is not *impossible* for murderers and incendiaries both to break the law and to escape the penalty.   Judges may order a mother to deliver up her child to the custody of such and such a person; but, if she chooses to disappear, or, in the last resort, to destroy either the child or herself, they cannot compel her to obey.   Nobody, however, cites these obvious facts as evidence that the general body of our laws is without powerful sanctions.   In like manner, nobody ought to cite the fact that the sanctions to authoritative decisions about wages are imperfect as evidence that they are non-existent.[2]   They are real and potent.   With their help interference to raise wages *can* be made operative in practice.

[1] Cf. my *Principles and Methods of Industrial Peace*, pp. 191-2.
[2] *Ibid.* p. 185.

CHAPTER XII

METHODS OF ENGAGING LABOUR

§ 1. BEFORE the effect of interference to raise wages is examined, it is necessary to make a preliminary inquiry into the methods of engaging workpeople; for the effect produced by interference depends in part upon what these methods are. The reason for this dependence is that, when wages in any occupation or place are raised, an influence is set at work which, according to circumstances, may draw new workpeople from outside into the occupation or place, or, *per contra*, may push out workpeople who are already there. This influence acts through the change which the wage movement brings about in the attractiveness of the industry, on the one hand, to people ·outside it,_ and, on the other, to those already belonging to it. But the change in attractiveness to these two sets of people ˙is not determined solely by the amount of the change in wage and the nature of the demand for labour in the industry, but also by certain other conditions associated with the methods of engagement in vogue. This can be proved as follows. The mathematical expectation of earnings in any place or occupation is measured by the aggregate annual earnings of all the workpeople of given quality attached to it at any time divided by the number of those workpeople. If the methods of engagement are such that everybody of given quality, whether already engaged in the industry or at present outside it, has an equal chance of obtaining a share of employment in it, the attractiveness of the industry to outsiders and insiders alike corresponds to this mathematical expectation, and, from the standpoint of both these classes, changes in the mathematical expectation correspond roughly to changes in

attractiveness. This correspondence. is not, indeed, complete,
because to many men a given " expectation of earnings " made
up of a higher nominal wage coupled with a worse prospect of
employment is more attractive than an equal expectation made
up of a lower nominal wage coupled with a better prospect of
employment. Thus, the Poor Law Commissioners report : " In
Liverpool it is freely said that the nominally high wages
attract men from the country and from Ireland, under the
impression that they can get regular work at these rates." [1]
Mr. Dearle speaks to like effect of the London building trades.[2]
And Mr. Beveridge puts the point strongly thus : " Men can
be got to follow up work which gives them five shillings a day
about four times in a fortnight, when they would repudiate
with scorn a regular situation at fifteen or eighteen shillings
a week." [3] But this consideration need not be pressed here.
It is enough that, in the conditions contemplated, there is a
rough general correspondence between changes in the mathematical expectation of earnings and changes in the attractiveness of the industry both to outsiders and to insiders. If,
however, the methods of engagement are of such a sort that
anybody of given quality, who has already been employed in
the industry, will be taken on rather than a new man from outside, the attractiveness to outsiders of the industry, when the
rate of wages there is forced up—and the quantity of
employment available thereby reduced—is necessarily zero,
whatever the effect of the change may be upon the mathematical expectation of earnings. Yet again, if the methods of .
engagement are such that, among the workpeople of given
quality, who have already been employed, men are always
selected for employment · in accordance with a formal or informal ·preference list, an enforced rise in the wage rate must
press the attractiveness of the place or occupation to those
insiders who are near the bottom of the list down to zero.
Of course, divergencies in the methods of engagement are
more or less blotted out from the point of view of people considering a long time beforehand for what industries their

[1] *Report of the Royal Commission on the Poor Laws*, p. 353.
[2] *Unemployment in the London Building Trade*, p. 127.
[3] *Unemployment*, p. 197.

children shall be trained.   This, however, does not lessen their relevance to the effect produced by interference designed to raise wages.   In the face of an enforced rise there are three possibilities: (1) the attractiveness of the occupation or place affected may correspond after the change, both for outsiders and for insiders, to the mathematical expectation of earnings there; (2) for all insiders it may correspond to this mathematical expectation, but for all outsiders to zero; and (3) for displaced insiders as well as for all outsiders it may be zero. The first of these possibilities will be realised if the method of engagement of labour is entirely haphazard and engagements are for short periods; the second if the method is such that all insiders are preferred to any outsiders, but among themselves are on an equal footing; the third if all workpeople interested in the occupation are implicitly or explicitly arranged, for purposes of engagement, upon some sort of preference scale.   Of the three methods thus distinguished the obvious label for the first is the *casual* method and for the third the *preference* method. For the second no satisfactory label is available, and it is necessary to invent a name: I shall call it the *privileged class* method.

§ 2. The distinction between these three methods can be made clear by examples.   The casual method reigns when all comers of given quality (not necessarily all comers of different quality) are accepted indifferently.   The general nature of the method is obvious.   It is sometimes supposed that, when workpeople for a number of firms are engaged through a central institution, it is necessarily ruled out by that fact. But this is a confusion.   It is open to Employment Exchanges, just as much as to single firms, to engage men by the casual method; and in fact the rules often in effect provide that they *must* do so.   Thus, in many Employment Bureaux organised by trade unions in France, the officials " allot situations to their members strictly in order of *priority of application*." [1]   " The Antwerp Bureau adopts the rule of sending workmen to situations in the order in which they apply at the office—a method which has been the subject of much criticism." [2]   And in the Labour Bureau of the Berlin brewers, " a workman must wait his turn before he is placed, *i.e.* on

---

[1] *U.S.A. Bulletin of Labour*, No. 72, p. 761.   [2] *Ibid.* p. 766.

registration he gets a number and must then wait till all the numbers on the list prior to his own have been satisfied."[1] Under all these arrangements the method of engagement that rules is the casual method. The privileged class method is formally established under the Liverpool docks scheme of 1912. All workmen who were dockers at a given date were furnished with a tally, possession of which gave them preference over workmen not holding tallies, while leaving certain classes of them still equal among themselves.[2] The preference method, whether formally or informally applied, is of wide scope. It implies that different workpeople of given quality are not hired indifferently but in some sort of more or less definite order, so that whatever work there is tends to be concentrated upon certain individuals while the others get nothing. When an actual preference list is used it does not matter, from the present point of view, upon what basis this list is drawn up. One made by placing the names of applicants in order of their length of service in the industry—a specially good arrangement in a decaying trade—or even in alphabetical order, would answer the purpose. In practice, when preference lists among similar men exist, they are always a mere bye-product of lists designed to set in order of capacity a number of workpeople presumed to be dissimilar. Thus, the Central (Unemployed) Body for London suggested, among its model rules, that "the superintendent will recommend applicants for employment according to suitability, but employers may select from the registered applicants any one whom they consider suitable."[3] Broadly speaking, this policy is pursued by the Berlin Central Labour Registry.[4] It involves incidentally the placing in order of precedence of a number of men of *equal* capacity, and this implies preference of the kind relevant to this discussion.

§ 3. It need hardly be said that the methods of engagement ruling in different places and occupations are not

[1] Schloss, *Report on Agencies and Methods for dealing with the Unemployed*, p. 84.
[2] Cf. Williams, *The First Year's Working of the Liverpool Docks Scheme*, chapter i.
[3] *U.S.A. Bulletin of Labour*, No. 72, p. 803.
[4] Cf. Schloss, *Report on Agencies and Methods for dealing with the Unemployed*, p. 87.

sharply separated into the three types that have just been described. Rather, actual existing arrangements are, in general compromises tending towards, but not identical with, one or another of them. The influences which determine the choice made between them are very similar to those which were discussed in Chapter X. in connection with the choice between different ways of meeting periods of depression. Many of the considerations which make employers unwilling to resort to a reduction of staff in these periods—fear of losing men who for any reason have a special value to them and so on—also make them hostile to the casual method. Therefore this method is likely to be adopted only when the men are so unskilled, and the detailed conditions of particular plants or works so similar, that a man's value to an employer is not appreciably increased by his having been employed by him before. The preference method is favoured when, the conditions are such that continuity of work by the same man is important, while to retain in bad times a larger number of men than is necessary by resort to short time would be costly or otherwise injurious. When the technical difficulties in the way of short time are less serious, the way is open for the privileged class method. It will be readily perceived that in a "stationary state" the last two methods would lead to identical results.

§ 4. It is interesting to observe that there is a connection between the casual method and the custom of short engagements. Long engagements are not, indeed, incompatible with some degree of casualness, because, even with annual engagements, provided the hirings of different people terminate irregularly, there will always be a certain number of jobs on offer; whereas, if the hirings of different individuals all terminate at the same time, at those times all the jobs that there are will be on offer. With very short engagements, however, practically all the jobs there are will be continuously on offer. Since it is only in respect of jobs on offer that casualness is possible, it follows that the casual method cannot be developed so completely when long engagements prevail as when short engagements do; or, more generally, that every increase in the length of the normal period of engagement, in an industry in which the casual method prevails, will to some extent undermine that method. In great measure, long engagements are a bye-product of the same causes that make employers prefer the preference or privileged class method to the casual method, and have not themselves any causal influence. Sometimes, however, long engagements are fostered by causes other than these, and then the long engagements, or, more strictly, the causes which bring them about, operating through them, are properly regarded as additional factors making against the casual method. Among skilled manual workers, in industries where continuous service to the public is extremely important, long engagements have sometimes been introduced as a device for obviating strikes. An example is afforded by the agreement of the South Metropolitan Gas Company with its "co-partners." "The agreement is a definite engagement on our part to give a man work for a period varying from three months to twelve months, and the great bulk of our men work under such agreements. The origin of it was, as perhaps you may have heard, in order to prevent a large number of men giving notice to us at the same time. At the time of our strike in 1889 all the stokers gave notice at one time. In order to obviate that, we instituted a series of agreements, to fall in so many every week. It is not compulsory. The men can sign them or not as they please, but those who do sign partake in the prosperity of the Company. At present, the men who have signed are getting 10 per cent on their wages as a result of being under agreement, so you may realise that there is no difficulty in getting the bulk to sign."[1] Among unskilled workpeople, not only is this positive motive for long engagements generally weak, because, in the event of a strike, their work can be more easily replaced, but there is sometimes a negative motive working definitely in the opposite sense. For, whereas, among skilled men, their own greater intelligence and the existence of strong union organisation make disciplinary machinery unnecessary, among the rougher class of the unskilled, foremen may find it impossible to enforce a

[1] *Report of the Charity Organisation Society's Committee on Unskilled Labour,* 1908, p. 170.

fair day's work unless the weapon of instant dismissal is ready to hand.[1] Moreover, it must be remembered that, among all classes of workers, short engagements *may*, as was indicated in § 1, be preferred by the men themselves, just because they make casualness possible. The majority of the Poor Law Commissioners write: " The ' docker's romance,' as it is called, is that he, alone of all tradesmen, can take days off when he likes, without suffering for it. . . . At Southampton docks several cases have come under notice, where permanent hands have asked to be given casual employment." [2] Mr. Walsh, in like manner, writes that a large percentage of men have taken to the docks, " because the work there is intermittent and, therefore, more congenial to them than other occupations, where regularity in attendance is required." [3]

.§ 5. It is possible for the Government, by direct action designed to encourage the re-engagement of the man whose engagement has just terminated rather than of a new man, to combat the casual method in the same way that the establishment of a system of long engagements would do. Thus, the Poor Law Commissioners write: " One method of discouraging casual labour would be the imposition of what we might call an ' employment . termination due.' That is to say that, to the termination of an engagement, either by the master or by the man, should be attached a small payment, both by the master and the man, in the nature of a fine or stamp duty to the State. The tax, or ' employ- ment termination due,' could be very easily levied by means of stamps placed upon a ' termination of employment ' form, which it might be made incumbent upon every workman to produce to the labour exchange upon registration. It is urged that the advantages of this system, if it could be adopted, would be threefold. In the first place, it would discourage the, so to speak, wanton termination of employ- ment either by the employer or the employee. In the second place, it would discourage also the employment of casual labour, inasmuch as, the more casual the labour

---

[1] Cf. Messrs. Pringle and Jackson's *Report to the Poor Law Commission*, Appendix, vol. xix. p. 15.

[2] *Report of the Royal Commission on the Poor Laws*, pp. 335 and 354.

[3] *Report on Dock Labour*, p. 19.

employed in a concern, the greater would be the amount of 'employment termination due,' which would have to be paid. And, thirdly, to the extent to which it did not deter either of these practices, it would afford a source of revenue, which might be devoted to defraying the cost of one or other of the proposals which we shall make."[1] Devices of this sort, if introduced, would undoubtedly strengthen the desire of employers to keep posts occupied as far as possible by the same men, and so would enhance the stimulus, which this desire affords, towards the adoption of methods of engagement other than the casual method. The provision of the National Insurance Act, to the effect that, "when an employer has employed a man continuously throughout a period of twelve months, he may recover one-third of the contributions paid for that man"[2] is a device of the kind contemplated. We must not forget, however, that all such devices not only encourage employers to fill posts, which they have decided in any event to fill somehow, with the same man continuously, but also encourage them, in some slight measure, to keep men on in posts which otherwise they would have been inclined temporarily to close down. *Pro tanto*, the effect of this is to check the free movement of labour from centres of falling demand to centres of rising demand, thus impeding its most profitable employment. The direct injury which these devices would in this way inflict on the national dividend needs to be set against whatever indirect benefit they may confer upon it.

[1] *Report of the Royal Commission on the Poor Laws*, pp. 410-11.
[2] Explanatory Memorandum [Cd. 8911], p. 5.

§ 1. THE way is now prepared for a direct inquiry into the probable effect upon the national dividend of interference to raise the rate of wages at any point above the "natural level." As a preliminary to this attempt it is convenient to set out Dr. Marshall's definition of a fair rate of wages. Real wages in any occupation are fair, according to this definition, when, allowance being made for differences in the steadiness of the demand for labour over a year in different industries, "they are about on a level with the payment made for tasks in other trades which are of equal difficulty and disagreeableness, which require equally rare natural abilities and an equally expensive training."[1] It is easily seen that, provided the wages paid to workpeople in all occupations are equal to the values of the marginal net products of their work, fair wages in this sense are a necessary correlate of what I have called in Chapter IX. the ideal distribution of labour. This circumstance enables us to state our problem in such a way that some of the results obtained in Chapter IX. can be utilised in the discussion of it. I shall ask first whether, and, if so, in what circumstances, the national dividend will be benefited by interference—in the form, for example, of the legal enforcement throughout a district or occupation of real piece-rates equal to those paid by reputable firms there— designed to raise wages that are unfairly low; and secondly, whether, and, if so, in what circumstances, it will be benefited

_____
[1] Introduction to L. C. Price's *Industrial Peace*, p. xiii.

by interference designed to raise wages that are already fair. In the present and following chapters I shall endeavour to answer these questions upon the assumption that the reactions produced by the earnings of workpeople upon their efficiency can be ignored, and I shall reserve for Chapter XVI. the inquiry how far our results must be modified when that assumption is removed. Let us turn then to the theme of the present chapter, namely, the effect, apart from the reactions on workpeople's efficiency, of interference with *unfair* rates of wages.

§ 2. In real life, when the wage rate ruling at any point is unfairly low, the unfairness may be the resultant of two or more separate elements of unfairness, produced by different causes, which operate, perhaps in the same, perhaps in contrary directions. In the practical treatment of a case of this kind, the consequences of interference against each of the different elements of unfairness would need to be examined separately, since it might happen that interference was desirable against one element and undesirable against another. But, though this consideration creates a difficulty for practice, it makes no difference to the form of our analysis. For purposes of exposition, therefore, we are justified in ignoring it and in confining attention to those forms of unfair wages in which the unfairness consists of a single element. This is the method that I propose to adopt in the following discussion.

§ 3. It is of the utmost importance to distinguish between two principal sorts of unfair wage. On the one hand, wages may be unfair in some place or occupation, because, though they are equal to the value of the marginal net product of the labour assembled there, this is not equal to the value of the marginal net product, and, therefore, to the wage rate, of the labour assembled elsewhere. On the other hand, wages may be unfair in some place or occupation, because workpeople are exploited, in the sense that they are paid less than the value which their marginal net product has to the firms which employ them. The effects of interference with these two kinds of unfairness are by no means the same, and the discussion of them must be kept sharply separate. In the next three sections I shall be considering exclusively

interference with wages which, though unfair, are equal to
the value of the marginal net product of the workers directly
affected, and thus involve no exploitation.

§ 4. One preliminary observation of a general character
should be made.   Given that the number of workpeople
assembled in a particular place or occupation is such that, in
the existing conditions of demand there, the value of the
marginal net product of labour, and, therefore, the wage rate,
is unfairly low, the effect which interference would have on
the national dividend is entirely independent of *the reason
why* the conditions of demand there are what they are.   On
reflection this point is obvious.   But in popular argument
it is frequently ignored.   Thus, manufacturers in out-of-the-
way districts often urge that the inferiority of their machinery
or the magnitude of their freight-charges (factors which
depress the level of their demand for labour) "justify" the
payment of a wage lower than that paid by their competitors.
In an agreement made in the coal industry of Illinois, Indiana,
Ohio and Pennsylvania, the validity of this plea was formally
recognised, and "the scale nicely adjusted so that the districts
with the better quality of coal and the lower railway charges
are required to pay enough higher wages than other districts
to counterbalance their superior natural advantages."[1]   In
like manner, employers in towns often urge that it is "justifi-
able" for them to pay lower real wages than are paid for
similar labour in the country, because the payment of fair
real wages would involve a greater cost to them than it
involves to their country competitors; or, in other words,
because the level of the real demand for labour is forced
down by the high price of workpeople's food.   Much argument has been expended upon the question whether pleas of
this type are sound or unsound.   The truth of the matter
is that they are neither the one nor the other, because they
are irrelevant.   The effect which interference with unfairly
low real wage rates at any point produces on the national
dividend will be good or bad according to the way in which
it reacts on the distribution of labour power between different places and occupations (including the occupation of

[1] Clause 8 of agreement, *U.S. Bulletin of Labour*, January 1897, p. 173.

idleness). The character of this reaction is not made different by any difference in the causes through which the existing conditions of the demand for labour at the point affected have come about. It depends exclusively on the causes which have prevented the number of workpeople attached to that point from so adjusting itself to the existing conditions of demand there as to make the real value of the marginal net product of labour equal to what it is elsewhere. We have, therefore, to distinguish the principal causes to which failure of adjustment may be due, and to examine in turn the effect of interference with each of the different types of unfair wages for which these several causes are responsible.

§ 5. First, the wage rate in some place or occupation may be unfairly low because the costs of movement prevent workpeople there from moving to other places or occupations where the wage rate is higher. Among unfairly low wages of this kind are included the abnormally low wages that may rule (1) in some country distant from others, and differing, from them in race, language and religion; (2) in some occupation; movement from which to other occupations would involve much loss of skill; (3) in some occupation mainly filled by low-grade unskilled workpeople, the failures of higher classes, who have spent their energies in attempting a skilled trade or in confidential service to a particular firm, and are, consequently, incapable of becoming either high-grade unskilled labourers or skilled workers of another kind; (4) in some district, movement away from which would involve for the workmen who move the loss of special opportunities for earnings which that district offers to their women folk, or, for women workers, to their men folk; and (5) in some form of work, to wit, home work, to which more people are tied by the non-economic compulsion of family cares—a very large proportion of home workers are married women or widows[1]—than, in the existing highly developed state of factory manufacture, economic considerations alone would warrant. It can be shown in a summary manner that interference designed to raise any of these forms of unfairly low wages will, apart from reactions on efficiency, be injurious to

---

[1] Cf. Vessilitsky, *The Home Worker*, p. 13.

the national dividend. The only part of the effect that even *appears* to be advantageous is the movement of certain workpeople from points of lower productivity to points of higher productivity; for the diminution of work available to those workpeople who do not move from the point where the wage rate is raised obviously involves nothing but loss. But the argument of Chapter IX. has already shown that that movement of workpeople, though it appears to be advantageous, is not really so. For no doctoring of the wage rate can alter the costs of movement; it can only cause the obstacles set up by them to be leapt over or forced. So long, however, as the costs of movement are what they are, that distribution of labour which differs from the absolute ideal only on account of the costs of movement was shown in Chapter IX. to be the ideal distribution *relatively to the fact of those costs.*[1] Any change of distribution, therefore, so long as those costs remain, must actually make the dividend smaller than it would otherwise have been. Plainly, therefore, no loop-hole is left for any gain.[2]

§ 6. Secondly; the wage rate in some place or occupation may be unfairly low because ignorance retains there workpeople who, if costs of movement alone were in question, would find it advantageous to move. To determine the effect of interference in these conditions is more difficult than it was in the conditions discussed in the preceding section. For, as was shown in Chapter IX., while the forcing of obstacles set up by costs of movement involves a loss to the dividend, the forcing of those set up by ignorance involves a gain. Hence, so far as the effect of pushing up wages in a low-wage trade or district is to transfer workpeople from employment in that trade or district to employment elsewhere,

---

[1] It should be noted, however, that, as old employees die off, these costs will disappear ; for to young men contemplating a choice between the occupation we are considering and others there will be no costs. Hence, if wages there are still unfairly low after a number of years, this will presumably not be because of costs, and the above argument against interference does not apply.

[2] Thus, in so far as home workers earn a wage equal to their marginal worth — which is often low because they are in direct competition with machinery of great efficiency — and are prevented from moving into factory work by family necessities, the national dividend, apart from possible reactions on efficiency, would be injured by any forcing up of their wage rate.

the national dividend will be increased. The apparent advantage involved in movement, where movement occurs, is also a real advantage. Before, however, any conclusion can be drawn as to the *net effects* of interference, we need to inquire how far, and in what circumstances, the pushing up of wages will transfer superfluous workpeople elsewhere.

When the method of engagement that prevails is the preference method, it is plain that, whether the demand for labour is elastic or inelastic, no superfluous new employees will be tempted to attach themselves to the place or occupation where the wage rate has been raised, and that all persons dislodged from employment there will know themselves to be definitely and finally dislodged. For, under this method, certain men are formally preferred to others, and it is known that whatever work is available will be wholly concentrated upon them. In these circumstances, since, if these others do not move, they must expect to earn nothing at all, they will be under a very strong inducement to move. Hence, the whole effect of the enhancement of wages will consist in the transference of some workpeople from points of less productive employment to points of more productive employment. No unemployment or partial employment will be created anywhere as a set-off against this gain. Consequently, interference designed to force up wages to the fair level *must* benefit the national dividend.

When the method of engagement of labour is either the privileged class or the casual method, the effect on the national dividend is different, according as the demand for labour, in the place or occupation where the wage rate is raised, has an elasticity less than, or greater than, unity. If the elasticity is less than unity, the attractiveness of that place or occupation to workpeople already assembled there will be increased, because the mathematical expectation of earnings will be increased. Consequently, under either of these two methods of engagement, there is no reason to anticipate any movement of workpeople away from there to more productive places or occupations; and under the casual method there will probably be some movement in the opposite direction. It is certain, however, that the amount of work available in that place or occupation will be diminished. Hence, the national dividend will necessarily suffer. If the elasticity of the demand for labour is greater than unity, the attractiveness of the place or occupation to the workpeople assembled there, as well as to the outsiders, will, under both these methods of engagement, be diminished when wages are raised. Therefore, it is *prima facie* probable that some workpeople will move away; though it should be remembered that, in so far as workpeople are better acquainted with, and so attach more importance to, the nominal wage than to the prospect of continuous employment, the tendency to move may meet with considerable obstruction. To the extent that movement does occur, the national dividend will be made larger. But, on the other hand, some workpeople, who formerly were fully employed, are likely, at all events for some time, to remain in the place or occupation in partial employment. The injury which the national dividend suffers from this cause may either exceed or fall short of the benefit which it receives from the movement of the other workpeople. It is impossible to say generally whether the net result will be advantageous or disadvantageous. It will be different in different circumstances. There is, however, one case in which a definite solution is obtainable. Where the elasticity of demand is so great that the raising of the wage rate to the "fair" level reduces the demand for labour to zero, the attractiveness of the place or occupation to all workpeople is also reduced to zero, and those assembled at it *must*, therefore, move away. This condition is satisfied when individual employers are so incompetent, or individual factories or mines are so badly situated, that the enforcement of fair wages causes them to collapse altogether before the competition of others. When it is fulfilled, the national dividend is bound to be increased by interference designed to enforce fair wages.

§ 7. We now turn to the second main class of unfair wage rates that was distinguished in § 3, namely, wage rates that are unfair, not because the value of the marginal net product of labour at the places where they occur is different from what it is elsewhere, but because exploitation

on the part of employers forces workpeople to accept in
payment for their services less than the value which the
marginal net product of their services has to these employers.
There is, indeed, something artificial in this statement of
the problem, because, if any employer, or body of employers,
exploits the workpeople in his service, he will, in general,
not be able to hire as much labour as would have been
available for him otherwise, and, consequently, the value
of the marginal net product of such labour as he does
hire will be indirectly raised. Hence, in general, if an
employer exploits his men by paying them 5s. a week
less than the value of their marginal net product to him,
this will not mean that they are getting 5s. a week less
than the fair wage obtainable for similar work elsewhere,
but perhaps only 4s. or 3s. less than this.[1] This being
understood, we may proceed to investigate the way in which
unfairly low wages due to exploitation may be brought
about.

It was explained in Chapter VI. that, if perfectly free
competition prevailed everywhere, the wage rate paid by any

[1] This point, and the general relation of the discussion that follows to the
analysis of Chapter VI., can be most easily understood by the help of a diagram.
Let DD' be the employers' demand curve for labour and SS' the workers' supply

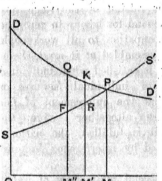

curve in the district under review. Let
PM be the wage that would result from
free competition and is equal to the general
rate of wages for workpeople of the grade
concerned; QM" the wage most profitable
to the workpeople if they were combined;
and RM' the wage most profitable to the
employers. Then the range of indeterminateness described in Chapter VI. is
constituted by all rates between QM" and
RM'. There is necessarily exploitation
if the employers succeed in paying any
wage less than PM. Let us suppose
that they succeed in paying a wage
RM'. It follows that, if they obtain
an amount of labour represented by
OM', then the measure of *unfairness* in
the wage is the excess of PM over RM',
but the measure of *exploitation* is the excess of KM' over RM'. If the workpeople succeeded in establishing a wage larger than PM, the exchange index
would necessarily fall on the demand curve to the left of P, say at the point Q,
and we might speak of an exploitation of employers by workpeople measured
by the excess of QM" over FM".

employer in any occupation would be determinate at a definite point. The value of the marginal net product of labour of given quality would be the same to all employers, and, if one employer offered a man less than others, that man would know that he could at once get as much as this value of his marginal net product from others. In so far, however, as movements of workpeople are hampered by ignorance and costs, a monopolistic element is introduced into the wage bargain. Consequently, there is created *a range of indeterminateness,* within which the wages actually paid to any workman can be affected by individual "higgling and bargaining." The upper limit of this range is a wage equal to the value of the marginal net product of the workman to the employer engaging him, it being understood that this value is not fixed from outside, but depends in part upon how many men the employer concerned chooses to engage. The lower limit is a wage equal to what the workman believes he could obtain by moving elsewhere *minus* an allowance to balance the costs of the movement. The width of the gap between the workers' minimum and the employers' maximum varies in different circumstances. It is made larger when the employers in a district tacitly or openly enter into an agreement not to bid against one another for labour, since, in that event, the alternative to accepting terms from them is to seek work, not near by, but in a perhaps unknown district. For example, in some districts the rate of pay to agricultural labourers had, before the war, become a matter of tradition and custom. Though conditions had become quite different from what they were when this tradition crystallised, nobody ventured to take the initiative in breaking away from it. "The farmer," says the *Report of the Land Inquiry Committee,* "has been accustomed to pay a certain wage and to feel that the conditions of farming would not allow him to go beyond that limit, and we have found instances of his going without labour for a time rather than grant a rise in wages. . . . His line of defence is greatly strengthened by the solidarity of interests among farmers. If an employer in the town wishes to make a substantial advance in wages, he can afford to be indifferent to

the resentment, if any, among other employers. But the
personal bonds between farmers are extremely close, and the
best employer of labour is sensitive to social ostracism. From
many parts of the country we have heard of cases where
farmers would willingly raise wages but for fear of local
opinion. Thus, a farmer told us that, to avoid the appearance
of paying higher wages than the farmers round him, he had
actually resorted to subterfuge and adopted a bonus method
of payment."[1] The width of the gap is also greater the more
free employers are to make use of devices likely to aggravate
the ignorance of their workpeople as to the real amount of
the earnings they are receiving—such devices as are combated
by the "particulars clause," the Truck Acts and the other forms
of protective legislation that were discussed in Chapter IX.,
§ 6. Whenever any gap exists, exploitation of the workpeople up to the measure of this gap is *possible*.[2]

Whether and how far, when the extent of the gap is
given, exploitation will actually take place, depends partly
on the relative bargaining power of the employers and workpeople concerned and partly on the willingness of the stronger
party to exercise its power. Even when the gap is large, the
occurrence of exploitation is not certain, and, in occupations
where the workpeople have been able to organise themselves
into strong Trade Unions, supported by a reserve fund and
bargaining for their wage rates as single collective wholes, it is
not even probable. But in occupations in which the workpeople—whether because they are widely scattered in space,
or because they are poor and ignorant, or because they are
women who do not expect to continue in industry after
marriage, or for any other reason—are unorganised, there are
grounds for fearing that exploitation will often occur. The

[1] *Report of the Land Inquiry Committee*, 1914, vol. i. p. 40.
[2] It is sometimes thought that an employer's power of exploitation is
always greater under a piece-wage than under a time-wage system. But this is
not so. Workpeople engaged in operations, the pace of which is dependent upon
machinery controlled by employers, often prefer piece-wages on the ground that,
under that system, they will be subjected to *less* overstrain through speeding-up
than they would have to put up with under time-wages. The cotton operatives
and the operatives in those sections of the boot-trade where machinery is
largely employed appear to take this view. (Cf. Lloyd, *Trade Unionism*, pp.
92-4.)

chief of these is that, when workpeople are unable to combine, an employer generally possesses considerably greater strategic strength than his opponents. First, the actual process of bargaining is one to which he is accustomed and to which he is, in a sense, trained, while these things are not true of the generality of workpeople. Women workers and children are especially weak from this point of view. Secondly, partly because he is generally richer and partly because he generally employs a considerable number of workmen, an employer stands to suffer a smaller *proportionate* loss of well-being when a bargain with an individual workman fails to be consummated than that individual workman stands to suffer. He is, therefore, in a better position to push things to extremes. The significance of the number of people employed is brought out by the comparative weakness of employers in bargains about domestic service: "The alternative to the well-to-do woman of doing without a servant for a single day is perhaps as disagreeable to her as the alternative to the servant of being out of a place; and the worry and inconvenience to the mistress of finding another servant is at least as great as the discomfort to the servant of getting another situation."[1] Thirdly, in some circumstances for a workman to refuse an employer's terms involves for him further evil in addition to loss of wages. This will happen if, besides being a workman, he is also a tenant to his employer, and so liable to eviction from his house. In view of these considerations, if an employer of unorganised workpeople chooses to exercise his bargaining power, he *can* pay wages much nearer to the workman's minimum than to his own maximum. Where employers reckon to keep the same workpeople for a long time, fear of injuring these workpeoples' future efficiency may induce them in their own interest to concede terms more liberal than they need have done. Furthermore, it is to be expected that feelings of generosity and kindliness will often prevent employers from fully exercising their power. But, when they are themselves very poor, there is little scope for generosity: and, even when they are not very poor, if they work through foremen or sub-contractors employed

[1] Webb, *Industrial Democracy*, p. 675.

upon piece-profits, there is little prospect of it.[1] It follows that, among unorganised workpeople unable to bargain collectively, a number of men and women are likely to be paid wages approaching much more nearly to the lower than to the upper end of the range of possible rates. Such wages are, in general, lower than the wages for similar work that are paid elsewhere, and are, therefore, "unfair."[2]

§ 8. The establishment anywhere of unfair wages of this type does not involve, at all events directly, any divergence in the actual distribution of labour from the most advantageous distribution. All that it involves directly is that in some places certain workpeople, who would in any event have been employed there, are mulcted of part of their possible earnings by the greater strategic strength of opposing bargainers. Thus, it appears *prima facie* that, though the abolition of this type of unfairness would presumably benefit economic welfare as a whole by preventing the relatively rich from taking money from the relatively poor, it would make no difference to the magnitude of the national dividend. This *prima facie* conclusion omits, however, to take account of certain important indirect effects. These are three in number, and have now to be noticed in turn.

First, the forcing down of wages in particular places or occupations, though it does not reduce the labour supply sufficiently to compel employers to refrain from it, does reduce it to some extent. When this happens, the quantity of labour

---

[1] There is reason to believe that the excessive pressure to which children were subjected under the old factory system was partly due to the fact that overseers were paid piece-wages. (Cf. Gilman, *A Dividend to Labour*, p. 32.) In like manner, the "sweating" that is sometimes found among the employees of sub-contractors is probably traceable, not to the system of sub-contract, but to the fact that sub-contractors are generally small masters on piece profits.

[2] It may possibly be argued against the above analysis that, though an employer may succeed, by bargaining, in forcing upon workmen, *other than the man most expensive to him*, a wage below the value of their marginal net product, it cannot pay him to treat *this* man so. For it will be to his interest to go on engaging fresh hands till the wage and the value of the marginal net product of the workman most expensive to him are equal. Hence, it is impossible for any employer who pays to all his workpeople the same efficiency-wage to pay to any of them less than the value of the marginal net product of their work. This argument, however, tacitly assumes that an employer, whom it *would pay* to engage fresh hands at an exploited wage rate, *will be able* to do this to an indefinite extent. No such assumption is warranted.

employed there will be so far contracted that the value of the marginal net product of labour there is greater than it is elsewhere. This involves injury to the national dividend. Consequently, a forcing-up of the wage rate, by bringing in men from other occupations which yield a smaller marginal return, would benefit it. In so far, for example, as the wages of agricultural labourers before the war were kept down by tacit understandings among farmers, the legal enforcement of a higher wage would have increased the number of these labourers in a way unambiguously advantageous to the national dividend.[1]

Secondly, it was pointed out in Part II. Chap. VI. § 14, that, "when their clients, be they customers or workpeople, can be squeezed, employers tend to expend their energy in accomplishing this, rather than in improving the organisation of their factories." To prevent them from seeking profit along the line of bargaining power indirectly impels them to seek it along that of technical improvement. Thus, Mr. Mallon writes: "An employer, compelled by the Trade Board [through the institution of a minimum wage] to scrutinise his factory, found that, through lax organisation, its workers were often kept waiting for work to their, and his own, considerable loss. Applying himself to the removal of this cause of waste, he was soon able to provide for the steady and continuous employment of the workers, the outcome being substantial gain to them, and, in at least an equal degree, to himself. Such cases could be multiplied indefinitely. In many factories and workshops for the first time methods and equipment are being overhauled, with results at which many of the employers, not at the outset in favour of the Act, are pleased and

---

[1] It is thus perfectly correct to attribute a portion of the transference from arable to grass farming that has taken place in England since the 'seventies to the low rates of wages driving the labourers off the land. (Cf. Hall, *Agriculture after the War*, p. 121.) Another and a larger portion of it is, however, due to the cheapening of imported food, which has rendered the employment of British resources in direct food production less profitable relatively to other employments than it used to be. To substitute grass farming for arable farming is merely one way of reducing the resources devoted to food production in this country, as against the production of other things by the sale of which food can be purchased from abroad; for, as Mr. Hall observes, "land [apart, of course, from special sorts of land] under arable cultivation produces nearly three times as much food as when under grass and employs ten times as many men" (*ibid.* p. 127).

astonished."[1] With this passage may be compared a kindred
observation of Mr. Hunter's: "Through cheap labour, manufacturers are often able to retain and perpetuate methods
of manufacture which are unnecessary and antiquated.
Mechanical ingenuity and inventive skill are enabled to lie
dormant, because the labour of women and children is cheap
and plentiful." If the cheap labour were excluded, "a
thousand devices latent in inventive brains would quickly
make good any momentary loss."[2] Other writers emphasise
the same point. Miss Black argues: "Low-priced labour is a
great obstacle to improvement. It discourages invention and
removes or prevents the growth of a great stimulus to progress
and efficiency. . . . It has been shown over and over again
that, when employers are prevented from developing their
business along the lines of cheap labour or bad conditions,
they proceed to develop it along the lines of improved methods,
and that the improved methods tend both to increased output
and to greater cheapness."[3] In like manner, Mr. Rowntree
believes factory equipment and so forth to be worse in
Belgium than in England. As the employer, he writes,
"finds ready to his hand a large supply of badly organised
labour willing to work very long hours for exceedingly low
wages, he naturally takes the line of least resistance, and
makes use of this instead of striving after improved methods
and investing in labour-saving machinery."[4] Care must,
indeed, be taken to avoid confusion in this matter. When
workpeople are paid the full value of their marginal net
product, no less than when they are exploited, employers are
likely to introduce a larger amount of machinery, the more
expensive is hand labour. It might, therefore, seem at first
sight that the forcing up of exploited and of unexploited
wage rates is on all fours. But this is not really so. For
the forcing-up of unexploited wage rates causes employers to
resort to machinery as a *second-best* alternative to the labour
which they are compelled to forgo; whereas the forcing up of
exploited wages leaves the quantity of labour which it pays

[1] *Industrial Unrest and the Living Wage*, p. 155.
[2] *Poverty*, pp. 244-5.
[3] Black, *Makers of our Clothes*, pp. 185 and 192.
[4] *Land and Labour*, p. 530.

them to employ unaffected, and simply adds a stimulus to their inventive energy. Hence, the general statement set out at the beginning of this paragraph gives a correct representation of the facts.

Thirdly, if particular employers outbargain their workmen, in such wise as to compel some or all of them to accept a wage below the value of their marginal net product, it necessarily happens that these employers are receiving more than the normal earnings of persons of their degree of competence;— a state of affairs which, in view of the imperfect mobility of employing power between occupations, may continue for some time. If the exploiting employers were persons of the ordinary competence of their grade, interference which forced up the wages paid by them to the fair level would simply compel them to hand over to workpeople profits formerly exacted from them by *force majeure*, and would have no other effect. As a matter of fact, however, exploitation of this kind is much more often practised by incompetent or badly situated employers, who, without it, could not maintain themselves in business, than by competent and well-situated men. The small masters have, throughout history, been always the worst exploiters. Hence, exploitation provides, in the main, a bounty at the workers' expense for relatively incompetent and badly situated employers; and the prevention of exploitation would tend to hasten their defeat at the hands of more efficient rivals. This consideration, in conjunction with the others that have preceded it, makes it plain that external interference to prevent that type of unfair wages which I have described as exploitation is desirable in the interest of the national dividend as well as upon other grounds.

§ 9. All that has been said hitherto, both of unfair wages that are equal to the value of marginal net product, and of unfair wages that are exploited below the value of marginal net product, is of quite general application. It holds good equally of men's wages and of women's wages; and, of course, in view of their inferior organisation, the danger of exploitation is especially great with women. Any specific plea that the wage of either sex in any place or occupation is unfair would need to be reviewed in the light of it. There still remains, however, a somewhat special problem arising out of *the relation between men's wages and women's wages,* which our analysis does not cover. It may happen that women's wages in some place or occupation are fair relatively to women's wages in other places or occupations, but unfair relatively to men's wages in that place or occupation. This statement has not, of course, anything to do with the well-known fact that women's day wages on the average are considerably lower than men's day wages. Women, looking forward, as they do, to matrimony and a life in the home, are not trained to industry as men are, and do not devote to it that period of their lives when they are strongest and most capable. Thus, between the age-periods of 18—20 and 25—35 there is a great decrease in the percentage of women who are engaged in wage-earning occupations, and this is due, no doubt, to the withdrawal of many of them at marriage. In the period 45—55, and still more markedly in the period 55—65, while the percentage of "occupied" men declines very rapidly, the percentage of "occupied" women hardly declines at all, the explanation being that many women return to industry after the death of their husbands.[1] In these circumstances, even though women's natural endowments of mind and muscle were equal to those of men, which, on the average, they are not, it would be surprising if their day wages were not lower. Certainly, the fact that they are lower involves no unfairness in the sense in which that term is here used. In some places or occupations, however, it may happen that, not only the day wages, but also the piece wages, or, more accurately, the efficiency wages, of women are lower than those of men. This state of things may come about because women's wages in those places or occupations are unfair relatively to women's wages elsewhere. In that event there is nothing special about it, and the analysis relevant to it has already been given in preceding sections.

---

[1] Cf. [Cd. 4671], p. 23. Professor Chapman refers to this point in connection with home work, pointing out that much of this work requires only such skill as can be acquired by anybody at any time of life, and is taken up by untrained persons, who "suddenly find it necessary to do something, or have to make money" (*Home Work,* Manchester Statistical Society, Jan. 1910, p. 93).

But it may also come about because women's wages in those places or occupations are unfair relatively to men's wages there, although they are fair relatively to women's wages elsewhere. It is this state of things that constitutes our present problem.

In order to understand the matter rightly, analysis is necessary. The common idea is that women are normally paid less than men, because men's wages have, in general, to support a family, while women's wages have only to support the women themselves. This is very superficial. The correct line of approach would seem to be as follows. The productive efficiency of a representative woman relatively to that of a representative man is different in different occupations: in some, such as nursing and the tending of infants, it is much greater; in others, such as coal-mining and navvy work, it is much less. If we knew enough of the facts, we could draw up a list of all occupations, giving for each of them the amount of normal man's labour to which a day or week of normal woman's labour is equivalent. The relation between the demand schedules for women's work and for men's work is determined by the facts embodied in this list, in conjunction with the general conditions of demand for the products of the several occupations. The relation between the supplies of women's work and of men's work is determined partly by the physiological fact that male and female children survive in nearly equal numbers, whatever the comparative wages ruling for men's work and women's work may be; and partly by the economic fact that the proportions, respectively, of the men and women in existence who offer their work in industry depends, not only on the wages offered to members of either sex separately, but also, since women are the less likely to work at industry the more money their husbands are earning, on the aggregate amount of the joint family income. These two sets of influences together govern and determine the relation between the general level of the wages per day paid to representative members of the two sexes.[1] In equilibrium there is one

[1] This analysis may be formulated mathematically as follows:

Let w_1 be the rate of women's wages per day,
w_2 the rate of men's wages per day.

Then, since the amount of women's labour offered in industry at any given

general rate of representative men's day wages and one general rate of representative women's day wages, the one or the other being higher according to the circumstances of supply, and according as the commodities demanded by the public are chiefly commodities for the manufacture of which the one or the other sex is specially well fitted.[1] Men alone are employed in all occupations where the ratio of their efficiency to women's efficiency exceeds the ratio of

---

wage depends in part upon the rate of men's wages—being, in general, smaller the larger these are, the supply of women's labour may be written $f_1(w_1, w_2)$. In like manner, the supply of men's labour may be written $f_2(w_1, w_2)$.

And we know that $\dfrac{\delta f_1(w_1, w_2)}{\delta w_1}$ and $\dfrac{\delta f_2(w_1, w_2)}{\delta w_2}$ are positive, and $\dfrac{\delta f_1(w_1, w_2)}{\delta w_2}$ and $\dfrac{\delta f_2(w_1, w_2)}{\delta w_1}$ are negative.

Again, since the amount of women's labour demanded in industry at any given wage depends upon the rate of men's wages—being, in general, smaller the smaller these are — the demand for women's labour may be written $\phi_1(w_1, w_2)$, and the demand for men's labour $\phi_2(w_1, w_2)$. And we know that $\dfrac{\delta \phi_1(w_1, w_2)}{\delta w_1}$ and $\dfrac{\delta \phi_2(w_1, w_2)}{\delta w_2}$ are negative, and $\dfrac{\delta \phi_1(w_1, w_2)}{\delta w_2}$ and $\dfrac{\delta \phi_2(w_1, w_2)}{\delta w_1}$ are positive.

The two equations, which suffice to determine our two unknowns, are:

$$(1) \quad f_1(w_1, w_2) = \phi_1(w_1, w_2)$$
$$(2) \quad f_2(w_1, w_2) = \phi_2(w_1, w_2).$$

It may be added that, if the proportion of women and men offering work in industry were determined solely by the proportion of women and men in existence, we should have to do with a straightforward problem of joint-supply; for, obviously, the comparative numbers of the two sexes are determined by physiological causes outside the range of economic influences. In these conditions, therefore, both the supply of women workers and the supply of men workers would be functions of one variable, this variable being some symbol of a normal family income, such as $(w_1 + w_2)$. For $f_1(w_1, w_2)$, and $f_2(w_1, w_2)$, we should have to write $f(w_1 + w_2)$ and $kf(w_1 + w_2)$: and in countries where males and females survive in equal numbers, k would be equal to unity.

[1] It is interesting to note that in the European war, while the withdrawal of men from industry for the army naturally tended to raise men's wages relatively to women's wages, the character of the commodities demanded by the public was changed in a way tending in the opposite direction. Ordinary tailoring and munition making, the demand for both of which enormously expanded, appear to be better adapted for women's work than the general run of industries. In the Report of the Conference of the British Association on *Outlets for Labour after the War* it is suggested that, on the whole, the special war demand of the Government was "a demand for a class of goods in the production of which a greater proportion of women rather than men can be more usefully and economically employed than under normal peace conditions" (*Report*, 1915, p. 8).

their day wages to women's day wages; women alone in all
occupations in opposite case; and men and women indifferently
in the marginal occupations in which their respective efficiencies
bear to one another the same ratio as their respective day
wages. In these marginal occupations, that is to say, the
efficiency wages of the two sexes are equal. This equality
of efficiency wages means, with certain allowances, equality
of piece wages. The principal allowances are, first, a small
extra for men because, since, at need, they can be put on
night-work and can be sworn at more comfortably, it is
rather more convenient to employ them; secondly, a small
extra to the more skilful workers, whether men or women,
because they occupy machinery for a shorter time than
less skilful workers in accomplishing a given job. In equilibrium the piece wages paid to the members of the two
sexes in the marginal occupations are, with these limitations,
equal.[1] This is the state of things which the play of economic
forces tends to bring about; and, so far as it in fact brings it

[1] It so happens in fact—as indeed is probable *a priori*—that the range of
these marginal occupations is in this country small. The Poor Law Commissioners report: "About four-fifths of the occupied male population are
engaged in employments which they monopolise, or in which women are a
negligible factor as regards possible competition, such as agriculture, mining,
fishing, building, transport, wood, gas and water, and the staple metal and
machine-making trades, all of which are virtually male preserves. Only one-
fifth of the males are engaged in trades where women enter to the extent of 1
per cent of the whole number of occupied females" (*Report*, p. 324). Mr. and
Mrs. Webb witness to the same effect: "There are a very small number of
cases in which men and women compete directly with each other for employment on precisely the same operation in one and the same process" (Webb,
Industrial Democracy, p. 506. Cf. also Smart, *Economic Studies*, p. 118.) When
one sex appears to be invading the province of the other, the fact generally is
that the process, as well as the workers, is being changed. Thus, machinery
and males have come into lace and laundry work: machinery and females into
boot-making and tailoring. The Poor Law Commissioners report: "In the boot
and shoe trade—which has been distinctively a male industry—women are
certainly obtaining a relatively stronger hold, owing to the division of labour
which now furnishes certain lighter processes, suitable for women, that were
formerly done as part of the general work of male shoemakers. Slipper-making,
for instance, is now passing entirely into female hands" (*Report of the Royal
Commission on the Poor Law*, p. 324). Also, on the authority of the Board of
Trade inquiry into the *Cost of Living of the Working Classes*: "The same
phenomenon occurs in other fields; for instance, in Sheffield, file-cutting, an
occupation which used to be largely done by female out-workers—the work
requiring rather dexterity than strength—is now being done by heavy
machinery requiring male attendants" (*ibid.* p. 324). The Commissioners
summarise their views thus: "The conclusion is that, while women and

about, it is not possible for women's wages in any place or occupation to be fair relatively to women's wages elsewhere and yet unfair relatively to men's wages there.

In real life, however, it happens from time to time that economic equilibrium in this matter is not attained. In particular occupations employers may pay to women workers an efficiency wage which, though fair relatively to women's wages elsewhere, is less than the efficiency wage they are paying to men workers, and yet may still employ some men. They may do this either for a short time, while they are in process of substituting the one sex for the other; or for a long time, because trade union pressure or custom either compels the retention of some men, or vetoes the entry of more than a limited number of women. In these conditions is the claim "equal pay for workers of equal efficiency" justified? In what way would interference to raise the women's efficiency wage to the level of the men's affect the national dividend?

If the power of tradition, custom or trade union pressure is such that neither the number of women attached to the occupation under review nor the number of women employed there will be different if employers are allowed to pay them the

---

juveniles are now engaged in many industries in which the specialisation of machinery enables them to take part, they are not, in any considerable trade or process, displacing adult males in the sense that they are being more largely employed to do work identical with that formerly done by men. The great expansion of women's labour seems to have been in new fields of employment, or in fields which men never occupied. It should also be borne in mind that, even when women are employed where men used to be employed, this is largely due to the men going into more highly paid industries. Mining, machine-making and building have of late years attracted an abnormal number of men and boys" (*ibid.* p. 325). This view is fully borne out by what occurred during the European war. The British Association Conference of 1915 on *Outlets for Labour after the War* reported : "Even during the present time of stress, when women are to a certain extent doing work which would normally be done by men, the work, as shown in the detailed portion of this Report dealing with separate trades, is very rarely similar either as regards process or conditions. With the introduction of women the work has often to be sub-divided, and the men generally have at least the arduousness of their work increased, with oft-times the addition of over-time and night-work and a larger amount of work entailing a greater strain. Where workshops have been recently built for women workers, they have been equipped with machines of a different type from what would have been installed had the management been able to procure trained men" (*loc. cit.* p. 15). Cf. also *Report of the War Cabinet Committee on Women in Industry*, 1919, pp. 21-2.

lower rate from what it will be if they are forced to pay the higher rate, the national dividend will not be affected at all. This, however, is a very improbable state of affairs. For, even though the number of women who may be *employed* in the occupation is rigidly limited, it is likely that the number trained for and attached to it will be made greater by the higher wage rate; and, if this happens, the dividend obviously suffers from the enforced idleness of those who are attached but not employed. Furthermore, in real life permission to pay the lower wage rate will seldom be without effect on the number of women who are employed there and take the place of men. For example, "in Stoke-upon-Trent it appears that women and girls are very largely employed in the pottery industry. In some branches of this trade they are being employed to an increasing extent upon work which, a few years ago, was performed almost exclusively by men; they are now acting in competition with male labour; and, as they are able to do similar work for lower wages, they are gradually driving men from certain sections of the trade." [1] This consideration confirms Professor Cannan's contention, that "the most powerful lever for increasing the opportunities of women is taken away if they are not allowed to do the work cheaper." [2] It follows that, generally speaking, to compel the payment to them of an efficiency wage equal to that paid to men in occupations which they are seeking to enter, and in which such a rate would give them higher earnings than similar women can obtain elsewhere, must obstruct their entry either directly, or indirectly by relaxing employers' efforts to break down the customs and rules that hinder it. But, since, *ex hypothesi*, they are more efficient, relatively to men, in these occupations than they are in marginal occupations common to both sexes, their entry would necessarily be beneficial to the national dividend. Hence, generally speaking, interference designed to enforce the payment to them of a "fair" wage, as compared with the wages paid to men, in circumstances when this means an unfairly high wage as compared with women's wages elsewhere, would injure the national

---

[1] *Report of the Royal Commission on the Poor Laws*, p. 323.
[2] *Wealth*, p. 206.

dividend.[1] Interference may still conceivably be advocated by those who wish to exclude women from industry, as far as that can be done, on general social grounds. Such a defence for it is, however, insecure, because interference of the type here discussed, not only lessens the aggregate number of women in industry, but distributes them among different occupations in a wasteful manner. The social argument for excluding women from industry generally cannot sustain a policy which has this effect.

§ 10. In view of the distinctions that have been found, in the course of this chapter, to exist between different forms of unfair wages, it is plain that interference directed indiscriminately against all forms must do harm as well as good. The procedure, which, if practicable, would most advantage the national dividend, would be to examine and deal separately with every place or occupation where there was *prima facie* reason to believe that wages were unfair in any of the senses studied in the text. It may, however, be argued that this plan is an impracticable one, and that it is necessary either to interfere against unfair wages by broad general rules, or else not to interfere at all. Thus, it may be said, it is practicable to pass and administer a law like the French law of 1915, which provides that female outworkers shall be paid a piece wage that will yield the average outworker earnings equal to those of an average factory worker;[2] but it is not practicable to enact that a wage lower than this shall be permitted when it is due to the ties which restrain home workers from going into factories, and forbidden when it is due to exploitation. When the issue raised is of this type, policy must be based on a balancing of conflicting considerations.

---

[1] It is possible to employ the term "unfair" wages in reference to women's wages in a somewhat different sense, and to hold that women's wages in general are unfairly low, because they fall short of what they would have been, were it not that custom and tradition permanently exclude women from certain occupations suited to their powers, and so force some of them to take up work for which they are relatively ill-fitted. As was shown in Chapter IX., the removal of all artificial barriers of this kind would benefit the national dividend. But, so long as the barriers are left standing, reasoning analogous to that employed in § 5 of the present chapter proves that any attempt to force up women's wages towards what they would be if the barriers were removed, will injure the national dividend.

[2] *Labour Gazette*, Sept. 1915, p. 357.

CHAPTER XIV

THE STATISTICAL DETERMINATION OF FAIR WAGES

§ 1. Our analysis has shown that interference designed to substitute fair wages for unfair wages will sometimes benefit the national dividend. This theoretical result must, however, remain barren until we can ascertain whether the actual rate of wages in any place or occupation is in fact fair, and, if not, what rate would be fair. Paraphrasing Dr. Marshall's definition in shorter form, we may say that the wage paid to A is fair relatively to that paid to B, when it bears to the wage paid to B the same ratio that A's efficiency bears to B's efficiency.[1] Hence, the wage that is fair to one workman or group of workmen relatively to the wage paid to another workman or group of workmen can be determined if, and in so far as, the comparative efficiencies of the two workmen or groups of workmen are known. I propose to inquire how far know-

---

[1] The term efficiency contains ambiguities and difficulties which it is not possible to investigate fully here. Two uses of it we may definitely exclude. Efficiency does not mean for us, as it means for engineers, the ratio of the output of energy to the intake of fuel, or, in other words, the ratio of the value of a workman's product to his wage. And it does not mean for us, as it means for Mr. Emerson, the ratio of a man's actual output to the output which the task-setter holds that he ought to be able to produce without undue strain ; a man of 100 per cent efficiency being one who produces exactly the allotted task. What it does mean, however, is much more difficult to state precisely. Roughly, we may speak of it as *exercised capacity*. But in this definition there is an unsolved perplexity. On the one hand, it seems imperative to find some measure of efficiency independent of the value which a unit of it is capable of producing. But, on the other hand, it is difficult to see how this can be done, while at the same time the proposition that wages tend to correspond to efficiency is maintained. For a person with a units of moral force, b of mental, and c of physical force tends to earn more or less than a person with b units of moral force, c of mental, and a of physical force, according to the comparative popular demand for things in the production of which these different qualities are respectively most important.

ledge on this subject is attainable, first as between different
workmen engaged in a single industry where piece-wages are
paid; secondly, as between different workmen engaged in a
single industry where time-wages are paid; and thirdly, as
between different workmen engaged in different industries.

§ 2. As a preliminary to this investigation, it must be
made clear that the wage, in the "fairness" or "unfairness" of
which we are interested, is not the nominal money wage, but
the real wage. The point is important, because the comparative money wages ruling in different places or occupations
frequently, do not afford a true measure of the comparative
real wages. In some occupations, notably agriculture, very
considerable payments in kind are made in addition to payments in money. Again, even when no payments in kind are
made, equal money wages do not necessarily imply equal real
wages, because the purchasing power of money in terms of the
things that workpeople are accustomed to purchase—principally food and house-room—is different in different places.
Furthermore, in some occupations special "amenities" exist
which it is proper to count as a part of the real wage. The
home worker, for example, "cares very much about being able
to settle her own times of work, and about being able to go
out in the afternoons and to have visitors." [1] Whenever, for
the above or any other reason, money wages are not truly
representative of real wages, allowance must be made for whatever discrepancy may exist. That this may be done properly,
elaborate inquiries as to the methods of wage payment that
are in vogue in different occupations and as to the relative
levels of retail prices in different places must be made. Unless
information on these subjects is to hand, any accurate statistical determination of fair real wages is out of the question.
There is, however, no reason to doubt that the greater part of
the information required can be obtained; and, indeed, for the
United Kingdom, large masses of it are already available in
various official publications. We may, therefore, pass away
from this aspect of the problem, and concentrate attention
upon more difficult matters.

§ 3. If in a piece-wage industry all workpeople rendered

[1] Miss Collett, Evidence before the Committee on Home Work, Q. 793.

their services under exactly similar conditions, their comparative efficiencies would be reflected in their comparative outputs, and, therefore, their wage rates would be fair relatively to one another if, subject to the extra for fast work referred to in § 9 of the preceding chapter, they were all paid at the same piece rate. In real life, however, all the workpeople in an industry do not, in general, render their services under exactly similar conditions. When they do not do this, their comparative efficiencies are not reflected in their comparative outputs, and, therefore, in order that wages may be fair, the piece rates must be so adjusted that different outputs representing equal efficiencies shall receive the same reward. The nature of the necessary adjustments and their susceptibility to statistical estimation may most conveniently be indicated under three separate heads.

§ 4. First, allowance must be made for differences in the assistance which different men receive in their work from machinery or, from nature. Thus, the piece rate must be higher for men working with obsolete machinery, or in mines where the easiest seams have been used up, than it is for men assisted by the most modern appliances, or hewing coal from a face that is easy of access. Allowances of this kind have frequently been provided for in the wage-agreements of important industries. For example, "in mining the tonnage rates paid to hewers vary almost indefinitely, not only from colliery to colliery, but from seam to seam within the same pit, according to the nature of the coal and the conditions under which the coal has to be won in each place; yet in some districts (as, for example, in Northumberland and Durham) the agreement, which governs wages, requires that the tonnage rates throughout the county shall be so fixed that each collier shall be able to make certain agreed earnings, i.e. the "county average."[1] There is abundant evidence that men of local and trade experience can calculate with very close accuracy what this kind of allowance ought in different circumstances to be.

§ 5. Secondly, allowance must be made for differences in the exact character of the article which different workpeople in the same industry are engaged in making. These allowances

[1] *Report on Standard Price Rates*, 1900, p. xiv.

2 M

also have often been provided for in important industries by means of piece-wage lists. The general method by which they are arranged is well described in a report of the Labour Department as follows: "A close inspection will show that, notwithstanding the variety of detail which these lists exhibit, there are certain salient features of construction and arrangement common at least to the more important among them. The most noteworthy of these common features will be seen to be the definition of a 'Standard' article or process, with a corresponding piece-price fixed in relation to this unit. From this point of departure the whole wage-scale starts, all other articles or processes having their price fixed by means of extras, deductions and allowances, specified in the 'list, and corresponding to clearly defined variations from the standard. In this manner it is possible to provide for a very large number of processes with very fine shades of difference under a single price-list. As an example of a standard unit we may take the basis of the book-work scale for compositors in the London printing trade:

All works in the English language, common matter, including english and brevier, are to be cast up at $7\frac{1}{2}$d. per 1000 [ens]; minion $7\frac{3}{4}$d., nonpareil $8\frac{1}{2}$d., ruby 9d., pearl $9\frac{1}{2}$d., diamond $11\frac{1}{2}$d., head and white lines included.

Here we have the piece-rates for the simplest form of the work; if the language be foreign, if the matter involve special difficulty, if any other variation or extra be required, the scale will be found to provide for the case, and to specify the amount of extra remuneration due in respect of the particular departures from the standard work which the compositor may be required to make."[1] In industries whose "output consists of a limited range of staple articles, more or less uniform in character, and produced in considerable quantities, year after year, by identical or very similar processes of manufacture,"[2] experience shows that technical experts can calculate with

[1] _Report on Standard Price Rates_, 1900, p. xvi.
[2] Schloss, _Report on Gain-sharing_, p. 113. For a detailed account of the arrangements by which piece-scales in the United States are adjusted to variations in the sizes and patterns of products, the materials used and the physical conditions of the work, cf. McCabe, _The Standard Rate in American Trade Unions_, Chapter i.

close accuracy how large the various allowances ought
to be.

§ 6. For operations which have not been standardised by
frequent use, such as the great bulk of repairing work and,
during the period of their novelty, all new operations of which
experience is lacking, the task of calculating these allowances
correctly is naturally much more difficult. But of late years
it has been made easier by the device of "elementary rate-
fixing." This device is based on the fact that the great bulk
of industrial operations consist of some out of a comparatively
small number of elementary movements combined together in
various ways. As a consequence of this fact, it is possible, by
determining from experience the time appropriate for each
elementary operation, to calculate beforehand the time appropriate for new complex jobs which have never been done
before. Of course, the process of combining any set of elements
can be performed more rapidly by men who undertake it
frequently than by those to whom the task falls on comparatively rare occasions, and, therefore, our reckoning of the
efficiency implied in any job will be somewhat different according as it is, or is not, carried out often enough to make it
worth while for a group of workmen to become specialised upon
it. But this difficulty is *comparatively* unimportant. The
general character of the device of elementary rate-fixing is
illustrated in the following description: "Suppose the work to
be planing a surface on a piece of cast iron. In the ordinary
system of piece work, the rate-fixer would look through his
records of work done by the planing machine until he found
a piece of work as nearly as possible similar to the proposed
job, and then guess at the time required to do the new piece
of work. Under the elementary system, however, some such
analysis as the following would be made:

WORK DONE BY MAN.

Minutes.

Time to lift piece from floor to planer table
Time to level and set work true on table
Time to put on stops and bolts
Time to remove stops and bolts
Time to remove piece to floor
Time to clean machine

Work done by Machine.

Time to rough off cut $\frac{1}{4}$ in. thick, 4 ft. long, 2$\frac{1}{2}$ in. wide ...
Time to rough off cut $\frac{1}{8}$ in. thick, 3 ft. long, 12 in. wide, etc. ...
Time to finish cut 4 ft. long, 2$\frac{1}{2}$ in. wide ...   .   .
Time to finish cut 3 ft. long, 12 in. wide, etc. .   .
     Total   .   .   .   .   .
Add — per cent. for unavoidable delays. .   .

It is evident that this job consists of a combination of elementary operations, the time to do each of which can be readily determined by observation, and, while this exact combination of operations may never occur again, elementary operations similar to some of those given will be performed in differing combinations almost every day in the same shop. The rate-fixer soon becomes so familiar with the time for each of the elements that he can write them down from memory. For the part of the work which is done by the machine he refers to tables, which are made out for each machine, giving the time required for any combination of breadth, depth and length of cut."[1]   This method is not, of course, perfect, for to determine what interval shall be allowed for passing from one elementary process to another is still a matter of more or less arbitrary judgment.[2]   Nevertheless, the method undoubtedly makes it feasible to ascertain what rate of wage is a fair one in a number of jobs, for which, apart from it, this could not possibly be done.

§ 7. Thirdly, allowance must be made for differences in the assistance which different workpeople receive in their work from the co-operation of managing power.   When the organisation of a factory is bad, so that men are kept waiting for their material and so on, a man of given efficiency will be able to produce a smaller output, and, therefore, ought to be paid a larger piece-wage, than when the organisation is good. That this point is very important is suggested by the following comment of an experienced observer: " The methods and distribution of work vary surprisingly in different places, and the real wage received is greatly affected by the degree of organising and administrative ability that may happen to be possessed

---

[1] *Engineering Magazine*, 1901, p. 624.
[2] Cf. Hoxie, *Scientific Management and Labour*, p. 51.

by the person in command.   It is a common thing for groups
of workers employed in different rooms of the same factory,
doing precisely the same work under identical outward conditions, and at the same piece-work rates, to show weekly general
averages, one of which will be always steadily larger than the
other." [1]   It is obvious that very great difficulties—not the
least of them being that the quality of the management in all
firms is liable to vary from time to time—must be met with
in any attempt to calculate with accuracy the allowances that
ought to be made under this head.   These difficulties cannot
be completely overcome.   When, however, they seem likely to
be serious, they may, to some extent, be met by the establishment, as an adjunct to the piece-wage system, of a minimum
time-wage, below which the earnings of workmen of average
quality shall, in no circumstances, be allowed to fall.   Strong
trade unions generally aim at securing this,[2] and the Minimum
Wage (Coal Miners) Act enforces it by law.   This arrangement,
in effect, makes an allowance for *extremes* of incapable management.   It also makes an allowance for accidental fluctuations of management.   Within any factory or mine, in
which managing ability stands on the whole at the average
level, there will necessarily occur from time to time accidental
variations in the facilities afforded to individual workmen in
the conduct of their operations.   " Suppose a gang is unloading
coal cars at so much per ton, and the switching crew is tardy
in moving away empties and setting in loaded cars, and so
keeps them idle for considerable periods, or suppose that, in
setting in the new cars, it places them badly, so that the men
have an extra long throw and work at a disadvantage.   Again,
the workmen may be unable to make fair wages through no
fault of their own.   Suppose, once more, a working gang is
made up by the foreman so that green men are mixed with
skilled, and these green men by their awkwardness cut down
the output of the whole gang.   Here, again, if they are
working at piece-rates, their earnings are reduced without
their fault." [3]   On the average of a long period, no doubt,

---

[1] Black, *Makers of our Clothes*, p. 145.
[2] Cf. Cole, *The Payment of Wages*, p. 4.
[3] Going, *Principles of Industrial Engineering*, p. 123.

accidents of this kind would be spread fairly evenly among
all the workpeople employed, so that everybody would get
approximately fair wages on the whole. Wide occasional
variations from a man's ordinary weekly wages are, however,
injurious and ought, if possible, to be prevented. The addition of a properly constructed minimum time-wage does prevent
them. In order that it may provide against extremes of bad
management and against these accidental fluctuations, without
also bringing about other and unintended consequences, it
must possess the following characteristics. First, when the
minimum time-wage is introduced, the general level of the
prevailing system of piece-rates should be slightly lowered;
for, if this is not done, the average efficiency-wage paid in the
industry is, in effect, raised; and that is an unintended consequence. A corollary is that the minimum time-wage should
change when the general average piece-rate of a district
changes. Secondly, the minimum time-wage should be
such as to yield somewhat lower day earnings to the man of
normal efficiency than such a man might expect to earn, with
average good fortune, upon piece-wages. For, otherwise, the
stimulus to effort, which piece-wages are designed to afford,
will be in great measure destroyed, and, as a consequence,
output may be much reduced; and this is a second unintended
consequence. Thirdly, provision should somehow be made to
secure that the full minimum time-wage is only payable to
workmen of normal efficiency. If it is a perfectly general
minimum, it will imply—yet a third unintended consequence
—an enforced enhancement, above the general level, of the
efficiency wages of incompetent men. There is, therefore,
required a rule, such as is provided under the British Minimum
Wage (Coal Miners) Act, that those workmen who frequently
fail to turn out a stipulated amount of output in a normal
week, when they are not hindered by accident, sickness or
abnormality in their workplace, shall be placed outside the
scope of the minimum time-wage.

§ 8. In an industry where time-wages are paid, in order
to know what wage rates are fair between different groups of
workpeople, we need, as before, a knowledge of the comparative
efficiencies of different workpeople. Whereas, however, in piece-

wage industries this knowledge was sought indirectly by calculating the comparative difficulty of different individual tasks, under time-wages it must be sought directly by observing the capacity and energy of different individual men.   Sometimes these direct estimates are assisted by records of output ; but often no extraneous aid is available.   Nevertheless, persons of technical knowledge and experience are able to make fairly close estimates of the relative worth of different men whom they observe at work in an industry familiar to them.   Our knowledge, therefore, need not be limited to such generalities as that the agricultural labourers of the north of England are more efficient, and should, therefore, receive higher real wages than those of the south.   By making use of the direct judgment of specialists, we can often say, not indeed that the fair wage for a given group of workpeople would fall at a rate which can be specified, but that it would fall between limits which can be specified, and which are not very wide apart. Thus, though it is not generally possible to make so close a statistical determination of the wages that will be fair to any particular workman or group of workpeople in a time-wage industry as in a piece-wage industry, it is generally possible to make a *reasonably* close one.

§ 9. To ascertain the comparative efficiencies of workpeople engaged in different industries, and, thereby, to determine what wage in one of them would be fair relatively to that prevailing in others, is much more difficult.   The centre of the problem is the appropriate relation between the wages of *average* workpeople in different industries.   For, when the wage that is fair for an *average* worker anywhere is known, to discover the allowance that should be made for those above or below the average is a comparatively simple matter.   But how is relative efficiency, and, therewith, the fair rate of wages to be ascertained as between an average worker in one industry and an average worker in other industries ?   The judgment of technical experts is difficult to employ, because practically nobody is a technical expert in more than one industry ; and, apart from their judgment, no direct way of reaching a decision seems to be possible. Any attempt, for example, to use value of product as a test plainly involves circular reasoning, since the value of anything is itself partly determined by the wage that is paid to the people who make it. Frequently, however, an indirect method is available. It may be possible to find some model, or standard, year, in which there was a general agreement among employers and employed in an industry that the wage rate there bore the same proportion to efficiency as that ruling in other industries, and was, therefore, fair. This wage rate will be our starting-point. Having ascertained it, we try to discover by statistical inquiry in what proportion wage rates in other industries have changed since our standard year. Suppose that they have risen by 20 per cent. Then, if no obvious change has occurred in the comparative average quality of the workpeople in our industry and in other industries, we may conclude that the fair wage for our industry now is the wage that ruled there in the standard year *plus* a rise of 20 per cent. This method, which was, in effect, pursued for a long time by Conciliation Boards in the coal industry, often enables a reasonably close determination of fair wages to be made.

CHAPTER XV

§ 1. UP to this point attention has been confined to the effects of interference designed to force up wages in places and occupations where they are unfairly low to a rate equivalent to that paid for similar labour elsewhere. It is sometimes claimed, however, that wages which are low and fair, as well as those which are low and unfair, may often be forced up with advantage to the national dividend. We have now to inquire how far and in what circumstances this claim is valid.

§ 2. First, as was implied at the beginning of Chapter XIII, fair wages at particular points may sometimes emerge as the result of a conflict and cancelling among two or more unfair elements. Thus, in some place or occupation the value of the marginal net product of labour may be abnormally high because the number of workpeople there is kept down by custom or by heavy costs of entry. If this circumstance operated alone, the wage rate would be unfairly high. But it may also happen that these workpeople are outbargained by their employers, and compelled to accept a wage less than the value of the marginal net product of their work. If this circumstance operated alone, the wage rate would be unfairly low. Conditions are *possible* in which these opposing tendencies exactly balance one another, so that the resultant wage stands precisely at the level of fairness. But this fairness embodies two elements of unfairness, interference with one of which would not benefit, while interference with the other would benefit, the national dividend. The interest of the dividend requires that the wage rate should not be fair, but should be put at a level that embodies the former of the two cancelling elements of unfairness. Interference, therefore, is desirable in spite of the fact that the wage is fair. It is obvious, however, that an exact cancelling of elements of unfairness that act in opposite senses is, in a high degree, improbable. ·Consequently, wage rates that, as wholes, are fair cannot reasonably be suspected, except on very special grounds, of embodying any element of unfairness. Hence, the considerations set out in this paragraph are only of academic interest and need not be taken into account in practical discussion.

§ 3. Secondly, in order that in any particular industry or place a wage that is *fair* as compared with other industries or places may also be *right* from the point of view of the national dividend, a certain definite condition must be fulfilled. This· condition is that in industries or places in general work-·people are receiving as wages the value of the marginal net' product of their work. If they are receiving less than this, they are without the normal inducement to give as much' work as the general interest demands.[1] The pushing up of their wages to a level that equates demand price and supply price would lead to an increase in the national dividend more than sufficient to compensate them for their extra sacri-·fice of leisure. Now, when things have settled down in more or less stable conditions, the play of economic forces tends to secure that in industries in general wages do correspond to the value of the marginal net product of labour. But conditions are liable to change, on account, for example, of new mechanical discoveries, the accumulation of capital, the opening up of foreign trade, or an expansion in the supply of the substance used as money. Any one of these changes necessarily tends to raise the value (in money) of the marginal net product of labour throughout occupations generally. The old wage, therefore, though still fair, will, nevertheless, be too low. It is to the interest of the national dividend that all wages should be raised. If, however, fairness in every individual wage rate was regarded as a conclusive reason against altering it, this change could never come about. Suppose, for example, that

[1] Cf. the diagrammatic footnote to Chapter XIII. p. 512.

wage rates over the whole of industry were settled by Boards of Conciliation and .Arbitration, whether wholly voluntary or partly controlled by State authority; and that the principle which each of these Boards followed was that of making its own wage rate equal. to that paid for similar work in other occupations. The result, in the face of changing general conditions, would be a complete *impasse.* In like manner, it is conceivable that workpeople might, even in stable conditions, have their wages "exploited" everywhere to exactly the same extent, and for this reason might be everywhere receiving less than the value of their marginal net product. Here again a rigid rule against interfering with fair rates would make any correction of the abuse impossible. Hence, it follows that fairness in a wage rate must not be taken as a conclusive reason against interference to raise it.

§ 4. If it were the fact, either that workpeople were exploited over the general body of industry, or that, over the general body of industry, wages were settled by Joint Boards whose sole principle of action was to establish fairness, the results of the preceding section would be of great practical importance. There would be a wide field over which interference to raise wages that are already fair would benefit the national dividend. As a matter of fact, however, the general body of industry is not controlled by Joint Boards actuated by the single principle of fairness, and there is good reason to believe that the occupations and districts in which workpeople are exploited form but a small part of the whole. Hence, these special reasons for interfering with wage rates in particular industries, in spite of their being "fair," are not of wide application. It must, however, be conceded that, when a large and sudden change, such as might be brought about by the issue of a large quantity of paper money, takes place in the money costs of living, money wages in general will not respond immediately, and, therefore, for a time real wages all round will tend to be too low. Hence, a policy which only interferes to raise unfair wages will lose opportunities for speeding up the required adjustment. If an external authority could force wages in any industry or group of industries from that old level, which is at the moment still

" fair," to the new level which will be " fair " in a short time,
it would benefit the national dividend. It will, of course, be
understood that, when the money cost of living undergoes a
large and sudden change, the response on the side of money
wages, which it is the function of the authority to expedite,
is not the same in all circumstances. If a given rise in the money
cost of living is a part of an equivalent rise in prices generally,
caused by a banking or currency change, the proper response
is a rise in money wages sufficient to make real wages equal to
what they were before. If the given rise in the cost of living is
a part of an equivalent rise in prices generally caused by
diminished facilities for production, such as might result from
the destruction of real capital in war, the proper response is
either no rise in money wages, or, at all events, a rise less
than sufficient to establish the old real wage; for the real
demand for labour will have fallen off. Lastly, if the given
rise in the cost of living is the result of a real rise in the cost
of producing the things on which wages are predominantly
spent, unaccompanied by any similar rise in the real cost of
producing other things, the proper response is a rise in
money wages less than sufficient to establish the old real
wage, but more nearly sufficient to do this than the response
proper to high general prices due to a general shortage; for
the real demand for labour in terms of general value will not
have fallen off so much.

§ 5. We have now to consider a much broader claim.
This is that in any occupation where wages are low,
whether or not they are fair (relatively to the degree of
efficiency among the workers engaged in them), they ought
to be raised far enough to yield a decent subsistence to
the average worker. Some approach to a recognition of
this claim was made in a modification introduced into the
British Trades Boards Act, of 1918, as against the original
Act of 1909. Whereas under the original Act a condition
precedent to the establishment of a Trade Board in an industry
is that wages there are *exceptionally* low, under the new Act it
is sufficient that the trade be unorganised and, therefore, likely
to be in receipt of wages *unduly* low. Elsewhere the claim
has been accepted explicitly. Thus, the South Australian

Industrial Arbitration Act 1912 provides that "the Court shall not have power to order or prescribe wages which do not secure to the employees affected a living wage. 'Living wage' means a sum sufficient for the normal and reasonable needs of the average employee living in the locality where the work under consideration is done or is being done."[1] In the Western Australian Act it is laid down that "no minimum rate of wages or other remuneration shall be prescribed which is not sufficient to enable the average worker to whom it applies to live in reasonable comfort, having regard to any domestic obligations to which such average worker would be ordinarily subject."[2] Obviously, since the price of the things on which workpeople spend their incomes varies, the sum of money required to yield a "living wage" must vary also. In terms of money, therefore, a living wage will not be a fixed amount, but an amount that changes at short intervals in accordance with changes in the prices of ordinary articles of food, clothing and housing accommodation. A special "cost of living" index number might be computed by the Board of Trade at monthly intervals, and wage awards for low-grade industries might be given in the form of a standard to be varied automatically every month in correspondence with variations in this index number.

§ 6. In popular discussion the issue which these proposals raise is sometimes blurred by a confused idea that a living wage implies, for workmen of normal efficiency in any industry which enjoys it, a "living income." This, of course, is not so. A living wage, as ordinarily conceived, is a wage that will enable the working man who receives it, if he has an average family to maintain and if he has average good fortune in the matter of sickness, to earn an income sufficient for a good life. But a rate of wages that will achieve this end in these conditions obviously will not achieve it for a man with a family in excess of the average or subjected to an unusual amount of sickness.[3] Nor can the "living wage" take account of

---

[1] *Bulletin of the U.S. Bureau of Labour Statistics*, No. 167, pp. 165-6.

[2] *Ibid.* p. 167.

[3] During the Great War the payment made to soldiers in effect varied with the size of their families, when account is taken of the maintenance allowances; and war bonuses on account of the increase in the cost of living were paid to

the fact that some workpeople need to support parents who are past work as well as their own children, or of the further fact that the wives of some workpeople contribute nothing towards the family income, while those of others contribute largely. Moreover, a wage for the breadwinner, which would provide a "living" for his family at one stage of its growth, would be quite inadequate at another stage. This consideration is very important. Dr. Bowley, for example, on the basis of his investigations into. the condition of the poor at Reading in 1912, estimated that the minimum expenditure necessary for the attainment of a reasonable standard of living "at marriage would be 16s. weekly and would rise gradually to about 25s. in five years and 28s. in ten years, provided that there were four children all surviving. It would remain at 28s. for another five years, and then fall back to 16s. as the children became self-supporting." [1] Yet again, when the industry under review is one that employs women, the notion of a living wage to a worker in "average" circumstances is almost meaningless, in view of the great differences between the positions of women mainly supported by their husbands, self-supporting single women, and women who are themselves the principal breadwinners of a family. These various considerations taken together make it plain that the enforcement in any industry of a living wage, in any plausible sense of that term, would go a very little way towards ensuring a "living income" even to those workpeople who regularly received it. Our natural desire to ensure in every industry a living income is thus not really relevant to the "living wage." The policy of forcing up wage rates in industries employing workpeople of such a low grade that fair rates, as defined in Chapter XIII., are less than living rates—however we may choose to define these—has, therefore, to be considered separately on its own merits.

§ 7. An argument by which it is widely supported is as follows: "An industry, which uses up the human capital

members of the police force on the same principle. It is, of course, in the power of the State to decree *for itself* arrangements of this kind even in normal times. But plainly no such adjusted living wage could be imposed on industry generally without setting up a powerful tendency to throw persons with large families out of employment altogether.

[1] *The Measurement of Social Phenomena*, pp. 179-80.

without replacing it, is not self-supporting and does positive harm to the community. When, therefore, a woman is partially maintained by some other source, such as by a father, husband, etc., the industry which employs her is being subsidised from these other sources to the extent by which her wages fall short of proper maintenance."[1] In other words, to allow the low wages, which make this subsidisation necessary, to continue, is to allow a process to go on by which productive power, and, consequently, the national dividend of the future, is steadily eaten away. This argument is invalid. It depends upon an ambiguity in the phrase "uses up." If the setting to work of people at some industry wears out and destroys productive powers which, had they not been set to work in that industry, would be available to augment the national dividend, then the destruction of this productive power ought strictly to be debited against that industry. Its social net product falls short of its trade net product to that extent. But there is no general presumption that an industry employing low-grade workers and paying them a wage equivalent to what they could obtain elsewhere is using up human capital in this sense. For, if it did not employ them, they would either be employed in another industry at the same wage or they would not be employed at all; and in either event there is no reason to suppose that their productive powers would be worn out any less soon. The industry, therefore, only uses up their productive powers in the sense of using or employing them, not in the sense of wearing them out. Hence, there is no difference between the (marginal) social and the (marginal) trade net product of the work done in it, and no damage is caused to the national dividend by its continuance. Nor is this conclusion affected by the fact—when it is a fact—that the workers engaged in the industry are "subsidised" from other sources; because, if they were not engaged in this industry, they would still have to be "subsidised" to at least as great an extent. It is true, as was argued at length in Chapter XIII., that, if an occupation or section of an occupation is maintaining itself in being by its power to pay to workpeople of a given grade of

[1] Women's Supplement to *New Statesman*, Feb. 21, 1914.

efficiency less wages than such workpeople *could*, and, apart from the existence of that occupation or section of occupation, *would* earn elsewhere, then the continuance in existence of that occupation or section involves a waste of the resources of the community. Here there is true parasitism. The essence of it, however, lies in the fact that workers are paid less than they could and would earn elsewhere. When this is not happening, there is no parasitism, even though workers are being paid much less than is required to maintain them in independent self-support. The thesis that industries which pay less than "fair wages" ought to be forbidden by law to do this, even though such prohibition involves their destruction, is quite different from, and lends no support to, the thesis that industries which pay less than a "living wage" to workpeople who are in fact worth, for all purposes, less than a living wage, ought to be subjected to a similar prohibition. This common argument, therefore, breaks down, and our problem must be studied without reference to it.

§ 8. We suppose that a particular industry is employing low-grade workers, and that these workers are being paid a wage which, in view of their comparative inefficiency, is fair relatively to that paid in other industries; and we suppose further that equality of efficiency wages in this industry and elsewhere is accompanied both by equality in the values of marginal net products there and elsewhere and also by a general equality between wages and these values. In these conditions, if the wage rate in our industry is forced up, a strong inducement is offered to employers to distribute inferior workpeople away from the occupations in which they are specially privileged, leaving these occupations to be occupied exclusively by more efficient men. For example, the establishment of different (real) trade union rates of wages in different towns is met, in the main, by the gravitation of the abler workpeople to the towns with higher real wages, just as the establishment of the "dockers' tanner" in 1889 was met by the substitution, in part, of strong immigrants from the country for the weaker men among the old dockers. If this class of reaction occurs, it will not really happen to any substantial extent that the workers aimed at are paid higher wages than before. All that will be accomplished will be a redistribution of workers of different grades between different occupations. Consequently, no significant effect, either favourable or adverse, will be produced upon the volume of the national dividend. The attempt at interference in favour of particular workpeople will, in fact, be parried by evasion. Let us suppose, however, that for some reason this reshuffling of workpeople is impracticable. Then, unless, of course, the demand for labour is perfectly inelastic, it must happen that some labour is ejected from employment in the industry where wages have been raised, with the result that, according to circumstances, it is either not employed at all or is employed elsewhere in conditions such that the value of the net product of most of it is less than it was. That this must be so follows directly from the analysis sketched out in Chapter XIII. The inevitable inference is that, apart from reactions on efficiency, interference to force up wages to a "living" standard in an industry where the fair wage is less than a living wage, must injure the national dividend.

§ 9. At first sight it is natural to suppose that the damage done will be roughly proportionate to the number of occupations to which the interference extends; so that the dividend will be reduced three times as much, if a living wage is enforced in all of three similar industries, where the fair wage is less than a living wage, as it would be if only one of them was touched. This, however, is an underestimate. When labour—and, consequently, capital also—is driven out of one occupation, it moves, in the ordinary course, into others; and, though it produces there less than it was producing before, it still produces a good deal. If only a little labour and capital are thus sent seeking a new home, and there is a large field open to them, the new contribution of each unit will be worth very nearly as much as the old contribution. But if, with a given field open to them, more labour and capital are sent to seek work, they will have to be pushed into less productive uses, and the new contribution made by each unit will be less. Hence, a doubling or trebling of the amount of interference, and, consequently, of the quantity of labour and capital turned loose, will involve more than a doubling or

2 N

trebling of the damage done to the dividend. This consideration must be borne in mind when any inference is attempted from Australian experience as to the probable effect of forcing up the wages of low-paid industries in this country. For "industrialism is relatively simple in form and limited in extent in the Australian colonies. Agriculture is the chief occupation, and this, being untouched by the arbitration laws, is a vent for any labour or capital driven out of the industries."[1] In this country the proportionate part played by agriculture is enormously smaller, and, therefore, the vent available, if a wide-reaching policy of forcing up industrial wages were attempted, would be far less extensive. Moreover, it is practically certain that in the United Kingdom this policy could not be applied to industry without being applied to agriculture also. The danger to the national dividend would, therefore, be very much greater than Australian experience suggests.

[1] Chapman, *Work and Wages*, vol. ii. p. 263. Since the passing of the Industrial Arbitration (Further Amendment) Act of 1918, this is no longer wholly true of New South Wales.

CHAPTER XVI

WAGE RATES AND EFFICIENCY

§ 1. THE whole of the analysis of the three preceding chapters has been conducted without reference to the effects which interference to raise wages may produce upon the efficiency and, therefore, the productiveness of the workpeople. But, as we have just seen, certain industries exist whose operations require little or no skill, and in which even the normal so-called able-bodied workers are of an exceedingly low grade of efficiency. In these industries—simple sewing at home is one of them—even a fair rate of wages, and, still more, an unfair rate, is necessarily an exceedingly low rate. In such industries it seems probable *prima facie* that interference designed to force up wage rates would react upon the efficiency of the workpeople and so might indirectly increase the national dividend, even though the direct effects, taken by themselves, would have been adverse. The reaction to be expected is partly physical, resulting from increased capacity due to better food and better conditions of life. It is also partly psychological, resulting from a sense of fair treatment, an increased feeling of hopefulness, and the knowledge that, with the increased wage, slack work is more likely to lead to a loss of employment. Hence, in occupations employing exceptionally inefficient workpeople—and an argument of the same kind, though of less force, can be advanced about those employing better workpeople—there would seem to be a stronger case for interference to raise wages than the considerations advanced in the preceding chapters by themselves suggest. This presumption has now to be examined.

§ 2. It is sometimes thought that light can be thrown

upon it by comparing the efficiencies of workpeople employed
in occupations or firms where the earnings are high and low
respectively. It is found that people who earn good money
are very much more efficient than those who earn bad money,
and it is inferred that, if the latter were paid as much as the
former, they would thereby be raised to their standard. This
reasoning is inadequate. The fact that workpeople in high-
wage districts are, in general, more efficient than workpeople
in low-wage districts does not prove that high wages cause
high efficiency; for there is available the alternative explanation that high efficiency causes high wages. Nor does the fact
that workpeople, who have moved from low-wage to high-wage
districts, are soon found to be earning the wages proper to
these latter districts, prove this; for the people most likely
to undertake such journeys are just those who feel themselves
already more efficient and worth a larger wage than their
neighbours. All statistical arguments of the above type must
be regarded with the greatest suspicion. In order to discover
experimentally how increased earnings react upon efficiency,
we should need to investigate the output of *the same individual
workman in the same environment* under both low-wage and
high-wage conditions. It is only thus that we could ascertain
the extent of the reaction which improved pay would produce
in workpeople of different income grades. Unfortunately,
investigations of this kind are not available. The rapid
improvement which took place in the appearance of the men
recruited and trained for the new armies in the great war does,
indeed, suggest that human quality is more rapidly and completely plastic, at all events in youth, than we had been
accustomed formerly to suppose. The effects, as reported by
those who have studied them, of the increased wages that have
been awarded by the Trade Boards in the tailoring and box-
making industries points in the same direction.[1] These things

---

[1] Cf. Tawney, *Minimum Wages in the Tailoring Trade*, pp. 121-134; and
Bulkley, *Minimum Wages in the Box-making Trade*, p. 51. In the box-
making industry the workpeople's efficiency has also been benefited in an
indirect way, because the enforcement of higher rates has induced employers to
pay more attention to their training; "every worker has to be trained to earn
the minimum, whereas formerly it did not matter how little they earned"
(*loc. cit.* p. 51).

give ground for hope, but they do not enable us to formulate any precise conclusions. We are thus in the end thrown back on the vague guess-work called common sense. This suggests that the reaction will be most marked among work-people who are exceedingly poor, and in whom, therefore, there is large scope for physical improvement through better food, clothing and house accommodation; that it will vary with the age of the people affected and with their previous condition; that it is more likely to occur where employment is fairly regular, so that a definite standard of life can be built up, than it is among people whose employment is "casual" and intermittent; and that the longer the improved payment lasts, the greater is the chance that efficiency will benefit to an appreciable extent.

§ 3. In industries and places where wages are low, because low-grade workpeople are being "exploited" by employers and paid less than they are worth, there is no reason to expect that the forcing of the wage rate up to a fair level will cause any of the people affected to lose their jobs for any length of time; for it will not pay employers to dispense with their services. Consequently, all that has to be considered is the direct effect upon the efficiency of the people who actually receive the better wage. It is, therefore, practically certain that there will be some net benefit to the national dividend. Moreover, there is reason to expect that this benefit will be cumulative. If exploitation is allowed, and a bad bargain by workmen leads to a reduction of their efficiency and so to a diminution in the value of their marginal net product, they will start for the next round of bargaining from a lower level; if they again get slightly the worse of the deal,— and, being weaker, they are now more likely to do so,—they will again, in the same manner, be driven yet lower. Thus, their efficiency, as well as the wage they receive, is cumulatively and progressively reduced, and the national dividend suffers thereby a serious injury. If, however, exploitation is prevented and wages are forced up to a fair level, the benefit to efficiency will start an upward movement exactly analogous to this downward movement. High earnings will lead to greater efficiency; greater efficiency will lead to the power of obtaining higher earnings, both because the

workers'·,services ·are ·worth more and because, being better
off, they are in a stronger· position for ·bargaining ; the higher
earnings so obtained will· react· again to increase efficiency ;
and so on· cumulatively. ·This·consideration is of special importance among those extremely poor·workpeople, whose ·very
poverty, so long as·it continues, makes them easy·victims to
the superior, bargaining power of employers. In these circumstances, therefore, the conclusion reached in Chapter XIII. that
the .national dividend· will be ·increased by the forcing up
of wage rates, which are rendered unfairly low by exploitation,
is confirmed and ·enforced·when account is taken of reactions
upon efficiency.

·§ 4. By similar reasoning it ·is·easily shown that, when
conditions are such that the forcing up of ·wage rates, which'are
either already fair or are unfair from other causes than exploitation, would .benefit the national dividend apart· from reactions on efficiency, these reactions are likely.to make the
benefit still greater. When, ·however, conditions are such
that, apart from .reactions on efficiency, the forcing up of ·a
wage rate would damage the national dividend, the way in
which these reactions will work is much more difficult to
determine. The reason is· that, in these conditions, some
workpeople are necessarily .ejected from employment in the
industry or place·where the wage·is raised, and either reduced
to unemployment or,· at best, set to.work where the value of
·their output is less than it was· before.· For, unless this
happens, the .dividend will not be damaged, and we are now
assuming that, apart from reactions on efficiency, it is damaged.
But, if some workers are made worse off than before, the net
effect on efficiency will not· consist merely of benefit done
to those who actually receive the· better wage rate, but also
of injury done to these others. *Prima facie* it seems reasonable to suppose that, if, after the' increase of wage rate in
one particular industry, the aggregate sum .paid in · wages
throughout the grand total of industries is less than before,
the aggregate efficiency of the workpeople as a whole will not
be enhanced. The conditions in which an increase of wages
in a particular industry may increase the real earnings of wage-
earners as a· body in spite of damaging the national dividend

will be examined at length in the course of Part V. It is evident that the prospects are best when the demand for labour in the occupation whose wage rate is forced up is highly inelastic. From the standpoint of a short period, which alone is relevant to reactions on efficiency, the causes making for inelastic demand are, in general, much more powerful than they are from that of a long period. For example, if the wage of any group were forced up, employers would not generally dismiss many of their workpeople so long as existing orders were still in hand. If, then, the "reaction time" of wages upon efficiency is fairly rapid, the chances of a favourable reaction may be taken, at all events when the commodity affected by the increased wage rate is not one largely purchased by working men, to be reasonably good. They are particularly so if the rate fixed for any group of workpeople is not raised suddenly much above the existing rate—in which event a large number of dismissals might take place—but is pushed up gradually by small stages. Hence, it may not infrequently happen that, in circumstances where, apart from reactions on efficiency, the forcing up of a wage rate would inflict damage on the national dividend, the damage will be at least partially cancelled by these reactions. When a State authority is available to help people who may have been incidentally thrown out of work, the extra State contribution, which is an indirect effect of the forcing up of the wage rate, will make this cancelling benefit somewhat larger than it would have been otherwise. Whether the cancelling benefit will be large enough to outweigh the direct damage to the dividend, against which it has to be balanced, cannot be determined generally, but will depend on the detailed conditions of each separate problem.

§ 5. It should be added that, in any event, such interference to raise wages as is warranted by the considerations set out in the preceding section is essentially a temporary interference. Where wages are paid by the piece it is temporary in form as well as in substance. For, though an enhanced piece-wage, by providing large earnings, may so improve a workman's efficiency that he can produce more pieces in the day, and is thus enabled permanently to make larger earnings at the old piece-rate, it cannot cause him to become worth the new piece-rate. Hence, there is no case for retaining that rate for a longer time than is necessary for its reaction upon efficiency to be completed—no case, at least, from the standpoint of the national dividend. If it is maintained for longer than this, it will add nothing further to efficiency, but will injure the national dividend by preventing labour from distributing itself among different uses in the most advantageous manner. When wages are paid by time, the interference warranted is no longer temporary in form, and there is no reason why the enhanced time-wage should ever be reduced. But it is temporary in substance, because, after a while, the workpeople, in consequence of their improved efficiency, will become worth the new time-wage, and, therefore, this wage will become the "natural" wage, for the maintenance of which no interference is necessary.

CHAPTER XVII

§ 1. In Chapter XV. we considered the effects of interference designed to raise the wages of a low-paid industry or part of an industry above the "fair" level. The centre of the problem was the wage of the "average" worker, and it was tacitly supposed that the rates paid to workers above and below the average would be adjusted according to their comparative efficiencies. We have now to consider a different type of interference, directed not so much towards trades as towards individuals. Granted that the average worker in all — or in most — industries is suitably remunerated, the very inefficient worker in some of them will, on account of his inefficiency, if paid on a like scale, often earn so small a sum of money that the public conscience is shocked. It is widely held that this state of things ought to be prevented by the legal establishment of a national minimum day-wage, below which no workman whatever can be legally engaged. This type of policy is illustrated—though very imperfectly, since the minimum fixed was very much below the worth of anybody except an extraordinarily inefficient apprentice—by certain of the labour laws of Australasia. The Parliaments of Victoria and South Australia "have decided that no person whatsoever can be employed there in a registered factory, without receiving some minimum remuneration—in Victoria 2s. 6d. a week, and in South Australia, 4s."[1] In like manner, the New South Wales Minimum Wage Act of 1908 provided that no workman or shop assistant shall be employed, unless in receipt of a weekly wage of at least 4s., irrespective of any

[1] Aves, *Report on Wages Boards*, p. 88.

amount earned as overtime.[1]   Again, in the Factory Act of
New Zealand, it is enacted that every person who is employed
in any capacity in a factory shall be entitled to receive from
the occupier payment for the work at such rate as is agreed
on, in no case less than 5s. per week during the first year of
employment in the industry and, thereafter, an annual increase
of not less than 3s. weekly till a wage of 20s. per week is
attained.[2] This clause in its original form—the form given
above is the slightly modified form of the 1907 amendment—
was passed in order to prevent persons being employed in
factories without "reasonable remuneration in money." Payment is always to be made irrespective of overtime, and
premiums are forbidden.[3] The same idea is embodied in the
statute by which the State of Utah in 1913 fixed a minimum
wage for all "experienced" adult women of 1·25 dollars per
day, no exceptions to this minimum being allowed even for
defective workers,[4] and in a flat-rate law of the same general
character enacted in the State of Arizona in 1917.[5] A more
elastic form of the same policy is expressed in the third section
of the Minimum Wage law of the State of Washington.
This section runs: "There is hereby enacted a Commission
. . . . to establish such standards of wages and conditions
of labour for women and minors employed within the State
of Washington, as shall be held hereunder to be reasonable
and not detrimental to health and morals, and which shall
be sufficient for the decent maintenance of women."[6] The
Industrial Arbitration Act (1918) of New South Wales, in a
similar spirit, provides: "The Board of Trade shall, from year
to year, after public inquiry as to the increase or decrease in
the average cost of living, declare what shall be the living
wages to be paid to adult male employees and to adult female
employees in the State or any defined area thereof."[7]

---

[1] *Labour Gazette*, March 1909, p. 103.
[2] Cf. Aves, *Report on Wages Board*, p. 88 ; and Raynaud, *Vers le salaire
minimum*, p. 335.
[3] *Ibid.* p. 88.
[4] *The World's Labour Laws*, Feb. 1914, p. 77.
[5] Douglas, *American Economic Review*, December 1919, p. 709.
[6] *Bulletin of U.S. Bureau of Labour Statistics*, No. 167, p. 81.
[7] *Loc. cit.* Paragraph 79 (1).

§ 2. Now, as was shown in Chapter XV. § 8, any attempt to force the wage rate of low-grade workpeople above their "fair" level, so long as the area over which it is extended is narrow, may be rendered inoperate by a perfectly legal form of evasion, namely, a reshuffling of workpeople of different grades between this area and occupations not included in it. When, however, the State interferes to establish a national minimum time-wage, the area affected by its action will not be a narrow one. On the contrary, it will be more or less nation-wide, leaving no field free into which low-grade workers can be pushed to be paid a derisory wage. Evasion by way of a redistribution of work among workers of various qualities is, therefore, altogether excluded. Hence, the effect produced upon the national dividend may prove serious and substantial.

§ 3. It is probable that the enactment of a national minimum time-wage will incidentally prevent the payment of certain low wages that are unfair, in the sense that they are the result of exploitation or the payment by employers of less than their workpeople's services are worth to them. The forcing up of *this* sort of low wage will, as was explained in Chapter XIII.; react favourably upon the volume of the national dividend, by strengthening competent employers in their competition with incompetent rivals. Nor is it only in this field that advantage will be won. Even when low wages are fair wages, in the sense of being proportioned to efficiency, it does not necessarily follow that a higher wage will not be fair also. For, as was shown in the preceding chapter, if only an inefficient worker can be secured good payment for a little while, he or she may be so far improved in efficiency as to become worth the higher wage. In so far as these things happen, the national dividend will be *pro tanto* benefited. Obviously, however, these are mere incidents, by-products as it were, of the establishment of a national minimum wage, and not the main consequence of it.

§ 4. This main consequence is the expulsion from private industry of a number of low-grade workers—the number being greater the higher the level at which the national minimum wage is fixed. When it is enacted that low-grade workpeople shall not in future be paid rates as low as many of them are now receiving, it necessarily follows that some of them will no longer be worth employing. Of course, not all those who are now worth less than the new wage will be affected in this way, because the withdrawal of some workers from private industry increases the worth of those that remain. Some, however, of those not now worth the new wage will still not be worth it when it is established. The proportion that these make of the whole will be greater or less according as the demand for labour is elastic or inelastic. It is sometimes argued that this demand is highly inelastic, upon the ground that in certain special industries, such as the chain trade, there is statistical evidence that the demand is of this character. But, when it is a question of a general minimum wage, it is the demand for labour as a whole, and not merely in particular industries, that is relevant; and, whether from a short-period or from a long-period point of view, there can be little doubt that the elasticity of this aggregate demand is much greater than the elasticity of the special demand of the chain trade.[1] Hence, the number of low-grade workers that the establishment of a national minimum wage substantially higher than the wage they are now worth will render not worth employing in private industry, is likely to be considerable. Some of these, no doubt, employers will still keep on from kindliness or old association. But many will lose their jobs, and, consequently, will have no opportunity to reap improved efficiency from improved earnings. As far as they are concerned, therefore, there will be no indirect gain to the national dividend. And there will be the obvious direct loss that their labour is withdrawn from production in private industry. No doubt, some of them might be set to work in State controlled institutions. But the enforced labour of assisted persons in institutions invariably yields but little product; and, therefore, the main part, at all events, of their capacities would be wasted.

§ 5. Under a regime of complete aloofness and passivity on the part of the State this effect would be dominant, and there can be no doubt that the national dividend would be injured. In the actual world, however, it must be remembered that a

---

[1] Cf. *post*, Part V. Chapter II.

well-organised system of care for the poor may rebuild the
strength of persons who, through unemployment, fall in need
of public relief, and may accord to them, in farm colonies or
elsewhere, an economic training of which they can afterwards
make use.. It follows that the establishment of a national
minimum time-wage, though it will, for a time, cause the
withdrawal of some persons from effective production, need
not, even in respect of·these persons, harm the national dividend in the long run, provided that it is associated with a
well-organised State policy towards the poor on the pattern
that will be exhibited in Part V. of this volume.

A little reflection shows, however, that the benefit to
be looked for in this connection is more apparent than
real. The establishment of a national minimum time-wage
would really accomplish very little more than could be
accomplished without it. If there is not·a well-organised
system of care for the poor, there is no reason to suppose that
any of the persons expelled from private industry by the
operation of the minimum will be trained and rehabilitated;
and, even if there is such a system, only those persons
will come in contact with it and so secure its benefit who
do not belong to·families able and willing to support them
without State help. But, if there were no national minimum,
most of the people, whom the minimum expels from private
industry, would, since the minimum itself will presumably
be a low one based on a consideration of what is essential for
subsistence, be earning so little that they would be nearly
sure, in one way or another, to come into contact with the
State organisation for looking after poor persons. This
organisation, therefore, will have much the same opportunity
for withdrawing from private industry those suitable for
training or those needing treatment for sickness as it would
have if there were no national minimum wage.

Nor is this all. It has to be remembered, further, that
by no means·all those persons who are prevented from
working at ordinary industry by the establishment of a
national minimum time-wage will be in a position to derive
benefit from State training. There will be no hope of this
kind for old men who have hitherto done a little work

and have derived the remainder of their support from their families and friends. These men will simply be precluded from rendering those partial and occasional services to industry which they are both able and willing to render. Elderly women home workers and younger women workers in factories, who are of low efficiency and are partly supported by husbands and fathers, will be in like case. So also will State pensioners and others who would gladly work up to their capacity and thus help to support themselves if they were permitted to do so. The driving of these persons into idleness will inflict definite and uncompensated damage upon the national dividend. Consequently, if damage is not to be done, it is essential that, in any law establishing a national minimum time-wage, provision shall be made for excepting from its operation would-be workers of the above type whom there is no serious prospect of rendering more efficient by training. But a satisfactory arrangement effecting this, which should not at the same time effect a number of other things that are not desired, is extremely difficult to devise. Until it is devised we may fairly conclude that the establishment of an effective national minimum time-wage (effective in the sense of being substantially above what a considerable number of people are earning now) is likely, on the whole, to damage rather than to benefit the national dividend. No doubt, in the absence of such a minimum a number of low-grade workers, particularly low-grade women workers with families, will be left in private industry with earnings insufficient to maintain a decent life. This evil, as will be urged with emphasis in Part V., it is imperative to remedy. But the cure for it consists, not in establishing a national minimum time-wage at a level that will drive low-grade women workers out of private industry altogether, but by the direct action of the State, in securing for all families of its citizens, with the help, if necessary, of State aid, an adequate minimum standard in every department of life.

CHAPTER XVIII

§ 1. WHEN in practice it is decided to interfere with wages in any industry, either because they are "unfair" or for any other reason, there is at once presented a new problem. Effective interference involves either the authoritative award of a new wage rate or encouragement to employers and employed to agree upon a new wage rate. Equally whether an award or an agreement is made, it would be ridiculous that the terms laid down should be fixed for ever. The industrial situation generally, no less than the circumstances of particular trades, is in a continuous state of flux. Every award and agreement, therefore, must be restricted, either explicitly or implicitly, to a short period of time. How short the period shall be before revision can be called for depends entirely upon the practical difficulties that revision would have to face. Apart from this, it would seem, on the face of things, that, since conditions may change fundamentally at any moment, revision should be permitted whenever either side desires it. In practice, however, considerations of convenience alone would make it imperative that some minimum interval should be provided for. But there are also other considerations. Except where the relations between employers and employed are exceptionally good, it is dangerous to reopen fundamental wage controversies more frequently than can be avoided. In view of this it often happens that the governing decisions are given a currency of not less than, say, two years from the date when they are launched. For the purpose of this discussion we will suppose that that practice is adopted

559

generally. It does not, however, follow from this that, whenever a governing award or agreement about wages is made, the rate must, thereafter, be fixed rigidly for at least two years. For it may be possible to devise methods by which the governing award or agreement shall provide for variation in wages in response to temporary changes of circumstances during the period that it covers. A choice, therefore, has to be made between a rigid arrangement and a plastic arrangement, and our investigation is not complete until the comparative effects of these have been ascertained.

§ 2. Let us postulate a trade in general equilibrium, which is neither expanding nor decaying on the whole, but in which the demand for labour—for the present we ignore fluctuations in the supply of labour—now falls below and now rises above its mean level. The argument of Chapters XIII. to XV. has shown that, allowance being made for certain obstacles and for possible reactions on efficiency, the wage rate that will most advantage the national dividend will be a rate that, taking one thing with another, is equal, over the period of the agreement or award, to the rate paid for similar work elsewhere. Ought this rate to be single and constant; or ought it to vary about a mean?

In the first place, let us consider a rise in the demand for labour. If a fixed wage system is adopted, this implies that the nominal rate remains unaltered. Hence, we should expect that the amount of labour provided will also be unaltered, and, consequently, that the aggregate amount of work done will be less than if the wage fluctuated. It must be remembered, indeed, that, though the wage per man remains the same, the wage per efficiency unit of labour is, in effect, raised for new employees. An adjustment is brought about, either by employers taking on inferior men at the wage formerly paid to good men only,[1] or by resort to overtime at special rates.

---

[1] It may be suggested that under a piecework system this device is impracticable, since a given wage bears the same relation to a given output, whoever the worker may be. But (1) equal pieces are not always of the same quality, and are not always obtained with the same amount of injury to the employer's property (e.g. in coal-mining, a ton of coal badly cut may damage the general conditions of the mine in the neighbourhood); and (2) even when two pieces are similar in all respects, one man, in finishing his, may occupy the fixed plant of his employer for a longer time than his neighbour.

In either event more is paid for the new labour units than for the old. It is conceivable, if the rise in demand is small, that the same addition is made to the aggregate amount of labour employed as would have been made had the general wage rate been raised in an equal proportion. The difference is that the employer, by fixing what practically amounts to two prices as between his new labour and his old, preserves for himself a sum of money, which, under a one-price system, would have been added to the remuneration of the latter. This result is best illustrated under the method of overtime. Suppose that the normal working day was six hours at sixpence per hour—sixpence being the equivalent payment for the disenjoyment caused to the workman by the sixth hour's work. Suppose, further, that the disenjoyment of an extra hour's equally efficient work, to a man who has already worked six hours and received three shillings pay, is measured by sevenpence. Then the employer can obtain seven hours' work from that man, either by raising the general rate per hour to sevenpence, or by paying the same as before for a six hours' day, and offering sevenpence for one hour of "overtime." The amount of work done is exactly the same on either plan; the only difference is that, if the former is adopted, the employer pays over to the workman an extra sixpence, which, under the latter, he retains for himself. This point is of some importance. As a general rule, however, particularly if the rise in demand is large, not all the extra labour that employers would like to have can be got by working overtime and taking on inferior men. Though, therefore, there will be some expansion in the dividend under the fixed wage plan, the expansion is not likely to be so big as it would be under the fluctuating plan.

In the second place, let us consider a fall in the demand for labour. If the wage rate remains at the old level, the quantity of labour which it will pay the employer to keep at work will be diminished. If the rate is lowered, it may still be diminished, but not in so high a degree. The point is well illustrated by a comparison, made shortly before the war in a Report of the British Board of

Trade, between conditions here and in Germany. "Trade Union standard rates of wages do not prevail in Germany to the same extent as in Great Britain. In consequence workpeople have greater liberty in accepting work at wages lower than those at which they have previously been employed, especially in bad times. A more speedy return to employment of some kind and a consequent reduction in the percentage of trade union members unemployed results from this."[1] The general result is that in bad times more work is done under the plastic than under the rigid form of wage system.

From a combination of these results it follows that, over good and bad times together, a wage system fluctuating on both sides of the mean level in accordance with temporary movements of the demand for labour means more work and, therefore, a larger national dividend than one permanently fixed at that level. This gain arises directly out of superior adjustment between demand and supply. It is the fruit of improved organisation, and is similar to the gain produced by improved machinery. It is not retained for long as an exclusive possession of the industry which first secures it, but is distributed over the community as a whole, with the result that a new general equilibrium is established somewhat more advantageous than the old. The interest of the national dividend thus requires that the wage should not stand at the mean level for periods as long as two years, but should undergo short-period oscillations about this level, in such wise as always to make the demand for labour and the supply of it equal.

§ 3. To this conclusion there is an objection, the limits of whose validity require careful investigation. It has been urged that fluctuations in the wages of individual workpeople tend indirectly to impair both their moral character and their economic efficiency. Thus, Professor Chapman writes: "It may be argued that there is far more chance of a somewhat steady wage, which varies infrequently and by small amounts only, contributing to build up a suitable and well-devised standard of life, than a wage given to sudden

---

[1] *Report on the Cost of Living in German Towns* [Cd. 4032], p. 521.

and considerable alterations."[1] If this is true, it follows that the direct advantages of a wage rate fluctuating with fluctuations of demand may be more than counteracted by indirect disadvantages. For, though the national dividend will, indeed, be enhanced for the moment, it may ultimately be diminished, in a more than corresponding degree, through the injury done to the quality of some of the nation's workers.

In examining this argument we at once observe that the term "wages" ought to be deleted in favour of the term "earnings." It is stability of earnings that enables a well-devised standard of life to be built up, and not stability of wages. Hence, if, for the moment, questions connected with distribution between different individuals are left out of account, we may put aside, as unaffected by Professor Chapman's argument, all occupations in which the earnings are not liable to be pushed to so low a point under a fluctuating wage as they are under a fixed wage. The occupations thus excluded comprise all those in which the elasticity of the demand for labour is greater than unity. It may, indeed, be objected that, though, in these occupations, the workpeople collectively earn more in bad times under the fluctuating system, yet the particular workpeople, who are so skilful as to command employment always, earn less, and that it is stability in *their* earnings rather than in those of others that is of especial importance. Since, however, these superior workpeople are presumably better off than their less skilful fellows, this latter statement is highly disputable. For there can be little doubt that fluctuations in the income of a poor man cause more suffering, and, hence, more loss of productive efficiency, than fluctuations of the same size in that of a rich man of similar temperament. Hence, the rejoinder fails, and it follows that, where the elasticity of the relevant part of the demand for labour is greater than unity, Professor Chapman's argument is of no force against a fluctuating wage.

In occupations where the demand, from a short-period point of view, is highly inelastic, the result may be different. In these conditions, the total earnings of the workpeople will

[1] *Economic Journal,* 1903, p. 194

touch a lower level in bad times under the fluctuating system. If it were the fact that in good times adequate provision were regularly made for bad times, the consequent evil effects on efficiency, and, therefore, on the national dividend, would not be great. But, as everybody knows, the ordinary workman does not " conform his expenditure and his savings to the standard wage, and regard what he sometimes gets above that standard as an insurance fund against what he will at other times get below it." [1] Hence, it is probable that there is a considerable net evil effect on efficiency. Against this, however, there has to be set the fact that, under a fixed wage, unless the demand is perfectly inelastic, the available employment in bad times will be smaller, and more workpeople are likely to be thrown out of work altogether. It is not, of course, certain that this will happen. In some industries, as was seen in Chapter X., a constriction of employment is met by short time all round instead of by a reduction in the numbers of the staff, and, in others, by a sharing of work more or less in rotation. But, in general, the actual number of unemployed persons in bad months will be greater under a fixed than under a fluctuating wage system; and the efficiency of totally unemployed persons is likely to suffer in a very special measure. Hence, even in occupations where the demand for labour is highly inelastic, so long as it is not absolutely inelastic, the evil effect on efficiency due to a fluctuating wage is matched by another due to a fixed one. This does not, of course, show that circumstances can never arise in which fluctuating wages are, on the whole, more injurious to efficiency, and so indirectly to the national dividend, than fixed wages. It does, however, throw the burden of proof upon those who maintain, in any particular instance, that such circumstances have arisen. For the two evils noted above are so vague and indefinite that it will often be practically impossible to weigh them against one another. In the absence of special detailed information our decision must then be based upon the one fact which is known,

---

[1] This is the advice given him by Smart, *Sliding Scales,* p. 13. It may be noted that the pawn-shop and the power to get credit afford, for short periods of unemployment, a partial, though probably an injurious, substitute for saving.

namely, that a wage fluctuating with fluctuations in the demand for labour has the better *direct* effect upon the national dividend. In general, therefore, the defence of a system of rigid wage rates examined in this section must be adjudged to have failed.

§ 4. The preceding analysis has reference only to fluctuations in the demand for labour in any industry. It is easily seen that analogous conclusions hold good as regards fluctuations in the supply of labour. No formal demonstration of this seems to be necessary.

§ 5. These results carry with them the implication that, if economic considerations alone are taken into account, the wage level ought to fluctuate from moment to moment, never remaining the same over a period of more than infinitesimal duration. For, even though changes in the conditions of demand or supply occur only at intervals, yet, in strictness, the wage appropriate to any given change varies in accordance with the period which has elapsed since the change occurred. It is, in short, a function of the time since which, as well as of the amount by which, demand or supply has oscillated.

This point is brought out very clearly when attention is directed to the reactions on the side of supply induced by oscillations of demand. A diminished wage in any occupation will command a smaller number of labour units per week after a little than it does at first, because men will gradually seek and find work elsewhere. Similarly, an increased wage will command more labour units when time has been allowed for new men to come into the trade, and when, therefore, labour units can be furnished by them as well as by the overtime exertions of the "old gang." Hence, the only correct adjustment to a given oscillation of demand would consist in a movement of wages most considerable at first, and, thereafter, gradually falling back towards its old level.

When it is supply that oscillates, similar considerations apply to the reactions upon demand. So soon as we take account of the element of time, it becomes necessary to allow for the working of the law of substitution. If the price of one factor of production, labour, is raised, the amount of it demanded gradually diminishes with the growth in the employment: of other factors—whether different kinds of labour or mechanical tools—in its stead. In like manner, if the price of one factor is lowered, the amount of it demanded gradually increases as it is introduced into uses to which it could not, hitherto, be profitably put. Hence, the only correct adjustment to a given oscillation of supply would consist of a wage at first abruptly altered and then slowly moving back towards its previous amount.

Thus, it appears that, whenever the unit of time over which wage adjustments are made is of more than infinitesimal length, there is a failure to reach the position most advantageous to the national dividend. This circumstance is, however, for several reasons, inadequate to justify a perpetually fluctuating wage. For to the establishment of such a wage there are insuperable practical obstacles. Time is required for the collection and arrangement of the statistics upon which the changes must be based. Considerations of book-keeping and ordinary business convenience come upon the stage, and fix a lower limit, beyond which the interval between successive adjustments must not be reduced. Of course, this limit is not always the same. In a small local industry, for example, it will probably be lower that in a great national one. But in every industry it must lie considerably above the infinitesimal level which pure theory recommends. So far as it is possible to judge from the practice of those industries in which the interval is determined, as under a sliding scale, by considerations of convenience alone, it seems as though this interval should not be less than two or three months.[1]

§ 6. Having thus satisfied ourselves that the interest of the national dividend requires a wage system fluctuating within the normal period of agreement or award, and having determined the intervals that should elapse between successive fluctuations, we have now to discover on what plan the fluctuations themselves should be organised. A preliminary solution of this problem can be given in the form of six fundamental propositions. The first of these is that, *when a given fluctuation occurs in the demand schedule for labour in any occupation, the wage fluctuation, which is required to*

---

[1] Cf. for illustrations, L. L. Price, *Industrial Peace*, p. 80.

*equate demand and supply, and which, therefore, in accordance
with our principle, ought to· be introduced, will be smaller the
more elastic, from the standpoint of a short period, is the supply
of labour in that occupation.* This proposition, when set out
in diagrammatic form, is self-evident. It is readily applied
to practice. The supply of labour is elastic in occupations so
situated that a small change in the wage rate offered in them
suffices to divert a considerable quantity of labour between them
and other occupations. In general, therefore, the following
results hold good. First, when, as with the Scottish shale
and coal-miners,[1] a small industry is neighbour to a kindred
and very large one, the wage change corresponding to a given
oscillation of demand should be less than in an isolated industry.
Secondly, a set of circumstances, which would justify a given
change in the wages of workmen specialised to a particular
industry or locality, would justify a smaller change in those
of labourers, whose lack of skill, or managers, the general
character of whose skill, renders them more mobile.[2] Thirdly,
among workmen trained to a particular job, the wage fluctuations corresponding to given changes in the demand of one
industry employing them should be smaller when there are
other industries in which their services are required. Thus, in
a boom or depression in the coal trade, the wages of mechanics
employed in the mines should fluctuate less than those of
hewers. Fourthly, when wages are paid by the piece, the
percentage fluctuation corresponding to a given fluctuation in
demand should be smaller than when they are paid by the
time. For, since, under the latter system, a rise of pay has

---

[1] Cf. Sheriff Jameson's award in a shale-miners' arbitration (*Economic
Journal*, 1904, p. 309).

[2] When specialisation, either to trade or place, is very high, the labour
supply will, for considerable variations of wage, remain practically constant.
The workman may know that his skill is useless in other districts or occupations,
and may, therefore, be driven to accept a great drop in wages before leaving.
Nor (except for navvies and other labourers the muscular character of whose
work makes it specially dependent upon their nourishment) need his efficiency
suffer appreciably. Thus, the supply may be perfectly inelastic. It may also
be inelastic on account of conservative feeling among the workers affected. For
example, Dr. Clapham writes of the decline of the hand-loom industry: "The
independence and professional pride of the old race of weavers made them hate
the thought of the factory, and stick to their home work with a tenacity that,
in the long run, did them no good" (*Bradford Textile Society*, June 1905, p. 43).

not the same effect in inducing workmen to pack more labour into an hour, the elasticity of the supply of efficiency units is lower. Fifthly, any general change, such as the spread of information, improvements in communication, or an increased willingness on the part of workpeople to work at a distance from their homes, will tend to increase the elasticity of the labour supply and so to diminish the wage change appropriate to any given fluctuation of demand. Lastly, in industries subject to regular seasonal fluctuations, many of the workpeople will have prepared themselves for their slack periods by acquiring some form of skill for which the demand at these times is apt to increase. Hence, within the normal limits of seasonal fluctuations, the supply of labour will be fairly elastic, and, therefore, seasonal demand changes should not seriously alter wages. Thus, despite the great fluctuations in the demand for gas stokers in summer and winter, wages do not fluctuate much, because these workers are often also employed in making bricks, the demand for which expands in the summer.

§ 7. So far of the general problem. We have still to inquire whether the wage fluctuation that corresponds to a given change in labour demand is related to it in the same way, whatever the direction and magnitude of this latter change may be. The answer must be in the negative, since the supply of labour will not have the same elasticity for all amounts. We may, indeed, presume that the elasticity will not vary greatly for changes in demand fairly near to the mean. The entrance and the exit to most trades are about equally open. In the North of England mining districts, for example, " the migratory miners include a large number of skilled mechanics, who divide their time between mining and their other handicraft according as either industry offers a better chance of profit." [1] A moderate upward movement in demand should, therefore, in general be met by about the same percentage of wage change as an equal downward movement. But for large upward and downward movements this symmetry no longer obtains. When the labour demand falls considerably, there is a limit beyond which the wage cannot be reduced without reducing the available amount of the labour in question to zero. This limit will be determined, for unskilled men, by the conditions of life in the workhouse, and, for skilled men, by what they can earn in unskilled occupations. Thus, if the labour demand has fallen in more than a moderate degree, a further fall should be accompanied by a less than proportionate fall, and eventually by no fall, in wage. These considerations justify the establishment, in connection with sliding scales alike for skilled and unskilled work, of a minimum wage uncompensated by any corresponding maximum. On the other hand, when the labour demand rises considerably, the effect upon unskilled wages should be proportionate to that produced when it rises a little. For skilled labour the percentage of wage increase should be even greater. For, while the power of those already in a trade to work extra hours, and the probable presence of a floating body of unemployed, will enable a moderate addition to the labour supply to be made fairly easily, these resources will be ineffective when a large addition is required. This consideration affords an argument in favour of the device of the "double-jump" after a certain point has been reached, which found a place in a former scale in the South Wales coal industry and also in certain English sliding scales.

§ 8. The second fundamental proposition is that, *when a given fluctuation occurs in the supply schedule for labour in any occupation, the wage fluctuation which is required to equate demand and supply, and which, therefore, in accordance with our principle, ought to be introduced, will be smaller the more elastic, from the standpoint of a short period, is the demand for labour in that occupation.* This proposition, like the preceding, is self-evident so soon as it is set out in diagrammatic form. In order that it may be fruitful of practical application, the principal factors on which the elasticity of the demand for labour in different occupations depends must be kept in view. It will be more convenient to examine them in Chapter V. of Part V. There remains, as in the preceding discussion of supply conditions, the minor question whether the labour demand is equally elastic for all quantities demanded. The answer is that it is likely to be least elastic when un-

usually small or unusually large amounts of labour are being
employed. If the number of workmen is reduced below a
certain minimum, there is a danger of organisation deteriorating,
or machinery being spoilt, or the place of work injured. This
point is important in the industry of iron-smelting, for, if
a blast-furnace is once allowed to go out, heavy expense is
involved in relighting it. It is important, again, in industries
that employ a large quantity of delicate machinery. Thus,
Mr. Brooks writes: "A very large proportion of capitalistic
investment is now embodied in machinery of the most delicate
and costly character. When the complex enginery is once
started, it has to be 'tended' precisely as if it were the most
frail human life or plant. It is as safe to shut up and
desert a hothouse of dainty flowers as to close up and desert
modern machinery. Every hostile element attacks it as if
bent on instant destruction."[1] Again, of coal-mining it has
been said: "So much loss and damage are incurred, or at all
events risked, by the shutting down of pits otherwise healthy,
that a coalowner will rather go on year after year working
at a loss than shut down at what may be a much greater
loss."[2] Finally, in some instances, considerations akin to the
above hold good about the more specialised part of the labour
staff; for, if the staff is once broken up, it may prove very
difficult to reconstitute it. For this reason, if the number of
workmen is reduced below a certain minimum, the relevant
demand on the part of employers is apt to be exceedingly inelastic. In like manner, if the number of workmen is
increased beyond a certain maximum, physical difficulties will
be encountered in mere lack of floor-space and will make the
employers' demand for further labour highly inelastic. Hence,
other things being equal, a considerable oscillation, either up
or down, in the supply schedule for labour should lead to a
change in wage rate more than proportionate to that which
is proper when a moderate oscillation takes place.

§ 9. The third and fourth fundamental propositions are
respectively as follows: First, *other things being equal, the
more elastic the demand for labour in any industry, the larger*

---

[1] *The Social Unrest*, p. 188.
[2] *Economist*, 25th October 1902, p. 1639.

is the wage change appropriate to any given oscillation of demand. Secondly, *other things being equal, the more elastic the supply of labour in any industry, the larger is the wage change appropriate to any given oscillation of supply.* These propositions again are self-evident when expressed diagrammatically. Their practical implications can readily be worked out in the light of what has already been said about the circumstances on which the elasticities of demand and of supply depend.

§ 10. The fifth fundamental proposition is that, *when the short-period elasticities of the demand and supply of labour in any occupation are given, the wage fluctuation appropriate to any given fluctuation of the demand schedule is larger the larger is the fluctuation of that schedule.* This proposition again is self-evident. In order that it may be fruitful in practice the principal factors upon which the magnitude of demand fluctuations depends must be described. These fall into two divisions: (1) movements in the employers' demand schedule for the commodity, which the labour we are interested in is helping to produce; and (2) movements in the supply schedule of the other factors that co-operate in production with that labour. These two sets of influences will now be reviewed.

§ 11. Movements in the employers' demand for the commodity the labour is helping to make are derived directly from movements in the public demand for the commodity. The liability to oscillation of that demand is, of course, different for different classes of commodities. The most obvious distinction is between articles which are desired for immediate personal use " for their own sake " and articles which are desired largely as means to distinction through display. The demand for articles of the former sort is likely to be the more stable, because, as Jevons suggests, people's desire for them is generally steady for a longer period. For example, we may notice the stability of the pinafore industry: "No clothing trade (in Birmingham) suffers so little from short time."[1] On the other hand, commodities that are largely display articles are liable to fluctuations of desire, as opinion transfers the

[1] Cadbury, *Women's Work and Wages*, p. 93.

distinction-bearing quality from one thing to another. Thus, the demand would seem to be less variable for common objects of wide consumption than for luxuries. To these special considerations should be added the more general one, that an industry which supplies a wide market made up of many independent parts is likely to enjoy a steadier demand than one which supplies a narrow market. This is merely a particular application of the broad proposition familiar to statisticians, that "the precision of an average is proportionate to the square root of the number of terms it contains."[1] It is well illustrated by the interesting study of M. Lazard on *Le Chômage et la profession*. Using figures from the French census of 1901, he takes the percentages of unemployment there recorded in a number of industries, and sets them alongside of the average number of men (*moyen effectif*) per establishment in the several industries, and finds, on a method of his own, an inverse correlation. Connecting large unemployment with variable demand, he explains this correlation by the relation, which he believes to subsist, between a large *moyen effectif* and *l'extension des debouchés commerciaux*. "The connection between this latter phenomenon and the size of the personnel is evident. Large establishments exist only when the markets to be served are considerable. Now, a large market must also be a relatively stable market, because in it considerable decreases in the consumption of some customers have a chance of being balanced by increases in the consumption of others; and this stability, implying, as it does, stability of production, implies at the same time the absence or, at all events, a diminution of unemployment."[2] In like manner, he argues: "If unemployment seems to grow as we pass upward from primary towards finishing industries, this circumstance is

[1] Bowley, *Elements of Statistics*, p. 305.

[2] *Le Chômage et la profession*, pp. 336-7. M. Lazard adds: "A ce premier avantage, propre aux grandes entreprises, du fait de leur organisation commerciale, il s'en ajoute d'autres, résultant du mécanisme de la production. Lorsque la direction de l'industrie est concentrée dans un petit nombre de mains, les chefs d'entreprises connaissent le marché qu'ils fournissent mieux que ne font, dans leurs sphères respectives, les petits ou moyens entrepreneurs des autres branches industrielles. Sachant sur quelle consommation ils peuvent compter, ils règlent leur production en conséquence. . . . Notre hypothèse demanderait d'ailleurs à être vérifiée, car plus d'une industrie fait apparemment exception à la règle indiquée; on remarque, par exemple, que l'agriculture,

explained by the fact that the industries at the top of the scale, being more specialised, have narrower markets. On the other hand, the industries that deal with raw products provide the material needed by numerous other industries, and, therefore, enjoy the advantages which a multitude of outlets confer."[1] The same principle may, of course, be invoked to explain the stability of the demand for railway transportation as compared with the demand even for such things as coal, sugar or iron. In like manner, an industry which sells largely in foreign markets as well as in the home market is likely, other things equal, to have a more stable demand than one which sells in the home market only—except, indeed, when it is disturbed by changes in the rate of duty imposed on its products by an important foreign customer.

§ 12. When the oscillations of the public demand for any commodity are given, it is natural to suppose that the oscillations of the employers' demand for it will be exactly equivalent to them. As a fact, however, the employers' demand usually oscillates through the smaller distance of the two. The reason for this is the common practice of making for stock. In bad months the employer is glad to acquire and warehouse more goods than he wishes, for the moment, to sell, while in good months, because he has these goods to fall back upon, his demand for new ones rises less for them than that of the public whom he supplies. His demand this month is, in short, derived from the anticipated public demand of a considerably longer period, thus divesting itself to some extent of temporary oscillations. Naturally the extent to which making for stock takes place is different in different industries. The practice is less attractive to employers, the greater is the cost of carrying a unit of the commodity affected from one point of time to another. This cost depends, of course, in part, upon a circumstance affecting all commodities equally, namely, the

---

l'industrie humaine par excellence, est assez épargnée par le chômage, bien que l'effectif moyen des établissements y soit très réduit. Il semble que l'on puisse attribuer cet état de choses au fait que les débouchés sont plus stables dans l'agriculture que dans l'industrie proprement dite ; en outre, le nombre des entreprises agricoles est naturellement limité par l'inextensibilité de la surface cultivée" (*ibid.* pp. 337-8).

[1] *Le Chômage et la profession,* p. 337.

rate of interest. For all carriage through time implies a loss of interest through holding commodities unsold. It also depends upon a number of circumstances which differ for different commodities. Of these the most obvious is the expense of storage. One important determinant of this expense is the resistance that the commodity makes to *physical* wear and tear in transit across time, or, more broadly, its durability, in respect both of decay and of accidental breakage. In this quality the precious metals and hard materials, like timber, are specially favoured. As we should expect, things that are extracted from the earth are, in general, more durable than things that are grown on it. It is interesting to note that, in recent times, the development of refrigerating and other preserving processes has rendered a number of commodities, chiefly articles of food, much more durable than they used to be. The Committee on Hops, for instance, wrote in 1908: "At the time of the previous inquiry in the year 1856, attention was called to the fact that 'the deterioration which hops suffer when kept prevents the superabundance of one year from adequately supplying the deficiencies of another.' The advent of cold storage has effected an adjustment between years of plethora and years of scarcity, with the resultant effect upon prices." [1] It may be added that such things as the direct services rendered by missionaries, doctors, teachers, train-drivers and cab-drivers are wholly incapable, and such things as gas and electricity are in great measure incapable, of being stored. A second important determinant of the expense of storage is the resistance that the commodity makes to *psychical* wear and tear in transit across time, or, more broadly, its steadiness of value. The contrast I have in view is between staple goods of steady demand—Charles Booth once cited philosophic and optical instruments as instances of this class of goods [2]—and fashion goods of unsteady demand. Clearly, there is a higher cost of carriage and less inducement towards storage for a commodity which, next week, nobody may want, than there is for one for which a constant market is assured. Thus, the turned and pressed parts of bicycles, which are much the same what-

---

[1] *Report*, p. x.   [2] *Industry*, v. p. 253.

ever type of frame is in vogue, are largely made for stock, whereas this is not done with completed bicycles, the form of which is liable to fashion changes. An extreme instance of unfitness for stock-making is afforded by commodities, such as ball-dresses, which every purchaser will wish to have constructed to her own special order, and which, when "ready-made," have practically no appeal for her. It is possible that things at one time customarily made to individual order may, subsequently, become more generalised; and *vice versa*. Houses are sometimes built to the order of would-be private owners, and sometimes as a speculation. The boot industry has developed from an earlier stage, in which the individual order method predominated, to the present condition, in which most boots are ready-made. In certain textiles, on the other hand, there is evidence of a movement in the opposite direction. A recent Report on unemployment in Philadelphia observes: "Twenty years ago a manufacturer made carpet or hosiery or cloth and then went out and sold *that* carpet or hosiery or cloth. To-day the order comes in for a particular design, with a certain kind of yarn or silk and a certain number of threads to the inch, and the manufacturer makes that particular order. Formerly a manufacturer produced standard makes of his particular line, and simply piled up stock in his warehouse in the off-season. . . . To-day manufacturers make, as a rule, very little to stock and run chiefly on orders."[1] It is evident that every development towards the standardisation of products renders making for stock more practicable, while every development away from standardisation renders it more difficult.

§ 13. There is another point to be made in this connection. Granted that the practice of making for stock causes the oscillations of employers' demand for any commodity to be less than the associated fluctuations in the public demand, it might be thought by the hasty reader that the relation between these two oscillations can be expressed by a constant fraction, different in different industries, but the same in any one industry whatever the size of the oscillation. This is a

---

[1] "Steadying Employment," *Annals of the American Academy of Political Science*, May 1916, pp. 6-7.

mistake. If, in response to a given percentage elevation or depression of the public demand, the employers' demand is elevated or depressed through a percentage five-sixths as great, it is not to be expected that the same proportion will hold good for larger changes of public demand. As a rule, making for stock is carried up to a certain point for a small inducement, and, after that, is extended only with great reluctance. Hence, the public demand is apt to undergo slight oscillations without producing on the employers' demand any appreciable effect. But, after a point is passed, further oscillations in it tend to be accompanied by further oscillations in employers' demand, the magnitude of which rapidly approaches towards equality with theirs. These considerations justify the provision, which is found in most sliding scales, that alterations in the price of the commodity must exceed some definite amount before any alteration takes place in wages.[1] They also serve as a ground for the rule, which in practice is universal, that, when wages are conjoined to prices under a sliding scale, the percentage change in wages shall be smaller than the percentage price change to which it corresponds.[2]

§ 14. Let us now turn to the second determinant of fluctuations in the demand for labour in any occupation, which was distinguished in § 10. Among the co-operant agents whose supply schedule is liable to move the most obvious are the raw materials used in the occupation. In extractive industries, such as coal-mining, these do not play any significant part; but in the majority of industries they are very important. In accordance with what was said in § 11, it is evident that, when they are obtained from a large number of independent sources, the oscillations of supply are likely to be less than when reliance has to be placed on a single source. For this reason the imposition of high protective duties upon any material, with a view to ousting foreign sellers, may be expected to bring about increased fluctuations. In addition to raw materials, the co-operant agents include the services of auxiliary labour and the services of machines. Mechanical improvements, for example, involve, in effect, a lowering of

[1] Cf. Price, *Industrial Peace*, p. 97.
[2] Cf. Marshall, *Economics of Industry*, p. 381 n.

the supply schedule of the services rendered by capital invested in the occupation that is affected by them. Moreover, in some industries, Nature herself, as represented by the light and heat received from the sun, is a very important cooperant factor in production. Thus, there is a high degree of seasonal variability in the demand for labour in the building trades, because the advent of frost in winter seriously interferes with brick-laying, masonry and plastering, while the shortening of the hours of daylight, by necessitating resort to artificial illumination, adds to the costs and further handicaps such work. No doubt, recent developments, such as the substitution of cement for mortar, are doing something to lessen the influence of climatic changes upon this industry,[1] but their influence is still very important. The same remark applies to the industry of discharging cargoes at the London Docks, which is liable to serious interruptions by frost and fog. On the other hand, indoor trades and trades little dependent on weather conditions, such as engineering and shipbuilding—dress-making is obviously not relevant here—display a relatively small amount of seasonal variability. Thus, according to a study by Sir H. Llewellyn Smith extended over some years, the mean difference in the percentage of unemployment between the best month and the worst month was $3\frac{1}{4}$ per cent in the building trades and only $1\frac{1}{3}$ per cent in the engineering and shipbuilding trades.[2]

§ 15. The sixth and last fundamental proposition is that, *when the short-period elasticities of the demand and supply of labour in any occupation are given, the wage fluctuation appropriate to any given oscillation of the supply schedule is larger, the larger is the oscillation of that schedule.* Like all the rest, this proposition also is self-evident. The oscillations to which it refers will, as a rule, be caused by temporary expansions or contractions of neighbouring or kindred industries. A depression, for example, in the contiguous agricultural districts, or in the Northumberland mines, necessarily increases the number of men on the look-out for employment in the Durham mines. The extent of the oscillations caused in this

---

[1] Cf. Dearle, *Economic Journal*, 1908, p. 103.
[2] Cf. *Committee on Distress from Want of Employment*, Q. 4580.

way can be roughly inferred from the wage movement which has occurred in those allied industries. Some guidance on the matter can also be obtained from the figures for unemployment in the industry with which we are primarily concerned.

§ 16. In the light of this general analysis, we have now to inquire how far it is possible to provide, in the terms of a governing award or agreement, automatic machinery for adjusting the wage rate to changes in conditions occurring within the period covered by it. The best-known instrument intended for this purpose is a sliding scale connecting the wage rate of an industry with the price of its finished product. This instrument makes no attempt to take account of fluctuations in the supply of labour, and is, therefore, limited in range. It is, nevertheless, very important. *Other things being equal*, changes in price serve as an index of changes in the demand schedule for labour, and, with sufficient knowledge, it would be possible so to frame a scale that under it exactly the right wage movement would come about in reference to any given movement in this demand schedule.

§ 17. The prices made use of may be "average," "typical," "realised," "quoted," or "newspaper" prices of the commodity concerned, or even of some different commodity, in which it forms an important ingredient.[1] "Newspaper" prices are rightly suspect, since they are apt to be collected on a different basis on different occasions. "Quoted" prices are doubtful, since the freaks of speculation "on Change," which help to mould them, scarcely have time to eliminate one another during the short periods intervening between successive adjustments.[2] Prices realised by a single typical firm may be influenced sporadically by fluctuations in managing ability, good fortune, and so forth. But, when the firms of whose prices account is taken are fairly numerous, inconstant causes of this kind are likely to be eliminated; for an exceptional increase of competence in some managers will

---

[1] *e.g.* the Cleveland iron-stone workers' wages are determined by a scale based upon fluctuations in No. 3, Cleveland pig-iron (Price, *Industrial Peace*, p. 90).

[2] Nevertheless, the West Cumberland pig-iron industry bases its scale on the prices declared on the Glasgow Exchange (Jeans, *Conciliation and Arbitration*, p. 79).

probably be balanced by a corresponding decrease in others.[1]
The consensus of practice in taking the average realised price
of a good number of firms appears, therefore, to be justified
by theory.

§ 18. The same remark applies to the practice, embodied
in all sliding scales, of making wage changes depend, not upon
contemporaneous, but upon antecedent price changes. For the
connection between the employers' and the public's demand
for any commodity always bridges an appreciable interval.
Oscillations in the employers' demand lag behind the primary
oscillations to which they correspond. It is generally only after
prices have remained up for some little while that employers
think seriously of expanding their business, and they hesitate in
a similar manner about reducing production when a depression
sets in. Their demand for labour at any time is thus derived
from the public demand for the commodity which existed at
an earlier time. It follows that the supposed defect in sliding
scales, that they fix *future* wages by *past* prices,[2] is really an
advantage. It is, indeed, sometimes objected that an intelligent anticipation of events before they occur is coming to
influence more and more the conduct of industrial concerns;
and that, so far as this tendency prevails, the adequacy of past
prices as an index of future demand necessarily diminishes.
"Why, then, should wages automatically fall when the leaders
of industry have cast their eyes over the future, and pro-
claimed the need of an enlarged output and more hands? Or
why should wages rise when employers see that good trade is
behind, and are preparing for a period of marking time?"[3]
The answer to this argument is found in a closer analysis of

---

[1] In view, presumably, of considerations of this kind, the renovated
Staffordshire sliding scale in 1888 was established, not on the old basis of
a single brand of Lord Dudley's coal, but "upon the average selling price
of all qualities of coal throughout the district." (Labour Commission, "Digest ·
of Evidence," p. 95.) When, however, an industry is dominated by a combine,
the divergence between the qualities of the men at the head at one time and at
another cannot be eliminated by any process of averaging. It is difficult
in that event to see how those fluctuations of fortune, which are due to fluctuations of managing ability, can be distinguished in practice from those due to
general causes.

[2] Cf. Ashley, *Adjustment of Wages*, pp. 56-7.

[3] Chapman, "Some Theoretical Objections to Sliding Scales," *Economic
Journal*, 1903, p. 188.

the phrase "public demand." In the present connection it signifies the demand, not of the ultimate consumers, but of those intermediate dealers who buy from the manufacturers, and whose operations are the proximate cause of changes in wholesale prices. Where such persons are present, it is extremely improbable that prices will fall when the anticipation of the leaders of industry are roseate, or rise when they are gloomy. For these anticipations will generally be shared by the dealers, and, if so, will be reflected in their present demand and, hence, in present prices. The foregoing objection is, therefore, only relevant on occasions when the forecasts of manufacturers and of dealers are at variance. Since, however, the former forecasts are, in the main, based upon the latter, these occasions will be exceedingly rare.

§ 19. At this point it is necessary to revert to the condition *other things being equal*, which has underlain the whole of the reasoning of the two last sections. In real life other things are often not equal. For the present we are not concerned with the assumption of stable conditions in the supply of the labour whose rate of wages is directly in question. Apart from that, "other things" embrace all the remaining factors which are required in the manufacture of the commodity. These are raw material, the services of auxiliary workpeople and the services of machinery. We have now to take account of possible changes in the circumstances attending the supply of these things. It is evident that a given oscillation in one direction of the supply schedule of any one of them causes the employers' demand for the labour, whose wages we are considering, to oscillate in exactly the same manner as an equal oscillation in the opposite direction in his demand schedule for the finished commodity. Hence, in order to infer the oscillations in labour demand from those in the employers' commodity demand, we need to subtract from the latter whatever oscillations occur in the supply schedules of the other factors of production. It is true that no provision has to be made for corrections under this head (1) when the supply schedules of the other factors are certain not to oscillate, and (2) when the part they play in the cost of the commodity is so small that their oscillations can be neglected.

without serious inaccuracy. It is not easy to imagine an industry in which the former of these conditions could be postulated; but the latter holds good in extractive industries, such as coal-mining, where nearly the whole cost of production is labour cost. Except in these industries the index afforded by price changes is seriously defective. A fall in price will occur in consequence of a fall in the demand for the commodity, and also in consequence of a *cheapening* in the supply of the raw material. Thus, there are two routes connecting changes in price with changes in labour demand. A price movement caused in one way indicates a fall; caused in another way, a rise. If, for example, the price of iron goes up on account of an increase in the public need for iron, there is a rise in the demand for iron-workers' services; if, however, it goes up because a strike in the coal trade has rendered one of the constituents used in making it more expensive, there is a fall in this demand. It is obvious that, in the latter event, wages ought not to follow prices, but should move in the opposite direction.

§ 20. As a way of escape from these difficulties, it is sometimes proposed that the index should be, not the price of the finished commodity, but the margin between its price and that of the raw material used in making it. "Margins" are utilised with apparent success by the officials of the Cotton Workers' Union, who obtain them by "subtracting the price of raw cotton (calculated from the five leading sorts) from the price of yarn (of eleven kinds) or of calico (of twenty-three kinds),"[1] and order their wage negotiations accordingly. This index has the advantage of moving in the same way in response to a fall in the demand for the commodity and to an increase in the expense of obtaining raw material. The solution it affords is not, however, perfect. Among the contributory factors to the production of the finished article raw material is only one. The conditions of supply of auxiliary labour and of the services of machines are also liable to vary, but their variations are not reflected in any change in the "margin." Mechanical improvements, for example, mean, in effect, a cheapening of the help rendered by machines. When such improvements

---

[1] Schultze-Gaevernitz, *Social Peace*, p. 160.

are occurring, margins are liable to mislead in the same
manner as, though in a less degree than, crude price statistics.
Furthermore, margins, equally with prices, and, because prices
enter into their construction, are subject to a serious practical
inconvenience. They are not likely to afford a good index in
industries where the general level of elaborateness and so forth
in the goods produced is liable to vary. In these industries
an apparent change in price may really indicate nothing more
than a change in the kind of article manufactured. This difficulty is specially likely to occur when prices are deduced from
the quantities and values of exports, since there is reason to
expect that the cheaper varieties of goods will gradually
yield place in foreign trade to the finer and more valuable
varieties.

§ 21. These considerations suggest that a still better index
is afforded by output or profits. Since these indices take
account of factors which margins ignore, a plea for a reduction
of wages based upon a fall in the margin can always be met
by a proof that the output or profit of the industry, or of the
representative firm in it, has increased. There are, however,
obstacles in the way of both the above indices. The employment of output is rendered difficult by considerations affecting
the element of time. As has already been observed, a given
change in labour demand is generally correlated with a change
in public demand occurring previously. This change in public
demand is, in turn, correlated with a contemporaneous change
in prices, margins and profits (in the sense of net receipts).
Therefore, changes in any of these indices, determined on the
record of the past two or three months, may fairly be used as
data for wage changes in the next two or three. A change
in the output, however, consequent upon an oscillation of
public demand, occurs, not contemporaneously with, but subsequently to, this oscillation—at the same time, in fact, as the
change in labour demand itself. Therefore, since statistics
take some time to collect, output is necessarily a very inconvenient index. In like manner, it appears, from the report of
the negotiations for conciliation in the cotton trade in 1900,
that there are very great practical difficulties, at all events in
that trade, in arriving at a satisfactory estimate of "repre-

sentative profits."[1] One obvious difficulty, for example, is the reckoning, that ought to be taken, of firms which have failed altogether. The net result of these considerations is that attention should, when practicable, be directed, not to one, but to all of the available indices, and that these should be employed mutually to check one another.

§ 22. At this point it is necessary to advert to a fundamental objection, which, if it holds at all, applies equally to the employment of all of the indices of demand change discussed in the preceding sections, though in practice it is generally urged only against regular sliding scales based upon prices. This objection is, in essence, that either party can, if it chooses, "rig" the index.

On the side of the workpeople it is often urged that a scale tempts employers to cut prices in the hope of recouping themselves out of the pockets of their employees. This argument is, in the first place, invalid generally, whether employers are combined or not, since under no practicable form of scale would the gain on reduced wages equal the loss on reduced price. Secondly, in trades comprising large numbers of competing employers, it is doubly invalid, since the effect on the index brought about by the action of any one firm must be negligibly small. Of course, it is conceivable that, if the index were obtained from the sales of a "typical firm," other firms might combine to bribe it into selling below the market rate. This rather "academic" danger can, however, easily be met by an enlargement of the basis upon which the index rests.

On the side of the employers it may be argued that the workpeople under a scale are tempted to work slackly or to adopt a policy of stop-days, in order to make prices rise, and so, for the moment, to benefit themselves. This form of argument is invalid unless the men are rigidly combined. For to act

---

[1] Mr. L. L. Price, in discussing these negotiations, speaks of a "profits" scale in the cotton trade as a "closer approach to the conception of profit-sharing than that made by the usual type of sliding scale" (*Economic Journal*, 1901, p. 244). This view appears to be erroneous, so long as the "profits" of the *representative firm* are taken as the index. Of course a system which should make the wage paid by individual firms fluctuate with their own particular "profits" would be an entirely different thing.

in the way suggested would not be to the direct advantage
of any one man, since his effect upon output would be
negligible, and he would lose, under piece wages in pay, and
under time wages in prospects of employment. In a rigid
combination the danger contemplated is real. The stimulus
to monopolistic action is, however, no greater when wages
are arranged with the help of an index than when they are
arranged otherwise. On the contrary, if anything, the danger
is diminished, since the adoption of "ca' canny" devices
would be exceedingly likely to lead to a rupture of the
industrial agreement, by the maintenance of which the men
are presumably benefited.

§ 23. The preceding discussion, while it has revealed explicitly or implicitly many difficulties in the way of constructing
an effective sliding scale; has, nevertheless, made it plain that
scales adequate to take account of all changes in the demand
schedule for labour are theoretically possible. In favourable
circumstances, when, for example, as in coal-mines, labour is
by far the most important element in the cost of production,
there is no reason why a fairly close approach to the theoretical ideal should not be made. Obviously, when this can
be done, an award embodying a scale is much superior to one
embodying a single fixed wage for the whole period covered
by it. But, while this is so, we have to recognise the very
serious disability from which even a perfectly constructed scale
must suffer. A given rise or fall in the price of the commodity covered by it may be brought about either by a
change in the real demand for the commodity or by an
expansion or contraction of money or credit, which affects
the general level of money prices but leaves real conditions
substantially unaltered. It is plain that, if the price of coal
goes up, say 50 per cent, as a part of a general 50 per
cent rise due to a purely monetary cause, the proper response
in the wages of coal-miners is a 50 per cent rise. But, if
the price of coal goes up 50 per cent in consequence of an
increase in the real demand for coal, the proper response,
as indicated in § 13, will be a rise of considerably less than
50 per cent. It follows that any scale, which provides for
the right adjustment of wages when the price of coal changes

from a cause special to itself, must provide a wrong adjustment when it changes from a general monetary cause. Something might be done to remedy this defect by making wage changes depend *both* on changes in the price of coal *and* on changes in general prices. Thus, there might be a scale of the type described in previous sections, but referred not to absolute changes in coal prices, but to differences between the changes in coal prices and in general prices; and, superimposed upon this, there might be a second scale making wages vary in the same proportion as general prices. Thus, if coal rose 50 per cent while general prices rose 20 per cent, wages should rise 20 per cent *plus* whatever fraction of 30 per cent (the rise peculiar to coal) the special coal scale might decree. This arrangement, however, though it would work satisfactorily when changes in general prices were due to monetary or credit causes, would not, as was shown in Chapter XV. § 4, give a right result when these changes were due wholly or in part to such causes as the destruction of capital in war, bad harvests, general improvements in transport methods, and so on.

§ 24. There is yet another disability, even less open to remedy, from which sliding scales necessarily suffer. As was indicated in § 16, they cannot from their nature recognise or in any way allow for alterations of the supply of labour in the industry to which they refer. In the course of this chapter, however, it has been made abundantly clear that, for complete adjustment, notice must be taken of these alterations equally with alterations of demand. The necessary failure of scales to do this has sometimes led to results so plainly unreasonable that it has been necessary for one party to a scale agreement voluntarily to concede to the other terms more favourable than those which the scale decreed.

§ 25. From these considerations it appears that, though we may expect from scale awards better adjustments than could be got from wage awards covering fixed periods of equal length, better adjustments still will be obtained if the relations between employers and employed are good enough to allow the two-monthly or quarterly variations of the wage rate, which take place during the currency of the governing agree-

ment or award, to be based, not exclusively upon the variations of price or some other mechanical index, but also upon
any other relevant considerations that may present themselves.
There are several examples of this type of settlement. In
the Scottish coal agreement of 1902, the relevant portion of
which remained unchanged till 1907, it was provided " that the
net average realised value of coal at the pit bank for the time
being, *taken in conjunction with the state of the trade and the
prospects thereof*, is to be considered in fixing miners' wages
between the minimum and the maximum for the time being,
and that, in current ordinary circumstances, a rise or fall of
$6\frac{1}{4}$ per cent in wages on 1888 basis for each $4\frac{1}{2}d.$ per ton of
rise or fall in the value of coal is reasonable."[1] In like
manner, in the agreement entered into in the Federated
Districts in 1906, it was provided that "alterations in the
selling price of coal shall not be the sole factor for the decision
of the Board, but one factor only, and either side shall be
entitled to bring forward any reasons why, notwithstanding an
alteration in the selling price, there should be no alteration
made in the rate of wages."[2] Even under this type of
arrangement wage rates are not perfectly plastic; for, as was
explained previously, perfect plasticity involves fluctuations
from moment to moment instead of at intervals of two or
three months. Evidently, however, schemes fashioned on the
model of the Scottish and the Federated Districts agreements
carry with them a greater measure of plasticity than is to be
found in sliding scale agreements, and, therefore, *a fortiori*,
than is to be found in fixed wage agreements. Moreover, they
have the great advantage that they enable allowance to be
made for fluctuations in the supply of labour in the industries
they cover as well as for fluctuations in the demand for it.
Under these schemes reasoned and agreed action, instead of
automatic action, is required every two or three months. The
successful introduction of them is, therefore, only practicable in
industries where cordial relations prevail between employers
and employed.

[1] *Report on Collective Agreements* [Cd. 5366], 1910, p. 32.
[2] *Ibid.* p. 27.

PART IV

THE NATIONAL DIVIDEND AND GOVERNMENT FINANCE

CHAPTER I

§ 1. In normal times the main part of a Government's revenue is required to meet current expenditure on the army and navy, civil service, education, administrative services, and so forth. There can be no question that in a well-ordered State all ordinary recurrent expenditure of this type will be provided for out of taxation, and not by borrowing. To meet it by borrowing, whether from foreign or domestic lenders, would involve an ever-growing national debt and a corresponding ever-growing obligation of annual interest. In the end, more would have to be spent in providing the interest every year than would have been required if the Government had paid its way out of taxes from the beginning. The national credit would suffer heavy damage, and ultimately the Government might find itself forced into bankruptcy. These considerations are not, indeed, incompatible with the financing by loans of abnormal expenditure. If a certain class of expenditure occurs, not annually, but at intervals of a number of years, it is admissible, so far as the present argument goes, to meet it by borrowing, provided that a sinking fund is established to discharge the debt out of taxes within the limit of each interval. And, if an expenditure has to be undertaken which is reproductive, in the sense that it yields an annual return to the Government adequate to pay full interest and also to provide its own sinking fund, taxation will not need to be resorted to at all. These matters will be discussed later on. It is evident, however, that the main expenditure of Governments in normal times is of a sort that must be provided out of taxes levied contemporaneously with the expenditure. Our task in the first nine chapters of this Part is to study that portion of the general problem of Government finance which is concerned with the levying of these taxes.

§ 2. This task is complicated by the fact that the collection of revenue by a Government is not an act complete in itself. It is one side of a complex operation, of which the other side is the expenditure of the revenue that has been collected. It would seem, therefore, that any attempt to discuss the relation of the national dividend to the levying of taxes, in isolation from the use to which the proceeds of the taxes are put, must be incomplete and one-sided. The question that ought to be asked is, rather; "How will the national dividend be affected by the collection of so much revenue by this means and the expenditure of it in that way?" To obtain any adequate answer to this question, we should need to compare what is in fact done with the resources that the taxes represent and what would have been done with them, if they had been left "to fructify in the pockets of the people." Thus, *other things being equal*, if the Government takes resources, which would have been employed in making plant and machinery, and uses them to make, instead, guns and shells destined for immediate destruction in war, the dividend afterwards will be smaller than it would have been if this had not been done. On the other hand, if the Government takes resources, which would have been used in wasteful consumption, and uses them to build railways, the dividend afterwards will be bigger than it would otherwise have been. Again, if it takes resources, which would have been used for the creation of some sort of capital, and uses them to make another sort of capital either more or less productive than this, the dividend afterwards will be; in the one event, benefited, and, in the other, injured. Yet again, if it takes resources from the taxpayers generally to pay interest to those among them who are also holders of national debt, it increases or diminishes the national dividend of the future, according as the average holder of national debt or the average taxpayer devotes the larger proportion of his income to capital uses. This aspect of things, though it is partial and incomplete and does not enable us to gauge the total effect produced on the national dividend, is, plainly, very important. *Prima facie* it appears as though the effects of collecting and spending revenue could and should be discussed in such a way as to place it in the foreground.

§ 3. That plan, however, would not really serve. One reason is that the quantity of revenue to be spent by Government on particular services (*e.g.* interest on the national debt, army and navy, education, police, and so on) is often determined already apart from economic considerations, so that the practical issue on which light is required is, not how the dividend would be affected by the collection of so much revenue and its expenditure on such and such an object, but, *given the expenditure,* how it would be affected by collecting the revenue in *this* way as compared with *that* way. Sometimes, indeed, the other issue is raised, and in Part V., when we are studying the effects of raising money from the rich for investment in the quality and capacities of the poor, some study of it will be attempted. Generally, however, the practical problem is to compare different ways of raising money with one another, rather than to balance the effects of collecting revenue and of spending it.

§ 4. This, however, is not the only reason that renders the method of analysis sketched out in § 2 unsuitable for our purpose. There is also another reason. That method is concerned exclusively with the effect of the *fact* of collecting (and spending) money. But, as a general rule and apart from special circumstances, such as the outbreak of war, the bulk of a Government's tax revenue is not very greatly different in one year from what it is in neighbouring years. In these circumstances the *fact* that a tax is levied in one year carries with it the expectation that it will continue to be levied in later years. This expectation modifies people's conduct, inducing them to act differently in the matter of work and saving than they would have done if there had been no tax, with a view, when the form of the tax allows this, to withdrawing themselves, in greater or less degree, from its impact. This type of reaction must be given a dominant place in any adequate discussion of taxation. For these reasons in the present Part the line of analysis suggested in § 2 will not be followed. Instead, several principal types of taxation will be discussed, in such a way as to bring out the comparative effects which they themselves, apart from the spending of the revenue they yield, tend to produce on the national dividend; and in this discussion the distinction between the fact of an impost and the expectation of its continuance will be made fundamental. It will be understood that the chapters which follow do not profess to contain a complete account of the problem of Government finance. Many aspects of that problem, which are not directly connected with the national dividend, are omitted altogether; and others are only touched upon very lightly. In particular, the very important subjects of method of levy and administrative machinery and technique, which, as regards one part of the tax field, were investigated at length by the Royal Commission on the Income Tax, have been, of set purpose, ignored.

CHAPTER II

§ 1. The fact of taxation reacts on the national dividend in two principal ways. Both of these are independent of the *object* through which taxes are levied, and are associated with the total quantity of money taken, not by particular single taxes, but by the tax system as a whole, from the persons affected. Consequently, the discussion of this part of our problem can be made compact and self-contained.

§ 2. The first way is by altering the marginal desiredness of money to the taxed person. Since a part of his income is taken away, the last unit of income that is left to him will be desired more urgently than the last unit of income that would have been left to him if there had been no taxation. But the last unit of energy that he devotes to work will not affect him differently from what it did. Consequently, there will be a tendency for him to work a little harder, and so to make a slightly larger contribution to the national dividend, than he would have done otherwise. This tendency may be strong from the point of view of a short period, when heavy taxation is suddenly laid upon people who are accustomed to live nearly up to their income, and whose standard of life has become more or less fixed. They may then work a good deal harder in the hope of maintaining this standard, just as miners upon piece-wages often work harder when the piece-rate is suddenly lowered. But, when a system of taxation has been in vogue for some time, the standard of living is itself likely to have been modified, and the tendency to increased effort on the part of persons subjected to taxation will become less.

Among the very poor, indeed, whose standard of living is already near the minimum of subsistence, there is little room for any further lowering, and, therefore, the tendency to increased work may, so long as their physical capacity is not reduced, continue in full force. Among better-to-do persons, however, there is considerable scope for a lowering of the standard. Furthermore, there is generally an alternative way, besides extra work, by which, if it is so desired, their standard may be maintained. For better-to-do people generally either make a certain amount of annual saving, or at all events possess a store of capital; and it is possible to meet taxation by saving less or by selling capital. Broadly, therefore, we may conclude that, except among the very poor and possibly some proportion of the middle classes, the fact of taxation is not likely in the long run to have any substantial effect in increasing the contribution of work that taxed persons make towards the national dividend.

§ 3. The second way in which the fact of taxation reacts on the dividend is more complex and needs longer discussion. Let us assume, for the moment, that the taxes are not large enough to drive anybody to provide for them by actually selling existing capital goods. The essence of the matter then is that, of the money collected in taxation, some is withdrawn from, or held back from, consumption and some from investment. Now, investment by one person, though it may take the form of buying existing property, *implies* the creation of equivalent new capital, because the property, if not sold to this person, would, in general, have been sold to some other would-be investor, who, apart from its coming on the market, would have had to find a place for his money in new creations. When, therefore, money is held back from investment in order to meet taxation, it is, in effect, held back from creating new capital, which would have enabled a larger dividend to be produced in future years. It is essential, however, that our terms should not be misunderstood. Expenditure upon food, clothing and house-room is not usually spoken of as an investment of capital. Nevertheless, if a man's expenditure on these things were reduced below a certain level, his efficiency would deteriorate and the contribution that he makes to the national

dividend diminish. Hence, for the present purpose, we ought
to regard all expenditure on "necessaries for efficiency" as
equivalent to investment, and, therefore, as included within
that portion of a man's income which is devoted to producing
capital in the widest sense; and consumption should be taken
to mean that part of consumption which goes beyond what is
necessary for efficiency. With this explanation of terms it is
plain that the fact of taxation upon any taxpayer causes an
injury to the dividend of future years, which is greater or less
according as the money for paying the tax is withdrawn to a
larger or smaller extent from investment in the widest sense
instead of from consumption. We have now to apply this
general conception to practice.

§ 4. First, when taxation is raised from persons who have
no surplus beyond what they spend for efficiency, the whole of
the taxation *must* be taken out of investment in the widest
sense; for there is no other source out of which it can be
taken. Nor does it make any real difference if a part of the
income of the taxed person is spent on things which are not
really necessary for efficiency, but to which insistent conven-
tion gives precedence over these things. For in that event
the conventional necessaries are likely to be retained and the
real necessaries cut short. No doubt, as was explained in
§ 2, a part of what taxation takes away from investment
in the widest sense may be replaced from the fruits of extra
work; but that is not the present point. The broad fact
remains that, of taxation raised from persons so poor that they
have no surplus above what is necessary for efficiency, practically the whole must come out of investment in the widest
sense.

§ 5. Secondly, let us consider taxation raised from better-
to-do persons who normally devote some income to consumption
beyond what is productive of efficiency, and some to investment in the ordinary narrow sense of the market place.
The natural presumption is that the taxation will come out of
unproductive consumption and out of investment respectively
more or less in proportion to the amounts of income which the
taxed person is devoting to these two uses. No doubt, when
a large new tax is put on, the standard of living of the taxed

person will, for a time, be very resistant to change, so that a larger proportion will tend to be taken out of income that would have been invested. But, if we have in mind a system of taxation that is more or less permanent, the standard of living may become modified; and, broadly speaking, the presumption that taxes will be withdrawn from income spent on unproductive consumption and on investment roughly in proportion to their respective amounts appears to be a reasonable one.[1] Now, we may fairly suppose that, as incomes increase, the proportion of them that is invested increases also; for, after a point, the attractiveness of further expenditure upon consumption must become very slight. Hence, other things being equal, capital, and, therefore, the national dividend of the future, will be hit more severely by taxes upon the rich than by taxes upon the moderately well-to-do, and by taxes upon the very rich than by taxes upon the rich.

§ 6. So far we have assumed that the taxation contemplated is moderate in amount relatively to the income of the taxed persons, so that the practical choice is between taking it from income that would have been spent and from income that would have been invested. It remains to consider taxation on a higher scale. Such taxation may be paid out of capital in a different sense, namely out of the proceeds of a sale of capital already existing. Of course, the sale of capital does not mean the direct destruction of capital, or, unless it is sold to foreigners, the loss of it to the nation viewed collectively. But, as was indicated in § 3, since the buyer was presumably intending to invest his purchase money, it means that he buys old capital with resources that would otherwise have gone to create new capital. Hence, the total stock of the nation's capital is diminished to the same extent as it would have been if the capital, by the sale of which the taxes are paid, had been literally melted down. When taxes are placed on anybody,

---

[1] Analytically, if A be the amount of his income that a man normally turns into capital (whether in a wide or narrow sense), B the amount he normally "consumes," and e_a and e_b the elasticities of his desire for these two uses respectively, it is easily shown that a given levy will be withdrawn from the two uses in the proportion of e_aA to e_bB. The conclusion of the text, therefore, implies that, from a long period point of view, $\frac{e_a}{e_b}$ differs from unity to a much less degree than $\frac{A}{B}$ does.

so large that they exceed or approach the sum of his normal savings and his unproductive consumption together, they are certain, in the year of levy, to be taken, in the main, from income that would have been saved and from capital in the above sense; for, though unproductive consumption may be reduced a little, the standard of living will almost certainly be too rigid to allow it to be reduced a great deal, in preference to trenching on these resources. It is possible, of course, in accordance with the argument of § 2, that, when a large amount of a man's capital has been taken away in taxation, this fact may cause him to make efforts and savings in later years, in order to reconstitute it, that he would not otherwise have made. If this happens, the proportion of the tax levy that is taken out of capital on the whole is less than the proportion that is so taken at the moment. In general, however, it does not seem likely that this kind of reaction will be very important. We may conclude, therefore, that, for any given class of taxpayer, very large taxes will trench upon capital, and, therefore, will injure the national dividend of the future in a greater proportion than moderate taxes.

§ 7. There remains one somewhat special point. It is possible to obtain any given revenue either by relatively small taxes levied annually or by relatively large taxes levied at long intervals. For example, the annual collection of, say, twenty millions from a given group by income tax on incomes derived from investments involves a comparatively small annual levy on each member of the group; whereas the annual collection of the same sum by death duties involves a comparatively large occasional levy from the estates of that small proportion of the group who die during the year. Let us suppose the income-tax method to raise an annual twenty millions by collecting £100 every year from each of a group of 200,000 people; and the death-duty method to raise the same sum by collecting £2000 from each of these people once in twenty years. We have to inquire which of these two methods is likely to trench the more seriously upon capital in the widest sense. Clearly, things *might* be so arranged that there would be no difference whatever between them. Under the death-duty method each person might furnish about £100 annually to insurance com-

panies, to be handed over by them in payment of the estate-
duties falling due during the year, instead of furnishing it, as
under the income-tax method, to the Treasury.   In actual life,
however, it is not likely that a tax falling due from any estate
every twentieth year will be fully provided against in the
untaxed years that precede or follow..   Consequently, it is
probable that under the death-duty method a good deal more
than £100 will have to be furnished towards the tax from the
resources accruing in the actual year of the tax, and a good
deal less from those accruing in other years.   It is fairly clear,
however, that, as the amount withdrawn from the resources of
any year grows, people will be less and less willing, owing to
the wrench threatened to their habits, to take it out of consumption.   If this be so, it follows that, in general, the death-
duty method is likely to trench on capital somewhat more
than the income-tax method.   The fact that death duties are,
in fact, levied on estates, not merely at long intervals, but at
the particular moment when property is changing hands
through death, and when, therefore, payment out of capital is
often specially easy, constitutes a further influence favouring
this tendency.

§ 8. The general result of this discussion is to show that,
though there are differences of detail, and though, especially
among the moderately well-to-do, unproductive consumption
may yield some contribution, yet a considerable part of the
money taken from the public in taxation is likely, especially if
the rate of taxation is high, to come out of what would otherwise have been, or become, capital in the widest sense.   To
that extent, therefore, the national dividend of the future is
injured. This injury, as was said at the outset, is quite independent of the *object* through which taxes are raised; and it
will, furthermore, be wiped out if the Government either itself
uses the money that it has raised for equally effective capital
purposes, or transfers it to State creditors who so use it. This,
however, is not the whole injury. Even if the money raised
in taxation were employed by the State or its creditors in
exactly the same way as it would have been if allowed to
" fructify in the pockets of the people," the national dividend
will, in general, still suffer. It will suffer, not directly from the

fact of taxation, but indirectly, because the fact creates the expectation of taxation, and this expectation often, though not always, tempts people to modify their conduct with a view to avoiding the threat of a tax. How far they are tempted to act in this way, and how far, therefore, the national dividend is injured, depends upon the objects through which taxation is assessed. In the following chapters certain principal forms of taxation will be studied from this point of view.

CHAPTER III

TAXES ON WINDFALLS

§ 1. THE expectation of a tax may lessen the national dividend by inducing people to work less in the taxing country, to save less in the taxing country, or to divert their purchases from one commodity to another. It is only in these ways that the expectation of a tax can affect the dividend at all. Consequently, the dividend will escape injury from this side under any tax so constructed that the impact of it upon the taxpayer is not lessened if he works less or saves less or alters the direction of his purchases. Taxes based on personal peculiarities, the natural colour of people's hair or eyes, their age or their height, or other qualities fixed by nature, would fall into this class. But all such taxes, since they treat people who are essentially alike in an unlike way, and since, furthermore, they make no attempt whatever to adjust the burden to the strength of the back, are inequitable, and, therefore, strictly limited in scope. There is, however, one kind of tax, which is as satisfactory from the standpoint of the national dividend as any of these, but which also has the great merit of not running counter to any canon of equity. I mean taxes upon accretions to the value of people's property that are not foreseen by them and are not due in any degree to efforts made, intelligence exercised, risks borne, or capital invested by them. These accretions of value may suitably be called windfalls and taxes upon them taxes upon windfalls. It is desirable to undertake a brief study of this type of tax.

§ 2. At the outset an observation must be made on the point of equity. It is necessary to distinguish between what may be called integral windfalls and partial windfalls. By an integral windfall is meant an accretion in the nature of a windfall to the aggregate value of a person's property reckoned relatively to the whole period of his life; by a partial windfall an accretion of this nature occurring at some definite moment to some definite part of a person's property. The equity of a tax upon integral windfalls needs no proof. Such a tax would merely do away with accidental accretions of wealth, for the maintenance of which no defence can possibly be given. The knowledge that it will be imposed *if* a windfall occurs has no appreciable effect on the value of any property now. But with partial windfalls the issue is less clear. For a windfall increment to one part of a man's property in one year may be offset by a windfall decrement to another part of it in another year. If there were a presumption that an observed windfall increment would in fact be balanced by a windfall decrement that is not observed, equity would point against the taxation of partial windfalls. Integral windfalls would be equitable objects of taxation, but partial windfalls would not. Since in practice it would be quite impossible to ascertain by direct inquiry whether or not an integral windfall had occurred,—for this would imply knowledge of the future as well as of the past,—or, if it had, how large it had been, this conclusion would, in effect, rule all windfall taxation out of court. There is not, however, in fact, any presumption of the kind contemplated. When a partial windfall increment is observed, it *may*, of course, be cancelled by a partial windfall decrement to the same property; but there is no presumption that it will be. Consequently, in the absence of definite knowledge that it is in fact so cancelled, there is nothing inequitable in taxing it. Those windfalls that are observed are not rendered improper objects for taxation by the fact that windfall decrements and other windfall increments occur, which cannot in practice be brought into account.

§ 3. The exceptional circumstances of the great war brought into being a new and very important class of windfall, in the abnormal profits made by certain businesses as a direct consequence of it. The values of certain sorts of goods and services were enormously enhanced, with the result that, as was shown in Part II. Chapter IX., those persons who had a store of these things or the means of making them quickly,—shipowners, iron and steel makers, munition makers, farmers, and many others—were in a position, except in so far as the Government interfered, by fixing maximum prices for the commodities in which they were interested, to reap undreamt-of fortunes. In these fortunes there was a large element of windfall. In order to isolate that element it was necessary to determine what the normal profit of the business was, to add on to that an allowance for extra profit due to new capital investments and additional work, and to take account of the fact that machinery set up and adaptations made specially for war purposes would be of little use, and might even be in the way, after the war was over. The estimate of normal profits ought strictly to have taken account, not merely of what the profits in the years immediately preceding the war actually were, but also of the prospects that then existed of their increasing; and it ought to have taken account both of the high level of general prices prevailing during the war, in consequence of which a given money profit represented a much smaller real profit than before, and also of the probability that prices would be high for some time after the war, in consequence of which larger reserves should properly be held against depreciation. The English excess profits duty aimed, in a general way, at isolating the windfall element in war profits on these lines and at taxing this element at as high a rate as possible; the only restraining influence being the fear that, since it was not possible completely to isolate the windfall element, a tax above, say, 80 per cent would discourage enterprise in a dangerous degree.[1]

[1] The original American excess profits duty was based on the absolute rate of profit, not on the excess above the profits obtained before the war. It was, therefore, much less nearly a true tax on windfalls than the English tax. It was, moreover, open to the serious objection that it penalised inventions, the skilful seizing of opportunities and good management. "Something can be said for a graduated tax on income; something can even be said for a graduated tax on capital; but it is difficult to say anything in defence of a tax which is graduated on the varying percentages which income bears to capital. To penalise enterprise and ingenuity in a way that is not accomplished by a tax on either capital or income—that is the unique distinction of the law" (Seligman, "The War Revenue Act," *Political Science Quarterly*, March 1918, p. 29).

§ 4. Windfall taxation, as an instrument for raising revenue in normal conditions, was until recently practically unknown. . Some years before the war, however, several attempts were·¡made on the Continent of Europe:to tax windfalls of a particular kind, namely those in respect of ·the public value of land, by means of increment duties. In Frankfort-on-Main, "if, since the·previous change of ownership less than twenty years have elapsed,· and if there has been an increase in value amounting to at least 15 per cent of the previous purchase price, after allowance has been made ,for expenditure on improvements, loss of interest and costs of transfer, increment duty is levied on the following scale: 2 per cent on the increase· in value for increases between 15 and 20 per cent, 3 per cent for increases between 20 and 25 ·per·cent, and so on, 1 per cent being added to the rate of duty for every 5 ·per cent· increase of value, up to a maximum rate of 25 per cent."[1] In Cologne the general arrangements are similar. ·'The scale of duty starts at 10 per cent for increases of value of ·more than 10 and less than 20 per cent, and the rate increases by· 1 per cent for every additional 10 per cent in the increase of value, up to the same maximum rate of 25 per cent. This scale is charged in its entirety when not more than. five ·years have elapsed since the previous change of ownership, two-thirds of the scale when not more than ten years have elapsed, and one-third in respect of any period exceeding ten years.[2] In 1911 the Conservative party in the Reichstag carried a proposal for the introduction of kindred arrangements into the imperial fiscal system, but "by the amendment of the law in 1913, the revenue accruing from the Wertzuwachssteuer was relegated entirely to the states and local authorities."[3] · In the United Kingdom a cruder form of duty upon increments of land value was imposed by the Budget of 1909. It might be thought at first sight that these duties satisfy the conditions required of windfall taxes, and that nothing more complicated is necessary. This, however, is not really so; and it is desirable to show why it is not so. We shall thus be able to bring into clear light·the

---

[1] Cf. Cd. 4750, p. 21.   [2] *Ibid.* p. 18.
[3] Scheftel, *The Taxation of Land Value,* p. 145, footnote.

practical difficulties by which any attempt to devise effective windfall taxes is confronted.

§ 5. To begin with, there are two classes of increment which are apparent and not real. One of these arises in this way. If the general level of prices during one decade is 50 per cent higher than in the previous decade, then the money value of unimproved land may increase 50 per cent and yet not experience any real increment. The income that the owner derives from it, or the capital sum that he would obtain by selling it, though 50 per cent larger than before in terms of money, is exactly the same as before in terms of the things which this money enables him to buy. This sort of difficulty does not exist as against *ad valorem* taxes, but it must exist wherever the taxed object is the difference between the money value which a particular thing has at different points of time. The only way to avoid it is to revise the valuation assigned to the basis period in the light of the new level of general prices, which exists in the period when the amount of increment liable to duty has to be determined. This revision would be a difficult task. The method of performing it that naturally suggests itself is to multiply the original site value by the ratio which an ordinary index number of general prices in the assessment year bears to the corresponding index number in the original valuation year. This method, however, would not be satisfactory, because the capital value of an instrument of production does not vary in correspondence with the income derived from it in a single year, but depends upon the expectation of income for a number of years. Nevertheless, by a reasonable, and not a mechanical, application of index numbers, it would seem that a competent authority could eliminate from the field of taxation the main part of the merely apparent increments of this class that come into being. By a similar process, though here much popular prejudice would have to be overcome, a competent authority might be able, in times of depressed prices, to bring into the field of taxation real increments of value which appeared as decrements.

§ 6. The other class of apparent increment arises when the general rate of money interest on long-period investments falls. This kind of change means that an investment yielding exactly the same annual return must rise in capital value. Such a rise is of no advantage to the owner of the investment—unless, indeed, he wishes to turn the proceeds into consumable income—because, even if he sells it, he will not be able to invest the proceeds in anything that will yield, on equal security, a higher annual return than he was obtaining before. Here, again, adjustment would be difficult. But, if account were taken of the place occupied by the year of the original valuation and the year of assessment in their respective credit cycles, it would seem that a competent authority could so qualify the original valuation that the increments assessed to taxation should not include this class of apparent increment.

§ 7. Our task, however, is not completed when apparent increments have been eliminated. For even real increments, when they are anticipated and discounted, are not windfalls. The point may be put in this way. The capital value of a site is the present worth of the annual income which it is expected to yield. Increments in capital value must, therefore, arise regularly as the period at which an increase in annual value will begin draws nearer. For simplicity of illustration, let us imagine an estate, which is not expected to yield any income at all for the next twenty years, but is, thereafter, expected to yield an income (apart altogether from expenditure on the land) of £500 a year. This example is typical of the condition of much land in the neighbourhood of towns, which is expected at a future date to become valuable for building purposes. Interest being reckoned at 5 per cent, a simple calculation shows that the capital site value of our imaginary estate will progress approximately as follows:

Value in 1920	.	.	.	.	£3800
Value in 1925	.	.	.	.	4800
Value in 1930	.	.	.	.	6100
Value in 1935	.	.	.	.	7800
Value in 1940	.	.	.	.	10,000

The increment of value over the fifteen years following 1920 is thus £4000, and a duty of 20 per cent on this increment, payable in 1935, is £800. A further simple calculation shows that, with interest at 5 per cent, £800 in 1935 is equivalent to a little less than £400 in 1920. This means that, if an owner wished to sell the estate we have been considering in 1920, the existence of a 20 per cent increment duty payable in 1935 would cause him to get some £3400 for it instead of £3800. The tax, in short, would be a direct impost on the present owner, and not in any sense a windfall tax.

§ 8. In practice, of course, many actual increments of value are partly windfalls and partly increments of this kind. When the element of appearance in actual increments has been removed, it is possible to distinguish the windfall element in the real increment in the following manner: If a piece of land in 1920 has a total value $(x + y)$, made up of a value x due to its present (agricultural or other) use, and a value y due to expectations of building rents after 1940, there should, interest being reckoned at 5 per cent, be a non-windfall increment in the value of the land by the year 1935 equal to about 108 per cent of y. In order, therefore, that increment tax may be confined to windfalls, it ought only to be levied on the excess of the then value of the land over its present value *plus* 108 per cent of that portion of its present value which is due to its prospects as building land. For periods of greater or less length than fifteen years similar calculations could, of course, easily be worked out. The root idea of this plan was embodied both in the increment duties established at Frankfort and Cologne and also in the German imperial increment tax. The fourth section of the Frankfort bye-law, for example, provided that, "in the case of unbuilt land which the vendor does not himself use for purposes of agriculture or industry," before the increment which has accrued at any time is calculated, there shall be added to the original basis valuation interest to the extent of 4 per cent.[1] Compound interest was, however — it would seem incorrectly—not allowed.

§ 9. Yet one more point remains. In some circumstances an increment, which is not definitely expected, nevertheless enters, in some measure, into present value, and is, therefore, not

---

[1] Cf. Cd. 4750, p. 21.

true windfall. I may, for instance, have a piece of land which
is expected to yield for a long while £500 a year, but in regard
to which it is recognised vaguely that either a rise or a fall
may take place. This land—with interest at 5 per cent—
will have a capital value of £10,000, and it, therefore, seems
at first sight that the possibility of its rising in value is not
being discounted. In reality, however, this possibility does
enter into present value, acting there as a counterweight to
the possibility of a fall. The measure of influence which this
possibility, reckoned over the ensuing fifteen years, exercises
upon present value is given by the sum for which the right
to all increment of *this class*—I am not, of course, now
referring to the *anticipated* increment already discussed—
accruing during the said fifteen years could be sold. It is
fairly certain that the sum obtainable would, in general, be a
very small fraction of the capital value of the land. Consequently, these increments, when they accrue, are *predominantly*, though not entirely, windfalls; and the passing of
a law for their taxation would not strike present owners to
any substantial extent. In order, however, to reduce the
risk of this to a minimum, it might be well to provide for
the exemption from duty of increments amounting to less
than 10 per cent. This provision, combined with that
suggested in the preceding section, would exempt from
increment duty all increments arising in a fifteen-year period
amounting to less than 10 per cent of the value x, plus, say,
120 per cent of the value y.

§ 10. The various safeguards, which this discussion shows
to be required in an increment tax that is to strike windfall
increments only, are probably too complicated for practical
politics. The cause, however, is not yet lost. For it is still
possible—at the expense, indeed, of letting some real windfalls
go free—to avoid serious danger of taxing increments that
are not windfalls by the simple device of exempting all
increments other than those which are very large indeed. In
normal circumstances, apart from war and its aftermath, we
may reasonably expect that no enormous variations in general
prices or in the general rate of interest will occur in the
course of fifteen years. If, therefore, we decree that increment

duty shall only be levied on land which in fifteen years has trebled in value—or, if our period be of some other length, has improved in a proportionate degree—it is very unlikely that anything other than true windfall increments will be enmeshed by our scheme. Nearly the whole amount by which, at the end of fifteen years, the unimproved value of any man's holding of land—it seems necessary to take the total holding as our unit—exceeds treble its original unimproved value might safely be taken by the State. If the unimproved values of land are periodically estimated for some other purpose, with a view, for example, to a direct tax on the body of these values, it would not appear to be a very difficult or expensive matter to collect a tax of this kind also. But the various complications, to which attention has been called, make it plain that such a tax is never likely to yield a large revenue from windfalls that accrue in landed property. The task of constructing a tax to catch analogous windfalls in other kinds of property, with the single exception of treasure trove, is so difficult that no attempt has yet been made to cope with it.[1]

[1] There is no resemblance between the arrangement discussed above and the German "property increment" tax introduced in 1913, which hit increments of property, whether inherited or saved, while exempting the general corpus of possessed property. (Cf. Cohn, *Economic Journal*, 1913, p. 543 *et seq.*).

CHAPTER IV

TAXES ON THE PUBLIC VALUE OF LAND

§ 1. A TAXABLE object, which, from the point of view of the national dividend, is closely analogous to windfalls, is that part of the annual, or of the capital, value of real property which is not due to the efforts or investments of owners or occupiers. In this country, apart from the small "undeveloped land" duty of the 1909 Budget, no resort has been had to this taxable object. In New Zealand and the Australian colonies, however, it has for many years played an important part both in local and in national finance; and the municipalities of Western Canada have made considerable use of it for local purposes. "In Queensland practically all the local revenue is raised from this source. All rates, general, special, and separate, are levied on the unimproved value."[1] In South Australia a special national tax on unimproved land values has existed since 1884. One halfpenny in the £ is levied on all unimproved (capital) values; an extra halfpenny on unimproved values exceeding £5000; and an absentee tax, amounting to 20 per cent on absentee owners.[2] In New South Wales: "The land tax of the State is levied on unimproved value at the rate of 1d. in the £. A sum of £240 is allowed by way of exemption, and, when the unimproved value is in excess of that sum, a reduction equal to the exemption is made; but, when several blocks of land within the State are held by a person or company, only one amount of £240 may be deducted from the aggregate unimproved

[1] Scheftel, *The Taxation of Land Value*, 1916, p. 49.
[2] [Cd. 3191], p. 20.

value. In cases where land is mortgaged, the mortgagor is permitted to deduct from the tax payable a sum equal to the income tax paid by the mortgagee on the interest derived from the mortgage on the whole property including improvements."[1] In New Zealand: "In 1891 the Property Tax Act then in force was repealed and replaced by the Land and Income Assessment Act, under which a land tax was imposed on land and mortgages of land, and an income tax on all income other than income derived from land and mortgages of land. Improvements on land were exempted up to £3000. In 1893 an amending Act was passed by which all improvements on land were entirely exempted, and in 1896 an Act was passed by which the principle of taxation on the 'unimproved value' was extended to local rating, by enabling local authorities to adopt the system on a poll of the ratepayers being taken and a majority voting in favour of its adoption."[2]. The amount of the national tax in this colony is ordinarily one penny in the £ on unimproved (capital) value. "Land in possession of natives is treated specially, and, out of consideration for small peasant farmers, plots worth less than £500 are exempted, and plots worth less than £1500 are allowed an abatement. In addition to the ordinary land tax, the same Act imposed a graduated State tax on large estates, commencing at one-sixteenth of a penny in the £ on land of an unimproved value of £5000, and rising to threepence in the £ on land of an unimproved value of £210,000 or more.[3]

§ 2. In all these arrangements the essential matter is the distinction between improved and unimproved value respectively. Some light on the precise way in which this distinction is drawn may be gathered from a very interesting explanatory memorandum furnished by the Valuer-General of New Zealand, Mr. G. F. C. Campbell. Mr. Campbell cites the definition clauses of the Government Valuation of Land Act, 1896, and adds certain comments of his own. The principal points to be noted are the following:

First: "The increased value attaching to any piece of land due to the successful working of other lands in the district or

[1] [Cd. 3191], p. 21.   [2] *Ibid.* p. 24.
[3] Chorlton, *The Rating of Land Values*, p. 160.

to progressive works effected by the State, the general prosperity of the country, high markets for produce, &c., form a portion of the unimproved value under the New Zealand law. Any increased value, however, which is represented by the improvements effected by the individual possessor, either past or present, does not form part of the unimproved value." [1]

Secondly : "Improvements can only be valued *to the extent to which they increase the selling value of the land.* This fact should not be forgotten; the valuer must, therefore, value an improvement at the proportionate sum which it represents in the selling value of the whole property. We sometimes find a large house built on a small area of farming land. The ordinary farmer who would purchase such a property would not be likely to pay for the house anything approaching its cost—he would only pay the price of a house which suits the requirements of the farm. The selling value of the house must, therefore, be valued at what the ordinary purchaser would be likely to give for it, or, in other words, at the sum by which it increases the selling value of the property. Sometimes an owner will expend his capital and labour injudiciously, and the result will prove detrimental to the land instead of being an improvement. Some lands hold grass better without first being ploughed than they do after the plough. The effect of ploughing in such cases would not be to improve the selling value. Some improvements, such as ornamental shrubbery, orchards, lawns, vineries, etc., rarely increase the selling value to the full extent of their cost, and should, therefore, be valued accordingly. . . . No work can be considered an improvement if the benefit is exhausted at the time of valuation. . . . The amount at which improvements are to be valued is defined by the Act as the sum by which they increase the selling value of the land, *provided that the value must not exceed the cost,* although it may be below the cost if their condition warrants it. The cost of an improvement is not necessarily its selling value, as its suitability and condition must be taken into consideration." [2]

Thirdly : "It is the actual improvement which is valued, not the effect of that improvement. For instance, suppose

[1] [Cd. 3191], p. 37.   [2] *Ibid.* pp. 39-40.

that the expenditure of a small sum in cutting an outlet for water has converted a swamp into first-class agricultural land. The fact that the swamp was capable of easy drainage would enhance its unimproved value, and the cost only of cutting the drain would be valued as the improvement." [1]

Lastly: An improvement, to be classed as such, must be made by the owner. Suppose that there are two pieces of land adjacent to one another, and that the cutting of a drain or the erection of a fence upon one of them would enhance the total value of both. If the two pieces are owned by the same person, their unimproved value, both before and after the drain is cut, would appear to be equal to their total value *minus* the cost of cutting the drain. If, however, they are in different hands, the unimproved value of the piece on which the improvement is not required is enhanced so soon as the improvement on the other piece is carried out. The same point arises in connection with collective improvements. Thus, Mr. Campbell observes: "It has been argued that public works done by small communities, and for which those communities agree to rate themselves, shall be valued as an improvement" for the purpose of the national land tax.[2] The New Zealand Act, however, does not accept this view.[3]

§ 3. The general nature of the distinction between improved and unimproved value has long been familiar to economists. It corresponds to the Ricardian distinction between true economic rent and profits from capital invested in land. Unimproved value is the capitalised value of the true rent, and improvement value that of the profits. A terminology for some purposes more convenient has been suggested by Professor Marshall. True rent is, of course, that part of the annual value of land which arises from its position, its extension, its yearly income of sunlight and heat and rain and air. "This (annual) value of the land," he writes, "is sometimes called its 'inherent value'; but much of that value is the result of the action of men, though not of its individual holders; and, therefore, it is perhaps more correct to call this

---

[1] [Cd. 3191], pp. 40-41.   [2] *Ibid.* p. 40.

[3] For an account of some of the difficulties of valuation, cf. Scheftel, *The Taxation of Land Value*, pp. 69 *et seq.*

part of the annual value of land its 'public value,' while that part of its value which can be traced to the work and outlay of its individual holder may be called its 'private value.'" [1] Public value capitalised corresponds to the unimproved (capital) value, and private value capitalised to the improvement (capital) value of the Australasian laws.

§ 4. It is easily seen that taxes assessed on the public value of land, whether annual or capitalised, will, like taxes on windfalls, leave the national dividend wholly unaffected. The value of the taxed object, being due to public causes, cannot be made less by any action or abstention from action on the part of the owner. He cannot avoid the tax either by working less or by saving less. Nor can he avoid it by selling his right in the land and devoting the proceeds to buying something else; because, if he sells it, the tax will be discounted in the price that he gets for his right. The tax is, therefore, completely "unavoidable," and the expectation of it wholly innocuous, provided only that the technical difficulty of appropriate definition can be overcome.

§ 5. From the point of view of equity, however, the position is different. True windfall taxes are equitable between all citizens, because, in a sense, they touch none of them. But taxes on the public value of land single out a particular class of property-owners for a special and exceptional burden. The inequity is the more serious in that the capitalised value of the levies expected in future years, and not merely the actual levy of the moment, is concentrated on those persons who happen to own land at the time the tax is first devised; for, as has just been said, selling gives no escape. This is true equally whether the annual amount of the tax is fixed once for all or whether provision is made for a progressive increase as time passes. Naturally, therefore, owners of site-values complain that new site-value taxes constitute discriminating imposts upon a particular section of the propertied class. Their title, they argue, is as good as that of any one else. They have bought it, or inherited it, in exactly the same way as the present owners of furniture or of Stock Exchange securities. The proposal to subject them to a burden not borne by other

[1] [Cd. 9528], p. 115.

persons of equal wealth is, therefore, fundamentally unjust. Let it be granted that for the State to have allowed its land to become the property of private persons was a grave error. None the less, the faults of a national institution ought not to be paid for at the cost of arbitrarily selected individuals.

Against this class of criticism some answer can be made along the lines of " betterment." Dr. Marshall has written : " There may be great difficulty in allocating the betterment due to any particular improvement. But, as it is, the expenditure of such private societies as the Metropolitan Public Gardens Association, and much of the rates raised on building values for public improvements, is really a free gift of wealth to owners who are already fortunate." [1] It is true, no doubt, that those who have purchased urban land recently may have partially discounted this betterment in their purchase price ; but they are not likely to have discounted it entirely ; while those owners who are not recent purchasers will not have discounted it at all. Consequently, it is to be expected that the special burden which new taxes upon site-values would impose upon site-owners—at all events in urban districts—will be partially offset by a special increment in no way due to their own effort and expenditure. This answer, however, is obviously a plea in mitigation, rather than a rebuttal.

It may be supplemented in certain circumstances by the further plea that revenue requirements make it necessary that *some* new particular tax or combination of taxes shall be imposed, and that every particular tax regarded in isolation is unjust, in the sense that it strikes one group of persons more severely than other groups. The tea tax strikes tea-drinkers only; the tobacco tax smokers only. These persons, no doubt, can, if they choose, evade payment by abandoning the use of the taxed articles; whereas, as was remarked above, the landowner, since the tax would be discounted in selling price, cannot escape by parting with his land. But, though the smoker can evade a payment, he cannot evade a burden from the tax—for it is a burden to smoking— ; and, as a matter of fact, he is most unlikely even to make the change needed to evade any large part of the payment. In matters of taxation, therefore, a moderate degree of

[1] [Cd. 9528], p. 125.

injustice, since it exists everywhere, cannot be appealed to anywhere. Arguments founded upon it, since they would condemn all taxes, cannot be used to condemn any tax.

Plainly, however, these considerations, though valid in respect of small taxes upon site-values, do not provide an adequate defence for very heavy taxes. Unless, therefore, equity is defied, no very large amount of money, even in substitution for existing local rates, could be raised by this means. Site-values are, from the standpoint of the national dividend, very suitable objects of taxation, but their scope is strictly limited.

CHAPTER V

§ 1. AN equal *ad valorem* tax on all consumable goods and services would be equivalent to a general ungraduated tax on expenditure. The presumption is that the expectation of such a tax, by lessening the net reward of work, would tend somewhat to check work, and so, in part directly, and in part indirectly through the diminution caused in the funds available for saving, to contract the national dividend. But, as will be argued presently, unless the rate of tax were large, this effect would not be very marked. There would be no differential effect additional to this effect, either between rival forms of consumption, or, as will appear in Chapter VI., between "spending" in general and "saving" in general. It is not, of course, denied that a general expenditure tax will alter the proportion of his resources which a man spends on different things, because, with a smaller total to spend, he will naturally economise to a different extent in different directions. It may conceivably increase the absolute amount of his expenditure on some relatively cheap things (*e.g.* bread), which, with his diminished spending power, he finds it desirable to substitute in his budget for others. But these adjustments do not mean that productive resources are shifted in such a way that the values of their marginal net products in different uses become unequal. Rather, net spendable incomes having changed, resources are shifted in such a way that, in spite of the new conditions, the values of their marginal net products in different uses are still kept equal.[1] That is to say, a general

---

[1] *I.e.* the position of the various "desiredness" curves is unaltered, and all that happens is a movement *along* them due to a change in total resources.

expenditure tax does not cause any injury to the national dividend by creating inequality among the values of the marginal net products of resources employed in different uses. So far as that aspect of things is concerned no harm is done.

§ 2. In fact, however, a general expenditure tax, operated through equal *ad valorem* duties on all consumable goods and services, is not practical politics. It is ruled out of court by two fatal objections. The first is an objection of technique—the practical difficulty, to say nothing of the enormous cost, of collecting equal *ad valorem* duties on all commodities and services purchased for consumption throughout the country. To collect them through shopkeepers, though it may be worth trying in the special emergency of a great war, gives such an open invitation to fraud that an army of inspectors would be needed to combat it. And to collect them otherwise than through shopkeepers is even less feasible. For, besides the difficulty of securing the due payment of the tax on such objects as the services of professional musicians, doctors, teachers, and so forth, it would be necessary to set up a system of production in bond for all consumable articles made at home! Even for imported articles an *ad valorem* system is exceedingly difficult to work on the side of valuation. The customs duties of the United States and Canada are, indeed, arranged on this system, but the task of safeguarding it against fraud and evasion has proved so exacting that Germany, after trial, abandoned it, and France, Belgium, Italy, Austria, and Russia all fought shy of it.[1] Nor is there any way round the difficulty. Owing to the innumerable grades of quality in many commodities it is not feasible to get a common *ad valorem* rate by means of scales of specific duties. Each specific rate is bound to cover more than one quality, and, whenever this happens, the higher quality will get off with a lower proportionate tax. The second objection is of another class. If the technical difficulties could be got over, and it were found practicable to set up a system of equal *ad valorem* duties on all consumable goods and services purchased in the country, we should, indeed, have a general expenditure tax.

---

[1] Cf. Higginson, *Tariffs at Work*, Chapter iii.

But this tax would hit the expenditure of all people, whatever the aggregate amount of their expenditure, in exactly the same proportion. There would be no graduation whatever as between the poor, the moderately well off, the rich and the very rich; and it would be equally difficult to make the rate higher for a bachelor or spinster than for a man or woman with a large family. It is, however, generally agreed—the matter will be discussed more fully presently—that any fair tax system *must* be graduated and must be adjusted through family allowances to the ability to pay of various classes of taxpayers. Conceivably, no doubt, we might have a proportionate general expenditure tax as a part of a tax system into which graduation and allowances were introduced by means of other taxes. There would, however, be very little object in having an expenditure tax operated through uniform *ad valorem* duties, unless it constituted, at all events, a predominant part of the whole tax system; and, if it does this, graduation and allowances in the system as a whole cannot practically be provided for unless they are embodied in the expenditure tax itself. The inference is that, as a matter of real politics, the uniform taxation of all consumable commodities, so as to constitute a general expenditure tax, is not practicable, and, if it were practicable, would not be desirable.

§ 3. When consumable commodities are subjected to taxation, it may be expected, therefore, that the choice made among them and the rates imposed on one or another of them will be determined, not so much by a general plan as by detailed considerations of technical convenience and revenue needs. Some commodities will be taxed and others left exempt, and among those that are taxed the rates of taxation will vary. Generally speaking, since mass-goods are more convenient and more economical objects of taxation than goods purchased in small quantities, and since the method of specific duties involves lower rates on the finer qualities of goods in each general class, taxes on consumable commodities are likely, as a whole, to take a much larger proportion of income from the poor than from the rich. According to Mr. Herbert Samuel's estimate, in 1918–19 British indirect taxes took on the average 13·8 per cent from a £100 income and only 0·1 per cent from a £50,000 income.[1] This class of inequity can, however—at all events in theory—be compensated in other parts of the tax-system; and, since this is not a general work upon taxation, I do not propose to enlarge upon it. For my present purpose the important point is that in practice taxes on particular commodities are differential as between different forms of consumption. This fact modifies in an important degree their relation to the national dividend.

§ 4. Broadly speaking, we may reckon that, if a given sum of money is collected by a tax on a particular consumable commodity instead of by special levy on consumable commodities in general, the effect produced on the dividend, through the quantity of work that people do and the share of their income that they save, will not be substantially different. But, whereas a general expenditure tax leaves the relative attractiveness of expenditure on various sorts of commodities unaltered, a tax system, under which different rates of duty are imposed on different things, alters this relative attractiveness, and so modifies the way in which purchasing power, and, consequently, productive power is distributed. This shifting of the lines of production, reacting, as it does, upon the relation between the values of the marginal net products of resources in different occupations, affects the volume of the national dividend. The change which it induces is superimposed upon any change that a general expenditure tax yielding the same revenue would have brought about. If it is an advantageous change, the total effect on the dividend is less injurious than it would have been under such a general tax; if it is a disadvantageous change, the total effect is more injurious. Whether, as a matter of fact, it is an advantageous or a disadvantageous change can only be determined by a detailed study of the individual duties that are embodied in the general scheme.

§ 5. Since neither the demand nor the supply of any ordinary commodity—bread is sometimes an exception—is ever perfectly inelastic, taxes on particular commodities must, in general, discourage the employment of resources in pro-

---

[1] "The Taxation of the Various Classes of the People," *Statistical Journal*, March 1919, p. 177.

ducing the commodities that are taxed and divert them to producing other untaxed commodities. If, therefore, a taxed commodity is one to the production of which, apart from taxation, too small a volume of resources would have been devoted, so that the value of the marginal net product of resources there would have stood above the general level, taxation necessarily disturbs the distribution of the community's resources in a way injurious to the national dividend. All commodities produced under conditions of increasing returns fall into this class, and many commodities produced under conditions of diminishing returns, provided that the producer is exercising monopolistic powers, also fall into it. But commodities that obey the law of diminishing returns, and the production of which is not monopolised, are different. Apart from taxation, too much of the country's resources would have been devoted to turning out these commodities, in such wise that the value of the marginal net product of resources there would have stood *below* the general level. As was explained in Part II. Chapter VIII., taxation imposed upon a commodity in this class up to a certain definite rate, the amount of which is determined by the conditions of the demand and supply of the commodity, would disturb the distribution of the community's resources in a way beneficial to the national dividend; whereas a rate higher than this would be injurious. This fact suggests that, other things being equal, the national dividend will benefit most, or suffer least, if the commodity taxes which the tax system includes are all assessed upon articles obeying the law of diminishing returns, and if they are imposed at low rates upon a large number of objects rather than at high rates upon a small number.) Experience shows, however, that a large number of taxes of small amount are relatively far more costly and inconvenient to collect than a few taxes of large amount. For this reason there is a strong tendency to concentrate indirect taxes upon a small number of important mass goods. When this is done, the rate of taxation is determined, in the main, by the needs of the revenue, rather than by subtle considerations of the type now under review. Nevertheless, it is evident that these considerations afford relevant data, which, if a statesman should arise who enjoyed acquaintance with them, would have a part to play in the structure of the tax-system.

§ 6. What has just been said is applicable to taxes on imported commodities as well as to taxes on commodities manufactured or grown at home. For an imported commodity is, in effect, produced by the resources devoted to making the exports against which it is exchanged. There is, however, an incidental element of advantage in taxes upon imports that is not present in other commodity taxes. In so far as foreigners want our goods, a check, such as a tax causes, to our readiness to accept in payment any one kind of import makes them willing to offer all other kinds on slightly better terms. In other words, it indirectly adds something to the real productivity of those of our resources that are still devoted to making exports. As is well known, conditions are conceivable, in which foreigners have so urgent a demand for our goods that they will contribute the whole of any import taxes we may impose on the goods they send to us in payment, and will thus carry off the same quantity of our goods as they would have done if no tax had been imposed. Generally speaking, however, there are many rival sources of supply from which the goods we export can be obtained. Consequently, the foreign demand for these goods is highly elastic, and it is not possible to compel foreigners permanently to pay any substantial part of our import taxes. These taxes lessen our imports and divert resources from the production of those goods with which our imports used to be purchased—or, more compendiously, from the indirect production by exchange of these imports. The *main* effect of a tax on an import is, thus, precisely similar to that of a tax on any other sort of commodity. Resources are diverted away from the route which the tax obstructs. To what extent they are diverted and how precisely the national dividend is affected depends, in the manner explained in the preceding section, upon the general conditions of demand and supply (through exchange) of the particular commodity concerned.

§ 7. In what has been said so far it has been tacitly assumed that imports subject to tax consist of goods that are not also capable of being produced at home. In these circumstances the differentiation involved in import taxes would be simply differentiation against certain commodities as compared with others. There are also, however, protective import duties, namely, import duties unaccompanied by corresponding excise duties, on goods normally produced in this country as well as abroad. These duties are differential in a fuller sense; for they hit one way of getting the commodities affected, namely, making something else and exchanging it for them, while leaving the rival way, namely, making these commodities themselves, untouched. It is widely held that this sort of differentiation *must* cause some part of the commodities to be obtained by a more costly process than need have been employed, and, therefore, *must* injure the national dividend. The analysis of the fourth section of Part II. Chapter VIII. will, however, have shown that this reasoning, in spite of the high authority that can be cited in its support, is not valid. In that section it was proved that, when a commodity is being obtained from two independent sources of supply—and the same argument is obviously applicable when it is being obtained by two independent methods—there is a presumption that the national dividend would be increased by the imposition of *some* rates of differential tax upon the portion of the supply that is due to the less elastic of the two sources or methods. Though, however, customs duties unaccompanied by excise duties cannot be condemned out of hand merely upon the ground that they are differential, the subtleties of the chapter cited do not afford any basis for a defence of them. The elasticity of the supply of the commodity from direct home manufacture is equivalent to the elasticity of its production. The elasticity of the supply from the exchange method is approximately equal to the elasticity of production abroad *minus* the (negative) elasticity of the foreign demand.[1] Hence, except for commodities, the production of which abroad is very much less elastic than it is at home, the supply from the

---

[1] I say approximately, because the statement of the text requires that the real supply price of the things in general which we produce to exchange against the particular import shall not change in response to changes in the quantity of the import that is purchased. Since a large percentage change in this quantity could not involve more than a very small change in our production generally, this condition is sure to be approximately, though it need not be exactly, realised.

foreign source must be substantially more elastic than the supply from the home source. In general, therefore, our analysis, so far from justifying the imposition of customs duties unaccompanied by excise duties, points, if anything, to excise duties unaccompanied by customs duties! This conclusion does not, of course, by itself suffice to condemn protective duties; and, in view of the assumption of diminishing returns, which is implicit in it, it has no relevance to the problem of infant industries or of industries threatened with destruction from "dumping" at unremunerative rates by foreign trust or kartels.[1]

[1] Cf. Part II. Chapter XVIII. § 6. It is also arguable that, under protective duties, a little more of the sort of tribute from the foreigner, described at the beginning of § 6, is obtainable than under non-protective duties. This, however, is probably a very small matter.

CHAPTER VI

INCOME TAX

§ 1. WE now come to income tax. In earlier days, when
fiscal technique was less perfectly developed than it is now, it
was often found much easier to ascertain the size of certain
specified parts of a man's income than to ascertain the size of the
whole. Consequently, income derived from a particular source
was taken as representative of income generally, and taxation
was based upon it, in the hope that the indication of "ability
to pay" which it afforded would not be very seriously wrong.
This is substantially the principle upon which local rates have
been organised in this country. Lands and houses are forms
of property, the virtual and actual income from which a
local authority can ascertain relatively easily; and, consequently, they have been used as the assessable basis for rates.
From the point of view of the national dividend taxes of this
character are highly objectionable. They disturb the free flow
of investment under the influence of economic inducements by
differentiating against resources invested in buildings and land
improvements, as compared with resources invested in machinery
and stock in trade. Consequently, they tend to divert capital
away from agriculture and houses into other kinds of enterprise, with the result that the values of the marginal net
products of capital in different occupations are made more
unequal, and the national dividend is made smaller than it
would have been under a more scientific and less haphazard
arrangement. Nor is there, to put against this, any compensating advantage on the side of equity. On the contrary,
taxes based, either on a man's possessions of *immobilia* gener-

ally or on his possessions of any particular sort of *immobilia* are bound to be highly inequitable. The proportion of income that is derived from "lands and houses," as compared with the proportion derived from machinery and stock in trade, is necessarily different for people engaged in different kinds of business; while a man, the main part of whose property happens to consist in holdings of government securities, escapes entirely from any form of taxation based upon real property. Monsieur Caillaux brought out this point very well in the French Chamber in introducing his income tax bill: "We must understand that taxes founded on external signs of wealth, on the system of presumptions, have had their day; that their injustice condemns them, and that we must replace them by taxes on actual income or on capital, or part on one and part on the other."[1] Leaving aside for the present taxes assessed on capital, I proceed to consider certain general problems presented by a general income tax.

§ 2. From the standpoint of the national dividend the most important of these relates to the exemption of savings from taxation, an arrangement which would convert the income tax into a tax on expenditure. It will be remembered that in Chapter III. of Part I. attention was called to the difference between Dr. Marshall's and Professor Fisher's use of the term national dividend, the former applying it to what would be consumed in any year if sufficient were withdrawn to maintain capital intact; and the latter applying it to what actually is consumed in any year. Under a pure income tax the national dividend in Marshall's sense would be the object of taxation; under a pure expenditure tax the national dividend in Fisher's sense.

§ 3. The British income tax, we may note in passing, does not conform exactly to either of these ideals. It is not a pure expenditure tax, because it strikes the great bulk of income that is devoted to investment, and does not strike the great bulk of capital that is realised and "spent." It is not a pure income tax, because it exempts appreciations— even appreciations realised by sales—in the capital value of property, which are virtual income, and (within limits) income

---

[1] Seligman, *The Income Tax*, p. 309.

2 s

invested in life-insurance premiums, and, on the other hand, it strikes terminable annuities as wholes and does not exempt that part of them which represents a refund of capital. Plainly, however, these last discrepancies are much smaller than those that separate it from a pure expenditure tax. For a rough approximation, to speak of it as an income tax is not unreasonable.[1]

§ 4. It is easily seen that an expenditure tax derived from a general income tax by the device of exempting savings is not open to the objection which was urged in Chapter V. against an expenditure tax derived from a system of uniform duties levied on all commodities, *i.e.* that it is necessarily proportional and not graduated. On the contrary, expenditures of different magnitudes could be taxed at different rates, just as incomes of different magnitudes are taxed at different rates now. The rates could be made to depend upon the amount of the income, or, if that were thought preferable, upon the amount of the expenditure. Nor need the graduation be based solely upon amount. Arrangements could easily be made—just as easily as under an ordinary income tax—for different rates to be levied upon equal amounts of expenditure, according to the number of people in the families that they had severally to support. Moreover, it would be possible, if it were so desired, to exempt, not merely income that is saved for investment in the popular sense, but also income saved for investment in personal capital—the purchase of necessaries for efficiency, the education of children, and so forth. No doubt, there would be difficulty in doing this at all accurately. Some expenditures of this character, such as charges for education, might, indeed, be exempted *eo nomine*. But "necessaries for efficiency"

---

[1] It may be noticed in passing that, in so far as taxation is required by Government to provide interest for domestic holders of Government stock, the practice of taxing both the fundholders' dividends and the income devoted to paying these dividends involves an element of double taxation. Strictly, just as a private mortgagor is allowed to deduct the mortgage interest he has to pay before he is assessed to income tax, so taxpayers ought to be allowed to deduct that part of their tax payment which is needed to pay the fundholders. If this were done, however, the general rate of tax required to yield a given revenue would have to be considerably increased. Incidentally, the burden would be shifted to some extent away from persons who pay taxes but hold no Government loans on to the shoulders of large fundholders.

is a vague conception, which, it may well be supposed, represents different sums of money for persons engaged in different occupations; and it would hardly be practicable to allow for this fact. Still, some approach to the ideal could be made by deductions, not only of saved incomes in the popular sense, but also of an arbitrary sum, varying with the size of the family, somewhere perhaps in the neighbourhood of £50 per head per year, before a man's liability to the tax is assessed.

§ 5. An income tax modified into an expenditure tax along these lines would strike the national dividend in one way, and one only; namely, by diminishing people's desire to exercise the productive capacity that is already in existence, or, more especially, to exercise it for the benefit of the taxing country. Thus, a heavy general expenditure tax may have the effect of (1) driving propertied men to live and hold their capital invested abroad;[1] (2) driving able men to live and exercise their ability abroad; and (3) relaxing the productive efforts of other able men who are not driven abroad. Its influence along the two

---

[1] Some part of the popular fear that high rate of income tax in this country will drive capital abroad arises from an imperfect knowledge of the exact scope of the British income tax law. It is, no doubt, true that a tax striking the fruits of capital, in so far as it impinges on the investments of foreigners in England, lessens the advantage to foreigners of investment here, and, *pro tanto*, stimulates foreign individuals to withdraw their capital, and foreign corporations with plant abroad to withdraw their head offices. This, however, is a minor matter, for foreign investment here is admittedly small in amount. The substantial fear is that high income tax will drive British-owned capital to foreign fields. This fear is not well grounded. Since the English income tax, unlike the income taxes of the colonies, is levied on incomes *received* in England, and not merely upon those *earned or built up* there, there is, in general, no inducement for an Englishman resident in England to send his capital abroad for investment, in consequence of high income tax here. He will have to pay income tax when he brings the income derived from it home from abroad; and, under an amendment of the income tax law in 1914, he must even pay if he leaves it abroad for investment there. Nor is this all. As things are at present, the income from English capital invested abroad will often have to pay a foreign (or colonial) income tax as well as the British income tax; so that a man, by sending his capital abroad, so far from escaping taxation, would actually encounter more of it. Hence, apart from deliberate and purposed fraud, if English capital is to be driven abroad, English capitalists must be driven there also. Nor is it even true that the supposed indirect effect of high income tax, namely, the fear of "Socialism," could rationally drive capital abroad without driving its owners abroad also; for, presumably, "Socialism" would not fasten on British factory-owners and leave British owners of foreign securities unscathed.

former of these lines is exercised by modifying the comparative
incomes and general amenities obtainable, after taxes have been
paid, at home and in foreign countries. There is, however, some
danger of misapprehension on this subject. It is not *necessary*
that a tax diminishing the relative advantages of residence in
England should drive any one abroad. For, when, as between
two places, movement from one to the other involves cost or
inconvenience, the net incomes of persons of the same ability
or property may differ permanently by any annual amount the
capitalised value of which does not exceed the equivalent of
this cost and inconvenience. There is, in fact, a *locus*, or range,
of possible differences between net incomes in the two places,
such that any difference within the *locus* might exist without
movement between the two places being brought about.[1] If a
tax is imposed on the returns of ability or of property in one of
the two places, A, it is not certain that movement will occur,
unless the tax is larger than the difference between the maximum possible excess, compatible with equilibrium, of returns in
A over returns in B. It is not *probable* that movement will
occur, unless the tax is such that its capitalised value is
nearly equivalent to half the sum representing the cost and
inconvenience of the act of movement. If, therefore, the cost
and inconvenience of movement are large, a very large tax
would be needed to drive people abroad. There is reason to
believe that residence in their native land means so much to
many rich men—particularly, since the advantage of wealth
is largely social advantage—that the cost and inconvenience
of movement would be enormous. It does not seem, therefore,
that a moderate tax upon large incomes available for spending
would have any important effect in driving the owners of
capital and ability abroad, even if similar taxes did not exist
in other countries; whereas, of course, if the high taxation was
world-wide, the tendency to migrate would be wholly destroyed.
There remains the tendency of taxation to check the output of
ability on the part of the able men who are not driven
abroad. Here, again, it seems probable that the effect of a
moderate tax would be small. Such a tax could hardly affect
the training of ability, and, when an able man is actually

[1] Cf. Part II. Chapter II. § 6.

engaged in industry, his aim is so largely " success "—an aim in no wise interfered with by a tax absorbing part of his profits—that he is likely to work much the same whether it is imposed or not. Hence, I do not think that the expectation of a moderate system of taxation upon expenditure would check the supply of industrial effort to any important extent. That is to say, an income tax, from the purview of which savings are exempted, so long as it was moderate in amount, might be levied without serious detriment to the national dividend. When, however, the rates of taxation reach the extremely high levels now attained under the British income tax law, the damage is, of course, much more serious. This aspect of the matter will be examined at a later stage.

§ 6. We have now to compare an expenditure tax of the type I have been describing with an income tax under which savings are not exempt. The essence of the contrast between the two forms of tax is that the former does not, and the latter does, differentiate against saving. It might be thought at first sight that an expenditure tax actually differentiates in favour of saving as compared with consumption. If we had in mind a tax to be imposed for one year only, or for a short period only, at a given rate, this would be so. But, if we are thinking of a system of taxation that is expected to continue indefinitely with constant rates, an expenditure tax is neutral as between saving and spending, and not differential in favour of spending; for the only ultimate advantage a man gets from saving is the return from his investment that he and his heirs can afterwards consume. This means that, under a tax system based on expenditure, resources that are saved are taxed indirectly through their subsequent·yield to the same extent as resources that are consumed at once. There is, therefore, no differentiation of any kind. An income tax, on the other hand, differentiates against saving, by striking savings both when they are made and also when they yield their fruits. Thus, a general permanent income tax at the rate of x per cent strikes the part of income that is spent at this rate. But, if £100 of income is put away for saving, it removes £x from it at the moment and, thereafter, every year removes $\frac{x}{100}$ths of the fruit of the £$(100 - x)$ that are actually turned into the investment. The effective rate of tax per cent is, in fact, $\left\{x + \frac{x}{100}(100 - x)\right\}$; that is, $x\left\{2 - \frac{x}{100}\right\}$. Thus, the effective rate on saved income is practically double the rate on spent income when the tax is small, and substantially more than equal, though less than double, when it is large. For example, a general rate at 10s. in the £ implies a tax, not of 10s., but of 15s. in the £ on saved income. Of course, when there is steep graduation against large incomes, income which is saved by a rich man and left to a relatively poor man, on whose income the income tax (including super-tax) rate is lower, is not differentiated against so heavily as it would have been if the rich man's rate held generally; but it is still differentiated against to a substantial extent. This aspect of the problem need not be elaborated. Apart from it, there is a clear-cut contrast between an income-tax, which differentiates against saving in the way described above, and an expenditure tax, which puts saving and spending on an equal footing.

§ 7. This statement must, indeed, be qualified. The contrast I have drawn is strictly true only of an expenditure tax, which leaves free from tax such "expenditure" as is necessary for efficiency. For, as was explained in Chapter II. § 3, expenditure on real necessaries produces future income, and is, therefore, really capital, in just the same sense as expenditure devoted to the purchase of machinery. A general tax which includes it hits this sort of expenditure twice, while hitting expenditure other than that on necessaries once only. Therefore, a general expenditure tax that does not allow an abatement for necessaries for efficiency is not wholly non-differential. Obviously, how-ever, it does not differentiate against capital in the widest sense so largely as a general income tax under which savings are not exempt. Under this type of tax a man, by diverting income from saving to expenditure, is able to escape taxation that he would otherwise have had to meet. Consequently, we may presume that, if the raising of a given sum of money by a general expenditure tax would have checked the national dividend of the moment, and, through it, new investments in capital, by so much, the raising of an equal sum by a general income tax will check the national dividend of the moment to

about the same extent,[1] but will check the share of it that is
devoted to investment to a greater extent.

§ 8. How much more seriously the collection of a given
revenue by an income tax will check saving than the collection
of an equal sum by an expenditure tax would do, depends
upon (1) the amount of revenue raised relatively to the real
income of the country, (2) the proportion of the country's
income that is normally saved, and (3) the comparative
urgency, to those persons who make savings, of the savings
use and the spendings use respectively. In so far as people
save with a view to providing some definite sum to leave to
their children, and in so far as very rich people save merely
what is left over after their customary standard of life has
been satisfied, the amount saved will not be affected by the
fact that it is subject to differential taxation. On the whole,
I do not think that any *large* difference is made to the amount
of annual savings in this country by the fact that we have a
6s. standard income-tax instead of a standard expenditure
tax calculated to yield about the same aggregate amount of
revenue.

§ 9. It is important to remember, however, that the effect
of any continuing check to investment is, from the point of
view of the national dividend, cumulative. For let us suppose
that the annual creation of new capital amounts normally to,
say, $\frac{1}{50}$th of the existing stock of capital. Let the check to
the creation of new capital due to the tax be, say, $\frac{1}{20}$th each
year. Then at the end of the first year the check to the growth
of capital stock is equal to $\frac{1}{20} \times \frac{1}{50}$, *i.e.* $\frac{1}{1000}$th of its initial
amount. By the second year the check has become equal to
$\frac{2}{1000}$ths, by the third year to $\frac{3}{1000}$ths; and so on continuously.
This does not, of course, imply that the capital stock will
eventually become smaller than it is now. But it does imply
that the restriction of its amount below what it would otherwise have been becomes larger every year. In the limit, the
proportionate check to the capital stock of the country will be
equal to the proportionate check to the annual saving. We

---

[1] Probably very slightly more, since, people's free choice of the way to use
the income derived from their work being interfered with, the inducement to
get income is a little less.

may conclude, therefore, that the effect on the national dividend of maintaining a general income tax instead of a general expenditure tax as a means of raising a given revenue on the present scale, though very small at first, is likely in the end to be substantial.

§ 10. In practice the choice between income tax and expenditure tax must take account, not only of effects on the national dividend, but also of fairness between differently situated individuals. From this point of view two contrary arguments may be advanced. First, it may be urged that persons whose income terminates with their life will, in general, need to save more, in order to make provision for their families, than persons in enjoyment of equal incomes derived from permanent property. This implies that they have a smaller taxable capacity. An undifferentiated expenditure tax allows for this while an undifferentiated income tax does not, and it is, therefore, "fairer" between people with equal incomes derived from different sources. Secondly, it may be replied that, generally speaking, the richer a man is, the larger is the proportion of his income that he is able to, and in fact usually does, save. An ungraduated expenditure tax will, therefore, take a smaller proportion of his income from a rich man, as compared with a poor man, than an ungraduated income tax will do, and this will generally be judged to be unfair. These two arguments from equity thus point in opposite directions. But it is easily seen that, since the former can be neutralised by appropriate differentiation and the latter by appropriate graduation—if desired the graduation could be made to depend on amount of income and not of expenditure—there is little substance in either. Considerations of equity cannot, therefore, properly be urged as decisive either for or against the exemption of savings from income tax. As we have seen, considerations touching the national dividend point definitely, if not very strongly, in favour of it.

§ 11. There is, therefore, only the question of feasibility. From one point of view it would seem to be easier to exempt savings than to tax them; because, whereas "expenditure" is a concept fairly easy to define, the determination of "income," as conceived for income tax purposes, involves the difficult problem of making proper allowance for maintaining intact the existing capital fund.[1] Are royalty rents, for example, to be assessed for income tax at their full value, or should a deduction be made on the ground that the property from which they are derived is being gradually exhausted? If a deduction is conceded, in what way, particularly when the life of the royalty-yielding property is uncertain, should the amount of the deduction be determined? There are many similar problems connected with the difficult subject of "wasting assets," all of which are at once swept aside if we agree to exempt *all* savings, whether made for the purpose of creating new capital or of maintaining intact capital that already exists. This argument, however, is less powerful from the side of practice than it is from that of logical consistency; because, after all, compromise decisions can, and, indeed, have been made on wasting asset puzzles, which, however unsatisfactory and unsystematic, nevertheless allow an income tax on the British plan to work and to yield an enormous revenue. The opposing argument is of a different order. It is that a provision for exempting all savings would strike at the root of income tax administration by opening a wide door for evasion. Dishonest citizens might save one year, so escaping taxation, and secretly sell out and spend their savings next year. It is possible that the revenue officials would succeed in mastering this form of dishonesty as they have already mastered other forms. But on this practical issue it would be unbecoming for an academic student to venture any decided opinion.

§ 12. The next important problem is concerned with differentiation between the rates to be charged on income derived from the recipient's own exertions and income derived from property. The distinction between the two classes of income is not, indeed, quite so simple as it seems to be at first sight. Thus, the income which a man receives from a business controlled by himself would seem rightly to be divisible between the two categories; but, under the English law,[2] it is classed, along with

---

[1] Cf. for an analogous difficulty in the definition of the national dividend Part I. Chapter III. § 6.

[2] Under the Italian law the distinction between incomes obtained from different sources is carried much further than in England.

(1) Income from practically gilt-edged securities is assessed at full value.

the earnings of professional men, as exclusively earned income. There is difficulty, too, as to the right position in this classification of the ·incomes ·received· by pensioners and by tenants for life of land.   The general drift of the distinction is, however, plain enough.   It is widely held that, since earned incomes are dependent on the life and activity of the recipient, he·will be under a sterner obligation to save for his children and for his own old age than the recipient of an equal income derived from durable·property.   Consequently, his taxable capacity being smaller, he.ought to be taxed at a lower rate.   If the income tax.were so modified as to exempt all savings and to become in effect an expenditure tax, the extra provision, which the man with an earned income finds it necessary to make for·the future, would be fully allowed for in this exemption, and· no plea for further assistance by way of differentiation could be derived from this line of thought.   As regards income tax proper, however, the argument for differentiation to allow for the smaller taxable capacity of earned income is extremely strong.

§ 13. In endeavouring to estimate the consequences of differentiation upon the national dividend, we must, of course, assume that the aggregate quantity of revenue to·be raised is given.   Thus, a diminution in the taxation of earned income, due to a decision to differentiate, must be taken to imply an increase in the taxation of "unearned." or investment income. From a short period point of view it is almost certain that this shifting of taxation from earned to "unearned" income would benefit the national·dividend.   For·it would lessen the discouragement to earn· income by ·work, and, though it would also discourage saving, yet, since·annual saving is only·a small part of the ·total capital existing in any year, it would only lessen the aggregate amount of capital to a very slight extent. The relief, in short, would extend over the whole range of work, but·the new burden would ·fall, in the main, on capital that already exists and· so cannot be discouraged.   If, however,

(2) Income from other securities at $\frac{4}{9}$ of value.
(3) Temporary mixed revenues, *i.e.* business and trade, $\frac{7}{9}$ of value.
(4) Income purely·from individual earnings, *e.g.* professional, $\frac{1}{3}$ of value.
(5) Income from pensions and Government salaries $\frac{4}{9}$ of value.
(Seligman, *The Income Tax*, 1911, p. 348).

we look at things *sub specie aeternitatis*, imagining a long continued reign of the supplemental tax on unearned income, the
position is different. For, from this point of view, new capital,
or what would have been new capital, is large relatively to the
capital in existence when the tax is imposed, and so the check
which the tax puts upon saving has an effect on capital of the
same order as the effect on saving. It is no longer clear, therefore, that the advantage to the dividend from relieving work
is greater than the disadvantage from hitting saving.

Nor need we stop at this negative conclusion. From the
point of view of a very long period, the main part of unearned
income is the interest resulting from past saving; so that to
impose a special tax on unearned income is to differentiate in
favour of spending and against saving even more largely than
is done under a non-differential income tax. In accordance,
therefore, with the reasoning of the preceding sections, it would
seem that, from a long period point of view, the collection of
revenue with the help of what is, in effect, a surtax on unearned
income is likely to be more injurious to the national dividend
than the collection of an equal income by a general undifferentiated income tax. Probably, however, there is not very much
in this.

On the whole, I incline to the view that, unless either
savings are exempted, or property incomes are substantially hit
by special property taxes, the case for differentiation should be
conceded on grounds of equity. It seems reasonable, however,
that, after a certain limit of earned income has been attained,
the proportion in which earned income as a whole is relieved
relatively to unearned income should continually diminish.

§ 14. Akin to differentiation between equal incomes derived
from different sources is differentiation between equal incomes
received by persons in different economic situations. Equity
plainly demands that allowance should be made for the widely
different "ability to pay" of bachelors or spinsters, persons
with small families and persons with large families. When
the rate of taxation is low, the injustice that results if these
allowances are not made is small. But, when once the rate is
made heavy, it becomes glaring. If the basis of taxation was,
not income, but expenditure, the case for allowances for wife and

children would be still stronger, because, other things being
equal, a man with a family is bound to spend a larger proportion of his income than a bachelor, and so would have to pay, not
merely the same amount in taxation, but a larger amount. Even,
however, under an ordinary income tax, the general principle of
charging a given income with less income tax the more persons
it has to maintain is obviously equitable. No doubt, the proportion of the tax of which a family man is relieved as against a
bachelor should diminish as income increases. If, for example,
a married couple with one child at £500 a year has, say, half
the taxable capacity of a bachelor with the same income, a
similar married couple with £100,000 a year has more than
half the capacity of a £100,000 bachelor. But *some* relief
should in equity be given at all points of the income scale ;
and an appropriately diminishing *proportion* might be provided
by enacting that, for all incomes above a certain limit, the
absolute amount of the allowances of tax-free income should
be the same. Of course, whatever is done in this matter,
puzzles will be met with in the precise definition of what a
family includes—on what conditions dependent parents or a
widower's sister should be reckoned in it, and so forth. But
these are minor difficulties, and, once the general principle
is accepted, can be easily overcome. No danger to the
national dividend need be apprehended from the adjustments
required by this principle.

§ 15. I pass to the next point. When it is decided, as in
a modern State it is fairly certain to be, that a large portion of
the annual revenue shall be obtained by means of a general
income tax, whether or not savings are exempted, there is
general agreement that the rates of taxation should be graduated steeply as the incomes of persons otherwise similarly
situated increase, and that persons with incomes below a certain
minimum should be exempted altogether. This would be
desirable even though income tax constituted the whole of the
tax system of the country. The view that taxes which
take equal proportions from incomes of different sizes are
equitable as between richer and poorer persons is no longer
seriously entertained. It is, indeed, still sometimes held
that the actual burden of dissatisfaction involved to a

man with an income of £1000 in paying £100 is about the same as that involved to a man with an income of £10,000 in paying £1000.[1] But it is no longer assumed that equity in taxation must mean equality in burden imposed; it may mean equality in *situation left* after the tax has been paid. And, on the other hand, it is coming to be realised with increasing clearness that, when a total revenue of £1000 is wanted, the aggregate burden, which the collection of it inflicts, will be very much greater if it is raised in ten pieces of £100 from each of ten persons with incomes of £1000 than if it is raised in one piece of £1000 from one person with an income of £10,000; and smallness in the aggregate amount of sacrifice involved, as well as equality in the distribution of that sacrifice, is an important element, not perhaps in the equity in a narrow sense, but certainly in the general "propriety," of taxation. In the light of these considerations, some considerable measure of graduation is universally recognised as proper in any modern tax system. When, as in real life, an income tax constitutes only a part of a system, in which there are also included a number of taxes on commodities of wide consumption, the case for graduation is still stronger. For, as already observed, commodity taxes, if they are to be reasonably inexpensive to collect, must be levied, in the main, on mass-goods of fairly general consumption. These goods are, of course, purchased by poorer persons in much larger quantities *relatively to their income* than they are by richer persons. A man with £10,000 a year does not consume one hundred times as much tea or sugar or beer as a man with £100 a year. Hence, whatever part of the tax system of modern States is made up of taxes on commodities is apt

---

[1] If we ignore differences of temperament and assume that (1) for everybody alike the satisfaction derived from income is one and the same function of the amount of income, and (2) that the curve, whose ordinates represent the increments of satisfaction from successive increments of income, slopes downward towards the right, the condition required to make it true that proportionate taxation involves equal sacrifice is that this curve shall be a rectangular hyperbola. For, x being the income, $f(x)$ the satisfaction due to the xth increment of income, and h any constant fraction, in order that $\int_0^x f(x) - \int_0^{hx} f(hx)$ may be constant for all values of x, it is necessary that $xf(x) = hxf(hx)$, a condition which, in general implies that $xf(x)$ is constant for all values of x.

to be graduated inversely, in the sense that it takes a larger proportion of their incomes from poor than from rich persons. Even, therefore, if it was thought proper to make the whole tax system a proportionate one, it would be necessary for the income tax portion of it to be graduated progressively. If, as was argued above, the whole system ought to be progressive, the argument for progression in this portion of it is, by so much, strengthened. What has been said implies that the scale of graduation which is equitable in an income tax cannot be determined until account has been taken of the other components of the tax system. As regards small incomes, the part played by those taxes on commodities, which are commonly known as indirect taxes, is very important. As regards large incomes, on the present English system these taxes constitute so small a fraction of the sum total of taxation that little attention need be paid to them. But, on the other hand, great attention must be paid to the existing scale of death duties.

§ 16. It is evident that graduation has a bearing on the national dividend very much more intimate than either differentiation or family allowances. Equity in the widest sense might point to a scale so steep that practically the whole of the revenue would be raised from the highest incomes. But this arrangement, when the aggregate revenue required is large, would involve a rate of taxation upon those brought under it so enormous that it would be bound to discourage enterprise, check saving, and stimulate emigration. It must be remembered in particular that, if effective rates of taxation on total incomes are graduated very steeply, the rate on increments of income at some points is liable to be much greater than the rate on aggregate income. If, for example, the effective rate on £2000 was 6s. and on £2100 6s. 6d., a £2000 man, who by extra work added £100 to his income, would have to pay on the £100 not 6s. 6d. but 16s. 6d. in the £; and it is this rate that is really relevant to his decision whether or not he shall undertake the extra work. When the total revenue required is small relatively to the aggregate income of the country, steep graduation is compatible with moderate rates even on very high incomes, and is, therefore, relatively innocuous to the national dividend. But, when the total revenue required is large, a like degree of steepness is literally impossible. More generally, if we call R the standard rate on incomes of £2000 and m the multiplier (fractional or integral) to be applied to this, so as to yield the rate on any other income x, this multiplier cannot be simply a function of x, but must be a function of R also. To retain the same set of multipliers, whatever the standard rate, would imply, for example, that, if the present standard rate were doubled, the effective rate on the largest incomes—super tax, of course, being counted along with income tax—would rise to more than 20s. in the £; and this must inevitably cause these incomes, and the portion of the national dividend which they represent, totally to disappear. The conclusion to which we are forced is that, while graduation is in equity essential, and, moreover, when a large revenue is required, is the only possible means of raising such a revenue, nevertheless the interests of the national dividend are seriously threatened if the rates in the upper part of the scale become very large. The extremely heavy rates prevailing—and in view of the large volume of our national debt necessarily prevailing—in this country at the present time give cause for serious apprehension.

CHAPTER VII

§ 1. THE last important category of taxes requiring study consists of taxes assessed on property, whether annually, or at specified intervals, or on special occasions such as transfer or death. In a rough general way annual property taxes correspond to taxes on income derived from property; for to a man with an estate of £100,000 yielding £5000 a year, it is indifferent whether a tax at 10 per cent is imposed on the income or one at $\frac{1}{2}$ per cent on the capital. The correspondence between the two sorts of tax is not, however, complete. As compared with the tax on unearned income under the British system, a property tax has certain advantages of detail. First, the British tax on unearned income is not strictly a tax on income from property, because, as was observed in the preceding chapter, the incomes of private business men, which are, of course, partly derived from property, are defined in law as wholly "earned." Thus, the British system favours one form of industrial organisation (namely the private business) as against the chief rival form (namely the joint-stock company). A property tax would be free from this element of differentiation. Secondly, a property tax has the advantage of hitting the gain that a man makes when he buys property (land, pearls, or anything else) and holds it to re-sell after it has appreciated. Under any ordinary form of income tax this gain, which in equity ought to be hit, is not hit. On the other hand, a property tax has several disadvantages. First, on sorts of property, the income derived from which varies greatly in different years, its continuous incidence

640

may involve difficulty and inconvenience in the lean years. Secondly, on sorts of property, which have value because it is expected that they will yield income, say, ten years hence, a property tax will not only be inconvenient in the way described above, but will also, in effect, involve double taxation on incomes derived from these sorts of property, thus differentiating against them. Thirdly, it is less easy to make arrangements for graduation in tax rates when there is an income tax on earned income coupled with a property tax than when the whole of everybody's income is brought under review under some form of general income tax. Lastly, and probably most important of all, whereas the tax on unearned income can, by the device of taxation at the source, be levied easily and cheaply and without any opening for evasion, a property tax would involve expensive valuations, would be complicated by the fluctuations of stock exchange values, and would, in some branches, offer great inducements to, and considerable opportunities for, evasion. On the national dividend an annual property tax might be expected to have much the same effect as an annual tax on unearned income producing an equal revenue.

§ 2. An annual property tax is not, however, the only possible form of that tax. Resort may also be had to a property tax at long intervals in the form of death duties. This type of tax has an advantage over either an annual tax on unearned income or an annual tax on property calculated to yield an equivalent return. For, let us revert to the contrast set out in Chapter II. between raising an annual 20 millions by collecting £100 every year from each of a group of 200,000 people and raising the same sum by collecting £2000 from each of those people once in twenty years. The choice between the two methods is indifferent to the State. But it is not indifferent to the persons concerned. Since these persons discount future taxes precisely as they discount all future events, the expectation of taxes levied after the second method will have the smaller restrictive influence upon the quantity of capital created by them. The fact, that distance in time introduces a considerable chance that the investor may no longer be living when the postponed tax falls due, greatly emphasises this difference. The superiority of postponed over immediate taxes is further enhanced when the levy is made, not after a distinctive time, during which there is a *chance* of the occurrence of the investor's death, but definitely *at* his death; for, obviously, a certainty influences conduct more strongly than a probability. Moreover, there are additional reasons why this form of postponed tax should impose a relatively small check upon the supply of capital. A part of the stimulus to accumulation consists in the power and prestige that riches confer. In persons of only moderate fortune, who have, or hope to have, children, this motive is not, indeed, likely to play a dominant part. A desire to provide for their children will be the main motive, and, if it were removed, many of them would elect to "retire" from work much earlier than they do now. But, as Professor Carver observes: "After one's accumulation has increased beyond that which is necessary to safeguard one's offspring and to provide for the genuine prosperity of one's family, the motive to further accumulation changes. One then engages in business enterprises because of a love of action and a love of power. Accumulated capital becomes then one of the instruments of the game. So long as the player is left in possession of this instrument while he is one of the players, he is not likely to be discouraged from accumulation merely by the fact that the State, rather than his heirs, gets it after he is through with it." [1] In a like spirit the late Mr. Carnegie wrote: "To the class whose ambition it is to leave great fortunes and to be talked about after death, it will be even more attractive, and, indeed, a somewhat nobler ambition to have enormous sums paid over to the State from their fortunes." Hence, very heavy death duties could probably be levied on large legacies—particularly on legacies not in the direct line—without causing any important check to saving and the national dividend.

§ 3. One further point may be added. Signor Rignano has published an ingenious plan under which death duties would

---

[1] *Essays in Social Justice*, p. 323. Professor Fisher even writes: "The ordinary normal self-made American millionaire is rather disposed, I believe, to look on the inheritance of his millions by his children with some misgiving" (*Journal of Political Economy*, vol. xxiv. p. 711).

be levied, not only on the death of the original accumulator,
but also on that of the first and second inheritors. On this
plan resources would be taxed to the extent, say, of one-third,
when they descended from their original accumulator to his
successor, the remainder would be taxed to the extent of two-
thirds when this successor handed them on, while, at the
next succession, the whole of what was left would be absorbed.[1]
There would, of course, be some technical difficulty in enforcing
any plan of this kind, and it might even be necessary for a law
to be passed requiring all legacies to be settled in such a way
that the heirs could not touch the principal. But, if these
difficulties could be overcome, there can be no doubt that a
large revenue could be obtained from rich persons by this plan,
in such wise that the expectation of the levy of it would
involve an even smaller restrictive effect upon the supply of
capital, and an even smaller injury to the national dividend,
than is associated with the existing system of death duties.
Indeed, there is much force in S. Rignano's contention that
his plan would actually lead to an *increase* of saving. For,
"as regards one's own children, every sum saved by the heir
of a given patrimony would come to have, in his eyes, *a much
greater value, even three or four times greater*, than the same

---

[1] Cf. Rignano, *Di un socialismo in accordo colla dottrina conomica liberale.*
The plan is described by its author in detail thus: "Sia ad esempio A che alla
sua morte lasci un patrimonio di un ammontare complessivo *a*; lo Stato inter-
venga, come coerede, a prelevarne, ad es., il terzo; e i due terzi restanti vadano
a B, da A di suo pieno arbitrio designato come erede. B aumenti col proprio
lavoro e col proprio risparmio, o col semplice risparmio sui redditi del patrimonio
ereditato, o coll' uno e l' altro insieme, questo patrimonio ereditato 2/3 *a* di un
ammontare complessivo *b*. Alla sua morte lo Stato divida un tale ammontare
2/3 *a* + *b*, nel quale i due patrimoni siano venuti comunque a fondersi e a con-
fondersi, in due parti del valore rispettivo appunto 2/3 *a* e *b*, e su questa quota
b prelevi pur sempre il terzo, ma sulla quota 2/3 *a*, che rappresenta l'ammontare
del patrimonio che B ha ereditato di prima mano dal suo effettivo accumulatore
A, prelevi, invece, una frazione o percentuale maggiore, ad es., i 2/3 (assumendo
questa progressività particolare ¼, ⅔ e, come andiamo ora a vedere, ⅓, cioè il 33,
il 66, e il 100 per 100, naturalmente a semplice titolo d' esempio)" (*loc. cit.*
p. 60). It is pointed out, further, that an arrangement permitting duty-free
transfer from A to B, accompanied by the State absorption of everything which
A had left to B, when B in turn dies, can be brought under the same general
formula; "la progressività particolare venendo ad essere in tal caso ⅔, ⅓" (*ibid.*
p. 61). Rignano suggests that direct descendants, who come into being after
their progenitor is dead, stand, as regards his desire to save for their benefit,
in much the same position as distant connections among his contemporaries
(*ibid.* p. 87).

sum inherited by him; whereas to-day the heir of a great fortune is not much inclined to increase further the patrimony which he has inherited, for, as it is more than sufficient for him, he thinks it will be the same for his son."[1]

[1] *Journal of the Royal Economic Society*, 1919, p. 308.

CHAPTER VIII

THE COMPARATIVE EFFECTS ON THE NATIONAL DIVIDEND
OF TAXES AND LOANS

§ 1. In the first chapter of this Part it was pointed out that the reasons which make it imperative for the normal expenditure of Governments to be met out of taxation do not apply to abnormal expenditures that occur only at intervals, or to expenditures on reproductive investments, the proceeds of which would suffice to pay interest and sinking fund on capital borrowed to finance them. The mere fact, however, that loans for these purposes are not ruled out of court *ab initio* does not prove that resort, either exclusive or partial, ought to be had to them. That important question has still to be debated. To this end I propose in the present chapter to investigate the comparative effects on the national dividend of raising a given sum of money by taxation and by loan. I suppose the money to be required for the purchase of actual goods and services by Government, and not for the repayment of an internal debt or the purchase of some existing concern hitherto conducted by private enterprise. I suppose, too, for simplicity of exposition, that the emergency to be dealt with is one which nobody expects to recur, so that, if it is met by taxation, that finishes everything, and, if it is met by a loan, all that is left over to the future is the need for paying interest and sinking fund on the loan. On these suppositions it is plain that, under the tax plan, the only way in which the national dividend can be affected is through the fact of the tax, while on the loan plan it can be affected both through the fact of the loan and through the expectation of the taxes that have to be levied subsequently for its service. We may begin by ignoring this last reaction and compare simply the fact of a big tax levy with the fact of a big loan levy.

§ 2. Whichever plan is chosen, the *source* from which it is possible for the money to be drawn is much the same. What the Government wants is the services of men and certain materials. For this purpose a large part of the capital wealth of the country as ordinarily conceived is not available. What is available can be set out roughly as follows. Some of the materials wanted can be got out of capital stocks, but in the main they must, if the quantity needed is at all large, be grown upon, or dug out of, the ground at the time they are wanted. Existing capital can be drawn upon indirectly if people choose to sell claims to it in the form of securities, or actual pieces of it in the form of pictures and houses, to foreigners, in exchange for work on their part in providing materials and other sorts of income that the Government may need. Non-existing capital, to put it paradoxically, can be drawn upon by the creation of capital obligations abroad through borrowing on the part of individuals. New resources, which would normally have gone to the creation of new capital or to the maintaining in repair of existing capital, can be drawn upon. Resources that would normally have been devoted to consumption can be drawn upon. Lastly, new resources can be created for the purpose by extra effort, which, apart from the need for national expenditure, would not have come into existence at all. All these sources are available alike under taxation and under purely domestic loans. When the loan plan is so arranged as to admit of subscriptions by foreigners, and, still more markedly, when a Government directly negotiates a foreign loan, it is, by creating a new capital obligation from the nation as a whole, tapping a source, which, under the tax plan, is only available to a smaller extent through the indirect process of individual foreign borrowing or selling of securities.

§ 3. It is plain that, under either plan, in so far as the funds required are drawn from consumption (in excess of what is needed for efficiency) or from the creation of new resources (by means that do not diminish the efficiency of the people or machinery employed), the national dividend of the future is left intact. So far as they are drawn from any of the other sources, it is damaged to the full extent of the interest loss which the depletion of capital implies. Our first problem, therefore, is to determine how far the choice between the loan plan and the tax plan makes a difference to the source from which the funds raised are in fact drawn. It is supposed in some quarters, where the *source* and the *object* of taxation are confused, that under the loan plan the whole levy comes, in effect, out of capital, while under the tax plan the whole comes out of income. When loans are raised abroad, it is fair enough to suppose that the whole levy is, in effect, taken out of capital : that is to say, the raising of it involves to the nation a new capital obligation, such that the national income left over after interest has been paid on it will be less, to the extent of that interest, than it would have been if the loan had not been raised. Nor is this burden on the future alleviated if citizens of the country making the loan afterwards buy up the debt claims held by foreigners; for, when they do that, the funds with which they buy them are themselves withdrawn from what otherwise would probably have been income-producing uses in the country itself. But, of course, the bulk of the loans raised by Governments—or at all events by the British Government— will be raised by subscriptions from citizens of the country where the loan is made. For this sort of loan the above simple solution does not hold; and it is necessary to compare the effects of the loan method and of the tax method in a more careful manner.

§ 4. It may be well to clear the ground by remarking that on either plan the extent to which the various sources are drawn upon will be affected by the nature of the cause which renders the raising of the money necessary. If this cause is the opening up of some enterprise capable of yielding a large money income to the State, people will know that the taxes they will have to pay in the future will be by so much lower. Consequently, they will not feel themselves hit, and will not be inclined to economise in consumption or engage in extra work in order to provide the money. The position will be in some degree similar if the expenditure, though it does not actually yield a money income to the State, is of such a sort that large economic benefits for the public in general—in effect an increase in their real incomes—is anticipated from it. On the other hand, if the cause of the need for money is, not opportunity for constructive work, but the necessity of warding off a threatened evil,—as in a war of defence—no positive gain, as distinguished from the prevention of harm, will be expected from it, people will feel themselves hit, and will be inclined to economise more and work harder to meet the call. These considerations are applicable both to levies made by taxes and to levies made, by loans. It is important that they should be borne in mind; but they are not directly relevant to a *comparison* between the effects of these two methods.

§ 5. To carry out this comparison, let us begin by supposing that the loan contemplated as an alternative to taxation is not a voluntary but a forced one, and that it will take from each individual exactly the same sum as, under the rival plan, would have been taken from him in taxes; and let us suppose further that each lender is given to understand that, of the taxation required to pay interest and sinking fund on the Government debt created by the loan, he will have to provide a proportion exactly equal to his proportion of loan-holdings. It is possible to imagine a world in which the levy of a forced loan on these terms would have the same effect as the collection of an equal sum of money by taxation. To tell a man who expects to live for ever, in a country where the rate of interest is always 5 per cent, that he must surrender £1000 now, is approximately the same thing as to tell him that he will have to surrender £50 a year from now onwards for ever. Or, to put the point otherwise, to take from him £1000 now in taxation is approximately the same thing as to borrow from him £1000 on a loan at 5 per cent, at the same time informing him that the £50 interest to be paid on his loan will be collected every year by that amount of taxation levied on himself. I have said that these two things are *approximately*, and not exactly, the same, because the loan plan would leave the £1000 in our citizen's possession and thus available to fall back upon in an emergency, while, on the tax plan, he would be deprived of this stand-by. But, if we carry our supposition further and abolish all economic friction, it will appear that our citizen could not make use of his £1000 for an emergency without sacrificing £50 a year in interest afterwards, and—always apart from economic friction—if he were prepared to do this, he could, on the rival plan, borrow £1000 for the emergency. On these suppositions the two plans would work in *exactly* the same way, and no one who understood what was being done would act otherwise if confronted with the one than he would do if confronted with the other.

§ 6. Let us now return by degrees to the actual world. And first let us reintroduce economic friction. What this means from the present point of view is that, when a person has collateral to offer, even though he is subject to extra taxes equivalent to the interest on the securities which this represents, it is practically very much easier for him to borrow from bankers, not merely in an emergency, but on any occasion, than it would be otherwise. He is, therefore, likely to consider himself *slightly* more hurt by a tax than by an equivalent loan: and he may, in consequence, make slightly greater efforts to meet the impost by harder work and by economy of consumption. In view, however, of the fact that most people rich enough to be subject to large levies have securities, which, if they are prevented from borrowing, they can sell, this effect is probably too small to need serious attention.

§ 7. A more important distinction is as follows. In practice, when a man is forced to lend £1000 at 5 per cent, it is not possible to decree that the £50 required annually to pay him his interest shall be taken in taxes from himself. The tax system may be designed to effect this object, and may succeed in effecting it at first. But taxation cannot be worked by way of poll taxes; it must be based on some objects—income, expenditure, commodities or what not. Hence, whenever any given amount of future taxation has to be provided for, the portion of it that will fall on any particular individual cannot be determined beforehand. It will depend roughly on the ratio at the time between his income and the aggregate income of the community, and this ratio is liable to be modified, not only by what he does, but also by what other people do. The tax method of raising money, therefore, means to any citizen the loss in after years of the interest that he would have received on the money he is forced to give to the Government: the (forced) loan·method means the loss in after years of an amount of taxation, which may exceed or fall short of this sum, according as his income comes to constitute a larger or a smaller proportion of the aggregate national income. This necessary looseness· of connection between the loan burden and the future taxation that a lender will have to meet towards providing his own interest leads to too little attention being paid to the debit side of the account under the loan method. People in general may, therefore, be expected to *think* themselves considerably less hard hit under the loan plan than under the tax plan. Consequently, they will be appreciably less keen to meet the call upon them by economies in consumption and increased output of work. So far as this happens, the capital of the community will·be depleted appreciably more under the loan plan than under the tax plan, and the dividend in future years will suffer in proportion.

§ 8. Hitherto we have supposed the loan plan to be carried out by way of a forced loan taking from each citizen exactly the sum that would have been taken from him under the tax plan. In actual practice, however, loans are generally voluntary, and large subscribers have good reason to hope that the interest on their holdings will exceed the contribution in taxes which they will have to make to provide this interest; for experience has never yet revealed a tax system graduated for increasing incomes anything like as·steeply as loan subscriptions are likely to be graduated, at all events when the loan required is large. Hence, the richer classes, from whom, when a large amount of money is wanted, contributions under any plan must chiefly come, will think, and rightly think, that a loan hits them much less hardly than equivalent taxation would do. They are, therefore, less likely to be induced to check consumption or to work more strenuously, and more likely to subscribe to Government only such resources as they would otherwise have invested in industry. Consequently, the check to the provision and maintenance of capital will be more serious, and the national dividend of the future will be diminished to a correspondingly greater extent.

§ 9. So far we have left out of account the effects of the future taxation which the loan method implies. Whereas a levy raised by taxation, when once it has been made, is over and done with, a levy made by the loan method leaves an aftermath in permanent or, at all events, long-enduring taxes to raise the money with which to pay interest on the loan. These taxes, being long-enduring, are foreseen; and the expectation of them must tend, in ways that have already been described, to check production and injure the national dividend, so long as they endure. This aspect of the matter has been discussed at length in previous chapters, and there is no need to dwell upon it here. Our discussion has thus made it plain that, not in one way only, but in several ways, the levy of any given sum of money by a loan is likely to prove more injurious to the national dividend of the future than the levy of an equal sum by taxation.

§ 10. These results are clearly correct when the choice is between a single large loan levy and a single large tax levy. Caution is required, however, before they are applied to the controversy between advocates of loans and advocates of taxes as a means of financing war. If all wars were very short, and the funds needed for them could be raised at one single blow, what has been said above would be entirely applicable. But, in fact, wars may last for a number of years. When this happens, or there is fear of this happening, the tax plan acts, not merely through the fact of it at the moment, but also through the expectation of its continuance *during* the war. Just in so far, therefore, as it is thought by the people subjected to it to hit them more severely than the loan method would do, the knowledge that a large part of the fruit of any exertions they may make will be absorbed by the State may, in spite of the patriotic stimulus that wars provide, seriously lessen their exertions. Had that part of the expenses of the great war which was defrayed out of domestic loans—even apart from creations of bank credit—been defrayed instead out of taxation, not only would the standard rate of income tax have had to be enormously higher than the 6s. level which it actually attained, but a great mass of other taxation must also have been imposed. Such a state of things continuing for a number of years might well have relaxed effort very seriously during the war itself. This is an important consideration. It partially excuses what many economists considered the undue caution of the British Government in the use of taxation to finance the war.

§ 11. At first sight it might seem that yet another qualification is needed. If, it may be said, it becomes the established custom to finance abnormal expenditure out of taxation, there will be created a general expectation of these occasional levies, and this will check the accumulation of savings during the intervals between the levies, and so indirectly injure the national dividend. This argument, however, ignores the fact that the alternative to a tax levy is, not nothing at all, but a series of levies later on to provide interest on a loan, and that the expectation of these should *prima facie* react on saving at least as seriously as the expectation of larger levies at long intervals. Hence, we conclude generally that, from the standpoint of the national dividend, and apart altogether from political difficulties, taxation affords a *somewhat* better method than loans of raising money for emergencies. *How much* better it is, it is not, of course, possible to say. When account is taken of the fact that economies of consumption and extra work very likely react injuriously on the future productive power of the human capital of the community, it may well be that the presumed advantage of taxation in causing a larger proportion of the levy to be drawn from these sources is in part illusory, and that, on the whole, the dividend of the future will be only a little larger than it would have been had the method of loans been employed. Still, we may fairly conclude that *some* advantage is probable.

§ 12. One further point remains. A part of this advantage is looked for because, as has been explained above, the tax plan will cause the people actually living and working at the time the expenditure is being undertaken to contract their consumption and to increase their productive efforts to a greater extent than they would do under the other plan. In other words,

the dividend of the future is benefited at the cost of an
enhanced real burden upon the present. It is possible to
maintain that an improvement in the dividend brought about
by these means is not an improvement in any ultimate sense,
but really involves on the whole—apart from its effects on
distribution—an injury to economic welfare. When, however,
it is recalled that the reason—apart again from distribution—
why the loan method leads to less economies of consumption and
less extra work than the tax method is largely that under it,
as was shown above, people estimate their real position over-
optimistically, whereas under the rival plan they are forced to
estimate it rightly, the ground for this demurrer is cut away.

CHAPTER IX

DISTRIBUTION UNDER TAXES AND LOANS

§ 1. THE preceding chapter contains all that is directly relevant to the main theme of this Part—namely, the relation between fiscal methods and the national dividend. To stop at this point would, however, be highly misleading, because it would leave out of account all those considerations which must be dominant in any practical choice between the rival plans of taxes and loans. So far as effects on the dividend go, the tax method has, as has been shown, a slight advantage. But there is not very much in it. The really decisive factor is the comparative effect of the two plans on distribution. Though, therefore, to do so involves something of a digression, I propose in the present chapter to make some study of this aspect of the problem. It will be convenient to consider in turn distribution between the present and future generations, distribution between people of equal wealth in different situations, and distribution between people of different degrees of wealth.

§ 2. It is evident that, in so far as the loan method causes more of the monies required by Government to be taken out of what would have been capital and so injures the dividend of the future more than the tax method. does, it must throw a larger share of the real burden of suffering and discomfort upon future generations and less upon the present generation. It has been argued, however, that, over and above this, the choice of loans in preference to taxes to finance, say, a great war, throws a direct and special burden on the future. That is the contention we have now to investigate.

§ 3. In this task it is well to distinguish between the payment of interest on the Government debt and the repayment of principal through a sinking fund. As in the preceding chapter, we ignore foreign-held debt. So far as interest is concerned, it is obvious that what is taken from the income of taxpayers in taxes goes into the income of holders of loan stock, and that, therefore, all that happens is a transfer of income from one section of the community to another section, and, in so far as taxpayers and loan holders are identical, from one pocket to another pocket in the same coat. Plainly, in a transfer of this kind, it is impossible that any *direct objective burden*—I am not at present concerned with other sorts of burden—can be involved. There remains the money raised for repayment of principal through a sinking fund. As regards this, it has been claimed by certain writers that the preceding argument is inapplicable. They reason that, when a holder of loan stock has the principal of his loan paid off by the Government, he receives no benefit, but is simply left in his old position—possibly a slightly worse position, because he will have the trouble of finding a new investment—and that, therefore, there is nothing to set against the objective burden thrown on the taxpayer in the form of taxation to provide the money to pay him. Professor Seligman writes: "The fallacy involved in the contention that the sacrifice imposed upon the future taxpayer is counterbalanced by the benefit accruing to the bondholder consists in the failure to realise that there are no benefits thus accruing to the bondholder."[1] Professor Scott arrives by similar reasoning at the same conclusion: "Speaking quite generally, the effect of a loan (he is discussing an internal loan) is that posterity is rendered liable to do the amount of work which is necessary to pay it off."[2] The substance of this argument is that, since, in the main, repayments of principal made to holders of loan stock are certain to be reinvested, posterity as a whole will be forced by the process of debt repayment to create new capital, and so to refrain from consumption, to approximately the extent of the debt repayment. Let us provisionally accept this presentation of the facts.

[1] *Annals of the American Academy*, Jan. 1918, p. 64.
[2] *Economic Journal*, Sept. 1918, p. 258.

Even so, to suggest, as the language used by Professors Seligman and Scott seems to do, that there is a *direct objective burden* on posterity equal to the amount of the debt repayment is highly paradoxical. Posterity will possess the new capital which it has been induced by the fiscal expedients of the State to create. We have no right to ignore this possession. To do so is as though one should say that a man, who has been induced by circumstances to put £100,000 into a factory instead of into a yacht or a feast, was thereby made poorer to the extent of £100,000 than he would otherwise have been. If there were reason to suppose that the world would end immediately after the investment had been made, there would, indeed, be something to be said for this view. But at present no cosmical catastrophe is in sight, and posterity may be expected to reap the fruit of its investments in the same way as its ancestors. Thus, though it is true, as Professor Seligman asserts, that the bondholder gets no benefit from debt repayment, it is also true that the taxpayer suffers no loss. What he, in effect, does is to make an investment of certain funds, the proceeds of which will serve in future years to keep the bondholder's position intact and so to relieve him (the taxpayer) of the need for making annual contributions out of his income for this purpose. On posterity as a whole no *direct objective burden* is imposed by the repayment of an internal loan, any more than by payment of interest upon it. The payment of interest and the repayment of principal alike are transfers, not costs, and to whatever is somewhere lost there corresponds elsewhere an exactly equivalent objective gain.

§ 4. It does not, however, follow from this that no difference is made by the choice between the two methods in the *subjective burden* borne by future generations. There is reason to believe that it is of this rather than of *the objective burden* that both Professor Seligman and Professor Scott are really thinking —though to interpret them so involves a rather generous straining of their language. Let us, therefore, consider the effects upon subjective burden. To simplify the discussion I shall begin by studying a representative man so situated that, what he pays in taxes to finance the national debt exactly corresponds to what he receives in interest and in repayment of the principal of his loan holdings. In these circumstances it is plain that the money for interest merely comes out of one pocket and goes into another, and that a subjective burden is excluded as completely as an objective one. But with the part of the tax used to repay principal the position is a little different. In effect £100 has been taken from our representative man in taxes and then paid back to him as a price for cancelling his £100 bond. If this procedure had not been gone through, this £100 would have remained in his disposable income, and would, we may suppose, have been spent. As the procedure has been gone through, he realises that, should he spend the £100, his "capital" will be £100 less than before, and his future income, therefore, £5 less. He will, therefore, it would seem, need to save the greater part of that £100 and invest it, so as to keep up his capital and conserve his future income; and this new need will involve a real subjective burden. This reasoning, however, ignores the fact that, though, if he does not save that £100, his future income will be £5 less, his future taxes, out of which loan interest is paid, will also be £5 less, since the £100 of State loan, to provide interest on which the taxation is required, has, *ex hypothesi*, been cancelled. When account is taken of this fact, it becomes apparent that the representative man's *net* income, after taxation has been deducted, will be exactly the same in the future as it has been in the past. His position as a whole, therefore, is not damaged in any way, and there is no reason why, to safeguard himself, he should save that £100 which he would normally have spent. It may, perhaps, be replied that the prospective escape from taxation will not balance the prospective loss of interest, because he may reckon that, as general wealth increases, the amount of taxation which he personally will have to contribute will fall. But this reply is illicit, because he must be taken as a representative man, whose wealth and (in his family) numbers expand in the same ratio as that of the whole community. A second possible reply—that the tax will fall through loan conversion—is obviously irrelevant, since conversion would reduce loan interest equally with the taxation made to provide that interest. We may conclude, therefore, that, if he realises

2 ᴜ

the whole situation, our representative man will suffer no
subjective burden in consequence of debt repayment. No
doubt, it is probable that in practice he will not realise the
whole situation, and will not perceive that his loss of capital is
balanced by his relief from prospective taxation. So far as he
fails to perceive this, he *will* be pushed into saving part of the
£100 which he would normally have spent, and so *will* suffer
a subjective burden. This appears to be the leaven of truth
in Professor Seligman's and Professor Scott's reasoning. Plainly,
however, it is a small matter. The only really significant
way in which the choice of loans instead of taxes affects the
future is, as was explained in § 2, that it causes rather more
of the money needed when the levy is made to be drawn from
sources which would otherwise have constituted capital yielding
future income. It was argued in the preceding chapter that
this effect is not likely to be large. *Pro tanto*, however, it
makes relevant to the choice between taxes and loans arguments concerning the relative interest of present and future
generations in the object on which the resources required
by Government are to be spent.

§ 5. Turning to distribution between people of equal
wealth in different situations, we find, in favour of the loan
method, a very important practical argument. Under that
method, loans in general being voluntary, those persons tend
to subscribe who can do so with least difficulty. Of two men,
for example, of equal wealth, one of whom is half-way through
the building of a factory when the levy comes, while the other
has no special call on his income, the second will naturally
take up a much larger share of the loan. Under the tax
method both these men would be forced to make the same
contribution, and, though, no doubt, the factory builder would
probably be able to arrange things somehow by borrowing
himself, yet, unless he happened to have a considerable amount
of suitable collateral, he might find it very difficult, expensive
and inconvenient to do this. Under the loan method, those
who have free money contribute it naturally and simply;
under the tax method it may have to be got from them
through an elaborate roundabout process of loans to people
subject to the levy but lacking free money of their own.

When money is suddenly needed to finance, say, a war, the relatively small disturbance and agitation, which the loan method is likely, for this reason, to cause, is a clear point in its favour.

§ 6. After all, however, the main problem of a State levy is not to organise it conveniently as between people of equal wealth who happen to be differently situated at the moment, but to organise it fairly as between people of different grades of wealth. The fundamental point is this. The amount of resources which it is possible for a government by any plan to draw in a short time from the poor is strictly limited. The available margin among them is, both for individuals and for the poor as a group, small. Consequently, when a large sum has to be raised in, say, a single year, it is *necessary* that by far the greater part of it shall be raised somehow from better-to-do people. Furthermore, it is plain that, generally speaking, as we pass up the scale of wealth, every increase in an individual's income means, not merely an increase in the available margin of resources, but an increase which grows more than in proportion to the growth of income. If one man is twice as rich as another, other things being equal, his available margin is not twice as large, but more than twice as large. Hence, of the money needed by the State the rich man *must* provide, in one way or another, more than the poor man, and the very rich man more than the moderately rich man; and the amount provided *must* increase, not merely proportionately, but progressively as wealth increases. Now, if the practical choice was between the provision of money in these proportions by taxes and by loans, *the revenue to pay interest on which would afterwards be assessed on the different classes in these same proportions*, there would be no difference between the distributional effects of the two plans. But, if the italicised condition is not appended to the loan plan, there is a very important difference—one which in some circumstances provides an argument in favour of the loan plan, and in others an argument against it.

§ 7. Suppose that a Government proposes to raise money to develop a coal-bearing area, or to build a system of electric power stations, the products of which it will afterwards sell

at a profit on the market; and suppose, further, that the sum
needed is 'so 'big that it has to be 'drawn from the · richer
classes in a larger proportion than the ordinary taxes; are
drawn.   If, in these circumstances, the money. is raised by
a loan, the fees from the people who buy 'the Government's
coal or electricity will ! pay the interest on it, and the tax-
payers will not be affected at all. But, if it is raised by
a special tax—which we assume to fall on the rich in a larger
proportion than ordinary taxes—these fees will go in relief
of the ordinary taxpayer. The better-to-do classes will thus,
in effect, be forced to provide money for an investment the
fruits of which go to taxpayers in general. Now, it may be
a good thing—in the next Part it will be argued that it is a
good thing—for the Government to take money from the rich
for the benefit of the less rich. But there is no defence for
their doing this in the roundabout way just described. When,
therefore, large sums of money are wanted to build up an
enterprise whose products are to be sold at a profit, considerations of right distribution point to loans rather than to taxes
as the proper channel of finance.

§ 8. Let us next suppose that the money is required for
some work, the products of which will not be sold for money,
such as the establishment of national art galleries, libraries,
museums, or, more pointedly, the conduct of a war.   In
these circumstances the loan plan means that the costs of the
undertaking are borne by all classes roughly in proportion to
the shares of ordinary taxation which they respectively bear.
The tax plan means that they are' borne in proportion to 'the
shares in which an abnormally large levy has to be distributed
among them; in other words, that the very rich' and the rich
bear a share of the costs of this enterprise much larger than
their share of ordinary taxation.   Our judgment as to which
of these two arrangements is the better must turn partly upon
our general views about equity in distribution, and partly on
the purpose which the expenditure to be financed serves. If,
for example, its purpose is to remodel at the State's charge
the housing conditions of the poorer classes throughout the
country, there is less to be said for throwing a main part of
the burden on the better-to-do than there would be if the

purpose were, for example, to cover the country with a system
of roads adapted for motor-touring. In order, therefore, to
determine the comparative advantages of the tax method and
the loan method from the side of distribution, it is necessary
to know the nature and purpose of the expenditure that has
to be financed.

§ 9. I do not propose to pursue that inquiry into all its
ramifications. But the general character of the problem may
be usefully illustrated by reference to the finance of a great
war, such as that which has recently closed. There the object
aimed at by the expenditure is political—self-defence, the
enforcement of treaties, the security of small nations, or what
we will: and the costs of conducting the war are colossal.
Our problem is, assuming the distribution and the general
principles of graduation adopted in the tax system of
this country to be fair and proper for ordinary purposes, will
it be fair and proper also to apply these same principles to
the financing of war? For this is in substance what is done
if war costs are met from domestic loans, on which interest
and sinking fund are paid out of taxes based on these
principles. This somewhat complicated problem has now to
be attacked.

§ 10. In discussions which have taken place about it, a good
deal of attention has been paid to the effects which a great
war produces upon the relative economic position of various
classes of the population. Thus, it has been argued that the
very rich and the rich may well find in a great war an
opportunity for positive gain. For they possess large incomes
of free resources, and free resources can, in such circumstances,
demand that the rate of interest, which people (including the
Government) promise for the use of them, shall go up to a
very high level. In view of the high probability that prices
after the war will fall again considerably below their war
level, the real rate of interest which they may reasonably look
for is considerably above even the high nominal rate. The
very rich and the rich are, in short—like the owners of iron-
works—possessed of something for which the demand is
enormously enhanced, and, consequently, are in a position
to become, without any suggestion of illicit practice, "profiteers"

on a large scale. Furthermore, whenever the rich are thus advantaged, the poor, it is, urged, are likely to suffer damage. When the Government requires an abnormal amount of money, whatever method of finance it adopts, it is both likely itself to borrow largely from the banks, and, through its heavy taxes or calls for loans, to cause a number of private persons to do the same. The large expansion of bank credit thus brought about raises prices all round, and, consequently, acts like a general tax roughly proportionate to income. There being no graduation or abatement in this virtual tax, the poor are hit much more severely, as compared with the rich, than they are under the ordinary tax system. Thus, it is said, not only have the rich special opportunities for profiteering, but also the poor are subjected to a special detriment. On the other side it is answered that the peculiar circumstances of a great war place many important sections of the poorer classes in at least as strong a position for profiteering as anybody else; and play is made with the enormous wages earned in munition works and shipyards. In view of these high wages, it is said, the poor are better, rather than worse off, relatively to the rich during the course of a great war.

§ 11. The issue set out in the preceding paragraph is an important one. But it has no real bearing on our present problem. One very obvious reason for this is that the main extra burden which the loan method throws upon poor people falls on them—for the benefit of the heirs of present rich people—not in the actual years of the war, but in the later years, during which taxes are raised to provide interest and sinking fund on war loans. There is also another consideration. In so far as any part of the population are enriched during the course of a war, they are hit in respect of the taxes that are levied at the time; and, if it is desired, war profits can be specially aimed at through an excess profits duty so arranged as to cover workpeople as well as capitalists. But, after all, these are secondary matters. Fundamentally, the question how the income of different people is changed by a war has nothing to do with the more general question whether the relation between the imposts levied on incomes of different sizes that is proper for ordinary expenditure is proper also for war expenditure. This latter question only is relevant to the choice between financing war predominantly by loans or predominantly by special taxation. The solution of it depends, not on statistical, but on general considerations.

§ 12. These considerations are two in number. First, when, as in normal times, what is wanted is a regular annual revenue, it is natural to base taxation in a general way upon income. But, when a single and entirely abnormal expenditure has to be met, ability to pay is best reflected, not in the income that happens to accrue in that particular year, but rather in income-getting power or capital—this term being taken to include objects of wealth not used in trade, such as houses and pictures, and also the capitalised value of a man's mental and manual powers.[1] Since £100 of "earned income," being terminable with life, represents much less "capital" than £100 of income derived from the funds, and since funded and other property is held predominantly by the rich, this consideration suggests that war charges ought to be thrown upon the rich in a greater proportion than the principles appropriate to peace taxation would warrant. Secondly, there is a general feeling that, in a pre-eminent national emergency, the call from each should be for his *utmost* rather than for his *share*. Men are required to give of their physical strength, not in equal proportions, but from each his all. There is no question of proportionate sacrifice between men of fuller and emptier lives. Indeed, the strong are taken and the weak rejected. It is difficult to see what ground of equity there can be for any different distribution in the summons to financial strength. But this is certainly not the distribution

---

[1] It is not, of course, suggested that the costs of a war can be paid for *out of* capital, in the sense that a person's holdings of land or factories or railways (except so far as they are saleable abroad in return for "income") can actually be used for war purposes. The main *source* of the funds raised must be the real income of the country. None the less, it would be possible for the Government to collect a large part of what is required for war from persons who have no income at all but only property. If £1000 were taken from such a person, he would have, in effect, to buy with £1000 worth of property £1000 worth of real income from somebody else and to hand this over to the Government. He would be the *subject* of the tax, though his property would not be the *source* of it.

aimed at in the ordinary tax system; and, therefore, some departure from the principles that underlie that system seems to be called for. This suggests that, from the standpoint of a sound distribution, a great war ought not to be financed predominantly by loans, interest on which will afterwards be provided out of ordinary taxes. Rather, a large part of the costs should be met by taxation levied at the time, on principles calculated to throw a much greater proportion of the burden on the rich than they are accustomed to sustain under the ordinary forms of taxation.

CHAPTER X

§ 1. To make our discussion complete it is desirable that something further should be said of the type of borrowing alluded to in § 10 of the preceding chapter, under which loans are obtained through the manufacture of bank credits. This type of borrowing, supported by abnormal issues of fiduciary notes, was largely resorted to during the war in all the principal belligerent countries, including the United Kingdom. I propose in the present chapter to describe and discuss our national variant of this common method. In that way it will be easy to exhibit the general principles that are involved.

§ 2. It is customary for critics of British war finance to make use in connection with it of the term "inflation." It is, however, exceedingly difficult to find any definition of this term that is at all satisfactory. One popular definition asserts that inflation is an increase in money more than proportionate to the accompanying increase in production.[1] Since, however, this definition compels us to say that a bad harvest involves inflation, it is too far out of touch with the common understanding of words to be admissible. An alternative definition applies the term inflation to *that part of the rise of*

---

[1] This definition is incidentally thought to imply that "inflation is inherent in the flotation of a loan for purposes other than the construction of material reproductive capital," the idea being that, when the loan is employed productively, extra things are created to offset the extra money. Obviously, however, no more extra things are produced *at the time* when a factory is built than when a house is built, or even than when people are set to work to make fireworks or guns. More extra things are, no doubt, produced later on when the factory begins to operate, but this fact is not relevant.

*prices that is consequent upon governmental interference with
money and banking.* Practically, however, it seems impossible to disentangle this part from the part that would
have taken place, particularly in war, if the Government
had allowed monetary affairs to proceed along the usual
lines. Furthermore, the notion of Government "interference
with money and banking" is not precise. Certain Government
acts, of course, clearly constitute such interference, but certain
others—for example, the commandeering of foreign securities
to support exchange and propaganda to persuade people not to
present Treasury notes for encashment—are doubtful. Again,
certain things, which cannot take place in England without
very definite Government interference, are permissible in other
countries under the ordinary law. Thus, the fiduciary note
issue of the Reichsbank might, under pre-war legislation, be
increased beyond the normal maximum on condition that a tax
was paid on the extra issues. In view of these considerations it
would appear that the only really satisfactory way of defining
inflation along these lines would be to make an arbitrary
schedule of the various sorts of action, which, for the purposes of
the definition, are to be regarded as governmental interference
with money and banking, and the fruits of which, therefore, are
are to be called inflation. But, when we are driven to an
artificial plan of this kind, there is much to be said for
abandoning the term altogether, and in the following pages
I do not propose to make use of it.[1]

§ 3. During the Great War, and particularly during the
earlier stages of it, the Government, whether rightly or wrongly,
were unwilling to push overt taxation beyond moderate limits,
for fear of checking production and rousing powerful resentment. They were equally unwilling to put the rate of interest
offered for war loan subscriptions above a moderate amount,
lest our reputation for financial power should be damaged in
the eyes of the world. As a result of these two things the
amount of money obtained by overt taxes and public loans
fell in most weeks considerably below the exigent demands of
the army, navy, air force and munitions establishments. Given
these conditions and given the determination to cut our cloth

---

[1] Cf. my article on "Inflation," *Economic Journal*, December 1918.

according to our coat and not *vice versa*; the only course open
to the Government, apart from direct resort to the printing
press, was to fill the gap between income and expenditure by
causing the banks, and particularly the Bank of England, to
create credits in its favour.   The process by which these
credits were brought to birth and, thereafter, as it were,
expanded in stature, is described in the First Interim Report of
the Committee on Currency and Foreign Exchanges (1918) in
the following terms : " Suppose, for example, that in a given
week the Government require £10,000,000 over and above
the receipts from taxation and loans from the public.   They
apply for an advance from the Bank of England, which, by a
book entry, places the amount required to the credit of Public
Deposits, in the same way as any other banker credits the
account of a customer when he grants him temporary accommodation.   The amount is then paid out to contractors and
other Government creditors, and passes, when the cheques are
cleared, to the credit of their bankers in the books of the Bank
of England ; in other words, is transferred from Public to
" Other " deposits ; the effect of the whole transaction thus
being to increase by £10,000,000 the purchasing power in
the hands of the public in the form of deposits in the joint
stock banks, and the bankers' cash at the Bank of England by
the same amount.   The bankers' liabilities to depositors having
thus increased by £10,000,000, and their cash reserves by an
equal amount, their proportion of cash to liabilities (which
was normally, before the war something under 20 per cent) is
improved, with the result that they are in a position to make
advances to their customers to an amount equal to four or
five times the sum added to their cash reserves, or, in the
absence of demand for such accommodation, to increase their
investments by the difference between the cash received and
the proportion they require to hold against the increase of
their deposit liabilities.   Since the outbreak of war it is the
second procedure which has in the main been followed, the
surplus cash having been used to subscribe for Treasury bills
and other Government securities.   The money so subscribed
has again been spent by the Government and returned in the
manner above described to the bankers' cash balances, the

process being repeated again and again until each £10,000,000 originally advanced by the Bank of England has created new deposits representing new purchasing power to several times that amount." [1]

§ 4. Now, in normal times it is possible for the Government, like any ordinary customer, to persuade banks to create credits in its favour by the offer of a good rate of interest. It is well known that in times of growing confidence bankers are accustomed to expand their loans and liabilities, thus raising prices and transferring command over resources, from receivers of fixed incomes to the persons to whom these loans are made. In normal times, however, there are powerful forces at work to prevent this process from being carried far. The rise of prices, by encouraging imports and discouraging exports, turns the exchanges against us and threatens a foreign drain of gold. At the same time it makes it necessary for people to carry rather more money than before in their pockets and in their tills for the payment of expanded wages bills and for the conduct of retail business on the higher price level. In this way it sets up a domestic drain. These two drains together, by lessening the reserve of the Bank of England, compel the Bank to raise its discount rate and to take steps, by selling Government stock or otherwise, to make the new rate effective in the market. The higher rate tends to check borrowing. If it does not actually do this at first, it will have to be raised still higher until it does do it; for otherwise the Bank would see its resources completely exhausted. The financing of any customer, the Government or anybody else, by the creation of bank credits is thus, in normal times, held closely in check.

§ 5. A state of things is conceivable in which these limitations should be greatly widened and large credit creations in favour of Government made possible without any interference with the normal working of the monetary machine. If other countries outside England were to create paper money in large quantities, thus throwing gold upon the

[1] First Interim Report of the Committee on Currency and the Foreign Exchanges, p. 2. I have made free use of the Report of this Committee, of which I was a member.

markets of the world and greatly raising prices, gold would tend to flow here. This gold would constitute a basis for enlarged credits by the Bank of England and ultimately by the joint-stock banks. These credits when expended would, of course, raise wage-bills and prices here and so set up an internal drain. But the new gold brought in from abroad would be more than enough to meet this drain: and, so long as prices here were not raised more than foreign prices, there would be no tendency to an external drain. Consequently, there would be no reason for discount rates here to be raised and no obstacle to continued credit expansion. The Government could finance itself to its heart's content out of bank loans so long as the credit expansion set up here lagged behind that set up in the rest of the world.

§ 6. In actual fact, in spite of the large credit expansion of other countries, there was never, after the very early stages of the war, any question of the United Kingdom being in the position thus sketched out. The enormous Government demands for munitions and materials from abroad, coupled with the check imposed by war upon our export trade, dominated the exchange position. By exporting securities, negotiating foreign loans and stopping British investments abroad, we continued, with difficulty, to provide funds against our excess of imports, while still retaining a large holding of gold; but there was not, and in the circumstances there could not have been, any question of a net inflow of gold from the surfeited currencies of other countries. Consequently, no basis for enlarged credits could be obtained from these sources. If credits were to be enlarged sufficiently to fill the gap between the Government's outgoings for the war and its incomings from taxes and ordinary loans, the Government itself must create that basis. The external drain normally consequent upon credit creation did not, indeed, require to be specially countered. For the export of gold by private persons was sufficiently provided against by the submarine peril and the refusal of the Government to insure gold cargoes. But, unless a basis had been provided by direct State action, collapse must have come about through the internal drain. As the Committee on Currency and the

Foreign Exchanges observe : " The greatly increased volume of bank deposits, representing a corresponding increase of purchasing power, and, therefore, leading, in conjunction with other causes, to a great rise of prices, brought about a corresponding demand for legal tender currency, which could not have been satisfied under the stringent provisions of the Act of 1844. Contractors were obliged to draw cheques against their accounts in order to discharge their wage-bill—itself enhanced on account of the rise of prices." [1] To meet this situation and to provide the required basis of legal tender money, currency notes, at first devised for a quite different purpose in the early days of the war, were issued by the Treasury in continually increasing quantities. These notes were handed to the banks—not, of course, to the Bank of England—in exchange for a transfer of balances belonging to the banks at the Bank of England to the Government's currency note account; the Government, thereafter, substituting in that account their own securities, and thus, in effect, purchasing the banks' balances for its own use by the exchange of an equivalent amount of newly created notes. By this arrangement the banks were put in a position to convert at will their balances at the Bank of England, enhanced in the way described in § 3, into legal tender currency, without causing notes to be drawn, as they would have been under the pre-war system, from the banking reserve of the Bank of England, and so without compelling the Bank to apply the normal safeguards against an excessive expansion of credit. " Fresh legal tender was thus continually being issued, not, as formerly, against gold but against Government securities. Plainly, given the necessity for the creation of bank credits in favour of the Government for the purpose of financing war expenditure, these issues could not be avoided. If they had not been made, the banks would have been unable to obtain legal tender with which to meet cheques drawn for cash on their customers' accounts. The unlimited issue of currency notes, in exchange for credits (belonging to other bankers) at the Bank of England is at once a consequence and an essential condition of the methods which the Government

[1] Loc. cit. p. 5.

found it necessary to adopt in order to meet their war expenditure."[1]

§ 7. It is a matter of some interest to determine how far, if at all, this very complicated method of obtaining resources for the Government has different effects from those that would have been produced by a straightforward issue of currency notes in direct payment for the Government's purchases. Apologists of British war finance have made a great point of the fact that the printing press was not used in this way and that notes were only issued in response to business demands. At first sight it seems that this complacency is justified. For on the plan actually adopted the Government's credits have been obtained in the form of bank balances, and notes have only been issued sufficient to support these balances: whereas, if Government had simply created notes to pay for its purchases, these notes would have formed a basis for a very much larger creation of bank credit. This distinction, however, rests upon the assumption that, if the Government had issued notes in direct payment of its purchases, all the notes so issued would have remained, as it were, " alive." This assumption is not justified. If the Government, in any week had created and paid to contractors ten million one-pound notes, the contractors presumably would have deposited these notes with their bankers, only keeping in their own hands for wage payments the same number as, on the plan actually adopted, they drew out of their account for this purpose. The joint-stock banks in turn would have deposited these notes with the Bank of England, thus creating balances to their credit there equal to the balances that, on the other plan, they would have created by book transfers, and, equally with them, available for the purchase

---

[1] First Interim Report of the Committee on Currency and the Foreign Exchanges, p. 5. For simplicity of exposition I have assumed in the text that the whole of the balances due to credit creation which were transferred from the banks to the Government were transferred direct. In fact a certain proportion of them were transferred through the mediation of private persons who borrowed from the banks money to invest in war loans. The banks, however, did not, as a rule, make loans to customers for this purpose for more than a short period, and the proportion was probably small. In any event, the effects of the transaction were the same whether the created credits did or did not pass through an intermediary on the way to their final destination.

of Treasury bills. So soon, however, as currency notes enter the Bank of England, they are automatically cancelled and die. To make our comparison a fair one, we must suppose that this same rule would hold good under the printing press plan. But, if it holds good, that plan, though it would involve the *creation* of many more notes than the actual plan, would only involve the *survival* of an approximately equal number. The only difference would be that the balances of bankers at the Bank of England, instead of being created by simple book transfers, would be brought into being through the agency of extra notes marked for destruction, which, in their brief span of life, accomplished nothing except to bring those balances into being. The printing press method, combined with the proviso that in the atmosphere of the Bank of England no currency note can live, is thus, contrary to common opinion, identical in its operation and consequences with the more round-about policy that was in fact pursued by the British Treasury.

§ 8. On the financial, as distinct from the monetary, side that policy has the peculiarity that, whereas, from the point of view of the Government, the money raised under it (except those balances which are obtained in direct exchange for currency notes) is a loan, on which interest must be paid and the principal eventually liquidated, from the point of view of the public it is a tax. If we may suppose the total money value of the country's real income to have stood in any year at, say, £2400 millions, then the banks, by creating credits to the value of £200 millions, would get command over $\frac{2}{26}$th of the purchasing power, and so of the real income, of the country, at the cost of making every £ in the hands of anybody else worth $\frac{1}{13}$th less goods and services than it was worth before. Moreover, this levy, like a levy through a protective duty, would be accompanied by a large transfer from one set of people (mainly the receivers of fixed incomes) to another set of people, in addition to the transfer made to the Treasury. In substance the Government has asked bankers, and, by providing them with currency notes, has enabled them, to make a forced levy on the public, and then to *lend* the proceeds of this levy to itself. The public as a whole receives no interest, and will never get back any principal, but the banks, for their services as tax-collectors, achieve both these things.

§. 9. I shall not here inquire how far this obviously objectionable arrangement could have been avoided by a Government more careful in expenditure and more courageous in taxation. That question touches the competence of particular politicians, and not the general principles of finance. It is, however, desirable that something should be said of the aftermath of problems in the monetary sphere, which the financial methods adopted during the war left behind it at its close. So long as the war continued, the activities of enemy submarines and the refusal of the Government to insure gold for export made it possible for certain foreign exchanges to stand much below the ordinary export specie point without any export of gold taking place. Moreover, the most important exchange, that with the United States of America, was deliberately "pegged" and held up by the Government through sales abroad of foreign securities collected for the purpose, through the issue in America of British Government loans on extremely favourable terms, and, after the entry of the United States into the war, through credits granted by the American Government to the British Government. When the war ceased, the protection to our gold hitherto provided by the submarines was automatically withdrawn, and shortly afterwards the pegging of the exchanges —a process necessarily involving the continual piling up of further foreign debt—was also dropped. In these conditions the heavy adverse balance of immediate indebtedness, resulting from our large need for imported materials and the loans we were still making to some of our allies, at a time when our export industries were still disorganised, threatened to bring about a tremendous foreign drain of gold. We might have lost practically all our gold, and yet, in view of our imperative need for imports, equilibrium might not have been brought about. In these circumstances it was decided (in March 1919) to make the export of gold by private persons illegal. This regulation, coupled with the already established war-time regulation against the melting of sovereigns, opened the way, in spite of the legal convertibility of currency notes into sovereigns on demand, for a specific depreciation of these notes

2 x

in terms of gold bullion and a corresponding depreciation of the American exchange in terms of British currency. Thereafter, an extensive depreciation in this sense (over 30 per cent in January 1920, diminished to 18 per cent in April) soon made its appearance. This constitutes by far the most urgent currency problem bequeathed to this country by the war.

§ 10. It is generally agreed that, apart from a fundamental reorganisation of our monetary system on some such plan as that to be discussed in Chapter VIII. of Part VI.—a plan which might well be made the subject of international discussion, but is at the moment scarcely practical politics—the removal of this specific depreciation and the restoration of an effective gold standard are imperatively needed in the interest of national industry and trade. An effective gold standard does not necessarily imply the actual circulation of sovereigns. But it does imply the absence of all restrictions upon the import of gold, the free exchange for export of gold (though not necessarily of coined sovereigns) against Bank of England and currency notes at par value at the Bank of England, and the absence of all restrictions on the export of gold. Under those conditions our price level necessarily tends to equilibrium with the world (gold) price level; and the exchanges with gold countries cannot, except momentarily, move against us beyond the export specie point. In order that an effective gold standard in this sense and with these consequences may be safely re-established, an essential preliminary condition is such a reduction of our balance of adverse immediate indebtedness as to insure that the restoration of a free market for gold will not lead to an overwhelming foreign drain. This implies that the war-time practice of making repeated long-time loans to foreigners ceases, that our export trade is rehabilitated, that the rates for money here are maintained at at least as high a level as prevails in the United States, and, for security, that the main part of the short-time debt owing from us abroad is funded. It is further necessary that the automatic connection between our gold reserve and the rate of discount, which war-time practice broke down, shall be re-knit in such wise that, if, at any time after the restoration of a free gold market, a heavy foreign drain does set in, the discount rate will be immediately forced up and credits contracted. There can be full assurance that this will be done only if the practice of selling new currency notes on request to bankers in exchange for balances held by them at the Bank of England is definitely abandoned. An important step in this direction was taken in December 1919, when the Chancellor of the Exchequer, by Treasury Minute, fixed the maximum fiduciary issue of Treasury notes in 1920 at 320 millions. The policy thus inaugurated implies, if it is to be successfully maintained, that the authorities are prepared, at need, to face a substantial rise both in the Bank rate and in the rates offered for Treasury bills. For, if they are not prepared to do this, conditions may arise in which bank loans to industry become so large that new currency has to be created to support the high prices caused thereby, while at the same time the Government finds itself unable to renew its Treasury bills, and so is forced to apply for further Ways and Means Advances from the Bank of England, thus still further expanding credits, forcing up prices, and enlarging the need for currency in the pockets of the people.

§ 11. Assuming that an effective gold standard is restored, the most urgent of our problems would be settled. It would still be necessary, however, before the situation could be regarded as completely stabilised, that some decision should be taken as to the permanent relation between the note issue of the country and the gold basis on which that issue rests. All notes being legally convertible into gold on demand, it is essential that a sufficient gold reserve should be held to afford an adequate guarantee that this legal obligation will always be met. Some authorities desire that this should be done by fixing a *proportion* of note issue to gold reserve, which it shall be illegal to exceed. But this plan is open to a serious objection. If, say, the proportion was fixed at three to one, every drain of £1 of gold from the reserve would, in certain conditions, involve a forced contraction of £3 in the currency; and this could hardly fail to cause a great deal of disturbance and difficulty. For this reason it seems clear that the thing limited by law should be, not the *proportion*, but, subject, perhaps, to special arrangements to meet emergencies,[1] the *amount* of the fiduciary issue. It is not practicable to determine now in a direct way at what figure this limiting amount, for the period when things have settled down after the war, should be put. But it is practicable to lay down a rule determining this indirectly. This point is explained in the Interim Report of the Committee on Currency and Foreign Exchanges, as follows: "Assuming the restoration of an effective gold standard, and given the conventional standard of banking practice and the customs of the public as regards the use of currency, the amount of legal tender currency (other than subsidiary coin) which can be kept in circulation, including the currency holdings of the banks and the banking department of the Bank of England, will determine itself automatically, since, if the currency becomes redundant, the rate of discount will fall and prices will rise; notes will be presented in exchange for gold for export and the volume of the currency will be reduced *pro tanto*. If, on the other hand, the supply of currency falls below current requirements, the rate of discount will rise, prices will fall, gold will be imported and new notes taken out in exchange for it." It was contemplated by the Committee that virtually the whole amount of the currency gold in the country would be held in the central reserve at the Bank of England. In these circumstances, "the total circulation (in the above sense) being automatically determined, it will follow that, the higher the amount fixed for the fiduciary issue (including, of course, the fiduciary part of the Bank of England's notes), the lower will be the amount of the covered issue and, consequently, of the central gold reserve, and *vice versa*, while if the fiduciary issue was fixed at a figure which proved to be higher than the total requirements of the country for legal tender currency, the covered issue, and, with it, the central gold reserve would disappear altogether. It is clear, therefore, that the amount of the fiduciary issue must be fixed at a figure low enough to make sure, not merely that there will always be some covered issue, but that there will always be a covered issue of sufficiently substantial amount to secure that the covering gold,

---

[1] Cf. *post*, Part VI. Chapter IX. § 7.

which constitutes the central reserve, never falls so low as to give rise to apprehension as to the stability of the gold standard." The Committee suggest that a normal gold reserve of 150 millions would be a reasonable one to aim at; and they accordingly recommend that, "until this amount has been reached and maintained concurrently with a satisfactory foreign exchange position for a period of at least a year, the policy of reducing the uncovered note issue as and when opportunity offers should be consistently followed. . . . When the exchanges are working normally on the basis of a minimum reserve of 150 millions, the position should again be reviewed in the light of the dimensions of the fiduciary issue as it then exists."[1] Presumably, if the position was considered satisfactory, the volume of the fiduciary issue would thereupon be fixed permanently at the amount then outstanding. When this has been done, the monetary problems left over by the Government's use of bank credits as a means of war finance will have been finally cleared away.

[1] *Loc. cit.* pp. 9-10.

CHAPTER XI

WAR DEBT AND A SPECIAL LEVY

§ 1. IN the actual rush and difficulty of a modern war statesmen are certain for political reasons to rely predominantly upon some form of borrowing—we need no longer distinguish between loans through bank credits and normal loans—rather than upon taxation. This was the course followed in every country—even in the United States of America—during the Great War. The hurried decisions thus taken are not, however, necessarily final. Their consequences can be, in the main, undone, if, shortly after the war has closed, a special levy is made to pay off the whole or a large part of the internally held war debt. To complete the present Part some study of this policy will now be undertaken.

§ 2. From the standpoint of the national dividend there can be little doubt that its adoption would be advantageous, because the obstructive effect of the expectation of higher annual taxes, which strike new efforts and savings, would be lessened. This consideration holds good even if the levy is payable in instalments spread over a number of years, so long as the amount of the instalments depends on the amount of property held when the law is passed, and not on the amount held when each instalment is paid. It should be noted, indeed, that, since in this country interest on war debt is itself assessable to income tax, the wiping out of a portion of the war debt would lessen assessable income, and, therefore, the *rate* of taxation would not be reduced in quite so large a proportion as the *volume* of taxation. Evidently, however, this circumstance does no more than slightly weaken the force of my argument. A more important objection is that, if people fear the special levy will be repeated, this fear may have the same kind of obstructive effect as the expectation of large annual taxes. But, since the threat of repetition, if a levy is made, is, at the worst, distant and uncertain, whereas the obligation to pay high annual taxes, if it is not made, is perfectly sure, and since, moreover, if the levy is not made, there is always the fear that it may be made in the future, we may reasonably conclude that the net effect of wiping out debt by a levy will be to oil the wheels of production and increase the national dividend. If the amount of the annual taxation which the levy would cancel is small, this conclusion could, indeed, only be held somewhat tentatively. But, as the amount of this taxation rises, assurance rightly grows. It may be fairly easy to devise a scheme which will raise in taxation 10 per cent of the national income without seriously hampering production. But to devise an equally innocuous scheme for raising 20 per cent will be much harder; and to devise one for raising 30 per cent *very* much harder. More generally, when the amount of the national money income is given, every extra 50 millions of revenue which has to be raised is more difficult to arrange for satisfactorily and more likely to involve injurious reactions upon national productivity. *Consequently, every addition to the size of the Budget, which will be needed if no special levy is raised to wipe off debt, makes the chance greater than any given special levy will do more good by lessening the Budget requirements than it will do harm through the reactions which it itself sets up.* The volume of the debt left in this country by the Great War is so enormous that, even if it is converted fairly soon into a debt bearing a lower rate of interest, and even if the money income of the country grows very rapidly—a thing which, in view of the probable tendency of prices ultimately to fall as a result of post-war deflation, will by no means necessarily happen, despite the prospect of production being largely increased—the general *rates* of taxation associated with it are certain for a long time to be enormously high. For that debt, therefore, the conclusion that a special levy, so arranged as to wipe out a substantial part of it, would help the national dividend may be taken as tolerably well assured.

§ 3. In popular discussion these economic considerations are often swept aside with the general objection that any form of special levy is indefensible, because it would necessarily penalise people who have saved and, maybe, lent the proceeds of their savings to the State, while letting off those who, in a time of dire national need, squandered their incomes. This objection rests on a misconception. It is perfectly true that a special levy must hit the man who has saved in the way described. But so also must an income tax which, as all income taxes do, covers income from property. The only practicable alternative to a special levy to wipe off the principal of the war debt is a heavy annual income tax to provide interest on it. Whichever of these methods is adopted, the man who has saved cannot escape, and the man who has squandered his income must escape. Consequently, this general objection really misses its mark. So far as I am aware, there are no other broad objections, though, of course, there are many objections based on considerations of technique and practical working. From now onwards, therefore, I shall assume that the policy of a special levy is acceptable *in principle*, and shall proceed to inquire what exactly it implies in practice.

§ 4. The first thing to settle is the general basis of assessment. Apart from war fortunes, the taxation of which might, indeed, supplement, but in any event could not yield enough money to supplant, a more broadly based levy, the principal alternatives are current incomes and aggregate existing capitals. Neither the one nor the other of these rival bases is essential to the main idea of a special levy. The only essential thing is that, on whatever basis the levy is made, it shall be so framed that people in the future will not have to pay more under it if they make new contributions of work and saving than if they do not. Given this condition, the choice of the basis of assessment—the basis or object of taxation does not, of course, as was made clear in an earlier chapter, determine the *source* out of which taxation comes—is a secondary matter. But, though secondary, it is nevertheless important, and some decision on it must be reached.

The principal argument against income as a basis for the purpose of a special levy is one already referred to in another connection in Chapter IX. § 12, namely, that equal incomes do not always imply equal abilities to pay. For an annual tax, indeed, the fact that a man's income is variable does not matter; for the tax varies correspondingly whenever the income varies. But for a single special levy it does matter; because it means that, among people "worth" substantially the same amount, those whose holdings are paying specially well in the particular year of the levy are hit more severely than those who in that particular year happen to be doing badly. Moreover, among properties of equal present values, those in which the annual return is high now with the prospect of a later fall are hit more hardly than those—unripe building land, for example—in which the return is small or possibly nothing now, but is expected to become large in the future. These objections to the income basis are important even when attention is confined to incomes from property. When account is taken of incomes derived from personal work, they are still more serious; for, plainly, a man with £2000 a year received as a salary and terminating with his present employment is much less able to bear a levy of, say, £3000 than one with an equal income derived from £40,000 of war loan stock. Considerations of this character point strongly to capital rather than income as the proper basis, not, of course, for regular annual taxation, but for the imposition of a single special levy.

The principal argument on the other side is that, if capital is taken as a basis and the special levy turned into a levy on capital, wealthy people with large incomes earned in salaries and fees will, except in so far as they also own property, escape altogether. Why, it is asked, should a barrister with £50,000 a year, the whole of which he spends, contribute nothing, while a comparatively poor man, who, out of savings, has accumulated a capital of, say, £5000, has to pay his share? In point of equity there is no answer to this. Capital alone, as a basis for a special levy, is not a fair basis.

The practical inference is that the levy should be based on a double foundation. There should be a capital levy as ordinarily understood, based on capital, and, alongside of this, a subsidiary levy based on incomes derived from work. To work out a fair arrangement for this subsidiary levy would, no doubt, be very difficult. It is impossible to hope for more than a rough adjustment. Perhaps the simplest plan would be to make people in receipt of incomes from work liable to a levy of some multiple, adjusted with regard to the general scale of the capital levy proper, of the average of their income tax payment over the last three years. This levy might be payable in, say, ten annual instalments, later instalments to lapse if the income-receiver died, or if other cause deemed adequate by the Inland Revenue authorities could be shown. Of course, this plan is open to serious objections. But it seems clear that, if a special levy is decided upon, something of the kind ought to be attempted, in order to remove a legitimate sense of grievance from small owners of property and to emphasise the exceptional character of the levy, as a unique financial effort to meet an unprecedented situation.

§ 5. Whatever is done in this matter, there is no doubt that very much the larger part of the proceeds of any special levy that might be made would have to come from that part of it which falls on material capital as ordinarily understood, and not on brain capital. On the basis of such imperfect statistics as are available it may be hazarded that, of income falling within the province of the income tax in this country, probably as much as three-quarters is due to material capital. Since the largest "earned" incomes are likely to belong to elderly men, the number of years' purchase at which they should be capitalised is, presumably, small. Say it is, on the average, ten years. This, with interest at 5 per cent, will make the present value of the existing immaterial capital something like one-tenth of the value of existing material capital. Even, therefore, if no account is taken of the fact that a considerable part of the country's brain-capital belongs to people whose total capital is relatively small, and would, therefore, under a graduated scale, be subject to a low rate of levy, it will follow that the supplementary levy on brain capital would only yield about one-tenth of the whole, leaving the other nine-tenths to be provided by the capital levy proper. Necessarily, therefore, the principal *technical* problems connected with the general policy of a special levy centre upon that.

§ 6. The first of these problems is that of valuation. It is sometimes urged that this would prove so difficult that a special levy could not possibly be worked in practice. To determine the force of this objection we need to know in what forms the capital of the country is held, and what is the relative importance of the several forms. Upon this matter no direct information is available. But for this country the statistics of estates passing at death throw some light upon it. For the fiscal years 1913–14 and 1914–15 the gross capitals of which the Estates Duty Commissioners had notice were made up as follows:

DISTRIBUTION OF PROPERTY.

	Passing at death in 1913–14. Per cent.	Passing at death in 1914–15. Per cent.	Estimated at the present time. Per cent.
Stocks, funds, shares, etc.	45	39	60
Cash in home and bank	6	6	4
Money on mortgage, etc.	7	6	4
Policies on insurance	4	3	2
Trade assets, book debts, goodwill, etc.	5	5	3
Household goods, apparel, etc.	3	3	2
Agricultural land	5	8	6
House property and business premises	14	16	10
Ground rents, etc.	1	1	1
Other property	10	13	8
Total	100	100	100

Except in so far as some forms of property evade death duties more easily than others, the first two columns of the above table may be taken to represent roughly the distribution of property among different forms before the war. At the present time, however, in consequence of the enormous volume of war loan securities, the proportion of the whole represented in stocks, funds, shares, etc., must be very much larger. War loan by itself very probably amounts to one-third of the whole, so that, though there must be set against it a large diminution in our holdings of foreign securities, it may well be that the first item in the table should be raised to 60 per cent. If this is so, all the other percentages must be reduced to two-thirds of what they stood at in 1914–15, and the third column of the table will roughly represent the facts. In that column, then, in the absence of direct statistical information of more recent date, we have a starting-point for estimating the true scale of the valuation problem in this country.

Clearly, there need be no serious difficulty about the first four items, with the exception, perhaps, of those classes of securities which change hands so seldom that their quotations are more or less fictitious. These items together we have estimated to amount to some 70 per cent of the whole. Further, the most important of the other items, namely, house property, business premises and agricultural land, could be roughly assessed on the basis of the income-tax returns, appeal being allowed to any one who felt himself aggrieved. But for the trade assets group, household goods and apparel, and miscellaneous property, it would seem that the only available method is direct appraisement—a process which it would take years to apply over the whole country. On the figures given in the table, these items should work out at some 13 per cent of the whole. But, since they probably evade death duties to a considerable extent, and so are not fully counted, it would be safer to reckon them at, say, 20 per cent. Plainly, to leave them outside the purview of a special levy would be very unfair to owners of other sorts of property, and would be the more objectionable in that it would directly benefit those persons who, during the war, endeavoured to evade their obligations to the State by investing their resources in pearls and pictures, which were expected to appreciate in value and so to yield a return of a kind not liable to assessment for income tax.[1] On the other hand, the task of a general valuation is so prodigious and would prove so irritating that any Government would think many times before embarking upon it. Here, therefore, is a serious impasse. It would seem, however, that the difficulty might be got over by postponing the levy due from these items and storing it up, as it were, till the next occasion on

---

[1] Under the German capital levy law of 1919, a compromise arrangement exempts furniture and household stuff unless they form part of the accessories to real estate or of working capital ; but precious stones and precious metal goods are liable if their value exceeds 20,000 marks (Par. 11). The owner of buildings under this law may demand to be assessed on his own valuation ; but, in this event, the central Government or a municipality may buy in the buildings at that valuation (Par. 19).

which they pass at death, and have to be valued in the
ordinary course. No doubt, this postponement would offer
opportunities for evasion to unscrupulous persons. That,
however, cannot be helped. It would probably be better to
accept that loss than to undertake the gigantic task of an
immediate general valuation. The evasion and the loss to
Government that must result from it is regrettable. But it
is not a fatal objection to a special levy, any more than the
evasion of death duties and income tax that now takes place
is a fatal objection to these means of raising revenue.

§ 7. A second difficulty concerns the actual collection of
a special levy. It is often maintained that this cannot
practically be done, because, if it were attempted, a vast
number of people would be compelled to throw securities
and other property on the market in order to obtain the
wherewithal to pay the levy, and would find there no buyers.
The first and most obvious answer to this objection is that
the Government need not require payment of the levy in
cash. There is no reason why it should not accept all
Trustee securities, and many others in which there is normally
a free and fairly wide market, at their market value on some
specified day. Of course, if it did this, it would lose through
some of these securities falling in value before it itself disposed
of them, but, the field being wide, it would probably gain to
about an equal extent through others rising. Since then we
have reckoned that some 60 per cent of the capital of the
country is represented by securities, the great majority of
people subjected to the levy would probably be able to meet
it without making any sales at all. But, even if this were not
so, or if, for any reason, the Government decided to accept in
payment only a very limited class of securities, the argument
here under review would not be valid. For, after all, whatever
money is paid over to the Treasury will not be locked up there
in a box, but will probably be expended in buying up and cancelling war loan stock. The people from whom this stock is bought
will want other securities instead of it and will, therefore,
constitute a market for those that other people are offering
for sale in order to raise money for the levy. There should
be no difficulty about so arranging things, with the help of

temporary loans from the banks, that the Government purchase of war loan kept pace with the sale of the other securities, thus making the market for them effective and obviating the need of forced sales. No doubt, certain persons would not be in a position to raise either money or securities to meet the levy upon them; if they were compelled to pay the whole of it at once. Owners of private businesses, the greater portion of whose resources is locked up in their businesses and whose holding of securities is not more than sufficient to provide collateral for loans in case of need, cannot be expected to raise large sums quickly. Some landowners may be similarly situated. It would be necessary to allow these persons the option of payment by instalments, as is done at present for death duties, or even perhaps, in special circumstances, to accept the payment of interest on the levy, until such time as the property affected was broken up on the death of its owner or otherwise, and the payment of the principal thus became feasible. It should not be beyond the power of the revenue authorities to make satisfactory rules for overcoming technical difficulties of this kind. If this was done, the objection urged by Professor Dietzel, that different persons would be affected differently according to the facilities they have for borrowing cheaply, would be mitigated, though not entirely overcome. On the whole, therefore, it would seem that the problem of actually collecting the levy, as well as the problem of valuation, can be solved. The plea that a special levy would be unworkable in practice cannot be sustained.

§ 8. There remain certain questions concerning the rates at which the levy should be imposed upon different capitals. It is evident that, after provision has been made for the exemption of minimum capitals and for certain classes of capitals, *e.g.* charitable trusts, not belonging to individuals, the rates should be arranged on a graduated scale, increasing as capacity increases. It is equally evident that the precise scale of graduation can only be settled by a rough balancing of conflicting considerations. Apart from this main problem, one important minor matter needing

[1] *Economic Journal*, 1919, p. 359.

settlement is: Ought holdings of war loan to be placed, in the matter of rates, on the same footing as other capital, or should they be accorded specially favourable treatment? There is, clearly, no case for the special treatment of war loan stock which has been obtained by the conversion of consols or from the proceeds of the sale of other securities held before the war. But some of the war loan stock which has been purchased with new money has, no doubt, been the fruit of special and patriotic saving, for which some recognition might be claimed. Furthermore, it must be remembered that all capital created with new money during the war has been subjected to a burden, not experienced by the capital accumulated in earlier times, in consequence of the high war income tax; and war loan constitutes the predominant part of this war-time creation of capital. Against these considerations has to be set the fact that it would be practically very difficult to distinguish war loan holdings that have been bought with new money from other war loan holdings; and still more difficult to distinguish among them those that are the fruit of special patriotic saving from those that have been secured out of abnormal war profits. It has also to be remembered that a special levy on capital would be, to a large extent, a substitute for high continuous income tax on unearned income, and that nobody has proposed to give income from (ordinary) war loan any special abatement under income tax. Probably it would be convenient to privilege war loan to the extent of accepting it in payment of the special levy on terms somewhat more favourable than are accorded to cash and other securities, but, on the whole, particularly in view of the heavy reduction that any more substantial privilege must cause in the yield of the levy, the case for going further than this does not seem to be made out. A more difficult point to decide is whether the rates of the special levy should depend simply on the amount of people's holdings or should take account also of the size of their families. There can be no doubt that, under an annual income tax, to make bachelors and the fathers of a number of young children pay at equal rates would be exceedingly unfair. But, under a special levy there is the difficulty that a man who was a bachelor at the moment the levy was made might be a family man a few years later, while one who was a family man then might, in a little while, have become a childless widower. Under an income tax adjusted to family conditions these changes would be allowed for automatically; but, under a special levy, since this accomplishes itself once and for all, no allowance for them would be possible. Clearly, therefore, if it is decided to modify the rate of levy according to family conditions, the extent of the modification ought to be much smaller than is appropriate under income tax. Probably the best that can be done practically is to allow some slight modification where capitals are small, but none where they are large.[1]

[1] It may be noted that under the German law, in families where there are two or more children, a sum of 5000 marks in respect of each child is released from levy (Par. 25).

PART V

THE DISTRIBUTION OF THE NATIONAL DIVIDEND

CHAPTER I

THE GENERAL PROBLEM OF DISHARMONY

IN the three preceding Parts we have examined the way in
which the magnitude of the national dividend is affected
by three important groups of influences. It is not, of course,
pretended that *all* the influences that are relevant have been
brought under review. On the contrary, many of the more
remote *causae causarum*, such as those that determine the
general attitude of people toward work and saving, as well as
many less remote causes that affect the development of
mechanical inventions and improved methods of workshop
management, have been deliberately left on one side. This
deficiency I do not propose to remedy. There is, however,
another deficiency which cannot be thus lightly left unfilled.
From the propositions laid down in Chapter IV. of Part I.
it follows that, while, apart from incidental effects upon
temporal variability, anything that either increases the
dividend without injuring the absolute share of the poor,
or increases the absolute share of the poor without injuring
the dividend, must, in general, increase economic welfare, the
effect upon economic welfare of anything that increases one
of these quantities but diminishes the other is ambiguous.
Plainly, when this kind of disharmony exists, the aggregate
effect upon economic welfare brought about by any cause
responsible for it can only be determined by balancing in
detail the injury (or benefit) to the dividend as a whole
against the benefit (or injury) to the real earnings of the
poorer classes. No general solution of problems of that class
is possible. It is important, therefore, to determine how

far they are likely to arise in real life; to discover, in other words, whether causes acting discordantly upon the dividend as a whole and upon the absolute share of the poor are frequent or rare. When disharmonies are found, certain practical problems arising out of them will have to be examined.

CHAPTER II

PARETO'S LAW

§ 1. THE mere statement of this problem brings us into contact with an interesting thesis which, if valid, would immediately dispose of it. This thesis is that no cause operating in opposite senses upon the aggregate amount of the dividend and upon the absolute share of the poor can possibly exist. It is backed by an inductive proof. The data for the induction are derived from some remarkable investigations conducted by Professor Pareto and published by him in his *Cours d'économie politique.* Statistics of income in a number of countries, principally during the nineteenth century, are brought together. It is shown that, if x signify a given income and N the number of persons with incomes exceeding x, and if a curve be drawn, of which the ordinates are logarithms of x and the abscissae logarithms of N, this curve, for all the countries examined, is approximately a straight line, and is, furthermore, inclined to the axis of X at an angle, which, in no country, differs by more than three or four degrees from 56°. This means (since $\tan 56° = 1\cdot5$) that, if the number of incomes greater than x is equal to N, the number greater than mx is equal to $\dfrac{1}{m^{15}} \cdot$ N, whatever the value of m may be. Thus, the scheme of income distribution is everywhere the same. "We are confronted, as it were, with a great number of crystals of the same chemical composition. There are large crystals, middle-sized crystals and small crystals, but they are all of the same form."[1] These are the facts as found by Professor Pareto.

[1] *Cours d'économie politique,* ii. pp. 306-7.

The inference, which he appears to draw from them in the *Cours d'économie politique*, contains two parts. He defines diminished inequality among incomes thus: "Incomes can tend towards equality in two quite different ways; that is, either because the larger incomes diminish, or because the smaller incomes increase. Let us give this latter significance to the diminution of inequality among incomes, so that this will take place when the number of the individuals having an income less than an income x diminishes compared with the number of persons having an income greater than x." [1] On this basis he finds: First, "we may say generally that the increase of wealth relatively to population will produce either an increase in the minimum income, or a diminution in the inequality of income, or both these effects in combination." [2] Secondly, "to raise the level of the minimum income or to diminish the inequality of income, it is necessary that wealth should grow more rapidly than population. Hence we see that the problem of improving the condition of the poor is, before everything else, a problem of the production of wealth." [3] Now, on Professor Pareto's definition, "to increase the minimum income, or to diminish the inequality of income or both" is substantially equivalent to "to increase the absolute share of the national dividend accruing to the poor." Hence, what this thesis amounts to in effect is that, on the one hand, anything that increases the national dividend must, in general, increase also the absolute share of the poor, and, on the other hand—and this is the side of it that is relevant here—it is impossible for the absolute share of the poor to be increased by any cause which does not at the same time increase the national dividend as a whole. Hence, disharmony of the type referred to in the preceding chapter is impossible: we cannot be confronted with any proposal the adoption of which would both make the dividend larger and the absolute share of the poor smaller, or *vice versa*.

§ 2. Now it is quite evident that a sweeping proposition of this kind, based upon an inductive argument, requires very

---

[1] *Manuale di economia politica*, p. 371.
[2] *Cours d'économie politique*, ii. p. 324.   [3] *Ibid.* p. 408.

careful consideration. It is, therefore, necessary at the outset
to call attention to certain defects in its statistical basis.
The sum of what has to be said is that, though the various
distributions that are brought under review are similar in
form, the likeness among them is by no means complete. In
all of them, it is true, the logarithmic income curve—at least
for incomes of moderate size—is approximately a straight
line; but the inclination of this line, though it does not differ
widely, still does differ distinctly, for the different groups of
statistics that have been observed. Professor Pareto's lowest
figure from adequate data for the tangent of the angle made
with the axis of X is, for instance, 1·24 (Bâle, 1887), and
his highest 1·89 (Prussia, 1852). Nor is this all. As Dr.
Bowley has pointed out, in the most important set of figures
observed over a long period (those for Prussia) the slope of
the curve has been decreasing with the lapse of time. The
figures which Dr. Bowley gives differ slightly from those
of Professor Pareto, but the general effect is the same in both
sets. According to Pareto, however, a smaller slope of the
curve means a greater equality in his sense—a sense
the appropriateness of which, it will be remembered, is
matter for debate—in the distribution of income.[1] Dr.
Bowley, therefore, naturally offers as an explanation of the
Prussian figures: "The incomes are becoming more uniformly
distributed in Prussia, and the result is, from these figures,
that the Prussian income is getting to the more uniform distribution of the English."[2] Hence, interesting as Professor
Pareto's comparisons are, to build upon them any precise
quantitative law of distribution is plainly unjustifiable.

§ 3. But, if the position is to be fully understood, it is
well that this point should be waived. Let us suppose that
the statistical basis of Professor Pareto's reasoning is not
defective in the way that has been indicated. Even so, much
material for criticism remains. For let us consider what
exactly this scheme, or form, of distribution is, for the existence of which a mysterious necessity seems to have been
discovered. If we were to plot it out, not as Pareto does, but

---

[1] Cf. ante, p. 58.

[2] Select Committee on the Income Tax, 1906, Evidence, p. 81.

in the simpler form of a curve so drawn that the abscissae represent amounts of income, and the ordinates the number of people in receipt of these amounts, the curve would rise very quickly to its highest point and thereafter continuously fall. This would express in a picture the well-known fact that there are a very large number of people with incomes much below the average income, and, comparatively, a very small number with incomes above the average income. In short, the essential characteristic of current income distributions is that the great bulk of incomes are massed together near the lower end of the income scale. This fact is significant for the following reason. There is clear evidence that the physical characters of human beings—and considerable evidence that the mental characters—are distributed on an altogether different plan. When, for instance, a curve is plotted out for the heights of any large group of men, the resulting picture will not be, as with incomes, more or less like a hyperbola, but it will be a symmetrical curve shaped like a cocked-hat. It will, in short—to use a technical term —be the characteristic Gaussian curve or curve of error, symmetrical about the mean, in such wise that there is no massing near either end, but equal numbers of heights above the average and below it, and a lessening number of people at every height as the distance from the average in either direction is increased. Now, on the face of things, we should expect that, if, as there is reason to think, people's capacities are distributed on a plan of this kind, their incomes will be distributed in the same way. But in fact they are not distributed in the same way; and a little reflection shows at once why they are not. The reason is that income depends, not on capacity alone, but on a combination of capacity and inherited property, and inherited property is not distributed in proportion to capacity, but is concentrated upon a small number of people not selected in accordance with their own, or even, in many families, their parents' capacity, but owing their good fortune, perhaps to their being only sons or daughters, perhaps to some other "accident." The significance of this fact from the standpoint of our present problem is obvious. If the form of the income distribution is partly determined by the facts of bequest and inheritance, the particular form which is found to be dominant in current conditions cannot possibly be *necessary*, except upon the assumption that the general scheme of inheritance now generally in vogue is maintained. An alleged law, then, that should speak of any form as necessary in an absolute sense, runs counter to apparently irrefutable reasoning.[1]

§ 4. The statistics adduced by Professor Pareto do not provide a basis for any counter-argument. For, as a matter of logic, it is plain that, if all the different groups to which his statistics refer possess any common characteristic in addition to the fact that they are all in receipt of income, no general inference about income distribution, that is based upon them, can be extended to groups not possessing these characteristics. And, in fact, all these groups are communities enjoying the general type of inheritance laws common to modern Europe.[2] It follows at once that no inference can be drawn as to how the form of the income distribution would be affected if these laws were abolished or fundamentally changed. In his *Manuale di économia politica*, published some years after the *Cours*, Professor Pareto himself explicitly recognises this. He writes: "We cannot assert that the form of the curve would not change if the social constitution were to change radically; if, for example, collectivism were to take the place of the system of private property."[3]

§ 5. Nor is it necessary to imagine so large a change as the destruction of inheritance laws, in order that the form of the income-curve may be largely affected. There is ground for believing that a like result would come about in consequence of anything that affected, in a marked way, the proportion between "earned" income and income derived from investments. The reason for this opinion is twofold.

---

[1] Cf. Benini, *Principii di statistica metodologica*, p. 310.

[2] Of course it is not suggested that the inheritance laws of all modern European countries are exactly identical. They differ considerably in detail. The French laws, for example, force a more even division of estates among children than the English laws and deny special privileges to the eldest son. It is interesting to connect this fact with the observation of Benini (*Principii di statistica metodologica*, p. 191), that the distribution of wealth is more even in France than it is here. (Cf. also Ely, *Property and Contract*, vol. i. p. 89.)

[3] *Loc. cit.* pp. 370-71.

First, it is found by experience that incomes from property are distributed much more unevenly than incomes from either head-work or hand-work. Mr. Watkins, in his *Growth of Large Fortunes*, after printing an interesting table, comments on it as follows: "In making the comparisons made possible by this table, the criterion must be relative, not absolute. Convenient relative numbers are the ratio of the upper decile, or the upper centile, to the median. It will be observed that, in the statistics of wages, the upper decile is always somewhat less than twice the median, and, in one occupation of the nine, it is little more than one-fourth greater. In the distribution of salaries the upper decile is approximately twice the median, the inequality thus being not greatly different from that prevailing among wage-incomes. But there is a great gap between this and the prevailing distribution of income from property. In the Massachusetts probate statistics the upper decile is eight or nine times the median, and the error is doubtless in the direction of under-statement, since the figures are not net, so that large deductions for debts should be made from the smaller estates, and also since many very small properties do not pass through the courts. Among French estates the upper decile is thirteen times the median." [1] Secondly, the distribution of earned income itself is likely to be more uneven, the greater is the importance of the unevenly distributed income from investments. This result comes about because differences in income from investments make possible different degrees of educational training and afford different opportunities for entering lucrative professions. The correlation between the two sorts of income is illustrated by Benini in a table, in which he divides the figures for certain Italian incomes into two parts: "The one represents the income that people derive from property, supposed to be invested for all the different categories at a uniform rate of, say, 5 per cent, the other represents the strictly personal income, due to work, enjoyed by the same people. For example, a total income of 2000 lire, accompanied by a property of 9016 lire, may be regarded as composed of 451 lire, the fruit of investment, and

---

[1] *The Growth of Large Fortunes*, p. 18.

of 1549 lire, the fruit of professional activity.   Calculating in this manner, we obtain the following table:

Total Income (lire).		Income derived from Property.		Income derived from Personal Activity.
1,000	=	143	+	857
2,000	=	451	+	1549
4,000	=	1,458	+	2542
8,000	=	4,285	+	3715
16,000	=	11,665	+	4335
20,000	=	15,885	+	4115
32,000	=	28,640	+	3360
40,000	=	37,500	+	2500

It will be noticed, of course, that, so soon as total incomes begin to exceed 16,000 lire, the part derived from personal activity diminishes; but this does not mean that the remuneration of the profession followed diminishes; it only means that many will now live wholly on the income derived from their property without following any gainful profession, and that this conduct of theirs reduces the average of the income due to work for the class to which they belong." [1]   Moreover, there is yet another way in which the form of the income-curve might be modified.   A change in the distribution of training and so forth, that is, of investment of capital in people, may take place apart from variations in income from investments.   When this happens, the change must tend directly to alter the distribution of earned income, even though original capacities are distributed in accordance with some (the same) law of error.   It is perhaps some change of this kind that accounts for the conclusion, which Professor Moore derives from his study of American wage statistics, that the variability of wages (as between different people at the same time) was less in 1900 than it had been in 1890.

§ 6. When these points are conceded, the general defence of "Pareto's Law" as a law of even limited necessity rapidly crumbles. His statistics warrant no inference as to the effect on distribution of the introduction of any cause that is not already present in approximately equivalent form in

---

[1] *Principii di statistica metodologica,* pp. 336-7.

at least one of the communities—and they are very limited in range—from which these statistics are drawn. This consideration is really fatal; and Professor Pareto is driven, in effect, to abandon the whole claim which, in the earlier exposition of his formula, he seemed to make. In the *Manuale di economia politica* he insists that that formula is purely empirical. "Some persons would deduce from it a general law as to the only way in which the inequality of incomes can be diminished. But such a conclusion far transcends anything that can be derived from the premises. Empirical laws, like those with which we are here concerned, have little or no value outside the limits for which they were found experimentally to be true."[1] This means that, even if the statistical basis of the "law" were much securer than it is, the law would but rarely enable us to assert that any contemplated change *must* leave the form of income distribution unaltered. As things are, in view of the weakness of its statistical basis, it can *never* enable us to do this. Disharmony between movements of the national dividend as a whole and of the absolute share accruing to the poor cannot be proved by general statistical inference to be impossible, and a detailed study of the matter must, therefore, be made.

[1] *Manuale di economia politica*, pp. 371-2.

§ 1. IN undertaking that study we are forced to avail ourselves of a somewhat rough method of approximation. Our inquiry is concerned with the comparative effects of certain causes upon the magnitude of the national dividend and upon its distribution among rich and poor persons. No machinery exists by which effects upon distribution in this sense can be directly investigated. But economists have carried through, and have made common property, a very full analysis of the influences that affect distribution in another sense, namely, distribution among the various "factors of production." These two sorts of distribution are not the same. They *would be* the same if each factor were provided exclusively by a set of persons who provided nothing of any other factor. But, of course, in real life the same man often provides portions of several factors, obtaining part of his income from one and part from another. A landlord is not merely the owner of "the original and indestructible properties of the soil." On the contrary, he frequently invests a great deal of capital in his land, and sometimes also considerable mental labour in choosing his tenants, exercising a certain control over their methods, and deciding, it may be, upon the necessity of evictions. A shopkeeper provides capital, or waiting, to some extent, but he also provides, especially if his sales are on credit, much mental labour in judging the "standing of his customers" and not a little uncertainty-bearing in respect of bad debts. A large capitalist employer is still more obviously capitalist,

brain-worker and uncertainty-bearer combined. Finally, an
ordinary manual worker is frequently, in some measure, also
a capitalist. In view of these considerations, it is plain that
doctrines about distribution among factors of production
cannot be applied directly and unreservedly to problems
concerning distribution among people. The difficulty is not,
however, as it so happens, of decisive practical importance.
By far the largest part of the poorer classes in this country
consists of wage-earning workpeople. It is true, of course,
that "there is no definite line between wage-earners and
persons working directly for customers and small employers
and small farmers, . . . nor is there any clear and uniform
division between wages and salaries."[1] But the dominant
position of wage-earners among the poor is illustrated by the
fact that, whereas, before the war, they numbered some
fifteen and a half millions, persons other than wage-earners
with incomes below £160 a year numbered, say, three and
a half millions.[2] Moreover, it is reasonable to suppose that
a large number of persons earning small salaries or small
incomes from working on their own account are affected by
the main body of relevant economic causes in much the same
way as wage-earners proper. For the purpose of the present
discussion, therefore, though not, of course, for all purposes,
we shall not commit any serious error if we treat manual
workers and the poor as roughly equivalent classes. Furthermore, statistics show that by far the most important income-
yielding instrument actually possessed by the poor of the
United Kingdom, as thus defined, is manual labour. Persons
in receipt of wages number, as I have said, some fifteen and
a half millions, and it is probable that persons dependent
upon wages amount to 30,000,000, or nearly two-thirds
of the population. The accumulated property of these
persons before the war—it is, of course, a good deal larger
now—was estimated at £450,000,000, and the interest on it
might, therefore, be put at some £20,000,000 a year. This
was probably little more than $\frac{1}{35}$th part of the total income of
the wage-earners, all the rest being received as wages of

[1] Bowley, *The Division of the Product of Industry*, p. 12.
[2] *Ibid.* p. 11.

labour.[1] Hence, just as we have agreed roughly to identify the poor with the wage-earners, we may agree also to identify the earnings of wage-earners with the earnings of the factor labour. No appreciable error is introduced by this simplification. When we have made it, the familiar analysis of economists can be directly applied.

§ 2. We may divide the factors of production, from whose joint operation the national dividend results, into two broad groups, labour and the factors other than labour. Of course neither labour nor the factors other than labour constitute a homogeneous group made up of similar units. Labour embraces the work both of wholly unskilled workpeople and of numerous sorts of skilled artisans. The factors other than labour embrace, along with the work of Nature, the work of many kinds of mental ability and of various sorts of capital instruments. This circumstance is not, however, relevant to our present problem. That problem is to determine whether and how far economic causes, which affect the national dividend as a whole in one sense, can affect the receipts of the factor labour in the opposite sense. In the present chapter attention will be concentrated upon two sets of causes of the broadest kind, namely, those that act respectively on the supply of capital in general and on the supply of labour in general. It will be convenient to begin with capital.

§ 3. Capital, or to put the same thing in concrete terms, capital instruments, are the embodiment of labour itself, waiting for the fruits of labour and uncertainty-bearing. Consequently, apart from inventions and improvements, which will be considered presently, an increase in the supply of capital instruments can only mean that people have been willing to undertake more waiting for the fruits of labour and more exposure of those fruits to uncertainty. In other words, the supply of waiting, or of uncertainty-bearing, or of both has been increased. It is obvious that a cause of this kind will make for an increase in the national dividend as a whole. Can it at the same time make for a decrease in the real income of labour? The analysis relevant to this question has been developed by Dr. Marshall. Subject to certain important

---

[1] Cf. Chiozza-Money, *Riches and Poverty*, p. 49.

qualifications, which do not affect the present argument, this
analysis shows, first, that every factor of production, including
entrepreneurs' work,[1] tends to be remunerated at a rate equivalent to its marginal net product of commodities in general.
It shows, secondly, that, other things being equal, the marginal
net product, in this sense, of every factor diminishes as the
supply of this factor increases. This proposition expresses
what may be called the *law of diminishing returns to individual factors of production*—the law, namely, that the
increase of production due to the increase, by a small increment, of any factor of production, will, in general, be smaller,
other things remaining the same, the greater is the supply of
that factor already employed. This law must not be confused
with the law of *diminishing returns to resources in general
invested in a given occupation,* as defined in Part II. Chapter
II. § 8. This latter law is applicable to some commodities
only, and corresponds to the law of increasing returns, as
ordinarily understood, which is applicable to others. The *law
of diminishing returns to individual factors of production* is
quite different from this, and is valid, not merely in some conditions, but, apart from a few unimportant exceptions, in all.[2]
There is no law of increasing returns to individual factors of
production corresponding to it. The ground of it is the general
fact that, as the supply of any factor increases, it pushes
forward an irregular boundary along a great number of routes.[3]
The more of it there is, the smaller is the quantity of other
factors, with which to co-operate and from which to derive
assistance, that each new unit finds available. Consequently,
as the quantity of any factor increases, its marginal net product
in terms of commodities in general continually falls.

---

[1] The special case of the entrepreneur's earnings is discussed in detail by
Professor Edgeworth in the *Quarterly Journal of Economics* for February 1904 ;
it is also touched upon in his paper on "Mathematical Theories" in the *Economic
Journal* of December 1907.

[2] For a discussion on lines somewhat similar to the above, cf. Carver, *The
Distribution of Wealth,* pp. 65-6 ; and Wicksteed, *The Common Sense of Political
Economy,* bk. ii. ch. v.

[3] This idea is well expressed by Turgot in an elaborate figure (cf. Cassel,
Nature and Necessity of Interest, p. 22). In illustration, it may be noticed
that, as the rate of interest falls, instrumental goods come to be built more
solidly and to be repaired and renewed more readily when need arises.

§ 4. From this analysis an important proposition directly relevant to our present problem can be derived. This proposition has two sides, and is to this effect : If the quantity of any factor of production is increased, the reward per efficiency unit reaped by all factors completely rival to that factor (in the sense of being perfect substitutes) will be diminished, and the reward per efficiency unit reaped by all factors completely co-operant with it, and in no degree substitutes, will be increased. The former half of this proposition is obvious. The advent of Chinese immigrants in the retailing business *must* injure the British retail shopkeepers of New Zealand, and the steady flow of low-grade European immigrants *must* keep down the wages of unskilled workmen in the United States.[1] The latter half of the proposition is easily proved as follows. Since each unit of the increased factor must be paid at the same rate, and the rate for the new units is less than the old rate, a part of the product of the old as well as of the new units is handed over to the co-operant factors.[2] As an illustration, we may note that a high level of wages generally prevails in new countries because, first, there is a large quantity of land available, and secondly, by mortgaging the land to foreigners, the inhabitants can obtain a large quantity of capital also.[3]

§ 5. If, as is, of course, generally true in the concrete, different factors are partly co-operant and partly rival, the

---

[1] Professor Taussig points out that, whereas most money incomes in the United States have increased, "the wages of ordinary day labour and of such factory labour as is virtually unskilled seem to have remained stationary and sometimes seem even to have fallen" (*Quarterly Journal of Economics*, 1906, p. 521). Whether the unskilled immigrants are mainly rival or mainly co-operant with the skilled workers of America is another and more difficult question. Dr. Hourwich writes on this point : "It is only because the new immigrants have furnished the class of unskilled labour that the native workmen and older immigrants have been raised to the plane of an aristocracy of labour" (*Immigration and Labour*, p. 12). In the same sense Prof. Prato (*Le Protectionisme Ouvrier*, p. 72) maintains that, in general, the low-grade immigrant takes on occupations which native-born workpeople wish to leave, and that this is true not only of the Chinese and European immigrant into the United States, but also of the Italian and Belgian immigrant to France, Switzerland and Germany.

[2] It is not relevant to the present argument to note, though the point may be added for completeness, that, in response to the improved demand, the co-operant factors tend to increase in quantity, but, since their supply curve is inclined positively, not to a sufficient extent to reduce their receipts to the old level.

[3] Cf. Marshall, *Royal Commission on Labour*, Q. 4237-8.

effect of an increase in the quantity of one of them upon the
reward obtained by the others can be analysed in this wise.
Suppose that the quantity of factor A increases from A to
$(A + a)$, and that x of the new units are substituted in uses
formerly occupied by mx units of the other factor B.   Then
the effect produced on the reward per unit of B is equal to
that which would have been produced had the two factors
been entirely co-operant, and had the quantity of A increased
from A to $(A + a - x)$ and the quantity of B from B to
$(B + mx)$.   It is obvious that this effect *may* represent either
an increase or a decrease in the reward per unit of B, and that
it is more likely to represent an increase, the larger is
$\dfrac{A + a - x}{A}$ relatively to $\dfrac{B + mx}{B}$.   It is not possible, in the
absence of knowledge as to the form of the function repre-
senting the relations between the factors and their product,
to make any statement more precise than this.   Interpreted
roughly, the condition, under which, on the hypothesis taken,
an increase in the quantity of A would lead to an increase in
the reward per unit of B, is that the predominant part of the
extra units of A can be profitably turned to uses other than
those formerly occupied by units of B.   Hence, in general,
where two factors are partly co-operant and partly rival, an
increase in the quantity of the one will augment the reward
per unit, and, therefore, the absolute share of the dividend,
enjoyed by the other, if the relation of co-operation between
the two factors is more important than the relation of
rivalry.

§ 6. The question whether the relation between waiting
and uncertainty-bearing in general and labour in general is,
in the concrete, mainly co-operant or mainly rival is not one
to which an *a priori* answer can be given.   If the only sort
of capital instruments which mankind had learned how to
make were a kind of Frankenstein monster capable of exactly
duplicating the labour of manual workers, and not capable of
doing anything else, this relation would be wholly one of
rivalry.   What it is in actual fact, therefore, chiefly depends
on the nature of the things which people are able, by combining labour with waiting and uncertainty - bearing, to

create. If we consider realistically what these things in the main are—and, of course, when what is contemplated is a general increase in the supply of waiting and uncertainty-bearing, we must imagine the new supplies to be used in an all-round addition to existing capital instruments—it is apparent that their work is mainly co-operant. Railways, ships, factory buildings and machines, taken broadly, are tools for, and not rivals to, men. By giving help, they enable any *n*th worker to produce more stuff than he could have produced without them; they do not, by supplanting him, compel him to produce less. This is the general teaching of experience. In particular instances, indeed, the relation is predominantly one of rivalry. But, *comparatively*, these are unimportant. As Dr. Marshall well writes: "There is a real and effective competition between labour in general and waiting [to which should be added uncertainty-bearing] in general. But it covers a small part of the whole field, and is of small importance relatively to the benefit which labour derives from obtaining cheaply the aid of capital, and, therefore, of efficient methods in the production of things that it needs."[1] In other words, the relation between capital as a whole and labour as a whole is predominantly one of co-operation. It follows that the question set out for discussion in § 2 must be answered in the negative. It is not, in present conditions, practically possible that a cause (other than inventions and improvements which will be considered in the next chapter) operating to expand the national dividend by increasing the supply of capital generally should at the same time lessen the real income of labour. Similarly, of course, it can be shown that a cause operating to contract the dividend by diminishing the supply of capital generally cannot at the same time increase the real income of labour. In this field, in short, disharmony cannot occur.

§ 7. This conclusion leads up to the difficult problem of capital investments abroad. Apart from the special qualifications indicated on page 162, it may be presumed that, since nobody will invest abroad rather than at home unless he expects a better return, freedom to invest abroad will

---

[1] *Principles of Economics*, p. 540.

augment the national dividend. As against this, it seems at first sight that it will diminish the real income of labour. The funds for investment must be obtained either by exporting goods or by refraining from the import of goods to which we have a claim. It makes very little difference whether or not the granting of a loan is made conditional upon the proceeds of it being expended in purchasing the railway material, or other things, which it is destined to pay for, in the lending country. If this is done, the *kind* of goods that we export may be altered, but the volume of them will not be substantially affected. In any event the volume of things immediately available in this country will be diminished. This is practically certain to involve a direct injury to labour, either by making the things workpeople buy more expensive, or by reducing the supply of tools and machines that help them in production. It is true that, since some capital will have been withdrawn from home uses, the rate of interest here will go up, and this will encourage saving to create more capital. But this tendency can only mitigate, and not wipe out, the initial injury to labour. It follows that labour must be less well-off *in terms of things in general* than it would have been if the opening for investing capital abroad had been closed.

This result, however, is not decisive. In certain circumstances, even though this happens, labour may, nevertheless, be better off in terms of the particular things which workpeople are interested to buy. For, as an indirect effect of our foreign investments, these things may have been generally cheapened. In actual fact this has happened. Sir George Paish, writing in 1914, stated: "In the aggregate, Great Britain has supplied the world outside these islands with nearly £600,000,000 for the construction of railways in the last seven years (out of a total so supplied by her of upwards of eleven hundred millions), and all of the money has been placed in countries upon which we depend for our supplies of food and raw material."[1] When our foreign investments are of this character, the real income of labour, in the only sense

[1] "The Export of Capital and the Cost of Living," *Manchester Statistical Society*, Feb. 1914, p. 78.

that signifies, is fairly certain to be increased, so that no disharmony arises.   No doubt, if there were special reason to believe that, had the export of capital been forbidden, the funds set free would have been devoted to domestic uses specially beneficial to workpeople, such as the erection of a large number of healthy workmen's cottages, this conclusion would not hold good.   But there is not, in general, special reason to believe this.

Moreover, it is necessary to take account of certain more remote consequences of foreign investment.   When the export of capital is free, the opportunity to obtain higher interest abroad both causes more British capital to be created—in lieu of consumption—than would have been created otherwise, and also enables a part of it to be invested in enterprises yielding a larger return than would otherwise have been open to it.   Thus, freedom to export capital at one time exercises a twofold influence in enlarging the aggregate real income of the country at a later time.   It follows that, other things being equal, the amount of new capital that can be created there at a later time will be enlarged.   This effect will repeat itself cumulatively year after year.   In the end, therefore, if we suppose the amount of capital exported to remain constant, the extra capital created on account of past exportation must, it would seem, exceed the amount withdrawn by contemporary exportation.   This means that, in the end, labour as a whole will be benefited and not injured.   Though, therefore, disharmony may prevail from the point of view of a short period, in the higher unity of the long view it is likely to be resolved.   The practical inference is that all proposals to restrict the export of capital in the interests of labour—apart from the special reasons discussed on page 162 cited above—should be subjected to a very cautious and critical scrutiny.

§ 8. We turn to the second main group of causes distinguished in § 2, those, namely, which operate through the supply of labour.   It is evident that, if this supply is increased, whether the increase comes about through an addition to the number of workpeople or through an addition to their average efficiency, the national dividend must be increased.   Our problem, therefore, is to ascertain the effect that will be produced upon the aggregate real income of labour. The analysis set out in the preceding section shows that the marginal net product of labour, in terms of things in general, and, therefore, its real earnings *per unit*, must be diminished. Whether its aggregate income will be increased depends, therefore, on whether the elasticity of the demand for labour in general is greater or less than unity. If this elasticity is greater than unity, labour in the aggregate will receive a larger absolute quantity of dividend than before; whereas, if the elasticity is less than unity, it will receive a smaller absolute quantity.[1]

[1] The general proposition, of which the statement in the text is a special instance, is that, other things being equal, an increase in the quantity of any one factor of production will be accompanied by an increase in the *absolute share* of product accruing to that factor, provided that the demand for the said factor has an elasticity greater than unity. The condition on which it will be accompanied by an increase in the *proportionate share* of product accruing to the factor is different from this, and can be determined as follows. The supply functions of the other factors being given, the aggregate output P depends on the quantity of the variable factor, in such wise that, if x represents this quantity, $P = f(x)$. The *absolute share* accruing to the variable factor is, therefore, represented by xf', and the *proportionate share* by $\frac{xf'}{f}$. The condition that this latter magnitude shall increase when x increases is that

$$\frac{1}{f}\left\{ f' + xf'' \right\} + xf'\left\{ \frac{-f'}{[f]^2} \right\} \text{ is positive.}$$

Let e represent the elasticity of demand for the factor in question. Then, since

$$e = -\frac{f'}{xf''}$$

the above condition can be expressed, by easy substitution, in the form

$$e > \frac{1}{1 - \frac{xf'}{f}}.$$

This magnitude exceeds unity by a larger amount, the larger is the proportionate share of the product accruing, before the variation, to our variable factor.

The above formula, besides its general application, has also a subordinate one; for it gives the conditions under which an improvement in the methods of cultivation will increase the proportion that true rent bears to the gross produce of farm-land. When additional doses of capital and labour yield only slightly diminishing returns, when, that is to say, the elasticity of the demand for them in terms of product is very large, an improvement (which is equivalent to an increase in the quantity of capital and labour applied) generally accords to capital and labour a larger proportion, and, therefore, to true rent a smaller proportion, than before. When, on the other hand, diminishing returns act sharply, the proportion accruing to true rent will generally be increased by an improvement. When changes in the proportion of product accruing to different factors are considered historically, it is, of course, vital to note that an increase in the "share" of land, the amount of which necessarily remains stationary, may mean something very different from a similar increase in the "share" of capital, the amount of which may have been very greatly increased.

It is, therefore, necessary to determine whether in fact the elasticity of demand is greater or less than unity.

Let us begin by ignoring the fact that an addition to the supply of labour available in industry is likely to react upon the supply of other factors co-operating with it. It may then be observed that there is a certain. field of personal service where labour works practically unaided by other factors, where, therefore, its productivity per unit would not appreciably fall with an increase in its quantity, and where a good deal could be absorbed without greatly reducing the value of its product in terms of other things. This circumstance points, *pro tanto*, to a fairly low rate of diminution in the (real) demand for labour in general as the quantity of it increases; though exactly *how rapid* the rate of diminution would be, or, in other words, how elastic is the demand for labour, it is quite impossible to say. In real life, however, it is illegitimate to ignore reactions, indirectly brought about by an increase in the supply of labour, in the supply of other factors. In particular, the supply of capital is known to be very far from rigidly fixed. When the quantity of labour increases, and, hence, indirectly, the return per unit of capital is enhanced, people in general will be willing to save more and so to create a greater quantity of capital. Moreover, owing to the greater volume of the national dividend, their ability to save will be increased. The resultant increase in the supply of capital will react to increase the marginal productivity of any given quantity of labour. On the whole, therefore, it is probable that the demand for labour, even viewed from the general standpoint of the whole world, is fairly elastic.[1] And the probability is far stronger as regards the demand for labour in any single country. For capital is so mobile that a small increase in the return per unit obtainable by it in any one country must inevitably—apart from complications due to double income-tax, about which it may be hoped that international arrangements will soon be made—bring about a large influx from foreign countries, or, what comes to the same thing, a large contraction

[1] Cf. Edgeworth, "On the Use of the Differential Calculus in Economics," *Rivista di Scienzia*, vol. vii. pp. 90-91.

of the outflow that formerly went to foreign countries. Hence, the elasticity of the aggregate demand for British labour is greater than the elasticity of that part of the demand which depends on British capital alone. It is, indeed, so much greater that, with any reasonable assumption as to this latter elasticity, the elasticity of the aggregate demand is practically certain, from the standpoint of a long period, which is alone in question here, to be immensely larger than unity.

Hence, it follows that an increase in the supply of labour, whether through an increase in the number of units of labour of given efficiency that the average workman provides, or through an increase in the number of workmen providing, on the average, a given number of units of labour, must increase the absolute quantum of dividend that labour in the aggregate receives. It is, no doubt, true that, within the broad group labour, an increase in efficiency, which only affected some of the sub-groups, might involve injury to other sub-groups, whose efficiency has not been improved. Even this danger, however, is likely to be avoided where the different sub-groups are not strictly homogeneous, but are partly co-operant, and where, as occurs when some unskilled labourers are trained to trades, the group, which is not made more efficient, is diminished in numbers by the indirect operation of the change that has occurred. Furthermore, these incidents within the broad group labour are, in any event, of subordinate interest. So soon as it is shown that the absolute share of labour as a whole possesses, along with the aggregate dividend, the property of increasing with increases in the supply of labour, the only proposition that is of direct relevance to the present argument is established.

§ 9. When the increase in the supply of labour comes about through an increase in the efficiency of labouring people, it is obvious that the consequent increase in the absolute share of dividend accruing to them carries with it, in accordance with the argument of previous chapters, an increase in their economic welfare. When, however, the increase of supply comes about through an increase in numbers, the absolute share *per man* is lessened, despite the fact that the absolute share of the group as a whole is increased. If there were reason to believe that the loss per man were large, we should hesitate to conclude that an increase of this sort in the supply of labour involves an increase in the economic welfare of labour. In fact, however, it can be shown that, under the conditions now existing in this country, the loss per man would be very small. That it would be very small in terms of commodities in general follows from the fact already established, that the elasticity of the demand for labour in England is large. If the conditions were such that an increase in numbers would materially increase the real cost of producing food or other articles predominantly consumed by the working-classes, it might, indeed, be large in terms of the things that are of significance to them. At present, however, the fact that abundant supplies of imported food are available makes it impossible that an increase in the population of a small country such as ours should, to any important extent, evoke the law of diminishing returns in respect of food production. Hence, in all senses, the diminution of real wages per head of the working-classes would be very small.[1] Consequently, it seems reasonable to conclude that an increase in the absolute share of labour, even when it results from an increase in the numbers of the population, will carry with it an increase in the economic welfare of working people. It is not necessary, therefore, to qualify our conclusion, that causes impinging upon the supply of labour affect the aggregate amount of the dividend and the aggregate real earnings of labour in the same sense, by emphasising the caution that the welfare of labour is sometimes diminished by causes that increase its wealth.

§ 10. The conclusions that have been reached in this chapter serve to rebut two popular opinions. The first of these has to do with hours of labour, and is to the effect that a general shortening of the working day, because it will cut down the supply of labour, will enable workpeople as a whole to secure terms so much better than before that their aggregate real income must be increased. The truth is that, in so far as a diminution in the hours of work leads to a more than corresponding increase in efficiency, both the

---

[1] Cf. Marshall, *Principles of Economics*, p. 672.

national dividend and the absolute share of labour will benefit. But, if the reduction of hours is pushed beyond this point, so that it injures the national dividend, the real income of labour must, in view of the elasticity of the demand for labour, necessarily be injured also. The second popular opinion is that the compulsory withdrawal from work of persons in receipt of State assistance would increase the aggregate real earnings of the poor, and, therefore, from the point of view of labour, ought to be encouraged. Two schemes were submitted to the Royal Commission on the Aged Poor, one of which contained, as a condition for the receipt of a pension, " the abstention from all work of pensioners, male and female," while the other would have awarded pensions to " every one over sixty, and prohibited work beyond that age." [1] The defence proffered for those schemes was that, if pensioners did not abstain from work, independent workpeople would find their earnings diminished. From a long-period point of view, however, the interests of the poor should be identified, not with those of independent workpeople only, but with those of all workpeople; for all workpeople are liable to become dependent at some period of their lives. But it follows directly from what was said in the preceding section that, if the supply of labour is contracted, the aggregate earnings of independent and dependent workpeople together will be diminished. Hence, so far as the present argument goes, it is inadvisable to adopt the policy embodied in these two pension schemes. It should be noted, however, that the cessation of work by pensioners can be defended from a more special point of view. It may be held desirable that the qualification for a pension should be, not age, but declining strength. This cannot be tested directly, but, if abstention from work were made a condition for receiving, say, a 10s. pension, conformity to the condition would ensure that recipients were really incapable of earning much more than 10s. regularly. Hence, such an arrangement, though it would abolish work on the part of many persons below the 10s. line, might, nevertheless, be desirable as a means of preventing many other persons from obtaining pensions,

[1] *Report of the Royal Commission on the Aged Poor*, p. 72.

and, in consequence of obtaining or expecting them, from relaxing their efforts in industry. The pension policy pursued by certain friendly societies seems to be based on considerations of this order.[1] Clearly, however, this argument is not relevant where the condition for the receipt of a pension is, not declining strength, but the attainment of some definite age.

[1] *Royal Commission on the Aged Poor, Minutes of Evidence* (Q. 10,880).

CHAPTER IV

INVENTIONS AND IMPROVEMENTS

§ 1. WE have thus seen that in existing conditions causes acting through the supply of capital in general and also causes acting through the supply of labour in general operate harmoniously. They either increase both the national dividend and the real earnings of labour, or they decrease both of them. A more complicated problem has to be faced when the initiating cause is an invention or improvement in processes or methods. All developments of this kind, since they enable something to be produced which was not being produced at all before, or enable something which was being produced before to be produced more easily, must increase the national dividend. Unless at the same time they indirectly alter distribution adversely to labour, they must also increase the real income which falls to labour. Hence, of any invention considered in the abstract, there is an initial presumption that its effects will be harmonious, in the sense that it will benefit labour as well as increase the national dividend. But it is *possible* that any given invention may change the parts played by capital and labour in production in such a way as to make labour less valuable relatively to capital than it was before; and, if this happens, the absolute share received by labour *may be* diminished. Our problem is to determine in what, if any, conditions this result will come about. It is interesting to observe that exactly the same analysis is appropriate when the initiating cause is, not an invention in the ordinary sense, but a development which enables a country to obtain some commodity more cheaply than before by making some-

716

thing else with which to purchase it from elsewhere, instead
of making the commodity itself. Here too more of what
people want is made available ; and here too the proportionate
parts played by labour and capital in production may be
changed.

§ 2. The popular solution of our problem is very simple.
It is thought that workpeople will be injured if an invention
causes less labour to be employed in the industry to which it
refers, and benefited if it causes more labour to be employed
there. Such a view leads at once to optimism. Mr. Hobson
has, indeed, shown that inventions do not always cause more
labour to be employed in the industry where they are
introduced: "The introduction of spinning and weaving
machinery into Lancashire and Yorkshire afforded a considerable increase of employment, and a number of successive inventions and improvements during the second
and third quarters of the last century had a similar
result, but later increments of machinery have not been
attended by similar results; on the contrary, there has
been a decline in the number of persons employed in some
of the staple textile processes. The introduction of type-
setting machines into printing works has been followed by
a large increase of employment; the introduction of clicking
machinery into the shoe trade has been followed by a net
reduction of employment."[1] A broader illustration of a
diminution of employment in a particular sphere, in consequence of an invention in that sphere, may be found in
agriculture : for it is well known that agricultural machines
have displaced agricultural labourers. An occasional failure
of this kind is fully admitted by all. Still, broadly speaking,
inventions, as a general rule, are believed by those who have
studied the matter to increase, and not to diminish, employment at the point at which they act. Thus, M. Levasseur
writes: " The common opinion is that ' the machine drives
out the workman' and robs a part of the working-classes
of work. It is certainly true that a shop furnished with
powerful machinery yields in a given time a greater product,
with the help of a much smaller number of employees, than a

---

[1] Hobson, *The Industrial System*, p. 281.

shop where the same goods are made by hand. It is this that one perceives in the first instance. What one only perceives later, by dint of study, is that the goods made economically by machinery, being sold, in general, at a lower price, often find such a number of new purchasers that the increased production, thus made necessary, provides employment for a greater number of workpeople than were employed before the machinery was introduced."[1] Again, the Poor Law Commissioners are gratified to find among manufacturers a remarkable consensus of opinion concerning the effects of improvements in machinery. They believe that such improvements "do temporarily reduce the demand for labour within the department where such changes occur; that the displacement does not, as a rule, reduce the labour employed in each producing unit, the workers dispensed with being readily absorbed within the same business—particularly in shipbuilding, where changes are slowly introduced and affect only a few men at a time—and that the final result is that more labour is required instead of less."[2] Now, I am not concerned to deny the empirical part of these conclusions. I do not dispute the Poor Law Commissioners' assertion that the conditions necessary to secure that increased employment in any sphere will ultimately result from an invention in that sphere are, as a matter of practice, usually fulfilled. I do dispute, however, the very widespread opinion that these facts are directly relevant to the question whether inventions and improvements are beneficial allies or injurious foes to the fortunes of labour, and so of the poor as a whole. To elucidate that issue a different and more far-reaching analysis is necessary.

§ 3. Every invention or improvement either facilitates the manufacture of some commodity or service that is already being produced, or makes possible the manufacture of some new commodity or service. It is certain, therefore, to lead to a cheapening and an increased consumption of the commodity affected by it. With the differently made and enlarged output, a different amount of labour, and also a different amount of capital (or waiting), will be employed

[1] *Salariat et salaires*, p. 421. [2] *Report*, p. 344.

in the industry and in the subsidiary industries engaged in making machinery for it. Let us suppose that work-people purchase absolutely none of the product which the invention has cheapened. Then the effect of the invention upon their real income depends upon its effect on the marginal net product of things for which labour is responsible in other industries; for, when equilibrium is established, it will get, in the industry where the invention has taken place, the same real wage as it gets in these industries. For the present purpose we may reasonably leave out of account factors of production other than labour and capital. It will then follow that, if, as a result of the invention, the quantity of labour in industries other than the improved industry and its subsidiaries is diminished in a larger ratio, or increased in a smaller ratio, than the quantity of capital, the marginal net product of labour in terms of the things workpeople buy—and, therefore, the aggregate real income of workpeople—must be increased. In the converse event, this aggregate real income must be diminished. If the two ratios of change are equal it must be left unaltered. Inventions which have these several effects I shall call, respectively, capital-saving inventions, labour-saving inventions, and neutral inventions. It will, of course, be observed that this use of terms is different from the common use, according to which every invention which enables a given amount of product to be got with the help of less labour is labour-saving.

§ 4. It is easy to apply this analysis to practice, provided we have to do with an industry in which (and also in its subsidiaries) the proportion of the country's total labour employed is equal to the proportion of its total capital. In this class of industry anything which changes in one direction the ratio between the labour and capital employed there must change in the opposite direction the ratio outside. Hence, on my definition, an invention or improvement which reduces the ratio of capital to labour in the industry to which it applies will be capital-saving, one which increases it labour-saving, and one which leaves it unchanged, neutral. In these conditions, therefore, we are able with fair confidence to distinguish in the concrete the several classes of inventions. Thus, assuming the above conditions to prevail, the introduction of two-shift or three-shift systems, making possible the more continuous working of machinery, *must* be a capital-saving invention. For if, instead of only 12 hours being worked in each 24-hour period, the whole 24 hours are worked, a staff of 100 men, 50 working by day and 50 by night, will only require half as much machinery to produce a given output as they would need if the whole 100 worked by day only. Of course, the machinery will wear out more quickly when it is worked for a longer time per day. But for many kinds of machinery the working life is—on account of obsolescence—much shorter than the physical life. Consequently, though the substitution of two twelve-hour shifts for one twelve-hour shift would not reduce the capital required for a given scale of production by as much as a half, it would, in general, reduce it a good deal. In whatever way, therefore, the absolute quantity of output is changed, the ratio of capital to labour employed must be diminished. The same result holds good of developments that enable the manufacturers, wholesalers or retailers, who deal in any commodity, to conduct their business equally efficiently with a smaller amount of capital locked up in the form of stocks. For, here again, whatever happens to absolute amounts, the ratio of capital to labour employed must be diminished. This point is of some importance in view of the economy in the matter of stock-holding, which, as will be shown in Appendix I., modern improvements in communication have made practicable. Among developments more ordinarily named inventions, we might, still assuming the industries to which they apply to have previously employed capital and labour in normal proportions, count as capital-saving such things as Marconi's invention of wireless telegraphy, by which the need for cables is removed. Probably, however, the majority of inventions in the narrower sense would have to be reckoned as "labour-saving," because, as Dr. Cassell has observed, "almost all the efforts of inventors are directed towards finding durable instruments to do work which has hitherto been done by hand."[1] These results, it must be remembered, are not necessarily valid, unless, before the inven-

---

[1] *Nature and Necessity of Interest*, p. 112.

tion, the industry (and its subsidiaries), in which the invention is made, was employing labour and capital in the same proportion as the general average of all industries. If it was employing an abnormally large proportion of labour or of capital, an invention, which changed the ratio in it in any direction, might change the ratio in other industries in the same, and not in the opposite, direction. Suppose, for example, that in a particular industry 3000 units of labour and 1000 units of capital are being employed, and in the rest of industry one million units of each. In consequence of an invention in this particular industry only 2000 units of labour and 500 units of capital come to be needed there. The ratio of labour to capital there is, therefore, increased from 3 to 1 to 4 to 1. At the same time in the rest of industry it is increased from 1 to 1 to 1,001,000 to 1,000,500. It is thus evident that a knowledge of the effect on the ratio in the improved industry would not by itself enable us to determine whether the invention is labour-saving or capital-saving or neutral. But, plainly, we have no ground for supposing that labour-saving inventions in my sense are impossible. If they take place in the conditions contemplated up to this point of our analysis, disharmony must result. The national dividend will be increased, but the real earnings of labour will be lessened.

§ 5. The conditions so far contemplated are not, however, in conformity with the facts. It has been assumed that workpeople purchase absolutely none of the commodity or service which the invention or improvement has cheapened. Obviously, this assumption is highly unfavourable to the prospect of their obtaining an increased real income. When conditions are such that, even on this assumption, they would gain, in so far as in fact they do purchase the commodity, they will gain still more; and, when conditions are such that, on this assumption, they would lose, nevertheless in real life they may gain. In short, the more important is the part played by the commodity to which the invention refers in the consumption of poor people, the more likely it is that the net effect of the invention will be advantageous to them.

In the light of this result it is a very significant fact that the things principally purchased by the working-classes are relatively crude things which can be readily made on a large scale by machinery, while the things principally purchased by the well-to-do are of higher quality, and, therefore, involve a larger use of human labour. Dr. Marshall writes: "Probably about twice as much horse-power is used in providing for each pound's worth of expenditure on commodities by the poor as by the rich." But it is just in things of this kind that the readiest opportunities are found for mechanical inventions and improvements, and in which, as a matter of fact, these are most extensively made. No doubt, the consumption of the poor embraces a much larger proportion of houseroom and food than the consumption of the rich, and both building labour and agricultural labour are relatively little aided by those mechanical instruments, in respect of which technical improvements and devices of organisation have the widest scope. This qualification is especially applicable to the very poor. "The fall of prices does not benefit the various grades of wage-earners in direct ratio to their wages. Rent and certain other necessary elements of expenditure, such as fuel, which have risen in amount for the large majority of workers, play a relatively larger part in the budget of the lower grades of workers, reducing to that extent their gain from the general fall of prices. The poorest classes, whose retail purchases are made in very small quantities, also gain least from the lower prices of other commodities, than housing and fuel."[1] But these qualifications leave the main result untouched. On the whole, the poor spend a larger proportion of their income than other classes on things the manufacture of which specially lends itself to inventions. Thus, Leroy-Beaulieu finds: "The man of fashion, who is fitted for his clothes by a tailor, gains nothing from the great reduction of prices which shops selling clothes ready-made offer to the less comfortable section of the population."[2] And he contrasts with these things "all those objects which the mass of the people have hitherto done without, but which have now come into general use, and which contribute either to better hygiene or to increased decency and dignity

---

[1] *Report of the Royal Commission on the Poor Laws*, p. 309.
[2] *La Répartition des richesses*, p. 37.

in the homes of the workpeople. Stockings, handkerchiefs, more varied and more suitable garments, curtains for the windows, carpets on the floors, a less exiguous array of furniture, these things constitute democratic luxury, the fruit of the development of mankind's powers of production."[1] Nor is this all. It has to be added, as Dr. Marshall has strongly urged, that the staple articles of food mainly consumed by the poor are, so far as this country is concerned, largely brought from abroad, and that one of the most marked features of recent times has been the development of improvements in the machinery of transport, and the consequent heavy fall in transport charges. To this may be added the important improvement in the machinery for retailing goods to poor persons, which has been realised by co-operative stores, and the consequent heavy fall in the cost of the service of retailing.

Of course, the historical fact that recent inventions have largely affected commodities, which enter directly or indirectly into the consumption of the working-classes, is not a proof that further inventions will be predominantly of a like kind. It is, however, open to us to urge that this historical fact is conformable to *a priori* expectation, because, not only are the openings for profit, and, therefore, the stimulus to invention, exceptionally great among " mass-goods " of wide consumption, but also, as Dr. Marshall has pointed out, even those improvements which were originally designed exclusively for the luxuries of the rich are apt soon to spread themselves to the comforts of other classes.[2] These considerations lead to the conclusion that it is less likely than the argument of the preceding section alone would suggest that any given invention will injure the real income of labour.

§ 6. Yet another qualification must be added to the analysis of §§ 3-4. That analysis tacitly assumed that the invention, whose consequences were examined, had no effect on the quantity of new waiting or capital which people are prepared annually to create. This assumption, however, is not warranted. Certain sorts of inventions, by giving a new field for " spending," may cause rich people to save less and

---

[1] *La Répartition des richesses,* p. 440.
[2] Cf. *Principles of Economics,* p. 541.

so to provide less new capital to help labour in production. The invention of luxurious motor cars for private travel has probably had this effect, and the impending invention of comfortable private air cars probably will have it. Nor is the effect necessarily confined to inventions which create new articles of consumption. It may also follow from those that cheapen articles which are already known, provided that they are of highly elastic demand. People who could have saved and created capital may be tempted to spend instead. On the other hand, inventions that cheapen things for which the demand is highly inelastic, by enabling people to get what they want at less cost, will leave them a greater margin out of which to make savings, and so will indirectly increase the annual creation of new capital. Whether the tendency thus set up by inventions is towards a decrease or towards an increase of capital, it is cumulative, in the sense that in each successive year further effects of the same sort are piled up. For this reason it is more important than it might be thought to be at first sight. When the indirect effect of an invention is to diminish savings, it may injure labour even though it is capital-saving; and, when the indirect effect is to increase savings, it may benefit labour even though it is both labour-saving and also concerned with some product which does not enter at all into workpeople's consumption. There is reason to believe that hitherto the general body of inventions has had the effect of increasing, and not of diminishing, the opportunity and the will to accumulate new capital.

§ 7. From these various considerations it is plain that no rigid and exact conclusions can be drawn. The general impression created by our study is that, though inventions and improvements injurious to the real income of the working-classes *may* occur, they will not occur often. The great majority of inventions and improvements will increase the real income of labour as well as the aggregate national dividend. Disharmony, as a result of inventions, is a possible, but a decidedly improbable, contingency. Nobody would seriously propose to interfere with, or to obstruct, inventions in order to provide a safeguard against it.

CHAPTER V

§ 1. In the latter portion of Part III. I examined at length the conditions under which an enforced increase in the wages rate paid in a particular occupation or place would injure the national dividend. We have now to consider the effect that will be produced on the real income of workpeople, and so of the poor, as a whole. For simplicity we may take for examination—no difference is made in the substance of the argument—the state of things contemplated in Part III. Chapter XV. §§ 8-9. The wage rate was there supposed to be forced up in an occupation where it had formerly been both "fair" relatively to other industries and equal to the value of the marginal net product of the work for which it was paid. It was assumed that no difference was made to the efficiency of the workpeople to whom the increased wage was given: and, on this assumption, it was proved that the national dividend *must* be diminished. In what, if any, conditions will the real income of labour as a whole, nevertheless, be increased?

§ 2. The first step towards answering this question is to determine in what circumstances the enforcement of an uneconomically high wage—that is a convenient term for a wage that damages the dividend—will increase the real earnings of the particular group of workpeople in whose behalf it is won. It should be noticed in passing that an uneconomic enhancement of the wage rate in any occupation may take the form either of a special enhancement of the rate per unit of labour paid to inferior workpeople—*e.g.* such work-

725

people may be given the same time-wages as competent workers—
or of a general enhancement of the rate per unit of efficiency
paid to all workpeople. It is evident that an uneconomic
enhancement of the former kind must either throw all the
inferior workpeople out of work altogether, or must diminish
the aggregate quantity of labour employed to exactly the
same extent as an equal enhancement in the rate per unit of
efficiency paid to *all* the workpeople in the occupation. Hence,
it is bound to have a less favourable effect on the aggregate
earnings of the whole group of workpeople concerned than the
latter kind of enhancement. In what follows, therefore, it
will be sufficient to consider that type of uneconomically high
rate which affects equally the wages per unit of efficiency paid
to all workpeople in an occupation. To determine in the
abstract the conditions in which the establishment of this
type of uneconomically high wage will increase the real earnings of this group of workpeople is perfectly simple. It will
increase them if the demand for the labour of the group has
an elasticity less than unity, and it will diminish them if the
elasticity is greater than unity. This result—on the assumption, of course, that the workpeople concerned are not themselves purchasers to any appreciable extent of the commodity
they produce—is an obvious arithmetical truism, following
at once from the definition of elasticity. To fill it out in the
concrete, to investigate, that is to say, the conditions that
determine whether the demand for the services of any assigned
group of workpeople is likely to have a high elasticity or a
low one, is the task we have now to essay.

§ 3. In the fifth section of Part II. Chapter XI., an analysis
was given of the determinants of elasticity with reference
to the demands for different classes of commodities. This
analysis is applicable to the demands for different classes of
labour also. In that application it may be set out as follows.

First, we have the general fact that the demand for
anything is likely to be more elastic, the more readily substitutes for that thing can be obtained. This fact has an
important bearing on the relation between labour and
machinery; for, in some industries, a very small addition to
the cost of working a process by hand would induce employers

to adopt mechanical appliances. Mr. Aves, for example, quotes the statement of an ex-inspectress that, in the Victorian clothing trade, where minimum wage determinations have unintentionally discriminated against home work, employment was transferred to factories using machinery, and "practically all outside work was stopped."[1] In like manner, the tanners of Victoria, commenting on the effects of the Wages Board in their industry, state: "Labour-saving machinery is forced into use, so much so that the tannery trade has been practically revolutionised since the Wages Board system was applied to the trade."[2] In circumstances of this kind the high elasticity of demand for labour is, in effect, due to the fact that there is a readily available and closely competing substitute for its services in the rival factor capital, or, more strictly, other labour accompanied by a greater amount of waiting. Since it is easier to introduce this substitute after an interval than immediately, elasticity in demand due to this cause is greater from the standpoint of a long period than of a short period.

Secondly, we have the general fact that the demand for anything is likely to be less elastic, the less important is the part played by the cost of that thing in the total cost of some other thing, in the production of which it is employed. This general fact enables us to point out certain occupations in which the demand for a particular class of labour is likely to be especially inelastic. One of these is the occupation of women in sewing on the covers of racquet and fives balls.[3]

---

[1] *Report on Wages Boards*, p. 197. This "determination" fixed both an hour rate and a piece-work rate, compelling the latter to be paid to outworkers. The intention was that the two should be equivalent, but employers in practice found the hour, or wages, rate much the cheaper. The ex-inspectress added: "When the wages rate and the piece-work rate were nearly the same, as in the shirt and underclothing trade, the trouble did not occur, and, after ten years' working of the determination, these trades count many outworkers to-day." The choice between an out- and an in-worker is affected by the fact that, when employing outworkers, the employer escapes charges for working space, light, firing and so forth. "The savings upon factory rent, upkeep and superintendence appear to be larger factors in the cheapness of home work than the lowness of wages" (Black, *Makers of Our Clothes*, p. 44). Cf. also Marconcini, *L'industria domestica salariata* (pp. 432-3). On the other hand, of course, economies of superintendence and, sometimes, of power are to be obtained in factory work.

[2] *Report on Wages Board*, p. 179. Cf. *ante*, Part III. Chapter XIII. § 8.

[3] Cf. Lyttleton, *Contemporary Review*, February 1909.

Another is that of making trouser-buttons. Lord Askwith writes: "The rich man's trousers may be cut by an expensive tailor. The buttons on those trousers may be made by sweated industry. High payment for those buttons would be but a minute part of the cost of the whole article."[1] The engineering work done by engineers engaged by building firms, since these persons are employed only incidentally and as a trivial part of the total producing force, is in a similar position. In like manner, the part played by the original labour is small in commodities for which the addition to wholesale price made by the work of the retailer is large. "For example, when we find that the maker of a lady's costume is paid 10d. or 1s., while the article is sold for 25s. to 30s., it is obvious that the wage paid is so small in relation to the retail price that, even were the wage doubled, it need necessarily affect the price but little, if at all."[2] This condition, that the part played by labour in a particular act of production shall be small, is probably fulfilled fairly often, and it is likely to be fulfilled still more often as the relative importance of installations of plant and machinery in production increases. One writer has even suggested that "the labour cost of production in most industries is usually not sufficient materially to affect the price of the finished article." It should be noticed, however, that, in the important work of coal production, hewers' labour constitutes a very large part of the total cost, and the condition stipulated for is, therefore, not fulfilled.

Thirdly, we have the general fact that the demand for anything is likely to be more elastic, the more elastic is the supply of co-operant agents of production. This fact makes it evident that the demand for labour will be specially inelastic in industries which make use of raw materials of highly inelastic supply. Apart from raw materials, the principal co-operant agents working with labour in any industry are capital, instruments, managing ability and other labour. From the standpoint of a long period the supply of these to any single industry is, beyond doubt, exceedingly

---

[1] *Fortnightly Review*, August 1908, p. 225.
[2] Cadbury and Shann, *Sweating*, p. 124.

elastic. But, from the standpoint of a short period or a period of moderate length, it is likely to be inelastic; for specialised machinery and managing skill, and even other labour, can neither be created or brought from elsewhere, nor yet destroyed or carried off elsewhere, in the twinkling of an eye. Here again, therefore, the forces making for elasticity of demand are stronger from the standpoint of a long period than of a short period. It should be added that in some industries, notably coal-mining, Nature herself acts as a very important co-operant factor of production. In times of expanded demand new men have to be set to work on seams much more difficult and less productive than those ordinarily worked.[1] This means, from a short period point of view, a highly inelastic demand for labour.

Fourthly, we have the general fact that the demand for anything is likely to be more elastic, the more elastic is the demand for any further thing which it contributes to produce. This fact implies that the demand will be specially inelastic for the services of workpeople engaged in the manufacture of commodities of highly inelastic demand. When the elasticity of the public demand for any commodity is given, it is obvious that, from a short period point of view, the elasticity of the demand for new production of it will be greater or less, according as the thing can or cannot be readily made for stock. Apart from this, the circumstances upon which the elasticity of demand for various classes of commodities depends were discussed in the eleventh chapter of Part II. The most significant of them for our present purpose is the presence or absence of foreign competition. Thus, a critic comments on some of the effects of New Zealand wage regulation: " In some trades employers have not been able to cope with the extra cost of production owing to competition with the imported article. They have, therefore, had to give up the producing part of their business and increase their importations. In the tanning and fellmongering business some serious results have followed the fixing of a minimum wage. I will mention two instances. Some years ago a firm in the district of Dunedin closed down its works and removed its plant to

---

[1] Cf. Hooker, *Statistical Journal*, 1894, p. 635 *n.*

Australia, largely owing to the conditions imposed by the Arbitration Court. A member of a Christchurch firm has informed me that, since the Court's award in the Canterbury district was made about six years ago, a much larger proportion of sheepskins have been shipped to London, without being handled by the local fellmonger, than was formerly the case. Hides which should have been tanned here have been shipped raw. Prior to the award, my informant's firm paid from £10,000 to £15,000 in wages; now the wages sheet amounts to only about £5000. The number of bales of wool scoured annually by the same firm since the award came into force has not been more than 2000; formerly the number was from 6000 to 8000."[1] In connection, however, with this matter of foreign competition a word of caution is necessary. Let us imagine that there are a dozen industries in this country, all of about the same size and all subject in about equal measure to foreign competition in the home market. Looking at any one of these industries singly, we conclude, perhaps, that the elasticity of demand for its product is such that an increase of 10 per cent in the cost of making it in this country would reduce the demand for it by 50 per cent. It is natural to infer that a 10 per cent increase in costs in all twelve industries together would reduce the demand in all of them by 50 per cent. This, however, is not so. Foreign imports collectively constitute the demand for British exports. When, therefore, for any reason it becomes advantageous to increase the sendings of one kind of import, other kinds of import will tend to fall off, the adjustment, being brought about *through*—but not *by*—a change in price levels. Thus, when extra imports cause the demand in one industry to contract by 50 per cent, the contraction will be, in great part, cancelled by an expansion, made possible by lessened imports, in other industries. In other words, the demand for the whole body of British products subject to foreign competition is less elastic than the demand for a single representative item among these products. It follows that, other things being equal, the workpeople immediately affected are more likely to be benefited by interference to raise their wages if the inter-

[1] Broadhead, *State Regulation of Labour in New Zealand*, p. 215.

ference is extended to several industries subject to foreign competition than they would be if it were confined to one.

§ 4. With these results in mind we may proceed to the next stage in our inquiry, and ask in what conditions the establishment at one point of an uneconomically high wage, which raises the real earnings of the workpeople there, will also raise the real earnings of workpeople as a whole. Let us still suppose that the commodity, to the makers of which an uneconomically high wage has been assigned, is exclusively consumed by persons other than workpeople. It may be noted, in passing, that, when a factor making for inelasticity in the demand for the services of the particular group of workpeople in whom we are interested is inelasticity of supply and, therefore, "squeezability" in some co-operant group, a part of the gain to the first group will be offset by loss to the second. For the purpose of a general analysis, however, we may neglect this rather special point.

If the elasticity of demand for labour in the occupation where the wage rate has been raised is less than unity, the aggregate earnings of labour as a whole, and not merely the earnings in that occupation, will be increased, provided that either the casual method or the privileged class method of engaging labour, as described in Chapter VIII. of Part III., prevails in that occupation. Under the casual method workpeople will be attracted into the occupation from outside until the prospect of earnings per man inside and outside are brought to equality : and, since the number of workpeople left outside is diminished by this drain, the wage rate there will be raised. This proves that aggregate earnings inside and outside together must be raised. Under the privileged class method of engagement no one will be attracted from outside and no one will be driven out. Hence, earnings outside will be unchanged. Since, therefore, earnings inside are, *ex hypothesi*, increased, it again follows that earnings as a whole are increased. If the preference method of engagement prevails, conditions are conceivable in which earnings as a whole would not be increased. For some persons must be driven out of the industry where the wage is raised, and, though those left there will be getting more than they were getting before, the influx of labour into other industries might, if the demand in these industries had an elasticity less than unity, so lower earnings outside as to outweigh the gain inside. Since, however, as was shown in Chapter III., the demand for labour in industry in general is highly elastic, the conditions necessary to this result are not fulfilled. In real life, therefore, the earnings of·labour as a whole must be increased whenever an uneconomically high wage is enforced in a selected occupation, provided that the elasticity of the demand for labour there is less than unity.

If the elasticity of demand in the occupation where the wage rate is raised is greater than unity, analogous reasoning shows that earnings as a whole cannot be increased, provided that either the casual or the privileged class method of engagement prevails in the occupation. For some workpeople will be driven out of the occupation, and a new equilibrium will be established, with an expectation of earnings for every one equal to the earnings in other occupations; and these will have been made lower than before by an influx of new workers. If, however, the preference method prevails, earnings as a whole may be increased even though the elasticity of demand is greater than unity. Those who are left in the industry where the wage is raised will be getting more than they were getting before; and, though everybody else will be getting less than before, yet, if the demand for labour in other industries is sufficiently elastic, their loss need not be so great as the others' gain.

§ 5. It is now time to remove the assumption set out in § 2, that the commodity produced by the group of workpeople, whose wage is being interfered with, is exclusively consumed by persons other than workpeople. On the strength of that assumption we have been able, up to this point, to ignore the distinction between effects on money earnings and effects on real earnings. Where the assumption is unwarranted we are not justified in doing this. An increase of money earnings may be associated with a decrease of real earnings, and may, therefore, be delusive. If the commodities produced by the favoured workers are consumed by nobody except members of the working classes, it *must* be delusive, for it is bound to involve a more than equivalent loss to workpeople (those inside the privileged industry and those outside it together) in their capacity as consumers. If the consumers consist partly of workpeople and partly of others, it is not possible to say absolutely whether the workpeople's gain as producers or loss as consumers will be greater. All we can lay down is that, the more important the part of the consumption for which non-wage-earners are responsible, the more likely it is that the establishment of an uneconomically high wage rate will succeed in bringing about an increase in the real income of workpeople as a whole. When, therefore, the main part of the product of any group of workers is consumed by other workers, though the establishment of an uneconomically high wage rate may enhance the aggregate real income of the favoured workers, it is not probable that it will enhance that of all workers collectively. This point is important, because, in real life, it is rich people who make, or otherwise provide, a great part of the luxuries of the rich, while poor wage-earners make things for other wage-earners. Thus, Mrs. Bosanquet writes: "Nothing strikes one more forcibly in studying the position of the lowest-paid workers than that they are almost always engaged in producing goods for the consumption of their own class. . . . Badly paid tailors are making cheap clothing that no rich man would look at; badly paid servants are rendering services that would not be tolerated by any one of refinement and culture; while the real requisites of refinement and culture, if by these we mean such things as art, music and literature, are produced by professional people."[1]   Again: "*The great majority of wage-earners are engaged in producing for the benefit of other wage-earners*, and have no direct connection with the non-wage-earning classes. The majority of builders are building houses for wage-earners; the very large majority in the clothing trades are making clothing for the wage-earners; the majority of food-preparers are preparing food for the wage-earners. More especially of the sweated trades is it literally true, almost without exception, that they are working for the wage-earners alone, and that a rise in the price of their products would be paid by the wage-earners

[1] Bosanquet, *The Strength of the People*, p. 71.

alone. How would it be possible that the propertied classes should pay any share in the increased price of ready-made suits, or cheap blouses, or shoddy boots and shoes, or Pink's jams? The burden must fall on the consumers of these articles, and they are the wage-earners."[1] Mrs. Bosanquet would not, of course, pretend that there are no rich men's luxuries, towards which poor men's labour contributes an important part. It would seem, however, that not much of the labour of poor persons in the United Kingdom is devoted to the supply of luxuries of this sort.[2] It follows that the establishment of an uneconomically high wage rate for a particular group of workpeople is much less likely to involve a real increase in the earnings of workpeople as a whole than it appears to be when the distinction between money earnings and real earnings is ignored. So far, however, the possibility that it may involve this remains.

§ 6. But against the realisation of this possibility there is at work a corrective tendency, the general character of which has already been indicated in § 8 of Chapter III. A change, which, while it increases the real earnings of labour, also diminishes the national dividend, since it implies a decrease in the rate of interest, will decrease people's willingness to save, thus hindering the creation of further capital. Nor is the reaction on willingness to save the only reaction which will take place. The fact that the national dividend is diminished implies also a diminution in the *power* to save, for the simple reason that the fund available for possible savings is made smaller. Thus, every decrease in the national dividend is in itself a cause making for diminished capital and, therefore, for lower payment to labour. Here plainly is a tendency adverse to disharmony. Furthermore, this tendency is cumulative. For suppose a policy to be adopted, which, while increasing the real income of labour, causes the aggregate national dividend each year to be one per cent less, not necessarily than it was before, but than it would have been apart from this policy. The addition made to capital

---

[1] *The Strength of the People*, p. 294-5.
[2] For examples of things made by "sweated" workers and consumed by others than wage-earners, cf. Cadbury and Shann, *Sweating*, p. 123.

stock in each year is thus diminished. In any one year the loss inflicted on that stock is small. But the annual losses are *cumulative*. After, say, ten years, the capital stock that is available to assist labour in its activities may be considerably smaller than it would otherwise have been.[1] And the reduction of this stock is aggravated by the fact that it must itself cause a reduction in the national dividend; that, therefore, the transference to labour of any given annual sum must throw a continually increasing burden on profits; that, therefore, the diminution (or check to the growth) of the national dividend must be greater in the second year than in the first, greater in the third year than in the second, and so on; and that, therefore, the rate of fall in the capital stock must be progressively accelerated. As this stock falls in amount below what it would otherwise have been, the annual earnings of labour also fall continuously. In the end it would seem that, as against any policy, which, in the first instance, benefits labour at the expense of injuring the national dividend, this cumulative tendency is bound to prevail, and that, therefore, from the standpoint of a sufficiently long period, any disharmony that may have been set· up must disappear. Since, however, relatively to the stock of capital, the annual creation of new capital is small, and, consequently, any probable change in· the annual creation very small, the harmonising tendency will work slowly. This implies that for some time after·the establishment of an uneconomically high wage in particular occupations disharmony may prevail.

§ 7. Up to this point we have been concerned with the consequences of fixing an uneconomically high wage, as if this were a single self-subsistent act. In actual life, however, it is inevitably mixed up with State policy as regards the protection of persons in distress. If the enforcement of an uneconomically high wage in some occupation throws a certain number of people out of work for a long time, the State will have to help these people. Consequently, if we count as a part of the real income of the poor what the State provides for assisted persons, their real income in this wider sense may well be raised by a policy which lowers the earned

---

[1] Cf. Marshall, *Economics of Industry*, pp. 372-3.

part of their real income.   Thus, by a forcing up of the
wage rate in some occupations, we may suppose that the
national dividend is injured, and that those workers who are
left in industry gain a little less than those who are thrown
out of it lose.   There is then harmony between the effects
on the national dividend and on the real income of the poor
in' the narrower sense.   But, if, in consequence of increased
unemployment, the expenditure of State aid to poor persons
becomes £1,000,000 bigger than it would otherwise have
been, there may be disharmony between the effect on the
dividend and the effect on the real income of the poor in the
wider sense.   The way is thus opened for a somewhat special
argument in favour of forcing up wage rates in low-grade
occupations.   It may be granted that both the national
dividend and the real earnings of labour as a whole will be
diminished.   But, it may be claimed, at all events if the preference method of engagement prevails, that a number of people,
who otherwise would have earned too little to maintain independently a decent life, will now get adequate earnings.   A
number of others will, indeed, earn less than before—possibly
nothing at all—but, owing to the action of the State, they
need not *receive* less than before.   Thus, we shall have, instead
of a large body of people, all of them occasionally or partially
supported by the State, one moderate-sized body fully self-
supporting and another moderate-sized body scarcely self-
supporting at all.   From the point of view of economic
welfare as a whole, particularly if the conditions are such as
to make the fully self-supporting body much larger than the
other, the latter state of things may be deemed the better, in
spite of the fact that it involves a smaller national dividend.
It may be objected, no doubt, that the persons now rendered
fully self-supporting will really be sustained by the help of
what is, in effect, a special tax upon the people who purchase
the things they happen to make; and that the care of
relatively incapable citizens is an obligation upon the whole
community, and not merely upon those members of it who
buy racquet balls, or whatever the article may be.   It may
be replied, however, that, in so far as relatively incapable
citizens are responsible for products of general consumption,

or in so far as they do work for municipalities or the State
in connection with commodities or services not designed for
sale, this objection loses the greater part of its force; and
that, in any event, since every indirect tax must hit some
people "unfairly," it is not of *very* great weight. Moreover,
since the workers who benefit will not think of themselves as
being in any sense "relieved by their customers," there is no
danger that any injurious moral effect analogous to the "taint
of pauperism". will be produced upon them. Plainly, an issue
turning upon considerations of this kind is not susceptible of
any general solution. Whenever it is proposed to enforce
an uneconomically high wage in any occupation upon the
grounds suggested in this section, a decision can only be
reached by a careful balancing of conflicting tendencies, after
all the relevant circumstances have been studied in detail.

CHAPTER VI

§ 1. In Chapter X. of Part II. some discussion was undertaken of the policy of rationing, as an adjunct to State control over the prices of commodities produced under competitive conditions. A brief study of this policy is now required from another point of view. The rationing of essential commodities to the better-to-do classes, whether coupled or not with price control, may be advocated as a means of ensuring that sufficient supplies at reasonable prices shall be available for the poor. *Prima facie* it would seem that this policy may affect the national dividend in one way and the absolute share of it accruing to the poor in another, thus involving disharmony. The question whether or not this is in fact so will be examined in the present chapter.

§ 2. In the special emergency of the Great War supplies were short as a result of causes which could not have been got over, whatever prices sellers had been allowed to charge. Price regulation and rationing did not, therefore, as was argued in Part II. Chapters IX. and X., substantially reduce the volume of the national dividend. At the same time, they jointly saved the poor from a disaster that could not otherwise have been avoided. The grant of large bonuses on wages would not have enabled poor people to obtain essential articles of which the supply was short and the demand of the rich inelastic. The prices of these things would, indeed, have been forced up, but the rich, at the cost of paying more money, would still have obtained as much as before out of the shortened supply, and would have correspondingly cut

738

down the share available for ; the poor.' '' Moreover, the fixing
of maximum prices without rationing would not have been
sufficient; for the presumption is that the rich, by various
pulls, would still have skimmed the market. From the joint
facts that in the war price control coupled with rationing did
not injure production and did benefit distribution it has
sometimes been inferred that the same policy continued in
normal conditions would produce the same harmoniously
beneficial result. That is the issue we have to judge.

§ 3. In attempting to elucidate it we have first to make
clear, from the present point of view, the relation between
rationing and price-fixing. Clearly, in a brief period of
shortage it is possible, with a given system of rations,
to have any one of a large number of regulated price
maxima, because, for the time being, the output and (within
limits) the amount offered for sale are independent of the price.
But, when we are contemplating a policy for normal times,
the position is different. Suppose, first, that a given scale
of rations is established unaccompanied by any price restriction, and that everybody is purchasing the whole of the
ration to which he is entitled. This implies a definite
quantity demanded; and there is, in general, only one price
that will call out this quantity. If the State fixes a maximum
price higher than this, the sellers will not be able to realise
it, and the maximum price will become otiose. If, on the
other hand, the State fixes a price less than this, not enough
will be produced to enable everybody to get his ration:
and, consequently, if the rations are to be effective, in the
sense that whoever wants his allotted ration can obtain it,
the whole ration scale will have to be altered to fit the new
price. Suppose, secondly, that a given ration scale is
established, but that, while the scale limits the purchases of
some people, others are buying less than their ration allowance. As before, to whatever aggregate quantity is being
purchased there corresponds one single price that will call out
that quantity; and, as before, if the State fixes a maximum
price higher than this, the maximum will become otiose.
If the State fixes a maximum lower than this, it seems
at first sight that a new equilibrium may be established, in

which some of those now, buying less than their ration will buy the full amount. But, in fact, the lower price must mean a lower output, so that nobody can buy more, or even as much as before, unless others buy less. It must happen, therefore, that some of those who before were purchasing their full ration are now unable, although they still wish, to do so. Here again, therefore, the ration scale becomes ineffective, and a new and lower ration must be established to fit the new price. Hence, generally, to any *effective* ration scale only one price level can correspond; and it is impossible for the State to establish any other price level without at the same time establishing another *effective* ration scale. This conclusion is a very important one for my present purpose: because it makes it unnecessary to study both rationing by itself and also rationing accompanied by price regulation. The two things work out, when the numerical constants are adjusted, in exactly the same way; and the whole problem is exhausted when the consequences of rationing alone have been examined.

§ 4. It is evident that any rationing system, which aims at benefiting the poor, must be so designed as to cut down the consumption of the rich. Such facts as that, for example, a *uniform* bread ration on a scale tolerable to the poor would not accomplish this, because normally poor people eat more bread per head than rich people, are not really relevant. We are not concerned here with technique, but with principle; and any rationing scheme that pretends to increase the supplies available for the poor as a body *must* be so devised— the scale need not, of course, be uniform—that it cuts down those available for the rich. So much being understood, our analysis of rationing in normal times may proceed. It works out differently for commodities produced under conditions of increasing returns and of diminishing returns.

§ 5. Under increasing returns the ultimate consequence of extruding from the market a part of the demand of the relatively well-to-do is necessarily to contract the production of the commodity and, therefore, since, as was shown in Part II. Chapter VIII., too little of it is being produced anyhow, to lessen the national dividend. At the same time the rise in price, which a diminution in the supply of an article produced under conditions of increasing returns must involve, forces poor people both to buy less of the commodity than they would have done and also to pay more for what they do buy. Thus, they are unequivocally damaged. The aggregate dividend and their share of it alike suffer, and disharmony is impossible.

§ 6. Under diminishing returns the extrusion of part of the demand again, of course, contracts the production of the commodity.' But this time, since, apart from interference, its production would—as was shown in the chapter just cited—have been carried further than the interest of the national dividend requires, the contraction will, if it does not go beyond a certain definite amount, benefit and not injure the national dividend. The price of the commodity will, however, be reduced, so that the poor probably get more of it and certainly get it at a lower price. Hence, the poor must gain. If the slice cut off the demand of the rich is not too large, there is, therefore, harmony of an opposite sort to that which comes about under increasing returns; the national dividend and the slice accruing to the poor are both increased. But, if the check to the purchases of the rich is pressed beyond a certain point, there is disharmony, the poor still getting a benefit but the national dividend as a whole suffering loss.

§ 7. This analysis makes it plain that conditions *may* exist in which a system of rationing in normal times, if conducted with perfect skill and without any friction, might yield a net social benefit. It does not prove, however, that in practice the rationing of any commodity is in normal times desirable. Not only is the skill of Government officials limited, but also a large adverse balance of inconvenience and irritation would have to be neutralised before any positive advantage could begin. Moreover, it must be remembered that, since the rich are relatively few in number, and their consumption of common articles—with the exception of coal, the consumption of which is regulated by the size of a man's house and not by his bodily capacity—a small proportion of the whole, a very large percentage cut in their *per capita* purchases would involve only a very small percentage cut in the consumption of the country as a whole, and an almost negligible cut, for most things, in the production of the world. In general, therefore, its effect in cheapening the supplies of diminishing return articles to poor persons would be scarcely perceptible. The practical conclusion seems to be that, while it may redound slightly to the general interest for well-to-do persons voluntarily to restrict their purchases of these articles, yet, in the present state of economic knowledge and administrative efficiency, it would, in ordinary times, do more harm than good for the State to force them to do this by any system of compulsory rationing.

CHAPTER VII

DIRECT TRANSFERENCES FROM THE RELATIVELY RICH
TO THE RELATIVELY POOR

§ 1. WE now turn to what is in practice by far the most important field of possible disharmony. In a great number of ways, and for a great variety of reasons, poor people in civilised countries are given help, in the main through some State agency, at the expense of their better-to-do fellow citizens. *Prima facie* the transference, which this help implies, *must* increase, and it can certainly be so arranged that it *shall* increase, the real income available for the poor. Hence, the question whether any particular form of help to the poor involves disharmony is often equivalent to the question whether its indirect consequence is to increase or to diminish the national dividend. This question, in one or another of its various aspects, will be the theme of the next four chapters. But, before we embark upon it, a brief comment is needed upon two popular arguments, one of which asserts that no transference of resources to the poor is possible, because, in effect, all money taken from the rich is really taken from the poor, while the other asserts that it is not possible, because the beneficiaries will give back what they have received by agreeing to accept lower wages..

§ 2. The position taken up in the former of these arguments is that any levy of money, whether voluntary or compulsory, from the well-to-do for the benefit of some poor persons necessarily implies the infliction of a substantially equivalent burden upon other poor persons, through the reduction which the rich are compelled to make in their

purchases of the services rendered by them. The foundation
of this view may be set out as follows. It is obvious that a
great part of the expenditure of the rich involves, directly or
indirectly, the employment of labour; and it is equally
obvious that, if the incomes of the rich are diminished by,
say, £20,000,000 of taxation, their expenditure for consumption and for capital investment together must be contracted to
a corresponding extent. Some persons, concentrating attention
upon this fact, immediately conclude that the workpeople,
whose services this expenditure would have called into being
if the tax had not been there—and an exactly analogous
argument applies to a voluntary contribution—must suffer
a loss of income approximating to the twenty million pounds
levied in taxation. To argue in this way, however, is: to
ignore the fact that the twenty million pounds collected from
the rich is transferred to the poor, and that the expenditure
of it by them is likely to be no less productive of employment
than the expenditure of it by the rich would have been. No
doubt, if we are contemplating the immediate effect of the
addition of twenty millions to the taxation of the rich for the
benefit of the poor, it is relevant to observe that the men who
lose jobs on the one side will not be the same persons as
those who find them on the other; and that, therefore, a
certain number of men, who have been trained to special
aptitudes, may find their immaterial capital of acquired skill
rendered permanently worthless. This loss, however, is the
result, not of taxation, but of *change* in taxation, and would
emerge equally in consequence of a *reduction* by twenty
millions in imposts levied on the rich for the benefit of
the poor. Our problem is not concerned with incidents of
this character. The comparison we have to make is between
one permanent system, under which nothing is collected from
the rich and handed over to the poor, and another permanent
system, under which twenty millions is so collected and
handed over. To this comparison the incident we have just
been discussing is irrelevant. Speaking broadly and apart
from special circumstances, we may say that it makes very
little difference to the employment of, and wages paid for,
labour, whether twenty millions is annually transferred or not

transferred from any one class to any other class. The idea
that reactions in this field will render attempts at transference
of no effect is, therefore, illusory.

§ 3. The latter of the two arguments distinguished above
asserts that, if any group of poor persons are accorded any
form of subsidy, they will, in consequence, be willing to work
for less than the worth of their services to their employer,
and so will, in effect, transfer back the subsidy they have
received to members of the richer classes. This view rests,
partly, upon *a priori* reasoning and, partly, upon what is
called experience. It needs, therefore, a twofold discussion.
The *a priori* reasoning starts from the fact that a Poor Law
subsidy *enables* a person to accept lower wages than it would
be possible for him to accept otherwise without starvation or,
at all events, serious discomfort; and it proceeds to assert
that, if a person is *enabled* to work for less, he will be *willing*
to work for less. Now, no doubt, in certain special circumstances, when a workman, in receipt of a subsidy insufficient
to enable him to live up to his accustomed standard of life, is
confronted by an employer occupying towards him the position
of a monopolist, this inference may be valid. In general,
however, where competition exists among employers, it is
quite invalid. A person, who, by saving in the past, has
become possessed of a competence, is *enabled* to work for less
than one who has not. A millionaire is *enabled* to work for less
even than a relieved pauper. So far from this ability making
it probable that he will strike a worse bargain in the higgling
of the market, it is likely, in general, to have the opposite
effect. It is not the fact that the wife of a man in good
work is likely to accept abnormally low wages. On the contrary, the woman, who, for this or any other reason, can afford
to "stand out," is, in general, among those who resist such
wages most strenuously.[1] Let us turn, then, to the reasoning
from what is called experience. This starts from two admitted facts. The first fact is that old and infirm persons
in receipt of a Poor Law subsidy very frequently earn from
private employers considerably less than the ordinary wage

---

[1] For an illustration of this among home-working tailoresses, cf. Vesselitsky,
The Home Worker, p. 17.

per hour current for the class of work on which they are engaged. The second fact—given in evidence before the Poor Law Commission of 1832—is that the refusal of guardians to grant relief in aid of wages "soon had the effect of making the farmer pay his labourers fairly." From these facts the inference is drawn that, where a Poor Law subsidy exists, workpeople accept a wage lower than the worth of their work to their employers. This inference, however, is illegitimate. There is an alternative and more probable explanation. As regards old and infirm persons, may it not be that the low wage per hour is due to the circumstance that the work they can do in an hour is poor in quality or little in quantity? As regards the old Poor Law, may it not be that the un-reformed system of relief, so long as it prevailed, caused people to work slackly and badly, that, when it was abolished, they worked harder, and that this was the cause of the alteration in their wages? The view that the true analysis of experience is to be found along these lines, and not in the suggestion that relieved persons work for less than they are worth to their employers, is made likely by general considerations. It has been further confirmed by recent investigations, which tend to show that, where two people differ solely in the fact that one does, and the other does not, receive a Poor Law subsidy, their wages are in fact the same. Thus, investigators appointed by the Poor Law Commission of 1909, as a result of their enquiry into the effects of out-relief on wages, write: "We found no evidence that women wage-earners, to whose families out-relief is given, cut rates. Such wage-earners are invariably found working at the same rates of pay as the much larger number of women not in receipt of relief, who entirely swamp them. . . . We could find no evidence that the daughters of paupers accepted lower rates than others, or earned less than others, because of their indirect relation to pauperism."[1] This argument, therefore, like that set out in § 2, breaks down. The direct transference of resources from the relatively rich to the relatively poor, by way of philan-thropic or State action, whatever its ultimate consequences

[1] *Report of the Royal Commission on the Poor Laws*, Appendix, vol. xxxvi. pp. vi-vii.

may prove to be, is at least not impossible. Of course, this conclusion does not deny that *additional work* by assisted, or any other, workers slightly lowers the general *rate* of wages. But that proposition is quite different from the proposition that assistance to persons who are working anyhow has this effect.[1]

§ 4. In view of this result we may proceed undisturbed to our main problem — that of determining the effect of various sorts of transference upon the volume of the national dividend. Some sorts, it would seem, are likely to increase that dividend and others to diminish it. We have, therefore, to investigate the conditions upon which the occurrence of the one or the other of these opposing consequences depends. These conditions can be examined most effectively by means of an analysis, on the lines set out in Part IV., in which the distinction between the effect of the fact, and the effect of the expectation, of transference is made fundamental. Of course, when we have to do with a levy, which is made once and for all to meet some exceptional need, and the regular continuance of which is not anticipated, effects operating through expectation do not have to be considered. In ordinary times, however, the fact of a tax levy imposed one year carries with it the expectation that it will be continued in future years, so that both fact and expectation are relevant. I shall consider first the expectation of transferences *from* the rich; secondly the expectation of transferences *to* the poor; and thirdly the fact of transferences.

---

[1] Cf. *ante*, Chapter III. § 10. Dr. Hourwick, in his book *Immigration and Labour*, seems to miss this point; for, having shown that immigrants into the United States do not earn less wages for equally efficient work than native Americans, he treats this conclusion as implying that they do not *affect* the wages of native Americans.

CHAPTER VIII

THE EFFECT ON THE NATIONAL DIVIDEND OF THE EXPECTATION OF TRANSFERENCES FROM THE RELATIVELY RICH

§ 1. THE expectation of levies from the relatively rich, as from any other class, acts upon the national dividend differently according as the levy is voluntary or coercive. The contribution of a voluntary levy implies that a new use has been found, into which people wish to put some resources more keenly than they wish to put them into other available uses. This means that their desire to possess resources is enhanced, and, therefore, that the provision they are willing to make of waiting and effort, in order to obtain resources, is also enhanced. Hence, the expectation by the rich of voluntary transferences from the rich is likely to make for an increase in the volume of the national dividend. "Though it would have disastrous effects if the State should attempt to enforce universal benevolence, yet only beneficial results would follow if all men were to become wisely benevolent."[1] It is, therefore, important to consider briefly what scope there is in the modern world for this type of transference.

§ 2. The most obvious form which it can and does take is that of generous conduct towards their workpeople on the part of wealthy employers of labour. Since these workpeople spend a great part of their lives in buildings provided by their employers and in conditions largely under their control, the employers have the power to spend money in their interest with exceptional effect. Acting in careful collaboration with chosen representatives of the workpeople, they can

[1] Carver, *Social Justice*, p. 142.

748

contribute conveniences, opportunities for recreation and opportunities for education, and can make it a condition of employment for their younger workers that these things shall be used. Thus, Messrs. Cadbury at Bournville require all their employees under eighteen to take part in regular gymnastic classes and in regular and elaborate courses of education, in part provided by, and in part paid for by, the firm.[1] The special opportunities which they enjoy for effective action may well create in wealthy employers a special sense of obligation. This sense was admirably expressed by the well-known Dutch employer Van Marken, when he declared: " It seems to me the duty of an employer to aid his subordinates by every means at his command—his heart, his intellect, his money— to attain that highest stage which alone makes life worth living. My own conviction is that in doing so the employer will make no sacrifices. But, if he needs must make them, be it from the material or the moral point of view, let him make them up to the limit of his capacity. It is his sacred duty."[2] With the education of opinion among well-to-do employers of labour we may look increasingly for a growth of this sense of patronal obligation. Furthermore, this sense may be fortified and extended by the egoistic consideration that generous treatment of workpeople is often a splendid advertisement, leading indirectly to large profits. On this point I cannot do better than adopt Professor Ashly's excellent words: " Instead of cynically pooh-poohing it [employers' welfare work] for that reason, I think this is a particularly encouraging fact, and highly creditable to human nature. It shows that there is such a thing as a consumers' conscience. The whole essence of the Consumers' League work in America and of the White Lists of the Christian Social Union in this country is to make it 'good business' to be known to manufacture under satisfactory working conditions; and, with increasing publicity and an increasing fellow-feeling among all classes, I expect that this is going to be the case more and more."[3]

---

[1] Cf. Cadbury, *Experiments in Industrial Organisation*, p. 17.
[2] Meakin, *Model Factories and Villages*, p. 27.
[3] Preface to Cadbury's *Experiments in Industrial Organisation*, p. xiii.

§ 3. Voluntary transference of resources may also take the form of generous conduct on the part of the wealthy to those poor persons who are united to them through common citizenship of the same town. Here, too, there is a special relation and, consequently, a special spur towards generous action : for the wealthy donor of such things as public parks and playgrounds has the satisfaction of choosing the form of his gift, of directing the use of it in some measure, and of seeing the fruits of it develop before his eyes. This localised generosity may easily develop into a wider patriotism, which interests itself, not merely in fellow-citizens of a common city, but in fellow-citizens of a common country. Pure public spirit often leads wealthy persons voluntarily to provide, partly in their lifetime and partly by legacies at death, large sums for the service of the poor. Oftener still public spirit is reinforced by the craving, strong in some men, for that sense of power which the fact of giving conveys.

§ 4. The normal motives prompting men to these and other forms of voluntary transference of resources to public ends are already of considerable force, and it is open to us to stimulate them still further. "No doubt," Dr. Marshall writes, "men are capable of much more unselfish service than they generally render ; and the supreme aim of the economist is to discover how this latent social asset can be developed more quickly and turned to account more wisely."[1] Not much has yet been accomplished in this direction. It is well understood, however, that Government, if it so chooses, has power to harness to the nobler motives for generosity others of a lower order. Much will be done for the sake of fame and praise, and fame of a sort may be offered as a reward for private munificence. Thus, the transference of resources from the rich can be purchased, in a delicately veiled manner, by honours and decorations that cost nobody anything. These things are at once symbols and conveyers of reputation ; for, when a worthless man is decorated, those who feel, or pretend to feel, respect for the decorator, offer a vicarious respect to the decorated also. No doubt, in some degree, the issue of fresh decorations may diminish the value to their possessors of

[1] *Principles of Economics*, p. 9.

those already issued.   To confer the Order of Merit broadcast among excellent bricklayers would annihilate its attractive power for the class in whose behoof it was originally designed. This difficulty can, however, be overcome to a great extent by the creation of new orders, instead of the extension of old ones.   It is not impossible, therefore, that, along these lines, inducements might be provided, adequate to secure the transference of a good deal of income from rich people, without the expectation of the transference involving any diminution, but, rather, some appreciable increase, in the waiting and effort furnished by them towards the upbuilding of the national dividend.

§ 5. Unfortunately it is quite certain that, in present conditions, voluntary transferences will fall very much below the aggregate of transferences from relatively well-to-do people which the general sense of the community demands. A considerable amount of coercive transference is, therefore, also necessary.) This means, in one form or another, taxation, and probably, in the main, direct taxation graduated against large incomes.   The effect upon the volume of the national dividend of the expectation of various sorts of taxes has been examined at length in the course of Part IV. Here it is enough to observe generally that the expectation of indirect taxes tends to divert resources from more to less productive channels, and the expectation of direct taxes to lessen the inducement people have to work and save.   Broadly therefore, unlike the expectation of voluntary transferences, it will make for a diminution, though, as was shown in Part IV., not necessarily a very large diminution, in the volume of the national dividend.   Whatever injury is brought about in this way will need to be taken into account before a final reckoning of the effect on the dividend of any particular form of transference is made.

CHAPTER IX

§ 1. In turning to examine the effect on the national dividend
of the expectation of transferences to the poor, we come at
once into contact with a widely held opinion. The experience
of the old Poor Law has made people very much afraid that
any expectation of assistance from public funds will tempt the
poor into idleness and thriftlessness. It is common—or at
all events was common before the war—to hear proposals for
State aid towards housing accommodation, insurance premiums,
or even education denounced on the ground that they constitute
relief in aid of wages, and are, therefore, a reversion to the
discredited policy of Speenhamland. This reasoning is based on
defective analysis. Underlying it is the tacit assumption
that the expectation of any sort of transference to the poor
acts in the same way as the expectation of any other sort.
In reality, different types of transference act in different
ways, and nothing of importance can be said that does not
take account of this fact. The main lines of division are
between transferences which differentiate against idleness and
thriftlessness, transferences which are neutral, and transferences which differentiate in favour of idleness and thriftlessness.

§ 2. The first of these groups is made up of those transferences which are conditional upon the recipients making provision for themselves on a scale that is fairly representative of
their individual capacity. These transferences can be arranged
as follows. First, the poorer members of the community are

classified according to the amount of provision that they "could
reasonably have been expected to make " for themselves, apart
from any transference of resources in their favour. The
standard of capacity set up is, of course, different for different
sorts of people with different opportunities. For example, the
income from savings, which a man can reasonably be expected
to have secured at a given age varies with his situation in
life. If, before the war, a man on 12s. a week had secured
for himself an annuity of 1s. a week, his thrift was much more
real than if a man on 50s. had got an annuity of 3s. a week.
The classification of different people into different groups with
different standards may be carried out with any degree of
roughness or exactness, according to the scope and skill of the
various classifying authorities. In ideal conditions a separate
standard capacity would be estimated for every individual.
Secondly, the standard having been set up, resources are
transferred to poor persons on condition that their productive
activity comes up to the standard assigned to them, an extra
amount, perhaps, being transferred in recognition of any excess
above standard to which they may attain. It is not, of course,
necessary that the same grant should be made to all persons
who live up to their capacity ; and, in general, we may presume
that a poorer man satisfying this condition will receive more
than a less poor man who also satisfies it. The kind of
arrangement which this policy embodies has been advocated
for certain purposes by Dr. Marshall. "Should not indoor
and outdoor relief," he asks, " be so administered as to *encourage
providence*, and to afford hope to those whose means are small,
but who yet desire to do right as far as they can ? " [1] Practically
the adoption of this ideal would mean that persons coming
up to, or exceeding, the standard adjudged reasonable for them
would be treated more favourably than similar persons failing
to do this. A rough application of it is made in the rules
governing the grant of old-age pensions in Denmark. In
order to qualify for a pension, a man must have worked and
saved enough to keep off the rates between the ages of fifty
and sixty. Under this system, though, possibly, thrift, labour
and private charity are discouraged, so far as they touch the

[1] *Economic Journal*, 1891, p. 189.

provision for maintenance after sixty, "on the other hand, both thrift and private charity have been stimulated, so far as they are concerned with provision for maintenance, between the ages of fifty and sixty. The motive for maintaining independence during these years is strengthened, and its effectiveness · is greatly · increased, by the consideration that a limited task, the completion of which is not· so distant and uncertain as to deter men from attempting it, is all that is now imposed on the honest and industrious, though indigent, person, or on friends, former employers or others, who may be interested in helping him. Many shrink from trying what seems impossible of achievement, and much effort, which would otherwise have remained latent, has been evoked by bringing the task within the reach of a wider circle of persons."[1]   There can be little doubt that openings exist for a further application of methods of this kind.   It is plain that the expectation of transferences to poor persons, engineered by means of them, will stimulate, and will not diminish, the contribution which potential receipts make towards the upbuilding of the national dividend.

§ 3. The second group, neutral transferences, is made up of those transferences which are dependent on the attainment of some condition, not capable of being varied by voluntary action in the economic sphere, on the part of possible beneficiaries. It, thus, includes schemes for universal old-age pensions (dependent only on the attainment of a certain age), the universal endowment of motherhood (dependent only on the fact of motherhood), or the universal gift to everybody of a sum deemed sufficient to furnish by itself the essential means of subsistence. These wide-reaching arrangements are, hitherto, nowhere more than projects.   But less ambitious examples of neutral transferences have been embodied in actual law.   Under them grants of help are made to depend, not on the performance of the

---

[1] "Denmark and its Aged Poor," *Yale Review*, 1899, p. 15. The following sentence from the first report on the working of the British Unemployment Insurance Scheme is of interest in this connection: "Twenty of our Trade Unions, with an estimated membership of over 86,000 in the (compulsorily) Insured Trades, have begun to make provision for unemployment since the passing of the Act; while other Associations making such provision have much increased their membership" [Cd. 6965], p. iv. The help given towards insurance would thus seem to have stimulated private effort.

recipient, nor on the relation between performance and estimated
capacity, but upon estimated capacity itself. The root idea
of this system was approached in a Report made to the Poor
Law Authority in 1872 by Mr. Wodehouse, in which he
endeavoured to distinguish between relief in aid of wages
and relief in aid of earnings. "Relief in aid of earnings,"
he wrote, "is clearly inseparable from any system of out-relief.
Thus, in all unions, relief is afforded to able-bodied widows
with children, and it is clear that all such relief is in aid of
an income obtained by the widow by washing, charing, or
other similar employments. So, again, in almost every union
that I visited, relief is given to old and infirm men, who,
though past regular work, are from time to time employed on
occasional odd jobs of various sorts. Relief to these two
classes of paupers may, I think, be distinguished from that
system of relief in aid of wages, which was so generally
prevalent prior to the introduction of the present Poor Law." [1]
A closer approach to the above idea is made in the treatment
which many Boards of Guardians before the war accorded to
old and infirm women and to widows with several children.
They appeared to hold that, whereas most of the regular trades
followed by men provide persons of average capacity, in full
employment and without encumbrances, with fairly adequate
earnings, most women's trades do not do this. It is not at
all obvious that a widow of ordinary ability, even without
children, can, with reasonable hours and so forth, earn enough
to "maintain herself and provide for the ordinary vicissitudes
of life." [2] Hence, we read: "Once a woman is put on the
roll (for out-relief), provided she is not guilty of immorality or
frequent intemperance, she is not disturbed. Her earnings
may rise and fall, but the relief will not vary. The inquiry

---

[1] Quoted in Appendix vol. xvii. to the *Report of the Royal Commission on the
Poor Laws* [Cd. 4690], p. 355.
[2] Cf. *Report to the Poor Law Commission* by Mr. Steel Maitland and Miss
Squire, Appendix, vol. xvi. p. 5. The position of widows is, of course, especially
likely to be difficult in districts where there is no established women's trade.
In such districts "widows left destitute come at once for poor relief and remain
throughout their widowhood on the rates." Where opportunities for home work
exist, pauperism may be postponed—often at the expense of hours far longer
than a proper interpretation of the minimum standard, to be stipulated for in
chapter xii., would allow. (Cf. *ibid.* p. 182.)

as to her earnings is made at her first application and rarely
afterwards. . . . One officer put the common practice into a
few words : 'We never bother about what the women earn.
We know they never earn ten shillings. They can always
find room for half-a-crown.' It follows that, in unions where
minute inquiry is the exception—that is to say, in most
unions—the pauper worker is not discouraged from working
up to her full capacity."[1] The French law of 1893
concerning sick relief is of kindred character. It provides
that in every commune there shall be drawn up periodically a list of persons who, if they become sick, will be
entitled to assistance, the persons on the list being placed
there on the ground that they have not the capacity
to make provision against sickness for themselves. Yet
again, the same principle is embodied in the English
system of exacting payment (whether through recoverable
loans or otherwise) from persons adjudged capable of making
some contribution, to whom medical aid has been given, or
whose children have been fed by public authority. A charge
is made, based, not on what the actual service rendered to the
poor man has cost, but on an estimate of the provision, which,
apart from the hope of outside help, he might have been
expected to make. Thus, Circular 552 of the Board of
Education urges that, when the parents cannot pay the full
cost of meals provided for their children, "it is better that
they should pay what their means permit, rather than that
meals should be given free of cost."[2] In other words, an

---

[1] *Report to the Poor Law Commission* by Miss Williams and Mr. Jones,
Appendix, vol. xvii. p. 334.

[2] *Loc. cit.,* Par. 4. The Board's Report on the Working of the Act in 1910
shows that the amount of money actually recovered from parents is insignificant.
([Cd. 5131], p. 9.) This, however, is largely due to the facts (1) that many
local Education Boards deliberately limit their provision of meals to necessitous
children, and (2) that, when they do not do this, parents who can afford to
pay dislike sending their children to meals where no distinction is made between
payers and non-payers. (Cf. Bulkley, *The Feeding of School Children*, pp. 107-9.)
In these circumstances not many children whose parents are capable of paying
anything are likely to be affected. In respect of lunatics the conditions are
different, and considerable contributions from relatives are collected. (Cf.
Freeman, *Economic Journal*, 1911, pp. 294 *et seq.*) It must be admitted, however
that there are considerable practical difficulties in the way of exacting payment
for a service which it is understood will be rendered whether payment is
made or not. Further objection is often taken to the device of "recoverable

attempt is made so to arrange the State's contribution to different families that it shall depend upon, and vary inversely with, their estimated capacity to make provision for themselves.

§ 4. The way in which the expectation of a neutral transference will react on the volume of the national dividend depends on the kind of things in which the transference is made. As a general rule, of course, it is made in money. In these circumstances it might be thought at first sight that the contribution of effort and waiting which potential recipients make, and, therefore, the volume of the dividend, will be wholly unaffected. This, however, is not so. For, if a man of any given presumed capacity knows that he will receive, say, a pound a week as a gift, independently of anything that he may earn for himself, his desire for any nth unit of money earned by himself is lowered. But his aversion to any rth unit of work that he may do remains unaltered; or, since the extra money creates new opportunities for a pleasurable use of leisure, may even be increased. Consequently, if he continued to do the same amount of work as before, his aversion to the last unit of work done would exceed his desire for the money received in exchange for it. It follows that the expectation of a weekly grant will cause the recipient to contract the amount of work that he does, and, therewith, his contribution to the national dividend.[1] The extent of this effect varies with the magnitude of the grant and the forms of (1) the schedule representing his desire for various amounts of money and (2) the schedule representing his aversion from various amounts of work; but, in any event, *some* contraction in his contribution to the dividend is likely, *ceteris paribus*, to occur.

§ 5. The transference may, however, be made in the form, not of money, but of things. If these things are things which, apart from the transference, a recipient would have

---

loans," on the ground that they divert energy from industrial effort to attempts at evading payment. As Mrs. Bosanquet observes: "Many a shilling is recklessly wasted, because, if not spent, it will only go to the debt collector" (*Economic Journal*, 1896, p. 223).

[1] This reaction can alternatively, if it is so desired, be brought under review as an effect of the fact of transference, on the line of thought followed in Part IV. Chapter II. § 2. In the present connection, however, the form of analysis adopted above is more convenient.

purchased out of his own earnings, or if, not being such things, they are capable of being sold or pawned and thus converted into money, the effect is the same as if money had been transferred. But transference of objects, not capable of being sold or pawned, and designed to satisfy needs which, apart from the transference, a recipient would have left unsatisfied, have a different effect. The last unit of money which a man earns for himself in industry will be required to satisfy the same needs, and will, therefore, be desired with the same intensity as it would have been, if no transference had been made. Hence, no contraction will occur in the contribution which, by work and waiting, he makes to the national dividend. Thus, public parks for the collective use of the poor, or flowers for their private use, can be transferred to them, without the expectation of the transference reacting injuriously upon the dividend. The same remark holds good of general sanitary measures. The grant from State funds of the expenses involved in such things is on a different footing from the grant of funds for ordinary medical treatment. As the Poor Law Commissioners write: "Sanitary measures, for the most part, lie beyond the reach of the individual, and are a common need, which must be provided for in common; while medical treatment is essentially an individual need, and is, for the most part, easily attainable by the individual."[1] Similar considerations hold good, in some degree, of the gift of free school education, or of a portion of the costs of it— when the amount of education to be covered is authoritatively fixed—to the children of the poor. For some persons are so poor that, if left to themselves, they could not devote any of their earnings to the purchase of school education, and, therefore, the free provision of it by the State does not lower their desire for any unit of these earnings. Since, when children are taken to be educated, their parents are deprived of the wages they might otherwise have obtained, it may be that, even when to free education free meals are added, there is no net lightening of the costs of living to parents, and, therefore, no diminution in the contribution of work and waiting which they find it profitable to make. In these circumstances

---

[1] *Report of the Royal Commission on the Poor Law*, p. 231.

the expectation of this variety of neutral transference will leave the value of the national dividend unaltered.

§ 6. There remains the third possibility. There are some commodities and services, the demand for which is so correlated with that for certain other commodities and services that the gift of them increases the recipient's desire for these others; thus increasing his desire for any rth unit of purchasing power that he may be able to earn; and thus, finally, increasing the work and waiting that he is willing to provide in exchange for purchasing power. It is claimed, for example, that the gift of medical treatment to children in some elementary schools reacts beneficially on the energy of their parents by enlisting co-operation and thought from them. The possibility thus opened up is illustrated in the following passage from Mr. Paterson's *Across the Bridges*:

At present the difficulty of school dinners centres round the position of the mother. Her apathy towards the education of her child, her severance from any sense of partnership with the school, makes her sometimes ready to snatch advantages, but slow to bear her proper share. Her lack of responsibility arises, not from the fact that so much is done for her, but that so much is done without her. As long as the education of the boy is taken completely out of her hands, so long will she be apt to stand aloof, regard every committee as a natural enemy, and grasp at all that she can by any manœuvre hope to be given. The absence of home work, visiting, reports, and all natural ties between school and home are the real enemies of parental responsibility. No mother is harmed by kindness done to her child, so long as every such kindness exacts from her a higher standard and ensures her active co-operation with the school.[1]

A like suggestion is contained in the following extract from the *Letters of Octavia Hill*:

I sometimes dream about the time that shall come, "when we shall try to keep up the spirit of our poor," not by shutting up their hearts in cold independence, but by giving them others to help, and thus rousing the deepest of all motives for self-help, that which is the only foundation on which to build our service to others.[2]

And an illustration of what is meant is furnished by the late Canon Barnett thus:

[1] *Loc. cit.* p. 110.   [2] *Loc. cit.* p. 207.

The Children's Country Holiday Fund, for instance, by giving country holidays to town children, and by making the parents contribute to the expense, develops at once a desire for the peace and beauty of the country and a new capacity for satisfying this desire. When parents realise the necessity for such holiday, and know how it can be secured, this fund will cease to have a reason for existence.[1]

In undertakings of this kind there is a field for neutral transferences of resources, the expectation of which not merely leaves the national dividend undiminished, but, by creating a new inducement for work and saving, actually increases it.

§ 7. We now pass to the third main group of transferences—namely those which differentiate in favour of idleness and thriftlessness by making the help that is given larger, the smaller is the provision the recipients have made for themselves. Some resort to this type of transference is involved in all Poor Law systems that fix a state of minimum fortune below which they will not allow any citizen to fall. For, in so far as they raise to this level the real income of all citizens whose provision for themselves falls below it, they implicitly promise that any reduction in private provision shall be made good by an equivalent addition to State provision. It is plain that the expectation of these differential transferences will greatly weaken the motive of many poor persons to make provision for themselves. For, whatever the standard is below which the State has determined that nobody shall fall, any person, who could not provide as much as this for himself but could provide something, will be equally well off if he provides nothing. In so far, therefore, as what a person provides for himself corresponds to what he contributes to the national dividend, transferences that differentiate in favour of small provision threaten grave injury to the national dividend.

§ 8. A recognition of this fact has led many persons to consider plans for limiting the scope of this class of differential transference. Since everybody agrees that in a civilised State no citizen shall be allowed to starve, this can only be done by so enlarging the scope of neutral transferences that the

---

[1] *Practicable Socialism*, p. 237.

elementary needs of practically all persons, whatever their income, are met through them. The movement in this direction is well illustrated by the debate between advocates and opponents of a universalised system of old-age pensions.[1] If, say the advocates of this plan, all persons over a given age, irrespective of their income, are awarded a given pension, there will be no differentiation tempting people in old age to earn smaller incomes than they are able to earn; whereas, if only those persons above the given age, who are in receipt of an income below some specified maximum, say £26 a year, are awarded a pension of, say 5s., there will be a strong inducement for all persons who could earn anything between £25, 19s. 0d. and £38 to see to it that in fact they earn only £25, 19s. 0d. On the other side, however, it is pointed out, in accordance with the reasoning of the last chapter, that money cannot generally be collected through taxation without some injurious reaction on the national dividend being produced. This reaction is likely to be more extensive the greater is the amount of the money that is raised. Since, therefore, universal old-age pensions necessarily cost more than limited old-age pensions, the argument in favour of the universal form is confronted with an argument of the same order that tells against it. Exactly the same issue, somewhat complicated in this instance by eugenic considerations,[2] is raised between persons who wish to confine State aid for mothers to those families with young children in which the parents are unable, out of their own resources, to provide for their children adequately, and advocates of the "endowment of motherhood" generally. To strike a balance between the conflicting considerations in controversies of this kind is evidently a very delicate task, and one that need not be attempted here. If, however, the method of obviating differential transferences contemplated by the advocates of universal pensions and universal endowment of motherhood were itself universalised, in such wise that the minimum required for subsistence were paid out

[1] This controversy is presented in a clear-cut form in the Report of the Departmental Committee on Old-Age Pensions [Cmd. 410] 1919. The majority of the Committee recommend that the means limit for pensions be abolished, but the minority dissent from this recommendation.

[2] Cf. Darwin, *The Racial Effects of Public Assistance*, pp. 13-15.

by the State to everybody, whatever his income might be, the
task of balancing gain against loss would no longer be delicate.
In these circumstances there can be little doubt that the type
of reaction described in § 7 would operate so strongly that
the dividend would be seriously injured. In any event,
among practical politicians the device of universalising
grants to large categories of persons, irrespective of their
individual needs, is greatly disliked. There is no real
question of pressing it far enough to do away with the need
for differential transferences based directly on the poverty of
recipients.

§ 9. The expectation of these transferences must, as we
have seen, damage the national dividend. If, however, to the
receipt of the help they give deterrent conditions are attached,
the damage can be mitigated. Consequently, the question
arises, in what circumstances it is desirable, in the interest of
the national dividend, to attach deterrent conditions to State
aid, and what form the deterrent conditions, if decided upon,
can best assume. To answer this question correctly we need to
revert to the concluding sentence of § 7, in which it was indicated that differentiation in favour of people who make small
provision for themselves injures the national dividend, *only in
so far as what a person provides for himself corresponds to
what he contributes to the national dividend.* It is common
to assume that the provision which a person makes for
himself must correspond exactly to his contribution to the
national dividend, and that, therefore, the contraction of the
aggregate provision thus made—which results from the
establishment of a system of differential transferences to poor
people—implies an equal contraction of the national dividend.
This is substantially true of provision made through work
and through savings invested in industry and not subsequently withdrawn. But it is not true of provision made
through contributions to the benefit fund of any form of
mutual insurance society. For, as will be explained in detail
in the last chapter of Part VI., a large part of the income,
which a sick or unemployed member draws from this source,
is not the fruit of real investment, but is a payment made to
him out of the earnings of other members—a payment which

they are willing to make in return for a promise that they
themselves shall, at need, receive similar assistance. In practice the main part of the provision which poor people make
for themselves, otherwise than by contemporary work, is made
by way of some form of insurance, though it is loosely and
popularly credited to saving. Consequently, we may conclude
broadly that, while any check, caused by differential transferences, to the provision that poor people make for themselves
through contemporary work involves a corresponding diminution of the national dividend, any check to the provision they
make otherwise than through work involves a very much
less than corresponding diminution in the dividend. It
follows that there is little to be gained by imposing deterrent
conditions upon those recipients of State help who have failed
to make this sort of provision.

§ 10. But differentiation in favour of small provision
made through contemporary work is a serious matter.
If, for example, it is understood that everybody's income
will, at need, be brought up by State aid to, say, £2
a week, it will, generally and roughly, be to the interest
of everybody capable of earning by work any sum less than
£2 a week to be idle and earn nothing. This *must* damage
the national dividend. How much it damages it will, of
course, depend on how large the sum fixed on as a minimum is, and how many people in the country would
normally earn by work less than that sum. If the sum
exceeds the normal earning power of a large part of the
community, the damage done must necessarily be very
great. It is probable that this consideration lay behind the
recommendation of the 1832 Commission, that " the situation
on the whole of able-bodied paupers should not be made
really, or apparently, so eligible as the situation of the
independent labourer of the lowest class "—that is to say, of
the ordinary unskilled labourer of full age and in good health.
At that time unskilled labourers formed a very large proportion of the population. To have guaranteed to everybody
a situation better than these labourers could ordinarily earn
would, therefore, have threatened the nation with the withdrawal from work of a mass of people, whose aggregate efforts

were responsible for an important slice of the dividend. It may be observed, however, that to guarantee now a situation better than that represented by the earnings of an unskilled labourer of 1832 would inflict a much smaller proportionate injury upon the dividend, because the proportion of the population, who are not capable of earning a wage greater than this, has become much smaller. And even to guarantee now a situation represented by the situation of the unskilled labourer of to-day would have a smaller proportionate effect, because the proportion of the dividend contributed by unskilled labour now is smaller than it was in 1832. Plainly, however, for the State, tacitly or openly to guarantee any standard high enough to affect a substantial number of people must threaten considerable injury to the dividend. Here, therefore, there is real scope for the association with State help of deterrent conditions. Of course, there is no object in attaching such conditions to help given to a man who is idle because he is genuinely unable to find work. The knowledge that he cannot get help without these conditions will not remove this inability. But there is an object in attaching them to help given to those who are idle because they are unwilling to find (or to keep) work. The deterrent conditions will make them less unwilling. Until recently the practical difficulty of distinguishing between these two classes of persons, coupled with a general and justified unwillingness to deal hardly with the former of them, made it impossible to arrange these conditions satisfactorily. A compromise was accepted, under which, instead of no deterrence on the one class and strict deterrence on the other, mild deterrence was imposed on both. This plan did, indeed, save the innocent from gross tyranny, but at the expense of leaving the guilty relatively immune and, therefore, inadequately deterred. Of late years, however, the establishment of employment exchanges has provided machinery by which the truth of a man's plea to be out of work through no fault of his own can be, in some measure, tested. In trades where the jobs, once obtained, are of "presumed permanence," if the employment exchanges are unable to find employment for a man who applies to them, more particularly if that man has a settled home and has insured himself against unemployment, the plea that he is a victim of misfortune and not of laziness may be provisionally accepted. This test is, indeed, not easily applicable to casual trades where workpeople continually alternate between work and idleness; for in these trades a man might be prepared to accept work for a day or so, whenever it was offered through an employment exchange, and yet might deliberately spend a much longer period out of work than there was any need for him to do. This difficulty must be recognised; and it must be admitted, further, that in the exceptional period of free insurance granted by the British Government after the armistice of November 1918, a number of persons obtained unemployment donation, who might, had they wished, have been employed. But, in spite of this, there can be no doubt that the development of employment exchanges has made it possible, over a wide field, to distinguish directly those who cannot, from those who will not, find work. Consequently, since the former class can be withdrawn altogether from the range of deterrent conditions, it is now feasible so to stiffen up the conditions against the latter class —people who are in need because they *will* not work with reasonable continuity in private industry—as to make them really effective.

§ 11. Some guidance as to the form that deterrence should take can be obtained from English Poor Law experience. It is clearly suggested, for example, that some degree of enforced labour is an essential ingredient. The importance of this element is well illustrated in some of the evidence given before the Royal Commission of 1832. Thus, one witness, in a Memorandum on Liverpool, stated: "The introduction of labour thinned the house very much; it was sometimes difficult to procure a sufficient supply of junk, which was generally obtained from Plymouth; when the supply was known to be scanty, paupers flocked in; but the sight of a load of junk before the door would deter them for any length of time."[1] In the same spirit, the Comptroller of the Accounts for the township of Salford, stated: "Finding work for those who applied for relief in consequence of being short or out of work has had a very good effect, especially when the work

[1] *Report of the Poor Law Commission of 1832*, p. 161.

has been of a different kind from that which they have been
accustomed to. In Salford employment to break stones on
the highways has saved the township several hundred pounds
within the last two years; for very few indeed will remain
at work more than a few days, while the bare mention of it
is quite sufficient for others. They all manage to find
employment for themselves, and cease for a time to be
troublesome; although it is a singular fact that, when the
stock of stones on hand has been completely worked up before
the arrival of others, they have, almost to a man, applied
again for relief, and the overseers have been obliged to give
them relief; but, so soon as an arrival of stones is announced,
they find work for themselves again."[1] The information
given in a recent Report on the Poplar Union points in the
same direction. But, though enforced labour seems to be
an essential ingredient in deterrent conditions, it is not by
itself sufficient. The chief reason for this is the extraordinary
difficulty of making a man work for the Poor Law Authorities
with anything approaching the energy that he would need to
put forth for a private employer. It is practically impossible
to set relieved persons to work, each at his own trade. Consequently, some general form of labour has to be required:
and it is impossible to fix, for a miscellaneous assortment of
different people, any single standard of performance. Hence,
the standard exacted has to be measured to each man " with
due regard to his ordinary calling or occupation, and his age
and physical ability." Since this cannot be tested objectively,
"no specified task can be enforced. The capability of the
persons employed varies, and it can only be required that
each person shall perform the amount of work that he appears
to be able to accomplish. . . . The standard of accomplish-
ment is practically fixed by the unwilling worker."[2] The
fact that resort cannot be had to the ordinary practice of
dismissal leaves the Poor Law Authority without any real
defence against this tendency. Consequently, potential beneficiaries are aware that the labour, which will be imposed upon

---

[1] *Report of the Poor Law Commission of 1832,* p 162.
[2] *Report of the Committee on Distress from Want of Employment,* quoted by
Beveridge, *Unemployment,* p. 153.

them, if, through unwillingness to work in private industry, they become candidates for public assistance, will not be severe labour. Furthermore, even if this difficulty could be overcome, work for the Poor Law, because its certainty and continuity absolve those engaged in it from the risk, trouble and cost involved in occasional loss of employment and the need of finding a new job, might still prove more attractive than independent labour. Thus, for effective deterrence something more than enforced labour is required. The addition of disenfranchisement and the stigma of pauperism is, in the opinion of practical administrators, quite inadequate. Consequently, for those who need support, but will not work to get it, resort must be had to disciplinary measures. This implies detention under control without excessive leave of absence. On the Continent of Europe, able-bodied men, who fail to support themselves because they will not work, are subjected to long periods of detention in labour colonies. In Belgium such persons may be committed to the penal colony of Merxplas for not less than two years nor more than seven years.[1] The cantonal law in Berne provides for their internment in a labour institution for any time between six months and two years.[2] The German Imperial Penal Code has a similar provision.[3] The practice of the Continent is coming to be proposed seriously for adoption in this country also. Thus, the Committee on Vagrancy recommended "that a class of habitual vagrants should be defined by Statute, and that this class should include any person who has been three or more times convicted, during a period of, say, twelve months, of certain offences now coming under the Vagrancy Act, namely, sleeping out, begging, refusing to perform his task of work in casual wards, or refusing or neglecting to maintain himself so that he become chargeable to the poor rate."[4] There is no reason—much the contrary—why the conditions of deterrence should not be arranged with a view to "improving" the deterred persons, if that be possible; for to a man wishing to be idle the prospect of improvement, whether by training or

---

[1] Cf. Dawson. *The Vagrancy Problem*, p. 136.
[2] *Ibid.* p. 179.   [3] *Ibid.* p. 193.
[4] *Report of the Departmental Committee on Vagrancy*, vol. i. p. 59.

by education or in any other way, will be as deterrent as anything else. Detention, however, is essential. Its adoption—which the development of employment exchanges as a means of sifting the sheep from the goats has made practicable—would enable a far more effective system of deterrence to be associated with State aid to the deliberately idle than is at present known in this country. We cannot, however, seriously expect that the system will ever become perfect enough to prevent the expectation of differential transferences from contracting, in some degree, the volume of the national dividend.

CHAPTER X

§ 1. So far we have been considering transferences of a direct
kind. There remain transferences through bounties or devices
substantially equivalent to bounties. These take three principal forms: first, bounties, provided out of taxes, on the whole
consumption of particular commodities which are predominantly purchased by poor persons; secondly, bounties, similarly
provided, but confined to that part of the whole consumption
which is actually enjoyed by defined categories of poor persons;
thirdly, authoritative interference with prices, so contrived
that the richer purchasers of particular commodities have to
bear part of the cost of what is sold to poorer purchasers.
The first of these methods is illustrated by the special subsidies which were paid on bread and potatoes during the Great
War to enable prices to be kept down to what was considered a reasonable level. The second and third methods
are only practicable in connection with commodities and
services which are non-transferable in the sense explained in
Part II. Chapter XIV. The second is illustrated by the Irish
Labourers Act, under which, not all house-building in the
districts affected, but only house-building for labourers is
subsidised, and by the more general arrangements which
have been adopted to meet the post-war house shortage.
The third method is illustrated by special arrangements
often made in connection with the services supplied by
monopolistic "public utilities." Whether these services
are actually produced by private concerns or by the public
authorities themselves, public authorities can, if they choose,
compel sales to selected poor persons to be made at a

loss, and can arrange for this loss to be made good through charges to other persons higher than would otherwise have been permitted. This plan is adopted under a number of Tramway Acts, where provision is made for a convenient service of workmen's cars at specially low fares. Thus, " a recent report of the Highway Committee of the London County Council estimates that the loss involved by running the workmen's car service is £65,932 per annum." [1] The same policy is illustrated in another connection by the practice of the municipality of Wiesbaden, where gas supplied by means of prepayment meters—a more expensive method of supply—is charged for at the same rate as gas supplied by ordinary meters to all persons the annual rent of whose house is less than 400 marks. [2] It should be noted that this method is not necessarily confined to commodities and services produced under conditions of monopoly. Provided that the goods are, or can be made, non-transferable, it is open to public authorities to fix a charge at which anybody undertaking a named business or profession must sell whatever quantity of service is demanded by persons in a given category. The result will be to limit the number of persons entering that business or profession, till the expectation of earnings therefrom—derived jointly from sales to the poor and to other persons for whose purchases the charges are fixed by the normal play of demand and supply—becomes about equal to that ruling in other businesses or professions of a similar difficulty and disagreeableness and involving an equally expensive training. This, of course, implies that the low charges made to the favoured category of persons are associated with charges to other categories higher than would have prevailed if the low charges had not been enforced.

§ 2. To all these methods it has been objected generally that they necessarily benefit unequally different poor persons whose circumstances are substantially similar. Professor Knoop writes, for example: " It is difficult to see why artisans, mechanics and day labourers who travel in the early morning should receive privileges which men and women serving in shops, clerks and others, who are no better off financially,

1. Knoop, *Principles of Municipal Trading*, p. 266.　　2. *Ibid.* p. 213.

do not enjoy."[1] It may be replied that, if a thing is good in itself, the partial realisation of it cannot rightly be condemned on the ground that complete realisation is impracticable. We are not, however, concerned with the validity either of this objection or of the different and more forcible objection, from the side of fairness, which can be urged specially against the third method, namely that it throws the cost of helping the poor upon particular persons instead of upon the taxpayers generally.[2] For the present purpose it is enough to know that all three of the methods distinguished above have, as a matter of fact, been adopted over a fairly wide field.

§ 3. The first of the three necessarily, and, if the categories are so chosen that people cannot practically be drawn by the bounty into a benefited category, the other two also involve "neutral transferences" in the sense explained in § 3 of the last chapter, and not differential transferences. Hence, they operate on the productive activity of the poor only through their effect on the marginal desiredness which money has to them. But they differ from the kind of neutral transferences so far examined in one respect. They will check to a small extent the contribution of work made by the poor, if they are granted upon things for which the demand of the poor has an elasticity less than unity; but they will increase this contribution to a small extent if they are granted on things for which this demand has an elasticity greater than unity. For in the former event the marginal desiredness of money to the poor will be lowered, since more is left over for other things; and in the latter event it will be raised. As a matter of fact bounties are more likely to be given on things of urgent need and, therefore, of inelastic demand. The check to output resulting from the consequent relaxation of effort on the part of potential recipients means *some*, though probably a very small, diminution of the national dividend.

§ 4. So far it would seem that there is little to choose between help to the poor by bounties and by direct neutral transferences. If the amount of the bounty-fed commodity which each recipient is to consume is fixed authoritatively,

---

[1] *Principles and Methods of Municipal Trade*, p. 266.
[2] Cf. *ante*, Part III. Chapter V. § 7.

as under the British system of free and compulsory elementary education, this is in fact, so.   It is. so, too, if the
amount is not fixed authoritatively, but is, for other reasons, not
liable to change in consequence of the bounty.   Thus, poor
people are accustomed to buy some things through a common
purchase fund, so organised that the payment a member has
to make does not vary with the amount of his individual
purchases.   Sick clubs are arranged on this plan.   There will
be no inducement to a member of a sick club to increase
the amount of the doctor's services that he calls for in a year
merely because the fixed amount that he has been accustomed to
pay for membership of the club is taken over and paid by the
State. These conditions, however, are exceptional.   In general,
when a bounty, or the equivalent of a bounty, is given on any
commodity, the beneficiaries of the bounty will buy more of
it than they would otherwise have done.   In this way resources
are diverted out of the natural channels of production, and
there is a presumption—which may, of course, as was
explained in Part II. Chapter VIII., be rebutted by special
knowledge—that this diversion will inflict an extra injury on the
national dividend, over and above that set out in the preceding
paragraph.   If the bounty is large enough, it may happen that
the output of bounty-fed commodity will be expanded so far
that to the poor themselves the marginal supply price, not
merely in terms of money, but in terms of satisfaction, exceeds
the marginal demand price, or, in other words, that the
economic satisfaction they get from the last increment consumed is less than the economic dissatisfaction involved in
producing it.   In general, the expectation of a transference
through bounties on particular commodities is likely to
damage the national dividend rather more than the expectation of a direct neutral transference of equal magnitude.   In
spite of this, however, the bounty method may still sometimes
be better, not only because there may be special economic or
non-economic reasons for encouraging the consumption of the
particular thing on which the bounty is given, but also because
the element of "charity" is less obvious and, therefore, less
damaging to the *morale* of the beneficiaries, when it is concealed
in a bounty than when it is displayed in a direct dole.

CHAPTER XI

§ 1. IN the three preceding chapters we have been concerned
with the effect on the national dividend of the indirect checks
upon productive activity, which may be brought about by
the expectation of transferences from the rich to the poor.
Obviously, however, the whole story has not yet been told.
For, in the long run, it is not merely the size of the contributions made to the national dividend by the various parties
concerned, which affect its volume, but also the way in which
the dividend itself is employed. The reason, of course, is that
some of the dividend at any one time is the fruit of that part
of the dividend of earlier times that has been "invested" in
one or another means of future production. When resources
are transferred from the rich to the poor, the extent and the
character of this investment is modified. The fact of transference, as distinguished from the expectation of transference,
to which it gives rise, is, thus, equivalent to a redistribution of
the dividend between certain different uses. If things went
on "naturally" and no transference took place, a part of it
would assume the form of goods consumable by the rich, a part
that of machines to assist future production, and a part that
of goods consumable by the poor. When a transference of
resources from the rich to the poor takes place, the third of
these three divisions of the dividend is increased at the
expense of the other two. Our problem is to determine the
effect of this alteration in the distribution among different

773

uses of the dividend of one year upon the magnitude of the dividend of future years.

§ 2. If no transference had occurred, the portion of the dividend, which would have assumed the form of machines, would have contributed to enlarge the dividend in later years. The portion devoted to the consumption of the rich, in so far as it served to make them more efficient producing agents, would also have done this to some extent. Among rich persons, however, it is improbable that any practicable reduction of consumption—the effect might, of course, be different if a levy were imposed so large as to bring down incomes from £5000 to £100—would diminish efficiency in an appreciable degree. Hence, we may say roughly that that part of the dividend, which, if it had not been transferred to the poor, would have been converted into capital, is the only part that would have made a substantial contribution to the national dividend of the future. But, when any given quantity of resources is collected from the rich, it is practically certain that some of it will be taken from that part of their income which would have been consumed. This implies that the part which would have become capital will not be reduced by the whole amount of the levy. It follows that any given transference of resources from the rich to the poor is bound to increase the national dividend, provided that the return yielded by "investment in the poor," through additions to their industrial efficiency, is not less than the return yielded by investment in material capital, that is to say roughly, than the normal rate of interest.

§ 3. Now, it must be admitted at once that there are certain classes of poor persons whom no transference of resources could render appreciably more efficient. These classes include the great mass of those who are morally, mentally, or physically degenerate. The history of Labour Colonies both at home and abroad and the experience of our own special schools for the feeble-minded make it clear that, for this class of person, real "cure" is practically impossible. "The officials of the colonies, on being asked their opinion as to whether it could be said with truth that any large proportion of the men sent to Merxplas were rehabilitated, morally or socially, by their stay at Merxplas, replied that in very few cases is such reclamation effected:"[1] and this is the experience of more than one colony elsewhere devoted to the care of the worst class of the non-criminal population." The fact is that, in the economic as in the physical sphere, society is faced with a certain number of "incurables." For such persons, when they are found, the utmost that can be done is to seclude them permanently from opportunities of parasitism upon others, of spreading their moral contagion, and of breeding offspring of like character to themselves. The residue of hopelessly vicious, mentally defective and other unfortunates may, indeed, still be cared for humanely by society, when they come into being, and it would be wrong to neglect any method of treatment that might raise the lives of even a few of them to a higher plane. But our main effort must be, by education and, still more, by restricting propagation among the mentally and physically unfit, to cut off at the source this stream of tainted lives. To "cure" them in any real sense is beyond human power. The same thing is true of those persons who suffer from no inherent defect and have lived in their day the life of good citizens, but whose powers have been worn out by age or ruined by grave accident. Here again, from the standpoint of investment, the soil is barren. The transference of resources to these persons, in whatever form it is made, may be extremely desirable for other reasons, but it cannot yield any significant return in industrial efficiency.

§ 4. Fortunately, however, these classes constitute only a small part of the whole body of poor persons. With the poor regarded generally there is no frozen fixity of quality, but investment is capable of real effect. At a first glance we might, perhaps, expect the marginal return obtainable in this field to be equal to what it is in industry proper. There is, however, reason to believe that the ordinary play of economic forces tends unduly to contract investments in the persons of the normal poor, with the result that the marginal return to resources invested in the poor and their children is higher

[1] *Report of the Royal Commission on the Poor Laws*, Appendix, vol. xxxii. p. 17.

than the marginal return to resources invested in machines. The ground for this belief is that poor persons are without sufficient funds to be able themselves to invest adequately in their own and their children's capacities, while they are also so situated that other persons, who have sufficient funds, are, in great measure, debarred from doing this. Under a slave economy, or under a social system so organised that those, in whom alien money was invested, could somehow pledge their capacities as security for loans, the case would be different. But, in the actual world, there is no easy way in which capitalists can ensure that any considerable part of the return on money invested by them in the capacities of the poor will come back in any form to themselves. If they make a loan, they cannot exact security for repayment; if they invest directly, by providing instruction for their own employés, they have no guarantee—unless, indeed, they are manufacturers of proprietary goods requiring a more or less specialised kind of labour, which is of less value to others than to themselves—that these employés will not shortly quit their service; and, even when there is such security, the employers must expect that the workers, having become more competent, will endeavour to exact a wage increased proportionately to their efficiency, and so to annex for themselves the interest on the employer's investment. In fact, investment in the persons of the poor is checked in a way analogous to that in which investment in land tenanted by rich occupiers and owned by poor men may be checked. The owners cannot afford to invest, and the occupiers, living without proper security as regards tenants' improvements, and receiving, therefore, as trade net product, only a portion of the social net product of their investment, are unwilling to invest as much as the interest of the national dividend requires. In view of these considerations, there is strong reason to believe that, if a moderate amount of resources were transferred from the relatively rich to the relatively poor, and were invested in poor persons with a single-eyed regard to rendering the poor in general as efficient as possible, the rate of return yielded by these resources in extra product, due to increased efficiency, would much exceed the normal rate of interest on capital invested in machinery and plant.[1] Of course, however, in real life transferences from the rich to the poor are not all made subject to the condition that they shall be employed in the way most productive of efficiency. It is, therefore, necessary to examine separately the effects of certain principal sorts of transference.

§ 5. First, consider transferences in the form of industrial training to selected persons among able-bodied adult workers. In this class of persons there are always a number who are making exceptionally low earnings, because they are ill-adjusted to the job in which they are engaged, but who are, nevertheless, of good natural ability. Resources transferred to these persons in the form of training are likely to yield a large return. This fact was recognised, not merely in the special arrangements made for demobilised officers and men after the war, but also in the National Insurance Act of 1911. The hundredth clause of that Act provided that, if, after test and enquiry, "the insurance officer considers that the skill or knowledge of a workman (who repeatedly falls out of employment) is defective, but that there is a reasonable prospect of the defect being remedied by technical instruction, the insurance officer may, subject to any directions given by the Board of Trade, pay out of the unemployment fund all or any of the expenses incidental to the provision of the instruction, if he is of opinion that the charge on the unemployment fund in respect of the workman is likely to be diminished by the provision of the instruction." The class of persons to whom this policy is especially applicable are workpeople not too far advanced in years, whose special skill has been rendered useless by some invention enabling the work they have learnt to do to be performed more economically by unskilled labour in attendance upon an automatic tool. They include, too, those persons whom accident or illness has deprived of some specialised capacity, as well as the victims of permanent changes of fashion. Money spent in teaching these persons a new trade in place of the one they have lost is likely to yield

---

[1] It should be noted that, if the transference is very large, the shortage of material capital may cause the normal rate of interest to increase appreciably ; and that then the advantage of investment in the capacities of the poor will have to be balanced against the advantage of investment in machines yielding this increased rate.

a substantial return. The same thing is true of instruction given to those persons, if in practice they can be distinguished, who, with an aptitude for one sort of occupation, have accidentally, or through perversity, drifted into another. In this category should be included men bred in the country and well fitted for rural life, who have been enticed by the glamour of some city to abandon their proper vocation. It is, however, essential that the men selected for agricultural training should be carefully chosen from among persons with a real turn for agricultural life. Frequently this has not been done.[1] The comparative failure which has attended British experiments in farm colonies does not, therefore, afford a decisive argument against further experiments, or justify any condemnation of these institutions when used as training-grounds for persons well fitted by nature for agricultural occupations. Their prospects of success would probably be enhanced if they were not confined to the service of persons who have fallen out of employment, but were general training schools of agriculture, open to members of the public, and so endowed with an industrial rather than a remedial atmosphere.[2]

§ 6. Secondly, we may distinguish transferences in the form of medical attendance and treatment to persons suffering from temporary sickness. If these persons are not assisted in time—delayed help may be comparatively useless—they may well suffer a permanent break-down in health. Resources transferred to them in the form of medical care and appropriate food are likely to prevent a large loss of efficiency. Of course, in order that good results may be attained, the transferences must be adequate and the medical attendance or supervision must not be abandoned at too early a stage. On this point the Minority Report of Poor Law Commissioners made a serious complaint against the administration of English

---

[1] On the continent of Europe, "the Farm Colonies, as distinguished from penal workhouses, do not, in general, receive the genuine unemployed, i.e. those who are out of work against their will. The great majority of the frequenters are the shiftless loafers, who, in the severer seasons of the year or in times of special distress, seek the shelter they offer rather than expose themselves to continued want or run the risk of entering the penal workhouse" (*Bulletin of the United States Bureau of Labour*, 1908, No. 76, p. 788).

[2] Cf. *Report on The Transference of Functions of Poor Law Authorities* [Cd. 8917], p. 26.

Poor Law Infirmaries : "No attempt is made to follow into their homes the hundreds of phthisical and other patients discharged every week from the sick wards of the Workhouses and Poor Law Infirmaries, in order to ensure at any rate some sort of observance of the hygienic precautions, without which they, or their near neighbours, must soon be again numbered among the sick."[1]   Given, however, that the transferences to sick persons are reasonably made, there is good hope that they will lead to a large increase of efficiency.

§ 7. Thirdly, attention may be directed to transferences in the form of training and nurture to the normal children of the poor. Here there is immense scope for profitable investment. It is just when their children are young, and, therefore, in many ways afford the most fruitful soil for investment, that poor families find themselves in the greatest straits, and, therefore, least able to provide adequately for them. The proportion of *children* who pass their earlier years in great poverty is much larger than the proportion of *families* who are in this condition at any one time. Thus, taking a standard of life analogous to Mr. Rowntree's poverty line, Dr. Bowley found, just before the war, that "more than half the working-class children of Reading, during some part of their first fourteen years, live in households where the standard of life in question is not attained."[2] And the same point is brought out by Miss Davies's observation about the village of Cowley, that "from the insignificant one-eighth of the households in primary poverty, two-fifths, or nearly half, of all children in the parish are drawn, and that only one-third of all the children are in households above the line of secondary poverty."[3] Properly arranged help for these children may do much towards building up, in the most plastic period of life, strong bodies and minds trained, at least in general intelligence, and, perhaps, also in some form of technical skill.

Of course, if these transferences are to be fruitful, they must be reasonably conducted. It is useless, for example, to spend money on educating children while leaving them the

[1] *Royal Commission on the Poor Laws, Minority Report*, p. 867.

[2] *Journal of the Royal Statistical Society*, June 1913, p. 692. Cf. also *ante*, Part I. Chapter IV. § 10.

[3] *Life in an English Village*, p. 287.

prey to demoralising home conditions. If they are not properly looked after at home, a part of the transference to them must be utilised in boarding them out with carefully chosen families, or in sending them compulsorily to an institution or industrial school. Thus, both the Majority and the Minority of the Poor Law Commissioners agree that children, who are neglected in the homes of parents in receipt of relief, should be forcibly "sent to an institution or industrial school,"[1] and that, for the children of "ins and outs," "power should be taken to keep these children in institutions while the parents are detained in a detention colony."[2]

Again, it is useless, and may be even harmful, to spend money on educating children so ill-nourished that they cannot learn and merely exhaust their nervous system in trying to do so.[3] Underfed children must be provided with meals as well as with education, and, it need hardly be added, these meals must be regular and not spasmodically offered to different children twice or three times in a week. Probably the meals should be continued during the school holidays, for otherwise much of the benefit will be lost. In like manner, it is useless to spend money on educating children if, at the same time or immediately afterwards, they are permitted to engage in occupations which inquiry shows to be destructive of whatever benefit education might be expected to yield. There is reason to suppose that many of the forms of unskilled labour at present open to boys not merely fail to train, but positively untrain, their victims. In a report presented to the Royal Commission on the Poor Laws, Mr. Jackson well writes: "Mere skill of hand or eye is not everything. It is character and sense of responsibility which requires to be fostered, and not only morals, but grit, stamina, mental energy, steadiness, toughness of fibre, endurance, must be trained and developed." But these general qualities can ill withstand the conditions, if these are unalleviated, of many forms of unskilled boy-labour. Mr. Jackson reports the view that "the occupation of van-boys is very calculated to destroy industry," and

---

[1] *Royal Commission on the Poor Laws, Report*, p. 620.
[2] *Ibid.* p. 187.
[3] Cf. Bulkley, *The Feeding of School Children*, p. 179.

adds that " opinion is practically unanimous that street-selling is most demoralising to children. It is not so much a question of a skilled trade not being taught, as of work which is deteriorating absorbing the years of the boy's life when he most needs educative experience in the wider sense."[1] It is plain that, if investment in the children of the poor is to be truly fruitful, it must be accompanied by prohibition, or at all events by restriction, of the right of entry into these occupations.

Yet again, as with the sick, so too with the children, the care expended on them must be adequately prolonged. " It is not sufficient to send a child of fourteen to a situation which may prove unsuitable, and leave it there to look after itself."[2] In short, stupidly organised investments in children's capacities—like other stupidly organised investments—will yield little return ; but well organised investments, and, more especially, investments adjusted in amount to the natural abilities of the various children affected, hold out large promise. Nor is this promise exhausted when account has been taken of the effect produced on *average* children. Among the great number of working-class families there are sure to be born from time to time children of exceptional power. Investment in the education of children generally should be credited with the effect it produces in these children. This point and the implications of it are put with great force by Dr. Marshall in the following passage: " There is no extravagance more prejudicial to the growth of national wealth than the wasteful negligence which allows genius that happens to be born of lowly parentage to expend itself in lowly work. No change would conduce so much to a rapid increase of national wealth as an improvement in our schools, and especially those of the middle grade, provided it be combined with an extensive system of scholarships, which will enable the clever son of a working man to rise gradually from school to school till he has the best theoretical and practical education which the age can give."[3]

[1] *Royal Commission on the Poor Laws,* Appendix, vol. xx. pp. 23-7.

[2] *Royal Commission on the Poor Laws, Report,* p. 188.

[3] Marshall, *Principles of Economics,* p. 213. Furthermore, it should be noticed that such a policy will react to the advantage even of those members of

§ 8. Up to this point we have been considering transferences made in selected forms and to selected groups among the poor; and we have seen that for such transferences there are "openings," in which the return probably obtainable is very much superior to that offered by investment in machines. It follows that the fact of these transferences, when they are managed by competent persons, is practically certain to benefit the national dividend. The effect of transferences made in a general way, in the form of command over purchasing power, cannot be determined so easily. The main difficulty is that many poor persons are unable, through lack of knowledge, to invest resources in themselves or their children in the best way. Thus, in a recent report of the Board of Education, we read: "A large proportion of the badly nourished children suffer from unsuitable food rather than from lack of food. It is probably no exaggeration to say that the improvement, which could be effected in the physique of elementary school children in the poorer parts of our large towns, if their parents could be taught or persuaded to spend the same amount of money as they now spend on their children's food in a more enlightened and suitable manner, is greater than any improvement which could be effected by feeding them intermittently at the cost of the rates."[1] In like manner, Mrs. Bosanquet notes that some two-ninths, out of Rowntree's three-ninths, of poverty is "secondary" poverty. She writes: "The weight of the problem rests with the ignorance and carelessness of parents, who do not lack the means to do better; and this view is further enforced by the large amount of evidence that most of the malnutrition is due to misdirected feeding rather than underfeeding."[2] To charge the whole body of the poorer classes with ignorance and lack of capacity for management would, indeed, be to utter a gross libel. A sharp distinction must be drawn between poor

---

the manual working class who are not directly touched by the improved educational opportunities; for it will both increase the demand for their services, by increasing the number of persons capable of acting as business managers, and also diminish the supply of their services by withdrawing these men from among them.

[1] [Cd. 5131] p. 5.
[2] "Physical Degeneration and the Poverty Line," *Contemporary Review*, Jan. 1904, p. 72.

families whose income, though small, is fairly regular, and poor families where the fathers are in casual and intermittent employment. Families of the latter class, disorganised in their mental habit no less than in their homes, never knowing from day to day or week to week what their income will be, *cannot* arrange their expenditure well. But families of the former class are in a position, if they choose, to build up a fairly definite standard of life. Among them there are many whose spending is even now arranged with extraordinary competence and wisdom; and, if they were better off, so that the wife was less burdened with work and worry, it may be supposed that their present high standard would be still further raised. Still, though, as against some members of the poorer classes, the charge of incapable management is ridiculous, as against many members it is undoubtedly true. Nor from the nature of things could it be otherwise. The art of spending money, not merely among the poor, but among all classes, is very much less developed than the art of making it.[1] The investments which people make in industry are usually made with the help of specialists, who are in competition with one another and among whom bad judgement ultimately means elimination; but the investments which people make in their own efficiency are conducted by themselves—that is to say, by persons who are not specialists, acting in circumstances where the selective influence of competition is excluded. This distinction can be brought out by an illustration drawn from within the business sphere itself. Those entrepreneurs, who produce goods for the market, are subject, in general, to keen competition among themselves. The result is that the stupid and ignorant tend to be extruded, and those only continue to act as entrepreneurs, who approach fairly closely to the average level of intelligence among their class. In occupations where commodities are produced, not for sale in the market, but for domestic consumption, and where, therefore, the competitive struggle is relaxed, the standard of competence tends, other things being equal, to be lowered. This point is well illustrated by the history of the English textile industries. Wool and linen, at the time of the industrial revolution, were

[1] Cf. *ante*, Part III. Chapter IX. § 2.

associated with the ordinary routine of peasant life, but the treatment of cotton was not so associated. "Everywhere a professional employment, not a by-product, those who followed it did so for gain."[1] The result was that improvements developed and spread much more rapidly in cotton manufacture than in the other textiles. It is plain that the conditions under which the art of spending money is conducted are on a par with those prevailing in domestic, and not with those prevailing in professional, employments. It follows that the main stimulus making for competence and the power of wise choice between different ways of using resources is lacking. Thus, Professor Mitchell writes: "The limitations of the family life effectually debar us from making full use of our domestic brains. The trained intelligence and the conquering capacity of the highly efficient housewife cannot be applied to the congenial task of setting to rights the disordered households of her inefficient neighbours. These neighbours, and even the husbands of these neighbours, are prone to regard critical commentaries upon their slack methods, however pertinent and constructive in character, as meddlesome interferences. And the woman with a consuming passion for good management cannot compel her less progressive sisters to adopt her system against their wills, as an enterprising advertiser may whip his reluctant rivals into line. For the masterful housewife cannot win away the husbands of slack managers, as the masterful merchant can win away the customers of the less able. What ability in spending money is developed among scattered individuals we dam up within the walls of the single household."[2] The inevitable consequence is that among all classes, and among the poor along with the others, there is a very great amount of ignorance concerning the comparative (marginal) advantages of different ways of spending money. Consequently, it is idle to expect that resources transferred to poor persons in the form of general purchasing power will be employed by them exclusively in the openings that are likely to yield the largest return of efficiency.

---

[1] Cf. Clapham, *Cambridge Modern History*, vol. x. p. 753.
[2] "The Backward Art of Spending Money," *American Economic Review*, No. 2, p. 274.

When the mistakes made are very grave, the national dividend may gain less from the improvements wrought in the efficiency of the poor than it loses by the withdrawal from ordinary investment of that part of the transferred resources, which, if they had not been transferred, would have been invested in industry. There is a danger that resources transferred to poor persons, in the form of command over purchasing power, will, from the point of view of the national dividend, be wasted. The Royal Commission on the Poor Laws complain, for example, that out-relief, as administered in many parts of the United Kingdom, serves merely " to perpetuate social and moral conditions of the worst type." [1] Many Boards of Guardians take no measures to ascertain what recipients do with the relief granted to them.[2] " With significant exceptions, Boards of Guardians give these doles and allowances without requiring in return for them even the most elementary conditions. . . . We have seen homes thus maintained out of the public funds in a state of indescribable filth and neglect, the abodes of habitual intemperance and disorderly living." [3]

§ 9. The practical inference from this discussion is that transferences to the poor, made in the form of command over purchasing power, have a much better chance of benefiting the national dividend if they are associated with some degree of oversight over the persons to whom the transferences are made. This oversight, and whatever control it may be necessary to couple with it, must, of course, be very carefully guarded. It should be based on a full recognition of the fact that people are not machines, and that their industrial—not to speak of their human—efficiency is a function of their moral, as well as of their material, surroundings. If the arrangements are such that persons hitherto respectable are compelled, for any considerable time, to associate with vagabonds and ne'er-do-weels, their industrial character is endangered. If, on the other hand, the gift of material aid is accompanied by the interest, sympathy and counsel of friends, willingness to work and save may be largely and permanently encouraged. Out of a full experience Canon

---

[1] *Royal Commission on the Poor Laws, Majority Report*, p. 102.
[2] *Ibid.* p. 267.
[3] *Ibid., Minority Report*, p. 750.

3 E

Barnett wrote: "Many have been the schemes of reform I have known, but, out of eleven years' experience, I would say that none touches the root of the evil *which does not bring helper and helped into friendly relations.*"[1] A system of administration, in which, as in the Elberfeld and Bergen plans—copied in essentials by the voluntary Guilds of Help now growing up in many English towns[2]—the elements of personal care are largely utilised, is, thus, likely to prove, even from a purely monetary point of view, a better investment than one dependent on mechanical rules. This consideration emphasises the great importance of associating voluntary effort with the official machinery of State aid to the poor.

[1] *Practicable Socialism,* p. 104.

[2] Cf. Mr. Snowden's *Report of the Local Government Board on Guilds of Help* [Cd. 5664].

CHAPTER XII

A NATIONAL MINIMUM STANDARD OF REAL INCOME

§ 1. WHEN we desire to determine whether the fact, *plus* the expectation of the fact, of any given annual transference of resources from the relatively rich to the relatively poor is likely to increase the national dividend, all the various considerations set out in the preceding chapters must be taken into account together. There can be little doubt but that plans could be devised, which would enable transferences, involving a very large amount of resources, to be made with results advantageous to production. Since the generality of these transferences will also increase the real incomes of the relatively poor, they must redound to the advantage of economic welfare in a wholly unambiguous way. Transferences which diminish the national dividend, on the other hand, are liable, through various reactions which have been indicated in the course of this discussion, to diminish the real earnings of the relatively poor; and, if their amount is kept constant, they may do this to so great an extent that the earnings of the relatively poor *plus* the transference made to them will *ultimately* be less than their earnings alone would have been, had no annual transference been made. When this happens, these transferences also affect economic welfare in an unambiguous way: this time by injuring it. There remains, however, one further sort of transference, the results of which cannot be unambiguous. I refer to a system of transferences, varied from year to year in such a way as to compensate for any reduction that may come about in that part of the income of the poor which accrues to them through earnings. An arrangement of this sort is implicitly introduced, whenever a government establishes a minimum standard of real income, below which it refuses to allow any citizen in any circumstances to fall. For the establishment of such a minimum standard, implying, as it does, transferences to the poor of a kind that differentiate in favour of poverty, is likely to diminish the national dividend, while it will, at the same time, for an indefinitely long period, increase the aggregate real income of the poor. To determine the effect, which the establishment of this kind of minimum standard is likely to exercise upon economic welfare, involves, therefore, a balancing of conflicting considerations.

§ 2. Before this balancing is attempted, it is desirable to obtain a clear notion of what precisely the minimum standard should be taken to signify. It must be conceived, not as a subjective minimum of satisfaction, but as an objective minimum of conditions. The conditions, too, must be conditions, not in respect of one aspect of life only, but in general. Thus, the minimum includes some defined quantity and quality of house accommodation, of medical care, of education, of food, of leisure, of the apparatus of sanitary convenience and safety where work is carried on, and so on. Furthermore, the minimum is absolute. If a citizen can afford to attain to it in all departments, the State cares nothing that he would prefer to fail in one. It will not allow him, for example, to save money for a carouse at the cost of living in a room unfit for human habitation. There is, indeed, some danger in this policy. It is a very delicate matter for the State to determine authoritatively in what way poor people shall distribute scanty resources among various competing needs. The temperaments and circumstances of different individuals differ so greatly that rigid rules are bound to be unsatisfactory. Thus, Dr. Bowley writes: "The opinion is quite tenable that the poor are forced (by the effect of the law to enforce a minimum quality and quantity of housing accommodation) to pay for a standard of housing higher than they obtain in food, and that they would make more of their income if they were worse housed and better fed."[1] This danger must be recognised; but the public spirit of the time demands also that it shall be faced. A man must not

---

[1] *The Measurement of Social Phenomena*, p. 173.

be permitted to fall below the minimum in one department in order that he may rise above it in others. Again, if a citizen cannot afford to attain the minimum in all departments, but, by failing in one, can remain independent, that does not justify the State in standing aside. The State must not permit anywhere hours of child labour or woman labour above the minimum, or the acceptance of house accommodation below the minimum, on the ground that, by resort to them, some given family could, and, without resort to them, it could not, support itself; for, if that is the fact, the family ought not to be required to support itself. There is no defence for the policy of "giving poor widows and incapable fathers permission to keep their children out of school and take their earnings."[1] Rather, the Committee on the Employment of Children Act are wholly right when they declare: "We feel, moreover, that the cases of widows and others, who are now too often economically dependent on child labour, should be met, no longer by the sacrifice of the future to the present, but, rather, by more scientific, and possibly by more generous, methods of public assistance."[2] The same type of reasoning applies, with even greater force, to the common plea that women should be allowed to work in factories shortly before and shortly after confinement, because, if they are not allowed to do this, they and their children alike will suffer shocking poverty. In these circumstances it is the duty of the State, not to remit the law, but to defend those affected by it from this evil consequence.

§ 3. There is general agreement among practical philanthropists that *some* minimum standard of conditions ought to be set up at a level high enough to make impossible the occurrence to anybody of extreme want; and that whatever transference of resources from relatively rich to relatively poor persons is necessary to secure this must be made, without reference to possible injurious consequences upon the magnitude of the dividend.[3] This policy of practical philanthropists

---

[1] Cf. Henderson, *Industrial Insurance in the United States*, p. 301.

[2] *Report*, p. 15.

[3] It is sometimes suggested that those very improvements in the efficiency of labour, which have been discussed in previous parts of this book, are calculated to push some men below the minimum standard. It is true, as a

is justified by analysis, in the sense that it can be shown to be conducive to economic welfare on the whole, if we believe the misery that results to individuals from extreme want to be indefinitely large; for, then, the good of abolishing extreme want is not commensurable with any evils that may follow should a diminution of the dividend take place. Up to this point, therefore, there is no difficulty. But our discussion cannot stop at this point. It is necessary to ask, not merely whether economic welfare will be promoted by the establishment of *any* minimum standard, but also by *what* minimum standard it will be promoted most effectively. Now, above the level of extreme want, it is generally admitted that increments of income involve finite increments of satisfaction. Hence, the direct good of transference and the indirect evil resulting from a diminished dividend are both finite quantities; and the correct formal answer to our question is that economic welfare is best promoted by a minimum standard raised to such a level that the direct good resulting from the transference of the marginal pound, which is transferred to the poor, just balances the indirect evil brought about by the consequent reduction of the dividend.

§ 4. To derive from this formal answer a quantitative estimate of what the minimum standard of real income established in any particular country at any particular time ought to be, it would be necessary to obtain and to analyse a mass of detailed information, much of which is not, in present circumstances, accessible to students. One practical conclusion can, however, be safely drawn. This is that, other things being equal, the minimum can be advantageously set higher, the larger is the real income per head of the community. The reason, of course, is that every increase in average income implies a diminution in the number of people unable by their own efforts to attain to any given minimum standard; and, therefore, a diminution, both absolute and

---

point of analysis, that increased efficiency of labour is, in effect, equivalent to an addition to its supply, and, therefore, involves a slight reduction in the real wage of a labour unit of given quality. In view, however, of the elastic character of the demand for labour in general, the number of the unimproved men whom this change would push over the line of self-support would almost certainly be very small.

proportionate, in the share of the dividend which an external guarantee of that standard threatens to bring about. It follows that, when we have to do with a group of pioneer workers in rough and adverse natural circumstances, the minimum standard may rightly be set at a low level. But, as inventions and discoveries progress, as capital is accumulated and nature subdued, it should be correspondingly raised. Thus, it is reasonable that, while a relatively poor country makes only a low provision for its "destitute" citizens, a relatively rich country should make a somewhat better provision for all who are "necessitous."[1]

§ 5. In this connection it is important that there should be no confusion as to what is meant by a rich country. For the present purpose country means, not Government, but people. There is a widespread impression that a nation's duty to make provision for its poorer citizens depends upon the amount of money that the Government has to provide for other purposes; and from this it is inferred that the great increase in the British Budget required to meet the annual charges on the war debt justifies, and indeed commands, large retrenchments in social expenditure. As the later chapters of Part IV. have already implicitly argued, this idea is, in great measure, illusory. It is true, of course, that the indirect effect in checking production of the expectation (as distinguished from the fact) of continuous taxation sufficient to yield 800 millions a year, is a good deal greater than that of the expectation of taxes yielding 200 millions. But no part of the real income of the country is directly *used up* when interest is paid to domestic holders of Government securities. Resources are merely transferred from one group of citizens to another. No doubt, when a nation has to provide funds for a large internal debt in consequence of a war, this is a *sign* that resources have been expended on war that might have been expended on building up capital equipment and so making the real income larger. It must not be forgotten, however, that a large part of the resources, that were lent, for example, to the British Government by its citizens in the great war, was not withdrawn

[1] This is the term employed by the Majority Commissioners of the 1909 Report on the Poor Laws.

from what would have been real capital, but was the result of
economies in consumption and special activities in production,
which, but for the war, would not have taken place.   Even,
therefore, as a sign of a country's capacity to give help to
its poor the magnitude of an internal war debt is of little
use.   The true test of this capacity is the direct one—aggregate real income compared with population.   It is, indeed,
proper to subtract from this the resources which are necessarily used up in unproductive ways.   Thus, when a country
is so situated that it has to devote an exceptionally large
proportion of its real income to the upkeep of powerful
armaments, or to the payment of interest to foreigners
who, in the past, have lent money to its Government, or
to machinery for preserving internal order, account must
be taken of these things.   As a rule, however, they are
relatively unimportant.   The amount of the aggregate real
income in relation to the number of the population is the
dominant relevant fact.

§ 6. For the United Kingdom the best available estimate
gives an aggregate national income, for 1913–14, represented
at then prices by some 2250 million pounds.   Deducting
some 250 millions for rates and taxes and some 230 millions
for new investments, we have left a sum sufficient, if it could
have been divided up equally without being diminished in the
process, to yield an income of £162 to each representative
family of $4\frac{1}{2}$ persons.[1]   Of course, as a matter of fact, it would
have been quite impossible to pool the national income in this
way without a large part of the flow of goods and services,
which this money figure represents, disappearing altogether.
Apart from great improvements in productive organisation,
which may, perhaps, be hoped for, but certainly cannot be predicted with confidence, there is no reason to expect that the
real income per head of the country—we need not trouble about
its swollen reflex in the glass of money—will be substantially
greater in the near future than it was in 1913–14.   In view of
these facts it is plain that, wealthy as this country is, as compared both with itself in the past and with most of its neighbours in the present, it is not wealthy in an absolute sense.   As

[1] Cf. Bowley, *The Division of the Product of Industry*, pp. 20 *et seq.*

things are, it is literally impossible for it, by any manipulation of distribution, to provide for all its citizens a really high standard of living. In so far, therefore, as social reformers rely upon improvements in the distribution of wealth, as distinguished from improvements in production, they are bound to chasten their hopes. The national minimum may rightly be set now much higher than it could have been set a hundred or fifty years ago. But, with the *national average* no larger than it is, it is inevitable that the *national minimum* must still be set at a deplorably low level.

§ 7. So far nothing has been said of the common view that, in determining the minimum standard which it will establish for itself, a country must have regard to the policy of other countries, because, if it moves too far ahead of its rivals, it will be beaten by them in the economic battle. This view has now to be examined. It is obvious that, if an injurious but cheap process, such as the use of white phosphorus in match-making, is forbidden in this country but is permitted in other countries which compete with us in our home market, the British industry affected by the prohibition will have less work to do. But the common inference that the country as a whole will have less work to do is not warranted, because, since imports are necessarily paid for by exports, an increase in one sort of import involves either a diminution in other sorts of import, which relieves the competitive pressure on other British trades, or a corresponding increase in British exports, which are, of course, produced by British trades. For the same reason the common view that the abolition in England alone of socially undesirable methods common to many industries, such as the night work of women, the use of unfenced machinery, or the building of factories without proper sanitary arrangements, would lead to a reduction, through foreign competition, of opportunities for employment here is illusory. It does not, however, follow from this that it is impossible for a country to be injured, however far it moves ahead of other countries in establishing minimum standards desirable from a general point of view, but not productive of economic efficiency. For, if a handicap is imposed on productive methods in one country only, there

will be a tendency for employing power, capital and labour to
leave that country.   If all leave in equal proportions, the general
scale of the country's industry will be correspondingly reduced,
the rate of pay per unit of every factor remaining much as
. before.   The national dividend need not fall as much as
production falls, because capitalists may still live and receive
income here while employing their capital elsewhere. ׀ Since,
in fact, capital—at all events if we suppose the obstacle of
double income-tax to be done away with by international and
intra-imperial agreement—is more mobile than labour, the
presumption is that capital will leave in a somewhat larger
proportion, and that, therefore, the earnings per head of workpeople will fall.   In whatever way the detail of the movement
is worked out, it is plain that economic welfare in
the country affected is likely to be lessened.   The injury
thus inflicted on it cannot, it should be observed, be prevented by setting up a tariff against imports from countries
where labour legislation is less advanced.   On the contrary,
such a tariff, by interfering with the normal distribution of
the country's resources among different occupations, would, in
general, make the national dividend smaller, and the injury,
therefore, worse.   If, however, the handicap of these high
minima is extended to all important countries by international labour legislation, the danger that our capital will
be driven abroad is removed—at the cost of some slight
damage to us in the terms on which our goods exchange
against foreign goods.

§ 8. From these considerations it appears that the extension by international labour legislation of regulations, which
are both desirable in themselves and also a real handicap to
industry, is likely, though in a way quite different from that
commonly supposed, to lessen the burden which these regulations would inflict on any country accepting them in isolation.
To this extent it will, therefore, really be easier for a country
to rule out injurious methods and processes, if it can persuade
other nations to move forward in company with it. Moreover,
when the injurious methods specially affect particular industries, an international agreement will really make it easier for
the persons engaged in those industries to accept a veto upon

injurious methods; and it will almost always be thought to make this easier both for those persons and for the community regarded as a whole. Hence, the development of machinery for international labour legislation may be expected to accomplish something solid in speeding up improvements in industrial conditions. The advantage to be looked for is the greater in that many improvements in method, which are not really handicaps at all, but, through their effect on efficiency, net benefits, are, nevertheless, popularly believed to be handicaps, and are, therefore, unlikely to be adopted by cautious statesmen without some outside stimulus. International negotiation may often furnish such a stimulus and give strength to reformers in a country where the social movement is slack or the power of vested interests strong. There can be little doubt, for example, that the Franco-Italian treaty of 1906 led indirectly to a general improvement in Italian practice in the supervision and enforcement of labour laws. At the same time it would be a mistake to expect from the lever of internationalism more than it has power to give. Inevitably, international minima, if they are to secure general or wide assent, must lag behind the practice of the most advanced nations. It would be disastrous if a custom should grow up of regarding these international minima as national maxima; for that would check the forward movement of pioneer nations, and so indirectly of the whole world. Just as a "good" employer, while welcoming the factory acts, will keep his own practice well in advance of the legal standards, so also a "good" nation will always maintain national laws more ambitious than those which at the time have international sanction.

§ 9. One word should be added in conclusion. It was implied in the argument of Part I. Chapter IV. that, in view of the probable reaction of improved fortunes upon the standard of living, the establishment of a reasonable minimum standard would not lead to any significant increase of births. We cannot, however, conclude with equal confidence that, if adopted in one country alone, it would not lead to a considerable increase in the numbers of the population through the immigration of relatively inefficient poor persons attracted by the prospect of State aid. If it did lead to this,

the new immigrants would consume more than they contributed to the dividend; and, as their numbers grew, the
portion of this dividend available for distribution among the
native-born citizens of the country concerned would, other
things being equal, continually and rapidly diminish. It is,
therefore, to the advantage of a State, which has established
a minimum standard above that enjoyed by its neighbours, to
forbid the immigration of persons who seem unlikely to attain
this minimum without help from the public funds. To this
end idiots, feeble-minded persons, cripples, beggars and
vagrants, or persons over or under a certain age may be
excluded, unless they are either accompanied by relatives able
to support them, or themselves possess an adequate income
derived from investments.[1] But it is exceedingly difficult to
devise machinery which shall be effective in excluding all
" undesirable " immigrants without at the same time excluding
some that are " desirable."

[1] For a summary of a number of laws on this matter, cf. Grünzel, *Economic
Protectionism*, p. 281 *et seq.*

PART VI

THE VARIABILITY OF THE NATIONAL DIVIDEND

CHAPTER I

THE ECONOMIC RHYTHM

§ 1. If anyone were asked to characterise the economic life of a modern community, he would probably answer that there is a general trend towards increased production, both in the aggregate and per head of the population. This, associated as it is with mechanical inventions and the growth of capital, is observable throughout the greater part of the civilised world. But, he would add, the upward trend is not a continuous and steady movement. Rather, progress takes place by a succession of jumps or spurts, periods of rapid increase being followed by periods of stagnation or even of decline; so that, if we were to represent the movement pictorially, our diagram would not show a straight line gradually sloping upwards, but a wavy, oscillating course with a general upward tendency. This is what is seen, and the interpretation of it is plain. The *income-getting power* of any community consists of its people, its machinery and its organisation. This expands with every expansion in adult population, mechanical equipment and industrial intelligence. But the changes in the volume of the community's *income-getting power* are not the only, or, indeed, the dominant factor in the oscillating movement. Superimposed upon them are variations in *the extent to which the income-getting power of the community is actually engaged in work*. Changes in the volume of income-getting power are like movements of the tide; they alone signify from a long-period general view. Changes in the proportion of the volume actually at work are like movements of the waves; they are of principal interest to students of short period effects. The interplay of the two together has an important practical consequence, which it is the business of the following paragraphs to display.

§ 2. But, before this task is attempted, it is well to observe that the volume of income-getting power actually set to work varies considerably less than it appears to do at first sight. The reason is that a diminution in the quantity of activity is often correlated with an increase in its *intensity*. In periods of depression the amount of *intelligence* put into production is, in general, larger, partly because relatively inefficient business men are compelled to sell out to others, but mainly because those persons who remain in business "are put on their mettle, and exert themselves to their utmost to invent improved methods and to avail themselves of the improvements made by others."[1] In like manner, workpeople, since they are earning less, are likely, if on piece-wages, to work harder and more intelligently. Thus, in coal-mining, the late Lord Rhondda has shown: "The better off men were, and the more easily they could obtain the means of subsistence, the less energy they put forward; there was a very considerable diminution in the output per man per annum. On the other hand, when prices fell and wages followed, the fact that the men worked harder accentuated the depression which followed from the number of mines opened during the period of boom."[2] These considerations must, of course, be borne in mind throughout the discussion which follows.

§ 3. When the contraction or expansion in the volume of income-getting power at work is given, it is, of course, not to be expected that the contraction or expansion in the aggregate product will be proportionate to this. Since machinery

---

[1] Marshall, Evidence before the Gold and Silver Commission [Cd. 5512], Q. 9816. Cf. Aftalion, *Les Crises périodiques de surproduction*, vol. i. p. 230.

[2] *Statistical Journal*, January 1914, p. 174. Cf. Mitchell, *Business Cycles*, p. 478. It should be remembered that output per man is not, in these circumstances, at all an adequate test of energy, since in good times inferior men will be added to the normal staff, and, after a point, many firms will be working beyond the output yielding maximum efficiency, and so under conditions of diminishing returns, the workmen having to work with too little machine power per workman. M. Aftalion quotes statistics to show that in coal mines, iron mines and blast furnaces, output per head is less in times of prosperity than in times of depression (vol. i. p. 195).

is not, in general, hired for wages, but is owned by the controllers of businesses, a contraction in the use of income-getting power takes the form principally of a reduction in the quantity of labour employed. But the relation between a decrease or increase in labour power and a decrease or increase in production depends on how far the firms affected are working on a scale corresponding to their maximum efficiency. If we start at a point of great depression, it may well be that the change in output would be proportionate to the change in labour power; but, if we start from a point of considerable expansion, when the normal firm is already employing more men than are really appropriate to its plant, the change in output would be much less than proportionate. A "critical point is reached in the affairs of any enterprise when it has already secured sufficient orders to keep busy its standard equipment and its regular staff of employees. To execute additional orders then requires overtime-work, the hiring of new and presumably less efficient hands, the starting of old-fashioned machines, the installation of new equipment, or some similar change."[1] These considerations are important. None the less, when the volume of income-getting power is given, variations in the extent to which it is set to work are, in general, correlated with variations *in the same direction*—though of smaller magnitude—in the aggregate volume of production.

§ 4. But this conclusion does not exhaust the facts. Carrying our survey further, we notice that the industries of a modern community fall roughly into two groups, industries—or professions—which serve the needs of consumption directly, and industries which serve these needs indirectly by the manufacture of instruments of production. It is not, of course, possible to make this distinction perfectly rigid and clear-cut. The building industry, for example, builds both dwelling-houses, which serve consumption directly, and factories, which are instrumental goods. But, blurred at the edges as it may often be, the distinction is still real. Any community's resources are devoted in part to making consumers' goods and in part to making producers' goods.

[1] Cf. Mitchell, *Business Cycles*, p. 458.

3 F

Furthermore, these two groups of industries behave in different ways. In the periods of spurt, both sorts expand, but the instrumental industries expand much more largely than the others. In the periods of decline that follow each period of spurt, the instrumental industries greatly contract their product, but the product of the consumers' industries merely ceases to expand. Thus, a diagram showing the output of the instrumental industries would be a curve with large rises and large falls, while one showing the output of consumers' industries would consist of rises interspersed with horizontal movements, like the outline of a flight of stairs. Evidence for this statement is afforded by railway statistics, which indicate general expansion in boom periods, but hardly any contraction in periods of depression.[1] The statistics of coal consumption [2]—in this differing from the statistics of iron consumption—and the statistics of the quantities of foreign trade are of like character. There may, indeed, be a momentary contraction due to shock in some crises, such as that of 1870, but this will not generally last long.[3] M. Aftalion, summarising a considerable inquiry, writes : "Perhaps reductions in the manufacture of objects of consumption have taken place on the morrow of crises. Perhaps also the production of goods of this kind declines in those industries which are only slightly capitalistic and make use of hand-work and home-work. But, during a good part of the depression, for a number of industries making consumable goods, manufacture progresses rather than diminishes."[4]

§ 5. The explanation of these facts is that, in the actual world, we have not to do simply with variations in the extent to which income-getting power is employed, the volume of this income-getting power remaining constant, but with a complicated combination of these variations and of secondary induced variations in the volume of income-getting power itself. In a period of expanded activity many instruments of production are being made and other constructions are being built up. It is true that some of the extra activity is devoted

---

[1] Cf. Aftalion, *Les Crises périodiques de surproduction*, ii. p. 23.
[2] *Ibid.* ii. p. 157.   [3] *Ibid.* ii. p. 26.   [4] *Ibid.* pp. 174-5.

merely to the exploitation of mares' nests, and is thus, sheer waste; but there remains a great deal that really adds to the provision of instruments. It follows that, when activity declines, such activity as is employed in consumption industries finds itself assisted by a much larger supply of machinery and plant than before. During the earlier part of a depression the quantity of machinery is still being increased through the completion of machines ordered in the latter part of the preceding boom period; for, of course, it generally pays to complete machines on which a good deal of work has been done, even when it does not pay to make new ones from the start. The creation and development of railways in a boom period acts in the same way as the creation of machinery in facilitating the production of all forms of consumption goods in the succeeding period. In practice, the process of events is as follows. In a boom period the amount of labour at work expands, the expansion being large in constructional industries and *comparatively* small in others. In the succeeding period of depression the amount of labour at work contracts, the contraction being large in constructional industries and *comparatively* small in others. In the constructional industries the large contraction in the amount of labour at work is accompanied by a large contraction in the output of producers' goods. But in the consumption industries the extra machinery and plant provided in consequence of the preceding boom so far facilitates production that the comparatively small contraction in the amount of labour at work does not reduce output appreciably below what it was in the preceding boom period.[1] Hence, industrial fluctuations involve large movements, not in the consumption of the community as a whole, but in the demand for the services, and, therefore, in the real income of the labouring classes. In view, therefore, of the analysis of Part I. Chapter IV., it is plain that industrial fluctuations are likely, other things being equal, to prove very specially injurious to economic welfare.

---

[1] It should be noticed in this connection that the turning-point from increase to decrease in the aggregate *supply* of machinery occurs somewhat later than the turning-point in the annual output of new machinery; for the aggregate supply does not begin to fall until the annual output has fallen, not merely below what it was before, but below the rate of annual decay.

Some study of them is, therefore, essential to complete the general plan of this volume.

§ 6. If our interest were primarily historical, we should be compelled to investigate every single incident that might *prima facie* be thought responsible for disturbing in any way the surface of the industrial stream. The standpoint of my book, however, is not historical but analytic. It does not seek a detailed explanation of every expansion and contraction in industry and in the demand for labour that has occurred from time to time, but rather a general explanation of the main tendencies of the industrial movement. Now, the dominant characteristic of that movement during the last half century in this country is that it has taken place in a series of waves, rhythmical in character and closely similar in length. Since 1860 the intervals between successive years of minimum employment, as recorded by British Trade Unions making returns, were 7, 10, 7, 10, 7 and 7 years respectively; the intervals between successive maxima, 6, 11, 7, 7, 11 and 5 years respectively; the average length of periods of lessening employment being $2\frac{6}{6}$ years, and that of periods of improving employment $2\frac{1}{6}$ years. It is with this regular rhythmical movement that I am concerned here to deal. For that purpose the study of obviously sporadic events, such as wars, fashion-changes and gold-discoveries, can only be of secondary interest.[1] There are only two sorts of causes in which we can reasonably hope that the real explanation may be found. First, there are causes, which, there is reason to believe, themselves recur with a periodicity corresponding in some degree

[1] To avoid misunderstanding it should perhaps be added that the only sort of fashion-change that could, in any case, cause an alteration in the general demand for labour would be what one may call a "net" fashion-change, that is to say, something more than the mere substitution of one taste for another. Mr. Robertson argues that in practice fashion-changes come to very little as causes of industrial fluctuations, and, in support of this view, points out, first, that even in France, the great luxury-producing country, only $\frac{1}{110}$th part of the normal production is subject to the influence of fashion; and, secondly, that France, though the chief maker of fashion-goods, is less subject to general industrial fluctuations than other countries, in which fashion-goods play a smaller part (*A Study of Industrial Fluctuation*, p. 72). In contrast to this type of movement we may set the enormous net change of taste that occurs on the outbreak of a war, when the demand for soldiering and munitions represents, in great part, not merely a transference, but an addition to the aggregate demand of the community for effort in general.

with the periodicity of the general industrial movement. Secondly, there are causes the occurrence of which may be sporadic, but which, once they have come into play, do not exhaust themselves in a single act, but start wave movements of a periodicity similar to that which our records display. In the following chapters we shall have occasion to consider causes belonging to each of these two types.

CHAPTER II

A FALSE SCENT

§ 1. BEFORE this task is seriously undertaken it will be well to notice two methods of approach which are plausible, but can be shown to lead to no result. The first of these is favoured by Mr. Hull in his interesting book on *Industrial Depressions.* Mr. Hull maintains that the "causes of booms and depressions must lie within the industries—by which he means the constructional industries—where great increases and decreases in the volume of business can and do take place." [1] The fact that the greatest fluctuations occur in this type of industry is easily established alike by indirect and by direct evidence. First, as M. Aftalion points out, England, the earliest seat of capitalistic industry, was also the first country to experience commercial crises, and these have spread to other countries as capitalistic industry has spread to them. [2] Moreover, Mr. Hull finds a remarkable correspondence between the rank of ten nations in the production of iron, which may be taken as a rough index of industrial development, and their rank in the severity of industrial depressions. [3] Secondly, there is direct contemporary evidence that the variations in the quantity, and, still more markedly, in the value, of output, which occur in works of construction, are much larger than those which occur elsewhere. [4] The exceedingly large cyclical fluctuations of employment in engineering and shipbuilding in this country afford further evidence of this. Concerning

---

[1] *Industrial Depressions*, p. 100.
[2] Cf. Aftalion, *Les Crises périodiques de surproduction*, ii. p. 190.
[3] Cf. *Industrial Depressions*, p. 83.
[4] *Ibid.* p. 82.

the fact, then, there need be no ·dispute. Does the fact warrant the inference that the source and cause of industrial fluctuations lies within the constructional industries?

§ 2. A definite answer can be given to this question. Instrumental goods in general, unlike the main body of consumable goods, are goods that are not destroyed by the process of being used. Therefore there is always in existence a much larger stock of them relatively to the annual output than there is of consumable goods generally. Hence, if it is decided to increase the production of cotton goods by 20 per cent in conditions such that, in order to do this, the supply of cotton machinery has to be increased by 10 per cent, the 10 per cent increase in the *supply* of cotton machinery will involve a very much larger increase, perhaps an increase of 80 per cent or 100 per cent, in the *new production* of that machinery. In like manner, when the demand for the services of houses, ships or rolling-stock increases or decreases by a given percentage, the demand for the production of *new* ships, houses, or rolling-stock necessarily changes in a much larger proportion. Thus, there is, *prima facie,* reason to expect that a given boom in the production of consumable goods will involve a larger (percentage) boom in the production of constructional goods. Nor is this all. For, if the boom of primary demand subsequently disappears and the old level is resumed, the reduced derived demand for instruments will find itself confronted with an increase in the supply—an increase whose magnitude varies directly with the average intensity, multiplied by the length, of the preceding boom period.[1] This, of course, means that the slump in the demand for the new production of instruments will be reinforced and augmented. Even, therefore, if the whole source of an upward movement were an increased demand for consumption goods, it would necessarily happen that credits are "transformed from liquid capital into fixed capital and investments,"[2] and that "the proportion which the capital devoted to permanent and remote investment bears to that which is but temporarily invested soon to reproduce itself"[3]

---

[1] Cf. Babson, *Business Barometers*, p. 96.
[2] *Lessons of the Financial Crisis*, p. 30.
[3] Jevons, *Investigations in Currency and Finance*, p. 28.

is increased.   Wherever, in short, the causes, of booms or
depressions originate, the fluctuations of demand that are
associated with them, would be abnormally large in the industries making fixed capital.   The fact, therefore, that they *are*
abnormally large is no evidence that these causes originate
within these constructional industries.

CHAPTER III

§ 1. THERE is a second false scent. The way in which varia-tions in industrial activity and the real demand for labour come about is sometimes explained as follows. Unused savings, it is said, are gradually accumulated, and, as soon as they are massed in sufficient quantities, are thrown forward into industry. Munitions are, as it were, built up during several years of trench warfare and then discharged in a great attack, and this attack, in turn, is followed by another period of quiescence and accumulation. Thus, M. Tugan Baranowsky draws a parallel for industry from a steam engine. Capital—in the sense of unused savings—accumulates, he says, like steam behind a piston; when the pressure attains a certain in-tensity, it drives the piston forward, and exhausts itself in doing so; then a new accumulation takes place, until the piston is again driven forward, and so on continually.[1] In like manner, M. Lescure writes: " There are periods when savings are employed in creating new means of production, others when they flow to the banks or the Stock Exchange to be employed in pur-chasing Government bonds or securities bearing fixed interest, or simply to slumber in the form of deposits."[2] Discussing this idea in detail, he adds: " The category of production which will first be vivified by the outflow of savings towards industry will evidently be that of the means of production. Of what means of production ? That will depend. At the beginning of the nineteenth century it was the means for sewing and

[1] Cf. *Les Crises industrielles en Angleterre*, p. 273.
[2] *Des Crises générales et périodiques de surproduction*, p. 505.

spinning, in a word, all kinds of textile machinery; a little later it was the formidable apparatus of railways and railway material and of steel steamships to take the place of wooden sailing vessels; in our own day it is electrical energy and its manifold industrial applications, tramways, electric railways, electric furnaces, electric light, and so on. Manifold in their origin, savings have always as their final goal the satisfaction of new or more intense needs, and the satisfaction of these needs exacts the production of new means of production."[1] The central idea is that savings are made; that, instead of being turned at once into industry, they are stored up in the form of non-industrial capital; and that eventually, when the due moment comes, they are converted into industrial capital by means of a process that involves greatly expanded industrial activity.

§ 2. If we had to do with a single individual in primitive conditions, this explanation, though not probing very deep, would be satisfactory so far as it went. Accumulated savings not yet turned into industrial capital would consist, and would consist only, of stored up consumable goods. These things might be accumulated over any period that we choose. They would be turned into industrial capital when our imaginary individual had resort to them for sustenance, while devoting his labour, not to the production of consumables, but to the production of some durable instrument of production. The stored consumable goods in their natural state would be savings, or, in one sense, capital, but not productive capital. When, at the cost of consuming them, Robinson Crusoe created his canoe or his barn or his factory, they would have been *turned into* productive capital. This process of conversion might occur in jerks, while the process of preliminary accumulation was gradual. There is no difficulty about this conception. But it will be perceived that, according to it, *the aggregate amount of industrial effort* is not different in the periods of conversion from what it is in other periods. All that happens is that a given aggregate of effort is directed, at one time to the production of consumable goods, at another to that of instruments of production.

---

[1] *Des Crises générales et périodiques de surproduction,* p. 412.

§ 3. We may get nearer to reality by supposing that, alongside of Robinson Crusoe on his island, there exist a number of men, who normally produce—perhaps with a little help from Robinson's charity—enough to maintain themselves alive, but who ordinarily possess a good deal of unemployed labour power. As before, Robinson saves, in the sense of accumulating a mass of consumable goods. When he has been doing this for some years, it occurs to him to entice his neighbours' unused labour power into activity by the offer of some of his accumulated goods in return for the manufacture of certain productive instruments. If he does this, his savings are, as before, converted into productive capital. On this occasion, however, the conversion means, not that industrial effort has been diverted from making consumables to making instrumental goods, but that new industrial effort destined to the production of instrumental goods has been called into play. This is what we might suppose to happen in the actual world, so far as the real wages paid to workpeople, whose activity in instrumental trades is increased in times of boom, are drawn from goods piled up in shops and stores during the preceding period of quietness.

§ 4. If this account gave a true picture of the facts, the inference drawn in the theories of Lescure and Tugan Baranowsky would be largely justified. For, the larger the volume of consumable goods in store becomes, the more willing Robinson Crusoe—our representative of the controller of industry—will be to " convert " a given quantity of them into productive capital. The store is useful to him because it constitutes an insurance against disaster in the event of bad harvests or of a sudden need to pay off debts. Consequently, when the store is small, the expectation of profit, which will be needed to induce him to convert a given amount of it into productive capital, will be larger than it is when the store is large. Hence, an expansion in the store of savings would be a true cause of a boom in the amount of labour that is hired to make productive instruments; and the using up of the store of savings would be a true cause of a check to this boom. So soon as the accumulated savings of the past have been " used up " by conversion into fixed capital—railways and so on

—the boom must break. There is no free capital—unhypotheticated savings—left, with which to carry it on, and it, thereupon, comes to an end.

§ 5. I shall argue immediately that the foregoing analysis cannot be reconciled with the facts of real life, for the reason that in practice unused savings are not accumulated in periods of depression and are not used up in periods of boom. Before, however, a direct argument in this sense is attempted, it is necessary to draw attention to an important confusion of thought. Everybody admits that in times of depression many people accumulate *purchasing power* and pay it into the banks, where, owing to the general atmosphere of caution that, in those times, prevails, most of it tends to stagnate rather than to be lent out again to finance industrial and business ventures. The gap between the volume of purchasing power that the public is surrendering to the custody of banks and the volume that the banks are handing over to the use of the business community is, thus, much narrower than usual. The extent of the narrowing is sometimes believed to measure the accumulation that has been made of "unused savings." The fact that the gap is narrowed is, it is claimed, complete proof that unused savings *must* have been accumulated. This reasoning is incorrect. By accumulating unused purchasing power people have not automatically accumulated also unused savings of real things. What they have done by not spending their money has been to reduce prices in general below what they would otherwise have been, thus making the money of other people worth more goods than it would otherwise have been worth; and thus enabling these other people to buy more goods. What they have accumulated by this proceeding is, not things, but the power, when they choose later on to spend the money, to raise prices, reduce the purchasing power of other people's money, and absorb for themselves the goods which have in this way been rendered inaccessible to others. The accumulation is, thus, an accumulation of claims upon other people. It is not an accumulation of things, and does not imply any accumulation of things, or, in other words, any real savings, on the part of those who make it. The question whether there is in fact an accumulation of real things on the part of the community in general cannot, therefore, be answered by any direct appeal to monetary and banking changes. The question must be examined on its own merits.

§ 6. It is plain that, when a boom is on the point of breaking, and immediately after it has broken, a very great check to purchases of all kinds will take place. The large output that is coming from the factories will find the public demand suddenly and greatly contracted. It must necessarily, therefore, pile itself up in warehouses and shops, just as the water in a lake would pile itself up, if the outflow were suddenly choked, while the inflow for the moment remained unaltered. But this is only the first stage. The blocking up of the exit from the lake where products are stored leads immediately to a blocking up of the entrance also. As the Poor Law Commissioners write: "The shops, with unsold goods on their shelves and diminished takings in their tills, cannot give the usual orders to the merchants and manufacturers who supply them."[1] All this is plain and simple. But it does not by itself throw light on the question whether, during a period of depression, unused real savings go on accumulating till their volume is so great that they burst their way, as it were, into productive industry. If that version of the facts is true, it *must happen* that, throughout periods of depression, the exit from our lake continues to be blocked up more thoroughly than the entrance to it. Does this in fact happen? For an absolutely conclusive answer statistical evidence is at present lacking. But what evidence there is suggests that it does not happen. The truth appears to be, in Professor Mitchell's words, that, as a depression proceeds, " the accumulated stocks of goods carried over from the preceding period of prosperity are gradually disposed of. Even when current consumption is small, manufactories and merchants can reduce their stocks of raw materials and finished wares by filling orders chiefly from what is on hand and confining purchases to the small quantities needed to keep full assortments."[2] If this view is correct, the later part of the period of depres-

---

[1] *Report of the Royal Commission on the Poor Laws*, p. 331.

[2] *Business Cycles*, pp. 565-6.

sion is responsible, not only for no accumulation of stocks, but for an actual reduction in the stocks left over from the preceding period of boom. Consequently, the theory that unused savings go on accumulating till their growing pressure bursts the dam that holds them back from industry is directly disproved by facts.

§ 7. The preceding paragraph does, indeed, ignore one aspect of a community's life, namely its trade relations with other communities. If account is taken of this, our conclusion is somewhat modified. When there is a depression in one country, not merely absolutely, but also relatively to the rest of the world, the low prices that rule in that country cause imports of goods to diminish and exports of goods to increase. They, therefore, cause either an import of gold, or an increase in the country's credit holdings abroad, or both these things together. The extra gold and foreign credits constitute real accumulated savings. In effect British manufacturers and others have sold goods to foreigners and taken gold and credits, instead of goods, in exchange for them. The gold and credits are not, of course, themselves, either consumable goods or instrumental goods; but they constitute a power to purchase from foreigners either sort of goods, when their owners choose to make use of it. Thus, when account is taken of foreign trade, the "unused savings" that accumulate during depressions—when the depressions are peculiar to particular communities—are not wholly imaginary; but are represented by a growing power in the community as a whole to make effective claims upon foreign communities. This qualification to our general conclusion is, however, clearly of no significance from the standpoint of industrial fluctuations that are spread over the world in general, as, in fact, in greater or less degree, most large movements are. And, further, since the change in the holdings of gold and foreign credits is always small relatively to the whole volume of industrial activity, the qualification is only of secondary importance from the standpoint of movements confined to a single country. The things that chiefly matter are goods stored in warehouses and shops. Of these, as has already been observed, not only does no continuing accumulation take place during periods of depression, but the stocks that are left over at the end of the preceding booms, if the scanty evidence which is available may be trusted, are dissipated rather than increased.

§ 8. The result of this analysis is not doubtful. The passage from the end of a depression to the beginning of a boom may, if we will, be compared to the discharge of a piston, but the pressure behind the piston is no larger when the passage is being made than it is at any other time; on the contrary, the strongest pressure (in the sense of masses of unused savings) is present when the piston is beginning to *return* to its starting point. It is, therefore, plain that accumulation of unused savings cannot rightly be regarded even as a proximate cause of booms, or the using up of these unused savings as even a proximate cause of depressions. Nor is this all. For, even if it were established that accumulation and discharge of savings took place in the way that the theory under discussion supposes, we should still be very far from an "explanation" of industrial fluctuations. It would still be necessary to ask *why* savings are accumulated gradually and then suddenly discharged in bulk, instead of being utilised in production as and when they are made; and, *why* the periods of industrial depression and boom, which, on this theory, must coincide with the periods of accumulation and discharge, cover the intervals of time that they do cover rather than any other intervals. A theory that left these fundamental questions unanswered could not, in any event, be accepted as an "explanation."[1]

---

[1] The separation between changes in real capital and changes in the purchasing power of the business community, which has been stressed in this chapter, must not, of course, be treated as absolute. When purchasing power is given to the business community, whether by the creation of bank credits in their favour or in any other way, the primary effect is merely to *transfer* command over the productive power of the country. But, if the business community is more willing than those from whom the transference is, in effect, made, to cause that productive power to be exercised, a secondary effect is that more real capital is created. So far as this happens, the creation of bank credits in favour of business men is not, indeed, itself a creation of capital, but it is a proceeding by which the creation of capital is facilitated. It has, or may have, the same sort of effect as the transference of the command of an army from a lethargic to an active general. This consideration does not, however, affect the argument of the text.

CHAPTER IV

HARVEST VARIATIONS

§ 1. I now propose in three successive chapters to discuss certain causes which, it can be shown, would, if operating by themselves, produce some kind of more or less rhythmical industrial fluctuation. The question how far each or all of them "explain" the fluctuations that actually take place is left over for separate study in Chapter VII. Before that question can be attacked, each of these causes must first be examined in detail. The first of them, which Jevons long ago brought into strong light, consists in harvest variations.

§ 2. To facilitate our analysis of the way in which this cause works, we may conveniently regard agriculture and industry as separate productive groups, between which, for the short periods relevant to industrial fluctuations, mobility is practically excluded. This assumption is warranted by the fact that a harvest boom or slump is not a durable change, and that, therefore, if labour and capital are to be transferred between agriculture and industry, they would need to be instantly responsive. No readiness to respond to slow and continued pressure would suffice to constitute mobility from the present point of view. It is well known that extreme sensitiveness to monetary impulses towards movement is not to be found in the comparatively massive and slow-thinking agricultural community. Furthermore, the richest parts of the agricultural world are, under present conditions, physically somewhat distant from the richest parts of the industrial world. This circumstance necessarily obstructs quick movement of labour and capital. On this basis we have to inquire in what way a given variation in harvest-yield might be expected to react upon the volume of industrial activity generally.

§ 3. If the products of agriculture were instantly perishable, it would be impossible for any reaction to occur, except in so far as the variations in their yield could be foreseen; for, apart from this, no group of non-agriculturalists would have time to alter their own output with a view to the altered opportunities offered for the purchase of agricultural products. Since, however, agricultural products are not in fact instantly perishable but are capable of being stored, variations in their amount must react upon industrial activity, even though they are not foreseen in any degree. Thus, the feasibility of forecast does not affect the nature of the reactions produced upon industrial activity. But it does affect the interval of time after which they occur. Clearly, this must depend on the *extent* to which crop prospects are capable of being foreseen. If no foreknowledge were possible, no reaction could occur until the harvest had actually been reaped. In modern conditions, however, some considerable measure of foreknowledge is possible. In the United States reports on the prospects of the crops are issued monthly on the basis of widespread official inspection.[1] Mr. Brace finds a close relation between prices on the produce exchanges and visible supply. He adds: "Furthermore, it is seen that prices have a tendency to move sooner than the visible supply, thus indicating that the market leaders, from the reports of crops and acreage, together with other indications of prospective change in demand and supply, were able to predict what the visible supply would be, and, hence, to initiate a price movement before the demand and supply of the actual commodity were reflected in the visible supply."[2] Nor is this all. Means of forecast additional to those furnished by inspection of the standing crops have recently become available. Thus, Dr. Shaw has shown that in England the wheat crop in any year depends upon, and can, within close limits of error, be deduced from, the rainfall of the preceding autumn;[3] and Professor Moore

---

[1] Cf. Babson, *Business Barometers*, p. 317.
[2] *The Value of Organised Speculation*, p. 133.
[3] "An Apparent Periodicity of the Yield of Wheat in Eastern England," *Journal of the Royal Statistical Society*, vol. lxxviii. pp. 69-76.

has found a similar correlation between the harvest and the rainfall of the preceding "critical period" in the principal grain growing areas of the United States.[1] As a result of this increased power of forecast, the interval between harvest causes and industrial effects appears in recent years to have diminished. Thus, Professor Jevons writes: " In the 'seventies it took two years for abundant harvests to work their full effect upon the iron industry. By the early·'nineties the activity of industry lagged but one year behind the harvests, while, in recent years, its movement has become simultaneous. At the present day, the growing crops are discounted—literally. turned into money as they stand—either by the farmers themselves or by the merchants to whom the farmers have sold their crops in·advance. Relying upon Government crop estimates, too, manufacturers and wholesale merchants anticipate the demand which will arise from an abundant harvest, and railways the call for rolling stock; and they place orders accordingly."[2]

§ 4. These considerations, however, lie outside the main drift of our investigation. For we are concerned, not with the time at which reactions·upon the volume of. industrial activity occur, but with the nature and scope of these reactions. The first stage in this inquiry is to analyse the actual process through which reaction takes place. A change in the output of agriculturalists is seen, or expected, by industrialists to involve a change in the aggregate amount of money which will be paid to agriculturalists, and which agriculturalists can; therefore, afford to offer for the products of industrialists, thus making it to the interest of industrialists to alter correspondingly their own output. This is, of course, merely a roundabout way of saying that industrialists will be ready to create an altered amount of their products (in the manufacture of which they will pay an altered aggregate amount of real wages) in return for an altered amount of agricultural products. It is, however, convenient to conduct

---

[1] Cf. *Economic Cycles*, Chapter iii.
[2] *Contemporary Review*, August 1909, pp. 177-8. Professor Moore finds for the average of the period he has examined an average lag of between one and two years (*Economic Cycles*, p. 110). This, of course, is not incompatible with Professor Jevons's view that the lag has now disappeared.

our analysis with reference to the money process. It is readily seen that the kind of effect produced depends exclusively upon the elasticity of the general demand for agricultural commodities. If this elasticity is equal to unity, exactly the same amount of money, and ultimately of goods, will be forthcoming to purchase any one quantity as would be forthcoming to purchase any other quantity. A variation in the harvest will, in these conditions, not affect the activity of other groups at all. If the elasticity of demand is less than unity, less of other things in the aggregate will be offered for an increased quantity, and more for a diminished quantity. If the elasticity of demand is greater than unity, more of other things will be offered for an increased quantity, and less for a diminished quantity. In any event, the magnitude of the change in the activity of other groups will be greater, the more widely the elasticity of the demand for agricultural produce diverges from unity.[1]

§ 5. Now, since agriculture embraces a large number of different sorts of crops, the question whether the demand for agricultural produce has in fact an elasticity greater or less than unity is both ambiguous and difficult. A further com-

---

[1] The problem discussed in this section presents a curious example of the way in which diagrams, if carelessly handled, may mislead. If, in an ordinary price-amount diagram, we represent the offer of the group whose output has expanded by a supply curve, and the offer of the other group by a demand curve, the conclusion of the text is immediately established. But, if we represent the offer of the group whose output has expanded by a demand curve and the offer of the other group by a supply curve, it appears, at first sight, that a raising of the demand curve must, in all circumstances, cause an increase in the output of the other group, and, therefore, that the conclusion of the text is invalid. This appearance is false. The explanation of it is that we are accustomed to employ the price-amount diagram to represent the quantity of a single commodity demanded and supplied at various money prices. Since variations in the supply of individual commodities (the case may be different with labour) cannot react appreciably upon the marginal desiredness of money, it is impossible for the supply curve in this type of diagram to bend backwards towards the left in such a way as to cut a vertical line more than once. In the face of a supply curve bound by this condition it is true that a raising of the demand curve must, in all circumstances, cause an increase in output. But, when this type of supply curve is used to represent the offer of things in general for some one thing, there is no presumption that the marginal desiredness of this thing will be approximately unaffected by variations in the amount of it that is purchased. Consequently, there is no presumption that the supply curve will not bend backwards towards the left, and no ground for the thesis that a raising of the demand curve must, in all circumstances, cause an increase of output.

plication is introduced by the fact that the elasticity of the demand of any group for the whole of any kind of produce is different from the elasticity of its demand for that part of the produce that is grown in a particular country. Since the supply from other countries can be substituted for the supply from any one country, the elasticity of the demand for the part that comes from one country is always greater than the elasticity of the demand for the whole. But, the relation between the two elasticities is not fixed. That relevant to the produce of one country falls more nearly to that relevant to the whole, as the proportion which that country's crop bears to the world crop increases. Thus, though the demand for wheat in the aggregate is probably less elastic than the demand for cotton in the aggregate, yet, since America provides a much larger share of the world's cotton than of the world's wheat,[1] the demand for American cotton is less elastic than the demand for American wheat. The most useful form in which the question of elasticity can be posited from our present point of view is probably the most general form. Would an expansion in harvest yields throughout the world generally cause industrialists as a body, and English industrialists in particular, to spend a larger or a smaller aggregate sum in the purchase of agricultural products? Obviously, no exact answer can be given to this question, because harvest yields in general may expand in a great number of different ways, sometimes through a crop of inelastic demand and sometimes through one of elastic demand. Perhaps, however, the difficulty is not really so important as it seems. For some degree of positive correlation appears to exist between the variations that occur in the yields of different sorts of crops in the same country.[2] On the whole, in spite of Mr. Hull's assertion that small crops often bring in as much money to farmers as large crops,[3] there would seem reason to accept Mr. Robertson's view that the elasticity of the demand for agricultural produce, in the rough sense indicated above, is somewhat greater than unity.[4] We should, therefore,

---

[1] Cf. *Quarterly Journal of Economics*, 1906, p. 340.
[2] Cf. Robertson, *A Study of Industrial Fluctuation*, p. 153.
[3] Cf. Hull, *Industrial Depressions*, p. 45 et seq.
[4] Cf. Robertson, *A Study of Industrial Fluctuation*, p. 135.

expect good harvests to make for an expansion, and bad harvests for a contraction, in the aggregate real payment made to agriculturists by other industries, and so in the aggregate real demand of those industries for the services of the workpeople whom they employ.

§ 6. We turn now to the *magnitude* of the reactions that may be expected. This depends partly, as has already been indicated, upon the extent to which the elasticity of the demand for agricultural products diverges from unity. About this no information is available. But the extent of the reaction also depends upon four other quantities—(1) the elasticity of the community's demand (in terms of effort) for goods and services other than agricultural produce; (2) the normal proportion between the community's expenditure on agricultural produce and on other things; (3) the extent of the variations that are liable to occur in the amount of the harvest yield; and (4) the extent to which these variations are balanced by converse variations in the quantity of crops held in store.[1]

§ 7. Concerning the first of these factors we do not know much. Plainly, however, the elasticity of demand in terms of effort for non-agricultural goods in general is likely to be fairly large, and the fact that many of these goods are capable of being stored and are not instantaneously perishable makes it larger than it would be otherwise. This circumstance tends to limit the magnitude of the reactions upon aggregate activity; because it implies that, when people increase or diminish the part of their activity which is directed to the purchase of agricultural products, they will offset this change to a considerable extent, by diminishing or increasing the part that is directed to satisfying their other wants directly and to making goods for store. But nothing at all precise is known upon the subject of elasticities, and we may, there-

---

[1] A careful analysis along these lines is given in Mr. D. H. Robertson's *A Study of Industrial Fluctuation*, pp. 129 *et seq.* Mr. Robertson adds the interesting suggestion that, since practice creates habit, and, therefore, demands are likely to be less elastic for backward than for forward movements of supply, a change that causes a given *increase* in the payment that has to be made to the group primarily affected is likely to modify the aggregate output of other groups to a greater extent than a change which causes an equal *decrease* in this payment. (Cf. *loc. cit.* p. 136.)

fore, pass at once to the other three factors that have been distinguished.

§ 8. We may begin with the proportion of the community's income that is normally expended upon agricultural products. If one-tenth of the whole income is expended upon the output of any one group, this means that the rest of the community normally devote one-ninth of their output to purchasing the output of that group. If, therefore, their output for other purposes suffers no reaction, they will be affected only in respect of one-ninth of their output. Hence, if the effect on that part of their activity, which is directed to purchasing the product of the one group, is, say, 5 per cent, the effect on their aggregate activity will be 5 per cent multiplied by one-ninth. Clearly, therefore, the percentage change in the aggregate activity of the other groups varies directly with the proportion of the community's resources that are normally spent on the product of the group primarily affected. If 95 per cent of the community look for a 10 per cent change in the output of 5 per cent of the community, the percentage effect will normally be very small; but, if 5 per cent of the community look for a 10 per cent change in the output of 95 per cent of the community, it will be very large. The comparative size of the community's expenditure on the products of agriculture and of industry is, thus, a dominant factor in determining the extent of the reactions on industrial activity produced by harvest variations. It is, therefore, important to our present purpose to know that, as man's powers increase, the proportion of these that he needs to expend in obtaining nature's raw products tends, through mechanical inventions and so on, steadily to diminish. As a result, a greater proportion of the community's total expenditure is devoted to non-agricultural goods than was so devoted in earlier times. The proportionate reactions on industrial activity due to harvest changes is, therefore, presumably smaller than it used to be.

§ 9. We come next to the variability of the harvests themselves. The magnitude of this variability, depending, as it does, upon "nature," appears at first sight to be outside human control. In fact, however, there are a number of ways in which "progress" tends to diminish it. First, it is plain that the variability of yield is different in different crops. For example, few, if any, agricultural crops fluctuate so greatly from year to year as hops. In the year 1878, when the largest number of acres was under hops, viz. 71,789, the home produce is estimated not to have exceeded 700,000 cwt., and in 1907, when the acreage had been reduced to 48,962, the home produce fell little short of 700,000 cwt.[1] As civilisation advances, mankind tends to substitute the use of less variable kinds of produce for the use of more variable kinds. The introduction of a type of wheat immune to the disease of rust is an instance in point. Secondly, the importance of natural forces outside human control, in bringing about variability, is itself, in some degree, subject to human control. As wealth increases, people are able to afford more expenditure to buy off irregularity and uncertainty, and so tend to introduce machines to undertake tasks that were formerly left to Nature. In India, for example, the development of irrigation works has done much to mitigate the effect of the vagaries of the seasons in rendering the crops variable.[2] Thirdly, the development of the means of communication tends greatly to diminish the variability of *that part of the world's agricultural produce that is relevant to any particular country.* For, as intercourse is opened up, different crops come to be so distributed among different countries that each country becomes the producer of that one which in it is relatively invariable. Moreover, there is a general tendency for fluctuations, which occur independently in different parts of the world, partially to compensate one another—a tendency which, as the general theory of probability proves, is stronger the more numerous are the different independent sources of supply. Yet again, as some think, there is a physical connection between different parts of the world, which directly and overtly makes for compensating movements. "The crop yield," it has been said, "depends largely on the moisture of the atmosphere," and "it is physically impossible that there should be at once in all

[1] Cf. *Report of the Committee on Hops*, p. v. Of course, as the Committee point out, allowance must be made for the introduction of more intensive methods of production. This consideration makes the illustration offered above less apposite than it appears to be at first sight.

[2] Cf. Morison, *The Industrial Organisation of an Indian Province*, pp. 155-61.

Europe, in Asia, and in all America excess of dampness or
excess of dryness." Furthermore, as was well pointed out by
the *Economist* some years before the war: "Sowing is taking
place in every month of the year, and a shortage of European
harvests is apparent early enough to influence the acreage put
under wheat in the southern hemisphere, in Australia, and
Argentina. The effect of this system on prices has been that,
whereas, prior to 1898, they showed big fluctuations, since
that date they have been remarkably steady, though with a
slight upward tendency." [1] The great practical importance of
these influences in combination is illustrated by the fact that,
whereas in the ten year period 1898–1907 the wheat crop of
the British Empire had a variability of 15 per cent, the
variability of the crop of the whole world was only 5½ per cent.[2]
The general effect of these considerations is to suggest that
the percentage range of variability in the annual volume of
agricultural produce is not very large.

§ 10. The last influence we have to consider is the cancelling
effect exercised upon crop variations by the practice of holding
much larger supplies in store when the crops are good than
when they are bad, and thus, in a measure, equalising the

[1] *Economist*, April 17, 1909, p. 811.
[2] *Economist*, April 24, 1909, p. 861. The details are given in the following
table:

	World's Crop.	Per cent Increase or Decrease compared with Previous Year.	Crop of British Empire.	Per cent Increase or Decrease compared with Previous Year.
	Million bushels.		Million bushels.	
1898	2948	...	453	...
1899	2765	− 6·2	377	− 16·8
1900	2610	− 5·6	428	+ 13·5
1901	2898	+ 11·0	411	− 4·0
1902	3104	+ 7·1	471	+ 14·6
1903	3190	+ 2·7	572	+ 21·6
1904	3152	− 1·2	458	− 19·9
1905	3321	+ 5·3	565	+ 23·3
1906	3435	+ 3·4	565	...
1907	3109	− 9·5	412	− 27·1

The greater variability of the imperial crop is not, of course, due merely to
the relatively small area of growth. It so happens that, owing to climatic
conditions, India and Australia are liable to almost complete crop failures, while
the Canadian harvest is also extremely variable.

quantities of harvest products that actually come upon the market in successive years. This cancelling effect is made greater by anything that causes people to act upon better forecasts of future crop yields, and is, therefore, enhanced by the development of any of the various means of forecast indicated in § 3. It is further enhanced by the development of a speculative market, in which persons specialised in the art of making forecasts come together and by their action affect, first prices, and, through prices, the stocks held back in stores and shops. No doubt, a speculative market may, on some occasions, be manipulated, and, on other occasions, may make mistakes. On the whole, however, we may safely conclude, that both the wheat pit and cotton exchange tend to bring about the holding of larger stocks in anticipation of shortages and of smaller stocks in anticipation of bumper crops. Institutions of this kind thus lessen the reactions produced upon the volume of industrial activity by variations in the harvests.

§ 11. The above considerations, though they do not enable us to establish any quantitative relation between harvest variations and consequential variations in industrial activity, nevertheless leave no doubt that good world harvests lead to expansions and bad world harvests to contractions in the activity of industry. If these harvest variations occurred in a purely chaotic and random manner, the industrial reactions caused by them would not, of course, be rhythmical in any degree. Harvest variations, in short, fall into the first of the two types of causes distinguished at the end of Chapter I., namely, causes which, to produce rhythmical effects, must themselves occur at more or less regular intervals. In actual fact there is *some* measure of regularity in harvest variations. It is true that on the problem of "periodicity" different writers have reached very divergent conclusions. Dr. Shaw's inquiry into "An apparent periodicity in the yield of wheat in Eastern England" appears to reveal the existence of an 11 year period there. Professor Moore's study of the central grain district of the United States suggests an 8 year crop period, closely correlated with an 8 year rainfall period.[1] Mr. P. G. Wright disputes

---

[1] Cf. *Economic Cycles*, Chapters ii. and iii.

Professor Moore's analysis of the rainfall period, insisting
that he has paid inadequate attention to the relation between
average annual rainfall and the critical period of the year, but he
does not quarrel about the crop period.[1] Professor Jevons claims
to have established a $3\frac{1}{2}$ year period for the world's harvests,
connected with a $3\frac{1}{2}$ yearly solar period of varying average
barometric pressure;[2] and Mr. Robertson doubts whether any
periodicity is really demonstrated by his figures.[3] All these
discrepancies and the general uncertainty as to whether any,
and if so what, crop period really exists have been the source
of a great deal of difficult discussion. But for our present
purpose the question whether or not a definite period can be
established is not important. All that we need is sufficient
regularity to afford the basis of a more or less loose rhythm.
That this exists there can be little doubt. Consequently,
harvest variations must be regarded as a true cause of the
observed industrial movement, in the sense that, if operating
by themselves, they would produce some kind of more or less
rhythmical scheme of industrial fluctuations.

[1] *Quarterly Journal of Economics*, May 1915, p. 631 *et seq.*
[2] *The Sun's Heat and Trade Activity*, p. 6.
[3] *A Study of Industrial Fluctuation*, p. 147.

CHAPTER V

INVENTIONS

§ 1. A SECOND true cause in this sense is inventions. An invention, such as that of steam transport, which led to our railway boom in the 'forties, or that of electric transport, which led to great iron and steel booms in Germany from 1895 to 1900, causes, it may be supposed, a rise in the demand for certain sorts of instrumental goods, which is not balanced by any equivalent fall in the demand for other sorts of instrumental goods. This involves an increase in the new production of these instrumental goods. It also involves an increase in the demand for a number of other goods which are subordinate to them. "To construct a factory or a railway it is necessary to procure materials of construction (wood, tiles, iron, etc.), machines and tools, and to engage workpeople. The materials of construction, like the machines, do not fall from the sky; they are furnished by other branches of production. Thus, the more numerous new enterprises are, the greater is the demand for means of production."[1] Further, the workpeople engaged in connection with the invention are paid more money and spend it in the purchase of more food, clothes and amusement. Therefore, the makers of these things, finding their manufacture more profitable than before, offer more money to their workpeople in order to evoke from them a greater volume of activity and a larger product. In this way invention booms cause approximately synchronous booms, not only in the industries that make materials, but also in those that make the goods ordinarily purchased by workpeople.

[1] Tugan Baranowski, *Les Crises industrielles en Angleterre*, p. 258.

§ 2. If this analysis exhausted the matter, it would have been shown that inventions are capable of causing industrial booms, but there would be no reason to regard them as a true cause of more or less rhythmical industrial fluctuations. There is, however, something further to say. The effect of an invention boom is not exhausted when the boom itself stops. On the contrary, there is initiated a continuing *series* of events into which rhythm does enter. In other words, inventions fall into the second of the two classes of causes distinguished at the end of Chapter I., namely, causes that are capable of setting up a rhythmical effect without themselves recurring rhythmically.

§ 3. The first phase of the process is as follows. During the invention boom itself, in response to the demand which the invention has set going, a great number of durable things are being created. So long as they are being created—as we may say, throughout the period of gestation—exceptional activity continues. Some of them, of course, are completed sooner than others. Even for the same sort of thing the period of gestation is not the same when factories are fully occupied as when they are slack. And for different sorts of things it naturally varies greatly. An invention boom involves, as it were, the sowing of a great number of different kinds of seed, the crops from which are scattered over a considerable range of time. Some of the seed will spring up and flower immediately; some in one year, some in two, some in three, some perhaps in ten. The period of gestation for ordinary consumable goods, such as cotton cloth, is very short. Construction goods in general take a good deal longer to make. Mr. Hull states that it takes a year to build an iron furnace. M. Aftalion suggests that the gap between ordering and completion is, for the rolling stock for railways some one and a half years, for locomotives some three years, and for shipping some two years. Houses, according to their size, may take from one to three years to build. Steam-engines for industrial works in France may take one, two, or three years. The period of gestation of a coffee plantation is some five years. That of a coal mine is probably, in present conditions, even longer. "There is nowhere," Mr. Robertson was told by the

representative of a large mixed iron-works, "we could sink a
new colliery except a few parts of Yorkshire and the south of
England, and, even so, we should not see any coal for years."[1]
The above are not designed to be more than illustrations. The
essential fact is that the period of gestation varies greatly for
different things, and is especially likely to be long for elaborate
constructional instruments. We cannot, therefore, say generally that the period will always be of such and such a definite
length. But we can say that, as the different things, for the
production of which an invention boom has called, come to be
finished, industrial activity dies down, and the first phase of
the rhythm comes to a close.

§ 4. The second phase is one of comparative quiescence.
The durable things called into being by the invention are there
in sufficient quantities, and there is no need, for the present,
to renew them. It is known, of course, that they will eventually wear out and will have to be replaced, and it is possible,
therefore, that some production may be undertaken in anticipation of that event. As a rule, however, this will not happen
at all extensively, partly because of the loss of interest involved
in it, and partly because technical improvements are likely to
be invented that will make machines and so forth manufactured
now obsolete before renewal becomes necessary.

§ 5. The second quiescent phase is followed by a third
phase of boom, when the life of the things made at the beginning draws to an end. Of course, different things have lives
of different lengths. Houses, for example, last much longer
than delicate tools. But there is reason to believe that many
different sorts of machinery enjoy the same sort of length of
life. Ten years seems to be, not merely the average, but also
the markedly predominant length. This, at all events, is the
view of the Director of the British Census of Production.[2]
Hence, it would seem that we can speak more generally of
length of life than we can of period of gestation, and can
suggest ten years as a reasonable allowance. If this be so, the
third phase of the rhythm set up by an invention will be a
second boom similar to the first, beginning about ten years

---

[1] *A Study of Industrial Fluctuation*, p. 17.
[2] *Report*, pp. 35-6. Cf. also *ante*, Part I. Chapter III. § 6.

later. This boom, like its predecessor, will be followed by a period of quiescence, and, thereafter, by yet another boom. Thus, a fairly definite rhythm is established, and invention is seen to be a true cause of industrial fluctuations. The difficulties which arise out of the interplay of a number of different inventions will be considered in Chapter VII.

CHAPTER VI

§ 1. A THIRD true cause of wave movements in industrial activity generally may be found in the psychological tendencies of the business community. The attitude of business men towards the signs of the times does not remain constant, but varies from period to period between errors of optimism and errors of pessimism. It is the purpose of this chapter to study these variations.

§ 2. One primary difficulty has first to be overcome. It might conceivably be thought that, if everybody at the same time formed the ungrounded opinion that everybody else was about to be prosperous (or the reverse), the very universality of this error would transmute it into truth. For A, thinking that B is about to be prosperous and so to exercise an increased demand for his products, increases his output, and B, dominated by the corresponding thought about A, does likewise. These increased outputs, created in error though they are, nevertheless constitute increased reciprocal demands for one another. Therefore, the argument runs, the fact of A's error causes A so to act that B's error becomes the truth; and the fact of B's error causes B so to act that A's error becomes the truth. The fact that *all* expectations have been false causes *each* expectation to be true! This reason, paradoxical as it is in form, is not obviously fallacious in substance. It is, however, in fact, fallacious. The nature of the fallacy involved can be set out as follows. It is perfectly true that an increase in the output of A, however caused, makes worth while, or "justifies," some increase in the output of B. In this sense Bagehot is right when he observes that

831

the prosperity of one industry reacts on all the others "and in a certain sense rebounds." [1] Professor Mitchell seizes the same point when he writes: "As it spreads, the epidemic of optimism helps to breed conditions which both justify and intensify it. The mere fact that a growing number of business men are gaining confidence in the outlook becomes a valid reason why each member of the group, and outsiders also, should feel confident. For the hopeful mood means greater readiness to make new purchases, enter into new contracts, etc.,—in fine, means that the incipient revival of activity will be supported and extended." [2] All this is true. But it is not true that a given false expectation on the part of A justifies an *equal* false expectation on the part of B, and *vice versa*. The two false expectations jointly do create for one another *some* justification, but not a *sufficient* justification. This can easily be proved. The general laws of demand inform us that A will be prepared to offer a lower price per unit for B's goods the larger the quantity offered becomes; and that B will stand in a like relation to A's goods. Hence, if A thinks that B is going to offer twice his normal supply of goods, A will reply by producing, not twice his normal supply, but, say, one-and-a-half times his normal supply; and B, under the influence of a similar opinion about A, will act in the same way. Hence, both A and B, as a result of their false opinions, produce one-and-a-half times their normal output. But, *ex hypothesi*, A is willing to give one-and-a-half times his normal product in exchange, not for one-and-a-half times, but for twice B's normal product; and B is in like case. Hence, the error of the one, though it makes the error of the other less glaring than it would otherwise be, does not convert it into a truth. A and B are both disappointed and both find that their expansion of output was a mistake. The situation is exactly similar if each of A and B falsely expects the other to contract his output, and contracts his own in consequence. In these circumstances, as Dr. Marshall observes: "The chief cause of the evil is want of confidence. The greater part of it could be removed almost in an instant if confidence could return, touch all industries with her magic wand, and make them continue their production and their demand for the wares of others."[1]   In lack of such revivification of confidence, both A and B will find, when their product comes to be sold, that the profit to be made is exceptionally large, and will realise that contraction of output was a mistake. Thus, the doubt whether general errors of business optimism and business pessimism are *possible* may be dismissed.

§ 3. Let us suppose the business world to be in a neutral position, not suffering from either type of error. On this situation there supervenes some real cause for increase in the demand for business activity; a good harvest, the cessation of a war, the sudden influx of new gold, a 'tariff change, a political rumour, or the need of replacing in some important constructional industry machines that have 'become worn out. If all business activity yielded its fruits immediately, these causes of increased demand could not lead to any appreciable error of optimism, because, should such an error emerge and be acted upon, it would instantly be detected and destroyed. But in actual life very little industrial energy yields its profit—not very much yields its actual physical output— immediately. For most consumable goods take some time to make, and still more time before, after passing through warehouses, and, perhaps, intermediate agents, they reach purchasers ready to pay; and the profits from instrumental goods are not, of course, realised by the persons who have bought them until the consumable goods they help to make have been produced and sold. In different occupations different intervals of time prevail, but in almost all occupations there is some interval of time—some element, so to speak, of prospectiveness.' This fact leaves the way open for the development of an optimistic error that is not immediately corrected: and several influences make it probable that this kind of error will in fact develop.

§ 4. First, the real cause at the back of the increased

---

[1] *Principles of Economics*, p. 711. Cf. Kinder (*The Effects of recent Changes in Monetary Standards upon the Distribution of Wealth*, p. 499): "In a community where the individual members are working only half their time, any inducement, though illusory in itself, which sets them at work their full time, may benefit all without necessarily injuring any." Mr. Kinder is thinking of the possible effects of a rise of prices due to monetary causes.

demand has probably brought improved present fortune to
the business men affected. There is, however, a psychological
connection between one's present fortune and one's attitude
towards evidence about future fortune. Happiness breeds the
expectation of future happiness, success the hope of more
success In this way a tendency is created among business
men in good times to look on the sunnier side of doubt.
Even in a country where each family or small group was
more or less self-sufficing and devoted the main part of its
activity to the production' of things to be consumed by itself,
there would be some scope for optimistic errors generated in
this way. For in the most primitive enterprises of hunting
or of cultivation it is easy to over-emphasise the'signs of a
good or a bad prospective yield. In modern conditions,
however, the opportunity for errors so generated is much
increased by the fact that industry is conducted on a basis of
division of labour and exchange of products. For, whereas
in primitive times the estimate relevant to the employment
of industrial energy in any field was a single estimate as to
the physical productivity of that energy, in modern times it
is a double estimate, envisaging both this physical productivity
and the rate at which the thing produced can be exchanged
against the products of other people. This circumstance
compels each business man to take account in his reckoning
of future prospects, not merely of his own industry, but also
of a number of other industries, many of which are necessarily
unknown to him. For very few sorts of goods are made to
order. "In the general wholesale manufactures production
in anticipation of demand is the almost universal rule." [1]
Furthermore, with modern developments in the means of
communication, the area of demand about which forecasts have
to be made has become extraordinarily wide. This circumstance, giving, as it does, large scope for ignorance, naturally
causes the optimistic errors generated by initial success to be
larger than they would otherwise be.

§ 5. Secondly, people do not fully realise that their own
response to a business inducement must presently lessen the
force of that inducement. When demand in some field

---

[1] Conant, *The Principles of Money and Banking*, ii. p. 387.

becomes good, the thing that is apparent to industrialists is the high profit that is being obtained by those who can sell various sorts of goods. This high profit continues in spite of the fact that new machinery is being built to enable supply to catch up demand, because the new machinery will not become available till it is completed, and its completion will take a considerable time. The demand for the goods being obviously unsatisfied, manufacturers often fail to realise that the means for its complete satisfaction are already in process of construction, and, therefore, unrestrainedly pile up still further investments in machinery. "If," writes M. Aftalion, "to remedy the deficiency of heat in a room, one revives the fire on the hearth, it will be necessary to *wait for some time* before the desired temperature is obtained. As the cold continues and the thermometer continues to register it, one would be led, if one were not instructed by experience, to throw more fuel on to the fire. One would do this even though the quantity already accumulated there were such that, when it is all ignited, it would give out an unbearable amount of heat. In letting oneself be guided by the sensation of present cold—by the present indications of the thermometer —one would fatally overheat the room."[1] This image exactly displays one aspect of the error to which the prospectiveness of industry leads those who are in control of it. Concentrating attention upon *present* facts, they anticipate profit from further new investment, when already so much new investment has been prepared that all real prospect of profit is destroyed. Plainly, the extent of the error that is liable to arise in this way is greater, the longer is the interval that technical conditions establish between the will to increase production and the manifestation of that will in fact. "Large errors are especially liable to occur in enterprises in new fields, whose limitations have not been accurately measured by investors, or even by capitalists of proved judgment and experience. . . . New discoveries and the opening of new continents have contributed greatly to these mistakes during the modern commercial age."[2] The

---

[1] Aftalion, *Les Crises périodiques de surproduction*, vol. ii. p. 361.
[2] Cf. Conant, *History of Modern Banks of Issue*, p. 461.

opening up, at the return of peace, of wide opportunities to make good the wastes of war, acts in a similar way. No less plainly, every development; of intelligence and capacity to learn from experience on the part of entrepreneurs, and of bankers from whom in part they draw their funds, is likely to lessen the magnitude of the errors that arise from this cause. It is alleged, for example, that France has suffered less from industrial crises than England, partly because her business houses are more conservative.[1]

§ 6. Thirdly, the likelihood that important optimistic errors will be generated is enhanced by the fact that, in the modern world, most industries are conducted by a large number of separate producers. In view of this fact, when the demand for the product of any industry changes in a given measure, the *appropriate* action for each producer in the group depends both on the magnitude of the change in the demand and also on the policy adopted by the other producers. In so far as the different producers act independently of one another, experience shows that each of them is likely to pay insufficient attention to the effect which the change of demand produces upon the output of his competitors. In the same spirit, new competitors—in industries where the capital required for a start is not too large to permit of this—come into the business without due consideration of the fact that those already in it are certain to increase their output. The result is that errors of optimism grow to larger dimensions than they would otherwise attain.

§ 7. A fourth cause fostering error is closely associated with that just described, and depends, like it, upon the fact that most industries are conducted by a number of separate and independent producers. These separate and independent producers are not, in general, integrated businesses completing the whole process of manufacture from raw material to finished article. For the most part the entrepreneur in control of an industrial concern has to buy raw materials and half-manufactured goods, to engage labour and to borrow capital; and the persons from whom these things have to be obtained are not exclusively *liés* to him. When undertakings, such as

[1] Cf. Burton, *Financial Crises*, p. 39.

works of construction, occupy a long time in execution, contracts are usually made in connection with them months, or even years, before much of the labour and material employed upon them will be required. Thus there arises the practice of "forward buying," firms engaged in the more advanced processes of production contracting to make at a future date certain purchases at certain rates from those engaged in the less advanced processes. It is not, however, in general, practicable for advanced contracts to be entered into for labour or for certain raw materials. Consequently, in reflecting on the terms at which they are prepared to sell for future delivery, most of the firms affected must be content with guess-work concerning a considerable part of their costs. Each firm, however, in making its guess, is, in general, without information as to the future contracts undertaken by other firms, and is, therefore, apt to ignore the effect which the execution of these contracts, when they fall due, will have upon the real price of labour and materials. Hence, a general movement towards optimistic expectations is likely to be carried further than it would be if the making and the execution of contracts synchronised. These tendencies, it will be observed, are not dependent upon the modern practice of manufacture in anticipation of demand, but occur also in respect of commodities that are made to order. An excellent illustration is afforded by the history of the English munition contracts in the earlier part of the Great War. Firms contracted to deliver large quantities of shells on the assumption that they would be able to sub-contract a part of their orders to other works, and then discovered that these works were also being sought after for a like purpose by rival firms; with the result, incidentally, that the aggregate of shells actually delivered fell enormously below the aggregate for which contracts had been made.

§ 8. It is readily seen that the influences making for error, which have been discussed in the two preceding sections, would be mitigated if full information were regularly issued concerning the amount of plant laid down, orders given, and constructions begun by all the various firms affected. Mr. Hull suggests that the State should publish monthly "all pertinent information in relation to the existing volume of construction under contract for future months."[1] This policy would necessarily do away with the ignorance of each concerning the conduct of all; and business men would have better warning of impending changes in the real price of labour and materials. A still more complete remedy would be provided if all the firms engaged in any given form of production were combined under a single head in a Trust or in a Kartel possessing a central office entrusted with the regulation of output.

§ 9. The above reasoning, however, must not be taken to prove that the "trustification" of industries makes for stability of output on the whole. There is, indeed, reason to believe that the *continuous* exertion of monopolistic power will lead to about the same degree of variability as perfectly intelligent competitive action;[2] and, therefore, presumably to a less degree of variability than the type of competitive action described above. In practice, however, it frequently happens that monopolistic power is exercised much more rigorously in bad times than in good times. A good illustration of this tendency is furnished by the practice of the master cotton-spinners of Lancashire, who, in periods of booming trade, compete freely with one another, but, in periods of depression, enter into a joint agreement to shut down for so many days per week. But it is not only under temporary joint agreements that monopolistic power is exercised with unwonted stringency in bad times. The same thing happens whenever an industrial combination or other monopolistic body decides, for any reason, to prevent the price of its product from fluctuating. Partly for convenience and partly for advertisement, monopolistic bodies in fact frequently do this. For example, according to the 1907 report of the British Consul-General for Frankfort, "syndicates prevented, during the boom, the prices from rising to the level to which they would otherwise have risen; again, during the beginning of the set-back,

---

[1] *Industrial Depressions*, p. 218.

[2] On the assumption that the curves of demand and supply are straight lines, it is easily shown that the output proper to monopoly is always one-half of that proper to simple competition; so that the percentage variations of output due to changes of demand or supply must be the same.

they have made for stability generally."[1] Again, according to the same authority, "the Coal Syndicate fixes its prices for a year, from April to April; once such base-prices have been fixed, they are only very exceptionally liable to modifications."[2] Finally, it is well known that the United States Steel Corporation have from time to time endeavoured with success to keep the prices of their products, and particularly the price of steel rails, absolutely stable in spite of large fluctuations of demand.[3] It is evident that a monopolistic body animated by this purpose must act "more monopolistically" in times of depression than it does in times of boom. Whenever this happens, output must vary more extensively than it would do if monopolistic power were either exercised continuously or not exercised at all. Of course, if in bad times prices are only maintained at home and are allowed to fall abroad, the variations of output will be smaller than they would have been had the policy of price maintenance been adopted in the foreign as well as in the home market; but they will not, in general, be as small as they would have been if there had been no price maintenance in either market. Thus, the intermittent monopolistic action found in practice may well cause greater fluctuations of production than even imperfect competition. Further, it must be remembered that attempts at trustification often lead to multiple monopoly rather than to simple monopoly. If this happens, fluctuations may be made extremely great by causes other than those specified so far. Even apart from cut-throat competition, we may get fluctuations over the wide range of indeterminateness indicated in Part II. Chapter XII.; and, if cut-throat competition supervenes, the range of possible fluctuations is still further enlarged. Finally, even if a true monopoly is formed for a time, it may presently break up again, and so cause a large fluctuation.

§ 10. When an error of optimism has been generated, it

---

[1] *Report* [Cd. 3727-167], p. 64.   [2] *Ibid.* p. 75.

[3] Cf. Jenks and Clark, *The Trust Problem*, pp. 168 *et seq.* The authors defend the policy adopted by the Steel Corporation on several grounds, principally the convenience of the railway companies, which are said themselves to have first suggested a system of fixed prices. The system continued for 15 years, and only broke down in 1916 after nearly two years of the European War.

tends to spread and grow, as a result of reactions between
different parts of the business community. This comes about
through two principal influences. First, experience suggests
that, apart altogether from the financial ties by which different
business men are bound together, there exists among them a
certain measure of psychological interdependence. A change
of tone in one part of the business world diffuses itself, in a
quite unreasoning manner, over other and wholly disconnected parts. An expansion of business confidence " propagates
itself by that sympathetic and epidemic excitement which so
largely sways communities of men."[1] There comes into play
a quasi-hypnotic system of mutual suggestion:

> One with another, soul with soul
> They kindle fire from fire.

" Perhaps the buoyancy of a grocer gives a lumber dealer
no adequate reason for altering his conservative attitude
towards the business projects upon which he must pass. Yet,
in despite of logic, he will be the readier to buy if his ac-
quaintances in any line of trade have become aggressively
confident of the future. The fundamental conditions affecting
his own business may remain the same; but his conduct is
altered because he sees the old facts in a new emotional
perspective."[2] This tendency is the more marked in so far
as business men are congregated in close physical proximity
to one another in the business sections of large cities.[3]
Secondly, as was explained at the beginning of this chapter,
an error of optimism on the part of one group of business
men itself creates a justification for some improved expectation
on the part of other groups. For the group primarily affected
has more product to sell, which means, in effect, that it offers
a higher real demand for the goods of other groups. The
real increment of prosperity thus given to these others
stimulates in them a spirit of optimism, and makes it more
probable than it would otherwise be that they too will lean
unduly to the sunnier side of doubt. The fact that A's
erroneous optimism is a ground of some small justified

---

[1] Kemmerer, *Money and Prices*, p. 83.
[2] Mitchell, *Business Cycles*, p. 455.
[3] Cf. Jones, *Economic Crises*, p. 204.

optimism on the part of B, C and D, adds a material link to
the link of sympathy which we have already seen to bind
business men in different occupations together. These two
links act, as it were, as conducting rods along which an error
of optimism once generated propagates itself with ever-gather-
ing force throughout the business world.

§ 11. For a time the error of optimism, the fortunes of
which we have been describing, will, thus, not merely maintain
itself, but will extend in scope and magnitude. But eventually the activity that has been devoted to industry under its
influence will materialise in the form of commodities seeking
a market. This will happen after an interval has elapsed
roughly equivalent to the "period of gestation" of the
principal new instrumental goods which have been made, *plus*
the time necessary to bring to market the products which
they help to make. After this interval the fact that an error
of optimism has been made and prospective profits exaggerated
is necessarily discovered; and by the fact of discovery the
error is destroyed. As a consequence, the flow of business
activity is checked. But the check does not operate instantaneously, because business men who find themselves in
difficulties are tempted to extend their borrowings and make
a desperate throw to restore their fortunes. After a little
while, however, those people, who have made and acted upon
errors of optimism, have to confess them—at least to themselves,—to sell a mass of products at a lower price than they
had anticipated, and to pocket the consequent loss. This
leaves them in no mood for any further error of optimism.

§ 12. But this is not all. In the modern world a debtor-
creditor relation subsists between different business men. In
fact, most firms are both borrowers and lenders. They borrow
from one set of people by buying materials from them on
credit, and they lend to another set by selling the fruits of
their workmanship on credit. Thus, we have, as it were, a
series in the form A, B, C, D, each member of which is debtor
to the one preceding, and creditor to the one succeeding, himself. Manufacturers of raw material are borrowers from the
banks and lenders to manufacturers of finished goods; manufacturers of finished goods are borrowers from manufacturers

of raw materials and lenders to wholesale dealers; wholesale
dealers are borrowers from manufacturers of finished goods and
lenders to retailers, and retailers are borrowers from wholesale
dealers and lenders to customers who buy on credit. This fact
implies that, if any good or evil chance happens to one, its
effects are likely to be passed on to the others. Furthermore, the measure of this financial interdependence among
business men is increased by every development of business
practice towards longer or larger credits between manufacturers of raw materials and manufacturers of finished
products, between manufacturers of finished products and
wholesalers, and between wholesalers and retail tradesmen.[1] Hence, it is significant that, as the tide of profits
advances, credits do in fact tend to become both larger and
longer. Some sorts (though not all sorts) of collateral,
being of higher price, will command a larger advance,
and, when no collateral is employed, A, looking more
optimistically on B's prospects, will regard with less critical
eyes his request for credit. Thus, Professor Chapman observes:
" The longer the period of good trade, the further is forward
buying drawn out and the more involved do traders become.
If normally the rule is to buy in October for January
deliveries, towards the end of a period of good trade dealers
will be buying for January deliveries, say, in July, under the
pressure of demands crowding in in the face of only slightly
elastic production."[2] In these circumstances it is evident
that the ill-fortune that has accrued to the victims of
optimistic error will react upon a great number of other
people. Traders who have done bad business find that they
can no longer hold up their goods from sale, are compelled to

---

[1] It may be noted that, as between brokers and their clients, credits are
kept low by the system of "short settlements." This system "aims at reducing
the risk of loss due to the assumption by weak dealers of risks greater than the
funds at their disposal enable them to cover, and, thus, at rendering business
more secure, and, being more secure, capable of being carried on with narrower
profits. The parties to the contract may (or in some cases must) deposit a sum
of money sufficient to cover any probable loss due to variation of price for a short
time, and, if prices vary beyond what the deposit can make good, must increase
the deposit." (*British Association Report*, 1900, p. 4.) This system, in effect,
prevails both among those who speculate on margins on the Stock Exchange
and among those who deal in futures on the Produce Exchanges.

[2] *Unemployment in Lancashire*, p. 95.

accept a loss on them, and, being thus impoverished, endeavour to draw in their debts from other houses directly associated with them. This action on their part causes the other houses in turn to adopt a like policy. Hence, a fairly general liquidation of bad business sets in. "Once begun, the process of liquidation extends rapidly, partly because most enterprises, which are called upon to settle their monetary obligations, in turn put similar pressure upon their own debtors, and partly because, despite all efforts to keep secret what is going forward, news presently leaks out and other creditors take alarm."[1] This movement inevitably reacts upon business confidence. Under its influence the dying error of optimism gives birth to an error of pessimism. This new error is born, not an infant, but a giant; for an industrial boom has necessarily been a period of strong emotional excitement, and an excited man passes from one form of excitement to another more readily than he passes to quiescence.

§ 13. The error of pessimism thus established implies an unduly depressed view in all industries of the prospective demand of other industries for their products. Therefore, in all of them but little activity is expended and dulness supervenes. After an interval, equal, as before, to the period of gestation of the principal instrumental goods employed *plus* the time necessary for their products to get to market, this error also is discovered. Because people have been shy of directing industrial energy into any but the very safest channels, a general shortage of a number of important commodities gradually makes itself apparent, and those persons who have them to sell are seen to be earning a good real return. Thereupon, certain of the bolder spirits in industry see an opportunity and seize it. The prices of materials and labour are low owing to the general unwillingness of industrialists to buy them, and, with the help of adequate security, capital also can be obtained on favourable terms.[2] The new pioneers undertake and expand enterprises, thus at once filling a real need and laying up good profit for themselves. Gradually, as no disaster happens to them, other

---

[1] Mitchell, *Business Cycles*, p. 576.
[2] Cf. Alberti, *Verso la crisi*, p. 101.

less bold spirits follow their example; then others and yet others. They are further encouraged by the fact, noted by Professor Mitchell, that, during the preceding period of depression, there has probably been an accumulation of "technical improvements of which new plants can take advantage, and therefore the greater becomes the inducement to invest in new equipment."[1]   Advance thus takes place all along the line. "There is, of course, no formal agreement between the different trades to begin again to work full time, and so make a market for each other's wares. But the revival of industry comes about through the gradual and often simultaneous growth of confidence among various trades; it begins as soon as traders think that prices will not continue to fall; and, with a revival of industry, prices rise."[2]   The first-comers make an addition to industrial energy that is really needed to correct the error that has hitherto prevailed. Perhaps those who come in and expand their business directly after the beginnings of revival are also in this class.   The first year or two, say, is taken up with a wholly justified expansion. But, after the first year or two, further expansion represents, not a correction of the past error, but the creation of a new one, and, thereafter, any further expansion represents a growth of unjustified optimism.   The turn of the tide from ebb to flow is a slow and gradual process.   Cautiously and hesitatingly the first steps on the return journey towards the correct route are taken; some time elapses before the route is reached; when it is reached it is passed, and a new false track on the opposite side is entered upon, down which industry runs at an accelerating pace, until once more the presence of an error of optimism is revealed and, on revelation, destroyed.   An error of pessimism is then again generated in the way we have described, and presently, when it in turn has died, a new wave of optimism begins to gather on the same pattern as before.

[1] Mitchell, *Business Cycles*, p. 567.
[2] Marshall, *Principles of Economics*, p. 711.

CHAPTER VII

§ 1. WITH the information at present accessible to students it is not possible to construct a complete explanation of the rhythmic industrial movements that are actually experienced, or to gauge the exact part played by the three sets of true causes examined in the three preceding chapters. But a rough outline sketch may be attempted.

§ 2. The part played by inventions is the easiest to determine. It is probably a subordinate one. If it were independent and dominant, since there is no reason to suppose that different sorts of inventions are all made together, we should have such a large number of discrepant wave-movements set up by different inventions that very little general rhythm would be likely to result from them. The fact is that the influence of inventions is subsumed under that of psychological movements. For, first, the adoption on a large scale of an invention in industry does not generally take place at the moment when the invention is made, but rather waits till business men are feeling confident and ready for enterprise. Thus, during slack periods technical devices and improvements accumulate, but they do not cause industrial activity to expand. It is confidence that causes this, and the new processes are merely the channels along which it directs itself. Secondly, the reflex boom, which was spoken of in Chapter V. as liable to occur after an interval equal to the length of life of the instrumental goods made in the initial boom, is probably not of great practical importance. For length of life does not depend in a rigid way upon physical conditions. It depends in great part upon what the owners of the instruments consider an *appropriate* length of life. There is, thus, a wide margin of choice as to the time at which renewals shall be made ; and the time chosen will generally be one in which confidence is high.   The renewal of plant due to inventions, like the original construction that embodies them, is, thus, a channel, rather than a cause, of expansions in industrial activity.

§ 3. The place to be assigned to harvest fluctuations is not settled so easily.   It is apparent that, if good harvests had, *no* causal influence in bringing about the expansions that occur in.industry, changes in the price of agricultural produce and of producer's goods respectively would be correlated positively. For industrial activity is, in general, associated with an expansion of credit, and this tends to bring about a rise of prices all round.   In fact, however, there are often downward kinks in the curve of food prices in the years that *start* upward movements of industry.   There is some degree of negative correlation between movements of agricultural prices and movements in the price of pig-iron.[1]   Furthermore, there is a fairly well-marked positive correlation between changes in the volume of the crops and immediately subsequent changes in business activity.   Professor Jevons writes concerning this matter: "The production of pig-iron is the best evidence of the state of the iron and steel trades, and these themselves vary with the general state of industry in the country (*i.e.* the United States), though perhaps in a somewhat exaggerated manner—I mean that fluctuations of the iron and steel business synchronise closely with those of other trades, but tend on the whole to be more violent.   On calculating the production of pig-iron per head of population in the United States year by year, and plotting it as a curve beneath that of the total agricultural production, the connection between the two sets of figures is obvious.   The abundant crops of 1870 and 1871 were followed by a great production of iron in 1872 and 1873 ; the big harvests of 1879 and 1880 were followed by an increased production of iron, which, again, culminated two years later, in 1882 ; and the bountiful harvest of 1884

---

[1] This inference is derived from Professor Moore's proofs of positive correlations between crop-yield and pig-iron production and between pig-iron production and pig-iron prices, and of negative correlation between crop-yields and agricultural prices.   (Cf. *Economic Cycles*, Chapters iv. and v.)

produced a spurt in the iron trade two years later. In the years 1888 to 1895 the curve of pig-iron production follows closely that of agricultural production, one year later; and, from 1893 onwards, the correspondence of the two curves is most remarkable, making due allowance for the rapid growth of the iron and steel industry."[1] The same point is made, as Professor Jevons notes, by Professor Piatt Andrew. Summarising a careful study of the influence of crops on business in America, that writer observes: "One cannot review the past forty years without observing that the beginnings of every movement towards business prosperity, and the turning-points towards every business decline (movements which frequently, it will be remarked, have antedated the actual outbreak of crises by several years), were closely connected with the out-turn of crops."[2] Lastly, Professor H. L. Moore has worked out, for the period 1870–1907, the correlation coefficient between changes in the yield per acre of certain American crops and changes (in the subsequent year) in the quantity of pig-iron produced, and has found this coefficient to be very high.[3] The existence of this high correlation clearly makes it probable that variations in the crops exercise a causal influence upon the process of industrial cycles. It must be noticed, however, that the observed correlation affords no evidence that this influence is exerted by way of the direct process described in Chapter IV. It may equally well be exercised through the medium of business confidence. This was fully realised by Stanley Jevons: "Periodic collapses," he wrote, "are really mental in their nature, depending upon variations of despondency, hopefulness, excitement, disappointment and panic. But it seems to be very probable that the moods of the commercial mind, while constituting the principal part of the phenomena, may be controlled by outward events, especially the condition of the harvests."[4] On this view, the influence of crop changes would be an indirect one, operating in the main by giving a fillip to optimistic and pessimistic tendencies in the business world. Their direct influence would be small.

---

[1] *Contemporary Review*, August 1909, pp. 177-8.
[2] *Quarterly Journal of Economics*, 1906, p. 351.
[3] Cf. *Economic Cycles*, p. 110.
[4] *Investigations in Currency and Finance*, p. 184.

§ 4. But whether their influence is direct or indirect, the fact that they exercise an influence at all makes it necessary to bring them into relation with the movement of business confidence described in Chapter VI. In my view, the dominant cause of the rhythmic fluctuations that are experienced in industry lies in these movements. But these movements are not rigid and self-contained. Thus, the normal period for the discovery of an error of optimism or pessimism may coincide with the occurrence of an exceptionally good harvest, which, in a sense, justifies the error retrospectively, and so cancels the effect of its discovery. If this happens, the turn of the tide may be delayed for a while; whereas, *per contra*, if a bad harvest, the outbreak of war, or other injurious event, occurs, it will be hastened and intensified. The length of the period of industrial wave movements is, thus, not fixed. Internal stresses do not determine the form of it in detail, but only in a rough general way. Chapter VI., in short, furnishes the backbone of the explanation of which we are in search, but other bones must be added from elsewhere. Of course, there is no absolute proof of the justice of this contention. Still, on a review of such evidence as is available, it appears to me that an explanation on these general lines is *probably* correct. By recognising the power of external events to modify the time-incidence and the magnitude of successive industrial waves, it leaves room for enough influence from the side of good and bad harvests to account for the observed correlations between crop variations and industrial movements. It should, thus, satisfy Professor Jevons, who, while he claims that bumper crops occur at intervals of from three to four years and give *some* impulse to industry each time they occur, admits that they only give *an effective* impulse at intervals of 7 or $10\frac{1}{2}$ years, when other conditions are ripe.[1] The kernel of the explanation is that optimistic error and pessimistic error, when discovered, give birth to one another in an endless chain, and that the interval between the successive generations is mainly, but not exclusively, determined by the period of gestation of industrial plant and machinery.

[1] Cf. *The Sun's Heat and Trade Activity*, p. 8.

CHAPTER VIII

§ 1. IN modern conditions the whole movement of industry and business is conducted in terms of, and, in large measure, through the agency of, money or some representative of money. The entrepreneurs, financiers and so forth, by whom the stream of goods that comes to completion every year is legally owned, sell these goods for money to wholesale houses and shopkeepers. The proceeds of this sale they employ, partly as personal income for their own use, partly in payment of interest to those persons from whom they hold loans, and partly in the hiring of labour to be employed in their enterprises. The money thus distributed is then used by all parties as a means of purchasing commodities from shopkeepers; and, in this way, the final distribution of the inflowing dividend is annually effected. In a perfectly stationary state the round-about character of this procedure would not modify in any respect the results ultimately achieved. The quantity of money passing from shopkeepers to entrepreneurs, as likewise the quantity of goods passing in exchange from entrepreneurs to shopkeepers, is the same every year; the distribution of the money by entrepreneurs is the same; and so also is the quantity of purchases effected by it when distributed. The quantity of commodities annually consumed by each several class and the quantity permanently held in store are not only identical with themselves in every year, but are also, at all times, identical with what they would have been had the process involved been direct. Furthermore, in a state of affairs which is not stationary, but in which the money system is so arranged that prices are invariable, the existence of a roundabout process would still leave the substance of what happens unchanged. For, though the motives at work operate upon goods through the medium of money instead of directly, yet, since a unit of money always controls the same quantity of goods, the medium is absolutely rigid, and always transfers power exactly as it is received. Finally, in a state of affairs, which, though neither perfectly stationary nor yet containing a money system so arranged that prices are invariable, is such that all changes in general prices are perfectly foreseen, the intervention of the monetary medium is still without effect; for full allowance will be made for future price changes in all industrial contracts, including those which deal with wages.[1] In actual fact, however, under the conditions prevailing in all modern countries, general prices, besides being variable, are also imperfectly foreseen. In these circumstances, there is clear *prima facie* ground for suspecting that the intervention of the monetary system may modify the effect of the forces whose application is mediated by it. Even if the monetary and banking aspects of industrial fluctuations were mere epiphenomena of the real process, caused by it, but not exercising themselves any reflex causal influence, it would still be necessary to study them, before that process could be fully understood. Since they in fact do exercise a reflex causal influence, the necessity for doing this is still more apparent.

§ 2. In normal times, when the general state of their

---

[1] It should be observed, to obviate misapprehension, that the above statement is strictly accurate only if we assume that both parties to all contracts purchase different sorts of commodities and services in the exact proportions in which these enter into the national dividend. If they do not do this, a knowledge of the way in which the price of "commodities in general" is going to move will not carry to any one a knowledge of the way in which the price of the particular collection of commodities interesting to him is going to move. This, however, lies beside our main argument. For, whatever imperfections of adjustment may result from the formulation of contracts in terms of "commodities in general," additional imperfections are practically certain to result if the standard actually employed is unstable relatively to commodities in general; and these additional imperfections will be larger or smaller, according as the variability of the standard relatively to "commodities in general" is larger or smaller.

income and their industrial activities is given, business men like to keep to their credit in their banks a certain balance upon which they can draw at need. How big this balance is depends, on the one hand, on how far, in their particular industry, a big balance is required for convenience in business and security against sudden calls, and, on the other hand, upon how high is the rate of interest which has to be sacrificed when resources are locked up in unproductive forms. For many men this balance will be the fruit of an actual loan from their bankers, so that its retention involves, not merely the sacrifice of interest that might have been secured by investment, but the actual payment of interest.

When confidence grows and the business community begins to look more optimistically at the prospective fruits of industrial activity, their desire to buy things and services (so transferring part of their balance to other people) relatively to their desire to hold a big balance expands. This tendency has a double cause. On the one side, business men want things and services more; on the other side, feeling increased confidence generally, they have less fear of bad debts and so attach less importance to holding a balance against sudden calls. Consequently, they are inclined to draw out funds and to offer them in effective demand for increased quantities of things and services. This procedure would, of course, by itself cause prices to rise. But in a modern community something further happens. Not content with drawing on (and so transferring) their existing balances, business men now think it worth while to offer a higher rate of interest to the banks to induce them to make new loans, to be used in still further demands for things and services. The banks consent to make these loans, partly out of funds which other people pay into them under the inducement of increased rates on deposit accounts, but mainly out of new bank money which they themselves are tempted by the higher interest to create, at the cost of permitting the ratio of their liabilities to their reserves to increase.[1]

---

[1] It is, of course, possible for an individual banker to increase his loans without thereby causing the aggregate liabilities of the banking system as a whole to increase. Thus, he may give a loan by crediting a customer with a deposit, and the customer may use this deposit to make a payment to somebody who uses it to discharge a debt to the same, or some other, banker. If this happens,

Plainly these new balances augment the volume of money that can be offered in purchase of things and services by the business men to whom in the first instance they are made over. Their creation, therefore, causes prices, which would, in any event, have moved up to some extent, to move up in a larger measure than would have been possible without them.

So far of the period of expanding confidence: it remains to consider the period of decline. As was explained in Chapter VI., when a boom draws towards its close, past investments are found to yield less than was looked for and many expectations are disappointed. Confidence is, therefore, shaken. Business men are no longer so anxious to buy things, and are much more anxious to contract their indebtedness to banks, and, if possible, to accumulate balances as a safeguard against possible disaster. This change of attitude does not, indeed, immediately cause prices to fall, because, as indicated in Chapter VI. § 11, most business men do not at once realise that the tide has turned. Finding that they cannot sell their goods at the high prices of a moment before, they try to hold them, in the hope of being able to do this in a little while. There is less money being spent, but there are also less commodities being offered for sale. This state of things may continue for some little while after confidence has broken. It explains the fact that the check to production is apt to *precede* the fall of prices. Soon, however, it is realised that further holding up of stocks is impracticable as well as useless. The hope that they will appreciate disappears. The business community's desire for them, relatively to its desire for bank balances, falls sharply. Captains of industry draw fewer cheques for new business. They spend less and accumulate more in the banks. Prices fall. Thus, just as the upward movement of business confidence was associated with a rise in

the deposit at once disappears. Again, the banker may agree to a customer's overdrawing his account, and the customer may, on the strength of this, draw a cheque which enables somebody else to wipe out an overdraft. When this happens no deposit is ever created. In general, however, when bankers make loans, whether by creating a deposit to a customer's credit or by sanctioning some form of overdraft, only a comparatively small part of the credit thus created will be used in wiping out other bank-credits. Though, therefore, it would be inaccurate to say that bankers' loans create *equivalent* deposit liabilities, it is exactly true that they create *substantial* deposit liabilities.

prices, so the downward movement is associated, after a short interval of lagging, by a downward movement of prices.

§ 3. Now, as has already been remarked, if the price movements described above were perfectly foreseen and allowed for, they would not react in any way upon the industrial movements out of which they spring. In fact, however, they are not perfectly foreseen and allowed for. When A, with new money, buys B's services, B thinks of a shilling as having for him the purchasing power over the things he is accustomed to buy that is shown in the prices *then* ruling, and does not take account of the fact that, when he (with others in a like position) comes to spend it, his act of spending will force up the prices of the things he buys. C, who sells to B, is, in turn, in like case, and so on throughout the industrial community. Nor is the failure of adjustment merely due to lack of foresight. When prices actually have moved, people do not for some considerable time realise and allow for the movement. Delay in the perception of facts and delay in the emergence of facts are both at work. The results are well known. As Professor Fisher has shown, contracts for interest are not adequately adjusted. If prices are going to rise 5 per cent during the year, in order to get 5 per cent real interest, we should need to contract for about 10 per cent nominal interest on a one-year loan. In fact we do not do this. Friction and ignorance intervene. Nor, except in the comparatively rare industries where a sliding scale or some well-organised and plastic system of conciliation exists, can contracts concerning wage rates be properly adjusted to price changes, till a good deal of friction has been overcome and a good deal of time wasted.[1] Money rates of interest and of wages alike

---

[1] Cf. Part III. Chapter XVIII. § 1. It may, perhaps, be objected that the price of most of the things purchased by wage-earners, since wage-earners purchase the bulk of them, can only be pushed up substantially in price in consequence of an increased offer of money for them on the part of wage-earners, this increased offer being, in turn, made possible by the extra payments which employers are prepared to make to wage-earners in periods of expansion. Hence, it would seem to follow that the prices of things of interest to workpeople cannot be pushed up in consequence of a confidence boom more than in proportion to the accompanying increase in their wages. This may well be true of *aggregate wages*, but, since in times of boom the number of workpeople employed is increased, it does not warrant the inference that these prices cannot rise more than in proportion to the *rate of wages*.

thus fail to rise sufficiently to prevent the rise of prices from
causing a fall in the real rates. In like manner, when, other
things being equal, there are forces at work making for
a decrease in the output of industrial energy, the business
world's borrowings from the banks decline, prices fall, and the
fall is not adequately allowed for. Consequently, money
rates of wages and interest fail to fall sufficiently to prevent
the fall in prices from causing a rise in the real rates. These
failures of adjustment tend in two distinct ways to accentuate
the fluctuations that occur in the volume of industrial energy
that is devoted to production.

§ 4. When the wave is mounting, business men, who are,
in the main, wage-payers and borrowers, are made more
prosperous, at the expense of wage-earners and sleeping
capitalists, than they would have been in a world ringing
perfectly true to the economic harmonies. Conversely, when
the wave is sinking, they are made less prosperous. Furthermore, besides the real change in their fortunes, there is also an
element of imagined change. For, when people have more
or less money than usual, even though prices have changed
in precise correspondence, the natural tendency to "think
in gold" is apt to make them imagine themselves really
richer or really poorer. But, as was observed in Chapter
VI., the judgments which people form are biassed by
their feelings. When they are, or believe that they are,
enjoying good fortune, they are apt to look on the brighter
side, and when they are suffering bad fortune, on the darker
side, of doubt. Consequently, anything which improves the
fortunes of business men constitutes a spur to optimistic
error ; just as anything which worsens their fortunes constitutes a spur to pessimistic error. In prosperity they
borrow more money, and, thereby, cause prices to rise still
further. By this rise, the real rate of interest payable on
their *past* loans is reduced still further, their fortunes are
again improved, and, in consequence, the error of their forecasts is again expanded. The process thus begun tends,
until it is interrupted by the shock of discovered reality,
to continue indefinitely. In periods of depression an exactly
converse process takes place. In both sorts of period the

error thus born out of monetary movements allies itself with the other more general error that was discussed in Chapter VI., and causes the output of industrial energy to expand in good times and to contract in bad times beyond what it would do in a community made up of perfectly cool intelligences.

§ 5. It is not, however, only as a cause of error that the monetary system affects the steadiness of the output of industrial energy. It also exercises an important influence of a more direct kind: For it offers to business men, if they choose to raise money and spend their balances in times of rising prices, a gain derived from the exploitation of other people, additional to that derived from their own productivity, and it threatens them, if they dare to do this in times of falling prices, with a loss due to the exploitation of themselves by other people. The reason for this is that changes in general prices are not merely imperfectly, but are also unequally, foreseen. The anticipations concerning them formed by the entrepreneur class are, in general, more nearly correct than those formed by either sleeping capitalists or the wage-earning class. This circumstance implies that business men, if they wish to raise new resources, can reckon, in periods of rising prices, on finding capitalists and wage-earners prepared—by error and quite unknown to themselves—to offer any assigned quantity of their services at a reduced real rate of payment; and, in periods of falling prices, upon finding them insistently demanding, for any assigned quantity, an increased real rate. When prices are rising, the business world's expectation of profit from investment is enhanced by an expectation of a kind of bonus at the expense of capitalists and wage-earners; when prices are falling, it is contracted by an expectation of a kind of toll, which will have to be paid in respect of the services of those classes. Thus, as Professor Fisher observes: "Inequality (as distinguished from imperfection) of foresight produces over-investment during rising prices and relative stagnation during falling prices."[1] In times of rising prices it is profitable for each business man to cause the group of productive factors over which he has control to put forth more industrial energy than it is profitable to the group as a

[1] *The Rate of Interest*, p. 286.

whole to put forth; and in times of falling prices it is profitable for him to direct less energy into industry than it would pay this group to direct there. This consideration, combined with that discussed in the preceding section, makes it plain that, the less general prices vary in conjunction with given variations in business confidence, the smaller the associated variations in the output of industrial energy are likely to be.

§ 6. Under a banking system of the type of the English system before the Great War price variations are held in check by a somewhat complicated process, which has already been summarily described in the fourth section of Part IV. Chapter X. When, in response to the demands of business, banks create new credits and prices consequently rise, it becomes convenient for members of the general public to carry, on the average, a rather larger amount of currency in their pockets than they have been accustomed to carry hitherto. Furthermore, in so far as the new bank loans are employed, either directly or indirectly, in the hiring of labour, they have necessarily to be broken up and taken out in the form of currency. In both these ways an internal drain, for currency purposes, is set up upon the reserves of the banks. At the same time an external drain also is set up. For, prices here having risen, or, in other words, gold here having become cheaper in terms of things, foreigners will be tempted to send more things here with which to buy gold. Imports are encouraged, exports are discouraged, and gold tends to flow abroad. The joint action of these two drains, by lessening the reserve, forces the Bank of England to raise the discount rate, and, if necessary, by selling government securities or otherwise, to make the rise effective in the market also. As a result of this, borrowing on the part of business men is discouraged; their expenditure is checked, and the upward movement of prices thereby restrained. In periods of depression, when, through slackened demands on the part of business men, prices are falling, a converse process is set up. Gold flows into the reserve both from the circulation and from abroad, discount rates fall, borrowing and expenditure are encouraged, and so the fall in prices is restricted.

§ 7. The speed and efficiency with which these processes operated were particularly great under the English pre-war system for two reasons. First, the quantity of fiduciary notes issued was, for practical purposes, absolutely fixed. To increase it was illegal and to decrease it always unprofitable. Under a system, which, by permitting extra issues on the payment of a tax, causes the note circulation to expand in times of boom and to contract in times of depression, the internal drain upon the reserve set up in periods of rising prices and the replenishment of it in periods of falling prices would both be checked. For in prosperous times people would carry extra notes—it should be observed that notes of large denominations would not serve the purpose—instead of extra gold. It is true that their action in doing this would add to the aggregate liabilities of the banking system. But the addition of, say, three million pounds to liabilities makes a very much smaller difference than the subtraction of this sum from the reserve to that *proportion* between liabilities and reserve, which determines the risks involved in the grant of further loans. Secondly, the English gold market was absolutely unhampered, and so the tendency to a foreign drain of gold acted with full force. Evidently any arrangement that obstructs the free export of gold, whether a confessed embargo, or informal discouragement by the banks, as practised in pre-war Germany, or the exercise of a right to offer depreciated silver for export in lieu of gold, as in pre-war France, or any arrangement that deliberately manufactures credit abroad to "protect the exchanges" in times of stress, must lessen the efficacy of the check exercised by foreign drains upon the expansion of bank loans and so upon the upward movement of prices.

§ 8. The English gold standard plan has thus been shown to accomplish a good deal in the way of limiting the price variations which oscillations in business confidence set up. Plainly, however, even apart from the lag that necessarily occurs in its corrective processes, it is impotent against fluctuations that extend over the commercial world generally. It tends to hold English prices in the neighbourhood of world prices and to prevent them from oscillating much *round* world prices. But it does nothing to prevent—on the contrary it assists—them to oscillate *with* world prices. The realisation of this fact has led thinkers to inquire whether it might not be possible to accomplish something more to keep prices steady by a manipulation of the monetary mechanism. The collapse of the gold standard throughout the greater part of the world, consequent upon the war, and the chaos of unregulated paper that has supplanted it, have rendered these speculations from one point of view more actual, but from another more remote. They have rendered them more actual, because, whereas before the war the then existing system, which it was proposed to supplant, at all events worked moderately well, the existing system of the present time, over the greater part of Europe, is altogether intolerable. They have rendered them more remote, because in a period of chaos one naturally seeks to find again the relatively firm ground one has left rather than some new Utopia. In most countries, certainly in such a country as England, effort and thought are likely to be concentrated upon re-establishing a definite relation, if possible the pre-war relation, between the currency and gold. Until this is accomplished, it will be widely felt that attempts to improve on pre-war monetary arrangements, which everybody recognises to have been enormously superior to the state of things existing now, are premature. Nevertheless, though it may well be that, at present, proposals to establish a currency stable in terms of things are not practical politics, it is the clear duty of economists impartially to study them on their merits.

§ 9. The general idea is to increase the currency when prices show signs of falling and to diminish it when they show signs of rising. Something on these lines was attempted under the German currency law of 1909, which, while fixing the normal untaxed limit of note issue at 550 million marks, provided that in the last week of each quarter—when an exceptional amount of currency is apt to be wanted—the limit should be raised to 750 millions. A much more elaborate and thorough application of this general idea is made in a plan originally suggested by Ricardo, which has been elaborated in detail by Professor Irving Fisher in the concluding chapter of his work on the *Purchasing Power of Money*. The proposal in broad outline is as follows. For simplicity we suppose provisionally that it is adopted in one country only. In that country the currency, whether made of paper or of gold or of anything else, should be so constructed that the value of the material in a unit of it is worth very much less as material than it is when turned into currency. A Government Department should publish month by month an index number representing the variations in the purchasing power of a unit of currency. The Mint, or some corresponding Government agency, should always be prepared to exchange currency into or out of gold bullion. But the quantity of currency given or taken in exchange for a given weight of bullion would not, on Professor Fisher's plan, be a fixed quantity; it would be increased or diminished according as the index number of general prices showed a tendency to fall or to rise. When general prices began to fall, the Mint would sell currency for bullion below. the market rate; and, therefore, more of it would get into the bank reserves (thus providing a basis for further credit) and into the circulation. The quantity of exchange instruments being thus increased, while the quantity of transactions against which they were required remained the same, an influence would be set up making for a rise of prices. In this way the fall of prices, which was threatening to come about, would be checked. In like manner, when general prices began to rise, the Mint would buy currency for bullion above the market rate, the supply of currency would be contracted, and the rise of prices, which was threatening to come about, would be checked.[1] In short, to employ Professor Fisher's terms, the Mint—or whatever governmental authority might be selected for the purpose—would buy and sell currency in terms of bullion, in such a way as to maintain, so far as possible, "a par, not with a fixed weight of gold but with such a weight of gold as should have a fixed purchasing power."[2]

[1] Of course the whole purpose of this arrangement would be upset if the Government were to deposit the coined gold, which it buys in order to lower prices, with the banks; it must withdraw it altogether from the money-providing machine. The Philippine legislation sets a bad example in this respect, in that it allows a certain portion of the Gold Standard Fund to be held on deposit in Manila banks. (Cf. Kemmerer, *Modern Currency Reforms*, pp. 375-7.)

[2] Fisher, *The Purchasing Power of Money*, p. 342.

§ 10. It might perhaps be thought at first sight that this plan, if it succeeded, would not merely prevent prices from fluctuating alongside of fluctuations in business confidence, but would also prevent business men in periods of optimism from making any larger investment than in other periods; because the process by which they are normally enabled to do this, namely additional bank loans, would be done away. This, however, is not really so. The rate of discount going up under the influence of business demand, business men would still get more loans than usual, partly at the expense of other would-be borrowers who would get less, and partly as a result of extra savings to which other people would be tempted by high deposit rates. Thus, Professor Fisher's stabilising plan would allow the *proportion* of purchasing power designed for investment to expand in good times, although it would prevent the absolute quantity of purchasing power relatively to things offered for sale from expanding. The fear that this plan would freeze industry, as well as general prices, into stationariness is thus seen to rest on a misunderstanding. There is no real ground for it.

§ 11. The same thing is true of a second important objection which naturally suggests itself. As will be made plain in the following chapter, it is of the utmost importance in times of panic that the banks should lend freely. It might be thought that Professor Fisher's plan would prevent them from doing this. That is a delusion. In ordinary times, of course, large bank loans mean large expenditure and, therefore, a rise in prices; and, when this happens, the plan attacks the reserve and so checks lending. But in times of panic people want money, not to spend, but to discharge debts and to hold against the danger of failure. To this end they offer, as in times of boom, a high rate of discount, but they also offer, at a greatly reduced rate, their holdings of commodities. In other words, the loans which business men seek when confidence collapses, unlike those which they seek when it expands, are associated with a fall of prices.[1] In these circum-

---

[1] Cf. Kemmerer, "A large demand for call money sometimes is a sign of low confidence and represents liquidation, and sometimes is a sign of high confidence and represents good opportunities for new investment" (*Money and Prices*, p. 124).

stances, the plan, so far from making it more difficult for banks to lend freely to check the panic, would, by creating new reserves for them, make it easier for them to do this. Thus this objection also is without substance.

§ 12. There remain certain minor difficulties, to which Professor Fisher's plan is exposed, and to which it is well that attention should be called.

First, if the supply of gold greatly expands, so that commodity prices in terms of gold bullion rise rapidly, the quantity of gold bullion which the Mint or Treasury would need to pay in order to withdraw any given quantity of currency from circulation will largely increase. This means that a much larger bullion reserve than was thought necessary at first will need to be established, and the Treasury will, therefore, have to buy or borrow in the market a large extra quantity of bullion. This circumstance, though not of first-class importance, threatens a certain amount of awkwardness and expense.[1] It will be noticed, however, that, though the quantity of bullion which the Treasury will need to hold will be increased, it does not follow that the aggregate value of it in terms of things in general will be increased.

Secondly, should the supply of gold fail to expand, in such wise that commodity prices in terms of gold bullion fall, then, if the currency has been constructed of token gold coins, it may happen that the token coin will cease to be a token, as in fact the Indian rupee did as a result of the war, and even that, in order to carry out Professor Fisher's plan, the Mint will have to give a greater weight of coined gold in return for a given weight of uncoined gold.[2] This it obviously cannot do except at great cost. Consequently, in order that the plan should continue in operation, it would be necessary to reduce the weight of gold in the token coin; and this would almost certainly involve a considerable shock to business confidence. We should, in short, be compelled, as the Government of the Philippines was compelled for this very reason in 1906, to recoin the whole of the currency into coins containing a smaller amount of bullion. The danger that this might

[1] Cf. J. M. Clark, *American Economic Review*, Sept. 1913, pp. 577 *et seq.*
[2] Cf. Patterson, *American Economic Review*, Dec. 1913, p. 864.

become necessary would, however, be very small if the original coins contained very little bullion and were issued at a high seigniorage. ·If the currency were made up, not of coins at all, but of those paper notes of low denominations with which the war has made everybody familiar, it would be done away with altogether.

Thirdly, for a single country to adopt Professor Fisher's plan would lead to difficulties in the business of persons engaged in foreign trade, since, apart from special arrangements, they might find themselves borrowers in terms of one standard and lenders in terms of another. In the present state of the European currencies these difficulties must, of course, be experienced by a gold standard country, and would not be any worse for a country with a stabilised standard. If, however, we suppose the rest of the world restored to a gold standard, a particular country, by adopting the gold standard, could avoid them, but, if it adopted the stabilised standard for itself alone, it would have to face them. Even so, however, the difficulties are liable to be exaggerated. They are in essence the same as those to which merchants in a gold standard country are exposed in their dealings with silver standard countries, and *vice versa*. They consist in the risk that, after a sale has been made in foreign currency and before payment has been received, the value of foreign currency in terms of native currency may have undergone a considerable change. In ordinary times this risk can be shifted—of course at a price—upon the shoulders of exchange banks, which will contract to buy from exporters their prospective foreign currency three months hence at a definite rate in native currency. In so far as the banks choose to hedge, by contracting at the same time to sell to importers the foreign currency which they expect to need three months hence at the same definite rate in native currency, the risk is, not merely shifted, but is actually destroyed.[1] Thus, the exchange difficulty is a less serious one than it is sometimes supposed to be.

Finally, apart from these technical difficulties, it is fairly plain that absolute stability of the standard money in terms of "commodities in general" could not be obtained in any

[1] Cf. Kemmerer, *Modern Currency Reforms*, p. 297.

country by the adoption of Professor Fisher's plan; for the corrective to price variations, which the plan introduces, must act through the quantity of money, and must, therefore, lag somewhat behind the errors which it seeks to overtake; and in the sudden changes of commercial crises the lag might be considerable.

§ 13. In spite, however, of these difficulties and imperfections, any country adopting this plan would almost certainly enjoy considerably greater stability of price levels than prevailed under pre-war arrangements, and, of course, incomparably greater stability than the unregulated paper currencies born of the war have afforded. Moreover, if one country would consent to Professor Fisher's proposal, any other country, by basing its currency on the currency of that country, on the pattern of the gold exchange standard, could also obtain a money whose purchasing power was fixed in respect of the same index number. No doubt, this kind of "derived" fixity would not be ideal, because stability in terms of the "things in general" consumed in one country is not likely to mean stability in terms of the "things in general" consumed in another. Still, it is probable that "a unit of fixed purchasing power in England gives a more nearly uniform purchasing power in any other civilised country than would an ounce of gold or an ounce of silver."[1]

§ 14. So far of the general consequences of Professor Fisher's plan. In order to carry it out in practice, the Board of Control, which it would be necessary to set up in the country operating it, would, of course, need to retain in store a large quantity of gold. The real annual cost of the scheme *to the country financing the Board* would be measured by the interest which it had to sacrifice through the retention of such part, if any, of this gold as was not formerly locked up in its own currency and bank-reserves. It would be exactly analogous to the real annual cost to the people of India of the exchange funds of gold and rupees, which they hold in London and Calcutta for the purpose of keeping the relative value of gold and rupees constant. The real annual cost of the scheme *to the world* would be somewhat less than its

---

[1] Marshall, *Contemporary Review*, 1887, p. 371.

cost to the country financing the Board, because, in so far
as the gold fund needed was taken from the monetary machines
of other countries, its withdrawal would not diminish the
efficiency of those machines. · This consideration, together with
the fact that the adoption of the scheme in one country would
make possible, in the way that has been explained, a steadying
of prices in other countries also, suggests that the Board of
Control might well be established and financed on an international basis. It cannot be rigidly proved that, even in that
event, the indirect gain accruing from steadier prices would
outweigh the direct costs, because there are no means of
estimating the magnitude of either of these quantities. I am
inclined, however, to believe that considerable net benefit to
the world would result even as against the pre-war system, and,
as against the chaos of the present time, enormous net benefit.

CHAPTER IX

§ 1. WE have not yet exhausted the influences upon which the amplitude of the wave movements of industry depend. The analysis of Chapter VI. has shown by implication that the extent of the revulsion towards pessimistic error, which follows when optimistic error is disclosed, depends upon the magnitude of the preceding optimistic error. But it does not depend only upon this. It is also affected by what we may call the "detonation," which accompanies the discovery of a given mass of optimistic error. The detonation is greater or less according to the number and scale of the legal bankruptcies into which the detected error explodes. These legal bankruptcies, or "business failures," are not, in themselves, of great industrial importance. It seldom happens that, as a result of them, any business enterprise is abandoned; the normal course is for it to pass, through sale or through a receivership in the interest of bond-holders, into the control of other—very probably more energetic and more able—men, with the net result that a relatively competent entrepreneur is substituted for one who was relatively incompetent. It is, thus, a true saying which Mr. Burton quotes from John Mills: "As a rule, panics do not destroy capital; they merely reveal the extent to which it has been previously destroyed by its betrayal into hopelessly unproductive works."[1] But business failures necessarily and always breed fear among industrialists that their own debtors may fail. The more extensive they are—that is to say, the louder the detonation—the more they shatter business con-

[1] Burton, *Financial Crises*, p. 20.

3 K

fidence. The influences by which the detonation that accompanies any given discovery of error is determined are, therefore, real causes affecting the amplitude of industrial fluctuations.

§ 2. Among these influences are the methods by which industry is normally financed. When people (not otherwise in debt) make unsuccessful investments with money belonging to themselves, the failure of their ventures cannot involve legal bankruptcy. But, when they employ borrowed money, failure may involve this. From this point of view, therefore, the highly developed credit arrangements of the modern world constitute a danger. The danger is especially great when loans have been taken up in a form that requires periodic renewal, so that the venturer may find himself, in his hour of need, forced to pay back the principal of his loan. In the United States a large share of the capital required in manufacturing establishments and in other enterprises " is furnished by discounts obtained from banks instead of by permanent capital or by long-time loans or bonds."[1] This is a risky arrangement. If businesses find it necessary to raise floating loans, prudence requires that they should fund them as soon as possible.[2] There is danger, again, when creditors are ill-advised enough, or when their fortunes are so far bound up with those of potentially insolvent debtors that they are practically forced, to add loan to loan for firms, which, whether by making new plunges of rash investment or by holding up goods against liquidation as prices fall, are heading for the rocks. When this happens—it is probable that the eventual collapse will be all the more severe, just because it has been delayed. For not only is there a presumption that a business house, which has committed errors large enough to render it potentially insolvent, is incompetently managed and is likely to commit further errors in the future, even if its business practice is not worsened; but also this practice is, in fact, likely to be worsened, because, since the house is already insolvent, further losses will fall, not upon it, but

[1] Burton, *Financial Crises*, p. 263.
[2] The increase in the issue of securities that often occurs after a crisis is due in the main to this process of funding. (Cf. Mitchell, *Business Cycles*, p. 405.)

upon its creditors. This danger can be partly mitigated by the embodiment in the bankruptcy laws of stringent provisions against various forms of fraud and sharp practice. In Germany an attempt is made to do more than this. As soon as the balance sheet of a company (the balance sheet must take account of depreciation of capital) shows an excess of liabilities over assets, compulsory winding-up is required and enforced by penalties. English law, of course, allows a company to continue in business till it actually becomes bankrupt.

§ 3. The above influences go far to determine over how wide a range, at any given turning-point of confidence, business failures will be threatened. They do not, however, by themselves determine what proportion of the threatened failures shall actually occur. This is settled principally by the capacity and willingness of the country's banking-system to save houses which are really sound—in the sense that their assets are more than sufficient to cover their liabilities—but which cannot at the moment secure sufficient money to meet obligations immediately payable in that form. For, of course, on these occasions it is money, and money only, that is wanted. Commodities and securities are both useless for the purpose. Money alone will save, and the repositories of money are the banks. Hence, other things being equal, the actual occurrence of business failures will be more or less widespread, according as bankers' loans *in the face of crisis demands* are less or more readily obtainable.

§ 4. At the time when errors of optimism are discovered, bankers are often beginning to realise, not merely that their liabilities relatively to their cash reserves have become exceptionally large, but also that an exceptionally large proportion of their loans are being used in financing constructional enterprises, as distinguished from commerce proper, and have, therefore, become, as it were, solidified, instead of liquid, assets. Therefore, it is natural that they should hesitate to swell their liabilities still further, whether by lending to sound houses or in any other way. They are themselves under contract to meet all liabilities with legal tender upon demand, and anything that widens the gap between liabilities and reserves lessens their assurance of being able to do this. It may, therefore, be

argued, and was argued, by earlier bankers, that, though the
public interest requires them to lend freely, their own private
interest commands, rather, a calling-in of their loans.   Under
a many-reserve system, when the separate banks are isolated
from one another, this reasoning *may*, on occasions, be sound.
Though it would pay *all* banks to lend freely, it need not pay
any particular bank to do so.   For, if it lends freely, the whole
of its reserve may be drawn out and paid over into the coffers
of its rivals ; whereas, if it holds its hand, it may possibly
stand a rare survivor amid the general ruin.   Even under a
many-reserve, system, however, and still more under a
one-reserve system, a selfish policy is dangerous to the banks
that practise it, as well as highly injurious to the community
as a whole.   If loans are withheld and sound houses fall, their
fall will drag down others.   Panic will grow wilder and wilder
and will eventually lead to distrust of the banks themselves.
When this happens and depositors begin to insist on their
legal right to actual currency, the safety of the banks generally
—of the selfish equally with the public-spirited—is threatened
far more seriously than it would have been, had loans been
made with sufficient freedom to nip the panic in the bud.   It
follows that the self-interest of the banks, looked at broadly
and generally, requires them to lend freely in the face of crisis
demands.   In other words, bank loans in these circumstances
are, so far as bankers recognise their own interest, readily
granted.   They will be refused only if bankers fail rightly
to analyse the situation and are timid by mistake.   They
must lend freely.   When, as in this country, there is a
central, banking institution, that institution especially must
lend freely.   This does not, of course, mean cheaply.   On the
contrary, since panic generally comes at the apex of an exaggerated boom, when high prices have led to expanded imports and
are inducing a heavy foreign drain, the rates charged must be
high.   But at high rates loans must be forthcoming.   This is
Bagehot's celebrated advice to the Bank of England : " The
end is to stay the panic ; and the advances should, if possible,
stay the panic.   And, for this purpose there are two rules.
First, that these loans should only be made at a very high rate
of interest. . . . Secondly, that at this rate these advances

should be made on all good banking securities, and as largely as the public ask for them."[1] The policy thus recommended has become a recognised part of Bank of England practice. It necessarily exercises a powerful effect in lessening the "detonation" of financial crises. It may, therefore, be credited with considerable influence in restricting the amplitude of confidence waves, and, therewith, of industrial fluctuations.

§ 5. It should be added that this policy carries with it an important practical corollary. In view of the danger that a domestic panic may be associated with a large foreign drain, it is imperative that, in a country where an effective gold standard is operating, the gold reserve of that country's banking system shall be sufficient, not merely to meet any probable demand upon it, but to leave such a margin that no serious fear of its exhaustion will ever arise. This is a necessary insurance against very severe panic. How large the reserve ought to be in relation to normal liabilities will, of course, be different in different circumstances. Under a one-reserve system it is not, of course, necessary to hold so much as under a many-reserve system, where all the banks are independent; for the maximum *aggregate* drain that is likely to occur at any one time is much smaller than the sum of the maximum separate drains that occur at different times. Again, the banks of a country where the proportion of bullion reserve is low may atone for this deficiency by a large net holding of foreign bills of exchange payable in gold and approaching maturity,[2] or by a large holding of first-class securities with an international market, or even by a great undocumented power to borrow bullion from abroad. The United Kingdom before the war was strong in all these respects. Not only were we large lenders both in the short and

---

[1] *Lombard Street,* p. 199.

[2] The special character of foreign, as distinguished from domestic, bills is recognised in the Swedish law, which allows the National Bank to issue notes beyond the authorised limit "to an amount equal to the funds of the bank held in foreign countries on current account with the banking and mercantile houses"; and also by the rule of the late Austro-Hungarian Bank, which recognised foreign three-months' bills as cover for notes. In Germany, on the other hand, no distinction between foreign and domestic bills is made in the rule compelling the Reichsbank to hold that part of its reserve against notes, which does not consist of gold, in discounted bills.

in the long market, but also it was very much against
the interest of foreigners to allow a crisis to develop here.
As the late Lord Goschen well observed, when the Bank of
France provided three millions to tide us over the Baring
crisis, "Paris was interested in saving the situation, let there
be no mistake about that."[1] It must be remembered, however, that our power to draw gold from abroad had been
weakened by the adoption by foreign countries, formerly on a
bimetallic or paper basis, of the gold standard; because this
meant that in crises they were as eager to obtain gold as we.
Moreover, the tradition of a free market for gold in London,
besides enabling us to obtain gold easily at need, also made us
liable to exceptionally large drains. A direct consequence of
the existence of that free market was that, when a foreigner
had a claim on London and wished to realise it, he was not
prevented from realising it in gold. An indirect consequence
was that many foreign traders, who expected to want gold to
finance their international transactions, regularly purchased
credits on London, while some Continental institutions, which
expected to want gold for their reserves, "always kept a port-
folio stocked with bills on London, constantly replaced as they
matured, so that, in time of need, they might take gold from
London to replenish the basis of their note issues."[2] A
further indirect consequence was that trade between England
and the rest of the world was, in general, financed by bills
drawn on London, and not on the places to which English
traders sell. In short, London was the regular centre to which,
along routes carefully prepared beforehand, foreigners, who
needed gold, were accustomed to present their claims. English
acceptors and discounters were, of course, paid for the services
which they rendered—some estimates put these services before
the war at eighteen millions annually—but, as a penalty
for rendering them, we were liable in a higher degree than other
nations to foreign drains of gold. In determining the proper
proportion of the normal reserve all these considerations had
to be borne in mind. It was often contended before the war
that in this country the proportion between the holding of

---

[1] Goschen, *Essays and Addresses*, p. 109.
[2] Withers, *The Meaning of Money*, pp. 171-2.

gold in the banking department of the Bank of England and the aggregate liabilities of the banking system of the country was dangerously low. When an effective gold standard is re-established and London again becomes a free market for gold, the question of the size of the reserve will resume its old importance. The relevant considerations will, however, be somewhat different from what they used to be. If we become less important lenders in the short loan market to foreigners, the need for a large reserve will be, *pro tanto*, increased. If certain foreign countries, which formerly had gold standards, go permanently on to an inconvertible paper basis, there will be fewer competitors with us for gold in times of crisis. We may, therefore, be able to reckon more confidently on getting gold' for emergencies when we want it, and we may not need so large a permanent store. On the other hand, if we decide to continue the circulation of notes instead of sovereigns, we shall, of course, need to keep in the central reserve a substantial gold backing for these notes, as well as for those in the ordinary banking reserve. As was indicated in Part IV. Chapter X., the Committee on Currency and the Foreign Exchanges tentatively looked forward to an aggregate central reserve in the neighbourhood of 150 millions as probably appropriate to our post-war normal condition. Plainly, however, no final judgment on this issue can be formed now; and plainly also, in a matter of this kind, security is a more important consideration than economy.

§ 6. In countries where the cheque system is little developed a large expansion of bank loans cannot practically be accomplished except with the help of an expansion in the note issue. Consequently, the normal treatment of a crisis must involve such an expansion. This is probably an adequate defence for the elastic system of note issue established in Germany. The loans required even in a quite ordinary crisis could not be provided otherwise. In this country, however, where bankers, as a rule, lend by crediting their customers with deposits on which cheques may be drawn, the position is quite different, and there is, in the ordinary course, no need to allow any extra issue of notes. It may happen, however, in the absence, or sometimes in spite of, a wise banking policy, that

a crisis detonates with sufficient force to affect public confidence
in the banks themselves. ; People, while still content with bank
notes, may become afraid that their deposits with bankers are not
safe, and may demand actual currency, . A panic of this kind
took place in the United States after the failure of the Knicker-
bocker Trust in 1907, and in this country after the Overend
and Gurney smash in 1866. The essence of it is fear that
the bankers have not enough money to meet their obligations
in currency, and consequent urgency on the part of each
depositor to draw out and hoard what is due to him, before it
is absorbed by other depositors.[1]   In a sufficiently severe panic
of this type a point may be reached beyond which further loans
of currency are impossible, because the currency is not there
to lend.   Then the only possible remedy is the creation of
currency.   This means in practice the creation of notes.   In
most modern States, however, the freedom of banks to create
notes is in some way limited by law.   When this is so
—and it does not matter for this purpose whether the limit
laid down for the fiduciary issue is an *amount* or a *proportion*—
it is impossible for bankers to give an assurance to depositors
that sufficient currency will be forthcoming to meet their
demands without the collaboration of the State. : Elasticity
of note issue, which is normally circumscribed, has, therefore,
to be specially expanded by the removal of the normal restrictions.   When people know that the State has intervened
and emergency issues are sanctioned, so that currency cannot
run short, nothing further is usually needed.   Knowing
that they can get currency if they ask for it, people do
not ask for it.   The explosion is finished and normal life is
resumed.

§ 7. On these grounds there is general agreement that, in
times of sufficiently severe crisis, the national Bank of Issue
must be given the power to add to the supply of notes
whatever extra amount may be necessary to stay the panic.
There is, however, difference of opinion as to the way in which
this power should be conferred.   In England the method

---

[1] A very similar effect is produced when the general public is not in fact
running on the banks, but when bankers are afraid that they will do so, and,
consequently, as in August 1914, themselves demand currency for their tills as
a safeguard.

adopted has been a suspension of the Bank Charter Act by emergency action, which was technically illegal, on the part of the Cabinet. In Belgium the same thing could be done, and technical illegality avoided, under a law which permitted the Finance Minister to set aside, at his discretion, the National Bank's obligation to keep specie in hand equal to one-third of the combined amount of its bank-note circulation and other sight obligations. In pre-war Germany and in the United States under the Federal Revenue Act extra issues of notes beyond the normal provisional maximum are permitted, on condition that a tax is paid on the excess. In criticism of the English system it was argued before the war that, when a crisis has actually begun, doubt as to whether or not the Bank Act will be suspended in time terrifies the market and intensifies panic. Under an automatic arrangement permitting excess issue on conditions defined beforehand — the payment of a tax on the excess, the establishment of a high discount rate, the prevalence of an adverse exchange—these unfavourable reactions could not, it was held, be set up. It was replied that the very rigidity of our system, and the solemnity of the step—a definite breach of the law—which was needed to release extra fiduciary notes, fortified the Bank of England in a policy of caution and conservatism towards the discount rate and the reserve well calculated to check at an early stage speculation that might otherwise have led to severe crises. Moreover, any automatic plan is faced with the formidable difficulty of so defining the conditions of excess issue that such issue shall always be permitted when required to check a panic and never permitted when not so required. The German system did not accomplish this, because, under it, it might pay the Reichsbank to issue notes while a boom was still under way, thus intensifying both the boom itself and the collapse to which it leads. After careful consideration of the whole matter the Committee on Currency and the Foreign Exchanges in 1918 unanimously recommended the following compromise: "The provision of Section 3 of the Currency and Bank Notes Act 1914, under which the Bank of England may, with the consent of the Treasury, temporarily issue notes in excess of the legal limit,

should be continued in force. It should be provided by
statute that Parliament should be informed forthwith of
any action taken by the Treasury under this provision by
means of a Treasury Minute, which should be laid before both
Houses. The statute should also provide that any profit
derived from the excess issue should be surrendered by the
Bank to the Exchequer. It will, of course, be necessary that
the bank rate should be raised to, and maintained at, a figure
sufficiently high to secure the earliest possible retirement of
the excess issue." [1]

§ 8. There remains a still severer form of banking panic.
People may lose confidence, not only in bank deposits, but
also in bank notes, and may threaten to present these in
large numbers for encashment in gold. For this malady it
is evident that the issue of extra notes is no sufficient remedy.
If nothing further is done, the notes will be presented for gold;
the gold in the reserve will not suffice for their encashment;
bank after bank will shut its doors: and the whole monetary
system of the country will be in chaos. In this type of
panic; if it goes far enough, free lending becomes no longer
possible. There will be no more of the only kind of currency
that people want available in the bank reserves. In these
circumstances one possible course of action is for the State itself
to create a new fiduciary currency—like our Treasury notes
—in the hope that the public panic will not extend to them.
Failing this *deus ex machina*, a breach of contract on the part
of the banks *cannot* be prevented. All that the State can do
is to mitigate the effects which this breach must have upon
business confidence by making it a legally allowable breach.
In 1907 in several of the Western States of America this was
done by the device of a series of legal bank-holidays. In most
of the other States of the United States the banks were
officially informed that they would not be held insolvent if
they paid their depositors a limited amount of cash and
settled the balance by certified cheques or drafts on corre-
spondents. This was, of course, an informal method of suspend-
ing specie payments; and Professor Andrew finds that " roughly
speaking, in two-thirds of the cities of more than 25,000

[1] *Report*, p. 9.

inhabitants the banks suspended cash payments to a greater or less degree." [1]   The same end can be accomplished in a more direct and straightforward manner by a law temporarily abolishing the issuing banks' obligation to convert their notes into gold.   Remedies along these lines are, of course, a *pis aller*. But nothing else is possible.   They make the detonation of the crisis less than it would have been without them, and, therefore, *pro tanto* lessen the amplitude of the movements of confidence and industry. [2]

[1] *Quarterly Journal of Economics*, 1908, pp. 501-2.
[2] In the text attention has been confined to banking panics that spring out of the wave movements of business confidence.   Of course, it is not pretended that these panics only, or even as a rule, arise in that way.   On the contrary, the most important source of banking panics is the outbreak of a great war, such as the Napoleonic wars or the war of 1914.   The detonation and the reaction upon industrial confidence when banking panics are engendered in this way are the same as they are in panics with an industrial origin; and the remedies required to mitigate their effects are also the same.

CHAPTER X

SPECIAL CAUSES AFFECTING THE REAL INCOME OF THE
MANUAL LABOURING CLASSES

§ 1. As was indicated in Chapter I. causes that bring about
variations in industrial activity are relevant to economic
welfare chiefly because they involve variations in the real
income of the manual labouring class. It has now to be observed that these causes are not the only causes of which
account needs to be taken. Besides those variations in the
demand for labour, through which they work, there are two
other important factors upon which the variability of the real
income of workpeople depends.

§ 2. The first of these is the content of the normal working man's family budget. In real life working men are accustomed neither to purchase the same things, nor to purchase
them in the same proportions, as members of the richer classes.
If there was no reason to suppose that the commodities which
play the chief part in their consumption are either more or
less variable in supply than commodities in general, this
circumstance would not be relevant to the present discussion.
As a matter of fact, however, observation brings out two
important points. First, the proportionate part played by
food products is much larger in the consumption of workpeople than in that of others. Secondly, raw materials also
play a relatively large part in their consumption, since rich
people desire goods of high quality, in the construction of which
human action, whether by way of manufacture or by way of
the organisation of retail distribution, and not raw material,
is of chief importance. Food and raw materials are, however,

in the main, grown upon the surface of the ground, and their output is, therefore, subject to the varying influence of climate. Consequently, to the causes which determine the variability of the real income of the working classes in terms of commodities in general, namely the variability of the real demand for labour, it is necessary to add, as a further cause, by which this variability is somewhat enhanced, the fact that the real income of the working classes is taken over in the form, not of commodities in general, but of certain specially variable commodities. This means that, when the variability of their income, in terms of commodities in general, has been determined, its variability in terms of the things which the working classes actually purchase—in the only sense, that is to say, which has interest for them—is likely to be somewhat larger than this.

§ 3. The second relevant factor is the degree of plasticity, in the sense explained in the last Chapter of Part III., which workpeople's organisations allow to their rates of wages. If the elasticity of the demand for labour is greater than unity, plastic wage rates will make the earnings of labour less variable than rigid wage rates; whereas, if the elasticity of demand is less than unity, rigid wage rates will make them less variable than plastic wage rates. Since, as has been shown in Chapter III. of Part V., the demand for labour on the whole is in fact highly elastic, it follows that, other things being equal, in a country where a system of plastic wage rates prevails generally, the aggregate real earnings of labour will be less variable than they will be in a country where a system of rigid wage rates prevails generally. The above two factors, though subordinate in comparison with the main determinants of industrial fluctuations, are, nevertheless, of real importance.

CHAPTER XI

PHILANTHROPIC AND STATE ACTION DESIGNED TO LESSEN THE
VARIABILITY OF INDUSTRIAL ACTIVITY AND THE DEMAND
FOR LABOUR

§ 1. AFTER this brief digression we may return to the main
trend of the argument. The problem to be considered is
that presented by interference with industrial fluctuations
deliberately undertaken with a view to increasing economic
welfare. Government authorities and private philanthropists
recognise that, other things being equal, economic welfare is
likely to be increased—both directly and also indirectly
through reactions on efficiency and, hence, on output—when
the variability of the real income of the labouring class is
diminished. They also recognise that the contributions to
welfare, which changes of this kind furnish, do not, in general,
enter into the calculations of private captains of industry.
Consequently, they decide, quite rightly, that there is ground
for philanthropic or governmental action designed to make
the earnings of labour more stable, even though such action
involves a certain amount of direct cost. The larger the
direct cost, of course, the less far it will be socially advantageous to press equalising action. When such action
involves the setting of men to work in times of depression on
something which is physically perishable, or is liable to lose
its value through a change of fashion, and, still more, when
it involves the making of employment that is avowedly
useless, the direct cost is large. When, on the other hand,
workpeople, who would otherwise have been unemployed, can
be turned to some task of "actual and substantial utility,"

it may be comparatively small. This class of consideration helps to determine from how large a quantity of equalising action economic welfare would benefit. Always, however, except in the special circumstances discussed in the next chapter, advantage can be obtained from *some* quantity of equalising action. So much public authorities and private philanthropists often understand. On the basis of this understanding, they sometimes deliberately transfer a part of their demand for labour from times of boom to times of depression, with the express object of making the real income of the working classes less variable. The purpose of the present chapter is to study the various ways in which this can be done.

§ 2. Before this study is entered upon, however, a preliminary objection must be met. This objection is akin to that considered in another connection in Part V. Chapter VII. It is that philanthropy and the State are necessarily impotent to reduce the variability of the real income of the working classes as a whole. The quantity of resources devoted to the purchase of labour at any time is, it is asserted, rigidly determined. Any resources, which the State or private persons turn to the purchase of extra labour at one point, are necessarily taken away from the purchase of labour at some other point. In the words of the Transvaal Indigency Commission: "Wealth is the only source from which wages are paid, and the State must levy taxation in order to pay wages to its workmen. When, therefore, a Government gives work to the unemployed, it is simply transferring wage-giving power from the individual to itself. It is diminishing employment with one hand, while it increases it with the other. It takes work from people employed by private individuals, and gives it to people selected by the State."[1] This contention is altogether erroneous. It is easily shown that the dividend of consumable products that comes at any time into the hands of the people in control of industry, is devoted to three purposes, *i.e.* immediate consumption by entrepreneurs and capitalists, storage, and the purchase of labour engaged to produce goods for the future. With this conception clearly

[1] *Report of the Transvaal Indigency Commission,* p. 129.

before us, we can no longer suppose that the labour-purchase
fund (in terms of real things), which is available at any
time, is something rigidly fixed; it can, obviously, be enlarged
or contracted by the transference of resources between it and
the two funds designed respectively for consumption by
entrepreneurs and capitalists and for storage. Such transference may be effected in times of depression without it being
necessary for any transference to be made in the aggregate, if
resources are borrowed by philanthropists or by the State in
bad times and repaid with interest in good times. It is, no
doubt, true that a part of the resources borrowed in bad times
would be taken from funds which would normally have been
devoted by private persons to investment involving the purchase of labour. Another part, however, would be taken from
funds which would normally have been stored and from funds
which would normally have been consumed by the relatively
well-to-do. Consequently, though the net alteration in the
aggregate resources devoted to labour-purchase will be less
than the alteration in the resources devoted to this use by
the State, there will almost always be some, and there will
often be a considerable net alteration in these aggregate
resources. Nor is this all. In civilised countries at the
present time there is a further source—wholly ignored by
the Transvaal Commissioners—from which a substantial part
of the requisite resources could be drawn without diminishing in any degree the quantity of investment in labour-
purchase by private entrepreneurs. This source consists in
the large sums annually devoted by Charity and the Poor
Law to the relief of persons who have been brought low
through the effects of intermittent employment. In so far
as the purchase of labour by the State in bad times checked
unemployment and the resultant pauperism, the expenses
involved in it would be balanced by a corresponding reduction
in the expenses incurred by these agencies. For these reasons
the objection referred to at the beginning of this section falls
to the ground.

§ 3. In passing to the main problem of the present
chapter, we may observe that no *essential* distinction exists
between policies under which public authorities manipulate

the demand for any sort of labour by modifying the conduct of industries directly related to themselves, and policies under which, by means of bounties and taxes, they modify the conduct of industries in which private persons are exclusively concerned. No doubt, it may sometimes be practically easier for them to take action in industries where they are themselves the employers, or where, through the placing of government orders, their demand plays an especially important part, than it is in other industries. This, however, is a secondary and subordinate distinction. So much being understood, the principal devices open to the State or to private philanthropists may be grouped into the following divisions. First, certain employers, producing for a market, in bad times deliberately manufacture at a loss for sale or stock, and in this way keep their hirings of labour more regular than, under the existing circumstances, is economically to their advantage. Secondly, certain purchasers of a commodity dovetail a demand that necessarily emerges at intervals into the interstices of the demands of other purchasers of the commodity, thus making the aggregate demand for it more regular, and, thereby, indirectly causing employers to obtain and use funds for investment in labour more regularly. Thirdly, certain purchasers, whose demand is continuous but fluctuating, take measures to stabilise that demand. Fourthly, certain purchasers, whose demand is normally stable, take measures to make that demand fluctuate in such a way as to compensate fluctuating movements of an opposite character in other demands. These four devices have now to be considered in turn.

§ 4. Efforts made by employers (whether of their own motion or under Government influence) to keep their investment in labour more stable than private economic interest suggests act somewhat differently, according as the redundant product in bad times is principally sold on the market or retained in stock. When the greater part becomes stock, even a single employer may produce a substantial—or at all events an uncounteracted—effect on the stability of work-people's earnings. When, however, the main part of the redundant product is thrown on the market, the action of the philanthropic employer, who keeps his hands at work, leads indirectly to other employers dismissing more hands than they would dismiss otherwise. The reason is that the larger sales by the philanthropic firm lower the price; and, therefore, cause a diminution in the output of the others. If the philanthropic firm constitutes only a small part of the total market, the negative effect will be *almost* as large as the original positive effect.[1] It is, thus, idle for the State to set men to work in times of depression at making and offering for sale things that are ordinarily made by private firms.[2] "Convincing testimony was given on behalf of the Firewood Trade Association that the adoption of wood-chopping as the task at the Labour Homes of the Church Army, as well as in many Workhouses, had definitely resulted in ruining independent wood-chopping firms, in throwing many men out of employment and in reducing some actually to pauperism."[3] The action of those philanthropic ladies, who in August 1914 started workrooms to give employment to women thrown out of work by the war in making garments for sale, can, in like manner, only have diverted work from the ordinary channels of trade and done no good to women workers as a whole.[4] No such difficulty exists as regards action taken by the general body of employers in any business. This point, if not obvious *prima facie*, becomes obvious on inspection of the mathematical note at the foot of the page. General action of this sort might, of course, be taken by voluntary agreement among "good" employers. It is, however, more likely to come about through the pressure either of trade unions or of the law. An example of the former

---

[1] A mathematical statement of this proposition is as follows : Let there be n firms, each with an output x and an elasticity of production e, and let the elasticity of the public demand for the commodity be η. Let the output for sale of one of the firms be increased philanthropically by hx units. It can be proved that the consequent net addition to the output of all the firms, including the philanthropic firm, will be equal (within the limits of a first approximation) to $hx\dfrac{\eta}{(n-1)e+\eta}$. When n is large, this is obviously small relatively to hx, unless η is very large and e very small.

[2] Cf. Pierson, *Principles of Economics*, i. p. 292.

[3] *Royal Commission on the Poor Laws*, Minority Report, p. 1099.

[4] Cf. *The War, Women, and Unemployment*, Fabian Tract, No. 178, p. 11.

sort of pressure is given by Mr. Schloss thus: "In Lancashire, if workmen are ordered to cease work owing to a furnace being put out on account of depression of trade, the agreement provides that an additional furnace shall not be started within three months, unless half-wages are paid to these men for the time which they have lost through the stoppage."[1] An example of the latter sort of pressure is afforded by enactments limiting the extent to which systematic overtime is permitted. In either case some steadying effect upon the aggregate demand for labour is almost certain to be exercised.

§ 5. I pass to the dovetailing of consumers' demands. Boards of Guardians in ordering stores, the Board of Admiralty in ordering ships, the War Office in calling up portions of the Special Reserve for training, and Municipalities in carrying through certain kinds of occasional work—such as the making of road surfaces—exercise a demand, which necessarily operates, not smoothly and continuously, but, as it were, in fairly large occasional jets. To a certain extent the public authorities concerned are free to choose at what times these separate intermittent masses of demand shall be brought into play. No doubt, in some circumstances, the moment of their incidence is practically dictated by influences which it is impossible to resist. When a war threatens, for example, there can be no question of allowing care for the steadiness of employment to affect the time at which the Admiralty orders ships. Often, however, it makes very little difference, either to public convenience or to the public purse, in what way the time-incidence of these irregular demands is arranged. When this is so, it is open to public authorities considerably to lessen the fluctuating character of the demand for labour by dovetailing irregular public, or publicly manipulated, demands into the interstices of the demands of private industry. Municipalities may build schools, or give orders for building them, when private building work is dull. The War Office may arrange for the periods of service of the Special Reserve to vary in different localities, in such wise that they shall everywhere occur in slack seasons.[2] On the same plan, educa-

[1] *Board of Trade Report on Collective Agreements*, 1910, p. xxviii.
[2] Cf. *Report of the Royal Commission on the Poor Laws*, p. 411, footnote.

tional authorities may enforce attendance at training schools upon all youths up to some defined age during periods of unemployment. "Up to a given age—say 19—[a youth out of employment] should return [to the training school] during any period of unemployment, and develop the knowledge and faculties gained in his previous work. As soon as he becomes unemployed, it should, therefore, be the duty of the employer, under penalty, to advise the head of the training school of the fact, possibly through the medium of the local Labour Exchange. It would forthwith become compulsory for the boy to re-enter the training school until he was again able to bring a certificate that he had secured employment."[1] A policy on these general lines is clearly implied in a "Circular concerning the Organisation of the Provision of Employment," issued by the Prussian Minister of Commerce in 1904, and quoted in Mr. Schloss's Report on foreign methods of dealing with the Unemployed. The Circular runs: "We further request you to have the goodness to direct your attention to those measures, which are calculated to prevent the occurrence of want of work on a wide scale or to mitigate its effects when it is unavoidable. Not only the State, but also the provinces, districts and communes, in their capacity as employers, are bound to do their utmost to counteract the evil in question by paying general and methodical attention to the suitable distribution and regulation of the works to be carried out for their account. In almost every industrial establishment of importance there are tasks, which do not absolutely need to be performed at a fixed time; just so in every State and communal administration there are works, for the allotment of which the time may, within certain limits, be freely chosen according to circumstances. If all public administrations, in making their arrangements, would take timely care to choose for such works times in which want of employment is to be expected, if, especially, works in which unemployed people of all kinds, including, in particular, unskilled labourers, can be made use of, were reserved for such times of threatening want of employment as have almost regularly recurred of late in winter in the larger towns and

[1] Rowntree, *Unemployment*, p. 21.

industrial centres, the real occurrence of widespread want of employment could certainly be prevented in many cases, and serious distress warded off." [1] The same policy is embodied in the proposal of the Poor Law Commission concerning irregular municipal work. They write: "So far as it may be inevitable to employ occasionally other than their own regular workers, or to place contracts, we think that it may be desirable for public authorities to arrange such irregular work so that, if possible, it comes upon the labour market at a time when ordinary regular work is slack. This point has been well put by Professor Chapman, who suggests that, so far as the public authorities' demand for labour fluctuates, it is desirable to liberate such demand from the influences of good and bad trade and seasonality, and then deliberately to attempt to make it vary inversely with the demand in the open market." [2] The policy thus sketched out is sometimes stimulated by the Central Government through a judicious use of grants-in-aid to municipalities in times of depression. It might conceivably be stimulated further by the establishment of a system of bounties, to be paid in such times on particular sorts of consumption, the funds required being raised, perhaps, by corresponding taxes in times of boom. A step in this direction was once suggested in the House of Commons by Mr. Balfour. He proposed that, when industry was depressed, a bounty should be given to firms making for foreign orders, in such wise as to enable them to accept contracts. Some persons of less cosmopolitan mind might, perhaps, prefer to see the bounty given to firms making for British orders, so that the proceeds of it should go to British rather than to foreign consumers; but this does not affect the general idea.

§ 6. The third of the devices distinguished in § 3 raises a more difficult problem. When the demand manipulated by a public authority is not one that recurs at intervals, but is more or less continuous, what will be the effect of action on the part of the authority designed to render its demand more

---

[1] *Report on Agencies and Methods of dealing with the Unemployed in Foreign Countries*, p. 108.

[2] *Report of the Royal Commission on the Poor Laws*, p. 411.

stable than it would naturally be? Generally speaking, the fluctuations, which, normally occur in the manipulated, demand, are not likely to be directly compensatory to those which occur in other demands for the commodity concerned. It is, therefore, probable that increased steadiness in the manipulated demand will carry with it increased steadiness in the manipulated and the other demands combined. When this happens, fluctuations in the aggregate wages fund *must* be diminished. Hence it follows, in general, that a policy designed to do away with, or to diminish, such fluctuations as would normally occur in the demand manipulated by a public authority for the things made by any class of labour will *probably* diminish the variability of the aggregate earnings of labour as a whole. Public authorities, like private persons, but in a much higher degree, have it in their power to lessen this variability by rendering, at a slight sacrifice of convenience or of money interest, their own demands steadier than they tend, in the ordinary course, to be.

§ 7. There remains the device of deliberately rendering a stable demand unstable in such a way as to compensate the instability of some other demand. More concretely, this device may be set out as follows. The main part of the demand affecting any particular sort of labour is outside of our control; but some part is within our control. Normally, we may suppose, the controlled part would be fairly steady, but the other part unsteady. The policy, we have now in view consists in the deliberate introduction of unsteadiness of a compensating kind into the controlled part, in conditions where the controlled part is not in its nature intermittent. This policy won the approval of the Royal Commissioners on Afforestation. They were concerned to satisfy themselves that " that part of sylvicultural work which requires most labour, namely, the establishment of the forest, is of a sufficiently flexible character to be capable of being pushed on when labour is abundant, and suspended when labour is scarce; "[1] and they advised that it should in fact be pushed on, and suspended, on those principles. The same point of view, in respect of a much more extended field, is adopted by the Minority of the Royal

---

[1] *Report of Royal Commission on Coast Erosion and Afforestation,* vol. ii. p. 13.

Commissioners on the Poor Law. They write: "We think that there can be no doubt that, out of the 150 millions sterling annually expended by the National and Local Authorities on works and services, it would be possible to earmark at least four millions a year, as not to be undertaken equally, year by year, as a matter of course; but to be undertaken, out of loans, on a ten years' programme, at unequal annual rates, to the extent even of ten or fifteen millions in a single year, at those periods when the National Labour Exchange reported that the number of able-bodied applicants, for whom no places could be found anywhere within the United Kingdom, was rising above the normal level. When this report was made by the Minister responsible for the National Labour Exchange —whenever, for instance, the Percentage Unemployment Index as now calculated rose above four—the various Government Departments would recur to their ten years' programme of capital outlay; the Admiralty would put in hand a special battleship and augment its stock of guns and projectiles; the War Office would give orders for some of the additional barracks that are always being needed, and would further replenish its multifarious stores; the Office of Works would get on more quickly with its perpetual task of erecting new post offices and other Government buildings and of renewing the worn-out furniture; the Post Office would proceed at three or four times its accustomed rate with the extension of the telegraph and telephone to every village in the kingdom; even the Stationery Office would get on two or three times as fast as usual with the printing of the volumes of the Historical Manuscripts Commission and the publication of the national archives. But much more could be done. It is plain that many millions have to be spent in the next few decades in rebuilding the worst of the elementary schools, greatly adding to the number of the secondary schools, multiplying the technical institutes and training colleges, and doubling and trebling the accommodation and equipment of our fifteen universities. All this building and furnishing work, on which alone we might usefully spend the forty millions per decade that are in question, is not in fact, and need not be for efficiency, done in equal annual instalments. There might well be a ten years' programme of capital grants-in-aid, made at the periods when the Minister in charge of the National Labour Exchange reports that the index number of unemployment has reached the warning point, for these works to be put in hand by the Local Education Authorities all over the kingdom to exactly the extent that the situation demands. At the same time the Local Authorities could be incited to undertake their ordinary municipal undertakings of a capital nature, whether tramways or waterworks, public baths or electric power stations, artisans' dwellings or town halls, drainage works or street improvements, to a greater extent in the years of slackness than in the years of good trade. This, indeed, they are already tending to do; and to the great development of municipal enterprise in this direction, setting up a small ebb and flow of its own to some extent counteracting the flow and ebb of private industry, we are inclined to attribute the fact that the cyclical depressions of the last twenty years have been less severely felt in the United Kingdom than were those of 1878–9 and of 1839–42."[1] The general scale of the adjustment needed was indicated some years before the war by Dr. Bowley thus: " In round numbers it may be estimated that 200,000 or fewer able-bodied adult males are out of work for non-seasonal causes one year with another, and have no sufficient resources, and that the number fluctuates between 100,000 in the best years to 300,000 in the worst. There is, consequently, a need in the worst year for wages to the extent of £10,000,000, to bring it to a level with the best, so far as these men are concerned; for the whole of the last ten years £40,000,000 would have sufficed."[2] It is evident that the above policy, which cannot, of course, in the concrete be always distinguished sharply from that discussed in § 5, would necessarily render the aggregate real earnings of the wage-earning classes less variable than they would normally be. As will appear, however, in the next chapter, the question whether it is on the whole desirable is not settled by this fact.

---

[1] *Royal Commission on the Poor Laws*, Minority Report, p. 1196.
[2] *Ibid.* p. 1195.

CHAPTER XII

THE RELATION BETWEEN VARIATIONS IN THE REAL INCOME OF
LABOUR AS A WHOLE AND VARIATIONS IN THE CON-
SUMPTION OF THE REPRESENTATIVE WORKING MAN

§ 1. HITHERTO attention has been concentrated upon the variability of the real income of the working classes as a body. This variability is, however, as was pointed out in Part I. Chapter IV., only related to economic welfare in an indirect manner. What is directly related to economic welfare is the variability of the actual consumption of the representative working man. The proposition, that economic welfare is greater the less variable is the real income of the working classes, is only true because it is true, in general, that the variability of the consumption of the representative working man is greater or less, according as the variability of the aggregate real income of the working classes is greater or less. It is thus seen that the discussion conducted so far does not exhaust the whole of what need be said. *Generally speaking*, the introduction of a cause that lessens the variability of the real income of the working classes will make for economic welfare; but it is possible to imagine causes whose introduction will not have this effect. In the light of this consideration it is necessary to look again at the several forms of remedial activity described in the preceding chapter.

§ 2. The essential point can be put briefly as follows. It is broadly true that the variability of the income of the representative working man is not susceptible of diminution, in an important degree, by any cause that does not, at the same time, reduce the variability of the aggregate income

of the working classes. But the converse of this proposition
does not hold good. Causes, which diminish the variability of
the aggregate income of the working classes, may not merely
fail to diminish, but may actually increase, the variability of
the income of the representative working man. If, indeed, all
labour were perfectly mobile between all places and occupations,
this result would not be possible. That it is possible under
existing conditions is, however, easily shown by an imaginary
example. Let us suppose that labour is demanded at two
points A and B, between which, in contradistinction to what
happens as between two complementary occupations, such
as gas-making in summer and brick-making in winter,
movement is absolutely impossible. If the demand at A is
unsteady, and the demand at B steady, the demand at A and
B jointly can be made more steady by the introduction of
unsteadiness at B, so arranged as to "compensate" the unsteadiness at A. The increased steadiness of the demand
of A and B together—implying, of course, increased steadiness
in the aggregate earnings of labour at A and B together—,
which is introduced in this way, does not, however, diminish
the variability of the earnings of any workman. Rather,
it has the contrary effect; for, while the variability in respect
of workmen at A is left unaffected, in respect of workmen at
B it is increased—a result implying, of course, an increase,
and not a diminution, in the variability of the income of the
representative working man. In real life, where labour is
neither perfectly mobile nor perfectly immobile, the result
of analysis is as follows. Causes, which steady the demand
for, and, therewith, the real earnings of, labour as a whole,
without unsteadying the demand for the labour of any group
of workpeople, always diminish the variability of the earnings
of the representative working man : causes, which steady the
demand for, and real earnings of, the whole, by unsteadying
the demand for a part, do not always increase, but sometimes
increase and sometimes diminish, this variability.

§ 3. The application of this analysis to concrete policies is
easily made. All the various ways of steadying the real
earnings of the labouring classes that were discussed in the
preceding chapter, except only the last, necessarily also

involve a steadying of the real earnings of the representative working man. But this last way, that of unsteadying a stable demand in such wise as to compensate fluctuations elsewhere, is uncertain in its result. The question whether, in any particular application, it will render the earnings of the representative working man more or less stable depends upon the degree of mobility that exists among the workpeople in respect of whom it is introduced. When a municipal enterprise controls the demand for only a part of the services of a particular class of workpeople, the variability of the earnings of the representative working man is likely to be diminished, if the demand of the municipal enterprise, which might have been constant, is made to fluctuate inversely with that of the other establishments employing this class of labour in the neighbourhood. On the other hand, it is not unlikely that this representative variability would be actually increased, if the demand for labour upon State forests, which might have been constant, were made to fluctuate inversely with that of city businesses employing artisans and mechanics.[1] Anything, such as the development of a national system of Employment Exchanges, or the development of jobs common to many industries, that makes for improved mobility, whether between places or between trades, thus increases the probability that causes, which steady the demand for the whole of labour by introducing compensating fluctuations into the demand for a part, would lessen the variability of the earnings of the representative workman. Furthermore, this probability will be enhanced if the authorities entrusted with the management of national and local investments do not take account merely of the general percentage of unemployment, but look to the detailed figures of separate industries, and distribute their expenditure among them in proportion to the extent of the depressions from which they are severally suffering.[2]

---

[1] The experience of Belgium seems to show that forest work is well adapted to give winter employment to *unskilled* workmen engaged in the building trade during the rest of the year. (Cf. Rowntree, *Land and Labour*, p. 507.)

[2] In certain instances the policy of compensatory fluctuations has been handicapped in practice by association with the different, and not necessarily connected, policy of employing in the compensatory work "unemployed persons" under non-commercial conditions. The *Local Government Board Report* for 1907-8 explains how the Board gave grants-in-aid to work proposed

by Distress Committees, when such work was work of "actual and substantial utility," in the execution of which unemployed persons, whose applications had been investigated by the Distress Committees, could be given employment (p. clxxiv). "When a grant was applied for in aid of works, which would be executed by the town council or urban district council in the ordinary course of events, and of which the cost would normally be defrayed by the council from their own resources, the grant made by us was, as a rule, limited to the excess upon the cost of the work estimated as likely to arise by reason of the employment of unemployed persons" (p. clxxvi). A policy of this sort suffers from the grave disadvantage of favouring inferior workmen, under conditions highly adverse to efficiency, at the expense of better workmen, who do not apply to Distress Committees. Thus, as the Poor Law Commissioners quote from the Bethnal Green Distress Committee: " Carrying out . . . ordinary work at an earlier period than is necessary is directly calculated to have the effect of causing at a future date a reduction in the number of men regularly employed. . . . This means that the better class of workmen . . . become unemployed for the sole reason that the work . . . has been done at an earlier period by the unemployed at a much greater cost and with far less efficiency" (*Report*, p. 383). This association with relief work conditions is not, however, any essential part of the policy of compensatory fluctuations.

CHAPTER XIII

§ 1. The discussion of the last chapter points the way at once to something that still needs to be said. When the variability of the real income of the representative working man is given, economic welfare can still be increased by arrangements which lessen the variability of his consumption. If the fortunes of the whole community varied in exactly the same manner, the only way in which steadiness in their consumption could be promoted would be by the accumulation of savings in the good times against the needs of the bad times. It makes no essential difference whether saving takes place after the bad times to pay back debts contracted in them, or before the bad times to provide a fund that will be drawn upon in them. In either event the steadying cause is saving and nothing else. Plainly, if this device were carried sufficiently far, it would reduce the variability of the representative working man's consumption to zero. A less complete resort to it acts *pro tanto* in the same way. It reduces the variability of the representative working man's consumption to some extent below the variability of his income. In real life the fortunes of different workmen vary differently. This circumstance opens the way for a second device for steadying the consumption of the representative worker. This is a mutual pledge that those who are fortunate at any time shall hand on part of their income to those who at that time are unfortunate. This device taken by itself is imperfect, because it makes no provision against the danger of common misfortunes affecting a large proportion of the workpeople at the same time. But, when it is combined with the device of saving, great advantages result. The reason is that, though the device of saving, taken alone, *can* reduce the variability of the representative workman's consumption to zero, it can only do this at the cost of withholding a very large quantity of resources from consumption. Each member needs to retain, on the average, a reserve large enough to make good the variations that occur in his individual income. In any group of persons, however, whose individual circumstances result from partially independent causes, the sum of the variations from the average of individual incomes in any year will be much larger than the variation from the average of the sum of individual incomes. It follows that, by saving collectively instead of individually, a group of people can greatly lessen the amount of saving that is required in order to reduce the variability of the representative man's consumption in any given degree. Hence arises that combination of the device of "mutuality" and the device of saving which is commonly known as Insurance. This method is a cheaper way than saving alone of producing a given increment of stability. Consequently, among the poorer classes, to whom cheapness is of vital importance, attempts to foster it have been successful, where— witness the subsidies given under the Ghent system to provision made individually against unemployment—attempts to foster individual saving have failed.[1]

§ 2. Now, in practice, insurance cannot readily be applied directly to correct variations in individual earnings; for, if it were arranged so as to do this, it would act as a bounty on practices conducive to small earnings. Hence, certain events are selected, the occurrence of which is likely to be correlated with diminished income, or increased needs, or, as in sickness, with both these things, for the individual affected by them, and insurance is taken out against these events. The events must be, so far as possible, of such a sort that insured persons

---

[1] "The supplementary provision made at Ghent and elsewhere for unorganised workmen has been either a total failure or a not altogether gratifying success. At Strassburg, and in most of the French towns, it has been omitted, and the benefits of the municipal subvention have been confined to members of Trade Unions, in spite of the objections raised on social and political grounds to thus forcing workmen to join such associations" (*Report of the Royal Commission on the Poor Laws*, Appendix, vol. ix. p. 737).

are not likely to be induced either to bring them about intentionally or to simulate them. The successful development of insurance systems depends largely upon the extent to which arrangements can be devised in conformity with this condition. Two events, namely, death and, subject to the existence of an adequate system of birth registration, the attainment of some specified age, are, broadly speaking, free from the risk either of voluntary creation or of simulation; and, with only slightly reduced generality, the same remark applies to definite forms of serious disablement, such as the loss of an arm or leg. The other two principal events, against which insurance on the part of poor persons prevails extensively, namely sickness and failure to find work in a man's accustomed trade[1] at some agreed-on wage,[2] are, however, subject to both the above risks. Consequently, insurance against these events has to be hedged round with numerous defensive devices. Of these the most obvious is a rule fixing the benefits connected with the occurrence of the event at a figure considerably less than the loss which the event is likely to inflict on the person subjected to it. Thus, in the organisation of out-of-work benefit by trade unions provision is always made (1) to place the benefit at a much lower sum than the insured man would probably be earning if at work, (2) to limit the duration of the benefit, and (3) to start the

---

[1] It should be noticed that unemployment insurance, arranged, as in practice it almost always is, with this proviso, will injure the national dividend on some occasions by checking the movement of workpeople in decaying trades away to others. This evil is probably of small importance in ordinary times, but it is interesting to note that, in the Great War, the official out-of-work pay provided for workpeople in the jute and cotton industry, who lost their jobs through the enforced closing down of machinery, was not given to persons who refused reasonable offers of other kinds of work. In Denmark the hindrance to mobility towards jobs outside a man's own trade is partly met by an arrangement allowing the unemployment fund to pay, to any one accepting work at a lower paid job, the difference between the wage on that job and the maximum of unemployed benefit (Schloss, *Insurance against Unemployment*, p. 61).

[2] When insurance is effected in a trade union, the wage named is, of course, the standard rate of the union. In wider systems of unemployment insurance the determination of this wage presents, however, some difficulties. The English National Insurance Act, 1911, determines it as not lower than that at which the man concerned habitually works, or, in the event of an offer of work in another district, than the rate current there. Strictly, it would seem that this latter concession is right when the lower rate in another district is due to the prevalence of a lower cost of living, but wrong when it is due to the existence there of a lower average of capacity among workpeople.

benefit some days after unemployment has begun.[1] Besides
indirect protective devices of this sort, it is often found
desirable to provide directly for supervision against fraud.
In England it has generally been held that no form of supervision is so effective as the informal inspection of the
applicants' colleagues on the fund. With a view to this, the
sick benefit funds of English Friendly Societies are, in general,
administered locally, even when they are national in character.[2]
In like manner, unemployment benefit, where it existed, was,
until recently, almost always organised through unions of
workpeople belonging to particular trades and working
together in groups. German experience in regard to sickness
insurance suggests, however, that supervision can also be
effectively undertaken by large centralised societies, through
the agency of an organised staff of inspectors. As regards
unemployment also new methods have been coming into
play. What is, in effect, supervision is exercised passively,
both in this country and abroad, by means of the offers of
work made through the growing system of Employment

---

[1] This policy of postponement does not always seem to fulfil its purpose.
Thus, the *Economist* (June 19, 1909) writes in regard to workmen's compensation : "One clause in the Act of 1906 especially encourages workmen to prolong
their illness by making compensation payable from the date of the accident, *if
the disability lasts more than a fortnight*. The effect is to put a premium on
illnesses of between a fortnight and three weeks, and a Mutual Indemnity
Society in South Wales shows that, since the Act, the following curious change
has taken place in its own experience :—

	First Half 1907.	Second Half 1907.
	Per 1000 Workmen.	Per 1000 Workmen.
Illnesses of more than 7 and less than 14 days	18·89	7·44
Illnesses of more than 14 days . .	35·08	69·26

These figures require no comment." But a comment is required ; namely that,
though a portion of the increase in the length of "illness" may be due to
malingering, a larger portion may well be due to the fact that a longer period of
rest and care for sickness is really needed than the urgency of earning wages formerly
made practicable. (Cf. Irving Fisher, *The Need for Health Insurance*, p. 12.)
[2] Cf. Willoughby, *Working Men's Insurance*, p. 334. In Germany sick
insurance was, by the law of 1883, "entrusted to a large number of separate
societies, each of which was made absolutely independent of the others as regards
its receipts and expenditures" (*ibid.* p. 37). A more recent law has changed
this. (Cf. Frankel and Dawson, *Working Men's Insurance in Europe*, p. 158.)

Exchanges. "In Cologne and Berne the Insurance Fund and the public Labour Exchange are practically amalgamated. In Strassburg, Milan and Antwerp, receipt of subvention by an unemployed person under the 'Ghent system' is conditional upon his registration at the Labour Exchange. . . . The State subvention to unemployed benefit in France can only be claimed by Unions having an organised method of finding employment for their members."[1] In like manner, the administration of Part II. of the National Insurance Act of the United Kingdom—the Part, that is, which deals with unemployment—is conducted in connection with, and through the agency of, the national system of Labour Exchanges. Mr. Beveridge attaches such importance to this point that he writes: "Once the community or the insurance fund undertakes the notification of work, the necessity of making relief allowances inadequate and degrading in order to drive men on the search for work disappears."[2] Thus, the informal supervision of co-workers is yielding place to more highly elaborated arrangements. Supervision of some sort, however, still remains exceedingly important.

§ 3. The obstacles, which the need of guarding against the creation or simulation of insured events places in the way of insurance, as a means of steadying consumption, reside more or less in the nature of things. Consequently, even if there were no technical difficulties, insurance would necessarily be carried a good deal less far than would suffice to render the representative working man's consumption stable. But, of course, in fact there are technical difficulties. It is not, indeed, as might at first sight be supposed, a real obstacle to insurance that all forms of it, whether against fire, accident, sickness, unemployment or any other "risk," imply a surrender of income from those who are fortunate and escape the evil insured against to those who are unfortunate and fall victims to it. For before the event, when the bargain is entered into, it is not, in general, known who the fortunate and who the unfortunate are going to be. In virtue of the law of diminishing utility, a chance of one in a thousand that I shall lose £10,000 is

---

[1] [Cd. 5068], p. 737.
[2] *Unemployment*, p. 229. Cf. *ante*, Part V. Chapter IX. § 10.

3 M

more burdensome to me than the actuarial value of the chance,
namely, £10, and I am willing, therefore, to pay a premium
of more than £10 to guard myself against this chance. Hence,
if there are enough people in a similar position to myself, to
make a mutual insurance arrangement fairly secure on the
basis of a premium of not much more than £10, it will pay
all of us to contribute the required premiums into a fund,
from which those who, in fact, suffer losses may be compensated.
Furthermore, it will pay all of us to do this, even though the
adjustment between the premiums paid and the risks carried
by different members is imperfect. Within limits, workmen
less liable to accident or, to unemployment will gain by combining for insurance, on an equal footing, with workmen more
liable to these evils. Moreover, the limits are further extended when persons not likely to draw much benefit from
insurance schemes come into them in the hope of inducing
less fortunate fellow members to adopt a line of conduct which
the more fortunate believe to be advantageous to themselves.
This class of consideration is largely responsible for the
willingness of good workmen to allow bad workmen to
associate with them in the enjoyment of unemployment
benefit in their unions. That bad workmen are a more or
less definite class is suggested by the figures cited in Part III.
Chapter VIII., which show that, in the engineering trade and
among the London compositors, most of the unemployment which
occurs is concentrated upon a comparatively small number of
persons. Bad workmen are, indeed, partially excluded from
trade unions by an initial test on admission, by limitation
of the period during which benefits will be paid (a long
period one year meaning, a shorter period in the following
year), and by the refusal of benefit till premiums have
been regularly paid for some time. This practice of exclusion is, however, generally exercised in a strikingly lenient
manner. The reason is that the event insured against is, not
simply failure to find work, but failure to find it in the man's
ordinary trade, *at the rate which the trade union considers a
proper rate for that trade.* Better workmen, being interested
to prevent inferior workmen from cutting into the standard
rate, are prepared to include many of them in their fund,

though they know that, by doing so, they suffer a direct loss. They have an indirect gain to look to, for which they are willing to pay. Hence, voluntary insurance against unem-. ployment, worked through a trade society, will tend to embrace, at the same premium, men of more divergent capacities than at first sight seems to be probable.[1] The fact, that "practically one set of men continually pay more than they receive, and another (smaller) number of men as continually receive more than they pay,"[2] is not fatal to the voluntary continuance of the arrangement by both sets of men. But—and this is the point—though it is not a conclusive obstacle, it is a very serious one. Though the limits, within which advantage may be derived from an insurance scheme by the less vulnerable among any group of insurers, are wider than might perhaps be expected, they are still narrow. The ratio between the premiums charged and the actuarial value of the different risks, with which they are connected, must not differ widely. We shall not, for instance, find a voluntary insurance fund, paying a uniform benefit for sickness or for accident, that includes among its members, at the same premium, workers in safe and healthy trades and also workers in dangerous and unhealthy trades. Nor shall we find voluntary life insurance associations accepting obviously healthy persons and obvious invalids on equal terms. Nor, finally, shall we find voluntary schemes of insurance against unemployment dealing in this way with workers in the railway industry and also with workers in the highly fluctuating building and engineering trades. Of course, the theoretical solution of this difficulty is obvious, namely, to build up an insurance scheme on a basis of premiums carefully adjusted to the varying risks included under it. But in actual life misunderstanding and friction may easily make this plan impracticable. The technical difficulty of constructing a

---

[1] For example: "The Cigar Makers' Union spends a great deal of money on out-of-work benefit, and the managers of this fund inform us that a large number of the recipients of this relief are infirm persons who cannot earn the average wages, and that many of these are advanced in years." (Henderson, *Industrial Insurance in the United States*, p. 92). It should be noticed that the danger to *competent* men from the acceptance of low wages by *incompetent* men is generally much exaggerated in popular thought.

[2] *Third Report of the Committee on Distress from Unemployment*, Mr. Booth's Evidence, Q. 10,519.

system that will include these adjustments considerably restricts the effective range of mutual insurance.

§ 4. Nor must we stop here. Apart altogether from the considerations set out in the two preceding sections, it is very improbable that insurance would be carried so far as it is socially desirable that it should be carried. There is good reason to believe that stability of consumption is one of those remoter objects, referred to in Part I. Chapter II., the value of which people contemplating the purchase of them generally judge to be less than it really is. "The indefinite need for an old age which many may never experience, and which is far distant for all, the opportunity for an advanced education whose benefits are generally unknown because experienced by but few, the opportunity for leisure, which they do not know how to use because of the necessity of daily and continuous labour, these, and many other causes, have all been responsible for the absence of thrift (and insurance) among the labouring class."[1] The failure of workpeople to attain, in this respect, to the ideal of perfectly rational economic men causes insurance to be pressed much less far than it might, even under existing circumstances, be advantageously pressed. This fact, together with the causes lying behind it, was brought out very clearly by Mr. Richard Bell. He wrote: "During the period of prosperity, when a large number of workers are earning good wages, it is regrettable to think that they do not take care of the few extra shillings they then receive, but indulge so freely in drinking and gambling, so that, when they are meeting with a little depression, they are entirely at the mercy of the employers, and have to put up with circumstances which they otherwise would not."[2] Failure of this kind to effect possible adjustments is common to the general body of the poorer classes and, indeed, of all classes. It is illustrated by the improvidence of those poor persons whose income is exceptionally irregular. The observation of a witness before the Charity Organisation Society's Committee on Unemployment is highly relevant: "If I may express an opinion about the dock district, it is that the greatest evil of all is that there is not

---

[1] Gephart, *Insurance and the State*, pp. 170-1.
[2] Rowntree, *Betting and Gambling*, p. 217.

what the wife calls a Saturday night. If a man gets a job, he is paid for it, and the chances are that the wife sees none of the money." [1] The same point is brought out, in a less direct way, by the obstacles to a proper adjustment of expenditure, which seem to be experienced by persons in receipt of payments made at long intervals. " Those who have knowledge of workhouses know how often the army pensioner drifts in only because his pension comes quarterly, and he cannot keep it till he needs it." [2] It is illustrated again by the claim, often made on behalf of fortnightly or weekly, as distinct from monthly, "pays," that they facilitate the organisation of the workpeople's homes. A workman told Mr. Carnegie that the change from the monthly to the fortnightly system was equivalent, through the saving it introduced by making cash payments more practicable, to an addition of 5 per cent to wages. [3] The point, it may be noted, is recognised in the British Coal Mines Act (1912) by the provision that colliers' wages shall be paid weekly. Further evidence of the inadequate appreciation displayed by workpeople for the advantages of stability can be produced from another side, by reference to the devices, which philanthropists and commercial companies alike find necessary, in order to persuade them to make provision for the future. Thus, Mr. Lee, in his interesting discussion of Thrift Societies, asserts that the cultivation of thrift among the people is best carried out by the establishment of a " society which seeks the family in its home by means of a collector, who calls at stated times, usually once a week. He reaches the people in whom the germ of foresight hardly yet exists, who, accordingly, will not save on their own initiative, however little is required, to whom thrift must come embodied in a person, and must come at regular intervals, intervals not so long but that his next visit is always within the brief range of their forward vision." [4] It is found necessary, in fact, to follow the lead given by betting agencies, with their

---

[1] Report on the Relief of Distress due to Want of Employment, p. 10.

[2] Bosanquet, The Strength of the People, p. 263.

[3] Cf. Carnegie, Problems of To-day, p. 63. Cf. also the argument of the Minority of the Poor Law Commissioners in favour of the compulsory investment of sums paid in compensation for accidents (Report, p. 925).

[4] Constructive and Preventive Philanthropy, p. 22.

elaborate staff of assistants, prepared to visit the wives of working men when their husbands are out, to tackle domestic servants, and to waylay workmen in the factory during the dinner hour.[1] The need for this kind of action is illustrated by "the great difference between the contributions to the burial societies and other forms of saving."[2] It is brought out still more vividly by the fact that the Post Office, though giving considerably better terms for insurance, yet, apparently because it dispensed with collectors, had before the war a much smaller volume of policies than the Prudential Assurance Company.[3] The history of War Savings Certificates in this country affords further evidence that thrift is apt to wait on propaganda.

§ 5. In view of the evident failure, on the part of the ordinary poor man, to press insurance for steadying his consumption so far as his own economic interests suggest, it is open to the State to increase economic welfare by applying some spur to him in this direction; and the case for doing this is, of course, made still stronger, when attention is paid to the indirect effect, which, as explained in Part III. Chapter IX. § 4, it may be expected to have in improving the distribution of workpeople, so as to render the values of the marginal net products of labour in different occupations more nearly equal. Broadly speaking, two forms of spur are available, bounty and compulsion. The spur of bounty has been adopted, in varying degrees, by a number of governmental authorities in relation to private systems of workmen's insurance. In its mildest form it consists merely in the supply of statistical material and tariffs of risks.[4] The importance of this matter is illustrated by certain defects in the arrangements of the numerous local mutual aid associations in the United States. "The principal evil in connection with these voluntary local societies is that they are generally organised and administered without the aid of competent actuaries and are utterly without scientific foundations. A new society copies the bye-laws of an older society, without any kind of understanding of the

---

[1] Cf. Rowntree, *Betting and Gambling*, p. 73.
[2] Miss Octavia Hill, Royal Commission on the Aged Poor, Q. 10,569.
[3] Jebb, *Cambridge*, p. 115.
[4] Cf. Lewis, *State Insurance*, p. 49.

probable outcome of the plan."[1] It is clear that this sort of difficulty could be partially mitigated by supervising aid from State officers—though, no doubt, the local societies might not always welcome very heartily such advice as was offered. A second stage of bounty is reached when the Government provides an institution through which insurances can be entered into, thus affording to insurers a guarantee against fraud or insolvency. In France, for example, there is a *Caisse nationale des retraites pour la vieillesse*, which, besides offering facilities for individual insurance, also offers them for collective insurance.[2] In like manner, the Massachusetts Savings Bank Insurance Act of 1907 and the Canadian Government Annuities Act of 1908 both provide for the sale of insurance or annuities at low rates under a government guarantee.[3] A third stage of bounty is reached when the State contributes a subsidy in money. This subsidy may be small and conceived on the pattern set out by M. Andrifford in his Report on the Proposed French Law on Mutual Insurance Societies in 1889. He wrote: "To be truly useful, the subsidy of the State ought to be restricted to certain limits, and its true purpose preserved. This purpose is to provoke saving and providence, to encourage the indifferent to affiliate themselves with mutual aid societies, to persuade the societies themselves to enter the field of old-age insurance, and, possibly, to come to the aid of the societies at the moment of their organisation, or in times of emergency or distress resulting from epidemics or other great misfortunes."[4] An example of this type of subsidy is that furnished in England by the exemption from income tax up to a certain figure of that part of income which is spent on premiums on life insurance policies. Finally, the most advanced stage of bounty is reached when the money subsidy granted is large. This is so with many of the contributions made to insurance against unemployment by towns that have adopted the Ghent system.[5] Such subsidies have amounted

---

[1] Henderson, *Industrial Insurance in the United States*, p. 80.

[2] Cf. Willoughby, *Working Men's Insurance*, p. 122.

[3] Cf. *Quarterly Journal of Economics*, 1910, p. 718.

[4] Cf. Willoughby, *Working Men's Insurance*, p. 180.

[5] This system, which has spread widely in Belgium, is also largely adopted elsewhere. "In France (1905), Norway (1906), and Denmark (1907), it has been adopted by the State. It is applied by many of the French towns in

to as much as 50 per cent of the benefits paid. In Belgium the State subsidy to old-age insurance amounts to 60 per cent.[1] The spur of compulsion, as applied to insurance, has been amply illustrated in the German compulsory insurance laws against sickness and accident and also in those against old age and invalidity. In the Hungarian law of 1884 there is an interesting example of partial compulsion, it being provided that, "where the majority of the employés decide to found an aid fund, the minority is also bound to join and to pay a certain percentage of their weekly wages for the maintenance of the fund."[2]   Our own Insurance Act of 1911 adopted the method of compulsion, in respect of sickness, for all trades, and, in respect of unemployment, for the building and engineering trades; and the range of compulsory insurance against unemployment is now being greatly extended.

§ 6. If it be granted, on the strength of the arguments advanced in earlier sections, that some spur towards workpeople's insurance is socially desirable, it becomes important to attempt a comparison of the two forms of spur that I have

---

making grants to unemployment funds. In Germany it has been adopted by the Municipality of Strassburg (1906), and has come into the region of practical politics in Munich (1905) and elsewhere. In Italy it has been applied by the Société Umanitaria of Milan (1905). In Switzerland it has been adopted, after the failure of direct compulsory insurance, in St. Gall (1905), and is now proposed in Basle (1907)" (*Report of the Royal Commission on the Poor Laws,* Appendix, vol. ix. p. 736). In England it appeared, in respect of voluntary insurance against unemployment, in the non-scheduled industries of the National Insurance Act of 1911.

[1] Cf. Frankel and Dawson, *Working Men's Insurance in Europe,* p. 321. From the point of view of economic welfare it would seem that schemes of this order would be improved if the aggregate amount of subsidy paid to insurance in any industry were made to vary, not only directly with the amount of benefit privately provided, but also inversely with the level of wage prevailing in the different industries; for, if this is not done, prosperous groups of workpeople will be assisted more largely than poor groups. A step in the direction indicated is taken in the law governing State subsidies in France, according to which, "if the unemployed benefit paid by a Fund is of greater amount than 1s. 7½d. per day, then no subsidy is to be paid in respect of such excess (over 1s. 7½d.)" (Schloss, *Insurance against Unemployment,* p. 44). It should further be noticed that a subsidy to unemployment or sickness insurance proportional to benefit paid is likely to differentiate in favour of dangerous and fluctuating industries as compared with others. This disadvantage can be obviated by arrangements modelled on the German sickness insurance law, under which subsidies might be made proportionate to the number of persons attached to any insurance fund, on condition that the fund provides a certain defined minimum rate of benefit.

[2] *Economic Journal,* 1908, p. 632.

been describing. In making this comparison we must, of course, assume that the method of compulsion, if adopted, will be worked out in such a way that the premiums charged to different insurers are adapted fairly closely to the actuarial values of the risks they run. For, if this is not done, some workpeople will feel that they are being taxed for the benefit of others, and, apart from compensation, in the way either of a State grant or of the enforcement upon these others of conditions prohibiting the offer of work below the standard wage, will resent the system, and will endeavour, as at St. Gall, to break away from it. Given, however, that the method of compulsion is developed on a scientific plan, it has the advantage of freedom from certain practical difficulties, which the rival method cannot completely escape. For, if bounties are given, they can hardly be given with effect except through the Trade or Friendly Societies voluntarily established by the workpeople. In all countries, however, a number of workpeople do not belong to these societies. Consequently, unless the bounty is to be discriminating in its incidence, a rule must be made compelling the societies to allow outsiders, who will not become regular members, nevertheless to become members in respect of the fund subsidised by the State. A rule of this sort prevails in Denmark and also in Norway,[1] but it is plainly unsatisfactory, and likely to lead—as, indeed, in Norway it has led—to considerable friction. A compulsory scheme is free from this difficulty. A more weighty consideration is as follows. Bounties and compulsion are, neither of them, ends in themselves, but both are means to induce people to insure. Viewed from this standpoint, there can be no doubt that compulsion is to be preferred, more particularly as regards the poorer groups of workpeople. For many of these are in such a situation that to " persuade " them to insure is almost impossible. Thus, of this country, it was said before the war: " The workers, to whom insurance is a possible actuarial proposition, are fast being restricted to men whose position is almost professional, the spinner, the power-loom overlooker, the joiner, the engineer, the compositor, the man, in fact, who is in charge of the very top section of the productive

---

[1] Cf. Gibbon, *Unemployment Insurance*, p. 192.

process. The whole army beneath him lives in constant danger of being 'economically transformed' out of self-supporting existence."[1] This point is illustrated by the fact that, in contributory schemes for insurance against unemployment, the large bounties frequently offered under the Ghent system, though they extended the range of insurance operated by unions already in existence, had practically no effect in building up trade union insurance among classes of workpeople hitherto innocent of it. " The great bulk of those claiming the public subvention are drawn from highly skilled and organised trades—such as printing, cigar-making, diamond working. The unskilled and semi-skilled occupations—in which the bulk of distress through unemployment is found in the United Kingdom—do not appear as yet to be touched by the Ghent system anywhere. In Strassburg the hope of reaching these classes in this way is expressly abandoned, and annual relief works are contemplated as the only resource for the seasonal labourers."[2] In this respect compulsory insurance is obviously a more powerful instrument. It does not, indeed, imply, as popular opinion supposes it to do, universal insurance. For, since in all systems, so far as they are concerned with sickness and unemployment, benefits lapse after a time, highly inefficient men must often become uninsured in spite of the compulsion. The English National Insurance Act of 1911, for example, provides that no workman shall receive unemployment benefit for more than one-fifth of the number of weeks during which he has paid contributions. Still, it is plain that, though compulsion does not mean insurance for *all* workpeople, it must, in general, approach much more nearly towards this goal than any system of bounties. " With compulsory insurance laws, the end is reached in a comparatively short time; while, even with State subsidies, voluntary plans have only helped a part of the population imperfectly, and those who most need the protection of insurance not at all."[3] Furthermore, it may well be that the bounty system, if it is to be seriously effec-

---

[1] Report of Messrs. Pringle and Jackson, *Royal Commission on the Poor Law*, Appendix, vol. xix. p. 10.

[2] [Cd. 5068], p. 732.

[3] Zacker, quoted by Henderson, *National Insurance in the United States*, p. 311.

tive, will need to be backed, as it is backed in commercial life insurance, by a large and expensive system of persuasion, and may, therefore, prove, not only a slower, but also a more costly, means of attaining the end sought by compulsion. We are not, indeed, entitled to draw the inference that compulsion is, in this matter, universally superior to bounties. What people *think* good in such a matter goes a long way towards determining what *is* good: and, in a country where the idea of State compulsion was violently unpopular, that fact might turn the scale in favour of the method of bounties. In fact, however, the unpopularity of compulsion appears to be imaginary rather than real, at all events among the workpeople of western Europe. The device of combining with compulsion a certain element of State aid, which has been adopted in the legislation of Germany, France and England, has apparently sufficed to make the "principle" of compulsion palatable.[1]

§ 7. But this conclusion does not exhaust the problem. The end sought is the provision of insurance benefit, so arranged as to make the consuming power of relatively poor persons less unstable than it would otherwise be. Hitherto, we have supposed that the funds out of which those benefits are paid must be constituted, in the main, from premiums paid by the insured. But is this really necessary? Would not the whole scheme be greatly simplified, and many difficulties avoided, if the funds were contributed from the general tax revenue? In the ninth chapter of Part V. it was indicated that the effect upon the national dividend of arrangements that discourage people from making provision for themselves by means of insurance is much smaller than the effect of equal discouragement to provide for themselves by way of contemporaneous work. This point may be developed as follows. Suppose that a group of persons, *prima facie* with similar prospects, agree to subscribe annually for the needs of any of their number who may suffer misfortune in the course of the year. Being ignorant as to which of them will so suffer, it is worth while for all of them to enter into the contract. It is plain, however, that income paid over in fulfilment of it is

---

[1] Cf. *Labour Gazette*, 1911, p. 116, for an account of the French law of 1910 on old-age and invalidity pensions.

simply income transferred, and does not imply any equivalent
of national dividend created : it is, in fact, exactly analogous to
income obtained 'from the gift of a friend. Of course, the
insurance arrangements of real life are not fashioned in this
simple way. One obvious difference is that, since, in any
ordinary insurance society, the annual payment of benefits
is, within limits, variable and uncertain, *some* capital funds
must be put by to guard against exceptionally bad years, and
the amount of these funds must be greater, the smaller is the
range the society covers and the less independent are the risks
it assumes. In fire insurance, for example, provision must be
made against the danger of heavy drains through widespread
conflagrations. This, however, is not the main point. Most
of the risks insured against by the working classes are of
a kind to which a man becomes more liable with advancing
years. But it is not convenient to set up systems of insurance
involving steadily increasing premiums. Such systems have,
indeed, been tried, but, in practice, they cannot compete in
attractiveness with systems based on uniform annual subscriptions. If, however, level-rate systems are to be solvent, in
the sense of being competent at any time to fulfil the contracts outstanding against them even though the influx of
new members were to cease, the annual premium must be
fixed at a rate exceeding the actuarial value of the annual
risk involved in the insurance of the younger among the
insurers. This means, in effect, that the insurance society
holds as reserve, and, therefore, presumably invests, a sum of
money equal to the present value of the obligations which
it has contracted in favour of its existing members, *minus* the
present value of the probable future premiums to be paid by
those members.[1] So much is necessary to maintain technical
solvency. Under schemes of compulsory insurance of guaranteed permanence the certainty that the inflow of young
members will not be checked enables the revenue to be safely
maintained at a level much below this. Thus, in the German
law of accident insurance, " provision is made only for payment
of the benefits falling due during the current year; leaving the

---

[1] For a good discussion of this matter cf. Gephart, *Principles of Insurance*,
chapter viii.

payment of sums falling due in subsequent years to be met out of the receipts of such years."[1]   In some compulsory schemes, e.g. in the Norwegian law for compulsory insurance against accidents, it is provided that the finance shall be based on "capitalised values," which means that reserves adequate to technical solvency have to be built up.   But, even under voluntary schemes and compulsory schemes where this rule prevails, the point made above in regard to simple assessment societies still holds good in great measure.   The reserve required for solvency is necessarily much less than the sum which would yield interest sufficient to pay the benefits as they fall due, because, for purposes of solvency, the accumulated capital must itself be regarded as a distributable fund.[2] In the most completely solvent society, therefore, the money paid over in benefits in any year will include, besides income derived from invested funds, a large slice of the subscriptions received during that year; and, in societies that are not completely solvent, the slice will be still larger.   In this country, combining the figures for accumulated funds and for benefits, given, in respect of our principal Friendly Societies, in the Abstract of Labour Statistics for 1907, we find that the "accumulated funds" amounted to $20\frac{1}{2}$ million pounds and the benefits to $3\frac{1}{2}$ million pounds.   But a capital sum of twenty millions could not then have yielded an annual return of more than one million.   Hence, of the benefits paid by these societies, much the greater part—some three-quarters of the whole—must have come, not from the fruits of invested

---

[1] Frankel and Dawson, *Working-men's Insurance in Europe*, p. 112. "Employers prefer this arrangement because they can thus retain the money in their business, which sums would otherwise have been collected by the associations and accumulated in the capitalised values" (*ibid.*).

[2] If i be the rate of interest and a a given annuity, to begin next year and last for n years, the sum required to yield that annuity at interest without exhausting the principal is $\frac{a}{i}$, but if the principal also may be called upon, the sum required, even without allowing for the future subscriptions of present members, is only $\frac{a}{i}\left\{1-\frac{1}{(1+i)^n}\right\}$; and when allowance is made for these subscriptions it is smaller than that.   It is, indeed, necessary that, besides the reserves just described, an insurance society should keep a further reserve to guard against the occurrence in any year of a quantity of claims in excess of the "probable" annual amount.   In large societies, however, the reserve needed for this purpose is, in general, small.

moneys, but from contemporary subscriptions by other insurers. We conclude, therefore, that the income, which workpeople provide for themselves against sickness, old age and so on by means of friendly societies, is not, in the main, income correlated with any substantial contribution to the national dividend. Consequently, for the State, by providing free insurance, to discourage people from making provision for private insurance, will not involve a large injury to the dividend. It will, of course, involve *some* injury, both because, as explained above, a part of insurance benefits are provided out of real savings, and because, as was shown in § 4 of the ninth chapter of Part V., the gift of anything that people would have bought for themselves, if it had not been given to them, will somewhat lessen their motive to work. Still, the injurious effect on the dividend is not likely to be large. In view of this conclusion a powerful plea can be built up for making insurance, like education, free. But here a distinction must be drawn. Some occupations are much more liable than others to unemployment, accidents and occupational diseases. Consequently, as was pointed out in Part III. Chapter IX. § 4, for the State to charge itself with the payment of insurance benefits all round would involve exceptionally large payments to, and, therefore, differentiation in favour of, workpeople engaged in the more dangerous, unhealthy and fluctuating occupations. This differentiation would push workpeople into these occupations beyond the point at which the value of their marginal net product there is equal to what it is in other occupations. Thus, indirectly, it would inflict a real injury on the national dividend. For this reason we conclude that, when a risk is greater in some occupations than in others, free insurance should only be extended to the minimum risk that is common to all occupations. This conclusion is applicable to unemployment, occupational accidents and occupational diseases.[1] But there are, of course, other very important "risks," such as old age

---

[1] In this connection it is interesting to note that a recent Swiss law distinguishes between occupational and non-occupational accidents, throwing the whole cost of compensation for the former upon the employer, while the workman and the State jointly provide against the latter (*Labour Gazette*, May 1912).

and general sickness, that do not vary to any significant extent in different occupations. Free State provision of insurance against these risks would involve no injurious reaction upon the distribution of labour. The main effect would be simply to transfer the burden of supporting the sick and aged from the shoulders of their fellow workers to those of the tax-payers as a whole. This in itself would be a good thing: and it would have the further advantage, as against compulsory contributory insurance, of administrative simplicity and cheapness. Mr. Sidney Webb writes: "Regarded as a method of raising revenue, compulsory insurance of all the wage-earning population, with its elaborate paraphernalia of weekly deductions, its array of cards and stamps, its gigantic membership catalogue, its inevitable machinery of identification and protection against fraud, involving, not only a vast and perpetual trouble to every employer, but also the appointment of an extraordinarily extensive civil service staff—is, compared with all our other taxes, almost ludicrously costly and cumbersome to all concerned."[1] For these reasons, within the limits indicated above, the case for free insurance is a very strong one.

[1] *The Prevention of Destitution*, p. 170.

APPENDICES

APPENDIX I

§ 1. It is customary in economic discussion to class together as factors of production, along with the services of Nature, waiting and various sorts of mental and manual labour. In a world in which all future wants were perfectly foreseen this catalogue would be substantially adequate. But in the actual world some future wants are not perfectly foreseen. On the contrary, in the vast majority of enterprises, in the conduct of which resources are waited for, they are also exposed to uncertainty; they are turned, that is to say, into a use, the result of which cannot be certainly predicted. In these circumstances it is proper that there should be added to the list of factors of production enumerated above a further group comprising various sorts of uncertainty-bearing.

§ 2. The principal reason why this arrangement is not usually adopted seems to be that, in practice, uncertainty-bearing is bound up in such intimate association with waiting that the possibility of separating the two in analysis is not immediately apparent. Reflection, however, makes it plain that the connection between them is not a necessary or inherent connection,—that they are, in fact, two things generally found together, and not a single thing. Thus, let us imagine a man in possession of a vase, which, as a vase, is worth £100, but, if broken, would be worth nothing; and let us suppose the owner to know that this vase contains something, whose value is equally likely to be anything between nothing and £250. If the owner breaks the vase, he is, then, equally likely to lose any sum up to £100, or to gain any sum up to £150. The actuarial value of his chance is, therefore, £25, and, if there were a million people in his position, and they all elected to break their vases, the aggregate wealth of them all would probably be increased by about £25,000,000. In other words, the services of these million people, in bearing the uncertainty of placing £100 each in a position where it is equally likely to become anything between nothing and £250, are responsible for an addition of £25,000,000 to national wealth. This example shows that uncertainty-bearing, though generally associated with waiting, is analytically quite distinct from it.   Nor was it really necessary to seek an illustration so far removed from actual life.   If a man contracts to deliver 100 bushels of wheat six months hence, with the intention of buying them for that purpose on the day of delivery at a price which he hopes will be lower than his contract price, that man, no less than the breaker of the vase, provides uncertainty-bearing without providing any waiting.   Uncertainty-bearing is thus seen to be an independent and elementary factor of production standing on the same level as any of the better-known factors.

§ 3. In the way of this general conception there are two serious difficulties.   The first of them can be set out as follows. It is well known that the ordinary factors of production are two-dimensional, in the sense that a unit of any of them can only be expressed as a quantity of stuff multiplied by a quantity of time. Waiting consists in the provision of a given quantity of resources, and labour in the provision of a given quantity of labour, during a given period.   Thus, the unit of waiting is said to be a year-pound, and the unit of labour a year-labourer.[1]   It would seem, therefore, that, if uncertainty-bearing, as a factor of production, is to stand on a level with waiting and labour, it must somehow bear a relation to time analogous to that which they bear.   But uncertainty-bearing, unlike waiting and labour, is in its essence, independent of time, and, so far as pure theory goes, capable of instantaneous consummation.   Consequently, the provision of a given quantity of uncertainty-bearing, of any sort for a given period seems at first sight, a mere phrase without substantial meaning.   The difficulty thus suggested is, however, obviated by the fact that, as a matter of practice, the consummation of any act of uncertainty-bearing is not instantaneous, but involves a process in time.   The uncertainty-bearing, for example, which a company promoter undertakes, is not completed until the public has come in and allowed him to unload, and this, of course, will not happen till a considerable interval has elapsed.   This circumstance enables us to fashion a unit of uncertainty-bearing on the same plan as the units of waiting and of labour.   This unit is the exposure of a £ to a given scheme of uncertainty, in an act the consummation of which occupies a year.   The exposure of a £ to a succession of like schemes of uncertainty during a year, in acts the consummation of which occupies on the average, say ten days, will thus embrace $\frac{365}{10}$ of these units.   We have in this way obtained a two-dimensional unit of uncertainty-bearing analogous to the units of waiting and of labour, and the difficulty, which this section was designed to discuss, has been overcome.

[1] Cf. ante, pp. 142-3, footnote.

§ 4. The second difficulty is in this wise. Labour and waiting are objective services, the aversion to providing which may vary with different people, but which, in themselves, are the same for everybody. Uncertainty-bearing, however, it may be said, is in its essence a subjective state, invoked, indeed, by external conditions but bearing a quite different relation to these conditions for people of different temperaments and with different information. It would seem, therefore, at first sight that the amount of uncertainty-bearing involved in carrying through any operation must depend, not only on the nature of the operation, but also on the temperament and knowledge of the people who bear the uncertainty. Such a conception, however, is fatal to the symmetry of our analysis. If there is to be any real parallel with labour and waiting, we *must* define uncertainty-bearing objectively. Thus, the uncertainty-bearing involved in the investment of any given amount of resources means for us the uncertainty-bearing which that investment would involve if it were made by a man of representative temperament and with representative knowledge. If the investment is actually made by a man who never feels subjective uncertainty, whatever the evidence, or by a man who possesses information adequate to destroy subjective uncertainty, we shall say not that less uncertainty-bearing has been taken up, but that a given amount has been taken up by a person who, from temperament or information, is an exceptionally ready bearer of uncertainty. There is, it must be admitted, an arbitrary and artificial appearance about this method of defining our key term; but there appears to be no way in which this can be avoided.

§ 5. Up to this point we have taken no account of the fact that uncertainty-bearing, like labour, is a term embracing a large group of factors of production, rather than a single factor. It must now be observed, however, that, just as there are many different sorts of labour, so there are many different schemes of uncertainty, to which, in the course of industry, resources may be exposed. A scheme of uncertainty can be represented diagrammatically in the following manner. Along a base-line OX mark off all possible yields that may result from the exposure of a £ to the scheme in question; and, through each point on OX, draw an ordinate proportionate to the probability, on the evidence, of the corresponding return. Join the tops of all these ordinates, as in the figure on the next page. Evidently any scheme of uncertainty can be represented by a curve formed upon this plan. Furthermore, the principal species of schemes that are liable to occur can be distinguished into certain broad groups. Find on OX a point B, such that OB represents the actuarial value of the chances of the returns indicated on the curve, or, in other words, such that OB is equal to the sum of the products of each several ordinate multiplied by the corresponding abscissa, divided by the sum of the ordinates; and let the ordinate through B cut the curve in H. In like manner, find on OX a point M, such that OM represents the most probable, or most "frequent," return relevant to the scheme of uncertainty under review; and let the ordinate through M cut the curve in K. On this basis, we may distinguish, in the first place, between curves which are symmetrical, in such wise that BH and MK coincide, and curves which are asymmetrical. The symmetrical group includes schemes of such a sort that, if r is the actuarial value of a pound exposed to any scheme, the chance of obtaining a return $(r-h)$ is equal to the chance of obtaining a return $(r+h)$, for all values of h. The asymmetrical group includes all other schemes. The symmetrical type is only possible when the conditions are such that the ex-

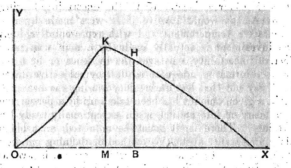

posure of a pound to uncertainty cannot yield a gain greater than a pound, since, from the nature of things, it cannot yield a loss greater than this. Secondly, within the symmetrical group we may distinguish curves which are spread out, like open umbrellas, and curves which are narrow, like closed umbrellas. The former sort represent schemes in which a wide divergence, the latter schemes in which only a small divergence, of the actual from the most probable return is probable. Thirdly, within the asymmetrical group we may distinguish curves in which MK lies respectively to the right and to the left of BH. The former sort represent schemes in which the most probable outcome is a moderate gain, but a large loss is more probable than a large gain. A scheme of this kind would be embodied in a lottery offering a great number of small prizes and one or two blanks. The latter sort of curve represent schemes in which the most probable outcome is a moderate loss, but a small loss is more probable than a small gain. A lottery of the ordinary kind, containing a few large prizes and many blanks, affords an example of this sort of scheme. Within each of the groups thus distinguished it is obvious that an indefinite number of further subdivisions could be made.

§ 6. The great variety of schemes of uncertainty, which uncertainty-bearing in general is thus found to include, might seem at first sight to vitiate the attempt, which was made in an earlier section, to treat "the factor uncertainty-bearing" and "the factor waiting" on the same footing. For, waiting is a single thing, while uncertainty-bearing is a group of different things. The meaning of a change in the supply of waiting is, therefore, clear; but how are we to conceive of a change in the supply of uncertainty-bearing? This difficulty, though it is a natural one to raise, is easily overcome. For, after all, uncertainty-bearing in this regard stands in exactly the same position as labour. Labour in general includes an immense variety of different sorts and qualities of labour. This circumstance does not prevent us from making use of the general concept labour alongside of the concept waiting. In order to render this procedure legitimate, all that we need do is to select in an arbitrary manner some particular sort of labour as our fundamental unit, and to express quantities of other sorts of labour in terms of this unit on the basis of their comparative values in the market. In this way all the various sorts of labour supplied or demanded at any time can be expressed in a single figure, as the equivalent of so much labour of a particular arbitrarily chosen grade. Exactly the same device is available for uncertainty-bearing. The exposure of a pound to a particular arbitrarily chosen scheme of uncertainty can be selected as a fundamental unit, and the exposure of resources to any scheme of uncertainty can be reduced, on the basis of comparative market values, to its equivalent in terms of this unit. Since, as experience shows, the desire for an extra unit of commodity diminishes as the number of units in our possession grows, and since, therefore, an even chance of gaining or losing $(x + \Delta x)$ units is less desired than an even chance of gaining or losing x units, it follows that, other things being equal, the exposure of £100 to a scheme of uncertainty-bearing whose range is broad will be sold at a larger price than the exposure of £100 to a scheme whose range is narrow. It should be added that the relative price of different schemes of uncertainty-bearing is not determined solely by their range, because, as with different sorts of labour, incidental associations may throw upon some of them a glamour that others lack. The uncertainty-bearing involved in gold-mining is, for example, offered cheaply because of the pleasurable excitement attaching to it. But the way in which the process of reducing various schemes of uncertainty-bearing to a common unit works out in practice is a secondary matter. The essential thing is that reduction is possible. So soon as this is understood, an apparently formidable obstacle in the way of assimilating uncertainty-bearing to the other factors of production can be successfully overcome.

§ 7. When the assimilation is accomplished, and all the various schemes of uncertainty, to which, in different industries, people submit resources, are translated into terms of some representative scheme of uncertainty-bearing, there will be a supply schedule and a demand schedule for pounds to be exposed to this scheme, just as there is a supply and demand schedule for pounds to be exposed to "waiting." The demand price or the supply price for the exposure of any given quantity of pounds is the excess of money offered or asked above the actuarial value of a £ so exposed.[1] For different quantities of uncertainty-bearing the demand price and the supply price will, of course, both be different. For some quantities the supply price will be negative. Up to a point, people will gamble, because they like it, though they know that, on the whole, they are likely to lose money. But, though some amount of uncertainty-bearing, like some amount of labour, would be forthcoming for industry, even though there were no expectation of reward, in present conditions more is wanted than can be obtained on those terms. Thus, in respect of such quantities of uncertainty-bearing as are actually made use of in modern industry, the supply price, like the supply price of the other factors of production, is positive; and the general conditions determining the value, or price, of uncertainty-bearing are similar to those determining the price of those factors.[2]

---

[1] The payment asked and offered for uncertainty-bearing is, thus, by no means the same thing as the exceptional profits obtained by persons who have succeeded in risky businesses. Even though no payment whatever were made for uncertainty-bearing, and the *average* earnings of these businesses were, therefore, equal to those obtained in safe businesses, the *successful* undertakers of a risky business would still need to make exceptional profits as an offset to the exceptional losses of those who fail. Otherwise the whole body of investors in the business, taken collectively, would be obtaining less than the actuarial value of investment in it. The payment for uncertainty-bearing, therefore, consists, not in the whole of the excess above normal profits earned by these successful undertakers, but only in that (generally small) part of this excess which is not cancelled by the corresponding losses of other undertakers who have fallen out of the race.

[2] It is easily seen that the quantity of uncertainty-bearing which any individual will provide at any given price depends, other things being equal, upon his wealth. For, if he has $(x+100)$£, to expose £100 to a 5 per cent range of uncertainty is to accept an even chance of receiving $(x+105)$£ or £$(x+95)$. But there is reason to believe that, not merely the desire for an extra unit of resources in general, but also the rate of diminution of this desire, diminishes as the number of units in our possession grows. It follows that the probable loss of satisfaction involved in accepting the above even chance instead of a certain $(x+100)$£ is smaller the larger is the value of x.

§ 8. Like any other factor of production, uncertainty-bearing may improve in technical efficiency. The central fact, upon which the improvements in it that have actually taken place depends, is that forecasts based upon existing knowledge are, in general, more certain when they are made about collections than when they are made about individual members of collections. This fact is expressed in technical form in the important corollary to the normal law of error, which asserts that the "precision of an average is proportional to the square root of the number of terms it contains."[1] It implies that, if there is an even chance that the investment of £100 in one assigned venture will yield a return greater than £95 and less than £115, there is an even chance that £100 scattered among a hundred similar investments will, if all the causes affecting the different investments are independent, yield a return lying between £104 and £106. If only some of the causes are independent and some common, the range within which it is more probable than not that the return will lie will be greater than that enclosed between £104 and £106, but it will still be smaller than that enclosed between £95 and £115. It follows, in accordance with the argument of § 6, that, in general, the investment of a sum of money in equal parts in a hundred similar enterprises involves less uncertainty-bearing than the investment of the same sum in one of these enterprises. It follows, further, that, if out of a hundred people, each of whom has £100 to invest, every one divides his investment among a hundred enterprises, the aggregate amount of uncertainty-bearing undertaken by the group is smaller than it would have been had every investor concentrated on a single enterprise. The physical results of the investments taken together must, however, be the same. Therefore, whenever more or less independent uncertainties are combined together, a given result can be attained by a smaller amount of uncertainty-bearing, or, to put the matter otherwise, the factor uncertainty-bearing has been made technically more efficient.[2] The principle thus explained is fully recognised by business men, and has long lain at the root both of insurance and of much speculative dealing on 'Change. Thus, the segregation of the speculative element in certain forms of business and its concentration upon a relatively small number of speculators have not only changed the distribution, but have reduced the aggregate amount, of uncertainty-bearing required in

---

[1] Bowley, *Elements of Statistics*, p. 305.

[2] This circumstance, of course, permits the release, partly for immediate consumption and partly for investment, of resources which must otherwise have been stored. For example, the combination of the community's gold reserves in a central bank lowers the amount of aggregate gold reserve necessary, increases the capital available for investment, and *pro tanto* lowers the rate of interest. (Cf. H. Y. Brown, *Quarterly Journal of Economics*, 1910, p. 743 *et seq.*)

industry.[1] In modern times the range over which this principle
can be applied has been greatly extended by two important
developments. Of these the one is a legal change, namely, the
concession to joint-stock companies of the privilege of limited
liability; the other an economic change, namely, the development
in the means of transport and communication. The ways in
which these two changes have facilitated the application of the
above principle may, therefore, now be examined.

§ 9. So long as liability was unlimited, it was often against a
man's interest to spread his investments; for, if he did so, he
multiplied the points from which an unlimited call on his resources
might be made. The English Limited Liability Act of 1862 and
its foreign counterparts enabled investments to be spread without
evoking this danger. Furthermore, intermediary organisations,
themselves fortified by limited liability, have been developed,
capable of spreading investments on behalf of persons whose
resources are too small to allow of their spreading them for themselves. Since the minimum share in industrial enterprises is
seldom less than £1, the small investor's capacity for direct
spreading is narrowly restricted. Savings banks, friendly societies,
trade unions, building societies, co-operative societies, trust companies and so forth—all of them limited liability associations—are
able, however, to put him in a position as favourable in this
respect as is occupied by the large capitalist. Nor is it only
the spreading of investments that the system of limited liability
has facilitated. It has also made possible the spreading or combination of risks in a wider sense. For, in general, each business
deals directly or indirectly with many businesses. If one of
them fails for a million pounds, under *unlimited liability* the whole
of the loss falls on the shareholders or partners—provided, of
course, that their total resources are adequate to meet it—
but under *limited liability* a part of it is scattered among the
shareholders or partners of a great number of businesses. Hence,
any shareholder in one business combines with the uncertainty
proper to his own business some of that proper to other businesses also. It follows that the range of uncertainty, to which
a normal £100 invested in industry is subjected by reason of
failures, is still further diminished in amount. This advantage
is additional to, and quite distinct from, any direct national
gain which limited liability may give to a country by throwing a
part of the real cost of its unsuccessful enterprises upon foreigners.

[1] In some circumstances the concentration together of divergent "risks"
would lead to their complete neutralisation, *e.g.* if outdoor entertainments were
insured against wet weather on a bank holiday and indoor entertainments
simultaneously insured for an equal amount against fine weather. (Cf. Marshall,
Industry and Trade, p. 255.)

§ 10. There remains the development in the means of communication. This facilitates the combination of uncertainties in one very simple way. It puts investors into contact with a greater number of different openings than were formerly available. This effect, though of great importance, is so obvious and direct that no comment upon it is required. There is, however, a more subtle way in which the development in the means of communication works. Dr. Cassel has observed that industrial firms have, in recent times, been lessening the quantity of stock that they carry in store waiting to be worked up, relatively to their total business. The improvement in this respect applies all round. As regards production, "there is, in the best-organised industries, very little in the way of material lying idle between two different acts of production, even if these acts have to be carried out in different factories, perhaps at great distances from each other. A modern iron-works has no large stock either of raw materials or of their product, yet there is a continuous stream of ore and coal entering, and of iron being turned out of it."[1] In like manner, factories are coming to keep a smaller amount of capital locked up in the form of reserve machines not ordinarily in use. The same tendency is apparent in retail trading. The ratio of the average amount of stock kept to the aggregate annual turn-over is smaller than it used to be. "Under modern conditions the trade of the country is conducted on a retail system which is growing year by year. The practice of keeping large stocks has almost ceased, and goods are ordered in quantities only sufficient to meet the current demands."[2] One reason for this is the improvement in the means of communication. "The trunk lines of America, with their wide-spreading branches, enable merchants in the cities and the larger towns to replenish their counters and shelves every day. Stocks, therefore, need not be so large as of old, when, let us say, a whole winter's goods were laid in by October. . . . The inter-urban roads are extending these advantages to the village storekeeper, who, in the morning, telephones his wants to Toledo, Cleveland, or Detroit, and, in the afternoon, disposes the ordered wares on his shelves."[3] Now, *prima facie*, this change of custom would seem to be of little significance. After all, a reduction in the amount of finished goods held by retailers, of reserve machinery held by manufacturers, and so on, does not necessarily imply a reduction in the aggregate amount of these things held by the whole body of industrialists. On the contrary, we are naturally

[1] *The Nature and Necessity of Interest*, p. 126.
[2] Inglis, *Report of the Board of Trade Railway Conference*, 1909, p. 33.
[3] Iles, *Inventors at Work*, p. 483.

inclined to suggest that the wholesaler and the machine-maker must increase their stocks *pari passu* with the decrease in the stocks of their clients. As a matter of fact, however, this suggestion is incorrect. The reason is that the wholesaler and the machine-maker represent points at which uncertainties can be combined. The development of the means of communication, therefore, in so far as it directly transfers to them the task of bearing uncertainty, indirectly lessens the amount of uncertainty that needs to be borne. Uncertainty-bearing, in short, is rendered more efficient. The same result as before can be achieved with a smaller quantity of it, or, what comes to be the same thing, with a smaller quantity of waiting designed to obviate the need for employing it.

APPENDIX II

THE MEASUREMENT OF ELASTICITIES OF DEMAND

§ 1. WITH the information at present available it is not possible to lay down any propositions about the elasticity of demand for different commodities beyond those general propositions that are set out in Part II. Chapter XI. As has been pointed out by Dr. Marshall,[1] attempts to determine the elasticity of demand for any commodity in any market by a direct comparison of the prices and the quantities consumed at different times are exposed to very great difficulties. If it could be presumed that the reactions exercised by price-changes upon quantity demanded came about immediately, and if allowance could be made for those upward and downward shiftings of demand schedules, for which movements of confidence and alterations in the supply of monetary purchasing power are responsible, a comparison of the percentage changes of prices between successive years with the percentage changes in consumption between the same years might, for commodities about which adequate statistics exist, yield a rough numerical measure of elasticity for amounts of consumption in the neighbourhood of the average actual consumption.[2] It seems that for certain com-

---

[1] *Principles of Economics*, p. 109 *et seq.*

[2] Professor Moore, in his *Economic Cycles* (Chapters iv. and v.), makes calculations of the "elasticity" of demand for certain commodities without resort to the allowances stipulated for in the text. But, as he himself fully recognises, the elasticity, which his method enables him to measure, is not the same thing as, and is not, in general, equal to, the elasticity of demand as defined by Dr. Marshall and employed here. Dr. Marshall's elasticity, if known, would make it possible to predict how far the introduction of a new cause modifying supply in a given manner would *affect* prices; Professor Moore's to predict with what price-changes changes in supply coming about naturally, in company with such various other concrete changes as have hitherto been found to accompany them, are likely to be *associated*. That this distinction is of great practical importance is shown by the fact that, whereas the elasticity of the demand for pig-iron, in Dr. Marshall's sense, is, of course, negative—that is to say, an increase in supply involves a fall in price—the elasticity in Professor Moore's sense, as calculated from his statistics, is positive. The reason for this is that the principal

modities the above presumption can reasonably be made.   On
the basis of it Professor Lehfeldt calculated, immediately before
the war, that the general elasticity of the demand for wheat
in the United Kingdom was about 0·6.[1] But there is little
hope that many elasticities will lend themselves to calculation in this direct way.   It is, therefore, important to inquire
whether any indirect method of calculation is available for
overcoming difficulties due to the slowness with which reactions
work themselves out.

§ 2. Some years ago I devised a method, the basis of which is
a comparison of the amount of a commodity consumed by persons
of different incomes at a given price, instead of a comparison of the
amounts consumed by persons of given incomes at different prices.
Statistical data needed for this method are found in family
budgets.   Much attention is now being paid both by State
Departments and by private persons to the study of these budgets;
and a number of tables have already been printed to show the
proportion of the income which families in different income groups
expend upon the various principal sorts of commodities.   It is
possible so to manipulate these data as to facilitate the determination of certain elasticities of demand.

§ 3. Let us suppose that the data are better than they are,
and that our tables give the expenditure of the group of workpeople whose wages lie between 30s. and 31s., of the group whose
wages lie between 31s. and 32s., and so on continually for all
wage levels.   With this close grouping we may fairly assume that
the tastes and temperament of the people in any two adjacent
groups are approximately the same.   That is to say, the desire
for the xth unit of any commodity (or group of commodities), the
demand for which is not markedly correlated with the demand for
other commodities, is equal for typical men in the 30s. to 31s.
group and in the 31s. to 32s. group.   Let the quantity of desire
for the xth unit of the commodity be $\phi(x)$: or, in other words, y
being the desire for the xth unit, let the desire curve for the commodity be represented by $y = \phi(x)$. We are entitled to assume
further, in the absence of special knowledge as to the existence
of correlation, that the desire curve of both groups for the com-

---

changes in the price of pig-iron that have in fact occurred are mainly caused by
expansions of demand (general uplifts in the demand schedule), and not by
changes in supply taking place while the demand schedule is unaltered. In
certain conditions it might be possible to *derive* Dr. Marshall's elasticity from
Professor Moore's elasticity, provided that the reactions exercised by supply
changes upon prices could be presumed to take place very rapidly. Apart from
this presumption derivation would be impossible, however ample the statistical
material.

[1] *Economic Journal*, 1914, pp. 212 *et seq.*

modity is independent of the quantity of other commodities consumed and, therefore, of the marginal desiredness of money. Let this marginal desiredness to the lower and higher income groups respectively be μ_1 and μ_2, and the quantities of the commodity consumed by these groups x_1 and x_2. Then, since the price paid for the commodity must be the same for both groups, we know that this price p is equal both to $\frac{1}{\mu_1}\phi(x_1)$ and to $\frac{1}{\mu_2}\phi(x_2)$. These two expressions are, therefore, equal to one another. But if, as it is reasonable to suppose when the incomes of the two groups are close together, x_2 differs only slightly from x_1, $\phi(x_2)$ may in general be written $\phi(x_1) + (x_2 - x_1)\phi'(x_1)$

$$\therefore \phi'(x_1) = \frac{1}{x_2 - x_1} \cdot \frac{\mu_2 - \mu_1}{\mu_1}\phi(x_1).$$

But the elasticity of the desire curve in respect of any consumption x_1 is known to be equal to $\frac{\phi(x_1)}{x\phi'(x_1)}$. Let this elasticity be written η_{x1}. It follows that

$$\eta_{x1} = \frac{x_2 - x_1}{x_1} \cdot \frac{\mu_1}{\mu_2 - \mu_1}.$$

But, since a small change in the consumption of any ordinary commodity, on which a small proportion of a man's total income is spent, cannot involve any appreciable change in the marginal desiredness of money to him,[1] the elasticity of the desire curve in respect of any consumption x_1 is equal to the elasticity of the demand curve in respect of that consumption. Therefore, the elasticity of demand, as well as the elasticity of desire, of the lower income group in respect of its consumption of x_1 units may be represented by the equation:

$$\eta_{x1} = \frac{x_2 - x_1}{x_1} \cdot \frac{\mu_1}{\mu_2 - \mu_1}.$$

§ 4. If we knew the relative values of μ_1 and μ_2, this equation would enable us to determine the elasticity of demand of the lowest income group for any commodity the demand for which is not markedly correlated with the demand for other commodities,

[1] Strictly, of course, such a change must involve *some* alteration in the marginal desiredness of money, unless the demand for the commodity in question has an elasticity equal to unity. If the elasticity is anything other than this, a change in the consumption of the commodity will be accompanied by a transference of money from expenditure upon it to expenditure upon other things, or *vice versa*. This must affect the marginal desiredness of money spent on these things, and its marginal desiredness, if affected in one field, is, since it must be the same in all, affected in all.

in respect of such quantity of the commodity as that group is consuming. Similar equations would enable us to determine the corresponding elasticities of each of the other income groups. If it is objected that our result would in practice be impaired by the fact that the higher income groups are apt to consume a better quality of commodity, and not merely a greater quantity, than the lower income groups, the difficulty is easily overcome by substituting in our formula for the quantities of the commodity that are consumed by the different groups figures representing their *aggregate expenditures upon it*. This device escapes the suggested objection by treating improved quality as another form of increased quantity. In order to obtain the elasticity of demand for the commodity as a whole, it would be necessary to calculate the separate elasticities for all income groups and to combine them on the basis of the quantity of purchases to which they respectively refer.

§ 5. Unfortunately, we do not know, and cannot ascertain, the relative values of μ_1 and μ_2. Consequently, we are estopped from using the above analysis to determine the elasticity of the demand for any commodity in absolute terms.[1] But this does not block our investigation. For, by the process indicated above, the elasticities of demand in any income group can be determined for all the things consumed in that income group in expressions into which μ_1 and μ_2 enter in exactly the same way, namely, as the term $\frac{\mu_2 - \mu_1}{\mu_1}$. If, then, the several elasticities be η_x, η_y, η_z, and so on, any one of them can be expressed in terms of any other without reference to μ_1 and μ_2. These unknowns are eliminated, and we obtain the formula

---

[1] Professor Vinci, in his very interesting monograph *L' elasticità dei consumi*, suggests that the method described above can be extended to yield an absolute measure of elasticity by reference to the distinction between nominal and real prices. The money price paid by the higher income group is the same as that paid by the lower income group. But the real price is, he holds, less than this, in the proportion in which the income of the higher income group exceeds that of the lower. Thus, if the higher income group has 10 per cent more income, an equal money price paid by it implies a real price $\frac{10}{11}$ths as great; and the elasticity of demand is obtained by dividing a virtual price difference of $\frac{1}{11}$th into whatever fraction represents the associated consumption difference (*loc. cit.* p. 22). This procedure is, however, illegitimate, because, on the assumptions taken, the virtual price of *all* commodities to the higher income group is $\frac{10}{11}$ths of what it is to the lower income group. Consequently, the difference in the consumption of *any particular* commodity is not due solely to the difference in price of that commodity, and cannot, therefore, in general, be inserted in the formula for elasticity of demand. Professor Vinci has, in fact, tacitly assumed that the marginal desiredness of money is equal for the two groups—an assumption which would only be warranted if the demand of both for the sum of commodities other than the particular one under investigation had an elasticity equal to unity.

$$\eta_y = \eta_x \cdot \frac{x_1}{x_2 - x_1} \cdot \frac{y_2 - y_1}{y_1}$$

This result, it should be observed, only follows directly from the preceding argument, provided that the commodities concerned are both such that only a small part of a typical man's income is normally spent upon them. In general, however, though the absolute formula for elasticities, from which the result is derived, is only valid on this assumption, the above comparative formula is approximately valid also for two commodities on which a large part of a typical man's income is spent, so long as the part spent on the one does not differ greatly from that spent on the other. The reason for this is that the errors in the two formulae for absolute elasticities, which have to be combined, will tend to balance one another. Our comparative formula is seriously suspect only when it is used to obtain the relative elasticities of the demands of a group for two things, on one of which that group spends a large proportion, and on the other a small proportion of its income. Apart from this, the formula, when applied to the statistics of quantities of, or expenditures upon, different commodities by neighbouring income groups, enables us to determine numerically the ratio of the elasticity of demand of any income group for any one commodity (in respect of the quantity of the commodity actually consumed by it) to the elasticity of demand of the group for any other commodity. This information will often be valuable in itself. It is important to know whether the demand of workers with 35s. a week for clothes is about twice, or about ten times, as elastic as their demand for food. But the information is also valuable indirectly. For, if we can in some other way—through the examination of shop-keepers' books or otherwise—determine the elasticity of demand of any income group, or collection of income groups, for one thing, we have here a bridge along which we may proceed to determine the elasticity of their demand for all other things.

§ 6. In explaining the above method I have, as indicated at the outset, assumed that our data are better than they are. This, I think, is legitimate, because there is no reason in the nature of things why these data should not be improved; and, indeed, there is little doubt that they will be improved. Even then, of course, any one attempting a detailed application of the method is certain to encounter serious difficulties, among which, perhaps, not the least will be that of deciding how far to treat different commodities separately and how far to group them together according to the purpose which they jointly serve. When put to the test, these difficulties may, no doubt, in some applications, prove insur-

mountable.   From the results of an experiment made upon figures
given in the second Fiscal Blue-book (pp. 215 and 217), I am,
however, tempted to hope for better things.   The figures refer to
the expenditure upon "food" and "clothing" of groups of workpeople whose wages were respectively under 20s., between 20s.
and 25s., between 25s. and 30s., between 30s. and 35s., and
between 35s. and 40s.   My method gave the ratio of the
elasticity of demand for clothes to that for food for the several
groups as follows :

Workmen under 20s.	.	.	.	.	1·16
From 20s. to 25s.	.	.	.	.	1·31
From 25s. to 30s.	.	.	.	.	1·62
From 30s. to 35s.	.	.	.	.	1·25
From 35s. to 40s.	.	.	.	.	2·46

Apart from the drop in the ratio for workpeople earning
from 30s. to 35s.—and it may be remarked in passing that the
instances from which the average in this group is made up are
only half as numerous as those in the two adjacent groups—these
figures are continuous and in no wise incompatible with what we
should expect from general observation.   It is natural that among
the very poor the demand for clothes should be nearly as inelastic
as the demand for food, and that, as we proceed to groups of
greater wealth, its relative elasticity should grow.   This small
experiment, therefore, is not discouraging, and it is much to be
desired that some economist should undertake a more extended
study along similar lines.[1]

[1] Cf. my article "A Method of Determining the Numerical Value of Elasticities
of Demand," *Economic Journal* of December 1910.

APPENDIX III

A

§ 1. SOME of the problems investigated in Chapters VIII., XII., XIII. and XIV. of Part II. are susceptible of treatment by an apparatus of diagrams. In the following pages the general character of this method will be explained and its uses illustrated. To simplify the discussion it will be assumed that the distinction between the intensity of a desire and the intensity of the satisfaction yielded by the fulfilment of that desire, which is discussed in Part I. Chapter II., may be ignored. It will also be assumed that the distinction between trade net product and social net product developed in Part II. Chapter VI. may be ignored. Throughout, the point of view taken will be that of a fairly long period.

B

A SYSTEM OF CURVES

§ 2. In what follows I shall employ four types of curve, a curve of marginal demand prices, a curve of marginal supply prices, a demand curve and a supply curve. These have now to be described.

In any occupation the *marginal demand price* of x units of output is the difference between the aggregate satisfaction (measured in money) to the consumers that is involved in the regular (say annual) purchase of x and of $(x + \Delta x)$ units respectively; and the *marginal supply price* of x units is the difference between the aggregate dissatisfaction (measured in money) to the producers that is involved in the regular (say annual) production of x and of $(x + \Delta x)$ units respectively.[1] Construct curves of

---

[1] It must be carefully observed that the difference between the aggregate expenses involved in the regular (say annual) production of x and of $(x + \Delta x)$

marginal demand prices DD_2 and of marginal supply prices SS_2, in such wise that, if a perpendicular be drawn from any point on DD_2 to cut the axis of X in M, this perpendicular represents the marginal demand price of OM units of production, and, if a perpendicular be drawn from any point on SS_2 to cut the axis of X in M, this perpendicular represents the marginal supply price of OM units of production. Let these curves intersect at a point Q, and let a perpendicular QM_2 be drawn from Q to the axis OX.

The *demand price* of x units of output is the price which in the long run tends to maintain an annual purchase of x units; and the *supply price* of x units is the price which tends in the long run to maintain an annual output of x units. Construct a demand curve DD_1, and a supply curve SS_1, in such wise that, if a perpendicular be drawn from any point on DD_1 to cut the axis of X in M, this

perpendicular represents the demand price of OM units of production; and, if a perpendicular be drawn from any point on SS_1 to cut the axis of X in M, this perpendicular represents the supply price of OM units of production. Let these curves intersect at a point P, and let a perpendicular PM_1 be drawn from P to the axis of X.

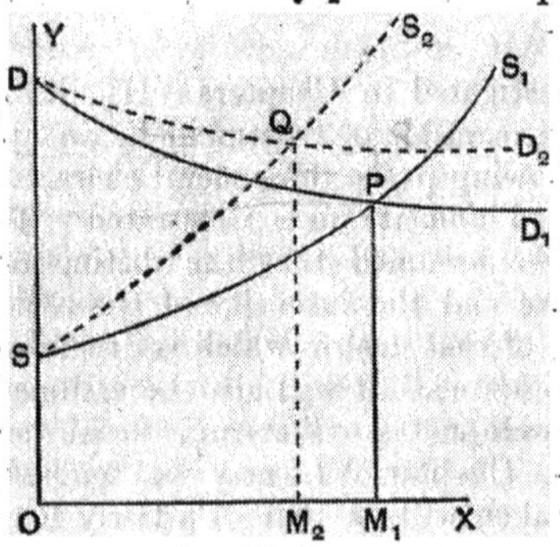

Fig. 1.

§ 3. The relation between the supply curve SS_1 and the curve of marginal supply prices SS_2 is perfectly definite, and can be deduced as follows.

---

units of output means the difference between the aggregate annual expenses of an industry when it is producing and is *fully adjusted to producing* x units, and when it is producing *and is fully adjusted to producing* $(x + \Delta x)$ units. It does *not* mean the difference made in any one year by the addition of Δx units to the output of an industry adapted to the production of x units. If it meant this, we should have to note that, when a railway is adapted for the transport of x units of traffic, an extra parcel will involve very little extra cost, a second will involve very little, until at last another extra parcel involves the putting on of another truck and has an enormous cost; the next parcel after this involves a very small cost; and so on. On our definition, however, we have not to deal with this kind of discontinuity. Whatever the flow of transport required, we conceive the organisation to be adapted to the flow. The loading of all the trucks will be different according to the total volume of the flow. The next step after 40 overloaded trucks would not be 40 overloaded trucks *plus* one truck containing one parcel, but 41 lightly loaded trucks. In like manner, the next step after one set of overcrowded lines is not one overcrowded set and one set carrying a very small traffic, but two moderately well-filled lines. (Cf. Part II. Chapter II. § 2.)

The supply price of any quantity of output is, by definition, the price which tends to call out the production of that quantity annually. But, if, in any industry, a price p_1 prevails for an output x, such that the total receipts of the industry exceed the total costs, including wages of management, interest at the normal rate and rent of the land used at the normal rate, the resulting surplus operates as a force drawing resources into the industry. Hence, equilibrium has not been established, and p_1 is not the supply price of x units, but is greater than this supply price. On the other hand, if, in any industry, a price p_2 prevails for an output x, such that the total receipts fall short of the total costs, the resulting deficit operates as a force expelling resources from the industry. Hence, here also equilibrium has not been established, and p_2 is not the supply price of x units, but is less than this supply price. It follows that the supply price of any output x must be such that the total receipts are equal to the total costs, and that there is no surplus either of a positive or of a negative character.[1] This means that the supply price of x units is equal to the sum of the marginal supply prices of each quantity from zero units to x units, divided by x. Hence, a perfectly

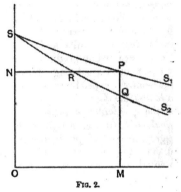

Fig. 2.

rigid relation exists between the supply curve and the curve of marginal supply prices in any industry. To exhibit this relation, from any point P on SS_1, draw PQM and PRN at right angles to the axes of X and Y respectively, and let PQM cut the curve SS_2 in Q. Then, if SS_2 is given, SS_1 is necessarily such that, for all positions of P and Q, the area PRQ is equal to the area SRN. It follows that, when SS_1 is a horizontal line, SS_1 and SS_2 coincide: when SS_1 is inclined positively, SS_1 lies below SS_2: when SS_1 is inclined negatively,

---

[1] At first sight it may, perhaps, be thought that this conclusion is inconsistent with the ordinary doctrine of economic rent, because the rent of land is, in that doctrine, regarded as a surplus. This objection, however, misconceives the argument of the text. It is obvious that, when land is one of the factors of production employed, there is, in conditions of equilibrium, a surplus of receipts over the costs of production incurred in respect of capital and labour. But it is equally obvious that there is no surplus over the costs of production incurred in respect of all the different kinds of resources, including land, of which use is made.

SS$_1$ lies above SS$_2$. Furthermore, the rapidity with which SS$_1$ and SS$_2$ diverge from one another, as they move towards the right, is greater, the sharper is the inclination of SS$_2$ in either a positive or a negative direction.

§ 4. Against the above analysis two objections, both of them focussed upon diminishing returns, have been made. The first is that, since, under conditions of diminishing returns, this analysis makes the supply price of any quantity of output less than the marginal supply price, it implies that the marginal unit is continuously produced at a loss to the producer of it; and that this is impossible and absurd. This reasoning derives its plausibility from an implicit assumption that the *curve of marginal supply prices* employed here represents the *particular expenses* of producing successive units of the commodity. That assumption is not correct. The marginal supply price of x units is, on my definition, the difference between the aggregate expenses of the annual production of x units and of $(x + \Delta x)$ units respectively. When x units are being produced—and the same thing is true when $(x + \Delta x)$ units are being produced—the particular expense to the representative producer of producing any one unit, *all costs, including the hire of the necessary land, being reckoned in*, is equal to the particular expense of producing any other unit. It is equal, not to the *marginal supply price* of x units, but to the aggregate cost of producing x units, divided by x, that is to say, to the *supply price* of x units. In other words, if the supply price is equal to p, the curve of particular expenses, in the sense here relevant, corresponding to the production of x units, would be a horizontal line drawn parallel to the base line at a height representative of p. Hence, despite the fact that the *marginal supply price*, as defined above, is greater than p, the marginal unit, when sold for a price p, is *not* being produced at a loss to the producer of it. This objection, therefore, breaks down.

§ 5. The second and more serious objection has been very ably developed by Professor Allyn Young in the *Quarterly Journal of Economics*. "The significance of the curve of marginal supply prices consists," Professor Young writes, "in the fact that the expense of producing $(x + \Delta x)$ units exceeds the expense of producing x units by more than the amount of expenses specifically incurred in producing the additional Δx units. This excess cost is due to the fact that increased production is only possible at an increased price per unit for the product, which makes possible and necessary an increased annual price for the land (and, under some conditions, for other resources) used in production. . . . Increased prices for the use of land and the other factors in production do not represent an increased *using up* of resources in the work of produc-

tion. They merely represent *transferences* of purchasing power." [1]
In other words, according to Professor Young's view, the excess of
marginal supply prices in industries of diminishing returns over the
corresponding supply prices is merely a nominal excess of money
paid, and not a real excess representing resources employed. This
criticism is, undoubtedly, very important. Furthermore, if it were
directed against an attempt to apply my duplex system of curves
to the output of the whole body of a country's resources lumped
together, as it were, into a single industry, it would, no less
evidently, be just. For the land available for all the industries
collectively in a country is fixed; any increase in the money paid
for it *is*, therefore, merely a transference of purchasing power;
and a large part of the additional money costs per unit resulting
from an increase in output generally might consist in money so
paid. But my analysis is not designed for application to the
output of the whole body of a coun-
try's resources lumped together into
a single industry. Its purpose, on the
contrary, is to provide machinery for
studying the distribution of resources
among a great number of different
industries and occupations, each one of
which is supposed to make use of only
a small part of the aggregate resources
of the country. Because every occupation is thus relatively small, the price
per unit of the several factors of production in each occupation is deter-

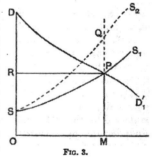

Fig. 3.

mined by general market conditions, and is not affected to any
appreciable extent by variations in the quantity of them that is
employed in that occupation. No doubt, the price of the factors
will not be *wholly* unaffected; and, no doubt, therefore, the
area QPS in the accompanying Fig. 3 will represent, in some
slight measure, nominal expenses and not real expenses. But
this error will *in general*, like the error that is committed in
all applications of the doctrine of consumers' surplus, be of the
"second order of small quantities." It must be admitted, indeed,
that the assumption that each industry only employs a small
part of the several factors of production is not completely true,
as regards land, of those divisions of agriculture which produce
the dominant crops. In wheat production, for example, it
may well be that a significant proportion of the area QPS

---

[1] *Quarterly Journal of Economics*, Aug. 1913, p. 683. A kindred objection
in a less fully elaborated form is suggested by Mr. J. M. Clark in the *American
Economic Review*, Sept. 1913, p. 624.

represents additions to the annual price of wheat land, instead of additions to the quantity of wheat land and of capital and labour applied to it. With this reservation, however, over the limited field to which it is intended to apply, the relation exhibited in my analysis between supply prices and marginal supply prices expressed in money affords an approximately true picture of the underlying relation that subsists between supply prices and marginal supply prices expressed in real resources. The reason why diminishing returns in terms of money appear when they do appear is, in general, not that the money price of the factors employed is increased, but that that proportionate combination of different factors, which it is most economical to employ when $(x + \Delta x)$ units of commodities are being produced, is a less efficient proportionate combination than that which it is most economical to employ when x units are being produced; and the extra cost involved in this fact is real, not merely nominal. For these reasons Professor Young's objection, as a general objection, fails; and the analysis set out in § 3 remains intact.

§ 6. It remains to examine the relations subsisting between the demand curve DD_1 and the curve of marginal demand prices DD_2, as shown in Fig. 1. There is here no rigid and general relation analogous to that which we have exhibited in connection with supply. It is plain, however, that, since the demand price of OM units of commodity measures the money value of the satisfaction directly conferred by the OM*th* unit upon the purchaser of it, while the marginal demand price measures the money value of this satisfaction, together with the satisfaction (or dissatisfaction) indirectly conferred upon the purchasers of other units, the demand curve and the curve of marginal demand price *may* diverge. For commodities, the desire for which is partly a desire for the uncommon, the curve of marginal demand prices will fall below the demand curve; for commodities, the desire for which is partly a desire for the common, it will rise above it; and for commodities which are desired solely on account of the direct satisfaction they confer, the two curves will coincide.[1]

[1] The dual system of curves was first suggested in my article on "Producers' and Consumers' Surplus" in the *Economic Journal* of 1910; but the argument in the text diverges from, and corrects, that employed in the article in some important respects. In what follows it is assumed for simplicity that the various curves slope either up or down *throughout their course.* In exceptional conditions they may run in one direction in one part of their course, and in the opposite direction in another part. These conditions can be examined without any essential change in the analysis developed in the text.

C

§ 7. On the average of "industries in general" we may presume that the earnings per unit of productive resources tend to equality with the value of the net product of their marginal increment. That is to say, the value of the net product of the marginal shilling's worth of resources in industries in general is equal to one shilling. It follows that the value of the net product of the marginal shilling's-worth of resources in any particular industry will be equal to the value of the net product of the marginal shilling's-worth of resources in industries in general, provided that it also is equal to one shilling. This condition is fulfilled if in that industry the product of the marginal PM shillings has a value equal to PM shillings; that is, if the marginal supply price (i.e. the difference made to aggregate supply price by the marginal increment of output) of the product of that industry is equal to the marginal demand price; that is, if the output of the industry is represented in Fig. 1 on p. 932 by the abscissa OM_2, corresponding to the intersection of the curve of marginal demand prices and the curve of marginal supply prices. This output we may conveniently call the *ideal* output. If the actual output is less than this, the value of the marginal net product of resources in our industry will be greater than the value of the marginal net product of resources in general; if the actual output is greater than this, the value of the marginal net product of resources in our industry will be less than the value of the marginal net product of resources in general. Our problem, therefore, is to determine the relation in which actual output stands in various circumstances towards ideal output. The solution of this problem depends upon the relations that subsist between the curve of marginal demand prices and the demand curve and between the curve of marginal supply prices and the supply curve, together with the choice that producers make among the methods of simple competition, monopolistic competition, simple monopoly and discriminating monopoly.

D

§ 8. Under simple competition it is plain that the actual output will be determined at the amount corresponding to the intersection of the demand curve and the supply curve. When, therefore, the demand curve and the curve of marginal demand prices coincide, it will be greater or less than the ideal output, according as the supply curve lies below or above the curve of marginal supply prices. In other words, the actual output will exceed the ideal output under conditions of diminishing returns, will be equal to it under conditions of constant returns; and will be less than it under conditions of increasing returns. From an inspection of suitably drawn curves it is easily seen that the extent of the difference between actual and ideal output will be greater, the more the supply curve diverges in either direction from the horizontal, that is to say, the more sharply either diminishing or increasing returns operate. When the supply curve and the curve of marginal supply prices coincide—a condition which only occurs under constant returns—the actual output

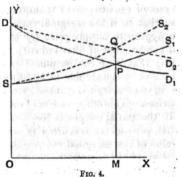

Fig. 4.

will exceed the ideal output if the demand curve lies above the curve of marginal demand prices; will be equal to it if the demand curve coincides with the curve of marginal demand prices; and will fall short of it if the demand curve lies below the curve of marginal demand prices. When both the curve of marginal supply prices diverges from the supply curve and also the curve of marginal demand prices diverges from the demand curve, it is possible that the two divergencies may cancel one another, and that the actual output may, therefore, be identical with the ideal output. This state of things is illustrated in Fig. 4. Evidently, however, such an exact cancellation is extraordinarily improbable, and it may be presumed that, when either or both sorts of divergence exist, the actual output will differ from the ideal output. Whenever this happens, some fiscal expedient can be conceived, the adoption of which, apart from practical difficulties, would increase the sum of economic satisfaction measured in money and, therewith, on our definition, the national dividend also. If X measures the actual output of the industry and Y the ideal output, *all* rates of tax or bounty which cause output to move from X towards Y, but not to pass to the other side of Y, would act in this way, and *some* rates which cause output to pass to the other side of Y would also act so.

E

MULTIPLE SOURCES OF DEMAND OR SUPPLY

§ 9. To complete our analysis it is desirable to add a study of certain problems that arise when a commodity is produced in a number of separate sources of supply. This study involves a preliminary conflict with commonly received opinion. In economic text-books it is generally assumed that an aggregated demand or supply schedule is always made up by the simple addition of a number of independent demand or supply schedules belonging to the separate sources. It is evident that, if and when this assumption is justified, the demand or supply schedule of every source of demand or supply can be represented by a plane curve, and the demand schedule of the market by a further curve obtained by the simple compounding of the curves representing the several sources. The assumption is in fact justified, for demand, only when the relation between the sources is such that the quantity obtained in any one of them has no effect on the demand schedule of any other; and, for supply, only when the relation is such that the quantity produced in any one has no effect on the supply schedule of any other. These conditions are necessarily fulfilled when the demand curves and the curves of marginal demand prices, and also the supply curves and the curves of marginal supply prices, are identical for every possible sub-division of the aggregated market. When some or all of the sets of companion curves are not identical, they may still be fulfilled if the aggregated market is divided up in certain ways; but there must be certain other ways of theoretically possible division for which they will not be fulfilled.

§ 10. When the aggregated demand, or supply, of a market is separated into a number of component sources, which are not independent in the sense contemplated above, it is evident that, though the demand (or supply) schedule of the market can be represented by a plane curve, the demand (or supply) schedules of the separate sources that make up the market cannot be so represented, and cannot be simply added together to constitute the aggregated demand (or supply) schedule. It, therefore, becomes necessary to inquire whether any other assumption of a reasonably simple nature can be employed, instead of the assumption of independent individual schedules with which it is usual to work. One such assumption readily suggests itself. It is that the price, at which any source demands (or supplies) a given quantity of commodity, is made up by the addition of two parts, one depending on the quantity that this source itself demands (or supplies), and the other upon the quantity that the whole market collectively demands (or supplies). On this assumption, if p be the price, y the aggregate quantity demanded (or supplied), and y_r the quantity demanded (or supplied) in the rth source,

$$p = \phi y_r + \psi y.$$

This formula is readily translated into the language of diagrams. The situation is the same as it would be if the commodity consisted of two physical constituents. For one of the constituents the market demand (or supply) curve is already in being, since the demand (or supply) price is known to depend in a definite manner on aggregate amount. The other constituent is demanded (or supplied) by the several sources in such a way that the demand (or supply) price in each source depends solely upon the amount in that source. The market demand (or supply) curve for the second constituent is thus found by a simple addition of the curves for the several sources. We have only then to superimpose this curve for the second constituent upon that for the first to find the complete market curve for the commodity.

§ 11. For certain problems of supply this instrument of analysis is valuable and enlightening. In applying it we are, it must be granted, ignoring the fact that the effect on the supply price of the rth source of supply brought about by a given change in the output of that source may itself be different, according as the aggregate output of the whole market is large or small. Nevertheless, we are approaching much more nearly to real life than we are permitted to do by the method usually adopted. In particular, we are enabled to fit our analysis more closely to the difficult problem of increasing returns. On the ordinary method, a market schedule indicative of increasing returns must be made up of a number of schedules for entirely independent sources, some, at least, of which also indicate increasing returns. A system of that kind, however, is necessarily in unstable equilibrium. Apart from obstructions due to the time element, to which Dr. Marshall has called attention, it would seem that one of the suppliers must drive all the others out of the market. In real life, however, when the commodity is one the production of which on a large scale is associated with "external economics," the separate sources are not entirely independent. Consequently, the presence of increasing returns in the market as a whole does not imply its presence in the parts. In the phraseology employed above, the "constituent" of the commodity, which the sources produce, as it were, on their own merits, may obey the law of diminishing returns in all the sources for any aggregate of production, while the other "constituent" obeys the law of increasing returns rapidly enough to give the character of increasing returns to the supply schedule of the two constituents jointly. It is thus seen that the apparent conflict between mathematical analysis and experience, which has sometimes perplexed the treatment of increasing returns, may be resolved even without reference to the time element, if the assumptions from which the mathematical analysis starts are brought more nearly into conformity with the facts.

§ 12. For the present purpose it is not necessary to follow this line of thought further. Let it be supposed that we have to do with a unified source of demand and with two sources of supply which are entirely independent, so that the aggregate supply curve is made up by a simple addition of their separate supply curves. The problem could, indeed, be treated equally well if the kind of dependence considered in the preceding section were postulated; but the exposition would be more complicated. Construct two supply

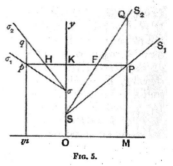

curves SS_1 and $\sigma\sigma_1$, each accompanied by their corresponding curves of marginal supply prices SS_2 and $\sigma\sigma_2$; and let the diagram be completed as in the annexed figure. Let the demand be such that OM and Om are the quantities purchased from the two sources at a price PM, which, of course, is equal to pm. The difference between the supply price and the marginal supply price in the two sources is then represented, in the

FIG. 5.

one by 'QP, in the other by qp. QP is such that the area QFP is equal to the area SFK: and qp is such that the area of qHp is equal to the area σHK. If, therefore, the curves are straight lines, QP is equal to SK and qp to σK. Hence, QP is equal to qp, if, and only if, the points S and σ coincide. Furthermore, if the curves are not straight lines but are of precisely similar shape, QP is equal to qp, if, and only if, the points S and σ coincide. If the two curves are not of precisely similar shape, there will, in general, be some one value of Sσ, and one only, that will make QP and qp equal. It follows that equality between these two magnitudes is exceedingly improbable. That is to say, when a market draws any commodity from several sources, or regions, of supply, in which production does not obey the law of constant returns, it will generally happen, not only that the marginal supply price in each source will differ from the supply price, but also that the amount of this difference will vary in extent from one source to another. It follows that, in general, no single rate of tax or bounty could so change the actual output as to make it equivalent to the ideal output. That result could only be brought about by the establishment of different rates of tax or bounty in the several sources—the rate being heavier in any source the more steeply, given the output and the price, the supply curve is inclined to the horizontal; or, in other words, the smaller is the elasticity of supply in respect of the quantities that would be produced if there were no tax or bounty.[1] It will be noticed that, if the curves are straight lines, the same absolute amount of differentiation in the rate of tax is appropriate between the two sources, whether a heavy tax or a light tax is imposed upon them. If the curves are not straight lines, this proposition does not, of course, in general, hold good.

§ 13. To these general conclusions it is, possible to add more particular results concerning rates of tax and consequent price changes. Let there be two sources of supply separated from one another in such wise that, when differential duties are imposed, evasion through false certificates of origin can be prevented. Let P be the price in the absence of any tax. Let the taxes contemplated be small, so that the elasticities of demand and supply may be regarded as approximately constant for the relevant parts of the demand and supply curves. Let there be one source of demand, D, of elasticity, η (η is necessarily negative) and two sources of supply, S_1 and S_2, of elasticities, e_1 and e_2; and let D, S_1 and S_2 be the quantity demanded and the quantities supplied from the two sources in the absence of any tax. Let T_1 represent a tax at a rate T on S_1, T_2 a like tax on S_2, and T_{1+2} a like tax on both S_1 and S_2. Let ΔP_1, ΔP_2 and ΔP_{1+2} be the corresponding changes of price to consumers. Then it is easily shown that

$$(1) \qquad \Delta P_1 = T_1 \cdot \frac{e_1 S_1}{e_1 S_1 + e_2 S_2 - \eta(S_1 + S_2)},$$

$$(2) \qquad \Delta P_{1+2} = T_{1+2} \cdot \frac{e_1 S_1 + e_2 S_2}{e_1 S_1 + e_2 S_2 - \eta(S_1 + S_2)}.$$

It follows that, other things being equal, when one source of supply is taxed and the other left free, the rise of price will be greater, the greater are the output and elasticity of the taxed source relatively to the untaxed source. In the special case of perfectly inelastic demand and equality of elasticities in the two supplies the above formulae reduce respectively to

---

[1] If e_1 and e_2 are the respective elasticities of supply and PM the price apart from taxation, it can be proved, on the assumption of straight lines, that $S\sigma = \text{PM}\left(\frac{1}{e_1} - \frac{1}{e_2}\right)$. Hence, the condition for no differentiation being needed, namely that S and σ coincide, is equivalent to the condition that $e_1 = e_2$.

$$(1) \quad \Delta P_1 = T_1 \frac{S_1}{S_1 + S_2}.$$

$$(2) \quad \Delta P_{1+2} = T_{1+2}.$$

§ 14. With similar assumptions it is possible to elucidate the comparative effects of raising a given (small) revenue by taxes imposed equally upon both sources and upon one source only. On the latter plan the rate of duty required to yield a given revenue is evidently higher, but, owing to the mitigating effect of the presence of an untaxed source, the proportion of the rate of duty by which the price rises is smaller. These two considerations point in opposite directions, and it is not obvious under which plan the absolute price change will be greater. Mathematical analysis, however, shows that a differential duty upon one source raises price more than a non-differential duty upon both sources, yielding the same revenue, provided either that the supply from the taxed source is more elastic than that from the other, and, therefore, than that from both together, or that, being less elastic, its defect of elasticity falls short of a given small amount. The proof is as follows:

Let R be the revenue required.

Let T_1, T_{1+2} be the duties per unit necessary to yield this revenue when one source (*i.e.* S_1) or both sources respectively are taxed.

Let both sources obey the law of diminishing returns and let both T_1 and T_{1+2} be small relatively to P.

It is easily proved, as a first approximation, that

$$\frac{\Delta P_{1+2}}{\Delta P_1} = \frac{e_1 S_1 + e_2 S_2}{e_1 S_1} \cdot \frac{T_{1+2}}{T_1}.$$

Therefore, the price rises more when both sources are taxed, if

$$T_{1+2} > \frac{e_1 S_1}{e_1 S_1 + e_2 S_2} T_1.$$

We know that

$$R = T_1 S_1 \left\{ 1 + e_1 \frac{\Delta P_1 - T_1}{P} \right\}$$

$$= T_1 S_1 \left\{ 1 + e_1 \frac{e_2 S_2 - \eta(S_1 + S_2)}{e_1 S_1 + e_2 S_2 - \eta(S_1 + S_2)} \frac{T_1}{P} \right\}.$$

Similarly

$$R = T_{1+2} \left[S_1 \left\{ 1 - e_1 \frac{-\eta(S_1 + S_2)}{e_1 S_1 + e_2 S_2 - \eta(S_1 + S_2)} \frac{T_{1+2}}{P} \right\} \right.$$

$$\left. + S_2 \left\{ 1 - e_2 \frac{-\eta(S_1 + S_2)}{e_1 S_1 + e_2 S_2 - \eta(S_1 + S_2)} \frac{T_{1+2}}{P} \right\} \right]$$

$$\therefore \ T_{1+2}^{2} \left\{ \frac{\eta(S_1 + S_2)(e_1S_1 + e_2S_2)}{P\{e_1S_1 + e_2S_2 - \eta(S_1 + S_2)\}} \right\} + T_{1+2}(S_1 + S_2)$$

$$- \left\{ T_1S_1 - T_{1+2}^{2} \frac{e_1\{e_2S_1 - \eta(S_1 + S_2)\}S_1}{P(e_1S_1 + e_2S_2) - \eta(S_1 + S_2)} \right\} = 0.$$

The problem is to find under what conditions the root of this equation when solved for $T_{1+2} > < \dfrac{e_1S_1}{e_1S_1 + e_2S_2} T_1$.

The equation may be written

$$-rT_{1+2}^{2} + qT_{1+2} - H = 0$$

where r and q and H are all positive quantities.

Consequently, it has two positive roots: and it can be proved that, if a given value γ be substituted in the left-hand branch of the equation, and if the resulting expression be positive, then γ must be $>$ the smaller root of the equation. If the resulting expression is negative, γ must be $<$ the smaller root of the equation: It is with the smaller root alone that we are concerned, since it may be assumed that the least possible tax capable of raising the revenue required will be imposed.

Hence, we have merely to substitute $T_1\dfrac{e_1S_1}{e_1S_1 + e_2S_2}$ for T_{1+2} in the left-hand branch of the above equation. If the result be positive, $T_{1+2} < e \dfrac{e_1S_1}{e_1S_1 + e_2S_2}T_1$, and, therefore, the price falls when both sources are taxed instead of one; if it is negative, the price rises.

Substituting, and writing $\{e_1S_1 + e_2S_2 - \eta(S_1 + S_2)\} = K$, we get

$$T_1^2\frac{1}{PK}.\left\{ \frac{\eta(S_1 + S_2)(e_1S_1)^2}{e_1S_1 + e_2S_2} + e_1S_1\{e_2S_2 - \eta(S_1 + S_2)\} \right\} + T_1\left\{ \frac{e_1S_1(S_1 + S_2)}{e_1S_1 + e_2S_2} - S_1 \right\}$$

$$= \frac{T_1}{e_1S_1 + e_2S_2}\left[\frac{T_1}{P.K}\left(\eta(S_1 + S_2)\{(e_1S_1)^2 - (e_1S_1)^2 - e_1S_1e_2S_2.\} + e_1S_1.e_2S_2(e_1S_1 + e_2S_2) \right) + S_1S_2(e_1 - e_2) \right].$$

This is positive, if the following expression is positive, namely

$$\frac{T_1}{PK}.\left\{ e_1S_1.e_2S_2 \{ -\eta(S_1 + S_2) + (e_1S_1 + e_2S_2)\} \right\} + S_1S_2(e_1 - e_2)$$

$$= \frac{T_1}{P}\left\{ e_1S_1.e_2S_2 \right\} + S_1S_2(e_1 - e_2) = S_1S_2\left\{ e_1e_2\frac{T_1}{P} + e_1 - e_2 \right\}.$$

The expression is positive if

$$e_1 > e_2 \frac{1}{1 + \left\{\dfrac{T_1}{P}\right\} e_2}.$$

Under these conditions, therefore,

$$T_{1+2} < \frac{e_1 S_1}{e_1 S_1 + e_2 S_2} T_1 \text{ and, therefore, } \Delta P_{1+2} < \Delta P_1.$$

In other words, under these conditions the price falls when both sources are taxed instead of one. That is to say, the price is raised less when the given revenue is collected from both sources than when it is collected from the more elastic source alone, or from the less elastic source alone, if its elasticity falls short of that of the other by less than a defined small proportion. From this result it is an easily deduced corollary that, when the choice is, not between the taxation of one source and of both sources, but between the taxation of one source and of the other source, price will be raised less if the source in which the supply is less elastic is selected.

§ 15. By similar methods it is possible to determine the effect upon price of imposing a tax upon one of two sources of supply and distributing the proceeds as a bounty to the output from the other source. The solution is as follows. Let the output in the taxed source be S_1, in the other source S_2. Let the tax per unit be T and of bounty V. Then the rise of price is found from our general formula thus:

$$\Delta P = \frac{e_1 S_1 T - e_2 S_2 V}{e_1 S_1 + e_2 S_2 - \eta(S_1 + S_2)}.$$

Cases of increasing returns are ruled out because the existence of two sources, in either of which increasing returns prevails, is incompatible with economic equilibrium. Hence, the price must rise unless $(e_1 S_1 T - e_2 S_2 V)$ is negative; that is, unless $V > \dfrac{T e_1 S_1}{e_2 S_2}$. But, since the taxed source must contract and the bountied source must expand its production, we know that $V < T \dfrac{S_1}{S_2}$. Therefore, the price must rise unless $\dfrac{e_1}{e_2}$ is < 1, that is to say, unless the bountied source of supply is more elastic than the taxed source. This conclusion does not, of course, imply that, when the bountied source *is* more elastic, the price *must* fall. On the contrary, conditions may well be such that prices would be raised *both* by the taxation of the source S_1 to provide a bounty for S_2 and by the taxation of S_2 to provide a bounty for S_1.

F

MONOPOLISTIC COMPETITION

§ 16. A condition of monopolistic competition exists when either of two or more sellers supplies a considerable part of the

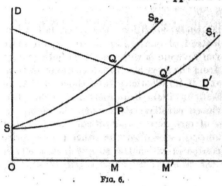

FIG. 6.

market with which they are connected. Let us suppose that two sellers only, A and B, are engaged in production in a given market. For this market construct a diagram, on the plan of those already employed, such that DD' represents the demand curve, SS₁ the supply curve, SS₂ the curve of marginal supply prices, OM the ideal output, and OM' the output normal to simple competition. Let it be assumed, for the sake of simplicity, that the demand curve DD' is also the curve of marginal demand prices. With the help of this diagram, that part of the argument of Part II. Chapter XII., which deals with competing monopolies, other than those that aim by sacrifice in the present at obtaining an advantage against rivals in the future, can be slightly extended. The reasoning of the chapter cited sufficed to show that the aggregate output is indeterminate; and that the range of that indeterminateness stretches from nothing at the one extreme up to the sum of the output that would maximize A's monopoly revenue in the absence of B and the output that would maximize B's monopoly revenue in absence of A. If the curves of demand and supply are all straight lines, these two outputs are respectively one-half of what A would produce under competitive conditions in the absence of B, and one-half of what B would produce under competitive conditions in the absence of A; for, as is well known, the largest rectangle which it is possible to inscribe in a triangle will touch the middle point of two of its sides. Their sum is, therefore, less than the output which would emerge under simple competition, if the larger of the two sources of supply were alone in existence. *A fortiori*, it is less than the output OM', corresponding to the intersection of the demand curve and the supply curve. If the curves are not linear, this result, though not certain, is still probable. Thus, the range of indeterminateness lies between nothing and some ascertainable quantity, which is different in different circumstances, but is, in general, smaller than OM'. When cut-throat competition of the type indicated in Part II. Chapter XII. is not excluded, the argument of that chapter shows that the output is no longer indeterminate between nothing and some quantity smaller than OM', but is liable to exceed OM' to an extent determined by the opinion of each of the combatants as to the staying power of his opponent, and by other considerations of a strategical nature. There is, obviously, no tendency for it to approximate to the ideal output OM.

G

SIMPLE MONOPOLY

§ 17. For the treatment of simple monopoly a similar diagram may be employed. We again assume, for simplicity, that the demand curve and the curve of marginal demand prices are identical. As before, OM repre-sents the ideal output and OM' the output that would come about under simple competition. The output under simple monopoly will be measured by OM″, where OM″ is such that the rectangle Q″FHK is a *maximum*. A study of the accompanying Fig. 7 enables us to reach the following results. Under constant returns and in-creasing returns, since OM' can-not be greater than OM, and

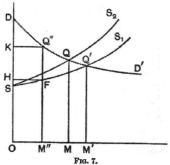

FIG. 7.

OM″ must be less than OM', OM″ must diverge from OM further than OM' diverges from it. Under diminishing returns, however, OM' is necessarily greater than OM, and, there-fore, OM″ *may* diverge from OM less far than OM' diverges from it. The conditions under which this possibility will be realised can be determined without great difficulty in the simple case where all the curves involved are straight lines. As already indicated, OM″ must then be equal to one-half of OM'. It is easily seen that OM must be greater than one-half of OM'; since it would be equal to one-half of OM' if DD' were a horizontal line. Hence, it is impossible for OM″ to have a value greater than OM. The condition that OM″ shall fall short of OM by a smaller amount than that by which OM' exceeds OM is equivalent to the condition that M″M shall be less than

MM'. This condition is satisfied if, in Fig. 8 below, the ∠HQK <∠Q'QK; that is, if the ∠DSS₂<∠SDQ. In other words, the required condition is that the angle made with the vertical by the curve of marginal supply prices is less than the angle so made by the demand curve. Of course, when the curves are not straight lines no such simple result can be obtained.

§ 18. When the State fixes a maximum price at the competitive level, it is obvious that, if conditions of increasing returns or constant returns prevail, it will pay the monopolist to increase his output up to the amount that would have been produced under free competition. If, however, conditions of diminishing returns prevail, the amount which it will pay the monopolist to produce, namely, the amount which will maximise output multiplied by the excess of the regulated price of sale over the supply price, is necessarily less than the competitive output. It *may* be either

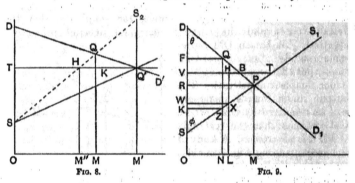

FIG. 8.   FIG. 9.

greater or less than the output that would result under un-regulated monopoly. If the curves of demand and supply are both straight lines, it will be exactly equal to this amount. This is readily seen by inspection of a suitably drawn diagram.

§ 19. If, under conditions of diminishing returns, the State fixes a maximum price, less than the monopoly price but greater than the competitive price, it is *probable* in general that the output will be intermediate between the competitive output and the output proper to unregulated monopoly. If the curves of demand and supply are both straight lines, it can be proved that this result is *certain*. Construct a diagram (Fig. 9), such that PM represents the competitive price and OM the competitive output; while QN represents the monopoly price, and ON the monopoly output. Let the State-controlled price, measured by OV, be greater than the competitive price, but less than the monopoly price. Through V draw a horizontal line VBT cutting DD₁ in B and SS₁ in T. It is easily

shown that the monopoly output ON is one-half of the competitive
output OM, and that the output which it will pay the monopolist
to produce when the price is fixed at OV will be measured by one-
half of the line VT, drawn horizontally through V to cut SS₁ in T, or
by the line VB, according as the one or the other of these lengths is
smaller. But, since OV is greater than PM, it is obvious that VT
is greater than OM. Consequently, one-half of VT is greater than
one-half of OM. This proves that the output at the controlled
price is greater than the monopoly output; and, since VB must be
less than RP, it is necessarily less than the competitive output.
That is, it lies somewhere between the two.

§ 20. An extension of the foregoing argument shows that, in
the conditions contemplated, when the demand and supply curves
are straight lines, the level of controlled price, which will make the
output larger than any other level would do, will be that which
causes the intersection points of VT and DD₁, namely the point B,
to be identical with the middle point of VT, namely the point H.
If the ∠ SDP be θ and the ∠ DSP be φ, this output can be shown to
be equal to the output proper to simple competition multiplied by
the fraction

$$\frac{\tan\theta + \tan\phi}{2\tan\theta + \tan\phi}.$$

H

DISCRIMINATING MONOPOLY

§ 21. Once more, as in the two preceding sections, we assume,
for simplicity, that the demand curve and the curve of marginal

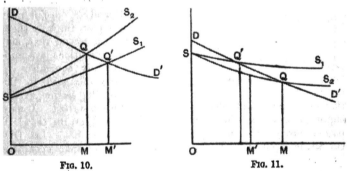

Fig. 10. Fig. 11.

demand prices are identical. Our first problem has to do with
what I have called in Part II. Chapter XIV. ideal discrimination, *i.e.*

discrimination carried so far as to permit of a different price being charged for any unit of product sold. Construct Figures 10 and 11, like those already employed, it being understood, in the first instance, that the point D shall stand above the point S. It is evident that, under monopoly *plus* ideal discrimination, output will be equal to OM units, the quantity, namely, which corresponds to the intersection of the demand curve and the curve of marginal supply prices. In industries obeying constant returns this result is also attained under simple competition, but in industries of diminishing and increasing returns, that is to say, in the generality of industries, the output OM' must under simple competition diverge from OM. The extent of the divergence that discriminating monopoly thus enables us to obviate is necessarily greater, the less far DD' diverges from the horizontal, that is to say, the more elastic is the demand for the commodity in question. It is also necessarily greater, the further SS_2 diverges from the horizontal, that is to say, the more markedly the conditions of supply depart from constant returns, either on the side of diminishing, or on the side of increasing returns.

§ 22. Hitherto it has been assumed that the point D lies above the point S. Let us now consider an industry in which D lies below S. If DD' lies throughout below both SS_1 and SS_2, it is obvious that no output can occur under monopoly *plus* ideal discrimination, just as none can occur under simple competition; whereas, if DD' passes through both SS_1 and SS_2 once, it must also pass through them both a second time, and the conditions are substantially equivalent to those discussed in the preceding section, except that there may be difficulty in getting the industry started. It may happen, however, in some industries of increasing returns, that DD' passes through SS_2, but does not pass through SS_1. Let DD' cut SS_2 in R and Q. Then, under conditions of simple competition, no output can occur. Under conditions of monopoly *plus* ideal discrimination, however, provided that the area RQ is greater than the area DRS, an output OM will yield aggregate receipts in excess of aggregate costs and will, therefore, be forthcoming.

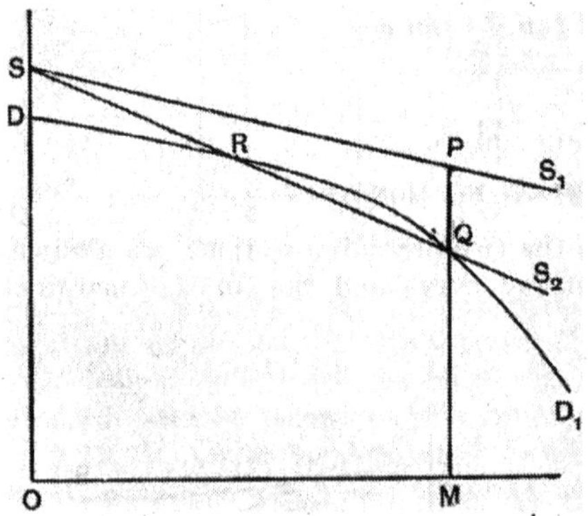

FIG. 12.

This result is more likely to be achieved, the more steeply the curve SS_1 slopes downward (that is to say, the more strongly the law of increasing returns works); because, the steeper is SS_1, the larger, when the distance OM is given, is the area PQS, and, therefore, the greater is the range of demand curves that will make the area RQ greater than the area DRS. Given the inclination of SS_1, it is also more likely to be achieved, if the demand curve does *not* slope downward steeply in its earlier stages (that is to say, if the demand is elastic till fairly low price levels have been reached).

§ 23. Monopoly *plus* discrimination of the second degree, as defined on p. 244, approximates in its effects towards monopoly *plus* ideal discrimination, as the number of different prices, which it is possible for the monopolist to charge, increases. This result, which is obvious in general, can be worked out exactly in a particular case. Let the output proper to ideal discrimination be a, and let n be the number of different price-groups. On the hypothesis that DD' and SS_2 are straight lines, it can be shown that, when the supply of the commodity obeys the law of constant returns, so that SS_2 lies horizontally, the output will be equal to $\frac{n}{n+1}a$ for all values of n. That is to say, if one price only can be selected, the output will be $\frac{1}{2}a$: if two prices can be selected, $\frac{2}{3}a$, and so on. When the supply of the commodity obeys the law of increasing returns, the output, if n is equal to 1, will still be equal to $\frac{n}{n+1}a$, but, if n is greater than 1, it will be somewhat less than this.

§ 24. Our next problem has to do with the relative outputs under discriminating monopoly of the third degree—again as defined on · p. 244—and of simple monopoly respectively. Let conditions of constant returns prevail, and let there be two markets only. Then, if the curves of demand in both markets are straight lines, pre-cise results can be obtained.

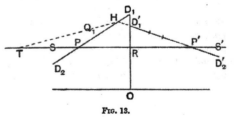

FIG. 13.

Let D_1D_2 and $D'_1D'_2$ represent the demand curves of the two markets, and let SS' be drawn at a vertical distance OR above the base line, where OR measures the constant cost of production. Produce $D_2'D_1'$ to cut D_1D_2 in H, and, through H, draw a straight line HT, such that PT is equal to RP'. Then, under discriminating monopoly the output for the two markets will be respectively $\frac{1}{2}$RP' and $\frac{1}{2}$RP. Under simple monopoly, *if PH is greater than HD_1*, the output will be $\frac{1}{2}$RT. But, since PT is equal to RP', $\frac{1}{2}$RT $= \frac{1}{2}$RP' $+ \frac{1}{2}$RP. Therefore, subject to the condition italicised above, the outputs under simple monopoly and under discriminating monopoly will be the same. If PH is less than HD_1, the output under simple monopoly will, *in some conditions*, be $\frac{1}{2}$RP, and there will be no consumption in the less favourable market. When these conditions prevail, so that under simple monopoly nothing would be consumed in one of the two markets, the substitution of discriminating for simple monopoly increases the output; but except in these conditions the output is not changed.

When the assumption of constant returns is removed and it is allowed that diminishing or increasing returns prevail, the results reached above are not modified, since it is only through a change in the quantity of output that diminishing or increasing returns can be called into play.[1] Increasing returns, however, open up a possibility referred to in Part II. Chapter XIV. § 13 and analogous to that examined in § 22 of this Appendix, to which the preceding discussion has no relevance. This is that, in some conditions under which neither simple monopoly nor simple competition would have led to *any* output, discriminating monopoly may lead to *some* output.

I

FLUCTUATIONS OF DEMAND

§ 25. In conclusion an illustration may be offered of the diagrammatic treatment of problems of fluctuation. Let DD' and SS' be the long period demand and supply curves respectively, and let S_1S_1' be the short period supply curve, drawn on the assumption that the fixed plant of our industry has been adapted to a normal output OM. For the present purpose we may assume, though, in view of the attention which producers

---

[1] In conditions such that a simple monopoly would sell in market A only, while a discriminating monopoly would sell in B also, it can easily be shown that the introduction of discrimination will affect consumption and price in A as follows. Under constant returns both will remain unchanged; under diminishing returns consumption will be diminished and price increased; under increasing returns consumption will be increased and price diminished. These considerations are of practical importance to a Government considering whether native cartels should be allowed to sell abroad at less than the home price.

in fact pay to the danger of "spoiling the market,"[1] the assumption is unreal, that the short period supply curve represents the prime costs of successive units of production. It is evident that DD' and SS' and S_1S_1' intersect at one point P. Through P draw PM and PR parallel to the axes of Y and X respectively. Then PRS_1 represents normal returns to sup-

plementary costs, and is equal to the average of the producers' surpluses (from a short period point of view) that result from the various positions assumed by the demand schedule from time to time. Let D_1D_1' represent the short period demand curve at any one moment, and let it cut S_1S_1' in Q. Through Q draw QM' parallel to PM. Then QM' represents the price proper to simple competition corresponding to this short

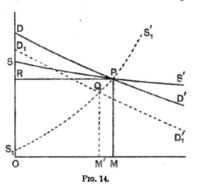

Fig. 14.

period demand. For a given variation of D_1D_1' from DD', the variation of QM' from QM is greater, the steeper is S_1S_1'. But PRS_1 represents normal returns to supplementary costs, and $PMOS_1'$ normal returns to prime costs. Therefore S_1S_1' is steeper the more important is the relative part played by supplementary costs. It follows that, under competitive conditions, the variations of price which correspond to given variations of demand are greater in any industry, the larger is the part played by supplementary costs relatively to prime costs.

[1] Cf. Marshall, *Principles of Economics*, pp. 374-6.

INDEX

THE END

Printed by R. & R. CLARK, LIMITED, *Edinburgh.*